# THE BLUE GUIDES

*The window in the west front of the church at the Convento de Cristo, Tomar*

BLUE GUIDE

# Portugal

## Ian Robertson

**A & C Black**
London

**W W Norton**
New York

Fourth edition 1996

Published by A & C Black (Publishers) Limited
35 Bedford Row, London WC1R 4JH

A CIP catalogue entry for this book is available from the British Library

ISBN 0-7136-4234-7

Published in the United States of America by
W W Norton & Company, Incorporated
500 Fifth Avenue, New York, NY 10110

Published simultaneously in Canada by
Penguin Books Canada Limited
10 Alcorn Avenue, Toronto, Ontario M4V 3B2

ISBN 0-393-31416-2     USA

The publishers and the author have done their best to ensure the accuracy of all
information in *Blue Guide Portugal;* however, they can accept no reponsibility for
any loss, injury or inconvenience sustained by any traveller as a result of information or advice contained in the guide.

**Ian Robertson** was born in Tokyo in 1928; and educated at Stowe. He has been
associated with Blue Guides for 25 years, since being commissioned to rewrite
*Spain* in 1970. He has compiled or rewritten several editions of Blue Guides, among
them those to France, Austria, and Switzerland. He is the author of *Los Curiosos
Impertinentes* (a study of English travellers in Spain), and *Portugal: a Traveller's
Guide,* and has written introductions to reprints of Richard Ford's *Hand-Book for
Travellers in Spain,* Joseph Baretti's *Journey from London to Genoa,* Gleig's *The
Subaltern,* and the Spanish translation of Joseph Townsend's *A Journey through
Spain.* He now lives in France.

Printed and bound in Great Britain by The Bath Press, Avon.

# CONTENTS

## Maps and Plans

Maps of Portugal on the inside front and back covers
Provinces and Districts 73

# PREFACE

This fourth and last edition by the present author of *Blue Guide Portugal* has been considerably revised and several routes rearranged and entirely rewritten. In general it follows the successful pattern set by the previous editions, the demand for which confirmed the revival of interest in the country. Younger, 'democratised' generations, now integrated into the European Union, have already done much to bring about this revival.

Several factors had affected Portugal's accessibility earlier this century: the Spanish Civil War; the Second World War; the long dictatorship of Salazar, with which few found sympathy; and, in more recent decades—although the Algarve was beginning to be exploited—the 'Revolution' of 1974 and subsequent 'troubles'. These caused it to be avoided temporarily by many travellers, in favour of other European countries. As a consequence, one may still find much in this very beautiful and individual country which has been commercialised elsewhere.

This Guide is devoted entirely to the mainland: Madeira and the Azores are *not* included, as it was thought that most travellers to those islands would prefer separate and slighter guides.

The listing of hotels and restaurants has been limited to a representative selection of hotels in Lisbon and Oporto only, although information concerning the *pousadas* of Portugal, to *turismo de habitaçaõ*, etc., is included in the practical section.

Only twenty years have passed since Portugal had her 'Revolution', which although bloodless, shook the country to its foundations. Some hundreds of thousands of Portuguese had to be resettled in Portugal on being forced to leave her colonies. Meanwhile, many Portuguese workers in the more affluent countries of Europe have returned to rebuild their homes in an extraordinary variety of styles. While it is easy to criticise apparently uncontrolled speculative building, it is hoped that those responsible for the preservation of the environment will be able to protect the country's shores and forests from the further encroachments of an increasingly materialistic age; certainly every encouragement should be given to those entrusted with the task of conservation and restoration of the nation's cultural heritage: there is still much work to be done. In the past much of this was unskilful or misplaced, the Church having already mutilated too many buildings in its care (by the application of 'gold paint' to gilded woodwork, for example); but at least the erection of tasteless statuary in the 'dictatorial style' has ceased.

Regrettably, at the time of writing, many of the museums of Portugal are closed or partially so for major reformation (notably in Oporto, Coimbra, and Castelo Branco), while others have now been entirely transformed, among them the Museu de Arte Antiga, and the Museu do Chiado in Lisbon: and the slow process continues.

To acknowledge all the hospitality and assistance I have received would swell these paragraphs inordinately, for many have gone out of their way over the years to offer advice and otherwise ease my path. However, I must thank in particular Pilar Pereira at the Portuguese National Tourist Office in London; Maria de Céu Sá Lima at Ponte de Lima; Ana Maria Horta, Nuno Jardim Fernandes, and João Custodio (ENATUR, Lisbon); José Luís Porfírio (Museu Nacional de Arte Antiga, Lisbon); Claudio Torres in Mértola; and Eugénio Lisboa, for many years Cultural Counsellor at the Portuguese Embassy in London; and

Malcolm Jack. Among many others are Paulo Lowndes Marques; Iria Esteves Caetano (Instituto Português do Primónio Arquetectónico e Arqueológico); Margarida Arçada, Maria Inácia Teles Grilo, and João Viera (Direcção Geral dos Edifícios e Monumentos Nacionais); Simonetta Luz Afonso, and Margot Fonseca (Instituto Português de Museus); Frederico de Freitas Costa (ICEP, Lisbon), António Carona (ICEP, Oporto); Paula Araújo da Silva (CRUARB, Oporto); Miguel Pessoa, and Vergilio Correia (Conímbriga); António Tavares (Museu Machado de Castro, Coimbra); António Seabra (Coimbra); Arminda Vidal (Guimarães); Teresa de Jesus Alves Silva (Tibães) and, if it is not invidious to mention individuals at municipal tourist offices—who have been invariably helpful—Maria Manuela Pessoa Ferreira da Silva, and Armandina Gonçalves (Évora); and Teresa Torres (Sintra).

I must also refer here to the help and encouragement I have received over the last two decades from the late Bernard Bevan, which will be sorely missed. His knowledge of the Peninsula, and its architecture in particular, was extraordinary.

My wife Marie-Thérèse, has again done all the driving—several thousand more kilometres—on the most recent of many extensive tours of exploration made during the last sixteen years—no mean contribution—continuing to share the vexations and pleasures of intensive travel.

# How to use this Guide

The way this guide is organised will be familiar to readers of previous editions or of other *Blue Guides*, describing Portugal in a series of route and sub-routes. They are not designed as suggested tours with some particular attraction in view, but as journeys between two major points on the map. It should be emphasised that in most cases it is impossible to visit on the same day all the places and monuments described in a route, but they suggest a general direction which it may be convenient to follow. Towns are described for sightseeing on foot, most of the larger being provided with a plan. In many cases the routes follow long-established roads, and which are likely to be the most interesting. Some have been split into alternative approaches (A, B, etc.), which offer different ways of driving between destinations (which naturally may be followed in reverse), and of touring the intermediate area, and several detours or excursions are suggested when appropriate.

Although it involves some overlapping or routes (indicated by cross-references), this well-tried system has the merit of grouping places in close proximity on a map close to each other on a page, which well serves the purpose of pointing out both to the habitual traveller and the tourist those places worthy of attention or detour. The comprehensive index will help and should encourage readers to plan their own itineraries.

Those travelling by car are recommended to acquire the latest edition of the Red Michelin Guide to Portugal, a very useful companion to the present volume, containing many more town plans, detailed indications of points of entry or exit, one-way streets, car parks, garages, tourist offices, post offices, and a representative selection of hotels and restaurants: but see also pp 83, 101 and 285.

**Type**. The main routes are described in normal width type. Indented type is used for historical and practical detail; excursions or deviations are described between rules.

**Abbreviations**. In addition to generally accepted and self-explanatory forms, the following occur in the guide:

| | |
|---|---|
| C | century |
| cf. | compare |
| N.-D. | *Nossa Senhora*, Our Lady |
| São or Santa | Saint (male or female) |

Note that Esq. (*esquerda*) and Dto. (*direito*) in Portuguese, indicate left and right respectively.

**Asterisks** indicate sites or monuments of special interest or merit.

**Distances** total and intermediate, are measured in kilometres (km), but, with the realignment of roads and bypasses, it is almost certain that these will vary slightly from those measured by motorists on their milometers, and are at best approximate. Altitudes, and the measurements of buildings, are given in metres (m).

**Maps and plans**. The town plans included in the text give fairly detailed guidance to areas of particular interest in them.

The author has found Michelin's spiral-bound *Motoring Atlas of Spain and Portugal* indispensable. Recently published, its maps are reproduced at 1:400,000, and it includes town plans and an index; however, the traveller is advised to obtain at least one of the following two maps for general planning: the Michelin Map 990 (Spain and Portugal, at 1:1,000,000), or preferably, Map 440 (Portugal, at 1:400,000). It is essential to acquire the *latest* editions, which will incorporate recent changes, but even they will not always give an accurate idea of the contours or windings of every road; but see pp 79–80. They are usually readily available at good bookshops or at Stanfords, 12–25 Long Acre, London WC2E 9LP, but in case of difficulty, one may apply to Michelin Tyre PLC, 38 Clarendon Road, Watford, Herts WD1 1SX.

**Population** figures, based on the latest available demographical statistics, should give some idea of the likely amenities of a town which the visitor may expect to find. They are not provided for places with fewer than 5000 inhabitants.

**Anglicisations**. Most place-names and personal names have been given their Portuguese form, except in a few cases where the English form is much more familiar, such as Lisbon (Lisboa); Oporto (Porto); Braganza (Bragança); Busaco (Buçaco); and the river Tagus (Tejo), etc. When the place itself is described, the Portuguese is given in brackets, as above. Likewise, certain names of persons have been given their English equivalent, such as Henry the Navigator, for instance, rather than Henriques, and Camoens rather than Camões. Some Christian names are not always obvious, for example: Duarte (Edward), and João (John). Note that Wellesley is referred to throughout as Wellington, although he did not receive his title until after the Battle of Talavera (July 1809).

**National Tourist Offices**. General information may be obtained gratis from the Portuguese Trade and Tourism Office at 22–25 Sackville Street, London W1X 1DE (tel. 0171–494 1441), preferably in writing; but see also pp 77 and 82.

Most of the larger and even some smaller towns in Portugal have local tourist offices, usually well indicated by sign-posts, which can provide information on accommodation, entertainments, museums, etc.

**Opening times** for museums and historic buildings, are very likely to vary from year to year, if not more frequently, so that times specified in anything except an annual publication rapidly become dated. Those intent on visiting a particular museum or monument are urged to check with a tourist office in advance of any proposed visit concerning times of admission, noting that some museums may be closed on Mondays, also between 12.00 and 14.00, and on public holidays. But see pp 88 and 91.

## Principal Sights

While this is a very subjective matter, some visitors may find it useful to have a certain number of places pointed out for them, which in the author's opinion are most worthwhile seeing. This may be of help when planning tours or walks. They have been listed under subjects, and apart from Lisbon itself (detailed below), have been placed in order working roughly from the north to the south of the country, and from west to east.

Reference should be made to the index in each case.

**Cities and towns**: the **old centres** of Braga, Guimarães, Braganza, Oporto, Amarante, Aveiro, Viseu, Guarda, Coimbra, Tomar, Abrantes, Santarém, Portalegre, Évora, Beja, Lagos, and Faro.

**Smaller towns and villages**: Monção, Valença do Minho, Caminha, Viana do Castelo, Ponte de Lima, Barcelos, Miranda do Douro, Lamego, Freixo de Espada à Cinta, Trancosa, Pinhel, Castelo Rodrigo, Almeida, Linhares, Oliveira do Hospital, Penacova, Belmonte, Montemor-o-Velho, Monsanto, Idanha-a-Velha, Obidos, Castelo do Vide, Marvão, Avis, Sintra (and Quinta de Monserrate gardens), Estremoz, Elvas, Borba, Vila Viçosa, Monsaraz, Serpa, Mértola, Silves, and Tavira.

**Convents, churches, and buildings other than those in the above**: Bravães, Bouro, Tibães, São Frutuoso, and stair of Bom Jesus (near Braga), Rates, Rio Mau, Sta Clara (Vila do Conde), Travanca, Solar de Mateus (near Vila Real), Paço de Sousa, Arouca, São João de Tarouca, Vila da Feira (castle), Lourosa, Lorvão, Leiria (castle), Batalha, Alcobaça, Almourol castle (west of Abrantes), Mafra, Queluz (palace), Evoramonte (castle), Quinta da Bacalhoa (north-west of Setúbal), Igreja de Jesus (Setúbal), and that of São Lourenço (north-west of Faro).

In addition, there are individual **pousadas** in restored buildings of interest, else-where than in any of the above-listed places, among them those at Vila Nova de Ceveira, Flor da Rosa, Palmela, and Alvito; but see pp 83–5.

**Archaeological sites**: **citânias** at Briteiros, and Sanfins, Chaves (Roman bridge), Conímbriga, Centum Cellas (Belmonte), Bobadela (near Oliveira do Hospital), Quinta da Torre de Palma (Monforte), Vila Formosa (Roman bridge), Cétobriga (Tróia, opposite Setúbal), megalithic remains near Évora (cf.), São Cucufate (near Vila de Frades), Miróbriga (Santiago de Cacém), Pisões (south-west of Beja), Castro da Cola (south of Ourique), Quarteira (near Vilamoura), Milreu (Estói, north of Faro), also Sagres.

**Museums**: Viana do Castelo, Braga (Biscainos, and cathedral museum), Guimarães (Martins Sarmento, and Alberto Sampaio), Braganza (Abad de Baçal), Oporto (Soares dos Reis), Vista Alegre, Aveiro (Convento de Jesus), Lamego, Viseu (Grão Vasco), Guarda, Figueira da Foz, Coimbra (Machado de Castro), Castelo Branco (Tavares Proença Junior), Obidos, Alpiarca, Évora, Beja (N.S. de Conceição), Mértola, and Faro (N.S. da Assunção).

**Military associations**: Almeida, Fuentes de Oñoro (just across the Spanish fron-tier), Freneida, Busaco (also museum, and forest), Roliça, Vimeiro, view of Oporto from N.S. da Serra do Pilar (although much changed), Lines of Torres Vedras, Campo Maior, and Cape St Vincent.

**Lisbon**: a selection only of the more notable and characteristic attractions in the main areas, even if pressed for time:

**Centre and east of centre**: Bairro Baixa and Praça do Comércio (Black Horse Square), Casa de los Bicos, N.S. da Conceição Velha, the Sé (cathedral), Espìrito Santo museum (Decorative Art), the Castelo de São Jorge (for the view), São Vicente de Fora, Santa Engrácia, and further east, the former Madre de Deus convent (Azulejos museum).

**West of centre**: the Chiado and Bairro Alto (and the Chiado museum), São Roch (and museum), the English Cemetery, and Aguas Livres aqueduct; and further west, the outstanding Museu Nacional de Arte Antiga (Janelas Verdes).

At **Belém**: the Coach museum, Jerónimos, the Archaeological and Marine museums, and the Torre de Belém.

**North of centre**: Gulbenkian museum, Museu da Cidade (City museum).

# Introduction to the History of Portugal

By **Richard Robinson**

Portugal emerged as an independent kingdom in the 12C, and its frontiers were established in the following century, so that the country can properly boast of being one of the oldest in Europe. The history of this territory before that period is open to much conjecture, while its prehistory is likewise largely speculative.

## The Romans, and before

Traces of habitation in the west and south-west of the Iberian peninsula date back to **Palaeolithic** times. After the last glaciation the area would seem to have been host to primitive shell-gathering folk (c 7000 BC), but settled communities only developed in the **Neolithic** period. Evidence remains of a dolmen culture, most prevalent in coastal districts, in the 2nd millennium BC. Especially in the north, this megalithic culture was succeeded by a *castro* culture, apparently originating in Neolithic times, but surviving through to the Roman era.

Based on fortified hill-top settlements, some of which appear to have fought shy of the Copper Age and the Bronze Age, this culture would seem to have merged during the Iron Age with that of **Celtic** invaders (c 700–600 BC). An excellent example survives in the *citânia* of Briteiros (in the Minho), although from the evidence of place-names it is suggested that Celtic settlements extended much further south. In the far south there were settlements, possibly from Africa, by people known as **Iberians**, who founded Tharsis. The relationship of these people, as indeed that of the Celts or the Ligurians, to the warrior tribe of the **Lusitani**, based between the Tagus and Douro, is obscure. Like the Bracari, living north of the Douro, they were probably Celts. In the earlier part of the 1st millennium BC the **Phoenicians** were active as traders, setting up coastal stations in the south and exploiting the metals mined inland. They were joined by Greek traders in the 6C BC, but from c 535 the **Carthaginians** held sway, possibly recruiting mercenaries here in the 3C during their wars with Rome.

The peninsula as a whole passed from Carthaginian to **Roman** domination as a result of the Second Punic War (218–202 BC). What was later to become Portugal formed part of their province of Hispania Ulterior, but it took some time for the Romans to overcome resistance. A general rising of the Lusitani in 154 BC led to massacres, and a prolonged guerrilla war in which the Lusitanian leader Viriatus was assassinated by three of his followers who had been bribed by the Romans (139 BC). The Consul Decimus Junius Brutus then set up a 'capital' at Olisipo (Lisbon), and embarked on a campaign to pacify the north.

Lisbon was likewise Julius Caesar's capital in 60 BC, and it was he who was really responsible for incorporating the area into the Empire. Colonists were settled at Scallabis (Santarém), and Pax Julia (Beja) was founded. Other major centres were Ebora (Évora), Myrtilis (Mértola), and Bracara Augusta (Braga). Pacification was not entirely achieved until 19 BC, by which time Hispania Ulterior had already been divided by Augustus (27 BC) into Baetica (Andalucía) and Lusitania (covering the territory of future Portugal south of the Douro, and Spanish Extremadura), with its capital at Emerita Augusta (Mérida). The area between the Douro and the Minho became the *conventus bracarum* of the province of Tarraconensis (created in 2 BC), which in the 3C was to be combined with the north-west corner of the peninsula to form the new province of Gallaecia. Although the boundaries of the provinces had little similarity with the frontiers of what was to become Portugal, the area covered by four of the lesser administrative units (*conventus*) largely conformed to its future extension.

While the effects of Roman rule over this area should not be overestimated, nearly four centuries of their presence left a most important legacy: their language (modern Portuguese being derived from Latin); their traditions of urban civilisation; a network of main roads; precedents for the exploitation of minerals; a legal system; and the establishment of farms on a large scale (*latifundia*) in the south. Evidence of their occupation may be seen at Conímbriga, Évora, Miróbriga (Santiago do Cacém), and elsewhere.

The last century of Roman rule saw the establishment of bishoprics at Braga, Évora, Faro, and Lisbon (the last three dependent on the see of Mérida); and also the appearance of the Arian and Priscillian heresies.

## Suevi, Visigoths, and Moors

With the demise of the Empire, the Peninsula was invaded after AD 409 by four groups of 'barbarians', all from beyond the Pyrenees. The **Vandals** settled in northern Gallaecia, and Baetica; the **Alans** occupied Lusitania, later (in 429) moving across to Africa on the arrival of the Arian Christian **Visigoths**, who c 415 had entered as agents of the Romans. The other group, who remained in the Peninsula, were the **Suevi** (or Swabians), who c 411 had settled between the Minho and Douro, as confirmed by the place-names. Strongest in the countryside, the Suevi co-existed and eventually merged with the urban Hispano-Romans, notably in Braga and Portucale (Oporto). Rechiarus, their king (448–57), although converted to Christianity, was attacked and killed by the Arian Visigoths. The Suevi were reconverted by St Martin of Dume after 550, but their kingdom was suppressed by the Visigothic King Leovigild in 585, whose successor, Recared, was converted to Catholicism.

The unstable elective monarchy of the Visigoths went unchallenged until internal disputes led to the invitation into the Peninsula of **Muslim** forces from Africa, commanded by Tarik (Tariq ibn Ziyād; 711). They advanced rapidly, probably occupying the southern half of the country up to the Mondego by 714/16. Settlement followed c 750, with Egyptians in the Beja-Faro region and Syrians between Faro and Seville, jointly known as al-Gharb al-Andalus, the western part of Muslim Andalucía, from which it became autonomous after a rebellion in the 9C. This area south of the Douro was relatively prosperous under the Muslims, but that to the north, being a battle zone, suffered depopulation.

The Moors introduced new forms of irrigation; rice fields and fruit farms were established in the Algarve (al-Gharb); mineral resources were exploited; handicrafts flourished. And the land, although theoretically owned by the 'State', or by mosques, continued to be worked by Christian smallholding peasants paying rent to urban landlords, who were in turn taxed by the 'State'. These subject Christians (known as Mozárabs), together with the Jews, lived in semi-autonomous quarters, and in comparative tranquillity, at least until c 1099, when a further wave of Muslims, the **Almoravids** (who had landed in the Peninsula from North Africa in 1086) reached the Algarve, to be followed in 1146 by the more fanatical **Almohads**. Meanwhile the Muslims were faced with Christian incursions from the north, before which a proportion of the upper and middle class fled; others were enslaved or were obliged to congregate in Moorish quarters, or *mourarias*, where they could be more easily taxed. During the next three centuries they were absorbed, but in turn left a legacy of hundreds of Arabic words to enrich the language.

## Reconquest, and the emergence of Portugal

The Christian reconquest may be said to have commenced in 718 with Pelayo's symbolic 'victory' over a small force of Moors at Covadonga, in the Asturias. During the next 150 years the kings of Asturias-León made further incursions into Gallaecia (Galicia) and the 'land of Portucale' between the Minho and the Douro. Oporto fell to them in 868. By the 11C Portucale had become established as a county in its own right, although those who ruled it were dependent on Asturias-León. In 1050 **Fernando I** of Castile (1036–65, who had become king of León in 1037) commenced the consolidation of his empire. An incipient 'dynasty' of Portucale was ousted, and in 1064 Coimbra was put under the control of Davidiz, a Mozárab.

In 1065 **Alfonso VI** succeeded his father, Fernando; by 1073 he was also king of Castile, Galicia, and Portugal. Among foreign crusaders who answered his call for support after his defeat by the Almoravids in 1086 was **Raymond of Burgundy**, who later married Alfonso's daughter Urraca. By 1095 Raymond was also lord of Galicia and count of Coimbra. In 1097, **Henry of Burgundy**, Raymond's cousin, was given the County of Portucale, and Coimbra, as *tenente* (feudal possessor).

On the death of Alfonso, a war of succession broke out. Galicia went to Urraca and her son Alfonso Raimúndez (later Alfonso VII). Henry retained Portugal until his death (1112/14), when his wife **Teresa** (illegitimate daughter of Alfonso VI) became 'regent' for their son, **Afonso Henriques**. Teresa fell out with local barons and veered towards subjection to Galicia, which since 1126 had been ruled by Alfonso VII. Young Afonso was more independent, and in 1128, at the battle of São Mamede, near his capital, Guimarães, he defeated his mother's faction. By 1137 his authority in the Minho was recognised by **Alfonso VII** (Pact of Túy), although Afonso Henriques acknowledged his vassalage; and in 1143 this was confirmed by the Treaty of Zamora, in which Alfonso recognised Afonso Henriques's title as *rex* (king) of Portugal.

Complete independence came with the break-up of León-Castile at Alfonso's death, and this was formally recognised by Pope Alexander III in 1179 (on payment of an increased tribute). Afonso Henriques was also supported by João Peculiar, Archbishop of Braga, whose right to a diocese independent of Toledo and Santiago de Compostela had been won by his predecessor, St Gerald of Moissac.

In Portugal, the Reconquest took a century and a half to complete, far faster than in the rest of the Peninsula. Santarém and Lisbon had been first captured in the 11C, but the Christians had been pushed back to the Mondego by the Almoravids; and the pattern of advances followed by reverses repeated itself during the reign of Afonso Henriques, who in 1139 inflicted a decisive defeat on the Moors at Ourique during one of his periodic raids. Santarém was retaken in 1147, while Lisbon likewise fell to him with the assistance of crusaders from northern Europe en route via Dartmouth to the Holy Land. Gilbert of Hastings was the first bishop of Lisbon, but dependent on Braga. Alcácer do Sal was captured in 1158, and in 1162 and 1165 both Beja and Évora were seized by Fernão Gonçalves and Gerald 'sem Pavor' (the Fearless); but in 1171 the Almohads pushed the Christians back to Santarém.

The Western Algarve was invaded by **Dom Sancho I** (1185–1211), who captured the Moorish capital at Silves in 1189 with the help of another contingent of passing crusaders, but all this territory south of the Tagus, except for Évora, was lost to him during al-Mansur's campaign the following year. **Dom Afonso II** (1211–23) recaptured Setúbal and Alcácer do Sal, likewise with the assistance of crusaders, while during the anarchic reign of **Dom Sancho II** (1223–48) the Alentejo and eastern Algarve were incorporated into the expanding kingdom. **Dom Afonso III** (1248–79) moved the capital from Coimbra to Lisbon, and occupied Faro and the western Algarve in 1249. Definitive recognition by Castile of the frontiers of the Portuguese kingdom was endorsed by the Treaty of Alcañices in 1297.

## Political and Social Organisation

The new kingdom had a population estimated at 400,000, with the northern half of the country much more heavily populated than the reconquered area. Internal colonisation followed in the wake of the reconquest. Communities were planted in Trás-os-Montes and Beira, and much land south of the Tagus passed into the hands of the military orders, the Templars, and the Hospitallers (from c 1128), and from the 1170s into those of Santiago and Calatrava. The religious orders also played an important part. The Cistercians were given land at Alcobaça in 1153, and did much to develop the area immediately to the south. By 1263 the Algarve was settled, and the towns of Covilhã, Guarda, and Idanha were founded to guard the frontier with León; while stock-rearing, the cultivation of olives and vines, and the growing of cereal crops took the place of more belligerent activities.

The kings of the Burgundian line, advised by rudimentary royal councils, began to consult the opinion of assembled nobles and clergy, the first of such *Cortes* being held at Coimbra in 1211. Municipal representation was conceded at the *Cortes* of Leiria (1254), called to agree to an increase in taxation and to a devaluation of the coinage. Royal power was only theoretically limited by the *Cortes*, which was summoned more frequently in times of financial stringency. Although a free peasantry was the dominant characteristic of society, the rights of subjects, particularly those in the towns, were defined by the king in a charter or *foral* (Pl. *forais*). Moors were still segregated in their *mourarias*, and Jews in their *judarias*, which were both under royal jurisdiction.

The next most powerful body in the emergent country was the Church. The clergy, who were extremely wealthy, were at first dominant in the society of orders, and were in theory immune from taxation; they collected their own 'tenths' (*dízimos*), and from 1210 held their own courts. The king appointed bishops and abbots, and could prevent Papal decisions being applied in his realm. There were constant disputes over the extent of jurisdictions, and the king inhibited the acquisition of property by ecclesiastics and nobles by instituting periodic inquiries (*inquirições*), which might result either in confiscations or in the reconfirmation of title. The concordat of 1289 settled most outstanding conflicts, and to the king's advantage).

Lay society was controlled by about one hundred *ricos homens*, an aristocratic warrior class possessing estates, dependents, and jurisdictions. Then came perhaps one thousand *infanções*, or lesser nobles (without jurisdictions), apart from more numerous *fidalgos*, men-at-arms attached to the king or to nobles. Among the Commons (or 'third estate'), free peasants predominated. The better-off (*homens bons*) represented the municipalities (*concelhos*) at the *Cortes*, whose power grew with the growth of the economy, and provided the villein-knights (*cavalheiros vilãos*), who defended the newly-established frontier. Although juridically free, many peasants were tied to their lord's demesne or were long-term tenants. The need to repopulate the south blurred existing distinctions between Christian serfs and free settlers, and serfdom would seem to have disappeared by the 13C, except for numbers of Moorish slaves.

## Apogee and Decline of the Afonsin Dynasty

First among the last four Burgundian kings to perfect the administrative system, to boost agriculture and trade, and generally to consolidate Portuguese independence, was **Dom Dinis** (1279–1325), by then ruling over about one million subjects. The judicial systems, both lay and ecclesiastical, were brought under royal control; silver-mines, and those of tin, sulphur, and iron, were exploited; and his progressive afforestation schemes won him the nickname of 'El-Rei lavrador', the Husbandman King. He also cultivated music and poetry. The military orders were 'nationalised'. The Templars, suppressed by the Papacy in 1312, were refounded as the Order of Christ in 1319. Fifty forts were built along the frontier. The promotion of 'free fairs' encouraged internal trade, while Portugal's geographical position made her an ideal intermediary between the maritime powers of northern Europe and the Mediterranean. Both Lisbon (provided with a university in 1290, but transferred to Coimbra in 1308) and Oporto flourished.

The country was ravaged by the Black Death during the reign of **Dom Afonso IV** (1325–57)—it decimated the population in 1348–49. In 1355 the murder took place of Inês de Castro (the Galician mistress of the Infante Pedro), whose family was suspected of furthering Castilian interests.

**Dom Pedro I**'s reign (1357–67) saw further centralisation of the judicial system; by now Portuguese was the language of the law and administration. His successor, **Dom Fernando** (1367–83), while continuing to encourage maritime trade, attempted to combat the growing agricultural crisis, accelerated if not caused by the Black Death, for the demand for labour in the cities had attracted the peasantry away from the land and led to food shortages by the 1370s. The Law of the Sesmarias (1375) was accordingly promulgated, which sought to bring more land under cultivation and to control the movement of labour.

Portugal had become involved in the Hundred Years War. Castilian legitimists assumed that Dom Fernando would succeed to the Castilian throne on the death of Pedro the Cruel, but in the event it was seized by **Enrique de Trastámara** (Enrique II), who invaded Portugal and in February 1373 sacked Lisbon. Portugal was at this time allied with **John of Gaunt**, Duke of Lancaster, who also claimed the Castilian throne (for both he and Edmund, Earl of Cambridge, had married daughters of Pedro the Cruel).

Partly owing to the failure of the English to send troops, Dom Fernando was obliged to make peace with Castile at the Treaty of Santarém (March 1373), ostensibly switching his allegiance to Enrique, although he remained in touch with John of Gaunt. On Enrique's death in 1379, Dom Fernando started parallel negotiations, promising Beatriz (or Brites), his ten-year-old heiress, to Edward, six-year-old son of Edmund of Cambridge, at the same time suggesting that she might marry the infant son of Juan I, Enrique's successor. Edmund of Cambridge arrived at Lisbon in June 1381 with 3000 men to assist in the planned attack on Juan.

Edward was betrothed to Beatriz. But the troops were not supplied with the promised mounts, and the campaign collapsed. Edmund and his son returned to England late in 1382. Meanwhile Dom Fernando, disappointed and much debilitated, and by now under the influence of his wife Leonor Teles de Meneses (who had taken as her lover a Galician knight, Juan Fernández Andeiro, Count of Ourém), continued to play a double game. Beatriz was now to marry Juan I himself, who had recently become a widower. Portugal would be governed by a council of regency until any child of the marriage was old enough to succeed, while should they remain childless, the Castilian king would guarantee the autonomy of Portugal. Beatriz left for Castile in May 1383 and in October Dom Fernando died, aged 38. Leonor Teles, his unpopular widow, attempted to govern the country with Andeiro, but some six weeks later her lover was assassinated by João, an illegitimate son of Dom Pedro I.

João, who was also Grand Master of the Order of Avis (formerly Calatrava), became regent; Leonor, although she had the backing of the majority of the nobility and bishops (but not the archbishop), being driven out by a revolt of the mercantile and lower orders of Lisbon. João rewarded the citizens by allowing representatives of their guilds to form a committee—later known as the House of the 24—to share in the administration of the capital.

In the face of another Castilian invasion, Portugal again sought English aid in her defence. Another siege of Lisbon was only raised by plague spreading through the invader's ranks. In the countryside a sense of national independence was intensified by grievances against the pro-Castilian nobles who had acquired crown lands in previous decades. Few of the latter were to survive the decisive battle fought near **Aljubarrota** on 14 August 1385, when Nun'Álvares Pereira, the 'Holy Constable', aided by some English archers, defeated the army of Juan of Castile. João of Avis was shortly after crowned at Coimbra, the first ruler of the new dynasty.

# The House of Avis

The revolution of 1383 led to the replacement of the old nobility by a new landed aristocracy dependent on **Dom João I** (1385–1433), a change of personnel rather than a social revolution. Mutual interest led to the signing of the Treaty of Windsor in 1386, formally confirming the Anglo-Portuguese Alliance of 1373, which was still being invoked in the 20C.

In 1387 Dom João I married **Philippa of Lancaster**, daughter of John of Gaunt, Duke of Lancaster. The struggle against Castile continued until 1411, after which Dom João kept some of his closer supporters happy by adopting an aggressive policy in Morocco, and Ceuta was taken in 1415. His successor, **Dom Duarte** (Edward; 1433–38), hoping to capture Tangier in 1437, met with disaster.

An attempt by Duarte to revoke some titles to land, promulgated by the Lei Mental of 1434 (decreeing that in the absence of a son to inherit, estates would revert to the crown) not unnaturally brought about a reaction from the nobility, which continued during the minority of **Dom Afonso V** (1438–81). In 1440 the Duke of Coimbra, associated with the 'peace party', seized the Regency from Dom Afonso's mother, Eleanor of Aragón, to the chagrin of the Duke of Braganza's party, who sought to undermine royal power. Dom Afonso, however, supported the Braganza faction, and the Duke of Coimbra was killed at the internecine battle of Alfarrobeira in 1449.

Although there had been some unification of legal codes during Dom Afonso's minority, the young king was more concerned with martial glory to be gained by crusading in North Africa. In 1471 Tangier was eventually taken. On the death of his Castilian brother-in-law Enrique IV in 1474, Dom Afonso supported Juana (Enrique's daughter, whom he hoped to marry), in her claim to the throne, but, defeated at Castro Queimado and failing to enlist French support, he had to concede to the Catholic Kings his own pretensions to the Canary Islands at the peace treaty of Alcáçovas (1479).

## The Making of the Maritime Empire

In the 15C Portugal was in the vanguard of European overseas exploration and expansion, although it had little naval or ocean-going tradition, even if Dom Dinis had employed a Genoese admiral to found a navy, and his successor Dom Afonso IV had encouraged non-Portuguese voyages to the Canaries. The activities of **Prince Henry** (a younger son of Dom João I and Philippa), administrator of the property of the Order of Christ, and known to history as 'the Navigator' (although he never ventured beyond Tangier in person), were an extension of his dual concerns with crusading and profit. In the wake of the capture of Ceuta, he built up at Lagos an international team of pilots, cartographers, astronomers, etc. The motives of Henry and subsequent expansionists were mixed. They included the desire to spread the Faith; to outflank Islam in Morocco; to become purveyors of gold, spices and slaves (long the role of the Infidel); to win renown by the conquest of more territory; and mere curiosity.

The 'adjacent islands' of Madeira and the Azores were discovered (or rediscovered) in 1419 and 1427 respectively, and both were subsequently colonised. The psychological barrier represented by Cape Bojador was rounded in 1434, and a trading-post set up at Arguim in the 1440s became a prime source of slaves. The Cape Verde Islands, later colonised by the Order of Christ, were discovered c 1457, while Sierra Leone had been reached by Henry's death in 1460. There followed a significant lull in the process of exploration until the reign of **Dom João II** (1481–95). That maritime enterprise paid off was strikingly confirmed when the Crown's revenue doubled with the establishment of São Jorge da Mina (1482), source of Sudanese gold. In 1487 Bartolomeu Dias rounded the Cape of Good Hope. After Papal arbitration, Spain and Portugal divided the world at the Treaty of Tordesillas (1494) at a line 370 leagues west of the Cape Verdes.

## Dom Manuel I

**Dom Manuel I** (1495–1521) and **Dom João III** (1521–57) promoted such expansion as part of a royal enterprise, the Crown taking its 'royal fifth' of the trading profits, which made Dom Manuel for a time the richest ruler in Europe. Vasco da Gama opened the route to India in 1497–98; Newfoundland, Greenland and Labrador were reached and Brazil discovered in 1500, although the exploration of Brazilian resources hardly started until the second half of the 16C, its sugar plantations stimulating the South Atlantic slave trade and leading to the foundation of Luanda in 1575. Morocco was not forgotten—Dom Manuel campaigned there in 1513–15, and Dom João III continued to hold Tangier, Ceuta and Mazagan—but the main target was Asia. By 1513 the Portuguese had reached Timor and China, and sailed on to Japan in the 1540s. In 1519 Magellan, born in the Trás-os-Montes, although at that time in the Spanish service, set out on his voyage of circumnavigation, only to be killed in the Philippines.

It was the monopoly of maritime trade which was now their primary concern, and the Asian empire therefore depended on the founding of key trading-posts (from which missionaries could also operate) and strategically placed forts. Goa grew in importance from 1510; Malacca was occupied in 1511, and Hormuz in 1515. A trading-post was set up at Macau in 1557.

Yet the growth of this impressive maritime empire did not in fact improve economic conditions at home, for the profits of trade got no further than the royal household, some of the quiescent nobility, and a few foreign merchants. What was essentially a royal project did not lead to the emergence of an entrepreneurial class, as had happened in northern European countries. But although overseas trade was estimated to constitute two-thirds of Portuguese revenue in the 16C, the cost was such that even the Crown fell into debt. Falling prices in Europe brought about a deficit in the spice and allied trades from the 1520s, and the royal trading monopoly, the Casa da Índia, was bankrupt by 1560; more and more of the proceeds of empire went to pay foreign debts. By the 1570s the picture was one of exhaustion. Although agricultural production had picked up after 1450, by the 1540s shortages of meat and cereals were again experienced, partially as a result of the continuing drift to the cities. Despite the essentially commercial nature of the empire, the heavy drain on population and the high cost of the material upkeep of its fleets were among its negative consequences.

# The Decline of the House of Avis

When 'the perfect prince', **Dom João II**, ascended the throne, he set about reversing his predecessor's profligacy in granting land to the nobility. In 1483 the Duke of Braganza, head of a family whose estates covered a third of the kingdom, was executed, and his possessions seized by the Crown. In the following year the queen's brother, the Duke of Viseu, was also eliminated. The nobility remained submissive as royal power thus asserted became more centralised and bureaucratic. Dom João II turned the complaints of the commons with regard to Jews against the nobles in the *Cortes*, but the nobility were not arraigned there by the king; and under **Dom Manuel**, 'the Fortunate', both *Cortes* and nobility were eclipsed. The taxation of the *concelhos* was regulated and the *forais* reformed, while the exercise of justice was brought completely under royal control. In 1521 the promulgation of a legal code, the 'Ordenações manuelinas', brought all separate jurisdictions to an end. Royal patronage of the *misericórdias* (charitable institutions ministering to the sick and the needy) encouraged their spread both at home and overseas during the 16C.

In the Middle Ages Portugal's treatment of its Jewish minority was, by international standards, lenient, but by 1490 popular resentment of their tax-gathering and moneylending activities was being voiced in the *Cortes*. When the Catholic Kings expelled the Spanish Jews in 1492, some 60,000 of them took refuge in Portugal, but four years later Dom Manuel also decreed their expulsion. Although a minority left for the Netherlands, most of them ostensibly submitted to baptism as 'New Christians'. Anti-Jewish rioting in Lisbon in 1504 was followed by a pogrom in 1506. Although Dom Manuel had given the forcibly converted a twenty-year period of grace before investigating their religious convictions, it was not until 1531, prompted by the threat of the Protestant Reformation, that **Dom João III** personally introduced the Inquisition into Portugal, encouraged, it is said, by his younger brother, the Cardinal-Infante Dom Afonso. This was established with Papal permission in 1536, but was not properly organised until 1547, and then was as much an instrument to control the growing middle classes (particularly those intermarried with 'New Christians') as a tool for rooting out heresy. Of 24,522 people investigated over the next two centuries, 1454 were condemned to death; others suffered lesser fates.

The late 15th and 16C witnessed a flowering of the arts and literature under the centralised monarchy. Printing was introduced c 1487, and there were many contacts with the humanism of the Renaissance. Portugal escaped the Reformation, but not the Counter-Reformation. From the 1560s the control of education passed into the hands of the Jesuits. A number of colleges were founded in the 1530s and 1540s, and in 1537 the University was reorganised at Coimbra. This was the epoch of the dramatist Gil Vicente, while in 1572 Luís de Camões published his national epic, *The Lusiads*. The arts and 'Manueline' architecture of this period are described in the Introduction to Art and Archtecture.

The reign of **Dom Sebastião** (1557–78) saw a disastrous reversion to the crusading ideals of Dom Afonso V. Morocco was the obsession of this unstable, chivalric dreamer, who came of age in 1568. Sensing his opportunity when the succession to the sultanate of Fez was in dispute, he raised a force of 18,000 (including a contingent commanded by Sir Thomas Stukely, a papist), and in 1578 set sail from the Algarve with high expectation. Dom Sebastião himself was killed and his army decisively defeated by a superior force at Alcácer-Quibir (al-Qasr al-Kabir), some 8000 Portuguese, including the flower of the nobility, being left on the field; and only 100 or so escaped capture. The raising of ruinous ransoms for the rest was the primary preoccupation of Cardinal Henrique, Dom Sebastião's elderly great-uncle.

# Habsburg Domination

The succession to the childless Cardinal-King Henrique (1578–80) was disputed, and **António, Prior of Crato**, a royal bastard, had himself proclaimed king; but he failed to emulate the precedent of 1383. A Spanish army under the 3rd Duke of Alba, supporting the claim of Dom Sebastião's uncle, Philip (Felipe) II of Spain, defeated the prior's troops at Alcántara, and in 1581 the *Cortes* at Tomar proclaimed the Habsburg king as **Dom Felipe I** (1581–98). Although the Crowns were thus united, Portuguese autonomy was to be 'respected'.

An attempt by the Prior of Crato to regain the throne in 1589 with the support of Drake (taking his revenge for the 'Armada' of the previous year, a proportion of which had set sail from Lisbon), was unsuccessful. Dom Felipe suppressed the challenges of various 'false Sebastians' who presented themselves. (There was a popular messianic belief that Dom Sebastião was still alive, and would on his return inaugurate a 'fifth empire' of Portuguese dominance, there being some confusion with earlier prophecies with regard to the advent of a *rei encoberto* or 'hidden king'.)

The union with Spain brought some short-term advantages. Spanish wheat made up for Portugal's deficiency, and Portugal found a protector for her vulnerable empire, while Habsburg generosity in granting titles benefited those few who could afford them. But the Spaniards were unpopular with the lower orders, who blamed them for the country's decline. The closure of Lisbon to Dom Felipe's Dutch rebels was held responsible for Dutch attacks in the East, but the defence of their maritime empire was by the 17C beyond the capacity of the Portuguese alone. During the 'Spanish captivity', Hormuz was lost to the English (1622), while the Dutch invaded both Ceylon and African territories. After the return to independence, Salvador de Sá chased the Dutch from Luanda and São Tomé (1648), and although Brazil was recovered by 1652, the Asian empire continued to shrink: the Dutch took Malacca in 1641, and Ceylon in the 1650s.

Although Dom Felipe I carried out certain administrative reforms, he respected Portuguese autonomy; but his successor, **Dom Felipe II** (III of Spain; 1598–1621) violated these undertakings by appointing Spaniards to the Council of Portugal in Madrid. Nevertheless, the *Cortes* gave him a tolerably warm welcome in 1619, and agreed that his son should succeed, but under **Dom Felipe III** (IV of Spain; 1621–40) the erosion of Portuguese autonomy continued. During the Thirty Years War Spain's lack of men and money led to increasing centralisation under the Count-Duke of Olivares, which provoked discontent in Portugal and elsewhere, even if the need for cash necessitated a more lenient attitude towards the 'New Christians'.

Hispanicisation of the élite; the absorption of the army and navy into the Spanish forces; increased taxation: all lent force to the latent spirit of independence in Portugal. Popular disturbances occurred at Évora in 1637, while in June 1640 Catalonia revolted. Olivares attempted to use Portuguese resources to crush this rising, which partially provoked the coup of 1 December 1640 in Lisbon. The Duchess of Mantua, the governor, was overthrown, and Miguel de Vasconcelos, her strongman, was defenestrated. The nobility, office-holders, and the clergy, were divided in their loyalties, but with popular support the movement for independence succeeded under the leadership of the reluctant but powerful Duke of Braganza, grandson of a female claimant of 1580, who became **Dom João IV** (1640–56).

## Restoration

The continuing revolt of the Catalans enabled the Portuguese to consolidate their newly won independence and, in the context of the Thirty Years War, Spain was also preoccupied with France until the Treaty of the Pyrenees in 1659. Meanwhile the English had renewed their old alliance with Portugal regardless of changes of regime: to the pledges of Charles I (1642) and Oliver Cromwell (1654) was added the Treaty of 1661, by which Charles II married Catherine of Braganza and Portugal ceded Tangier and Bombay. In 1659 Spain attacked and captured Elvas, but the Portuguese army, reorganised by the Duke of Schomberg, with a modest English contingent, won the battles of Ameixial, Castelo Rodrigo and Montes Claros (1663–65). In 1668 Spain, while retaining Ceuta, recognised Portuguese independence at the Treaty of Lisbon and the Papacy followed the Spanish lead.

Internally, Dom João IV endeavoured to create a centralised and bureaucratic administration run by secretaries of state. The demands of war had enabled him to force the *Cortes* to agree to a high level of taxation and to provide a defence levy, while the 'New Christians' and others were won over by the return of property confiscated by the Inquisition. His allies among the nobility were rewarded with lands, and some gained considerable power, which they attempted to consolidate during the confused reign of the paralytic **Dom Afonso VI** (1656–83). In 1667 the king's brother, Pedro, was persuaded by the Queen Mother and the French to oust the Regent, Castelo Melhor. Pedro ruled as Prince Regent, marrying his brother's former wife, Maria-Francesca d'Aumale, her marriage having been formally annulled. From 1683 to 1706 he ruled as **Dom Pedro II**, during which years royal authority was strengthened. Portugal was reconciled with the Papacy, and little recourse was had to the *Cortes*, summoned for the last time in 1697. For more than a century the Crown was financially independent of that body.

## The Age of Mercantilism

Dom Pedro II's most notable appointment was that of the 3rd Conde de Ericeira to the post of Superintendent of Finance in 1675. For the next fifteen years, until his suicide in 1690, this exponent of mercantilist ideas did much to improve the country's prosperity, by boosting exports and restricting the importation of luxury goods. Commerce prospered, being protected by tariffs, ranging from the textiles of Covilhã, Portalegre and Fundão to the production of hats and glass. But after his death the economy again deteriorated.

With a view to balancing trade as Brazilian sugar lost its markets, the famous Methuen Treaty of December 1703 was signed (called after its negotiator, John Methuen), not to be confused with the Anglo-Portuguese Treaty of May 1703 (signed by his son Sir Paul Methuen). England admitted Portuguese wines on preferential terms, which benefited Portugal in the short run. In the longer term it stimulated the port-wine trade, but arguably misdirected attention from the necessity of growing more wheat. English textiles were assured of a permanent market in Portugal, but the dominance of English goods, at first imported on the same terms as French and Dutch, was a product of the boom in Anglo-Portuguese trade made possible by the gold of Brazil. English merchants ran the carrying trade, and English competition adversely affected Portuguese industry in coastal areas, although not in the interior. The Methuen Treaty did not in itself prevent industrialisation in Portugal, although coupled with strategic factors it did in the long term increase Portugal's dependence on Britain. The Treaty was not revoked until 1842.

Portugal sided with Britain during the War of the Spanish Succession (1702–13) in supporting the Habsburg claimant to the Spanish throne in preference to a Bourbon. A Franco-Spanish invasion was repelled, and an Anglo-Portuguese force commanded by the Marquês das Minas entered Spain, even occupying Madrid briefly in the summer of 1706, but they were defeated at Almansa in 1707. With the accession of **Dom João V** (1706–50) the country took little further part in the conflict.

The absolutist monarchy built up by Dom João V and his successors was made possible by the exploitation and influx of gold from Brazil, which began in the 1690s and reached its peak c 1740. The Crown's revenue soared as it took its fifth, and every attempt was made to ensure that none was smuggled direct from Brazil to Britain, but as this gold had to pay for foreign imports, it had little direct beneficial effect on the country's economic development. Dom João V's ministers still followed Ericeira's practice in endeavouring to protect national industries, but measures such as the ban on buying foreign silk proved ineffective. Evidence of the 18C gold boom survives in the richly gilded woodwork adorning most Baroque churches, and in the gigantic Germanic palace of Mafra, on whose construction perhaps as many as 50,000 workmen were employed between 1717 and 1735.

Although the devout king had early in his reign sent a fleet to help the Papacy against the Turks, a fleet victorious at the battle of Matapan in 1717, the general tendency of policy was towards increasing royal control over ecclesiastical affairs. Dom João V favoured clerical reform and was opposed to the ossified educational practices of the long-dominant Jesuits. He therefore determined that the Papacy should agree to all bishops of Lisbon being Cardinal-Patriarchs, and a breach with the Papacy opened in 1728 was only healed in 1748 with Papal compliance to the king's wish. Reconciliation was complete when the Pope conferred on Dom João V the title of 'El-Rei fidelíssimo' (Most Faithful King). Meanwhile, he had exhibited a desire for cultural improvement by founding the Royal Academy of History in 1720; but the intellectual élite came increasingly under the influence of progressive ideas current in Britain and France, gaining for themselves the nickname *estrangeirados* ('foreignised ones').

Dom João V's successor, **Dom José** (1750–77) was more interested in the opera, introduced from Italy in the 1730s, and management of affairs of state was left in the hands of his ruthless minister, Sebastião José de Carvalho e Melo, **1st Marquês de Pombal**, who had been ambassador in London in the 1740s. Pombal's policies were initially pragmatic responses to circumstances. He endeavoured to improve the administration in order to extract the maximum profit from the colonies, and smuggling was inhibited. He created a tax-collecting bureaucracy and, in 1761, the Royal Treasury. State monopoly companies were founded to control the tobacco and port-wine industries, whaling, fishing, and the Asian and Brazil trades. It was the economic depression of the 1760s which prompted a more deliberate strategy for economic development. As Brazilian gold and diamond production declined, Pombal sought to boost agriculture and to build up industry at home, especially in the Lisbon area.

Like his father, Dom José was personally devout, but the *estrangeirado* Pombal went further down the road towards secular autocracy and Enlightened Despotism. He incurred the hostility of the Jesuits by emancipating their Indian protégés in Brazil, to the advantage of the settlers, while his methods for dealing with any opposition to reform became clear when the anti-monopolistic merchant association of the Mesa do Bem Comum was dissolved, and the taverners' (or Tipplers') revolt in Oporto was brutally put down in 1757.

On 1 November 1755 Lisbon was convulsed by an earthquake, in which a large part of the capital collapsed, and perhaps as many as 30–40,000 people died, not only in the earthquake itself but in the epidemics and famine that followed. During and after this calamity Pombal's position of power was supreme. For while Jesuits preached that the tremors represented Divine Judgement on the dictator's wayward policies, this, together with a mysterious attempt on the king's life in 1758, gave the minister an opportunity of neutralising any potential opposition. The Jesuits themselves, together with certain nobles, were held by Pombal to have been responsible for the attempted assassination, and the execution of members of the powerful Távora family followed, while Fr Malagrida, a leading Jesuit, was burned at the stake. In 1759 the Society of Jesus was dissolved and its members exiled. (In 1773 the Papacy was persuaded to suppress it altogether: at least for some decades.)

The rational principle of uniformity was applied to the juridical sphere. Slavery was abolished in mainland Portugal in 1761; Royal censorship replaced ecclesiastical; the Inquisition became a Department of State; and all distinctions between old and 'New' Christians were abolished. The Papal Nuncio was expelled. This secularisation of the State was accompanied by university reforms, and faculties of science were established. Royal schools were founded along the lines advocated by the exiled Portuguese philosopher Luís António Verney, and included one specifically for the nobility. In his authoritarian way, by dragging the country into the century of Enlightenment, Pombal laid the foundation of the modern Portuguese state. He was also responsible for the laying out of the present Baixa quarter of Lisbon, built in a Neo-classical style, and his rational attempts at town-planning may also be seen on a smaller scale at Vila Real de Santo António in the Algarve. Military reforms were undertaken, supervised by the Count of Schaumburg-Lippe, after Portugal had been again invaded following opposition to the Bourbon Family Compact of 1761 during the Seven Years War (1756–63).

On the succession of **Dona Maria I** (1777–1816), Pombal was immediately dismissed, tried, and confined to his considerable estates. Under this unduly devout queen (who also suffered from melancholia), his religious legislation was repealed, a concordat signed with the Vatican, and censorship again made an ecclesiastical concern. Although some monopoly companies were abolished, Pombal's economic policies were nevertheless implemented. Roads and canals were built, shipbuilding and mineral prospecting were encouraged, the textile industry was modernised, and attempts were made to improve agricultural methods. The Royal Academy of

Sciences was established in 1779, as were various technical academies. Full advantage was taken of Portugal's position as a middleman between Brazil (where cotton was replacing gold as a major export) and Britain, with which a trade balance was achieved. Dependence on Britain was offset by diversification of trade, and a trading and diplomatic alliance was entered into with Russia. Portugal seemed at last to be on the road to prosperity when in 1789 Europe was convulsed by the French Revolution.

## The Napoleonic Era

The reign of Dona Maria I united material progress with political conservatism. One of her ministers, the Intendant-General of Police, Pina Manique, brought security and street-lighting to Lisbon and founded an orphanage. But at the same time he was zealous in persecuting potential subversives, such as Freemasons, particularly after 1789, until to appease the French, he was retired. Fearful that revolution might be contagious and spread to Brazil, Portugal sent troops to fight revolutionary France on the Catalan front (1793), but after 1795 she stood alone with England against the Directory, and in 1801 was invaded by Spain during the so-called 'War of the Oranges', being compelled to cede the district around Olivença. Dependent for half her trade on Britain, and on British sea-power to protect her trade routes, more so after Trafalgar (1805), Portugal could hardly comply with Napoleon's demands that she close her ports to British shipping; and invasion by the French was the inevitable consequence.

General Junot entered Lisbon in 1807, but the royal family (with João as Prince Regent since 1799) had already embarked for Brazil, where they set up court. The Portuguese invoked the British alliance, and an expeditionary force, at first commanded by Sir Arthur Wellesley, later landed near the mouth of the Mondego. In August 1808 the French were defeated at Roliça and Vimeiro. By the reprehensible Convention of Cintra, signed soon after, the French were repatriated (with their booty) in English ships. Marshal Soult, turning south after Sir John Moore's retreating army had embarked at Corunna (16 January 1809), then invaded the north of Portugal, but on 12 May 1809 was driven out of Oporto by Wellesley, who had by then returned to Portugal after exoneration by a Court of Enquiry in London into the Convention he had been obliged to sign by his superiors. It was only after his victory at Talavera, in Spain, that July, that he was known as **Viscount Wellington**.

Meanwhile, he had ordered the secret construction of lines of defence, passing near Torres Vedras, to protect Lisbon from probable future French incursions, while William Carr Beresford was busy organising and imparting discipline to Portuguese forces, who at Busaco (27 September 1810) were able to take their place beside Wellington's seasoned troops in inflicting severe losses on another invading army, this time under Marshal Masséna. Portuguese troops continued to be integrated with the British until the end of the Peninsular War.

The French settled before the 'Lines of Torres Vedras', thoroughly frustrated, until, in the following spring, they were forced by sheer starvation to retire, hostilities being carried back into Spain (at the battles of Fuentes de Oñoro, and Albuera; May 1811). It should be remembered that numerous units of the British army were stationed along the Spanish frontier for several winters, mostly between the Douro and Guadiana. Wellington besieged and took the fortresses of Ciudad Rodrigo and Badajoz early in 1812, and in that July inflicted a stunning defeat on the French at Salamanca. After months of preparation during the following winter, in May 1813 he was able to surprise the French by swinging the bulk of his army north of the Douro, behind their right flank, and pursued them beyond Vitoria (21 June), where they were badly mauled, although the war did not end until after the battle of Toulouse in April 1814.

At the peace settlement, Olivença should have been restored to Portugal, but the decision of the Powers was conveniently forgotten by the Spaniards. The consequences of the French invasion and occupation were very much graver than this slight loss of territory. The process of industrialisation had been interrupted, and the vital links with Brazil (proclaimed a kingdom on equal terms with Portugal in 1815) were fatally weakened, although the court remained in Rio de Janeiro until 1821. Portuguese affairs were left meanwhile in the hands of Marshal Beresford, respected but not popular. Britain had preserved Portuguese independence, but the Anglo-Portuguese treaty of 1810, which allowed Britain to trade freely and directly with Brazil, removed the mainstay of the homeland's economy. The country was deep in debt and trade was bad. From 1808 until 1821 Portugal was in effect a British protectorate and a colony of Brazil. **Dom João VI** succeeded his deranged mother on her death in 1816.

# Constitutionalism

The growth of liberal ideas was for long associated with those who had served Napoleon. In 1817 a former commander of Napoleon's Portuguese Legion, and a Masonic Grand Master, Gomes Freire de Andrade, and 11 accomplices, were executed by Beresford for conspiracy, but this act of repression had little influence on the course of events. The large military establishment had not yet been disbanded and three-quarters of the national revenue was still spent on the army. Even so, officers resented not being paid regularly, and—as is their wont—complained of lack of promotion. In August 1820, while Beresford was visiting Brazil, soldiers in Oporto in touch with the Sinédrio lodge established by the liberal reformer, Manuel Fernandes Tomás, 'pronounced' against the government, ushering in thirty years of political turmoil, which did little to help the parlous economic situation.

As with similar risings in Spain, the rebel officers called a constituent *Cortes*, which proceeded to pass reforms, drawing up a constitutional document much influenced by Fernandes Tomás and the Spanish liberal constitution of 1812. Although ostensibly seeking a return to pre-absolutist times, the Constitution of 1822 was based on the ideals of the Enlightenment. Seigneurial rights and the *forais* were abolished, as were clerical privileges and the Inquisition: provisions which offended the Church. Despite a desire to promote agriculture in a climate of free enterprise, corporations and monopoly companies were not dissolved. Administrative and judicial decentralisation was decreed, and a single-chamber parliament instituted. The king, who eventually returned to Portugal in 1821, having been absent for 14 years, accepted the constitution which allowed him to suspend laws but not to dissolve the assembly. This was chosen every two years by an electorate excluding illiterates, women, and the clergy. Attempts by the constituent *Cortes* to restrict Brazilian autonomy led to independence being declared by Crown Prince Pedro on behalf of the creole élite in 1822, but Portugal only accepted the loss of Brazil in 1825.

In 1823 a rural reaction against liberal constitutionalism began, headed by Pedro's younger brother, Miguel, and his mother Carlota Joaquina (sister of the Spanish king, Fernando VII). The constitution was suspended, but Dom João VI sent his son Miguel into exile. On Dom João's death in 1826, his son Pedro (constitutional Emperor of Brazil) was appointed king by the Regency Council and, as **Dom Pedro IV**, he promulgated the Royal Charter (1826), the fundamental constitutional text of 19C Portugal—but a less advanced document than the Constitution of 1822—in which a Chamber of Deputies was partly elected on a restricted suffrage and partly nominated; an upper chamber consisted of hereditary peers. Dom Pedro conditionally abdicated in favour of his young daughter, Maria da Glória. It was planned that she would marry his brother, Miguel, who was appointed Regent. But immediately on his return from exile, Miguel abolished the constitution and convoked the traditional *Cortes*, and appears to have enjoyed considerable popular support for this move, although only the United States and Mexico recognised him when he proclaimed himself king.

Prior to his return, **Saldanha**, the War Minister, and a grandson of Pombal, had promoted a number of liberal officers, who were to lead military uprisings in Oporto and Coimbra. Saldanha himself, together with the Duke of Palmela, went into exile in England. In 1830 Dom Pedro IV was proclaimed Regent in the Azores, and with the backing of English and Spanish liberals, set up a government led by Palmela and José Xavier Mousinho da Silveira. Encouraged by France and England, a liberal expedition landed near Oporto in 1832, where it was besieged. The deadlock was only broken when the Duke of Terceira landed in the Algarve, under the protection of Charles Napier's naval squadron, and marched on Lisbon (1833). Miguel's forces then laid siege to the capital, but were defeated by Terceira and Saldanha and forced to capitulate at Évoramonte in May 1834. Miguel was again exiled, his supporters purged, and a liberal regime imposed on the indifferent population by the Quadruple Alliance (Britain, France, and Spanish and Portuguese liberals). Liberalism remained dependent for its survival on this foreign support throughout the 1840s.

# The Age of Revolution

Steps were taken to reduce the enormous debts accumulated during the 'War of the Two Brothers' or Miguelite War. Mousinho da Silveira drafted another blueprint for the regeneration of Portugal along the lines pioneered by Fernandes Tomás. The administrative and judicial systems were reformed on the Napoleonic bureaucratic model; tithes, *forais*, corporations, and monopoly companies were abolished. Joaquim António de Aguiar dissolved the religious orders, removed Miguelite bishops from their posts and seized ecclesiastical property, a move which naturally led to a breach with the Papacy. Most of the seized property was not distributed, but was sold to supporters of Dom Pedro in a desperate attempt to improve Portugal's financial situation. The land was mostly acquired by existing landowners or by the commercial bourgeoisie, some of whom were further gratified by receiving titles from the liberals. Thus ended the *ancien régime* in Portugal.

**Dona Maria II** (1834–53) ascended the throne at the age of fifteen on the death of her father. The prevailing state of political tension and confusion was exacerbated by her headstrong behaviour and by the poor advice she received, particularly from relations such as Leopold of the Belgians. The liberals soon divided into conservatives and progressives. The more radical of the latter became known as 'Septembrists', named after the revolt of September 1836 in Lisbon by the army and general populace, following the election victory in Oporto of the Passos brothers. Septembrists were mostly artisans and lower middle class, especially in Oporto; they demanded a return to the Constitution of 1822 and favoured protection and reform. Manuel Passos established a new educational system, modelled on French examples, and Sá da Bandeira took steps to end slavery throughout the Portuguese empire.

The Septembrists survived opposition from Terceira and Saldanha—who had supported the Charter of 1826—and in 1837 began to draft yet another constitution. It was more advanced than that of 1826, but still alienated some Septembrists by being less radical than that of 1822.

In 1842 the Septembrist Constitution of 1838 was replaced by the Charter of 1826. The 'Chartists' (supporters of this Charter) had come to the fore in the late 1830s under António Bernardo da **Costa Cabral**, an authoritarian ex-Septembrist backed by the Queen. He purged the National Guard—a paramilitary citizens' force—of leftists, re-established free trade, resumed relations with the Papacy, and reformed the administrative code, thus fostering a return to prosperity after 1839.

Discontent recurred when Costa Cabral's sanitary regulations forbidding further burials in churches provoked popular reaction in the countryside (the revolt 'of Maria da Fonte'). Economic recession returned, reviving urban discontent and by 1846 the country was again on the verge of civil war. Radical Septembrists supported the *patuleia* (their popular junta in Oporto) and co-operated with Miguelites against Dona Maria II and the Chartists. Peace was imposed by Anglo-Spanish intervention at the Convention of Gramido (1847), but there was still general resentment at the vengeful policies of Costa Cabral, who was returned to power.

An era of relative stability, coinciding with improvements in the international economy, began in 1851 when the Duke of Saldanha ousted Costa Cabral, a fellow Chartist but also a personal enemy.

# Liberalism

Under Saldanha, progressive and conservative liberals reached a new understanding based on the Charter of 1826 and the electoral reform of 1852. This restricted the suffrage to 36,000 electors. Dona Maria was succeeded by **Dom Pedro V** (1853–61), followed by his brother, **Dom Luís** (1861–89), who was a model constitutional monarch. The new political system was operated by an agreed rotation of power between the 'Regenerators' of Saldanha and Fontes Pereira de Melo, and the 'Historicals' of the Duke of Loulé (heirs of the Septembrists). It functioned smoothly enough until the end of the century, despite another revolt by Saldanha (an advocate of Iberian unity) and the creation of a Reformist party under Sá da Bandeira (who was intent on reducing public expenditure and the bureaucracy).

In 1876 the Reformists joined the Historicals to form the 'Progressists', under Anselmo José Braamcamp. Their programme emphasised gradual democratisation, administrative decentralisation and the development of primary education. The Regenerators gave priority to the country's economic development. The latter policies, known as 'Fontismo', were associated with Fontes de Melo, who created the Ministry of Public Works. He was responsible for the building of roads, bridges, and ports; the creation of an electric telegraph network; and for encouraging the construction of railways (the first line, Lisbon–Carregado, was opened in 1856).

The infrastructure of improved communications and the investment of foreign capital allowed a general expansion of the economy from the 1870s. Nevertheless, Portugal lagged behind the rest of western Europe. The growth of her industry was slow. Although interest had been shown in British engines from 1780, steam power was not used until the 1830s. Portuguese private banking developed only in the 1840s, but the State was always saddled with debts, and governments usually failed to balance budgets. An improvement in the balance of payments was largely due to the remittances received from emigrants from the Minho and the islands, who left for Brazil in large numbers from the 1880s. By 1900 a quarter of Portugal's trade and industry was foreign-controlled, and one sixth of industry was foreign-owned, half of this being in British hands.

The population of about three million in 1820 had risen to five million by 1900. The effect of the new industrialisation coincided with a quadrupling of Oporto's population, and a doubling of Lisbon's. In 1822 there were some 15,000 workers in the country; this figure had risen to 200,000 (a quarter of them in textiles) by 1914. Tobacco manufacture and sardine canning also became major industries in the late 19C, but the wine trade suffered from the ravages of phylloxera. Tariffs were raised in 1892, by which time the country was in the midst of a cork boom.

The drift of people from the land to the cities continued. Agriculture showed signs of improvement only towards the end of the century: more potatoes and rice were cultivated; and there was a fall in wheat imports. Agriculture may have also benefited from the eventual abolition of entailed lands (*morgados*) in 1863, the regulation of tenancy laws, and the abolition of primogeniture in the Civil Code of 1867. Under the new laws at least two-thirds of an estate had to be divided equally between the heirs. They also permitted civil marriages, and abolished the death penalty for civil crimes.

The 19C also witnessed a certain cultural regeneration, symbolically connected with political regeneration by the appointment to office of Almeida Garrett, poet and dramatist, by Saldanha in 1852. Other major Romantics included the novelists Júlio Dinis and Camilo Castelo Branco, and the historian Alexandre Herculano. A reaction set in from c 1865, manifested most obviously in realist novels by Eça de Queirós. Noteworthy among his contemporaries were the poets Cesário Verde and Antero de Quental, and the historian and reformer Oliveira Martins.

# From Monarchy to Republic

After the loss of Brazil in 1825, the Portuguese empire consisted of a number of islands, enclaves, and coastal settlements: Goa, Macau, part of Timor; and in Africa, the Cape Verde Islands, Guiné, São Tomé and Príncipe, Angola, and Mozambique. From the 1830s Sá da Bandeira was a constant advocate of the development of the African territories, but a revival of interest in imperial affairs only came during the last quarter of the century. This was especially true after 1885, when the international Conference of Berlin made effective occupation (rather than historical association) the criterion for ownership in the 'scramble for Africa'.

In 1887 the Portuguese announced their intention to bring all the land between the Angolan and Mozambican coasts under their control. This conflicted with British interests, however, by pre-empting British plans to link up their African possessions from Cairo to the Cape; and the Portuguese government of **Dom Carlos** (1889–1908) was humiliated by being forced to give way to Lord Salisbury's veto of the scheme in 1890. But the scheme did promote the 'pacification' of Angola and Mozambique by a generation of proconsuls such as António Enes and Mousinho de Albuquerque.

Britain renewed her pledge to defend the integrity of Portuguese possessions in the Treaty of Windsor (1899). During the late 19C and early 20C São Tomé became the chief cacao producer, but it was also notorious for the use of contract labour: outsiders considered the practice to be slavery in effect, despite Portugal's formal abolition of slavery throughout her territories in 1869.

Despite the progress described above, and the fall in illiteracy to 69 per cent by 1910 thanks to improved primary education, the liberal monarchy was in crisis from 1890. The state was virtually bankrupt, surviving on loans against the tobacco monopoly and on emigrants' remittances. From the 1880s there had been a decline in real wages, causing urban discontent. Industrialisation proceeded without legislation to protect the worker: trade unions were harassed by government and strikes were declared illegal. Socialist theories had begun to enter Portugal from France in the 1850s, but it was not until the 1870s that socialist organisations were founded. These remained small, and they were hopelessly divided into reformist, revolutionary, Marxist, and Anarcho-Syndicalist factions, and therefore did not represent a serious threat to government.

The real threat to the Monarchist establishment came from Republicanism, a radical and nationalist movement of the urban lower-middle class. This movement attacked governments for their corruption and inefficiency and held them responsible for the resurgence of clerical influence in society, led by the Jesuits. Troubles began with the Republican military revolt of 31 January 1891 in Oporto, protesting against the government's submission to British political pressure. It failed. The crisis reached a head when the system of alternating parties—allowing bankers, industrialists, traders and landowners to share political power—collapsed after the 1890s.

In rural areas elections were largely controlled by landowners or government officials, despite the extension of the suffrage to 500,000 by 1910. Nevertheless, Republicans gained strength in the cities with the growth of popular discontent. Governments vacillated between firm and conciliatory action. While the Regenerators and Progressists fragmented, Liberal-Regenerators, Dissident-Progressists, and Nationalist parties emerged with the new century.

In 1906 Dom Carlos placed the government in the hands of João Franco. Franco used dictatorial methods to put the regime back on its feet, but these proved counter-productive, driving more liberals into the Republican camp. The failure of another Republican revolt in January 1908 was followed by the assassination of the King and the Crown Prince on 1 February. Attempts to appease the Republican challenge by the ministers of **Dom Manuel II** (1908–10) also proved futile, and the Monarchy was violently overthrown on 5 October 1910 by a combined force of Republican military and naval personnel and the popular but clandestine, Masonic-led organisation known as the Carbonária. Dom Manuel, 'The Unfortunate', went into exile in England, where he died in 1932.

# The Republic

The Republicans gained an overwhelming victory in the elections for the Constituent Assembly of 1911. Although they promised universal suffrage, literacy requirements actually reduced the male electorate to less than it had been under the previous regime. There was only minimal popular support for the fallen monarchy during minor monarchist incursions from Spain in 1911–12. The Republicans created a bi-cameral parliament, but did not give the President of the Republic the power of dissolution. It legalised the right to strike, with the result that ensuing strikes alienated the middle classes from the protesting urban and rural workers who were sympathetic to the regime. The government dissolved the Jesuits and decreed the Law of Separation (1911), dividing Church and State. In effect, this was an attempt to put the Catholic church under State control and led to Portugal's second breach with the Papacy as well as widespread passive popular opposition. The introduction of military service was also unpopular, but it was the religious issue which was the key to political alignments. In the absence of social reform, anticlericalism was used as a means to retain popular urban support. Afonso Costa became leader of the majority Republican faction, the Democrats, largely because of his intransigence on this issue. The less radical minority Republican groups were led by Brito Camacho (Unionists), and A.J. de Almeida (Evolutionists).

Costa retained control largely by the manipulation of patronage. The havoc brought to the economy by the outbreak of the European war in 1914 ended any hope of financial stability. Discontent among Republicans and non-Republicans, both inside and outside the armed forces, increased. As the President could not dissolve parliament, and the Democratic party machine could win elections by patronage and intimidation, military intervention became the accepted way to change governments. There were 45 governments between 1910 and 1926.

In 1915 General Pimenta de Castro took power and sought to appease the opposition. He was overthrown by a Democratic revolution within four months. Costa returned to power, but economic conditions worsened and class conflicts became more acute. In 1916 Portugal officially entered the war on the Allied side, although it had been fighting in Africa since 1914. Costa formed a short-lived coalition with Almeida. Sidónio Pais, heading another coalition of the discontented, led a coup in December 1917. His 'New Republic', based on a strong presidency and universal male suffrage, was soon opposed by his Unionist and trade union allies and forced to rely increasingly on Monarchist and Catholic goodwill.

Sidónio Pais was assassinated in December 1918. There followed a confused period in which the Monarchist Admiral Canto e Castro became President but opposed attempts to restore the Monarchy by force. The Democrats returned in 1919. The years 1919–26 were marked by political instability, inflation and insolvency aggravated by the effects of the war, by frequent outbursts of violence, and by military interventions. Workers organised themselves into Anarcho-Syndicalist unions. Conservative Republican groups and Monarchists, members of the officer corps and the hitherto staunchly pro-Democratic urban lower-middle class were utterly weary of politics; while in the universities French anti-Republican theories became fashionable. On 28 May 1926 a bloodless coup was launched in Braga, overthrowing the Democratic government. Power passed first to Commander Mendes Cabeçadas, a leader of the revolution of 1910; then to General Gomes da Costa, who had commanded troops in Flanders; and finally to General Óscar Carmona. These changes reflected divisions within the anti-Democratic coalition. By 1928 Republican institutions were consolidated, following the failure of the Monarchist General Sinel de Cordes to improve the financial situation. Carmona then became President.

# The New State

In 1928 a new Finance Minister, the Catholic economist **António de Oliveira Salazar**, was given full powers to put the economy in order. He achieved this by balancing the budget, reducing the national debt, reducing the cost of living, and stabilising the currency. The prestige he gained by this success enabled him to outmanoeuvre his rivals for power. Carmona appointed him Prime Minister in

1932, a post which he retained until incapacitated by ill-health in 1968. In 1933 a new political constitution was promulgated, converting the military dictatorship into the 'New State', an authoritarian, nationalistic, pro-Catholic and corporative Republican regime. Salazar was made constitutionally responsible to the President and legislation was passed by the National Assembly, advised by a nominated Corporative Chamber. Only members of the National Union—successor to the coalition of conservative forces who supported the 'National Revolution' of 1926— were ever elected to the National Assembly.

Ostensibly a corporative Republic, the country was effectively ruled by the traditional bureaucracy and the police. The National Union was the political association of the regime. It was allied with a 'youth movement' known as the *Mocidade*, and with the Portuguese Legion, a paramilitary body. Workers were organised into national syndicates, but these never had the kind of power achieved by the employers' guilds. Agricultural workers and fishermen each had their own associations, but these were controlled by their employers. Education was nationalistic and Catholic. (The Church had been rehabilitated by the Concordat of 1940, but was ostensibly kept separate from the State.) The police forces had military commanders and a special secret police force, the Polícia Internacional e de Defesa do Estado (PIDE), relied on informers and its own sinister methods to break opposition. Although the armed forces were subject to the civilian regime they never in practice gave up the pretension (assumed in the 19C) of having the final word in national affairs.

Conspiracy was not unusual in the armed forces, and old-style Republicans attempted to seize power in 1927, 1931, 1946, 1947, 1958–59, 1961, and 1962. A revolutionary general strike was crushed in 1934; and Anarchists failed to assassinate Salazar in 1937. Salazar supported the Nationalist military rising in Spain in 1936 and cultivated close relations with Franco's dictatorial regime.

Portugal remained neutral during the Second World War but was sympathetic to Britain and gave generous credit. The Allies were able to place bases on the Azores in 1943; but it was not until 1944 that Portugal ceased to sell wolfram to Germany.

From the 1940s the clandestine Communist Party led the opposition, which still included old-style Republicans such as General Humberto Delgado (who contested the Presidential election of 1958, and was later assassinated). In the 1960s, Social Democrats, Christian Democrats, and some Monarchists added to the opposition. The Monarchists had hoped that Salazar would restore Duarte Nuno, who aspired to the throne after Dom Manuel's death in exile in 1932.

Limited peaceful dissent was permitted during election campaigns but such token freedom seemed at odds with Portugal's membership in the North Atlantic Treaty Organisation, a membership dictated by geo-strategic factors. Censorship was strictly enforced from 1926 to 1974.

The regime followed colonial traditions inherited from the liberal Monarchy and First Republic, although from the 1930s imperial administration was centralised in Lisbon. In 1951 Portugal's colonies (a term adopted in 1911) were re-styled 'Overseas Provinces', but this did nothing to stem the tide of decolonisation: Goa was occupied by India in 1961; local nationalist elements commenced military operations in Angola in 1961, in Guiné in 1963, and in Mozambique in 1964. Portugal managed to contain these guerrilla movements only at the price of international notoriety, a high level of military expenditure, and a continual drain on material and moral resources. In Angola, increasing exploitation of its natural resources contributed to the Portuguese economy. In general the international political cost was excessive.

# Social and Economic Change in the 20C

During the 1950s and 1960s Portugal experienced an unprecedented growth rate—almost 9 per cent a year in the industrial sector. But in the 1970s it was as low in the European economic league tables as it had been at the end of the Monarchy.

The population rose from five million in 1900 to almost ten million by 1991, although emigration to western Europe and elsewhere in the 1960s actually accounted for a decrease for that decade. The proportion of the working population in the agricultural sector fell from 72 per cent in 1864 to 57 per cent in 1911, and to 30 per cent by 1970. The drift to the cities continued throughout this period. The proportion of illiterates had dropped from 69 per cent in 1910 to 25 per cent in 1970.

The greatest economic progress occurred in the 'New State' period. The infrastructure of communications was extended and modernised, and dam construction boosted the production of hydro-electric power. These developments formed the base for Portugal's accelerated growth through the 1950s and 1960s, especially in metallurgical industries. Textiles remained the principal industry, but agriculture stagnated because mechanisation was slow.

As late as 1959, 13 per cent of the population still lived in villages inaccessible by road. Widespread subsistence agriculture persisted, largely sustained by remittances from abroad. Tourist receipts, however, helped to make up the chronic deficit in the trade balance. Internal migration continued towards the Braga-Setúbal coastal regions, and Lisbon and Oporto remained poles of attraction. The socio-economic divide between urban and rural areas deepened despite the advent of mass media.

The densely populated Minho remained deeply religious while in the larger cities and the illiterate South religion was a declining social force. In the secular field the present century produced only one literary giant, the poet Fernando Pessoa (1888–1935).

# Revolution and Democracy

Salazar was succeeded as Prime Minister by Marcelo Caetano (1968–74), who sought to reform the New State and find answers to Portugal's overseas problems. He attempted to widen the basis of the regime's political support by limited liberalisation. More intellectual freedom, however, only led to demands for further democratisation. This was stubbornly opposed by the diehards, including the President, Américo Tomás (1958–74). Theories of progressive autonomy for the overseas territories satisfied neither guerrilla leaders nor world opinion, while at home war-weariness increased. Rising domestic inflation offset the advantages gained by an improved but rudimentary welfare system. Limited democratisation of trade-union structures enabled the clandestine Communists to obtain further footholds. The necessity to find more officers to carry on the fruitless colonial war only provoked military unrest, and led to the creation of the Armed Forces Movement (MFA; *Movimento das Forças Armadas*) in 1973.

There was a premature and unsuccessful rising by the MFA at Caldas da Rainha in March 1974. On 25 April 1974 the junior officers, nominally led by General Costa Gomes (the Chief of Staff) and General António de Spínola (the former commander in Guiné), achieved a successful and nearly bloodless coup. The rest of the country followed the lead of the capital.

With this revolution there commenced a period of confusion and instability in which the political centre of gravity moved generally to the left until August 1975. General Spínola became provisional President and formed a coalition government comprising Communists, Socialists and centrists. The authority of the State had largely collapsed, however, and the more radical officers of the MFA remained the real arbiters of the situation.

Economic conditions deteriorated as the political confusion continued, but it was decolonisation which divided Spínola from the Left. The former favoured the creation of a Lusitanian community, including Brazil, while the latter insisted on a speedy withdrawal from the colonies. Spínola consented to the independence of Guiné in 1974, and of Mozambique in 1975, but demurred at handing over Angola to its most leftist local liberation movement. The organisation of a rally in support of Spínola led to a showdown on 28 September 1974, from which MFA radicals and the Left emerged victorious. In 1975 independence was granted to the Cape Verde Islands, São Tomé and Príncipe, and Angola, while East Timor was taken over by Indonesia.

General Costa Gomes became President of the Republic after Spinola, but power was still effectively exercised by MFA radicals and a coalition government led by Brigadier Vasco Gonçalves, himself a MFA radical. There was some uncertainty until 11 March 1975, when an attempted coup by Spínola failed, leaving Gonçalves and the radicals more firmly in power.

Private banks and insurance firms were nationalised, putting about half the economy in the public sector. Elections for a constituent assembly were held on 25 April 1975 and won by the Socialists and centrists, but Gonçalves remained keen on an alliance with the Communists, who dominated the trade-union movement. Still other MFA officers were in favour of more novel Third World-style revolutionary solutions.

In July there was a conservative backlash in the north of the country headed by Mário Soares and nine key moderate MFA officers, greatly strengthening the Socialist opposition. Opinions became polarised and the MFA disintegrated. Gonçalves was dismissed by Costa Gomes in August and the sixth provisional government of Admiral Pinheiro de Azevedo sought a return to normality. Opposition was organised by the Communists and the extreme Left. This period of revolutionary confusion finally ended on 25 November 1975 when the failure of a Leftist revolt against the coalition government permitted democratic and centrist opinion to assert itself.

In 1976 a new constitution, drawn up under MFA influence, attempted to uphold socialism and democracy. It gave considerable potential power to a popularly elected President. The Prime Minister and cabinet were responsible to the President and to the single-chamber Assembly of the Republic elected by universal suffrage on a system of proportional representation. The Council of the Revolution, a legacy of the now defunct MFA, controlled the armed forces and advised the President. Devolution was granted to the Azores, Madeira and to Macau, the only remaining overseas possession, which is to revert to China in 1999. General António Ramalho Eanes, leader of the government forces on 25 November 1975, was elected President. Mário Soares, leader of the Socialists, was appointed Prime Minister. Soares's party won the election of 1976 and he was appointed Prime Minister of a minority government.

Soares at first governed alone, and then in coalition with the Christian-Democrat CDS (Social Democratic Centre). Three attempts in 1978–79 at non-party government by independent Presidential nominees failed to stay the course, the last being led by Maria de Lurdes Pintassilgo, the first woman Prime Minister. In the elections of December 1979 the Socialists of Soares were still the largest party, and well ahead of the Communists led by Álvaro Cunhal, but both were defeated by the conservative Democratic Alliance (AD; a formation based on the Social Democrat, CDS, and Monarchist parties). The AD's controversial leader, the Social Democrat Francisco de Sá Carneiro, became Prime Minister and adopted a right-wing stance until his death in an air crash in December 1980. His successor, the Social Democrat Francisco Pinto Balsemão, attempted to steer a moderate course. Under his leadership AD reached agreement with the Socialists to revise the Constitution in 1982, when the Council of the Revolution was abolished. Other changes were minimal. But unrest within the parties of the AD coalition over policies and personalities led to Balsemão's resignation in December 1982. President Eanes (who had been comfortably re-elected in December 1980) vetoed the candidate chosen by Balsemão to succeed him as Prime Minister, and forced Balsemão to stay on in a caretaker capacity until new elections on 25 April 1983. The AD coalition disintegrated meanwhile into its component parties, which gave themselves new leaders.

The Socialists emerged from the elections as the largest parliamentary group, but without an overall majority. Their leader, Soares, formed a coalition government with the Social Democrats. This government's policies of economic retrenchment made it unpopular, and a new and more dynamic leader of the Social Democrats, Aníbal Cavaco Silva, withdrew his party from it, forcing elections in October 1985. The Social Democrats were victorious, although lacking an overall majority. Cavaco Silva's minority government was the tenth administration since 1976.

Early in 1986 the presidential elections were narrowly won on the second round by Mário Soares, who was installed as the first civilian Head of State for 60 years. Ex-President Eanes took over the leadership of the Democratic Renewal Party, which had obtained almost a fifth of the vote in the election of 1985, the first it had contested.

# Portugal in Europe

Having applied to join in 1977, Portugal became the eleventh member-state of the European Community (EC) on 1 January 1986. Membership followed of WEU (West European Union) and the EMS (European Monetary System). Portugal signed the Treaty of European Union at Maastricht without derogations and adhered to the Schengen agreement (on the abolition of internal EC frontiers). The first Portuguese presidency of the EC, in 1992, was a qualified success, being overshadowed by the Bosnian crisis. Entry into the EC, opposed only by the Communists, proved generally popular and coincided with the upturn in international economic conditions. EC funds, together with reviving tourist receipts, emigrant remittances and foreign investment, boosted prosperity and helped strong economic growth until the recession of 1992–93. Targets for EC aid included infrastructure (most notably roads and bridges), training schemes, and attempted modernisation and restructuring of the ailing textile and agricultural sectors.

The outcome of better economic performance were seen in longer-term changes in employment. The proportion of the working population in agriculture and fisheries fell from 29 per cent in 1973 to eleven per cent in 1993, while the service sector, which accounted for 37 per cent in 1973, expanded to 56 per cent in 1993. Portuguese living standards were estimated at 64 per cent of the EC average in

1993, with data for *per capita* wealth putting Portugal ahead of Greece but behind Ireland in the EC league tables of the early 1990s. The movement of Spain from low down to the top of the list of trading partners was a radical consequence of entry. In some quarters, suspicion of Spain, as of further European political integration, remains, yet entry into the EC did much to resolve the post-imperial crisis of national mission which had been troubling many intellectuals.

In 1989 the third revision of the Constitution of 1976 brought the text into line with open-ended EC norms by removing the clauses on the irreversibility of the nationalisations and land reform of 1975. Cavaco Silva's government embarked on a far-reaching programme of re-privatisation of the public sector: banking, insurance, brewing, steel, cellulose, cement, gas, electricity, telecommunications, etc. The public sector, estimated to have accounted for 60 per cent of Gross Domestic Product in 1976, accounted for 14 per cent in 1992: and the trend continues. By the 1990s only a few hundreds of people were still employed on agrarian collectives in the Alentejo set up in 1975. Broadcasting was further opened up to the private sector, with one or two new private TV channels being controlled by the Church, still a powerful influence in the land despite a shortage of clergy.

Neo-liberal economic policies were pursued with the goal of economic convergence for a possible single European currency by the end of the century. Efforts were made to control and reduce budget deficits and public indebtedness. Inflation fell from a peak of 30 per cent in 1983 to 6 per cent in 1994, while unemployment, 9 per cent in 1985, fell to 4 per cent in 1991 (low by EC standards), but with recession, rose again to 7 per cent by 1994.

Politically, Portugal enjoyed greater stability after the mid 1980s despite the sometimes uneasy cohabitation of Socialist President and Social Democrat Prime Minister. Mário Soares quickly established himself as a well-respected President, with opinion polls generally indicating two out of three citizens thinking he was doing a good job for most of his first and second terms of office: he was re-elected without serious opposition in 1991.

When Cavaco Silva's minority government was defeated in the Assembly in 1987, President Soares opted for new elections rather than a minority government of another complexion. Cavaco Silva's Social Democrats (PSD), who were allied at the European level with Liberal parties, were returned with a shade over 50 per cent of the vote and an absolute majority in the Assembly of the Republic, a remarkable result repeated in 1991. In 1987 the Democratic Renewal Party (PRD) was irretrivably shattered at the polls, so that politics reverted to the pre-1985 system of four parties, in which two were increasingly dominant. The Socialists (PS) remained the main parliamentary opposition under successive leaders who never managed to project their image as well as their former leader, Soares. The hardline Communists (PCP) and close allies declined electorally to under 9 per cent of the vote in 1991 and saw their hold on trade unionism shaken by non-Communist rivals. The share of the vote won by the Christian Democrats (CDS) fell to 4 per cent in 1987 and 1991, after which a new young leadership sought to revive its fortunes by turning it into a right-wing populist party.

It would now appear, two decades after the coup of 1974, that Portugal's democratic system was well consolidated in the context of the EU. In the three years up to 1994 the armed forces were halved in size and brought more firmly under civilian control. However, turn-out at elections was falling and politicians, conscious of their deteriorating image, began worrying about ways to make themselves more accountable to the electorate (rather than party headquarters) through reform of the electoral system.

# Rulers of Portugal

Some of the more commonly used nick-names are given. Dates in brackets indicate marriages. Kings are usually referred to by the title Dom.

## House of Burgundy (or Afonsin Dynasty)

| | |
|---|---|
| 1128/39–85 | Afonso (Henriques) I — Mafalda of Maurienne and Savoy (1146) |
| 1185–1211 | Sancho I — Dulce of Aragón (1174) |
| 1211–23 | Afonso II — Urraca (1208), daughter of Alfonso VIII of Castile and Eleanor Plantagenet |
| 1223–48 | Sancho II — Mécia López de Haro |
| 1248–79 | Afonso III — Matilde, Countess of Boulogne<br>— Beatriz de Guillén (1253), daughter of Alfonso X of Castile |
| 1279–1325 | Dinis, 'O Lavrador' (the husbandman) — Isabel of Aragón (1282) |
| 1325–57 | Afonso IV — Beatriz of Castile (1309), daughter of Sancho IV of Castile |
| 1357–67 | Pedro I (the Justicier) — Blanca of Castile (1328)<br>— Constanza of Castile (1340)<br>— Inês de Castro (1354?) |
| 1367–83 | Fernando — Leonor Teles (1372) |
| 1383–85 | (Interregnum) |

## House of Avis

| | |
|---|---|
| 1385–1433 | João I (John) — Philippa of Lancaster (1387) |
| 1433–38 | Duarte (Edward) — Leonor of Aragón (1428) |
| 1438–81 | Afonso V (the African) — Isabel of Portugal (1441) |
| 1481–95 | João II — Leonor of Portugal (1471) |
| 1495–1521 | Manuel I, 'the Fortunate' — Isabel of Castile (1497)<br>— Maria of Castile (1500)<br>— Leonor of Spain (1518) |
| 1521–57 | João III — Catarina of Spain (1525) |
| 1557–78 | Sebastião, 'the Regretted' |
| 1578–80 | Henrique, the Cardinal-King |
| 1580 | António, Prior of Crato |

## House of Austria (Spanish usurpation)

| | |
|---|---|
| 1580–98 | Felipe II of Spain (I of Portugal) |
| 1598–1621 | Felipe III of Spain (II of Portugal) |
| 1621–40 | Felipe IV of Spain (III of Portugal) |

## House of Braganza

| | |
|---|---|
| 1640–56 | João IV — Luisa de Guzmán (1633) |
| 1656–83 | Afonso VI — Maria-Francesca-Isabel d'Aumale of Savoy (1661; but unconsummated) |
| 1683–1706 | Pedro II (Regent from 1668) — Isabel d'Aumale (1668)<br>— Maria-Sofia-Isabel of Neuberg (1687) |
| 1706–50 | João V, 'the Magnificent' — Maria-Ana of Austria (1708) |
| 1750–77 | José — Mariana-Victoria of Spain (1729) |
| 1777–1816 | Maria (Francisca) I — Pedro III (her uncle; in 1760) |

| | |
|---|---|
| 1816–26 | João VI (Regent from 1792; formally from 1799)<br>— Carlota-Joaquina of Spain (1784) |
| 1826 | Pedro IV (who abdicated, leaving the kingdom to his daughter,<br>Maria) — Maria Leopoldina of Austria (1817)<br>— Maria Amelia of Leuchtenberg (1829) |
| 1828–34 | Usurpation of Dom Miguel — Adelaide-Sofia of Loewenstein-<br>Rosenberg (1851) |
| 1834–53 | Maria II, 'da Glória'— August of Leuchtenberg (1834)<br>— Ferdinand of Saxe-Coburg-Gotha (1836) |
| 1853–61 | Pedro V — Stéphanie of Hohenzollern-Sigmaringen (1858) |
| 1861–89 | Luis — Maria-Pia of Savoy (1862) |
| 1889–1908 | Carlos — Marie-Amélie of Orléans (1886) |
| 1908–10 | Manuel II, 'the Unfortunate' — Augusta-Victoria of<br>Sigmaringen |

## Republic

| | |
|---|---|
| | Presidents or heads of provisional governments |
| 1910 | Teófilo Braga |
| 1911–15 | Manuel de Arriaga |
| 1915 | Teófilo Braga |
| 1915–17 | Bernardino Machado |
| 1917–18 | Sidónio Pais |
| 1918–19 | Adm. João de Canto e Castro |
| 1919–23 | António José de Almeida |
| 1923–25 | Manuel Teixeira Gomes |
| 1925–26 | Bernardino Machado |
| 1926 | Commander Mendes Cabeçadas |
| 1926 | Gen. Gomes da Costa |
| 1926–51 | Gen. António Óscar de Fragoso Carmona<br>(with António de Oliveira Salazar as 'Prime Minister' from<br>1932 to 1968) |
| 1951–58 | Gen. Francisco Higino Craveiro Lopes |
| 1958–74 | Adm. Américo de Deus Rodrigues Tomás<br>(with Marcelo Caetano as 'Prime Minister' from 1968 to<br>1974) |
| 1974 | Gen. António Sebastião Ribeiro de Spinola |
| 1974–76 | Gen. Francisco da Costa Gomes |
| 1976–86 | Gen. António dos Santos Ramalho Eanes |
| 1986–96 | Mário Alberto Nobre Lopes Soares |
| 1996– | Jorge Sampaio |

# Introduction to the Art and Architecture of Portugal

By **J.B. Bury**

## General Characteristics

The Portuguese temperament is characterised by a down-to-earth realism generally incompatible with high flights of imagination or abstract ideas transcending the senses. In keeping with this uncomplicated, realistic outlook, Robert Smith has identified a 'pastoral' quality in Portuguese architecture—recognisable by such features as modest scale, simple constructional forms, and the neat facing of exterior walls with white plaster, against which the bare stone of the aperture frames and structural members provides a clean 'rural' contrast of texture and colour. The national temperament may also be seen reflected in the architecture of village churches, which almost invariably convey a welcoming impression. Inside, the same ingenuous and friendly spirit is maintained—the images of saints, for example, being always human and approachable, never withdrawn by the tragic intensity or abstraction which are found in the religious sculpture of some other Catholic nations. Nor are Portuguese towns completely dominated by huge cathedrals like those of northern Europe or Spain. In domestic architecture, equally revealing is the lack of those massive iron grilles or *rejas* which protect the ground-floor windows of Spanish houses, and emphatically assert their privacy.

The realistic approach of the Portuguese is also apparent in the very important status enjoyed by portraiture as a branch of painting, from Nuno Gonçalves onwards, and conversely, the relative weakness of their contributions to more imaginative artistic themes such as those of mythological, allegorical and history painting. It is worthy of note that the only Renaissance treatise on the art of portraiture was written by a Portuguese (Francisco de Holanda, *Do tirar pelo natural*; MS completed 1549); and perhaps no coincidence that in the distinguished succession of portrait painters of the Spanish House of Austria, Sánchez Coello (c 1531–88) came from a Portuguese family, and Diego de Silva Velázquez (1599–1660) was of Portuguese descent on his father's side.

Similarly in architecture, just as the Portuguese have produced no great philosopher or mystic, so neither the transcendental aspirations of Gothic nor the illusionism and theatricality of the Baroque have strongly appealed to their aesthetic sensibilities—despite superb examples, some of the finest in Europe, built in their country by foreign architects, at Alcobaça, for example, and at Mafra. Contrasting with this lack of enthusiasm for Gothic and Baroque, the Portuguese have positively favoured horizontal rather than vertical compositions, and they have shown an evident liking for the firmly based solidity of Roman construction, whether Romanesque or Renaissance, and even within the latter style have demonstrated a preference for the two most stable Orders, Tuscan and Doric.

In marked contrast to Spain, domes are rare in Portugal, and even barrel vaults are not common. This has not been due to lack of good craftsmen. 'Where shall we meet with such excellent stone cutters as in Portugal? Perhaps not in Europe', wrote a visiting professional architect two centuries ago (James Murphy, *Travels in Portugal*; London, 1795). Nor can Portuguese preference for rather low buildings of simple construction be attributed to seismic risk. It is true that Portugal has endured numerous earthquakes, and three during the past thousand years have been so severe and widespread in their effects as to be labelled 'great': 24 August 1356, 26 January 1531, and 1 November 1755). But Spain too has suffered considerably from earthquakes, and Sicily and Italy even more so, without any apparent inhibiting effects on the construction of complex systems of vaulting or cupolas, or tall towers.

The truth is that Portuguese builders and architects (as opposed to foreigners working in Portugal such as Terzi, Ludwig, or Nasoni) have seldom shown an interest in spatial composition, and have usually preferred stable rectangular forms to less stable curved shapes, a preference which is especially evident in ground plans. This is already to be seen in the chancels of Romanesque churches in North Portugal, with their usually square as opposed to Carolingian apsidal terminations. In this respect it might be said that the Portuguese resemble the English, among whom Sir Nikolaus Pevsner has detected a 'profound preference for the angular and dislike for full, rich, swelling architectural forms'. Thus the oval plan, a favourite of Italian, Austrian, and German church architects in the 17th and 18Cs, was almost completely rejected, or ignored, by the Portuguese, despite outstanding examples designed by Guarini for Lisbon (Divina Providência; never built), and built by Nasoni at Oporto (Clérigos; 1731–63).

In compensation, however, for the indifference to, or neglect of, spatial composition in their architecture, the Portuguese have demonstrated a remarkable creative talent for surface ornament—already noticeable in the decorative sculpture of their Romanesque churches; still more manifest in that of Manueline buildings; and visible again in the late Baroque and Rococo architecture of the Minho. The same genius is to be seen in the evolution of church reredoses of gilded wood, culminating at the end of the 17C in what Robert Smith has called the 'national style' of *talha dourada*. This was associated with the appearance of that astonishing, uniquely Portuguese phenomenon, the church interior entirely covered with carved and gilded wood (*a igreja toda de ouro*) of which spectacular examples are still to be seen at Aveiro (Convent of Jesus; before 1725), and Lagos (Santo António), although many of the finest perished in the earthquake of 1755. Further instances of this inventive interest in the treatment of surfaces can be seen in silver and furniture, and to it we may also assign another major Portuguese artistic achievement, the adaptation of blue and white *azulejos* to accommodate very large pictorial designs—an innovation evolved in the 18C after the Dutch and Chinese influences of the late 17C (which superseded earlier styles of Islamic derivation) had been fully absorbed and digested.

# Prehistoric and Roman

There is a fascinating example of the adaptation of a neolithic monument to Christian worship at Pavia (Alentejo), where the 16C chapel of São Dinis is constructed from a huge megalithic tomb or dolmen.

A good deal is known of **Ibero-Celtic** Portugal (5–1C BC) from the excavation of hill towns or *citânias*, notably those of Sabroso and Briteiros in the Minho, which had flagged streets, drainage systems, and numerous habitations, both rectangular and circular, some of the latter of helicoidal construction. (The finds are preserved in the Museu Martins Sarmento, Guimarães.)

Our knowledge of **Roman** Portugal has also been greatly extended by excavations, in particular those of the important town of Conímbriga (a few kilometres south of Coimbra), which was already recorded as an *oppidum* in the 1C AD. It was sacked by the Suevi in 468, and eventually abandoned. Here a number of buildings have been unearthed, including baths and houses with elaborate pictorial mosaic floors and hypocausts. A Roman bridge cited in the *Itinerary* of Antoninus Pius still exists at Vila Formosa, west of Portalegre. At Évora, part of a 2C or 3C AD Roman temple has survived on the central hill of the city, and the aqueduct completed in 1537 probably follows the course of the ancient Roman one; but most of Roman Évora has been destroyed over the centuries, some even relatively recently (e.g. in 1570 a large structure described as a triple triumphal arch was pulled down to enlarge the main square).

## Visigothic and Romanesque

A few examples have survived in Portugal of the small churches built prior to the 8C, when the **Visigoths** ruled the Iberian peninsula, and others which were built by Christian communities under Moorish domination in the style known as **Mozarabic**. To the first belongs the small Latin-type basilica of São Pedro de Balsemão, near Lamego in the Beira Alta, dating from the 7C or possibly earlier, which displays carved ornament including serrated and cord motifs, swastikas, rosettes, and lozenge patterns. To the second category belong São Pedro de Lourosa, near Oliveira do Hospital, dating from the 10C, and São Frutuoso, near Braga, probably of Visigothic origin, but rebuilt in the 11C: both these churches have been much restored and reconstructed in recent years, however. At São Pedro de Lourosa the nave is separated from the side aisles by rows of Tuscan columns supporting horseshoe arches, and there are *ajimeces* above the entrance and chancel arch: in ground plan São Pedro combines rectangle with Latin cross, and has a narthex at the west end. São Frutuoso has a Greek cross plan with apsidal terminations to the arms, a central dome (reconstructed), finely carved capitals and bands of carved ornament.

The independence of Portugal (from the Spanish kingdom of León) was proclaimed in 1143; but it cannot be said that the Romanesque architecture which survives from the formative years of Portuguese nationhood shows any really distinctive national features, except perhaps the aptitude for decorative sculpture. Like Spanish Romanesque, that of Portugal owed much to the inspiration and influence of the Benedictine monks of Cluny, sponsors and patrons of the pilgrimage to the shrine of Santiago de Compostela, some 90km north of the Portuguese frontier. Some of the more important 12C churches, the cathedrals of Braga, Oporto, and Lisbon, have lost much of their Romanesque identity owing to subsequent alterations and reconstructions. However, two major monuments have fortunately retained their original character, largely unspoilt: the 12C cathedral (*Sé Velha*) of Coimbra and the 12–13C cathedral of Évora—both continuing the Cluniac style with evident references to the 11C pilgrimage basilica type established at Clermont-Ferrand (N.D. du Port), Toulouse (St Sernin), and Santiago de Compostela.

Thus Coimbra's old cathedral is cruciform with three apses, a lantern over the crossing, side aisles and characteristic galleried triforia; while externally it presents a fortified appearance, as did Santiago. Subsequent additions in Gothic (cloisters; main reredos) and Renaissance styles (North door, and retable of northern apse) do not detract from the impressive 12C ensemble. Évora cathedral, although already transitional in its pointed arches, continues to follow the Cluniac architectural tradition constructively, and its porch is evidently modelled on the Pórtico de la Gloria at Santiago. The lantern cupola at the crossing, externally a conical dome, or low spire, follows the example of the old cathedral at Salamanca. The many subsequent additions and ornaments, in particular the splendid baroque chancel (*capela-mór*), co-exist harmoniously with the Romanesque body of the church without injuring each other's separate stylistic identity.

Two quite exceptional Portuguese Romanesque buildings of the 12C are the *domus municipalis* at Braganza, a very rare example of pre-Gothic civic architecture, and the hexadecagonal Templar church at Tomar—perhaps the best-preserved Templar church in Europe.

Literally dozens of small, usually very simple, Romanesque churches survive in northern Portugal, many of them decorated with rustic but striking and expressive carvings on their portals and on capitals. Two of the better known are São Martinho de Cedofeita at Oporto and São Salvador de Bravães on the river Lima.

# Gothic

Each of the main phases of Gothic architecture is represented in Portugal by examples which are unusually fine even by international European standards. The 'French church' (as W.C. Watson calls it in his *Portuguese Architecture;* London, 1908) of the abbey of Alcobaça, begun in the second half of the 12C, and Pontigny-in-the-meadows in Burgundy, are the two finest surviving specimens of Cistercian architecture in Europe. In the church at Alcobaça is preserved a series of medieval royal tombs including those of Inês de Castro and Dom Pedro I, outstanding masterpieces of Portuguese Gothic sculpture. Cistercian Gothic is also represented at Coimbra in the 13C cloister of Santa Maria de Celas, which has the best collection of decorated capitals in the country.

Other fine Gothic churches include Santa Maria dos Olivais at Tomar (begun second half 13C), which represents the most usual type of church built in the country until the end of the 15C. Also worth visiting is the fortified Templar church at Leça do Bailio, north of Oporto (rebuilt early 14C), and in the Alentejo the 14C fortified church of N.S. da Boa Nova at Terena, which has a Greek cross plan.

The masterpiece of mature Gothic architecture in Portugal is the monastery church of Santa Maria da Vitória at Batalha, begun in 1388. It is stylistically eclectic, combining French with some English influences, but the result is entirely successful. Over the following century or so there were added to this church a founder's chapel housing royal tombs, a great vaulted chapterhouse, a large cloister with remarkable late Gothic tracery, a second cloister, and at the east end the so-called 'Unfinished Chapels' (*Capelas Imperfeitas*), another example of the very late Gothic which is peculiar to Portugal and called Manueline because belonging mainly to the reign of Dom Manuel I (1495–1521), although several important Manueline buildings were completed in the reign of his successor Dom João III (1521–57).

Batalha, built throughout of an ivory coloured limestone, brings to our attention two aspects of Portuguese architecture which visitors should bear in mind. First, Portugal is a country unusually well supplied with building stone of various kinds—from marbles and limestones to granites, each of several different colours and textures. These have been regularly utilised in each locality where they occur, and their diverse appearance contributes to regional variety, adding interest, by contrast, to buildings of similar style in different parts of the country. Secondly, it is essential in order fully to enjoy the architecture and sculpture which Portugal offers in abundance to try to shed any prejudice against the close proximity in a single building of entirely different styles of architecture, decorative sculpture, furniture, and ceramic, woodwork, or other ornament.

A number of fine medieval castles survive in Portugal, although some of them have been rather drastically restored. Among the best known are those of Guimarães and of Lisbon (the two most historically significant); those of Monsaraz, of Almourol, on an island in the Tagus between Santarém and Abrantes, and of Óbidos (three of the most picturesque); that of Leiria (perhaps the most imposing); and the great keeps of Vila da Feira, between Oporto and Aveiro, and of Beja, and Estremoz.

# Painting: 1450–1550

There is nothing to suggest that Portugal possessed any flourishing native school of medieval painting; nor does Jan van Eyck's visit in 1428–29 appear to have created one. Apart from a few mural fragments, the earliest works are a series of panels attributed to **Nuno Gonçalves** (active 1450–71), court painter to Dom Afonso V. Of these the most remarkable are six panels in the Lisbon museum portraying the court and various ranks of Portuguese society praying in the presence of a saint usually identified as St Vincent, patron saint of Lisbon. The style is dry and powerfully realistic. There are similarities to contemporary Flemish painting, especially the work of Dirk Bouts, but also strong indications of Burgundian influence. The portraits, nearly life-sized, are of much historical interest, belonging as they do to the period when the Portuguese were on the threshold of their great overseas adventures. The identification of the portraits and the arrangement of the panels raise questions to which no convincing answers have yet been given.

During the first quarter of the 16C increased wealth resulting in more generous patronage persuaded a number of northern masters to emigrate to Portugal (e.g., the Flemish painter Frei Carlos, active 1517–29; and the Dutch miniaturist Antonio de Holanda, active in Portugal from c 1515, died c 1557). Pictures were also imported from Antwerp, and under these Netherlandish influences native schools developed. At Lisbon the circle of court painters included **Jorge Afonso** (active 1508–40) and his followers **Cristóvão de Figueiredo** (active 1515–38), Garcia Fernandes (active c 1514–65), and Gregório Lopes (c 1490–c 1550). With this circle we may also associate the anonymous painter of the charming Arrival of the relics at the Madre de Deus church (c 1520). To the important local school at Viseu belonged **Vasco Fernandes** ('O Grão Vasco', the Great Vasco; active 1506–42), and Gaspar Vaz (died c 1568). The prolific output of these so-called 'Portuguese primitives' is to be seen in the museums of Lisbon, Viseu, and Lamego. Their work is characterised by a realism not devoid of sentiment, exceptional skill in portraiture, and a predilection for brilliant colour schemes.

# Architecture: the Manueline Style

In architecture, the new wealth and accompanying patronage was demonstrated more strikingly. Late Gothic in the specifically Portuguese variant known as Manueline (a term seemingly invented by Almeida Garrett in his poem *Camões* of 1825, and given currency by the engineer Mousinho de Albuquerque in the 1840s) remained the prevailing style throughout the first quarter of the 16C. Certain features of the three-aisled, vaulted Gothic Church of Jesus at Setúbal (begun 1494) are generally considered to reveal the first manifestations of the Manueline style—in particular the dramatic use of twisted forms in the columns, ribs, and corbels. The builder of this church was a certain Master **Boitac** (active 1494–c 1520), probably a Frenchman, who was later employed at the Jeronymite monastery of Santa Maria de Belém, near Lisbon (from 1502 to 1517), and at Coimbra and Batalha (between 1509 and 1519). At Belém, Boitac was succeeded as master of the works by a Spaniard, **João de Castilho** (active in Portugal from c 1510, died 1552), who was responsible for executing the South Portal, the vault in the nave, and transepts of the church, as well as for the completion of the cloister. The work at Belém continued long after the death of Dom Manuel in 1521, so that Renaissance ornament of Lombardic type (introduced to Portugal via Spain and France) makes its appearance both on the pillars of the church and in the cloister. At Batalha the construction of the 'Capelas Imperfeitas' went on so long that Renaissance ornament began to creep in. The master builder in charge there until 1515 was **Mateus Fernandes**, and under his supervision it may be supposed there were executed the great Portal of the Capelas Imperfeitas (1509) and the tracery in the cloister windows, which are among the finest achievements of Manueline architectural decoration.

However, the most spectacular of all Manueline works are the apertures (two in the west wall, one in the south) of the chapterhouse of the Convent of Christ at Tomar—famous for their carved stone frames of twisted tree trunks, stumps of branches, artichokes, coral, knots, ropes, and sails. This Manueline masterpiece, begun in 1510, and the Tower of Belém (1516–21) on the north shore of the Tagus estuary west of Lisbon, were constructed under the supervision of **Diogo de Arruda** (active 1510–31) and his brother **Francisco** (active 1510–47), respectively. Other important manifestations of the Manueline style are to be seen in the metalwork of the period, notably the gold and enamel Belém monstrance (1506; Lisbon museum), commissioned by Dom Manuel from the goldsmith Gil Vicente.

The finest examples of Manueline civil architecture are the extensions made by Dom Manuel to the royal palace at Sintra, where some influence of Moorish (*mudéja*) crafts is visible in the elaborate wooden ceilings (*alfarge*) and glazed tiles (*azulejos*) imported from Seville. In the Alentejo and Algarve a series of curious 'gothic-mudéjar' churches with battlemented parapets and cylindrical cone-capped turrets was built at the end of the 15C—examples being São Bras at Évora and Santo André at Beja.

In general, however, *mudéjar* elements in Portuguese 15th and 16C architecture are much less prominent than in Spain and, apart from Sintra, virtually confined to the province of Alentejo—where the *mudéjar* craftsmanship was seemingly dependent upon influence from neighbouring Andalucía—the techniques being brought across the frontier perhaps by itinerant Moorish artisans.

Some more-or-less plausible efforts have been made in the interests of tidy classification by leading art historians, including Reynaldo dos Santos and Robert Smith, to identify common stylistic characteristics between the principal Manueline monuments. But it is probably more realistic to accept Vergílio Correia's conclusion that there were as many different schools of Manueline architecture as there were major monuments. The common factors which make the term Manueline useful are firstly that the buildings so categorised all date from between about 1490 and 1540, and secondly that they are all constructively Gothic and belong to the last phase of that style.

**Attributions**. A word of warning should here be interjected on the subject of attributions of the design of buildings and sculpture in Portugal by named artists. Little or nothing is known of Portuguese Gothic or Manueline sculptors. Usually we only have the name of the master builder (*mestre das obras*) who was in overall charge of construction. Sculptors, stonemasons, carpenters and woodcarvers would work under his supervision, but he might or, more likely, might not be responsible for the precise design to which each craftsman worked. There is no evidence for example that Diogo de Arruda designed the sculptural decoration of the chapterhouse at Tomar—the most striking and original of all Manueline achievements—although the window surrounds were carved while he was master of the works there. For the reign of João III the problem of identifying the designers of buildings becomes if anything even more difficult because the king was a keen amateur architect and from 1541 onwards had at court an artistic adviser, **Francisco de Holanda**, who had spent the years 1538–40 in Italy, sent there by the king himself, to study ancient and modern art and architecture and fortification. In Italy, Holanda was befriended by Michelangelo, Antonio da Sangallo the younger, and Sebastiano Serlio, and he brought back with him to Portugal an impressive collection of drawings (now in the library of the Escorial).

# Early Renaissance Architecture and Sculpture

Portugal began slowly to accept Renaissance art and architecture during the 1530s and 1540s. Although (according to Vasari) a leading Italian sculptor-architect, namely **Andrea Sansovino**, had spent some years in Portugal during the 1490s 'leaving behind him one who could complete his unfinished works', the influence of these two forerunners seems to have been negligible. A taste for Renaissance decorative themes was no doubt developed by the importation from Italy of illuminated manuscripts, illustrated books, woodcuts, and small works of art such as medals, ceramics, silver work, and perhaps small paintings. Dom Manuel possessed a magnificent example of Renaissance illumination in the seven-volume Jerónimos Bible (now in the Torre do Tombo National Archive, Lisbon), commissioned by his predecessor João II in 1494 from the Florentine shop of the celebrated miniaturist Attavante.

The first practitioners of the Italian Renaissance style in Portugal were a series of gifted French sculptors who introduced the highly ornate architectural decoration which had originally been developed in Lombardy in the 15C and acclimatised to France early in the 16C. These sculptors—**Nicolas Chanterène** (active in Portugal 1517–c 1540), **Philippe Houdart** (Filipe Hodart; active at Toledo 1522–26 and at Coimbra 1530–34), and **Jean de Rouen** (João de Ruão; active at Coimbra c 1530–70)—carved statues, portals, tombs, pulpits, retables, and whole chapels, in a style which from the 1530s to 1550s is more or less identical with the Plateresque style which was flourishing contemporaneously in Spain, and similar early Renaissance work elsewhere in Europe, in which great prominence was given to baluster columns, and in which vigorous invention compensates for imperfect knowledge of classical rules and proportions. Chanterène's altarpieces at São Marcos de Tentúgal (1522) and N.S. da Pena, Sintra (1529–32) exemplify this style. As also in Spain and France, there are only a few exceptional buildings, tombs, and retables prior to the mid century which reveal a more serious knowledge of the Renaissance style. In architecture this may be associated with Sagredo's valuable textbook of the classical rules (*Medidas del Romano*), first published at Toledo in 1526, then twice at Paris in the 1530s, and after that three times at Lisbon in 1541 and 1542. The third and fourth books of Serlio's *Architecture*, published at Venice in 1537 and 1540, would also no doubt soon have reached the Peninsula (they were translated into Spanish and published at Toledo in 1552).

Among the most elegant and harmonious of early Portuguese Renaissance works are the chapel of São Pedro in the Old Cathedral at Coimbra (1537), the tomb of Dom Afonso de Portugal at Évora (1537), and the very beautiful little church of

N.S. da Conceição at Tomar (dated on good evidence to the 1530s by Professor Rafael Moreira).

## Late Renaissance Architecture

For over 150 years from the middle of the 16C Portuguese architecture reacted slowly to the changes of style initiated in Italy—gradually developing a series of individual permutations of late Renaissance or Mannerist designs and resisting the advent of the Baroque until as late as the second decade of the 18C. Nevertheless, despite this retardataire aspect, if not because of it, Portuguese architecture during this century and a half offers a number of unusual, interesting, and beautiful buildings.

Among the most important monuments belonging to the third quarter of the 16C are the three new cathedrals constructed after new dioceses had been established in 1545 at Leiria, Portalegre and Miranda do Douro. These were all ribvaulted 'hall churches' with side aisles of the same height as the nave. Several fine churches in the Alentejo (e.g., Santo Antão at Évora, built 1557–63, and the slightly later parish churches of Estremoz and Veiros) follow a similar pattern. Centralised forms are represented by the octagonal chapel of the Dominican nuns at Elvas (1543–57), the *ermida* of São Gregório at Tomar, the chapel of Santo Amaro at Lisbon (1549), and the chapel of N.S. de Valverde near Évora, a 'crystalline' structure comprising five interlocking octagonal spaces (c 1550; attributed to Manuel Pires). Other complex plans include the palace chapel at Salvaterra de Magos (across the river from Santarém), which combines square, rectangular, and hexagonal spaces; and somewhat later the remarkable circular church and cloister (begun 1576) of N.S. do Pilar at Vila Nova de Gaia. At Belém a vaulted chancel in a severe classical style was added to the Manueline monastery church in 1571–72 (attributed to Jerónimo de Ruão). At Évora an astonishing sculptural façade was added c 1550 (according to Professor Moreira) to the church of N.S. da Graça, and a handsome new church dedicated to the Espírito Santo, built for the Jesuits (1567–74) by Manuel Pires and the royal architect **Afonso Alvares** (active third quarter 16C). This latter church, together with São Roque, Lisbon (also begun in 1567), provide early examples of Jesuit preaching churches and are important for the history of Jesuit architecture. At Viana do Castelo a new façade for the Misericórdia church was built by João Lopes the Younger (1589) with three storeys of open loggias, a design evidently derived from a Netherlandish or Rhenish architectural engraving.

The most remarkable building of the late 16C is the main cloister of the Convent of Christ at Tomar, begun in 1558 by the Spanish master builder **Diogo de Torralva** (1500–64). After Torralva's death construction ceased and was not resumed until 1584 when new designs were given by the Bolognese military engineer **Filippo Terzi** (1520–97) who had previously been ducal architect at Urbino (1559–74). Terzi's new design for the upper storey and alteration of Torralva's lower storey incorporate motifs derived from Girolamo Genga, Sanmicheli, and Palladio.

## Religious Architecture: 1580–1700

During the reign of the Spanish kings, Philip II and his son and grandson, in Portugal from 1580 to 1640, there was current what William Beckford described in *An Excursion to the monasteries of Alcobaça and Batalha* (London, 1835) as 'the majestic style which prevailed during the Spanish domination of Portugal'. He was specifically referring to N.S. da Luz at Carnide, in the environs of Lisbon, of 1575–96. The imposing monumental style of this edifice reflects the late Renaissance or Mannerist phase of architectural development which was in fashion in post-Tridentine Italy, and was closely paralleled by the *estilo desornamentado* in Spain. The two finest examples of this style in Portugal, both begun in the 1590s, are the Jesuit church (now Sé Nova, or new cathedral) at Coimbra, and São Vicente de Fora at Lisbon. It has been conjectured that Baltasar Alvares (active c 1575–1624), nephew of the royal architect Afonso, was responsible for the former. The design of the latter is usually ascribed to Filippo Terzi (see above) who perhaps received some assistance from Baltasar Alvares. It is improbable that any design contribution was made by the Spanish royal housekeeper (*aposentador*) and architect Juan de Herrera, who accompanied Philip II of Spain to Portugal and was with him at Lisbon during Philip's stay there in 1580–83.

Less famous, but still impressive, churches built in Beckford's 'majestic style' are to be seen throughout the country. The Dominican church (early 17C) at Bemfica near Lisbon is a good example, and the Augustinian church at Vila Viçosa (begun 1634) is another: and there are a whole series in and around Oporto, among them several Benedictine monastery churches—the one in the city itself (begun 1602) and those at Santo Tirso (first half 17C), and Tibães (begun 1628), near Braga; also the churches of the Augustinian monasteries of Moreira da Maia (1588–1622), north of Oporto, and of Grijó (late 16C), south of the city; and, in addition, the Jesuit church of São Lourenço (known as the 'Grilos'; begun 1614), and the contemporary church of São João Novo, which are both in the city and are remarkable for their powerfully monumental façades (which conflate designs by Serlio published in 1551 and 1575).

The considerable number of monastic establishments with fine large vaulted churches which were built during the sixty years of Spanish rule, seem to indicate that this was not a period of economic impoverishment for Portugal. The period of national penury, when art and architecture inevitably suffered from some neglect, was the second half of the 17C. The re-establishment of independence (1640) involved a twenty-eight-year war with Spain from which recovery was slow and spending resources therefore severely restricted.

It was not until the beginning of the 18C that the discovery of gold and, later, diamonds, in Brazil changed this situation, and patronage of the arts revived. Meanwhile the completion of buildings of religious foundations which had been begun under the Spanish kings was slowly pursued, and a very few new ones started—e.g., the domed church of N.S. do Carmo at Évora (begun 1670), the church of the Jesuit College at Santarém (now Seminary; begun 1676), and the convent of Santa Clara-a-Nova, Coimbra (1649–96), the design of which is attributed to the mathematician-architect Fr João Turriano (1610–79), Portuguese-born son of the Cremonese Leonardo Torriani (c 1559–c 1630), who had succeeded Terzi as Chief Engineer (*engenheiro-mór*) of the kingdom in 1598. To the very end of the 17C belongs the impressive convent of the Congregados do Oratório at Estremoz. The most original building of this period, Santa Engrácia, at Lisbon, was not completed (and remained unfinished until 1966). This centralised church of Greek cross plan with apsidal terminations to the arms, and towers in the four angles, was begun in 1682 by the architect **João Nunes Tinoco** (1631–90).

W.C. Watson, constrained by the prejudices of his time, described Santa Engracia as 'the real end of architecture in Portugal'. In saying this he ignored almost all the buildings of the 18C which was perhaps the richest and most varied period in the whole history of Portuguese architecture.

# Houses: 1400–1800

Although ecclesiastical buildings absorbed the principal architectural skill and resources of the Portuguese up to the end of the 18C, secular architecture was not entirely neglected, being represented, albeit usually rather modestly, by many charming town and country houses. A few late Gothic town houses and town halls survive; e.g., at Viana do Castelo, Caminhã, Barcelos, Alcáçovas (Alentejo), and Évora, most of them more or less altered by subsequent reconstruction. Houses of the regular and symmetrical kind which were usual in Italy from the 15C were almost unknown in Portugal before the 17C. The old, irregular, royal palaces remained virtually unmodified, indicating a curious indifference to Renaissance ideals of order and balance. Despite Vasari's story, the 'very beautiful palace with four towers' allegedly designed for the king of Portugal by Andrea Sansovino in the 1490s, may, Professor Moreira believes, have furnished the plan for the Castelo novo (Quartel de Dragões) begun by Diogo de Arruda (see above) at the southern entrance to the city of Évora. Dom João III received plans from Italy in 1550 for a new royal palace, and construction was begun at Xabregas, north-east of Lisbon, but the king's death in 1557 interrupted the work and it was never resumed. Small 16C town houses showing Italian influence survive at Lisbon (Casa dos Bicos, Rua dos Bacalhoeiros) and Braga (former Casa dos Expostos, Rua de São João); and eventually, towards the end of the century, a large square town house with four towers was built by the waterfront at Lisbon (palace of the marquesses of Castelo Rodrigo, begun 1585, burnt down 1751)—after which regular, symmetrical designs began at last to become more and more generally accepted.

The country house in Portugal developed from the medieval fortified tower, to which, as the land became more peaceful, low wings of one or two storeys were adjoined, in order to provide more commodious living quarters. Fine examples in the Alentejo are the **Torre das Aguias** (c 1500) of the Counts of Atalaia, near Mora, and the castle (c 1532) of the Dukes of Braganza at Évoramonte, which has vaulted Manueline state rooms on each floor. By the mid 16C the tower, now sometimes duplicated as a concession to Renaissance principles, had become a mere ornamental adjunct; but towers continued commonly to be incorporated in Portuguese country houses, until as late as the 19C.

Two important early country houses near Setúbal which reveal in their design a more than usually strong Renaissance influence are those of the Quinta da Bacalhôa (mid 16C), and the Quinta das Torres (late 16C). In both the layout includes a garden conceived as an extension of the house. Examples of houses dating originally from the 16C but enlarged and altered subsequently are the enormous Palace of the Dukes of Braganza at Vila Viçosa (begun 1501, and preserving its original Manueline arcaded courtyard), the Casa de Basto at Évora, and the Casa e Torre de Ribafria, near Sintra: the last two possess loggias, an important 16C innovation, and the Casa de Basto has exceptionally fine state rooms of c 1570, one of them oval, vaulted and ribbed, with lively frescoes signed by Francisco de Campos and dated 1578.

Among the architecturally more important 17C noble houses are the Palace of the Dukes of Aveiro at Azeitão, near Setúbal; the Palacio da Mitra, and the Almada, Galveias, Fronteira, and Palhavã palaces—all in or near Lisbon; the Calhariz house near Sesimbra (Setúbal), the Vale de Flores house near Braga, and the Palace of the marquesses of Ponte de Lima at Mafra. Although the five above-mentioned houses in or near Lisbon are now within the boundaries of the city, they were originally built (except for the Almada palace) in what used to be open country. The palace of the counts of Galveias and the Calhariz and Vale de Flores houses are built on the French plan (deriving from the Château de Bury, 1511) in which an entrance court formed by lateral wings projecting from the main house is closed in front only by a screen wall. The palace of the marquesses of Fronteira (c 1670) displays two storeys of Palladian loggias in front, and at the back it has one of the most beautiful formal gardens in Portugal, integrated architecturally with the house. The Fragosos-Barahonas *solar* at Alcáçovas, south-west of Évora, dating from the mid 17C, is square in plan with towers at the corners and a central arcaded courtyard. As the century advanced, the owners' private chapel became an increasingly prominent feature in Portuguese noble houses, especially in the country. In the Vale de Flores house the chapel, dated 1687, occupies the south wing.

The *solar* (that is, the manor house or seat of a noble family) of Bertiandos, which lies between Ponte de Lima and Viana do Castelo, admirably demonstrates the development of the Portuguese country house, from the massive medieval square tower (this one reconstructed in 1566) to the sophisticated arrangements of the 18C which here include a monumental approach stairway and first floor verandahs facing south-west: the Bertiandos *solar* in fact comprises two separate houses, joined by the tower, and a large private chapel extends outwards at the back. Likewise, in central Portugal, the development of the country house from the 16C to the 18C is admirably displayed in the beautiful house of the Quinta of Penha Longa, near Sintra, and the Quinta da Amoreira da Torre near Montemor-o-Novo (the word *quinta* means a country estate, and by association a country house).

There are numerous fine 18C country houses scattered throughout northern and central Portugal. In the north the baroque villas built by the Tuscan architect-painter **Niccolò** (or Nicolau) **Nasoni** (1691–1773) are especially remarkable: among these are the Palácio do Freixo (1750) to the east of Oporto, and the unfinished Quinta da Prelada (c 1747), north-west of the city. At the latter, Nasoni designed a garden with extraordinary vistas of the type which had been dramatically developed in the 17C at Cetinale, near Siena. The well-known *solar* of Mateus near Vila Real, and its fine baroque chapel dated 1750, have also been attributed to Nasoni, and they certainly seem to reflect his exuberant, colourful style. At Braga, notable examples of domestic architecture include the Casa dos Biscainhos, which has a charming formal garden incorporating four rococo fountains and an octagonal gazebo, and several striking town houses including the Archbishop's Palace (now Library), the baroque Town Hall designed by a local architect **André Soares da Silva** (1720–69), and the exceptionally picturesque Casa do Raio, which has been described as 'the most elegant, spontaneous and lyrical rococo exterior in Europe'. Among a number of fine 18C town houses at Oporto, the most splendid and imposing is the Bishop's Palace (Nasoni; 1734–1877). At Guimarães, the baroque town house of the region is paradigmatically represented by the Casa dos Lobos Machados, and the country house by the Palácio de Vila Flor, with its formal terraced garden, in the southern outskirts of the town. In and around Ponte de Lima there are also several fine baroque houses, among which the Casa Aurora in the town  and the Casa das Torres, a few kilometres to the south-west, are good examples.

In the small country town of Lousã, south-east of Coimbra, there is a particularly fine group of 18C town houses, among which that of the Viscondessa do Espinhal (c 1780–1818) is especially striking; while about 24km east of Viseu there are two outstanding baroque country houses, namely the Casa da Insua (near Penalva do Castelo) and the Casa Anadia (near Mangualde), the latter having a notably beautiful interior decorated with azulejos and mural paintings. The towns of the

Alentejo nearly all contain fine 17–18C houses, of which the charming Palácio Amarelo at Portalegre is a notable example.

In the Lisbon area, among the most architecturally distinguished country houses are that of the architect **J.F. Ludovice** (Quinta da Alfarrobeira, at Bemfica, 1727), the Galvão Mexia palace (at Campo Grande, 1746), the Quinta do Correio-Mór at Loures, Pombal's palace at Oeiras (both the last two exemplifying the so-called Pombaline style of the third quarter of the 18C), and several interesting mansions in the Junqueira district near Belém.

The **Neo-classical** style of the last years of the 18C is well represented by the Seteais palace (c 1790), Sintra, and the Casa do Conde Almeida Araujo at Queluz (after 1795).

The last great *solar* to be built in the 18C tradition was the Palácio da Brejoeira (c 1804–34) near Monção on the river Minho.

Unfortunately few Portuguese country houses are regularly opened to the public; but if asked beforehand, preferably in writing, the owner will often allow visitors to see the principal rooms of the house, and the garden.

# Gardens, Fountains, and Aqueducts

As we have seen, the concept of the garden as an open air extension of the house, which had been developed in Renaissance Italy, quickly found acceptance in Portugal. Several notable formal gardens have been mentioned above. Others include the Jardim da Manga (1528–35) adjoining the monastery of Santa Cruz at Coimbra, a remarkable architectural water garden, said to have been designed by Dom João III (and possibly the inspiration for the Four Evangelists fountain in the Escorial); the box garden of the Braganza palace at Vila Viçosa; the baroque garden of the former bishop's palace, now a museum, at Castelo Branco, famous for its statuary; the early 18C gardens of the old convent of Santa Marinha da Costa (now a *pousada*), near Guimarães; and of the *quinta* of N.S. do Carmo at Estremoz. To these should be added the garden of the former archiepiscopal Quinta da Palmeira, on the river Cávado, north of Braga (first half 18C); and the famous mid-18C gardens of the royal palace at Queluz. An especially characteristic and charming feature of Portuguese formal gardens is the large stone-bordered water tank or pool with *azulejo* wall facings. The level of water in these tanks is sometimes raised several feet above the ground to provide unexpected reflections and shimmering light effects. For botanists there are several remarkable gardens such as the unique forest-park of Busaco—surrounded by a wall 6km long. It was formerly a 'desert' of Carmelite monks, who in 1622 began importing exotic trees, particularly the beautiful 'cedar of Busaco' (*Cupressus glauca* or *lusitanica*) from Mexico. Secondly, there are the botanical gardens of Lisbon (1873), of Belém (Ajuda Palace, 1768) and Coimbra (1774). And thirdly, the 19C arboretum-park of the Pena Palace at Sintra.

The visitor to Portugal will soon become accustomed to the ubiquity of fountains. Some are ornamental, but the *chafariz* or public fountain was designed for the practical purpose of filling jars. As its importance merited, it was often given monumental form and sometimes sculptural ornament—providing one of the most attractive decorative elements in the Portuguese townscape. The Fonte do Idolo at Braga may originally have been a prehistoric sacred spring. The Chafariz dos Canos at Torres Vedras dates from the 14C and despite restoration in 1561 the Gothic arches supporting its roof still remain. There are other such Gothic fountain houses, one for example at Atouguia da Baleia, and another at Santarém, the latter, known as the Fonte das Figueiras, being crowned with pointed merlons and decorated with carved coats of arms. There is a superb Manueline fountain in the cloister of the monastery of Batalha, a smaller one in the cloister at Belém, and a charming triangular one, the Fonte da Rainha, at Montemor-o-Novo, in the garden of the Amoreira da Torre *quinta*. Fine Renaissance fountains dating from the second half of the 16C are to be seen in the main squares of Viana do Castelo, and Caminha (both by João Lopes) and at Estremoz (Fonte das Bicas). There are three at Évora: one at the Portas de Moura (1556), one at the Porta de Avis (1573), and the third in the Praça do Geraldo (1571), which latter has been described as 'the queen of fountains', and 'deserving to be crowned' (it is in fact surmounted by a crown). Most of the Renaissance fountains follow the design, probably going back to antiquity, which was preserved at Rome in the fountain of Santa Maria in Trastevere, that is a column or stem supporting one or more shallow circular bowls from which the water falls into a polygonal basin at ground level. This design remained popular in the 17C, being used for example at Évora in the cloister of the Cartuxa (c 1625), at Vila Viçosa (Fonte do Carrascal, c 1630); at Braga in the Campo das Hortas; at Coimbra both in the former Bishop's Palace, now museum (c 1677), and in the Claustro do Silencio of the monastery of Santa Cruz (c 1637); at Tomar in the principal cloister of the Convent of Christ, built by Pedro Fernandes de Torres; and at Barcelos in the Largo da Feira (18C). On the other hand, the medieval tradition of fountain houses persisted too in the guise of classical *tempietti*, rectangular but with twin cupolas at Alter-do-Chão (1556); also rectangular at Trancoso, with a pyramidal roof (Fonte Nova, 1589); and circular, with a cupola, at Elvas (Chafariz da Misericórdia, 1622, designed by Diogo Marques).

Some of the monumental fountains mentioned above were specifically installed to make available to townspeople the water brought by newly built aqueducts. During the 16C aqueducts were built to supply Elvas (1498–1622), Évora (1534–37), Coimbra (1568–70), and Tomar (1593–1614). Lisbon's aqueduct of the Águas Livres was also under consideration in the 16C, although not eventually built until the second quarter of the 18C.

Among many 18C baroque fountains, the handsome Fonte Nova at Coimbra (1725) occupies a site on which there has been a public source of water since at least 1137. The fountains designed by the Italian architects **Antonio Canevari** (at Santo Antão do Tojal, north of Lisbon, c 1730) and **Niccolò Nasoni** (the Tortoise Fountain in the Quinta da Prelada near Oporto, c 1750) are notably scenic; and there is an imposing monumental example dated 1789 at Arruda dos Vinhos, between Lisbon and Santarém. There is a strikingly elegant Neo-classical fountain at Borba, dating from 1781–84.

Among the many fountains of Lisbon, several possess artistic merit, including those in the Largo das Necessidades (1747), in the Largo da Esperança (designed by Carlos Mardel), in the Largo José Figueiredo (1775; with sculpture by António Machado), and in the Largo do Carmo (1786).

The most impressive and spectacular of all Portuguese fountains are however those which punctuate the stages of the ascent to the great 18C pilgrimage churches of Bom Jesus do Monte and of N.S. dos Remédios, situated on steep hillsides outside Braga and Lamego respectively. The fountain in the Court of the Kings below N.S. dos Remédios offers an astonishing dramatic spectacle. At Bom Jesus the central feature of the ascent is a staircase of five stages with late baroque and rococo fountains (completed c 1774) symbolising the five senses. This grand design is paralleled on a smaller scale by the early baroque fountain staircase situated a few kilometres away on the other side of Braga in the hillside garden of the monastery of Tibães.

The idea of the religious gardens of Bom Jesus and N.S. dos Remédios, in which octagonal and hexagonal domed chapels display life-sized groups of wooden figures, realistically painted, representing scenes from the life of Jesus, seems to derive originally from the sub-Alpine sanctuaries of north-west Italy, in particular from the Sacro Monte of Varallo, which was begun in 1486. Likewise the concept of a staircase of fountains in a hillside garden goes back to the 16th and early 17C villas of central Italy at Bagnaia, Tivoli, Frascati, etc. The achievement of the Portuguese designers was to combine these two Italian ideas and from them create a new and original species of scenic garden.

English visitors interested in gardens should not ignore those of the 'Terras de Basto'—the district in and near the river Tâmega above Amarante. Here a score or so of small country house gardens are famous for their architectural and sculptural topiary work and magnificent hedges of box, yew, and other evergreens. This fashion was introduced by two ladies of the locality, Dona Emília and Dona Justina Basto, in the second quarter of the 19C. They learned the art in England where they were educated, and taught it to their gardeners and those of their neighbours, who have passed it down to their successors over several generations.

# Bridges

Portugal is intersected by numerous rivers, including three large ones shared with Spain, the Tagus, Douro, and Guadiana. Consequently bridges are an important architectural feature of the country. The Roman bridge near Alter do Chão in the Alentejo has already been mentioned. Not far away there is another, situated in the parish of Marvão. In northern Portugal a 16-arched Roman bridge crosses the Tâmega at Chaves, and the 400m bridge spanning the beautiful river Lima at Ponte de Lima is partly of Roman construction. Fine examples of medieval bridges are the four-arched Ponte de Mucela crossing the river Alva near Arganil (dating from 1298) and the bridges at Mirandela, of 17 arches crossing the Tua (14C), at Barcelos, spanning the Cávado (15C), and the five-arched Ribeira de Tera bridge near Pavia in the Alentejo. A long 16C bridge crosses the Lima at Ponte de Barca, and there is another fine 12-arched one of similar date, incorporating an earlier structure, crossing the river Vouga at Lamas, east of Aveiro. Among numerous fine 18C bridges we may single out for its handsome appearance the Neo-classical one across the Tâmega at Amarante, built 1781–90 (replacing an original Roman bridge) and ornamented with obelisks. Portugal's splendid series of 19th and 20C steel bridges are noticed below, in the section on modern architecture.

# Painting: 1550–1800

The arts of painting and sculpture in Portugal from the 16th to the early 18C are distinguished by no well-known names. The work of the late 16th and early 17C Mannerists, such as **Francisco Venegas**, a Spaniard settled in Portugal where he was active c 1575–90, and **Simão Rodrigues** (active c 1580–1620), was uniformly undistinguished, as may be seen from the numerous canvases they supplied for retables of the period. **Josefa de Óbidos** (c 1630–84) painted senti-mental religious subjects and elaborate still lifes. **Félix da Costa** (1639–1712), a leading painter of the time, wrote a treatise entitled *The antiquity of the art of painting* (1696) in which he complained of the low esteem into which his art had fallen in

Portugal. To judge by engravings from his designs (no certain original work of his survives) his artistic talent was very modest: nor does his treatise, which was eventually published in 1967, possess any originality.

From this catalogue of uninspired work it is a relief to turn to portraiture, in which a considerably higher standard of achievement prevailed. To **Cristóvão Lopes** (1516–94), son of the royal painter **Gregório** (died 1550), are attributed the portraits of Dom João III and Dona Catarina in the Madre de Deus convent at Lisbon. Other fine 16C portraits are the Dom Sebastião by **Cristóvão de Moraes** (active 1557–71) and an anonymous Old Lady with a rosary, both in the Museu de Arte Antiga at Lisbon. The leading 17C portraitist was **Domingos Vieira** (c 1600–78), a tenebrist whose *chiaroscuro* technique earned him the nickname 'O Escuro'. The portrait of Dona Isabel de Moura in the Lisbon museum, which is attributed to him, suggests knowledge of Velázquez—whose influence is still more certainly apparent in a charming youthful portrait of Catherine of Braganza by an anonymous artist (Évora museum).

During the early decades of the 18C the art of painting in Portugal was dominated by Italian masters—notably the Savoyard portraitist **G.D. Duprà** (1689–1770; active in Portugal 1719–30) and the *trompe l'oeil* painters **Vincenzo Baccarelli** (1682–1745; active at Lisbon c 1710–20) and **Niccolò Nasoni** (1691–1773; active as a painter at Oporto and Lamego 1725–c 1740, thereafter working only as architect). Stimulated by the example of these foreigners, and benefiting from new opportunities to study abroad, Portuguese artists were soon able to compete for commissions. Among the most successful were **Francisco Vieira de Matos** (1699–1783), known as 'Vieira Lusitano', and **Pedro Alexandrino de Carvalho** (1729–1810), prolific painters of altar pieces, and the former also a skilful engraver. The **Morgado de Setúbal** (c 1750–1809) is best known for his powerfully realistic still lifes. *Fin de siècle* Romanticism had a talented representative in **Francisco Vieira** (1765–1805), known as 'Vieira Portuense', who spent twelve years in Italy and England, and painted religious, mythological, and historical subjects as well as portraits (e.g., Angelica Kauffmann painting; Lisbon museum). The work of Vieira's much more famous contemporary, Domingos Antonio Sequeira, is noticed below because it belongs mainly to the 19C.

# Sculpture: 1550–1800

As we have seen, during the first part of the 16C the leading Renaissance sculptors in Portugal were immigrant French masters, among whom the most distinguished was **Nicolas Chanterène** (active to c 1540), who was also a herald in the College of Arms and friend of the humanist scholar Clenardus. These sculptors worked mainly in marble and alabaster. During the last decades of the 16C a new type of retable, conceived as an architectural framework showing off a series of paintings, came into fashion, gradually superseding the stone reredos; and stone statuary was increasingly replaced by wood carved and painted figures. The most gifted of the *imaginários* who carved these figures was **Manuel Pereira** (1588–1683) who early in life emigrated to Spain where his most famous work is the St Bruno in the Miraflores monastery near Burgos. Other *imaginários*, whose statues were made of terracotta as well as wood, included **Frei Cipriano da Cruz**, active 1676–1716 at Tibães (near Braga) and at Coimbra, the **Rendufe sculptor**, active c 1720–34, and a certain Brother **Pedro**, active in the last quarter of the 17C at Alcobaça.

From the beginning of the 18C the international Baroque style began to influence Portuguese sculpture thanks largely to the arrival c 1700 of a French sculptor,

**Claude de Laprade** (1682–1738), to whom is ascribed the interior decoration of the University Library, Coimbra. He was employed at Mafra in the 1730s, at which time several dozen large marble statues, commissioned from leading Italian sculptors, were imported and installed in the monastery church where they presented an example to Portuguese artists of the best Italian late baroque work of their day.

The Portuguese sculptor **José de Almeida** (1700–69), who was trained in Italy, also executed commissions for Mafra; and in 1753 the Italian sculptor **Alessandro Giusti** (1715–99) set up a school for sculptors and architects there. The most famous 18C Portuguese sculptor is **Joaquim Machado de Castro** (c 1731–1822), who came from Coimbra (where the principal museum is named after him). He was trained by José de Almeida and worked under Giusti at Mafra (1756–70). His reputation principally derives from the splendid bronze equestrian statue of Dom José, with attendant figures, which he executed for the Praça do Comércio at Lisbon. Good examples of Portuguese Neo-classical sculpture are to be seen at Queluz and in the Ajuda Palace (Belém). The latter building was the main centre of Portuguese artistic, architectural and decorative activity during the first quarter of the 19C.

# Carved Woodwork: 1500–1800

From the 15C to the end of the 18C *talha*, or carved woodwork, principally for church interiors, represented one of the most popular and widespread of all forms of artistic expression throughout the Iberian Peninsula. Not only reredoses but also pulpits, organ-cases, frames of apertures, and choir stalls, were elaborately carved; and all this woodwork except such utilitarian elements as the seats of choir stalls was usually painted or gilded. After the discovery of gold in Brazil in the 1690s, the gilding of woodwork (talha dourada) became more or less the rule in Portugal.

**Late Gothic** woodcarving is well represented at Coimbra by the reredos in the Old Cathedral, which was begun in 1498 by two Flemish craftsmen, and by the choir stalls (c 1513) in the Santa Cruz monastery church. Good examples of **Mannerist** retables dating from the end of the 16C are to be seen in N.S. do Carmo at Coimbra, the cathedral at Portalegre, and N.S. da Luz, Lisbon; and somewhat later, the retable of São Domingos (c 1632) at Bemfica (Lisbon). The reliquary chapel at the monastery of Alcobaça exemplifies the early Baroque style. The reredos of the high altar (1698) and the transept reliquary retables in the Sé Nova at Coimbra are at last fully baroque in spirit, with Solomonic columns, and gilded all over. This Portuguese **High Baroque** mode of *talha dourada* has been named by Robert Smith the 'National Style'. Examples are to be seen all over the country. There are 12 retables carved in this style in the Jesuit church of the Espirito Santo at Évora for example, and 15 at Santa Clara-a-Nova (Coimbra; c 1696); while the high altar reredoses of São Bento at Oporto (c 1704) and of Santo António at Lagos (c 1715) may be cited as exceptionally fine specimens. The last named church exemplifies the peculiarly Portuguese invention of the *igreja toda de ouro*, the interior completely covered with gilded wood-work. Another example is the church of the Dominican Convent of Jesus at Aveiro (before 1725); while at São Francisco, Oporto (c 1720–70) the gilded woodwork displays a sequence of styles from High Baroque through Late Baroque to Rococo. The church of the nunnery of Santa Clara at Oporto is a late example of a golden church interior, its *talha* carved c 1730 by Miguel Francisco da Silva (active 1726–46). Indicative of conservative national taste was the rejection by Portuguese woodcarvers of the *estípite* (inverted obelisk) type of column shaft which achieved so much popularity among late baroque retable-makers in Spain and Spanish America, although they did develop a remarkable ornate pilaster known as the *quartelão*.

The change in style from High to **Late Baroque** is well demonstrated by the magnificent choir stalls of the nunneries of Arouca (1722–25) and Lorvão (1745). At the former rosewood has been used for the seats while the rest is *talha dourada*; whereas at Lorvão polished rosewood is used throughout. The Italianate Late Baroque or 'Joanine style' (named after Dom João V, who reigned 1706–50) is represented in *talha dourada* by the chancel of the church of the Paulistas at Lisbon, and the retables of the high altars of Oporto and Viseu cathedrals. Splendid examples of late baroque and rococo reredoses are to be seen at Tibães (1757–60) and Falperra (1763), both near Braga; at São Domingos (c 1763), Viana do Castelo; at the chapel of Queluz palace (c 1755) and at N.S. dos Remédios (c 1765) at Évora. The retable of the church of Bom Jesus do Monte near Braga, dating from the beginning of the 19C, is Neo-classical in style.

Among many fine baroque and rococo woodcarved pulpits we may single out for their high quality those in the Madre de Deus church, Lisbon; the monastery church at Tibães; and in São Marcos, Braga—which belong respectively to the early, mid, and late 18C. Splendid carved and gilded organ-cases are to be seen in Oporto cathedral (1727; design attributed to Nasoni), Braga cathedral (two organs, dated 1737 and 1738), Tibães (1785), and São Vicente de Fora at Lisbon (late 18C). The two fine baroque organ-cases (1767–73) in São Miguel de Refóios, Cabeceiras de Basto, together with most of the church's *talha*, including choir stalls, retables, and pulpits, were executed by the Benedictine woodcarver Frei José Vilaça (1731–1809), a follower of André Soares: the work of both of them reveals the influence of Augsburg prints, as Robert Smith has demonstrated in his monographs on the two masters.

# Architecture: Baroque, Rococo, and Neo-classical

Polygonal and other regular geometrical ground plans for churches, probably inspired by Serlio's *Fifth book of architecture* (1st edition Paris, 1547), were employed in Portugal throughout the 17C and 18C. The small 18C rustic church of Janas near Sintra is circular. Octagonal plans occur at Figueira da Foz, Belém, Pombal, Lisbon (Menino de Deus, 1711), Cascais, Braga, Aveiro (N.S. das Barrocas, 1722–32), and Oporto; hexagonal ones at Vila da Feira, Aveiro (two), and Caldas da Rainha (N.S. da Pedra, 1740–47; architect Rodrigo Franco); and Greek cross plans at Santarém, Lisbon (Santa Engrácia, 1682), and Barcelos (N.S. da Cruz, c 1705, attributed to **João Antunes**). These centralised-type plans for churches and chapels were especially popular in the first quarter of the 18C, reflecting Baroque interest in experiments with spatial composition. The most ambitious venture in this direction was the oval church of Bom Jesus do Monte near Braga (1722–25), but it proved unstable and was pulled down and replaced by the present Neo-classical structure (see below). The future for the 'unstable' oval form was to lie not in earthquake-prone Portugal but in Portuguese America.

Meanwhile the new wealth derived from Brazil, and the resulting revival of artistic and architectural aspirations, attracted to Portugal a series of gifted foreigners—among the most prolific and influential of whom were the goldsmith-architect **João Frederico Ludovice** (Johann Friedrich Ludwig, 1670–1752), a German trained in Italy, who arrived in Portugal in 1701 and was responsible for the monastery-palace of Mafra (begun 1717) and for the chancel of Évora cathedral (1718–c 1728); the French sculptor-decorator **Claude de Laprade**

(1682–1738), to whom is attributed the design of the Coimbra University Library (1716–28), one of the most colourful and original interiors of 18C Europe; and **Niccolò Nasoni** (1691–1773), a Tuscan painter, sculptor, and architect of remarkable creative genius—still much underestimated—who designed and rebuilt churches and town and country houses and laid out gardens in the north of Portugal between 1730 and 1770. **Luigi Vanvitelli** (1700–73) designed in 1742 and executed in Italy a complete chapel dedicated to St John—a masterpiece of neo-Palladianism—which was shipped to Lisbon and installed in 1747 in the church of São Roque—thereafter exercising a strong influence on design in the decorative arts of Portugal. Two Italian architects, Tamossi and Azzolini, were responsible for the Seminary (1748–65) at Coimbra. Another Italian, **Giovanni Carlo Bibiena** (died 1760) designed the beautiful Memória church (begun 1760) at Belém; the Hungarian **Carlos Mardel** assisted **Eugénio dos Santos** to rebuild the centre of Lisbon after the 1755 earthquake; the French silversmith and sculptor **J.-B. Robillon** (died 1782) enlarged the royal palace at Queluz from 1758 onwards; **John Carr** of York (1723–1807) designed the great hospital of Santo António (1770–95) at Oporto; Lt. Col. **William Elsden** designed the extensive new university buildings required at Coimbra after Pombal's reforms; and the Italian **F.S. Fabri** (died 1807) designed the Palacio Foz (1777) at Lisbon and was the principal architect of the Ajuda Palace at Belém (begun 1802).

These foreign masters together with several talented and original Portuguese architects were responsible for a series of monuments which are representative of almost all the principal European styles of the 18th and early 19Cs. The façade and plan of Mafra recall the great Central European monasteries of the early 18C, e.g. Weingarten and Einsiedeln; and Ludovice also introduced at Mafra various elements derived from his study of High Baroque buildings in Rome, which contribute to the creation of a remarkably successful eclectic composition. The huge towers flanking the façade derive from the late 16C tower of the royal palace on the waterfront of Lisbon destroyed in the 1755 earthquake. The basilica, which has the first fully developed dome, set upon a high drum, in Portugal, inspired several large churches of late baroque style—notably the pilgrimage shrine of N.S. de Aires at Viana do Alentejo (begun 1743), the church of the monastery of São Miguel de Refoios at Cabeceiras de Basto, and, most splendid of all, the Estrela basilica at Lisbon (1779–90), architects **Mateus Vicente de Oliveira** (1706–86) and **Reinaldo Manuel dos Santos** (1740–89).

Nasoni's near-oval church of the Clérigos at Oporto, with its magnificent *campanile* (inspired by the tower of the Palazzo Vecchio at Florence), belongs to a less conventional and more vigorously ornate variant of the baroque style than Mafra, reflecting the freedom of painted *trompe l'oeil* architecture (in which art Nasoni was well versed) and silver work and furniture. An example of the so-called *transparente*, or concealed lighting effect, which was one of the most sophisticated baroque inventions, is to be seen in the north transept chapel of the church of São Francisco at Évora. The fashion for *chinoiserie* is manifest in the University Library at Coimbra.

**Rococo** is exceptionally well represented in the Minho by a series of fascinating buildings such as the Falperra chapel, near Braga, designed by **André Ribeiro Soares da Silva** (1720–69), which reveal the ubiquitous influence of Italian and German engravings, here interpreted however in a startlingly original manner. In central Portugal **Mateus Vicente de Oliveira** (see above), who worked with Ludovice at Mafra, introduced important rococo elements into his design for the palace at Queluz (1747–52), which are absent in the slightly earlier and almost equally beautiful royal palace of the Necessidades (1745–50; architect **Caetano Tomás de Sousa**) in western Lisbon.

The rebuilding of the centre of Lisbon on a regular gridiron plan of uniform four or five storey blocks after the 1755 earthquake, following the master plan (1756) of **Eugénio dos Santos** (1711–60), was 'the greatest uniform architectural undertaking of the Age of Enlightenment'. The so-called **Pombaline** style generally employed by the architects associated with the rebuilding was characterised by an economical simplicity of form relieved by some baroque and rococo decorative details applied with restraint and discretion. The great set piece of Pombaline Lisbon is the Praça do Comércio.

The **Neo-classical** trend in late 18C architecture is represented in northern Portugal by the Law Courts or Relação (1766–96) at Oporto, designed by João de Almada e Mello (died 1786), under whose influence there were also built the stupendous convent of Santa Clara at Vila do Conde (begun 1777) and the Carrancas palace (c 1790) at Oporto. There is also the work of **Carlos da Cruz Amarante** (1748–1815) at Braga (notably the church of Bom Jesus do Monte, 1784–1811) and at Oporto (University, begun 1805). English Neo-classicism is represented at Oporto—both by John Carr's hospital, already mentioned, and by the British Factory House (begun 1785), designed by Consul John Whitehead (1726–1802).

At Lisbon, the Neo-classical Theatre of São Carlos was built in 1792 by the Italianised Portuguese architect **José da Costa e Silva** (1747–1819), who was also one of the architects of the Ajuda palace (begun 1802 to the designs of F.S. Fabri). Costa e Silva also completed in 1785 the rebuilding of the Italian church of N.S. do Loreto at Lisbon.

To sum up this section, the 18C was a golden period for Portuguese architecture and the decorative arts. Not only were the great monuments at and near Lisbon and Oporto, including the rebuilding of the whole centre of the capital, all admirably successful as sophisticated examples of their various styles, but innumerable smaller buildings in towns and villages throughout the country, and additions made to earlier buildings, as well as their interior decoration and furniture, were no less successful in their more humble way. It would seem as if even local builders, amateur architects, and rustic artisans and craftsmen were inspired, during these years, with instinctive sound judgement and sense of proportion, harmony, colour, and design.

# Fortifications: 16–18C

The new science of fortification based on polygonal bastions, capable of resisting gunpowder artillery, was invented in Italy at the turn of the 15C, and perfected by French military engineers in the 17C. A most interesting transitional style fortress at Vila Viçosa, dating from c 1530 and attributable to the military engineer **Benedetto da Ravenna**, has the massive round bulwarks recommended by Dürer in his treatise of 1527, and a fine rusticated main entrance. It follows exactly a design by Leonardo da Vinci (MS 'B', c 1490), which was by 1530 already old fashioned. So in 1537, when **Francisco de Holanda** was sent by Dom João III to Italy, he was particularly instructed to bring back information on the new science. By the end of the 18C nearly all the land and sea approaches to Portugal were defended by powerful fortresses built in conformity with the new principles. Of those which survive, the most interesting coastal forts are the ones guarding the mouths of the river Sado at Setúbal (late 16C and 17C); Tagus (São Julião da Barra on the north shore, and the circular Torre do Bugio on a shoal in the estuary; 16–17C); Douro

(Castelo de São João da Foz, c 1560–1647); Lima (the pentagonal Forte de S. Tiago da Foz, 1567–96), and Minho (Forte da Insua). On the land frontier during the 17C and 18C rings of fortifications were built round several border towns, including Caminha and Valença, defending the north, and Almeida (a new fortress town built to a regular hexagonal design enclosing a small 16C square fort with round towers of which only foundations survive), Campo Maior, and Elvas, defending the eastern approaches. The new fortified perimeter of the latter town was laid out in 1643, and with the construction of two adjacent forts, those of Santa Luzia (1641–87) and N.S. da Graça (1763–92), Elvas became one of the strongest places in Europe. To the same period belong the new defences of Estremoz and Vila Viçosa. The city of Évora, key to Lisbon, was also re-fortified in the 17C, and six bastions (1651–80) as well as the quadrilateral supporting fort of Santo António (1666–70) survive intact. Most of the 17C fortifications of Portugal were surveyed in 1666–68 by the French military engineer Manesson Mallet and are illustrated in his *Les travaux de Mars* (Paris, 1672).

# Architecture: 19C and 20C

Portuguese 19C and 20C architecture displays the typical stylistic variety which is characteristic of the period throughout Europe. The styles employed included traditional Italianate (Merchants' Exchange, Oporto, begun 1842; National Theatre, Lisbon, architect F. Lodi, 1842–46; Town Hall, Lisbon, architect Domingos Parente, 1867–75; Chamber of Deputies, Lisbon, architect Ventura Terra, begun 1896; Theatre of São João, Oporto, architect Marquês da Silva, 1912–18); Neo-Manueline (Palace Hotel, Busaco, architect Luigi Manini, begun 1888; Central railway station, Lisbon, architect J.L. Monteiro, opened 1889); cosmopolitan picturesque or eclectic (Pena palace, Sintra, designed by Baron Von Eschwege, 1840); Byzantine (Martins Sarmento Institute, Guimarães, architect Marquês da Silva, 1881); and functional (house in Rua Honório de Lima, Oporto, architect Viana de Lima, 1939; *pousada* near Venda Nova, river Cávado, architect Januário Godinho, 1948; Calouste Gulbenkian museum, Lisbon, architects Alberto Pessoa, Pedro Cid, and Ruy Athouguia, 1966–69). Other interesting examples of functional architecture at Lisbon built in the second quarter of this century include the cinemas designed by Raul Lino, Luis Cristino da Silva and Cassiano Branco in the 1920s, the Pavilhão-Radio (Carlos Ramos, 1927–33), the Institute Superior Técnico (Pardal Monteiro, 1927–35), the Edifício Standar Electrica (J.A. Cottinelli Telmo, 1940), the Lisbon Mint (J. Segurado, 1934–50), and the Estoril Estação Telefones (Adelino Nunes, 1938).

Portugal also offers one of the finest series of steel bridges to be seen in Europe—notably the bridge over the Tagus at Santarém (1876–81); the two over the Douro at Oporto designed by Eiffel and by Seyrig, inaugurated in 1877 and 1886 respectively; the one over the mouth of the Lima designed by Eiffel (1895); the one across the mouth of the Douro (1960–63); that across the Tagus estuary (1965), and those, recently completed, spanning the Minho at Valença, and the Guadiana at Castro Marim.

# Painting and Sculpture: 19C and 20C

During the first quarter of the 19C the Portuguese painter **Domingos António Sequeira** (1768–1837), who enjoyed an international reputation, was working in his native country. He returned to Lisbon in 1795 after a seven year sojourn in Rome, but left again in 1823 for France, thereafter returning to Rome where he spent the last ten years of his life. He painted historical, allegorical, and religious subjects as well as portraits—all adequately represented in the Lisbon museum. He was a brilliant draughtsman and his preparatory studies are often even more impressive than the finished paintings. Among his best-known portraits at Lisbon are: *The Viscount of Santarém and his family* (1805), *The young Count of Farrobo* (1813), and *The artist's children*; but his sketches for these portraits and for those of Beresford (c 1815) and Dom João VI (1826) are more memorable. In his late work he developed an increasingly impressionistic technique with the use of bright, shimmering colours.

Portuguese 19C art after Sequeira can best be studied in the Museu do Chiado at Lisbon, and in the Soares dos Reis Museum at Oporto. The latter is named after **António Soares dos Reis** (1847–89), a sculptor from Oporto whose work was much admired by his contemporaries, and has retained its popularity since (e.g., *O desterrado*, 1872; Oporto museum). Subsequently, the prolific Oporto sculptor **António Teixeira Lopes** (1866–1942) achieved almost as much popular success. Both these sculptors were competent portraitists.

The best portrait painters of the mid 19C were the **Visconde de Meneses** (1820–78) and **Miguel Angelo Lupi** (1826–83)—good examples of their work being the former's *Portrait of the artist's wife* (1862), and the latter's *Marquesa de Belas*. The topographical drawings and watercolours of **Carlos Vanzeller** (1811–39) are unusually lively and charming. The most brilliant and promising artist of the second half of the century was **Henrique César de Araujo Pousão**, who died aged 25 in 1884.

The most famous 20C Portuguese artist is **Maria-Helena Vieira da Silva** (1908–92), who lived and worked most of her life in Paris. Her paintings are to be seen in the principal museums of modern art throughout the world.

# Applied Arts

The Portuguese have always excelled in the domestic and practical arts. Wrought-iron balconies, although less striking than Spanish *rejas*, nevertheless distinguish the façades of most town houses in Portugal. The best representative collections of textiles, silver, porcelain, and furniture are those of the Museu de Arte Antiga at Lisbon, and the Machado de Castro museum at Coimbra. Ceramics and furniture are also well represented in the Soares dos Reis museum at Oporto, and there are smaller collections in regional and local museums throughout the country, e.g. those of Évora, Viana do Castelo, Guimarães, Lamego, and Viseu, to mention only a few: and in this context it is worth remarking that the smaller museums in Portugal seldom disappoint the visitor who is interested in the domestic arts, and they are often housed in architecturally important buildings which are worth seeing in their own right. The most famous specialised museum in Portugal is that devoted to cere-monial coaches at Belém, near Lisbon: these masterpieces of cabinet-makers' and decorators' art dating from the 16C to the 19C comprise the finest collection of the kind in Europe. Another important collection of carriages may now be seen at Vila Viçosa.

The development in Portugal of the very important Iberian art of **azulejos** (painted tiles) may also be studied in museums throughout the country, notably in Lisbon in the Museu de Arte Antiga and in the Museu do Azulejo (Madre de Deus convent), and at Coimbra in the Machado de Castro museum. The best examples of 16C *azulejos* still *in situ* are those of the palace at Sintra. There are particularly fine displays of 17C *azulejos* at Lisbon in the Fronteira palace, and in the chapel of Santo

Amaro, at Santarém (Marvila church), Elvas (Dominican nunnery chapel), Montemór-o-Novo (Convent of N.S. da Saudação), Évora, and Coimbra. 18C painted tiles are to be seen *in situ* all over the country, and nearly always enhance and enliven the interiors and the exterior walls to which they are applied.

Two principal trends should be noted in the development of the *azulejo*. First, colour: up to the end of the 17C a wide range of tints was employed (yellows, blues, and greens predominating); then, from the end of the 17C, the fashion changed to the use of blue and white only; after which, starting in the mid 18C, polychromy returned again to favour, although the blue and white fashion did not by any means die out. Secondly, design: until about the middle of the 17C patterns made up of repeated geometrical and other non-figurative motifs, resembling carpet patterns, were usual; but already by the later 16C tile pictures, often based on engravings, were created, occupying a whole block or panel of *azulejos;* and as the 17C advanced these pictorial designs, increasing in size, realism and variety of subject matter, gradually superseded the earlier two-dimensional repetitive patterns, and introduced perspective effects and chiaroscuro, even occasionally achieving effects of *trompe l'oeil.*

# Townscape

Few towns in Portugal fail to offer the visitor one or two attractive streets and squares; and sometimes there are whole quarters of exceptional merit. In Lisbon, for instance, the Alfama, the Bairro Alto and the Baixa admirably display the varied types of urbanism they represent—from the natural organic growth of the first to the imposed geometrical plan of the last. Interesting small-scale examples of regular town plans are to be seen at Vila Real de Santo Antonio (1774) in the Algarve, and Manique do Intendente (early 19C), south-west of Santarém. Among country towns noted for their exceptional architectural charm and urbanistic interest many would put Évora first. Other such towns are Elvas, Vila Viçosa, Portalegre, Obidos, Tomar, Santarém, Viseu, Guimarães, Valença, and Braganza; and less well-known, but at least equally remarkable for their charm and character, are Mirandela, Ponte de Lima, Lamego, and Linares in the north; Castelo de Vide, Borba, and Monsaraz, in the Alentejo; and Tavira, and Alcoutim in the Algarve—to cite only a few examples.

# Portuguese artists

As many of the names of the more eminent Portuguese artists, sculptors and architects (including foreigners working in Portugal) referred to in this guide are not generally known, they are listed below, with their dates, for ease of reference.

Afonso, Jorge (fl. 1508–40)
Almada e Mello, João de (d. 1786)
Almada Negreiros, José de (1893–1970)
Almeida, José de (1700–69)
Alvares, Afonso (fl. 1550–75)
Alvares, Baltasar (fl. c 1575–1624)
Amarante, Carlos da Cruz (1748–1815)
Arruda, Diogo de (fl. 1510–31)

Arruda, Francisco de (fl. 1510–47)
Baccarelli, Vincenzo (1682–1745; in Lisbon c 1710–20)
Bibiena, Giovanni Carlo (João Carlos; d. 1760)
Boitac, Diogo (fl. 1494–c 1520)
Bordalo Pinheiro, Rafael (1846–1905)
Carlos, Frei (fl. 1517–29)
Carr (of York), John (1723–1807)
Castilho, Diogo de (fl. 1525–75)

Castilho, João de (fl. c 1510–52)
Chanterène, Nicolas (fl. 1517–40)
Columbano, Bordalo Pinheiro
  (1857–1929)
Costa e Silva, José da (1747–1819)
Dos Santos, Reinaldo Manuel (d. 1789)
Duprà, Giorgio Domenico
  (1689–1770; in Portugal 1719–30)
Eiffel, Gustave (1832–1923)
Fabri, Francesco Saverio (1761–1807)
Fernandes, Garcia (fl. 1514–65)
Fernandes, Mateus (fl. 1480–1515)
Fernandes, Vasco ('Grão Vasco';
  fl. 1506–42)
Figueiredo, Cristóvão (fl. 1515–38)
Giusti, Alessandro (1715–99)
Gonçalves, Nuno (fl. 1450–71)
'Grão Vasco': see Fernandes, Vasco
Henriques, Francisco (fl. 1500–18)
Herrera, Juan de (1530–97)
Holanda, António de (fl. 1515–
  c 1557)
Houdart, Philippe (1530–34, in
  Portugal)
Laprade, Claude de (1682–1738)
Lopes, Cristovão (1516–94)
Lopes, Gregório (c 1490–c 1550)
Lopes, A. Teixeiro (1866–1942)
Ludovico, João Frederico (Johann
  Friedrich Ludwig; 1670–1752)
Lupi, Miguel Angelo (1826–83)
Machado de Castro, Joaquim
  (c 1731–1822)
Mardel, Carlos (fl. 1733–63)
Meneses, Visconde de (1820–78)
Morais, Cristóvão (fl. 1557–71)
Morgado de Setúbal (c 1750–1809)
Nasoni, Niccolò (or Nicolau;
  1691–1773)
Noël, Alexandre (1752–1834)

Óbidos, Josefa de (c 1630–84)
Oliveira, Marquês d' (1852–1927)
Oliveira, Mateus Vicente de (1706–86)
Oliveira Bernardes, Policarpo de
  (1695–1778)
Pillement, Jean (1727–1808)
Pires, Marcos (fl. 1517–27)
Pousão, Henrique César de Araujo
  (1859–84)
Ramalho, António (1859–1916)
Reis, Carlos (1863–1940)
Ruão, Jerónimo de (d. c 1593)
Ruão, João de (Jean de Rouen;
  c 1530–70)
Sardoal, Master of (fl. 1495–1525)
Sequeira, Domingos António de
  (1768–1837)
Silva, André Ribeiro Soares de
  (1720–69)
Silva, Miguel Francisco da
  (fl. 1726–46)
Soares dos Reis, António (1847–89)
Sousa, Aurelio de (1865–1922)
Sousa, Manuel Caetano Tomás de
  (1742–1802)
Terzi, Filippo (Felipe; 1520–97)
Tinoco, João Nunes (1631–90)
Torralva, Diogo de (1500–64)
Turriano, Fr. João (1610–79)
Vanzeller, Carlos (1811–39)
Vaz, Gaspar (c 1490–c 1568)
Vieira. Domingos ('O Escuro';
  c 1670–78)
Vieira, Francisco ('Vieira Portuense';
  1765–1805)
Vieira do Matos, Francisco ('Vieira
  Lusitano'; 1699–1783)
Vieira da Silva, Maria-Helena
  (1908–92)
Vilaça, Fr. José (1731–1809)

# Glossary of Architectural and Allied Terms

**Abóbada**, vault

**Adro**, precinct of a church

**Ajimece**, two-light Moorish window divided by a slender column

**Albufeira**, reservoir

**Aldeia**, village

**Almofadado**, (lit. pillows) rustication

**Alfarge**, *mudéjar* timber ceiling, usually hipped or domical

**Alpendre**, porch

**Anta**, megalithic grave

**Artesonado**, coffered wooden ceiling

**Azulejos**, glazed tiles, usually painted, of designs or scenes, or with floral patterns (*albarrada*), and about 13–15cm square; but see above

**Bairro**, district or quarter of a town

**Baixo**, lower

**Barragem**, dam of reservoir

**Beco**, alley, often a cul-de-sac

**Bilros**, elaborately turned finials

**Cabaceira**, apse

**Cadeiral**, choir-stalls

**Câmara municipal**, Town Hall

**Camarim**, shrine of an image

**Capela-mór**, chancel or sanctuary

**Chafariz**, public fountain, often monumental

**Charola**, ambulatory of centralised church; niche for image of saint

**Chave**, key, or keystone

**Cima**, top or summit

**Citânia**, prehistoric hill-settlement

**Claustro**, cloister

**Columna salomónica**, column, usually of Corinthian order, with twisted shaft

**Contador**, counter, desk, or cabinet

**Coro**, choir; the *coro alto* or upper gallery often containing the stalls

**Correio**, Post Office

**Cortes**, Parliament

**Cruzeiro**, cross; or crossing of a church

**Custódio**, monstrance

**Direita**, right

**Dourada**, gilded; see *talha*

**Entalhador**, carver, usually of wood

**Ermida**, hermitage or chapel, often isolated

**Esmalte**, enamel

**Espigueiros**, seen in the Minho, and equivalent to the *hórreos* of Galicia, these small granaries, corn lofts, or storehouses are raised on mushroom-shaped pillars to keep vermin from entering.

**Esquerda**, left

**Estalagem**, hotel or inn

**Fechado**, closed

**Feira**, fair; *férias*, a holiday

**Foz**, mouth of a river

**Guarita**, bartizan tower

**Horta**, kitchen-garden

**Igreja**, church, a parish church being an *igreja matriz*

**Ilha**, island

**Imaginário**, carver of images

**Janela**, window

**Jardim**, garden

**Joanine (Joanino)**, late baroque style in fashion during the reign of Dom João V (1706–50)

**Judiaria**, Jewish enclave, or ghetto

**Laceria**, Islamic geometrical decorative patterning of interlacing polygonal and star shapes

**Largo**, small square or market-place

**Manueline (Manuelino)**, final phase of Gothic in Portugal current during the reign of Dom Manuel I (1495–1521) and later

**Marfim**, ivory

**Mármore**, marble

**Marrano**, former derogatory name for a Jew ostensibly converted to Catholicism

**Mata**, wood or forest

**Mestre de Obras**, clerk of the works

**Miradouro**, belvedere or balcony

**Mosteiro**, monastery

**Moçárabe** or **mozárab**, Christian subject to the Moors: a term extended to their architecture

**Mudéjar**, Moslem subject to the Christians: a term extended to their architecture and decoration

**Muralha**, walls

**Nora**, water-wheel

**Paço**, country house or palace (usually *palácio*)

**Paragem**, a halt

**Pau preto**, Brazilian rosewood; also jacaranda. Among other woods (*madeira*) are *pau santo*, lignum vitae, and *mogno*, mahogany

**Pedra lioz**, calcareous white stone, resembling marble

**Pelourinhos**, stone columns serving the purpose of pillories, seen in numerous towns and villages in the northern half of Portugal, but less frequently south of the Tagus. They were the emblem of feudal or municipal jurisdiction, and the edicts of town councils were read from their steps. Near the summit of some, iron supports survive, from which were suspended chains, to which criminals were fastened: and it might in addition serve as a gibbet. Many were highly ornamented, while others are quite plain. In view of their ubiquity, only a few examples are specifically mentioned in this Guide

**Planicie**, plain

**Poço**, well

**Pombaline (Pombálino)**, architectural style employed in the rebuilding of Lisbon after the 1755 earthquake, while the Marquês de Pombal was virtually dictator of Portugal (1750–77)

**Portagem**, toll

**Praça**, place or square

**Prado**, field

**Praia**, beach or shore

**Quadro** or *pintura*, painting

**Quartel**, barracks

**Quarto**, room

**Quinta**, country estate, or the main residence on such

**Rés do chão**, ground floor.

**Retábulo**, reredos or altarpiece, often highly decorated

**Retrato**, portrait

**Saida**, exit

**Sé**, cathedral

**Século**, century

**Sobreiro**, cork oak

**Solar**, manor house, or seat of an armigerous family

**Talha**, carved work, usually in wood; *talha dourada*, gilded woodwork

**Tecto**, ceiling

**Torre de menagem**, castle keep

**Tremido**, parallel grooving in furniture

**Zimbório**, dome or cupola

# Introduction to Port and the Wines of Portugal

By the late **David Francis**; revised by **David Delaforce**

Although Portuguese wines are referred to by Chaucer, these came from Lisbon: those of the Upper Douro were described in the 1460s by a Czech traveller named Rosmital, who found there a strong wine made from over-ripe grapes dried like raisins, which was called 'Vinho da Grécia'. We find few allusions to a Port type of wine until 1700, when Thomas Woodmass, a young Yorkshireman, left an account of his trip up the Douro to a wild region still the preserve of bandits. By then there was in 'O Porto' a thriving and enterprising Factory, or community of British merchants, many of them engaged in importing Newfoundland cod, or cloth from England, who were eager to profit by the sudden growth in demand for Portuguese wines. They had in fact been anticipated by their colleagues in Viana do Castelo, who had found wines of a claret type near the Lima, which with other rivers in the Minho ran through a broad valley; whereas the Douro, although a much larger stream, flowed through a gorge above Oporto, and there was no easy way across the mountains it traversed. An occasional driblet of Upper or Alto Douro wine may have reached Oporto, but in general there was little knowledge of conditions there.

The entry of French wines into Britain had been prohibited from 1679 to 1685. During these years large quantities of wines had passed the British Customs as German, Spanish, or Portuguese, but it is difficult to say exactly where they came from. Portuguese wines averaged 5833 tuns, but in three of these years they fluctuated between 13,000 and 16,000 tuns, incredible if one considers that the figures for 1677 and 1686 were only 427 and 617 pipes, of which 407 and 253 pipes respectively came from Oporto, a pipe being a barrel containing 115 gallons, or 534 litres. A start had been made.

After the outbreak of war in 1690, when the prohibition was renewed, the import of Portuguese wines rose rapidly to 8000 pipes and to 10,000 during the War of the Spanish Succession (1702–13), after which exports from Oporto gained the lead over those from Lisbon, and the term 'Port Wine' tended to cover all Portuguese wines.

The wines which the British appreciated in particular were the product of vines grown on poor soil on small holdings high up in the mountains, where the schistose terraced slopes produced a crop of red wines of unusual strength, even if scanty. According to legend, Peter Bearsley and other adventurous men from Viana and Oporto had visited certain monasteries near the Douro which could sell them wines in quantity. But they were hard to discover, and Woodmass had much ado to avoid a rival party, which threatened to poach on his findings. The British continued to buy from the peasant farmers to their mutual advantage, but the larger landlords, realising that they were on to a good thing, had meanwhile banded together in an endeavour to corner the market.

In the reigns of William and Mary, and of Queen Anne, Port and claret were adopted as emblems of the Whig and Tory parties. The Whigs stood for Port; the Tories (who favoured an eventual rapprochement with France) supported claret. The Whigs enjoyed claret, burgundy, and champagne as well as anyone else, and while declaiming their political arguments in favour of Port, would admit in private that it had its defects: nevertheless it should be drunk as a patriotic duty, if for no other reason. Jonathan Swift, who in his *Journal to Stella* remarked 'I love white Portugal wine better than claret, champagne, or burgundy', composed the doggerel:

'Be sometimes to your Country true,
Have once the public good in view:
Bravely despise Champagne at Court
And choose to dine at home on port'.

The Tories had no hesitation in roundly denouncing Port, in the words of Richard Ames, who wrote *Search after Claret* and then in 1693, a satire against Portuguese wines:

'Mark how it smells. Methinks a real pain
Is by its odour thrown upon my brain.
I've tasted It—'tis spiritless and flat,
And has as many different tastes,
As can be found in compound pastes...'.

In 1693 William Salmon, somewhat of a quack, described Port or 'port-a-port' (in his *Compleat English Physician*) as a strong full-bodied wine with medicinal qualities, although not particularly palatable, for the earlier Port wines travelled from their eyries in skins on mule-back, which gave them a strong taste of resin, and much of the wine was bitter or turbid, or, alternatively, syrupy. The so-called 'ambrosia of the north' never really overcame these defects until the close of the 18C, when increased production and competition prompted an improvement, and the art of fortification became better understood. The best Port tended to become a rare commodity, and was generally acquired through recommendation. But the demand was growing for ever sweeter and stronger wines, to satisfy which the producers were obliged to lay hands on any liquors they could find.

The commercial interest in the Anglo-Portuguese trade was such that a Tory attempt to re-introduce French wines on equal terms at the end the War of Succession (1702–13), was roundly defeated in Parliament. After the war, it grew from strength to strength, and represented over 80 per cent of the total imports from Portugal. By now Port wine had ceased to be the emblem of the Whigs only, being regarded by the whole establishment as the only proper wine with which to wash down good English roast beef.

In the early days, the wines of the Upper Douro were a well-kept secret. Even in the 1690s the Portuguese minister Luís da Cunha (who had been a district judge in Oporto) could only suggest the Algarve as a possible source of sweet wine to meet the English taste, and made no mention of the Douro. More remarkably, John Methuen, author of the famous treaty of 1703 (which limited the duties on Portuguese wines to two-thirds of that paid by French wines, in return for the removal of Portuguese restrictions on British textiles), knew nothing of Port wines. He owned a vineyard himself and took a personal interest, but he had lighter wines and Lisbon wines in mind, and was helped to push through the treaty by the fact that several Portuguese statesmen had large vineyards near the capital. Nevertheless, in spite of the supremacy of Port at City and Academic dinners, the wines of Lisbon and Madeira, although neglected in the middle of the 18C, still continued to command somewhat higher prices.

Under the shelter of the **Methuen Treaty** the market in England for Port wine spread through the middle classes almost to the proletariat, but with more elder-berry being used as a colourant. Eventually things got to such a pass that Port began to lose its good name, and trade began to fail. It was then, in September 1756, that the future Marquês de Pombal intervened, to found the Company of the Vineyards of the Upper Douro (Companhia Geral da Agricultura das Vinhas do Alto Douro). [Kenneth Maxwell, in his recent study of Pombal, has stressed that even in Portuguese the word *Vinhas* in the title has invariably been mistranscribed *Vinhos* (wines, rather than vineyards), 'thus misrepresenting entirely the major objective of the company'. This 'was essentially to protect the upper Douro vineyard owners from the vast expansion of vine cultivation by smaller producers which had occurred over the previous decades'. Ed.] Its aims were also to correct abuses, to develop trade with Brazil, and to open up new markets in the Baltic, but it soon attempted to assume control of all wine for export to Britain, and the sale of brandy for fortification.

Not surprisingly, a long battle ensued between the Oporto Factory and the Company, which encroached on the trade in the Portuguese interest, and with considerable success, for they could count on the continuance of the political conditions which prevented the readmission of French wines, and they often inhibited Spanish competition. But it was the Company and the Portuguese middle-men who reaped the benefit rather than the farmers, whom the Company was intended to assist, and they also aspired to penetrate the market inside Britain itself, being in a position to pre-empt the best wines. They might have been able to compete in the quality market, but their connections were not good enough to sustain them very far, and beyond a certain point the Factory was able to hold its own, although such was the growth of counterfeit wines, and of spirit drinking, that the general importation of wine per head into Britain decreased.

Pombal encouraged the Douro trade at the cost of vineyards elsewhere in Portugal, which he considered might be more productive if turned over to corn, and vigilance was necessary to prevent the farmers of the Upper Douro from bringing in wines from outside the demarcated district, but production was increased meanwhile by an extension of the area in which Port wine could be grown. An extensive bureaucracy grew up within the Company, but in its first years, at least, it improved the standard of wines and regularised prices. The pure wine alleged to be the Company's aim was not altogether unfortified, for the majority of wines required the addition of some brandy—but not in inordinate quantities—to curb fermentation, but the use of elderberries as a colourant was diminished.

During this crisis the Oporto Factory was at one time reduced to thirty members, but by the last quarter of the 18C it had recovered, even if constant bickering continued. At one time it was thought that the Factory had become the helot of the Company, forced to take such wines as it was allowed to have, but the steady growth of the British market ensured that there was a living for all, both British and Portuguese.

Wines of a better quality were now being heard of, and in the 1770s 'vintage' wines were first publicly quoted at enhanced prices. In the previous century there had been talk of mature wines, but to what extent such wines, carefully selected and nursed for twenty years in the cellar, really existed, it is hard to tell. Those who had discovered how to produce Port wines of quality were naturally jealous of their secret, and sales were restricted to a few favoured customers, but even if not always easy to find, decent wines could still be bought through trustworthy sources.

In 1786 William Pitt's commercial treaty with France opened the market again to French wines, much to the indignation of Portugal. (Towards the end of his life Pitt, drinking it as a medicine and stimulant rather than as a connoisseur, practically subsisted on Port.) Nevertheless, the trade expanded, and suffered remarkably little during the Peninsular War, when duties were again raised, and Portuguese wines did not finally lose their preferential treatment until 1831.

The last decades of the 18C had seen a revival of interest in Lisbon wines, in those of central Portugal, and to some extent in the 'green wines' or **vinhos verdes** of the Minho. **Madeira** had never lost favour, but the small size of the island restricted production to an annual 2000 tuns or so, most of which was exported to America, for, as an African offshore island, Madeira escaped the prohibitions of the Navigation Act, and could trade with America direct. A good shaking, and the heat of a tropical voyage, helped to mature it, and much Madeira and some Port reached England by way of the West and even the East Indies, and then fetched a higher price.

From 1756 to 1801 John Whitehead was the British Consul at Oporto. He was a man of many parts, more of science and learning than of business, although closely connected with the wine trade through his nephew William Warre, the Elder. He maintained good relations with both the British and Portuguese, and was personally responsible for the planning and erection of the Factory House, completed by 1790, which is still owned the British Port exporters. At the end of the century the Oporto Factory had outstripped in importance that of Lisbon, which had suffered considerably in the 1755 earthquake. It even aspired to be a separate consulate general, but in spite of the recommendations of Robert Walpole, the Minister, these ambitions were thwarted. For a time during the French invasion, the building was in the hands of caretakers, but in 1811 the Port exporters resumed possession, although the Factories had by then ceased to be recognised by Portuguese law as public corporations. A long dispute followed as to its ownership. The wine exporters claimed that as they alone had borne the full burden of paying consulage, the Factory was theirs, while others argued that it belonged to the Consul and the British Community in general. Although the legal arguments rather favoured the latter, the matter was settled in 1834 by an agreement, which left the edifice in the hands of the Port men, the *de facto* occupants. Soon afterwards certain of the more notable members of the opposition, including the founders of the firm of Graham, originally importers of textiles and India merchants, were allowed into the fold.

The early days of the 19C were those of famous vintages, culminating in the 'Waterloo vintage' of 1815. Peninsular victories were celebrated with Port, while on Wellington's staff was General William Warre, an Oporto man, who could give knowledgeable advice on the subject. Meanwhile, the pure wine school, later led by **Joseph James Forrester**, engaged in heated controversy with those who preferred the more sophisticated product. Fortified Port eventually won the day, but we hear far less of blackstrap and of the various faults which had previously injured the good reputation of Port. In 1861 Forrester was drowned in the rapids of the Douro, and his cause foundered. Yet basically the two factions differed less than they appeared to do. Forrester did not object to a reasonable addition of brandy *at the proper time*, and both sides equally condemned adulteration. The best quality port could mature without fortification, but even that was liable to seasonal disturbance and the risk of deterioration. For most Ports some fortification was essential to mature the wine for the market without undue delay, and to preserve it by stabilisation.

While expensive and prestigious fortified wines were now the fashion, the bulk of the wine sold was still of the cheaper kind, the grocers' Port served by Mr Jawleyford to Mr Sponge, and the universal 'Port and lemon' served at every bar. In the same way, in later years, the market was sustained by the Belgian and French demand for Port as an aperitif.

Owing to the number of their Portuguese employees, coopers, artisans, boatmen, etc., and their position *vis à vis* the Portuguese authorities, with no legation to intervene, and being obliged to travel up country in their search for wines, the Oporto Factory were not quite so isolated from the Portuguese as the members of the Lisbon Factory, but their knowledge of the language was as sketchy, and few of them were ever guests in a Portuguese home, although in Whitehead's day there had been some mixing. Later, when the British community backed Dom Pedro during the civil war and siege of Oporto in 1832–34, some of the upper crust occasionally foregathered with the local gentry, and one or two even accepted Portuguese titles.

British firms also began to acquire *quintas* or country estates on the Douro. They had seldom done so before, partly owing to the stringency of the Portuguese laws on the subject of foreigners buying land. During the vintage they used them as offices, for they remained essentially export merchants resident in Oporto, and rarely became farmers of vineyards themselves. The Factory has continued on its prosperous course, entrenched in Portugal, yet self-contained and rarely participating in Portuguese society. There has been occasional friction, as in 1899 when Lord Salisbury intervened in Portuguese Africa, and more recently, in 1961, when the British failed to make any effective protest at the Indian occupation of Goa.

Apart from commercial and political problems to contend with, there have been the ruinous diseases of the vine to combat: firstly the *Oidium Tuckeri*; then the dreaded phylloxera. Vintage Port was not quite the same after the outbreak of phylloxera in the 1870–80s, but it was found that the vines of American root stock were resistant to the disease, and by grafting shoots on these the trade won a new lease of life. But even if Vintage Ports no longer enjoy the prestigious place they occupied in the days of Queen Victoria, when the birth of a son and heir was the signal to lay down a cellar full of Port to be ready for his 21st birthday, it has found favour again in recent years, although it represents only about one-fiftieth of the trade in value. This has been caused by an increase in demand for cheaper Ports, the export of which to Britain still exceeds that of Portuguese table wines (although they are being imported in large quantities), which have also grown in popularity elsewhere abroad.

Inflation and the general increase in the cost of labour have transformed the industry. Formerly, the bare feet of men trod the grapes during the necessary two or three days' period of fermentation, and the bitterness which would have resulted from the crushing of the pips was thereby avoided. But the old stone troughs or *lagares* are now largely replaced by metal or concrete tanks, with mechanical crushers. The days have passed when the treading of the must was a Dionysian scene, enlivened with music and song and numerous nips of brandy. Formerly, when enough fermentation had taken place, the *lagares* were unsealed, and the wine poured into great wooden vats or *toneis*. These are now largely superseded, but the quality wines are still pressed from the best black grapes, the basic process of vinification is unchanged, and the quality not impaired. The must is sealed off during fermentation, and not allowed to brim over into the next tank, as with the making of Sherry under the *solera* system. Only when fermentation has reduced the sugar content to the right point is the must drained off and fortified with up to 20 per cent of brandy to stabilise it.

There it remains until the spring, when it is taken down the Douro river to Oporto. Formerly it was carried in the picturesque sailing craft called *barcos rabelos*;

then by the serpentine single-track railway, drawn by vintage British-made engines. A road has replaced the narrow track with its numerous hairpin bends which wound steeply over the Quintela pass—a generation ago the only land route to the Upper Douro—and the wine is now transported by tanker-lorries.

Once in Oporto—or rather in the *armazens* of transpontine Vila Nova de Gaia—it is stored in large wooden vats, made of oak for the best wines, and of chestnut for the others. There it stays for about two years, being carefully watched and nurtured. Tasters test it from time to time, and add blends of other wines and small doses of brandy, up to a further 5 per cent in all, to direct the wine in the way it should go. Aeration and evaporation takes place at a rate of about 2.5 per cent a year, but the casks are regularly topped up.

After about two years the decision is taken as to whether the condition of the best wines justifies the declaration of a vintage year. Each firm decides for itself, but in good years, which occur about once in five, most of their colleagues follow suit. These **Vintage Ports**, which are not blended with wines from other years, are then set aside, and bottled. The introduction and general use of the modern straight-sided bottle facilitated the maturing of vintage wines, but until the last decades of the 18C the bottles were bulbous and flat-bottomed like modern decanters, and difficult to store on their sides, although it could be done with a packing of straw. But they had their advantages, for they could not be knocked over so easily, and the long neck could be 'cracked', which left a clean break-off, enabling the wine to be decanted without getting bits of cork into it. In the bottles the wines mature very slowly, and are left undisturbed to mature to perfection, resting on their sides for fifteen years or more. By then a deep purple colour, they are considered by many to be the doyen of wines.

Next come the **Tawny Ports**, so-called because they lose some of their colour in cask and become brown or even straw-coloured. They are kept in the cask for seven years or even longer, and during that period are carefully tended, and helped when necessary by blending with wines from other vineyards and other years.

**Ruby Port**, the main standard Port, made from a blend of lesser wines, is bottled early and drunk comparatively young. It is fuller bodied and sweeter than Tawny Port. Both are popular in Scandinavia and on the Continent, as is **White Port**, Port made from white grapes, which may be taken with ice, or chilled. White Port is also making headway in Britain, although in a country where Port has always been thought of as essentially red, it has had to fight something of a battle.

Except in Britain, the sale of Portuguese **table wines** (*de mesa*) now vastly exceeds that of Port. The best known are the green wines, *vinhos verdes*, so called from their youth and freshness, although they also have a green context, the shady Minho, where the vines grow profusely on high granite trellises (*bardos* or *cruzelas*), and even climb into the branches of adjacent trees (*arjoada*). This last method is an economy of land usage, as crops can grow beneath the trees, but the cost of labour in picking the grapes is now a disadvantage.

In Portugal there are red 'vinhos verdes' as well as white. They both have a slight natural effervescence, but they are somewhat hard to the taste and are less popular abroad. Other white wines are produced in the neighbourhood of Lisbon, and have been for centuries. *Bucelas* and *Carcavelos* (from Oeiras, where Pombal had his estate) were famous, but many vineyards have been swamped by encroaching urban development, and in any case most Portuguese table wines are now blended and are no longer sold under their regional names. The Lisbon area also produces red wines, including that of *Colares* (near Sintra), the vines of which grew in deep sand, and thus survived the phylloxera. But Colares—even more than

Carcavelos and Bucelas—has now been partly built over. *Setúbal* also produces a fortified wine from a blend of black and white grapes known as *moscatel*, and is still a demarcated district, although its production has diminished.

The red *Dão* wine, from an area centred on Viseu, is a full-bodied wine challenging comparison with Burgundy rather than claret, and is usually matured from five to seven years. There are white Dãos as well as red. A similar full-bodied red wine comes from the area of *Pinhel*, further east, between Guarda and the Douro.

An astonishing market success has been obtained by *Mateus Rosé*, a blended wine originating in the Vila Real district, but now drawn from all parts of the country. It is sold in shaped flagons, and may be drunk with anything. Made from black grapes with a white pulp, it is sweet and bubbly, but the bubbles come from carbonated gas and not from natural effervescence as in the *vinhos verdes*. Connoisseurs are supercilious about it, although Sacheverell Sitwell (who discovered it in 1951 before it was so well known) praised it highly, but then he was a man of eclectic tastes.

**Madeira**, which was known as a quality wine even before Port, retains its good reputation. No longer is it shipped to the tropics to aid its maturing, but undergoes a heat treatment ('*estufado*') in stoves to stimulate the process. Like *vinhos verdes*, it is grown on trellises. It is a blended wine matured in the cask, and fortified, but the must is not sealed off during fermentation, as is Port.

**Brandy**, which plays so important a part in the fermentation of Port, should be made from the distillation of pure fermented grape juice. It is mainly known for its own sake as French *cognac* or *eau de vie*, but the provenance and nature of the brandy used for Port is not much publicised. Much of it comes from the Douro region itself, but brandy can be distilled from common wines anywhere: nine pipes of wine make about one pipe of brandy. In Portugal it is called *aguardente*, but in Spain this term means what in Portugal is known as *bagaceira*, *bagaço* being the product of the pips and skins after the grapes have been pressed. The latter was initially very violent and spiritous, but modern methods have matured and improved it, although it is still very strong compared with some other *eaux de vie de marc*.

In recent years the wine trade of Portugal has greatly changed in character. It is no longer an Anglo-Portuguese affair concentrated on the British market, but an international business in which three times as much Port is exported to France as to Britain, and in value twice as many table wines as Port. Even the Portuguese, who in the past had feared—for the sake of their livers—to drink Port, are now taking to their product, but rather as part of the cosmopolitan scene. Nevertheless, Port wine is once again growing in popularity in Britain, especially with younger consumers, and Vintage Port still plays an important part in that trade. Many scions of the traditional family firms (despite some mergers with larger concerns) continue to work in Oporto, where the visitor will find much of the old flavour still, while, in the Factory House, Vintage Port continues to be drunk with the same ceremony and distinction as it always has been.

In the last decade or so the quantity exported annually has been in the region of 8½ million cases, a high proportion to France (37 per cent) and Belgium (16 per cent). That to the United Kingdom is 10 per cent, while the domestic consumption is now 14 per cent, but both the consumption in the United Kingdom and in the United States is definitely following the premium Port route and the positive traditions of this famous product are welcomed still, at the end of the 20th century.

# Geographical and General Introduction

Approximately one-fifth of the Iberian Peninsula is occupied by Portugal, which, situated at the south-western extremity of Europe, shares to its north and east a land frontier with Spain 1215km long. Its **area** is 88,550 sq. km (34,200 sq. miles), and it is rectangular in shape, 218km (137 miles) at its widest, and 561km (350 miles) from north to south. The 1994 estimate of the total **population** of the country, including the Azores and Madeira, was 10,076,184; that of mainland Portugal was 9,585,556, but very unevenly distributed, over one third of which being in the distritos of Lisbon and Oporto alone.

Many travellers to Portugal will have crossed Spain before reaching its frontiers. Although it may be invidious to make comparisons, it is almost impossible not to do so, for the differences are many and profound, and any tendency to regard Portugal as merely a geographical extension of Spain must be entirely discounted.

Although there are of course similarities, it is these differences which are immediately apparent. Perhaps the most striking of changes is that of vegetation, not merely that far more flowers and bushes are to be seen throughout Portugal, but also far more trees, including extensive areas planted (controversially) with eucalyptus, which are noticeably absent as one traverses the parched, windswept, high-lying Castilian plateau (as when descending from near Guarda to Celorico, for example). The roads, more often tree-shaded, are more pleasant to drive along; the landscape in general is softer, greener, and less austere.

Portugal is a far more scenically beautiful country than is generally imagined, although too often what might otherwise have been an attractive village has been spoilt by new houses built in execrable taste, bright with multicoloured *azulejos*, with exterior stairs and ornate ironwork. Many have been erected with hard-earned money gained in northern Europe. They are at least homes, and considering the conditions in which too many people existed in previous decades under the theocratic dictatorship, although disenchanted, one should not protest too much. Too many still live in poverty, particularly in parts of the larger towns, where the non-collection of garbage is also often evident.

In general the people are exceptionally obliging and helpful when their assistance is requested, and even when it is not. Numerous times when travelling in Portugal I have experienced unexpected courtesies increasingly rare in other countries. People will go out of their way to show one the exact whereabouts of a building, for example: the small acts of natural hospitality and kindness, the lack of pretension, an attitude of welcome rather than the negative reaction too often noticeable elsewhere—all these go to make a journey through Portugal memorable. Everywhere, sounds are more subdued than in Spain: the diminution in decibels is quite remarkable. Life is taken at a more moderate speed; indeed, for the traveller in a hurry there may be moments of exasperation. It should also be taken into consideration, particularly when among older folk in rural areas, that a higher proportion than might be expected may not be able to read or write, even if they make every effort to understand a foreigner's broken Portuguese. They do not particularly care to be addressed in Castilian—although they will understand it—unless the visitor makes it obvious that he or she is a non-Spaniard.

Even the police are usually noticeably more civil when applied to, and are more likely to give the traveller the benefit of the doubt, than elsewhere.

Portugal is a comparatively small and homogeneous country, unlike its neighbour, and there is less emphasis on regionalism: such nationalistic groups as the Basques or Catalans in Spain do not exist; there are, however, some unintegrated

Gypsies. The older **regions** are still referred to in this Guide as a convenient method of indicating parts of the country, although these were divided for administrative purposes into districts in the 1830s, and in 1936 partly sub-divided into provinces, but the boundaries between the *províncias* and *distritos* do not always coincide. The mainland divisions are approximately as follows:

| *Traditional regions* | *Províncias* | *Distritos*, named after their capitals |
|---|---|---|
| Minho, or Entre Minho e Douro (north-west coast) | Minho<br>Douro Litoral | Braga, Viana do Castelo<br>Oporto |
| Trás-os-Montes (north-east) | Trás-os-Montes (Alto Douro) | Braganza, Vila Real |
| Beira (below the former two) | Beira Alta<br>Beira Litoral<br>Beira Baixa | Guarda, Viseu<br>Aveiro, Coimbra, Leiria<br>Castelo Branco |
| Estremadura (centre west) | Estremadura<br>Ribatejo | Lisbon, Setúbal,<br>Santarém |
| Alentejo (south-east of the former) | Alto Alentejo<br>Baixo Alentejo | Portalegre, Évora<br>Beja |
| Algarve (south coast) | Algarve | Faro |

The province of Douro Litoral is comprised of the lower part of the Minho and the north-western part of Beira; that of Ribatejo is partly eastern Estremadura, and partly north-west Alentejo.

As far as the distribution of population is concerned on the mainland, the *distritos* of Lisbon, Setúbal, and Oporto together contain over 40 per cent of the total, inflated since the exodus from Angola and Mozambique, etc. In comparison, the eastern and southern districts (Braganza, Vila Real, Guarda, Viseu, Castelo Branco, Portalegre, Santarém, Évora, Beja, and Faro) contain merely 30 per cent of the population, although they make up over 70 per cent of the area of Portugal.

There are considerable physical variations between some of the provinces. The seaboard province of **Minho**, with a high density of population, originally settled by the barbarian Suevi, is named after the river separating it from Spanish Galicia. The conservative and prolific Minhotos still have much in common with their Gallegan cousins and, like them, provided a high proportion of emigrants—once to Brazil, and now more frequently to northern Europe. The Minho's high rainfall allows intensive cultivation, and the whole province is physically very green. Where it is not cultivated it is covered with woods, except on the bare upper slopes of some mountain ranges near Spain to the east, among them the Serras do Gerês and da Peneda. It is also divided transversely by the rivers Lima, Cávado, and Ave, whose valleys are dotted by *solares* or manor houses. It is in this early-reconquered area that a high proportion of the Romanesque churches of Portugal may be seen, even if a number of them have been transformed in later centuries, their 18C façades whitewashed between granite outlines. One may still see occasionally the notorious creaking ox-carts, their heavy wooden axles emit a shrill whine as they are dragged slowly along the narrow lanes by their lyre-horned oxen, which are often yoked in pairs by richly ornamented *cangas*. Also to be seen are the *espigueiros*, or small granaries on piles, like the *hórreos* of adjacent Galicia.

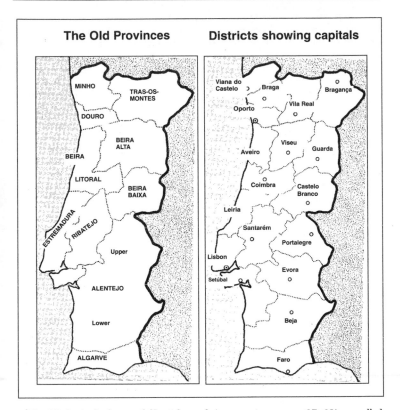

**The Old Provinces**

MINHO

TRAS-OS-MONTES

DOURO

BEIRA ALTA

BEIRA LITORAL

BEIRA BAIXA

ESTREMADURA

RIBATEJO

Upper

ALENTEJO

Lower

ALGARVE

**Districts showing capitals**

Viana do Castelo

Braga

Bragança

Oporto

Vila Real

Viseu

Aveiro

Guarda

Coimbra

Castelo Branco

Leiria

Santarém

Portalegre

Lisbon

Evora

Setúbal

Beja

Faro

The Minho is the home of the *vinho verde* (green wine: see pp 67; 69), so-called not so much for its colour as for its refreshing and slightly acid taste. The vines are seen trailing over granite props and trellises, even up into adjacent trees, and the fences of its smallholdings (*minifúndios*). Its traditional soup is the *caldo verde*, made from shredded cabbage. Traditional women's costumes are still occasionally seen, together with heavy gold earrings, particularly at the weekly markets held throughout the provinces, and are not donned merely as a tourist attraction. Minhotos are traditionally both superstitious and pious, the ecclesiastical capital long being Braga, a centre of reaction to Republican and Left-wing reforms.

The Minho is bounded on the south by the province of **Douro Litoral**, divided by the Douro, and densely populated around Oporto, its capital.

To the east, on the high mountainous uplands, which are an extension of the Castilian plateau, is the backward and empty province of **Trás-os-Montes**, literally that area 'across the mountains'. This is divided into the *terra fria* to the north, with its continental climate and long cold winters, and the *terra quente*, a warmer area to the south, where the summer sun is reflected off the schists of the Upper or Alto Douro valley, with its terraces of Port-wine vineyards, which provide the Trasmontanos with seasonal employment. It is divided diagonally (from north-east to south-west) by the rivers Tâmega, Corgo, Tua, and Sabor, all tributaries of the Douro, which, now dammed at numerous points, forms the frontier with Spain between Barco de Alva and Miranda do Douro. Until very recently, communication with the rest of Portugal was not particularly easy, Trás-os-Montes being divided from the Minho by the Serras de Barroso, da Cabreira, and do Marão. Only four decades ago 13 per cent of the population of Portugal lived in villages inaccessible by road, and even in 1970 one in four could be described as illiterate, especially in such sequestered districts.

Some distance south of the Douro, the province is abutted by the **Beira**, comprising three different areas. The eastern half of **Beira Alta** is geographically and climatically a westward extension of the Castilian plateau, but less monotonous. Once the descent is made from Guarda into the Mondego valley the difference is considerable. This river bears south-west parallel to the great transverse massif of the Serra da Estrela, the highest mountain range in Portugal, rising to 1991m (6530ft) at Torre, and then flows through Coimbra to Figueira da Foz, dividing the lower lying coastal **Beira Litoral** into two parts. To the north lies Aveiro, with its salt marshes and rice-fields, its lagoon fed by the Vouga, with its high-prowed *moliceiros* or seaweed-gathering craft. To the south are extensive pine forests planted to fix the coastal dunes. Some of the most beautiful countryside in Portugal is to be found in the valleys of the Mondego, the Dão (to the north, famous for its red wine), divided from the coast by the Serra de Busaco; and also in the valley of the Zêzere, flowing parallel to the southern flank of the Serras da Estrela and de Lousã. On the mountain sides pasture flocks of sheep and goats, whose wool is transformed into blankets at Covilhã, near the ski-slopes of the range. The **Beira Baixa**, lower as its name implies, is divided from the Alentejo by the Tagus, which, beyond Abrantes, veers south. On both banks of the Tagus extends the province of **Ribatejo**, the low-lying *lezírias* on the left bank, a bull-breeding district, being skirted to the north-west by hilly country, particularly attractive around Tomar.

Further west is **Estremadura**, comprising the square-ended peninsula west of the Tagus estuary, with Lisbon on its south side, the Sintra range further west, and Nazaré on the coastal strip further north. On the south bank of the estuary, more accessible since spanned by a bridge, it includes Setúbal and the Serra da Arrábida.

The **Alentejo**, once the granary of Portugal, and longer in Moorish occupation than areas further north, is another very different yet characteristic part of the country, being a vast undulating plain occasionally dotted by *montes* or farms, but largely given over to forests of cork oaks, desert heaths with a maquis of cistus, and extensive estates (*herdades* or *latifúndios*). The landowners of these estates—like those of adjacent Spanish Extremadura and Andalucía—have over the centuries exploited the peasantry, who became amongst the most communistically inclined in Portugal. Large flocks of sheep may be seen, guarded by *alentejano* shepherds, who in winter wear curious sheepskin coats (*pelico*) with a square tail and epaulette-like arms. Around Portalegre, to the north, the country is hillier and remarkably attractive, the straight, often still tree-lined roads providing some shade from the torrid summer sun. Throughout the region are seen low whitewashed houses surmounted by huge and ornate chimneys. The central half of this large area, the **Alto Alentejo**, has the river Guadiana forming its eastern frontier, which further south, in **Baixo Alentejo**, runs into Portugal between Beja and Serpa, while in the Algarve it again forms the boundary between Mértola and its mouth at Vila Real de Santo António. To the west, the Lower Alentejo is irrigated by the Sado and its tributaries.

The **Algarve** (the arabic *al-Gharb*; the West, or more specifically the western districts of Moslem al-Andalus) was the last part of Portugal wrested from the Moors; indeed the sovereign was first known, after the conquest, as King of

Portugal and the Algarves. It is divided from its neighbouring province by the Serras de Monchique and do Caldeirão, and further east by broken country—similar to the Spanish Sierra Morena—through which the Guadiana flows. The southern slopes of these ranges, with a scanty rainfall compensated for by Atlantic humidity, give way to luxuriant semi-tropical landscapes, with carobs, camellias and oleanders, and prickly-pear hedges, and to a rich variety of fruit: figs, almonds, and numerous citrus groves. The eastern half of the coast is known as the *Sotovento*; while to the west, beyond Faro, it is called the *Barlavento*.

Some sixty-five years ago a Blue Guide remarked that the Algarve was then 'so seldom visited by strangers, that the traveller will find himself an object of the greatest interest, and will probably walk about a town with a tail of 20 or 30 of the inhabitants', but which 'would be an ideal winter resort, superior to Málaga in the absence of parching winds, were it not for the inadequacy of accommodation'. Since 1945 a transformation has taken place, with colonies of villas and hotels strung out along the coast, which have not added to its natural attractions, its extensive beaches and occasional lines of cliffs carved picturesquely by the cold Atlantic breakers. The Algarve still provides employment for a large population of fishermen.

At its far west end projects the Cabo de São Vicente, and that of Sagres, 'where the land ends and the sea begins', in the words of Camoens. It was here that Henry the Navigator planned the exploration of the western ocean.

# PRACTICAL INFORMATION

## Formalities and Currency

### Passports

Passports are necessary for all British and American travellers entering Portugal.

### Consulates

There are consulates at the British Embasssy at Rua de São Bernardo 33, Lisbon (tel. 01 392 400, fax 392 4185); at Av. da Boavista 3072, Oporto; and at Largo Francisco A. Mauricio 7-1°, 8500 Portimão.

The British-Portuguese Chamber of Commerce (which publishes a monthly magazine) has offices at Rua da Estrela 8, Lisbon (also the address of the Royal British Club), and at Rua Sá da Bandeira 784, Oporto. The British Council maintains an office the British Institute (Rua de Luís Fernandes 3, 1200 Lisbon or Rua São Marçal 174, 1294 Lisbon; the British Hospital,Rua Saraiva de Carvalho 49, Lisbon; the British Historical Society of Portugal, Rua da Arriaga 13, 1200 Lisbon.

The US Embassy and Consulate is at Av. das Forças Armadas, 1600 Lisbon, with a consulate at Rua Júlio Dinis 826, Oporto. The Canadian consulate is at Rua Rosa Araujo 2, 1200 Lisbon.

The Portuguese Consulate in London is at 62 Brompton Road, SW3 1BJ, and its Embassy at 11 Belgrave Square, SW1X 8PP.

Other Anglo-Portuguese organisations in London include: the Anglo-Portuguese Society, 2 Belgrave Square, SW1X 8PJ (the address also of the Hispanic and Luso-Brazilian Council, and Canning House Library); the Anglo-Portuguese Foundation, 2 Bedford Square, WC1B 3RA; the Calouste Gulbenkian Foundation, 98 Portland Place, WN1 4ET; Portuguese Chamber of Commerce and Industry, 22–25A Sackville Street, W1X 1DE.

### Customs

Travellers have to pass the customs (*alfândega*) at the airport of arrival, or port of disembarkation. Provided that dutiable articles are declared, they will find the Portuguese customs authorities courteous and reasonable. It is better, unless one has a fluent knowledge of Portuguese, to commence any discussion in English rather than in Spanish (although the latter can later be of assistance).

### Money

The monetary unit is the *escudo*, written 1$00, divided into *centavos* (familiarly known as '*tostões*', originally called 'testoon' in Engländ). The sign $ is used to separate and differentiate escudos from centavos. Coins are issued by the Banco de Portugal of 50 centavos, and of 1, 2$50, 5, 10, 20, 50, 100 and 200 escudos; and notes of 500, 1000, 2000, 5000 and 10,000 escudos. 1000 escudos are known as a conto.

### Banks

Branches of Portuguese banks, which have been nationalised, and foreign banks in Portugal, are found near the centre of most towns. They are normally open from 8.30–15.00 from Monday to Friday, but times are liable to vary. Exchange facilities (Serviço de Câmbio) are also available from 18.00–23.00, and there is usually a

24-hour service at the main frontier posts and at airports. It is advisable to obtain a small supply of Portuguese currency for incidental expenses before leaving home. Banks provide all the normal facilities in accepting foreign bank cards, traveller's cheques, etc.

### Security and Hazards

With a reasonable amount of care, travellers will find their property respected, but it is advisable to take out some form of insurance before leaving home, and to keep a list of telephone numbers likely to be needed in an emergency: family, bank (including those for credit-card cancellation), insurance company, etc. Luggage, at ports and airports, railway stations, and on ferries, should not be left unattended. Cars should always be locked, and it is tempting providence to leave visible in a parked car anything which might be considered of value. Foreign number-plates are obvious. Normally, no problems should arise in the countryside, but there has been an increase of robbery in some of the main towns. Women should not display jewellery, and should wear their handbag straps across their body. However, they may rest assured that impudent sexual harassment, of the type still experienced in Spain, is unusual. Valuables should be deposited with the manager of one's hotel against receipt. The police should be contacted in case of any trouble: the Portuguese equivalent of ringing 999 is 115.

# Getting to Portugal, and Travel in Portugal

Portugal may be reached directly from Great Britain by a variety of ways, but it is recommended that the traveller intending to tour in the Peninsula should take his own car, or alternatively, fly-drive, as it is the only practical way to see large areas of the country.

Advice is given below on several alternative roads crossing Spain from San Sebastián (at the western end of the Pyrenees), and from the ferry ports of Bilbao and Santander. I have frequently been asked to suggest what roads might be followed if intending to make a tour of Portugal which would include a high proportion of the more interesting towns and monuments, together with a variety of landscape. I have therefore suggested such a route (see p 81), which should give the tourist a good idea of what the country has to offer. I have not made any recommendations regarding accommodation in that section, but the information provided on *pousadas* on p 83 may be of some assistance in planning such a tour.

### Tourist Offices

General information may be obtained free from the Portuguese Trade and Tourism Office at 22–25A Sackville Street, London W1X 1DE (tel. 0171–494 1441). Many of the larger and even smaller towns in Portugal have tourist offices, usually well indicated by signposts, which can provide information on accommodation, admission to museums, entertainments, etc.

The Direcção-Geral do Turismo is at Av. António Augusto de Aguiar 86, 1099 Lisbon codex.

Among branches abroad of the national tourist authorities, now known as ICEP (Investimentos, Comércio e Turismo de Portugal), are:
USA: 590 Fifth Av., 4th floor, New York NY 10036; and 1900 L Street NW, Suite 310, Washington DC 20036

Canada: 60 Bloor Street West, Suite 1005, Toronto ONT M4W 3B8; and 500
Sherbrook Street West, Suite 940, Montreal, QUE H3A 3C6
South Africa: 4th floor, Sunnyside Ridge, Sunnyside Drive, Parktown, 2193
Johannesburg, and P.O.Box 2473 Houghton, 2041 Johannesburg
Ireland: c/o Embassy of Portugal, Knocksinna, Foxrock, Dublin 18

## Tour Operators

Some tour operators based in the UK which specialise in holidays to Portugal are:

**Abreu Travel Agency Ltd**, 109 Westbourne Grove, London W2 4UL (tel.
0171–229 9905, fax 0171–229 0274)

**Caravela Tours Ltd**, 38/44 Gillingham Street, London SW1V 1HV (tel.
0171–630 9223, fax 0171–233 9680)

**Destination Portugal**, Madeira House, 37 Corn Street, Witney, Oxon OX8 7BW
(tel. 01993 773269, fax 01993 771910)

**Mundi Colour Holidays**, 276 Vauxhall Bridge Road, London SW1V 1BE (tel.
0171–828 6021, fax 0171–834 5752)

**Portugala Holidays Ltd**, 94 Fortis Green, London N2 9EY (tel. 0181–444 1857,
fax 0181–372 2274)

**Sunvil Holidays**, Upper Square, Old Isleworth, Middlesex TW7 7BJ (tel.
0181–568 4499, fax 0181–568 8330)

**Unicorn Holidays Ltd**, 2 Place Farm, Wheathampstead, Hertfordshire AL4 8SB
(tel. 01582 834400, fax 01582 831133)

## Air services

Air services between England and Portugal are maintained by Transportes Aéreos
Portugueses (TAP, or Air Portugal) working in conjunction with British Airways.
Full information on flights may be obtained from British Airways, 75 Regent Street,
London W1 (tel. 0181–897 4000), and from TAP, Gillingham House, 38
Gillingham Street, London SW1 (tel. 0171–828 0262 or 0171–834 2088).

In the USA they have offices in Boston, New York and Washington (tel.
1–800–221–7370). There are also offices in Montreal and Toronto, and in most
European and non-European capitals, from which there are regular flights.

Other airlines which fly to Portugal are TWA (tel. 1–800–221–2000), Delta (tel.
1–800–241–4141). Flights are also provided by charter companies. Internal or
domestic services, including those to Madeira and the Azores, are also maintained
by TAP, whose head offices are at Praça Marquês de Pombal 3A, Lisbon (closed
Sat/Sun). In addition to the Aeroporto de Lisboa (Portela de Sacavém), there are
airports at Oporto (Francisco Sá Carneiro) and Faro, to which there are regular
flights from London.

From airports there are bus services to the town termini, and in many cases
coach connections with other towns or resorts in the area. Taxis will also meet
planes, and many car-hire firms have offices at airports. TAP also provide fly/drive
facilities, together with fly/rail facilities in conjunction with Portuguese Railways.

## By Rail

While it may be convenient to travel to Portugal by rail (contact British Railways,
tel. 0171–834 2345), and to use the French Railways (SNCF), Spanish Railways
(RENFE), and Portuguese Railways (CP or Companhia dos Caminhos de Ferro
Portugueses) for long through journeys, they are not recommended as a means of
touring, except by enthusiasts.

Of interest to the latter are the two steam trains maintained by the CP: the 'Historical Train' running on a narrow gauge between Livração, Amarante, and Arco de Baúlhe (Tâmega line), pulled by a German locomotive of 1905 and with contemporary coaches; and the so-called '19C Train', with a British locomotive of 1875, running on a wide gauge between Oporto and Valença do Minho.

There are several *intercidades* (intercity) lines, among them, fanning out from Lisbon, is that leading north via Coimbra, Aveiro and Oporto for either Viana do Castelo or Braga (with a branch from Coimbra via Mangualde to Guarda); from Lisbon north-east via Castelo Branco to Covilhã; from Lisbon to Caldas da Rainha and Leiria; and from the south bank of the Tagus at Lisbon to Évora or Beja (to the south-east); and to Faro or Lagos in the Algarve.

For information on kilometric booklets, tourist tickets, Inter-Rail and Eurorail passes, and special fare rates, apply to tourist agencies or British Rail, Continental Section, Victoria Station, London SW1 (tel. 0171–834 2345), which provides travel tickets, sleeping-berth tickets, seat reservations, etc. on Continental (as well as British) transport services. Make certain that the 'global' price has been offered, including *all* supplements, etc., and check on the validity of return tickets. In Portugal it is essential to buy a ticket before travelling or a substantial fine is payable. Seats must be reserved in advance on international and express trains. Timetables for Portuguese trains are available from the Portuguese Tourist Office (in London, 0171–494–1441).

## By Coach

For travel between London and Lisbon, Oporto, or the Algarve, contact Eurolines at Victoria Coach Station (tel. 0171–730 8235).

There are a number of regular **bus services** (*autocarros*) in Portugal between the main towns maintained by several companies (among them Rodoviária da Estremadura, Av. Casal Ribeiro 18, Lisbon), apart from additional tourist services during the season, details of which may be obtained from travel agents and tourist offices. A bus-stop is a *paragem*.

## Driving to Portugal

Motorists will save much trouble by joining one of the automobile associations, which can provide any necessary documents, as well as information about rules of the road abroad, restrictions regarding caravans and trailers, advice on routes, and arrangements regarding delivery of spare parts, insurance, etc. Motorists who are not the owners of their vehicle should possess the owner's written permission for its use abroad. The Automóvel Club de Portugal has its head office at Rua Rosa Araújo 24, Lisbon, with branches at Oporto, Aveiro, Braga, Coimbra, and Faro. The insurance facilities offered by Europ Assistance or similar organisations should be used.

Continental rules of the road apply, and seat-belts are compulsory. Speed limits for cars are 90km per hour (55mph), slowing to 50km (31mph) in built-up areas, while the maximum speed on motorways is 120km (75mph). A word of caution: the road accident rate in Portugal is high, largely due to inexperienced drivers in fast cars.

Travellers approaching Portugal via France and Spain are advised to obtain the latest edition (showing motorways and other improvements) of the Michelin Map of France (No. 989) or the Carte Routière of France published by the French Institut Géographique National; for Spain, the Michelin Map No. 990. The *Blue Guide Spain* (6th edition) will not come amiss. For maps of Portugal see p 10.

Although it is possible that some visitors to Portugal will be touring the country as part of a general exploration of the Iberian Peninsula, this would take a long time. It is assumed that most people driving to Portugal will be taking the shortest route to the Franco-Spanish frontier, and continuing directly south-west towards the northern or eastern border of Portugal. Some may wish to take in the Asturias and Galicia (having landed from the ferry at Bilbao or Santander); or even Andalucía en route; or alternatively they may consider passing through those provinces of Spain on the return journey.

Motorways (*auto-estradas*) are prefixed by the initial **A**; the new highways, such as those between Bragança and Oporto, and between Vilar Formoso and Aveiro, by **IP** (*itinerário principal*), some approaches to which, among others, may be prefixed **IC** (*itinerário complementar*); and most other main roads by **N**.

Although the Geographical Introduction describes in general the main divisions of the country, it does not attempt to describe the intricacies of the roads in extensive regions. These are not by any means obvious even on the better and recently published road maps, and it cannot be emphasised too often that what appears to be the direct road between two points is by no means always the easiest or fastest, particularly off the beaten track. This is especially true in the scenically attractive centre and north of the country, which is remarkably hilly, and numerous apparently major roads, which might appear straight enough on a map, may well wind and climb through broken country for hours.

Communications are frequently easier in the Alentejo, for example, and in the higher-lying, but comparatively level *meseta* nearer the frontier with Spain. Some minor roads are in a perfectly satisfactory state (apart from the occasional rash of pot-holes), even if they are narrow and undulating; they may, however, deteriorate unaccountably into rough stoney tracks and continue so for some distance. Although there has been much improvement in recent years, certain roads remain in a lamentable condition.

Unfortunately, few maps give any detailed indication of contour, and very frequently roads leading through hilly regions are tortuous. This is almost always the case along the steep sides of the 'valley' of the Douro and its tributaries—such as from Entre-os-Rios to Lamego along its south bank, although some short stretches have been improved. (It is all very well to follow its south bank from Peso da Régua to Pinhão, for example, but should one wish to continue east to explore its upper reaches, this will entail a 15km steep climb to Alijó, an 11km steep descent to Tua, followed by another 22km ascent merely to reach Carrazeda de Ansiães: and winding all the way.)

Although tourists should plan to reach their destinations in daylight, particularly if travelling off the beaten track, when driving at dusk or after dark, a very sharp look-out should be kept for unlit carts, bicycles and scooters, and cattle.

**Petrol stations** are still comparatively few and far between off the beaten track, and motorists are advised to keep their tank 'topped up'. Unleaded petrol is *gasolina sem chumbo*.

### Routes by Car through Spain

The most direct and fastest roads are those from Irún (at the western end of the Pyrenees) and Bilbao, bypassing Vitoria, and Burgos, and that from Santander, which, bypassing Palencia, converge some 35km north-east of Valladolid. From Tordesillas, 30km south-west of Valladolid, both now bypassed, a number of routes radiate: see below.

Most of the minor frontier posts are open daily from 7.00 to 24.00, although the less frequented may close at 21.00 in winter. The main alternatives from Tordesillas are as follows:

(a) turning north-west via Benavente (also approached direct from Palencia) to Verín, there crossing the frontier for Chaves: see Rtes 31 and 32.

(b) continuing north-west from Verín via Celanova and Cortegada, to enter at São Gregório; or, from Celanova, turning south-west to Lindosa for Ponte de Barca; see Rte 34B.

(c) continuing north-west from Verín via Ourense and Tuí to cross the Minho at Valença: see Rte 34A.

(d) driving due east via Toro and Zamora; and from there to either Braganza or Miranda do Douro: see Rtes 28, 29, or 30.

An attractive road is the N364 driving west from Bilbao, skirting the coast and bypassing Santander before veering inland to bypass Oviedo, from which the A66 motorway crosses the mountains to approach León. Turn west on reaching the N120, which passes Astorga, Ponferrada, and Monforte de Lemos, for Ourense. From there one may make for Valença do Minho, turn south-west for Lindoso, or south via Verín to Chaves: see Rtes 34A, 34B, 31, and 32.

From Salamanca (south-west of Tordesillas) one may either cross into Portugal at Vilar Formoso for Guarda, and from their follow the IP5 west via Viseu to Aveiro, or drive south-west for Coimbra, or south to Castelo Branco (see Rtes 23, 21, and 22A); or bear south-west towards Cáceres and Mérida: see below.

Those wishing to take in Madrid, or driving from there, will follow the NV to Trujillo, and from there either continue due west to Cáceres, to cross into Portugal near Marvão (see Rte 16); or south-west via Mérida and Badajoz to Elvas for Lisbon or Évora; see Rtes 5A and B.

For those making for the Algarve, the route Elvas–Estremoz–Évora may be followed (Rte 5), and then either Rte 9, or 10 via Beja; or from Beja continuing south-west to meet the IP1 leading south towards Albufeira; see Rte 12.

From Andalucía, the A49 leading west from Sevilla via Huelva provides the fastest entry to the Algarve, while the N433 from Sevilla leads north-west via Rosal de la Frontera to Beja for either Lisbon or Évora (Rte 8). Évora may also be approached by the minor C4311 turning west from Zafra (between Sevilla and Mérida) via Jerez de los Caballeros (see Rte 7), while the N432 drives north-west from Zafra to Badajoz via Albuera.

**A very selective tour**, covering much of the country but by no means all, would be one entering northern Portugal at Valença do Minho (where there is a *pousada*), and leaving it at Vilar Formoso, between Guarda and Ciudad Rodrigo (in Spain). (Where there is a *pousada* in or reasonably near the place, this is shown in parentheses after the place-name. See below for a complete list of these establishments.) There are, naturally, several things of interest in the vicinity of most of the towns or villages through which this route leads (such as, near Braga: Tibães, São Frutuoso de Montélios, Bom Jesus, and the Citânia de Briteiros), and of course, one may make additional detours to take in, for example, Barcelos from Braga. No time scale is indicated, but note that in many areas the roads cannot be taken at speed. In my experience, two full days is sufficient to see most of old Oporto, while Lisbon itself will require a minimum of five, but obviously such factors depend very much on each individual's tempo and interests.

This recommended route leads through the following: Ponte de Lima—Braga — Guimarães (2 *pousadas*)—Oporto—Amarante (*pousada*)—Lamego—Viseu— Busaco—

Coimbra—Conímbriga (*pousada*)—Tomar—Batalha (*pousada*)—Alcobaça—Obidos (*pousada*)—Mafra—Sintra—Queluz (*pousada*)—Lisbon.

Then south-east to Beja (*pousada*), from there making a circuit south to Mertola and Serpa (*pousada*) before turning north to Évora (*pousada*)—Estremoz (*pousada*) —Vila Viçosa—Portalegre—Marvão (*pousada*)—Castelo de Vide—(Castelo Branco) —Idanha a Velha—Monsanto (*pousada*)—Fundão—Belmonte—Guarda—Almeida (*pousada*)—Vilar Formoso.

This may be extended north from Almeida to Barca de Alva—Freixo de Espada à Cinta—Miranda do Douro (*pousada*), and from there turning east to Zamora in Spain.

### Taxis

Taxis are still comparatively inexpensive and are numerous in the main towns. Formerly they were easily distinguished by their green roofs, but in Lisbon they are in the process of changing to a cream colour. In smaller towns there are cars which ply for hire, and charge by the kilometre. Surcharges apply for heavy luggage. A tip of 10 per cent is more than sufficient.

### Metropolitano

There is a limited underground railway system in Lisbon, the *Metropolitano* (see plan on p 104), for which a *caderneta* of ten tickets or a *Passe Turístico* may be obtained. The lines are slowly being extended, but it is not of great use for exploring the city. The rush-hour should be avoided.

A Tourist Ticket for a 7-day period may be bought for travel on public transport in Lisbon (apart from the underground) at most ticket offices marked CARRIS.

## Postal and other Services

### Post Offices

Post Offices (*Correios*) or CTT are normally open from 9.00 and 18.00 on Monday to Friday, and the main branches also operate a limited service on Saturday. Correspondence marked 'poste restante' (to be called for) may be addressed to any post office, and is handed to the addressee on proof of identity (passport preferable). A stamp is a *celo*.

Unlike in Spain, **telephones** are also to be found in post offices, apart from a number of public cabins, a few survivals of which will appear familiar to visitors from England, as the Portuguese telephone service was once maintained by a British company. Portugal is in automatic or STD communication with the rest of Europe and elsewhere.

### Press and Radio

Some foreign newspapers and a few magazines may be found, but at an inflated price, at kiosks in the centre of the main towns and in the main tourist areas during the season. The *Anglo-Portuguese News*, published since 1937, may be of interest to those intending to spend any length of time in the country, while English readers in the south have also the *Algarve News*. There is a brief radio programme in English every morning at 8.30.

### Tourist Offices

The main tourist office (*posto do turismo*) in Lisbon is at the Palácio Foz, on the west side of the Praça dos Restauradores, with posts elsewhere in the city, and they can provide tourists with information in English by telephone (706341). There are also national tourist offices in some of the larger towns, at the main frontier crossings, railway station, and airports, while most provincial towns also have their municipal tourist offices.

# Where to Stay

## *Hotels*

The standard of comfort, efficiency, and cleanliness of Portuguese hotels is comparatively high, and their sense of hospitality specially so. All have been officially graded by the tourist authorities, which produces an annual 'Guide to Hotels', which may be consulted at all tourist offices. A selection of hotels of all categories is included in the sections on Lisbon and Oporto.

Hotel accommodation falls into six categories: hotels, from 1-star to 5-star; apartment-hotels (2 to 4-star); *estalagens* (inns of quality; 4 or 5-star); *albergarias* (4-star); boarding-houses and pensions (*pensãos*), 1 to 4-star; and motels (2 or 3-star). In addition, there are some 40 *pousadas*, similar to the *paradores* of Spain but often more hospitable: see below.

Every bedroom should display a notice giving details of the maximum price applicable to the room, and this includes a 'Continental breakfast', all service charges and taxes. The maximum price may be increased by 20 per cent between 1 May and 31 October.

If no single room is available, a double room may be offered, for which the price is that of a double room less the price of a Continental breakfast, but as some hotels choose to assume that single tourists prefer a double room anyhow, this point should be checked. When accommodation is limited, it may be convenient to ask for an extra bed to be fitted into a single room, when an extra charge of 35 per cent may be made to the price of the room; or in apartment-hotels and motels, of an extra 25 per cent per person. The management must inform guests as to any reduced prices available, such as for children under the age of eight.

An official Complaint Book (*Livro de Reclamações*) is a requirement of every establishment offering food, drink, and accommodation (apart from travel agencies), and in the unlikely case of serious irregularity or indifferent service should be requested without compunction. Complaints may also be made to tourist offices, or directly to the Direcção-Geral do Turismo in Lisbon.

Up-to-date lists of local hotels are obtainable from any tourist office, the staff of which can also advise on which extra facilities are available (private swimming-pools, tennis courts, etc.).

## *Pousadas*

The first in the network of strategically situated hotels was established in 1942 by the government, which set out to provide hospitality and avoid the stereotype of international hotels. Since 1992 they have been run by ENATUR (Empresa Nacional de Turismo), a corporation set up with a view to future privatisation.

All the pousadas listed below were open at the time of writing; others are projected. For up-to-date information, and advance reservations, apply to ENATUR, Av. Sta Joana a Princesa IOA, 1700 Lisbon (tel. (01) 848 12 21, 848 90 78, 848 46 02; fax. (01) 80 58 46, 848 43 49).

Several of them are in buildings of architectural and historical interest (which are indicated by an asterisk in the following list), or convenient for visiting such sights as Batalha, or Conímbriga; and most of them are attractively or dramatically sited.

## North of the Douro

Valença do Minho: São Teotónio (within the enceinte, and with a view of Tuí)

Vila Nova de Cerveira (15km south-west of Valença do Minho): *Dom Dinis (within the castle ramparts

Viana do Castelo (Santa Luzia), a 1920s hotel overlooking the town

Guimarães: *N.S. da Oliveira (adjacent to the Colegiada), and *Santa Marinha da Costa (in a former monastery on a hillside south of the town)

Caniçada (c 33km north-east of Braga, off the N103): São Bento (with plunging views over the Peneda-Gerês National Park)

Amarante: São Gonçalo, just off the IP4 near the Alto do Espinho, c 20km east of Amarante, providing a fine valley view

Alijó (16km north-east of Pinhão): Barão de Forrester

Bragança: São Bartolomeu (with a view of the walled upper town)

Miranda do Douro: Santa Catarina (with a plunging view of the Douro)

## From west to east between Oporto and Coimbra

Murtosa (c 45km north-west of Aveiro; on the far side of the lagoon): da Ria

Serém (on the N1 east of Aveiro): Santo Antonio.

Caramulo (in the serra south-west of Viseu, and north-west of Tondela): São Jerónimo

Póvoa das Quartas (on the N17, east of Oliveira do Hospital): Santa Bárbara (with an attractive view across the wooded valley)

Manteigas (in the Serra da Estrela c 45km south-west of Guarda): São Lourenço

Almeida (within the fortified town, 25km north-west of the frontier at Vilar Formoso): Senhora das Neves

## Between Coimbra and the Tagus, from west to east

Condeixa-a-Nova: Santa Cristina, near the site of Conímbriga

Batalha: Mestre Afonso Domingues (close to the abbey)

Óbidos: *do Castelo (in the castle)

Castelo do Bode (13km south-east of Tomar): São Pedro (overlooking the Zêzere reservoir)

Monsanto: perched c 50km north-east of Castelo Branco, and conveniently near Idanha-a-Velha

## Between the Tagus and Évora

Sousel (18km north-west of Estremoz): São Miguel, a modern building with a wide view south

Estremoz: *Rainha Santa Isabel (in the castle)

Marvão: Santa Maria (with a fine view from the castle)

*Flor de Rosa (c 21km west of Portalegre), in the former monastery

Elvas: Santa Luzia, without the walls

Evora: *Dos Lóios (in the former monastery)

## Near Lisbon

Queluz: *Dona Maria I (in dependencies of the former palace)

Setúbal: *São Filipe (in the castle)

Palmela (8km north of Setúbal): *de Palmela (in the restored castle), with extensive views.

**South of Évora**

*Alvito (between Évora and Beja): within the castle

Beja: *São Francisco (in the former monastery)

Vale de Gaio (c 27km south-east of Alcácer do Sal, overlooking a reservoir)

Santiago do Cacém: São Tiago, near the site of Mirobriga); and 5km west, the Quinta da Ortiga

Serpa: São Gens (in the countryside south-east of the town, with a wide view)

Santa Clara-a-Velha (c 34km south-east of Odemira): Santa Clara (overlooking a reservoir)

São Brás de Alportel (20km north of Faro): São Brás

Sagres (33km west of Lagos): do Infante

Others are planned at the following sites: *Alcacer do Sal (in the castle); *Arraiolos (Convento dos Loios); *Bouro, north-east of Braga (monastery of Sta Maria); near *Sesimbra (Santuário N.S. de Cabo Espichel); and *Vila Viçosa (Convento das Chagas). Others were projected at Tibães, north-west of Braga (monastery of São Martinho), and Tomar (in dependencies of the Convento de Cristo), but they may not all materialise.

## Turismo de Habitação

The Portuguese tourist authorities rightly assume that not all travellers want to spend their holiday, or even part of it, in hotels: some might wish to meet the Portuguese in their own homes. In recent years they have encouraged owners of private houses to accommodate guests, and at the same time defray the cost of the upkeep of their property. The scheme has been developed throughout the country, but predominantly in the interior and north, particularly in the Minho, where there are more suitable and characteristic houses or *paços* able to offer such facilities. Some are *quintas* (usually associated with a farm or vineyard) or *solares* (a country seat), and vary from a simple but comfortable family home to the more palatial manor or mansion house; and naturally charges vary accordingly. This type of accommodation can offer attractive surroundings unlikely to be found elsewhere.

Home owners in the Minho have formed as association in order to insure standards and to advertise more effectively. Travellers looking for such accommodation as a base from which to tour the region should apply in advance to TURIHAB, Praça da República, 4990 Ponte de Lima (tel. 058 741672, 742827, or 742829; fax 058 741444), who can advise and will endeavour to suit individual requirements.

For more information on Turismo de Habitação elsewhere in Portugal, contact the office of the Direcção-Geral do Turismo at Av. António Augusto de Aguiar 86, 1099 Lisbon Codex, who can provide an illustrated official guide entitled *Turismo no espaço rural*.

Bookings should normally be for a minimum of three nights, and the price includes bed and Continental breakfast. Evening meals at houses some distance from towns and restaurants can be arranged if requested in advance. Some may provide cooking facilities; and some have tennis-courts and swimming-pools. Almost all have extensive gardens or estates, and there may be oportunities for fishing or riding. There is normally no language problem. If booking in advance from abroad it is preferable to deposit 50 per cent of the cost by sending a cheque in one's own currency directly to the owner.

A general prospectus illustrates each house or mansion, together with an outline map showing locations, and giving details of facilities at each place, and prices.

# Food and Drink

### Restaurants

While there are comparatively few 'de luxe' restaurants in Portugal, there are numerous less pretentious establishments offering better value than many places of a similar category in some other countries. While most of the larger hotels, particularly in tourist resorts, will also provide a safe 'international' menu, the visitor should not hesitate to savour the numerous local dishes. Portions are often generous, and a half portion (*uma meia dose*) is often enough, or one *dose* for two, and the differing prices are often so shown on the menu. 'S.P.' (*segundo o peso*) indicates that the food—usually seafood—is charged by weight. Service is now included on the bill or *conta*, but one may leave a small gratuity (*gorjeta*) for good service, although this is no longer expected.

Breakfast (*pequeno almoço*), lunch (*almoço*), tea (*chá*: both the beverage and meal), and dinner (*jantar*) are served at normal 'English' hours, particularly lunch: later than in France, but earlier than in Spain.

Among Portuguese words not immediately obvious when wanting the following, are: a spoon (*colher*; a knife (*faca*); a fork (*garfo*); a glass (*copo*); and a plate (*prato*).

Tap water (*água da torneira*) is usually perfectly safe, although bottled waters, available with (*com*) or without (*sem*; pron. sin) *gas*, are not expensive. Portuguese beer (*cerveja*) is very good; while the range of wines available is extensive. Even the ordinary *vinho da casa* is usually very palatable, and the prices of the quality *vinhos de marca* are in no way prohibitive. Local wines are known as *vinhos da região*, and may be red (*tinto*), white (*branco*), sweet (*doce*) or dry (*seco*); ice is *gelo*. See Introduction to Port and the Wines of Portugal, particularly p 69.

Coffee (*café*) may be ordered *simples*, black; or *com leite*, with milk.

Some of the more common dishes to be seen on a **menu** (*lista* or *ementa*) are the following; for their pronunciation, see p 89.

**Acepipes**, hors d'oeuvres; also *entrada*:
*Améndoas*, almonds
*Azeitonas*, olives; *azeite*, olive oil
*Manteiga*; butter
*Pão*, bread; *pão de broa*, rye bread
*Pimenta*, pepper; *sal*, salt

**Sopas**, soups:
*Caldeirada*, a fish soup or chowder, containing onions
*Caldo verde*, the ubiquitous finely shredded *couve* or Portuguese cabbage soup, with a mashed potato base
*Gaspacho à Alentejana*, a refreshing cold soup similar to the Andalucían *gazpacho*, but containing chopped ham or a hard spiced sausage
*Sopa de feijão*, bean soup
*Sopa à Alentejana*, garlic soup, with egg and coriander
*Sopa de marisco*, or *de peixes*, seafood bisque

**Ovos**, eggs
These may be ordered *cozido*, hard boiled; *mal pasados* or *quentes*, underdone or lightly boiled; *estrelados* or *fritos*, fried; *escalfados*, poached; or *mexidos*, scrambled *Tortilha à Espanhola*, Spanish omelette

**Peixe e mariscos**, fish and shellfish
*Ameijoas*, clams
*Anchovas*, anchovies
*Arenque*, herring
*Atum*, tuna or tunny
*Bacalhau*, cod, very often dried salt cod, a staple food served in various appetising ways
*Besugo*, Dory; also *dourado*
*Camarões*, shrimps
*Carabineiros*, deep-sea prawns; also *gambas*
*Caranguejo*, crab; *santola*, spider crab; *sapateira*, rock crab

*Carapau*, mackerel, a variety of which is *cavala*; also *sarda*

*Cataplana*, dish of stuffed clams with bacon and sausage; from the Algarve

*Cherne*, sea bream

*Chocos*, cuttlefish

*Eirós*, or *enguia*, eel

*Espadarte*, swordfish; *peixe espada*, scabbard fish

*Gambas*, prawns

*Garoupa*, similar to but with a whiter flesh than *cherne*

*Lagosta*, spiny lobster or crayfish; *lavagante*, lobster; *lagostim*, crawfish; *lagostino*, langoustine

*Lampreia*, lamprey

*Linguado*, sole

*Lota*, burbot

*Lula*, squid or inkfish

*Mero*, brill

*Mexilhões*, mussels

*Ostras*, oysters

*Pargo*, sea bream

*Perceves*, goose-barnacles

*Pescada*, hake

*Pescadinha*, whiting

*Polvo*, octopus

*Pregado*, turbot

*Raia*, skate

*Robalo*, sea bass; young ones being *robalinho*

*Ruivo*, gurnet

*Salmão*, salmon

*Salmonete*, red mullet; other mullet are known as *fataca*, or *tainha*

*Sarda*, mackerel

*Sardinhas*, sardines

*Sável*, shad

*Solha*, plaice

*Truta*, trout

**Carne**, meat (and some cooking terms)

*Anho*, lamb; also *borrego* or *cordeiro*, baby lamb; *carneiro*, mutton

*Bife*, steak of beef or cow

*Cabrito*, kid

*Costeleta*, chop

*Dobrada*, tripe; also *tripas*

*Fiambre*, cooked ham; *presunto*, smoked or spiced ham

*Fígado*, liver

*Língua*, tongue

*Lombo*, fillet

*Miolos*, brains

*Morcela*, black pudding; also *mouros*

*Perna*, leg

*Porco*, pork; *leitão*, sucking-pig; *paio*, smoked pork fillet

*Rims*, kidneys

*Salsicha*, fresh pork sausage; *chouriços*, smoked or spiced sausage

*Toucinho entremeado*, bacon

*Vitela*, veal

*Assado*, roasted; *cozido*, boiled or stewed; *fumado*, smoked; *grelhado*, grilled; *nas brasas*, on a charcoal grill; *no forno*, in the oven; *panado*, fried in breadcrumbs; *passado*, minced; *salteado*, sautéed; *guisado*, stew; *molho*, sauce

**Aves domésticas e Caça**, poultry and game

*Coelho*, rabbit

*Cordorniz*, quail

*Faisão*, pheasant

*Frango*, chicken; *galinha*, boiling fowl; *capão*, capon

*Ganso*, goose

*Lebre*, hare

*Pato*, duck

*Perdiz*, partridge

*Perú*, turkey

*Veado*, venison

**Legumes e hortaliças**, vegetables (and *especiarias*, spices)

*Agriões*, watercress

*Aipo*, celery

*Alcachofra*, artichoke

*Alface*, lettuce

*Alho*, garlic

*Alho-porro*, leek

*Arroz*, rice

*Batata*, potato

*Beringela*, aubergine

*Beterraba*, beetroot

*Bóculos*, broccoli

*Cebola*, onion; *cebolinha*, spring onion; *chalota*, shallot

*Cenoura*, carrot

*Chu-chú*, marrow

*Cogumelos*, mushrooms

*Couve*, Portuguese cabbage; *couve-flor*, cauliflower; *repolho*, white cabbage
*Ervilhas*, peas
*Espargos*, asparagus
*Espinafre*, spinach
*Favas*, broad beans
*Feijão*, dried beans; *feijão manteiga*, butter beans or haricot beans; *feijão verde*, French beans
*Grão*, chickpeas
*Grelos*, turnip tops, ubiquitous in the north
*Lentilhas*, lentils
*Nabo*, turnip
*Pastinaca*, parsnip
*Pepino*, cucumber
*Pimento*, red or green pepper
*Rabanetes*, radishes
*Salada*, salad

**Herbs and spices**
*Canela*, cinnamon
*Caril*, curry
*Coentros*, coriander
*Cominhos*, cummin seeds
*Piri-piri*, chilli seasoning
*Salsa*, parsley

**Queijos,** cheeses
*Queijo da Serra*, a ewe's milk cheese, mostly from the Serra da Estrela, and often served as an hors d'oeuvre, but not available in summer months
*Cabreiro*, goat's milk cheese
*de Tomar*, a small white cheese; also *de Castelo Branco*; *de Azeitão, de* Alentejo.

*Rabaçal*, from the region of Pombal.

**Sobremesa,** dessert
*Açúcar*, sugar
*Arroz-doce*, rice pudding
*Bolos*, pastries; also *pastéis*; *bolachas*, biscuits
*Flan*, cream caramel
*Gelado*, ice cream
*Mel*, honey
*Nata*, cream
*Pudim*, pudding
*Marmelada*, quince jam or *membrillo*; marmalade is *compota de laranja amarga*
*Compotas*, jams and preserves

**Fruta**, fruit
*Alperches*, apricots; also *damascos*
*Ameixas*, plums
*Ananás*, pineapple
*Avelãs*, hazel-nuts
*Cerejas*, cherries; *ginjas*, black cherries
*Figos*, figs
*Framboesas*, raspberries
*Laranja*, orange
*Limão*, lemon
*Maçã*, apple; *nêspera*, medlar
*Melão*, melon; *melancia*, water melon
*Morangos*, strawberries
*Nozes*, nuts
*Pêra*, pear
*Pêssego*, peach
*Tâmaras*, dates
*Toranja*, grapefruit
*Uvas*, grapes

# General Information

## Shops
Normally open from 9.00–13.00, and from 15.00–19.00, some remaining open during the lunch-hour, the time of which may vary. Many close at 13.00 on Saturday during the summer. Supermarkets, which are usually more expensive than local shops and markets, normally close at 20.00.

## Public Holidays
The main public holidays, when museums are closed, are:

1 January
25 April (commemorating the Revolution of 1974)

Shrove Tuesday
Good Friday
1 May

| | |
|---|---|
| 10 June (death of Luís de Camoens) | 1 November |
| 15 August | 1 December |
| 5 October (Proclamation of the Republic) | 8 December (Independence of Portugal, 1640) |
| Corpus Christi | 25 December |

The main festivals at Lisbon and Oporto are St Anthony's day (13 June) and St John's day (25 June) respectively. Tourist offices can provide details of other local festivals, but see also p 92.

## Climate and Season

The climate in general is much milder than that of neighbouring Spain. Except in the Trás-os-Montes and the frontier area near Guarda, and on such heights as the Serra da Estrela, it is rarely very cold. The Minho is inclined to be damp in the winter, with a heavy rainfall. In Lisbon this is 69cm (c 27 inches) annually, mostly falling between October and March. The heat in the Alentejo and Algarve is considerable in summer, particularly the inland regions, which are rarely tempered by evening breezes, and are perhaps best avoided—except by salamanders—in high summer. The early spring is perhaps the pleasantest time of year to visit the south, when the almond blossom is out, while areas north of the Tagus are perhaps at their best from May to November.

## Language

Although those who know no language other than English can get along quite comfortably anywhere on the main tourist routes, an attempt should be made to learn a few phrases. French is occasionally understood and, less frequently, German.

While there are similarities with Castilian, both being Romance languages, the pronounciation of Portuguese is very different, being softer in tone and less clear-cut. Consonants are apt to be slurred, and many of the vowels are nasal, so that it may take a foreign ear much longer to become accustomed to the sound.

**Vowels**: accented **ê** and **ô** are the ordinary long Latin vowels; unaccented, they have a short dull sound (the **o** is often replaced by **u**: e.g., Manuel rather than Manoel), while the final **e** is like the French e-mute. Dipthongs are pronounced separately, but the combinations **ei**, **ou**, sound almost the same as the **ê** or **ô**; the nasal vowels **ã**, **õ** (surmounted by a *til*), are pronounced as -**an** or -**on** in French; while in the combinations **ão**, **õe**, only the second vowel is nasalised (-**aon**, -**oen**); in the last syllable a vowel followed by -**m** or -**ns** is nasalised, but its tone is not changed (e.g., 'jardim' is not pronounced as 'jardin' in French, where the final **i** becomes a nasal **e**).

**Consonants** are pronounced more or less as in English except in the following cases: **ç** (before a, o, and u), as **s**; ch:, **g** and **j** as in French; **gu**, **qu** before **e** or **i** = hard **g** and **k**, before **a**, **o**, **u**, = **gw** and **kw**; **lh**, **nh** correspond to the French 'i-mouillé' and **gn** (Spanish ll and ñ); **s** before a consonant or in an unstressed final syllable is like **sh** (e.g., Cascais); between vowels is like **z**; **x** is usually like **sh**, but in certain words of classical derivation it is pronounced like **z** (e.g, exército).

**Accents**. Unless otherwise marked by an accent, the stress of words ending in a vowel, -**m**, -**s**, or -**ns**, is on the penultimate syllable (e.g., Leiria, Virgens); in words ending in other consonants it is on the last syllable (e.g., real).

One will soon pick up a number of everyday expressions and words, such as *sim*, yes, and *não*, no; *bom dia*, good morning, *boa tarde* and *boa noite*, good afternoon and good evening or night; *por favor*, please, and *obrigado*, thank you (or *obrigada* when the speaker is female).

Peculiarities, which will require a bit of getting used to, are the days of the week, apart from Saturday (*Sábado*) and Sunday (*Domingo*), which are respectively: Monday, *Segunda-feira*; Tuesday, *Terça-feira*; Wednesday, *Quarta-feira*; Thursday, *Quinta-feira*; and Friday, *Sexta-feira*. This system, different from other European countries, is probably Suevic in origin: a tombstone in the Minho is carved with the date 28 April, AD 616, SECUNDA FERIA.

Armed with a pocket dictionary or phrase-book, one should not meet with any great difficulty, although there are regional variations in pronunciation, between the Algarve and the Minho, for example.

Listed below are several essential words or phrases (see also previous pages):

*Fala inglês?*, Do you speak English?

*Não compreendo*, I don't understand

*Onde?*, Where?; *Porquê?*, Why?; *Quando?*, When?

*Um quarto de casal com banho*, a double room with a private bath; a single room being *um quarto simples*

*Onde ficam os lavabos?*, Where is the lavatory?

*Papel higénico*, toilet paper

*Que horas são?*, What time is it?

*hoje*, today; *ontem*, yesterday; *amanhã*, tomorrow

*agora*, now; *mais tarde*, later

*Vendem...?*, Do you sell...?; *Como se chama isto?*, What is this called?

*Quanto custa?*, How much is it?

*Comprido*, long; *curto*, short; *grande*, big; *pequeno*, small

*Caro*, expensive; *barato*, cheap

*Pode indicar-me o caminho para...?*, Can you direct me to...?

*Pode dar-me...*, Can I have...

*dinheiro*, money; *moedas*, coins; *notas*, notes

*Pode trocar?*, Can you change?; *Qual é o câmbio?*, What is the rate of exchange?; *Aceitam* (Do you take) traveller's cheques?

*o recibo*, the receipt; *a conta*, the bill; *o troco*, the change

*Quanto é a franquia?*, What is the postage?; *selos*, stamps

*Ponto de taxi*, a taxi rank

*Farmacêutico*, a chemist

Some colours are: *preto*, black; *branco*, white; *encarnado*, red; *azul*, blue; *verde*, green; *castanho*, brown; and *amarelo*, yellow

Numerals:

| | | | |
|---|---|---|---|
| 1 um | 11 onze | 21 vinte e um | 1000 mil |
| 2 dois | 12 doze | 30 trinta | 1001 mil e um |
| 3 três | 13 treze | 40 quarenta | |
| 4 quatro | 14 catorze | 50 cinquenta | |
| 5 cinco | 15 quinze | 60 sessenta | |
| 6 seis | 16 dizasseis | 70 setenta | |
| 7 sete | 17 dezassete | 80 oitenta | |
| 8 oito | 18 dexoito | 90 noventa | |
| 9 nove | 19 dezanove | 100 cem | |
| 10 dez | 20 vinte | 101 cento e um | |

## Visiting Churches, Museums, and Monuments

Most museums are open (*aberto*) daily, except Mondays and public holidays, from 10.00–17.00, or later in the summer, but some may be closed (*fechado*) at lunchtime. The guardians or guides are usually helpful when their assistance is sought.

One is advised to check times and days of admission with a tourist office in advance, if planning specific excursions, to avoid disappointment. For instance, while the palace at Queluz will be closed on one day of the week, that at Sintra is likely to be closed on another day, and thus it may not be possible to visit both on the same day as hopefully intended!

Churches may be open early, but are often closed between 13.00 and 16.00. Unlike so many in neighbouring Spain, the disinterested guardians of Portuguese churches—especially in the centre and south of the country—are proud of any treasures of art or architecture they may contain, are happy to show visitors around. In the north of Portugal, where more devotion is shown, the ecclesiastical authorities likewise display more interest: 'where every trifle may be turned into money, money will be expected for every trifle' (to quote Baretti), and this is noticeable particularly in the cathedral of Braga. When churches or other monuments are closed, it is usually possible to find the guardian and his key (*chave*), although in remoter districts it is advisable to make prior enquiries at the tourist post of the nearest town as to his likely whereabouts. Not all monuments are adequately signposted, and time can be wasted in an endeavour to track down some buildings, let alone obtain admission.

A pocket torch may be helpful when exploring the darker recesses of some churches, and a small pair of field-glasses will also be useful.

## Entertainment

While most towns of any size have cinemas, fewer have theatres, and concerts are not as frequent as they might be, in spite of the encouragement given to them by the Gulbenkian Foundation.

An entertainment promoted as being as 'typical' of Portugal as *Flamenco* is of Spain, is the *Fado*.

## Fado

Its origins are disreputable, it being generally accepted that it derived from the libidinous *lundum*, a dance which came originally from the Congo, and a popular activity among the slave population of Brazil. From Brazil also came the sentimentally lascivious songs known as *Modinhas*, which Beckford considered 'the most seducing, the most voluptuous imaginable, the best calculated to throw saints off their guard and to inspire profane deliriums'. Traditionally, it was taken over by the less than virtuous residents of the port quarter and the Alfama, some of them slaves before their emancipation in 1761, who thus entertained their clients. Among earlier *fadistas* known to polite society were the Brazilian creole named Caldas Barbosa, whose compositions were less than delicate, and later (c 1840) Maria Severa, who additionally became the mistress of the bullfighting Conde de Vimioso. Rarely referred to before the 1830s, *fado* became increasingly popular in the second half of the century, gaining a status similar to the can-can. Only comparatively recently has it been considered decent, and probably with respectability and professionalism (as in recent decades when performed by such artists as Amália Rodrigues, when it approached the status of an art form) it has lost much of its earlier spontaneity.

Nevertheless, a pleasant late evening may be spent at one of the better *casas de fado*, and local opinion should be sought as to where the best may be heard. They all serve food and drink and, apart from those on the tourist trails, are not over-priced. An interesting introduction is Chapter XI of Rodney Gallop's *Portugal: a book of Folk Ways*.

## Bullfights

Unlike the bloody spectacles of Spain, the Portuguese bullfight is a more civilised form of entertainment, but, apart from being promoted in Lisbon at the Praça de Touros do Campo Pequeno during the season (Easter to October) is little seen except in the Ribatejo, the traditional bull-breeding area of the country. Here also, at Vila Franca de Xira in July, the bulls run loose through the streets. In Portuguese bull-fights the interest is dependent on the dexterity and horsemanship of the *cavaleiro* (whose mount can in no way be compared with the poor hacks of Spain), who thrusts *banderillas* or *farpas* into the bull's neck muscles. An additional entertain-ment is the '*pega de cara*', the taking the bull by the horns (sheathed), which is done by the leader of a team known as the *forcado*, who will then pile on behind, the last one grabbing the beast's tail, bringing him down in a heap. The bull is not killed, merely immobilised. He is then enticed from the ring by a herd of gaily caparisoned and tintinnabulating tame bullocks, in whose reassuring company the fighting bull will trot out, probably wondering what on earth it was all about: and the next one will enter.

## Festivals.

Many towns and villages throughout the country have their local *festas* or *romarias*, some more promoted than others. Tourist offices can explain their manifestations and confirm their dates, during which period accommodation may well be in short supply. Among the more interesting are the following: mid June: agricultural fair at Santarém; June 12–13: Dos Santos populares, Lisbon; June 23–24: São João, Oporto; first week of July every two years: Tabuleiros, Tomar; early August: Gualterianos, Guimarães; August: de Santa Marta de Portuzelo, and da Senhora da Agonia, Viana do Castelo; August/September: de São Mateus, Viseu; September: São Paio da Torreira, Murtosa; and da Senhora dos Remédios, Lamego; early November: São Martinho horse fair at Golegã.

## Sports

Hunting, Shooting, and Fishing. Statements claiming that the wild game of Portugal was annihilated within days of the 1974 revolution are exaggerated, but more 'conservative' attitudes now prevail, and the National Parks offer some security to the surviving fauna. The Portuguese National Tourist Offices can supply the latest information on game and the regulations governing the importation of firearms; similarly concerning sea-fishing and underwater sports.

Tourist offices can also advise on local conditions in connection with the hiring of equipment, and what facilities are available for water sports and winter sports. The latter have a short season and are virtually confined to part of the Serra da Estrela. They may also be applied to for a list of golf courses and other sports grounds. Most of the larger resorts now have tennis courts, particularly in the Algarve and in the Cascais-Estoril areas.

# 1 · Lisbon

**LISBON** (663,315 inhab.), in Portuguese, **LISBOA**, is the capital and by far the largest city of Portugal, with the rapidly growing population of greater Lisbon estimated at well over 2,000,000. It has long been famous for its magnificent position on the north bank of the Tagus (Tejo in Portuguese). There is little doubt that since the estuary has been spanned by what is now known as the Ponte de 25 Abril, the most impressive approach to the city is from the south bank, as it was previously from the sea. (A new bridge and viaduct is now under construction from Sacavém, virtually a north-east suburb of Lisbon. It will span the Tagus towards Montijo, providing a more direct entry from the east, and is expected to ease communications when completed in 1998.)

Earlier travellers patronisingly claimed that Lisbon was only surpassed in beauty by Naples and Constantinople, but visitors today will find its impact sufficiently strong and the charm of the older town enticing enough without any gratuitous comparisons.

The hub of the city lies some 15km from the mouth of the Tagus at a point where the river has expanded to form a wide lake-like estuary, referred to as the Mar da Palha (Sea of Straw). As at Venice, the water laps the edge of one of the principal squares of the old town, the Praça do Comércio, familiarly known to the English as 'Black Horse Square', and formerly called the Terreiro do Paço.

Behind this extends the regularly planned lower town (Cidade Baixa), laid out ' after the Great Earthquake of 1755, framed by two of the legendary seven hills on which the city stands. Sightseers will soon find that the irregular and uneven contour of the site is perhaps its most characteristic feature, and a certain amount of stamina is required to clamber about: few would disagree with George Borrow, who remarked that 'the streets are in general precipitously steep'. Most of the steeper streets are those climbing uphill from the Cidade Baixa towards the Castelo São Jorge to the east, and to the Chiado and Bairro Alto to the west, above the quays stretching towards Belém. The wide Avenida da Liberdade ascends a gentler slope to the north and towards more modern quarters on a comparatively flat plateau to the north-east, beyond which proliferates a concrete jungle. In the last decade this has engulfed and ravaged almost all the outlying suburbs, including Queluz, and Belas, and threatens to spread far beyond.

The main thoroughfares are now much more congested by traffic, and visitors will find it sensible and preferable to use the buses, metro , or to take a green-roofed taxi (in the process of changing to a shade of cream) rather than negotiate a maze of steep one-way streets, some of which—as *travessas* or *becos*—peter out as steps. Along many streets yellow Edwardian-looking (and British-built) trams still run, while on certain slopes their place has been taken by funiculars, or inclined rack-railways.

The tessellated pavements are largely composed of a white limestone, relieved by a variety of designs in black basalt, a feature said to have been invented in the early 19C by the engineer Pinheiro Furtado. Both materials are readily available in the vicinity of Lisbon.

Street numbers mount rapidly, as ground-floor windows as well as doors are numbered separately. Still characteristic of the street life of Lisbon are the sellers of lottery tickets; the boot-blacks; the *varinas* or fishwives (cf. Ovar), balancing creels of fish on their heads and crying their wares (women also carry other goods on their heads); and the knife-grinders (many from Galicia, to the north of Portugal) playing their plaintive pan-pipes. A considerable number of refugees and emigrants from Portuguese ex-colonies in Africa and Asia will also be noticed; likewise gypsies, and occasional beggars.

Some of the older telephone boxes will also remind the English of home, for the telephone system was at one time British-maintained. The shop windows display a variety of exotic fruit, cheese, and fish—which is extraordinarily good here— including the inevitable *bacalhau* or dried cod. There are a remarkable number of shoe shops, but with those pavements and hills, they presumably find more than enough business. In the Ruas de Santa Paula and da Boavista (to the west of the lower end of the Rua do Alecrim) are ships' chandlers, exhibiting a bewildering range of tools, machinery, and nautical equipment.

## History, and the English in Lisbon

Ancient chroniclers (being marvellously exact at settling such remote dates— and even now the precise date, not merely the year, is placed on buildings to commemorate their inauguration) attributed the founding of the city to Elishah, grandson of Abraham, in 3259 BC. Others, in seeking a derivation for the name Olisipo, claimed Ulysses as its founder, but this is more probably of Phoenician origin (c 1100 BC). The **Phoenicians** made a permanent settle- ment on the hill of São Jorge. This the **Romans** occupied in 205 BC, after the Second Punic War, and in 137 BC Decimus Junius Brutus strengthened the Romans' hold on the place. Julius Caesar raised Olisipo to the rank of *municipium*, with the official title of Felicitas Julia, and under the Empire it became, after Mérida (with which it was connected by road) the most impor- tant city in Lusitania. It fell to the invading **Alans** in AD 409, who were followed by the **Suevi**, and in 457/8 to the **Visigoths** under Maldras, but it later defected.

In 714 the **Moors** overran Lusitania and fortified Lisbon, which later (798) was raided by Alfonso II of León. In 1093 it was briefly held by Alfonso VI, but it was not until 1147, after a four-month siege, that **Afonso Henriques**, son of Henry of Burgundy, aided by a motley force of crusaders, including an Anglo- Norman contingent sailing from Dartmouth, regained Lisbon. Gilbert of Hastings, an English priest, was consecrated bishop, and he established the Sarum Use, which continued in Lisbon until 1536. In c 1260 **Dom Afonso III** transferred the court from Coimbra (then the capital) to Lisbon, and the city began to increase in wealth and population. A university founded here in 1290 was twice moved to Coimbra in the following century, but returned to Lisbon in 1377, not being finally re-established at Coimbra until 1537.

Enrique II of Castile besieged Lisbon unsuccessfully in February 1373, but burnt the Rua Nova and Jewish quarter, after which **Dom Fernando** strengthened its fortifications by erecting new walls possessing 77 towers, 16 gates on the landward side, and 22 facing the Tagus. In July 1381 Edmund of Cambridge's fleet, with 3000 troops, entered the estuary as allies of Dom Fernando, before an abortive Anglo-Portuguese campaign against Spain.

Rabbi Eliezer set up a printing-press here in 1489 (the first eleven Portuguese incunabula are in Hebrew); but in 1498 the Jews of Portugal were forcibly baptised or deported. A pogrom of 'New Christians' took place in 1506.

The 16C saw many changes, for in 1497 **Vasco da Gama** had set sail from here on the voyage that opened up the sea route to India, and the subsequent discoveries of Portuguese navigators in Africa, Asia and America brought enormous wealth to the harbour. By the turn of the century the population was 85,000, which by 1527 had been reduced by plague to some 52,000; by 1557 it had risen again to 100,000, leaving the countryside depopulated.

By c 1550 tobacco had been introduced to Lisbon, at first used medicinally. Some leaves were sent from here by Jean Nicot (the French envoy in 1559–66) to cure Catherine de Médicis, which further disseminated the properties of the weed, and the name nicotine.

Lisbon experienced a severe earth tremor in 1531, and was again visited by the plague in 1569. The Inquisition was established here in 1536. Between 1580 and 1640 the city suffered under the domination of Spain. It has been suggested that had **Philip II**, who took up temporary residence there in the early 1580s, paid heed to his advisors, it might well have become the capital of the Peninsula. It was in the estuary of the Tagus that the Spanish Armada assembled under the Marquis of Santa Cruz, eventually setting sail (commanded by the 7th Duke of Medina Sidonia) in the spring of 1588. An Irish college was established here in 1593, and in 1621 Philip O'Sullivan Beare first published his history of Ireland in Lisbon; while in 1628 Simon Fallon of Galway wrote his treatise on mathematics and astronomy here.

After the revolution of 1640 much of Portugal's wealth was spent on erecting or strengthening its frontier fortresses. It was not until after 1690, with the discovery of Brazilian gold, that Lisbon achieved perhaps its greatest magnificence. **Dom João V** lavished this gold on its numerous churches, among other buildings; and Lisbon acquired at some cost the dignity of a patriarchate.

The poet Richard Flecknoe visited Lisbon in 1648, while in the following year Prince Rupert landed here with a small squadron and made it a base for naval operations against the Commonwealth, but was blockaded in the Tagus until October 1650 by Admiral Blake and Edward Popham. Sir Richard Fanshawe, Bart (1608–66), was ambassador here from September 1662—five months after Catherine of Braganza had embarked from Lisbon for England—until the following August; and his wife, Lady Ann, described Lisbon: 'with the river...the goodliest situation that I ever saw; the city old and decayed, but they are making new walls of stone which will contain six times their city. Their churches and chapels are the best built, the finest adorned, and the cleanliest kept of any churches in the world. The people delight much in *quintas*, which are a sort of country houses, of which there are abundance within a few leagues of the city, and those that belong to the nobility very fine, both houses and gardens. The nation is generally very civil and obliging ...'. (Fanshawe was also a translator of Camoens, and his version of *Os Lusíadas* was published in London in 1655.) In 1669 Lisbon was visited by Cosimo de Médicis.

With the Cromwellian treaty of 1654, the already long-established British merchants trading and resident in Lisbon—Thomas Daniel had been importing cloth from Bristol as early as 1378—set up what has been described as 'a kind of Chamber of Commerce-cum-Consulate...a Meeting house where the principal Merchants and Factors foregathered to discuss matters of trade, politics, and local interests of the British community.' This, for which Thomas Maynard (Consul from 1656–89) was largely responsible, was later to develop into a formal corporative body of traders which became known as the **British Factory**, and by the Portuguese as the Feitoria Inglesa, whose society a later urbane ambassador (in 1746–48)—Sir Benjamin Keene—was so much to enjoy, referring to it as the 'jolly free Factory'. They were also at one time to be condemned as a 'nest of Waspes'. Their heyday was probably in the 1730s, at a time when young David Garrick was in Lisbon, working for his uncle, a wine exporter. At a slightly later date the community included William Shirley, the dramatist turned merchant. In 1735 part of Admiral Norris's fleet was based in Lisbon for 21 months, and a number of his ships were careened here under the supervision of William Warden, a British subject and Dom João's dockmaster and naval architect, who held this important post for several years.

Meanwhile, since 1657, when the Rev. Zachary Cradock reached Lisbon to take up the post, the spiritual well-being of the British community had been supervised by a succession of chaplains, among them the Rev. Thomas Marsden, and the Rev. Michael Geddes (c 1650—1713; chaplain from 1678 to 1686, when his activities were forbidden by the Inquisition), author of *Miscellaneous Tracts*. From 1693 to 1700 the Rev. John Colbatch was chaplain, eternally wrangling with the then Envoy, John Methuen (father of Sir Paul Methuen, Minister at Lisbon from 1697–1702, and responsible for the important Commercial Treaty of 1703), whose scandalous relations with Sarah Earle (the Consul-general's young wife) Colbatch could not forgive. Neither could this worthy author of *An Account of the Court of Portugal in the Reign of Pedro II* much tolerate the laxity of life among the Factory in general: 'such a horrid crew, that he fancied himself in hell, while he was among them'. Colbatch likewise condemned royal morals, writing: 'I never heard that he [Dom Pedro] had any favourite of the sex, unless it were one Frenchwoman....Those he hath his commerce with are said to be of the lowest rank, and very many, and not all of the same colour.'

James O'Hara, Lord Tyrawley (1690–1773), the English Ambassador in 1728–41, was a popular figure, although Horace Walpole considered him 'singularly licentious, even for the courts of Russia and Portugal'. Not only did Dom João V give him 14 bars of gold on his departure, but Tyrawley returned to England with three 'wives', one Portuguese, Dona Anna, 'with long black hair plaited down to the bottom of her back', and no less than 14 illegitimate children. Another of his children, by Miss Seal, was to become the famous actress George Anne Bellamy. Tyrawley was certainly no fool, and he had many years of experience of Portuguese affairs and of members of the Factory (some of whom had treated him with 'disrespect and rudeness'). He condemned the majority of them: 'a parcel of the greatest Jackasses I ever met with, Fops, Beaux, Drunkards, Gamesters, and prodigiously ignorant, even in their own business.' In another of his memoranda he censured their relations with the Customs authorities. When discussing mutual problems with the Provedor d'Alfândega, the latter remarked that the members of the Factory 'were a set of *Casquilhos* (Petits Maîtres) that attended more to their Quintas, Balls, Masquerades & Gaming than to their business; that scarce one of them would give himself the trouble of going to the Custom House to dispatch their own goods, but left it to their Caixeiros (Book-keepers) who were all Portuguese Trapasseiros (Petty-foggers) and the greatest Rogues in the Country, and that there was neither Regularity or Fair dealing scarcely to be met with in our Factory. I did ask some of them (Merchants) why they did not goe to the Custom House to clear out their goods themselves as I had known all their Predecessors in the Trade constantly doe. I was answered that it was so dirty and mobbish a place that no Gentleman could set his foot into it.'

In 1727–28 General James Dormer (1679–1741) was resident in Lisbon as envoy extraordinary. Insanely jealous of the Consul, Thomas Burnet—more welcome at Court than he was—Dormer ordered his servants to drag Burnet from his carriage and beat him up. Burnet was wounded in the fracas, and Dormer was recalled to England in disgrace.

In October 1739 the dramatist António José da Silva, born of Portuguese-Jewish parents in Rio de Janeiro, was strangled and burnt in Lisbon at an *auto da fé*, for the Church, intent on stamping out all forms of heresy, was still powerful. During Lent in 1754 the Rev. George Whitefield spent some days in Lisbon, methodically in search of relics of their 'superstitious pageantry'. In August the ailing Henry Fielding disembarked, and here he spent the last two months of his life (cf. English Cemetery).

A year later, on the morning of 1 November 1755, Lisbon was shaken to its foundations by the **Great Earthquake** (whose effects were felt as far afield as Scotland and Jamaica), followed by a series of tremors, an even more disastrous fire, and a tidal wave which submerged the quay and overwhelmed the shipping. It has been estimated that five per cent of the population of 270,000 perished, among whom were some 78 British dead, and about 60 missing. It has been estimated that there were c 2000 British subjects there at the time. Many survivors of the Factory, while awaiting a ship for England, took shelter in the garden of Abraham Castres, the Envoy (who had himself escaped by jumping from a second floor window); and here, in the district known as Buenos Ayres, the Hon. Edward Hay, the Consul, afforded them every assistance. The royal family were likewise camping out in their garden at Belém.

The catastrophic situation was vigorously handled by the **Marquês de Pombal**, the only able minister, while the Marquês de Alorna announced to the king, Dom José: 'We must bury the dead, and feed the living, and shut the doors', words sometimes attributed to Pombal. Dom José's plan of removing the court to Rio de Janeiro was discouraged; military patrols were posted to check looting, and any damaged houses left standing in the lower town were demolished. (This area was later laid out by Pombal on the regular plan visible today.) The British Parliament had immediately voted £100,000 as an earnest of their solicitude, and sent out food, pick-axes, crowbars and spades. The cataclysm served as a text for an attack on the doctrine of a free and benevolent Providence in Voltaire's *Poème sur le désastre de Lisbonne* (1756), the pessimism of which provoked a letter of protest from Rousseau; it was also to suggest an episode in Voltaire's *Candide*, published in 1759.

Joseph Baretti, passing through Lisbon in 1760, described the scene, which still left 'a dreadful indelible image' on his mind. In one area 'nothing is to be seen but vast heaps of rubbish, out of which arise in numberless places the miserable remains of shattered walls and broken pillars.' Not much had been saved: fine libraries (including the remarkable musical library collected by Dom João IV), and irreplaceable works of art, were lost. Many people survived with only the clothes they were wearing at the time; some even less, having not yet dressed for Mass on that All Saints' Day.

'Our poor Factory, from a very opulent one, is totally ruined, at least for the major part...', wrote Tyrawley, admitting that they had in previous decades become 'Universal Traders', no longer merely 'respectable, regular & frugal merchants'. Yet Richard Croker, writing 25 years later, suggests that by then they had to a large extent recovered their fortunes, and again lived 'in a very sociable and pleasant manner', being 'particularly civil and hospitable', confirming Richard Twiss's description, when passing through Lisbon in 1772, who remarked that the members of the Factory and their families assembled once a week during the winter in two long rooms 'to dance and play at cards' (while Mrs May played the harpsichord with 'delicacy and taste'), and that any British stranger was admitted gratis. The Factory, having outlived its usefulness, was virtually disbanded by a treaty signed in 1810, but continued to subsist in a modified form until c 1825.

Several British officers, including John Burgoyne (the dramatist and later general, who capitulated at Saratoga in 1777), and Charles O'Hara, Tyrawley's son, were endeavouring to organise Portuguese resistance to the Spanish invasion of 1762. John Hunter, later the celebrated surgeon, was superintending the hospitals at Lisbon, Coimbra, and Santarém.

Among other **English travellers** of note visiting Lisbon at this period (when conditions had somewhat improved—the street lighting had been undertaken in 1780 by Martinho António Castro) were Nathaniel Wraxall (1772); Major William Dalrymple (1774); William Julius Mickle, the translator of The Lusiad in 1776 (in 1778–79); 'Arthur Costigan' (1779; Major James Ferrier, author of Sketches of Society and Manners in Portugal, published in 1789); Richard Cumberland, the dramatist and unsuccessful 'diplomat' (1780); and William Hickey (1782), the diarist. Hickey recorded that the Irish artist Thomas Hickey (no relation) was captured, while en route to India in 1780, by the French and Spanish fleets. After being released at Cádiz, he made his way to Lisbon where he painted numerous English ladies and gentlemen, as well as Portuguese of rank. He eventually reached Calcutta in 1784. Other visitors were William Beckford, England's notorious 'wealthiest son', for the first time (1787), where he was taken up by the Marquês de Marialva but not received by the Hon. Robert Walpole, the Envoy, and duly ostracised by the smug Lisbon British; Lady Craven (1791), openly accompanying the Margrave of Anspach; Dr Francis Willis (who had treated George III), summoned to Lisbon in 1792 to attend Dona Maria I, suffering from melancholia; and in 1804, Lord and Lady Holland. Many of them would put up at the hotel of Mrs Williams (an Irish widow), or at Mrs Duer's hotel (referred to by Twiss, who visited Lisbon in 1772, as 'an English inn, kept by one De War, on the hill of Buenos Ayres, where there is an ordinary every day, frequented by Englishmen, who reside in Lisbon for their health, and by members of the factory'). Four years later Robert Walpole reported to London that in Lisbon an English tavern-keeper named Dwyer (presumably the same man) had gone to London 'to seduce from England cotton manufacturers for this country'. Other visitors would have stayed at Reeves Hotel in the Rua do Prior (just south of the present British Embassy), although Beckford, who could afford it, and could only survive in a grand style, rented a quinta.

Mary Wollstonecraft was there briefly in the autumn of 1785 to nurse a female friend, but arrived too late. In 1796 Robert Southey visited Lisbon for the first time, staying with the Rev. Herbert Hill, his uncle, the then chaplain (from 1782 to 1807; he had been chaplain at Oporto during the previous four years). The high-minded young poet carped at his jolly congregation, complaining: 'The English here are the most indefatigable dancers and the most inveterate casino players in Europe.' He also disapproved of John Hookham Frere, who in 1800 had succeeded Walpole as Envoy: 'Frere is acting foolishly: he and the consul are slighting the English merchants, and establishing a little aristocracy with the quality-strangers, emigrants, and corps diplomatic'. The Hon. Robert Walpole (1736–1810), a cousin of Horace Walpole, and twice married to daughters of Factory merchants, and who had been envoy in Lisbon since 1772, was Beckford's bête noire: Beckford referred to him 'a blundering puppy', and complained of the 'abominable usage' he had received at his hands.

In December 1796 Sir John Jervis's squadron entered the Tagus, only a few weeks later decisively defeating a Spanish fleet off Cape St Vincent.

John Adamson, the Portuguese scholar, was living in Lisbon from 1803 to 1807, publishing his study of Camoens in London in 1820. During the same period Byron's 'Hibernian Strangford' (the 6th Viscount), in spite of his insipid—but popular—translations of Camoens (1803), was also resident here, having been offered the post of Secretary to the Legation. He later became Envoy, following the Court to Brazil in 1807. In 1802 Francesco Bartolozzi came to Lisbon from London to direct the National Academy, and here he died in 1815.

In April 1805 Géneral Junot visited the capital in a fruitless attempt to persuade the Portuguese to declare war against Britain. Six months later, the news of Nelson's victory at Trafalgar was celebrated in the Tagus by British ships there firing their guns all night. On 27 November 1807, as Junot again entered Lisbon—this time with the vanguard of a French army, which had marched across the Peninsula from Bayonne—the royal family (including Dona Maria I, incurably insane since 1792) hurriedly embarked for their long exile in Rio, the fleet setting sail with members of the government, together with perhaps as many as 15,000 other citizens, taking with them half the cash in circulation, and a vast amount of treasure.

After their defeat by Wellington at Vimeiro (cf.) the following August, by the disgraceful terms of the Convention of Cintra, the 24,000 French troops isolated here were able to sail back La Rochelle in British ships, boarding their transports to the execration of the populace.

On 22 April 1809 Wellington disembarked at Lisbon after some months of absence in England. Within 36 hours he was leading the occupying British troops north to evict Soult from Oporto (cf.). That July Lisbon was visited briefly by Lord Byron and John Cam Hobhouse en route to Greece.

In October 1810, having checked Masséna at Busaco (cf.), Wellington and his Anglo-Portuguese army retired behind the previously constructed defences known as the 'Lines of Torres Vedras' (cf.), some distance north of the capital. Lisbon remained the main port of supply for the allied forces until the closing stages of the Peninsular War. Here, officers on leave could find the most dissolute distractions. It was also the main base of the army contractors, among them Henrique Teixeira de Sampaio, later Conde da Póvoa (1774–1843).

In March 1817 a liberal conspiracy led by General Gomes Freire de Andrade (who had commanded a Portuguese contingent under Napoleon in Russia) was vigorously suppressed, and Gomes Freire was executed, which did not enhance the waning popularity of General William Carr Beresford, still the British commander-in-chief of the Portuguese army. In March 1821 Lisbon was illuminated to celebrate the passage of a draft constitution: the Papal Nuncio's window, remaining unlit, was forthwith stoned. Although Constitutionalism had come to stay, in May 1823 many of the Lisbon garrison deserted to the reactionary party of the Infante Dom Miguel, and during the subsequent civil war 'of the Two Brothers' it was frequently the scene of unrest: only with the entry of Marshal Terceira's forces (24 July, 1833) and the defeat of the Miguelites the following year, did the dust of constitutional conflict temporarily settle.

Lord Porchester (in 1827), George Borrow (in 1835), and James Holland, the artist (in 1838) passed through Lisbon, while in 1859 it was briefly visited by Francis Palgrave and Lord Tennyson, who drove around the city in 'a blazing heat'.

In 1864 Lisbon's population was 163,750, yellow fever and cholera epidemics having killed off over 8000 in 1855–57. In the second half of the century the suburbs were extended towards the north and west; railway stations were built, and the port facilities modernised, as they have again been since. By 1900 its population had risen to 356,000, and by 1910 to 435,000.

In 1908 Dom Carlos and his eldest son were assassinated in the Praça do Comércio; while on 4 October 1910, with the royal palace under fire from two rebellious warships in the Tagus, the monarchy was finally overthrown. Lisbon experienced a number of incidents during the early years of the Republic, among them the assassination of President Sidónio Pais as he entered the Rossio station in December 1918.

Being the capital, it was subsequently the scene of various revolts, among them that of General Gomes da Costa in 1926, precipitating the reaction of General Carmona; and more recently, that of 25 April 1974 (see Introduction to Portuguese History). During the Second World War (in the early years of which Norman Douglas, fleeing from Italy, spent several months there) it had the reputation of being a nest of spies.

Among eminent **natives of Lisbon** (*Lisboetas*) were St Anthony of Padua (1195–1231); Pope John XXI (Pedro Julião, or Pedro Hispano; died 1277); Fernão Lopes (c 1380–c 1458), chronicler; the soldier, merchant and adventurer Duarte Brandão (c 1440–1508), knighted by Richard III as Sir Edward Brampton, whose knowledge of the English court was put to use by Perkin Warbeck, at one time in his service; Francisco de Almeida (c 1450–1510), and João de Castro (1500–48), viceroys of India; Jerónimo Osório (1506–80), historian, and later Bishop of Silves; Francisco de Holanda (c 1518–84), artist and architect; Luis de Camões (Camoens; 1524–80), poet; Sebastião José de Carvalho e Melo, Marquês de Pombal (1699–1782), statesman; Francisco Vieira do Matos Lusitano (1699–1783), artist; Marcos Portugal (1762–1830), and Domingos Bontempo (1771–1842), composers; Domingos Antonio de Sequeira (1768–1837), artist; Alexandre Herculano (1810–77), historian; Fernando Pessoa (1888–1935), poet and author; José de Almada Negreiros (1893–1970), artist and author.

Domenico Scarlatti (1685–1757) lived in Lisbon from 1721–28 (except for a brief visit to Naples in 1725), with the Infanta María Bárbara de Braganza as his pupil. When she married Ferdinand, heir to the Spanish throne, she appointed Scarlatti court harpsichordist, and he remained in Madrid until his death.

Among those who died in Lisbon were Admiral Sir Richard Stayner (in 1662); Charles Mordaunt, the third Earl of Peterborough (1658–1735; he died only a week after arrival, but his body was returned to England); Henry Fielding (in 1754), author of *Tom Jones*, buried in the English Cemetery (cf.); Dr Philip Doddridge (1751), the Nonconformist divine; Francesco Bartolozzi (1815), the engraver; and Jeremiah John Callanan (1795–1829), the Irish poet.

- **Tourist Information Office**. The main office is in Palácio Foz at the south end of Avenida da Liberdade.

- **Airport**. Portela airport, north of the city, is a 20 minute drive from the centre of Lisbon. Those without their own transport can either catch a taxi (confirm the price before setting off) or a bus (Linha Verde No. 90).

- **Railway stations**. The main railway station is Estação do Rossio, just to the west of Rossio Square (Praça Dom Pedro IV). From here trains go to Sintra and elsewhere in Estremadura. Use Estação do Cais do Sodré by Praça Duque de Terceira for trains to Estoril and Cascais.

- **Ferry stations**. Estação do Sul e Sueste (or Fluvial) opposite the Bolsa on the Avenida Infante D. Henrique, from where car and passenger ferries cross the Tagus and also to Barreiro, the present terminus for trains to Algarve.

- **HOTELS**. Among a representative selection of 3 to 5-star hotels are the following, the more expensive being among the first listed in each section:

### Near the Parque Eduardo VII
*Diplomático*, Rua Castilho 74 (tel. 386 20 41, fax 386 21 55)
*Méridien*, Rua Castilho 149 (tel. 69 09 00, fax 69 32 31)
*Ritz*, Rua Rodrigo da Fonseca 88 (tel. 69 20 20, fax 69 17 83)
*Sheraton*, Rua Latino Coelho 1 (tel. 57 57 57, fax 54 71 64)
*Sol*, Av. Duque de Loulé 41 (tel. 353 21 08, fax 353 18 65)
*Capital*, Rua Eça de Queiroz 24 (tel. 353 68 11, fax 352 61 65)
*Dom Carlos*, Av. Duque de Loulé 121
*Eduardo VII*, Av. Fontes Pereira de Melo 5 (tel. 353 01 41, fax 353 38 79)
*Fénix*, Praça Marqués de Pombal 8 (tel. 386 21 21, fax 386 01 31)
*Flamingo*, Rue Castilho 41 (tel. 386 21 91, fax 386 12 16)
*Flórida*, Rua Duque de Palmela 32 (tel. 57 61 45, fax 54 35 84)
*Rex*, Rua Castilho 169
*Miraparque*, Av. Sidónio Pais 12 (tel. 352 42 86, fax 57 89 20)

### Near the Gulbenkian Foundation
*Real Parque*, Av. Luís Bivar 67 (tel. 57 01 01, fax 57 07 50)
*Carlton Lisboa*, Av. Conde Valbom 56 (tel. 795 11 57, fax 795 11 66)
*Dom Manuel I*, Av. Duque d'Ávila 189 (tel. 57 61 60, fax 57 69 85)

### Near the Av. De Liberdade
*Altis*, Rua Castilho 11 (tel. 52 24 96, fax 54 86 96)
*Tivoli*, Av. da Liberdade 185 (tel. 353 01 81, fax 57 94 61)
*Lisboa Plaza*, Travessa do Salitre 7 (tel. 346 39 22, fax 347 16 30)
*Sofitel*, Av. da Liberdade 125 (tel. 342 92 02, fax 342 92 22)
*Tivoli Jardim*, Rua Julio Cesar Machado 7 (tel. 353 99 71, fax 355 65 66)
*Veneza*, Av. da Liberdade 189 (tel. 352 26 18, fax 352 66 78)

### Near the Museu de Arte Antiga
*Da Lapa*, Rua do Pau de Bendeira (tel. 395 00 55, fax 395 06 65)
*York House*, Rua das Janelas Verdes 32 (tel. 396 25 44, fax 397 27 93)
*As Janelas Verdes*, at 47 in that street (tel. 396 81 43, fax 396 81 44)

### In the Barro Alta
*Boges*, Rua Garrett 108

### Near Rossio
*Mundial*, Rua Dom Duarte 4 (tel. 886 31 01, fax 887 91 29)
*Metropóle*, Praça Dom Pedro IV 30 (tel. 346 91 64, fax 346 91 66)

**North of the Castelo São Jorge**
*Albergaria Senhora do Monte*, Calçada do Monte 39 (tel. 886 60 02, fax 887 77 83)

**At Belém**
*Da Torre*, Rua dos Jerónimos 8 (tel. 363 62 62, fax 364 59 95)

- **RESTAURANTS**, listed in the order expensive to unpretentious:
**Central Lisbon**
*Consenso*, Rua da Academia das Ciências
*Alcântara*, Rua Maria Luisa Holstein 15
*Aviz*, Rua Serpa Pinto 12B
*Casa do Leão*, Castelo de São Jorge
*Conventual*, Praça das Flores 45
*Cais da Ribeira*, Armazén A, Cais do Sodré 2
*Gambrinus*, Rua das Portas de Santo Antão 25
*Michel*, Largo de Santa Cruz do Castelo 5
*Tágide*, Largo da Acad. Nac. De Belas Artes 18
*Tavares*, Rua das Misericórdia 37
*Cas da Comida*, Trav. das Amoreiras 1
*Pap'Açorda*, Rua da Atalaia 57
*Rex*, Rua Nova da Trindade 1B
*Sua Excelencia*, Rua do Conde 42 (near Museu de Arte Antiga)
*Bota Alta*, Trav. da Queimada 37

**Near the Gulbenkian Foundation:**
*Gôndola*, Av. de Berna 64
*Polícia*, Rua Masquês Sá da Bandeira 112
*Paco*, Av. de Berna 44A
*Lacerda*, Av. de Berna 36A

**At Belém:**
*Espelho d'Água*, Av. de Brasilia
*Vela Latina*, Doca do Bom Sucesso
*Guiseppe di Verdi*, Calçada Ajuda
*Caseiro*, Ru de Belém 35

- **Hours of admission to the principal museums**, etc. With certain exceptions they are *closed on Mondays* and on national holidays; many also close at lunchtime. It is always advisable to **check these times** with your hotel or a tourist office, as they are liable to vary from those published.

    The main monuments: the castle of São Jorge; São Vicente de Fora; the Monastery of the Jerónimos, Belém; the Sé (cathedral); and the Tower of Belém, are usually open daily from c 10.00.

| | | |
|---|---|---|
| *Arqueologia e Etnologia | Praça do Imperio | Tues 14.00–18.00 Wed–Sun 10.00–18.00/19.00 |
| *Arte Antiga | Rua das Janelas Verdes | Tues 14.00–18.00 Wed–Sun 10.00–18.00/20.00 |
| Azulejos (Tiles) | Madre de Deus Convent | Tues 14.00–18.00 Wed–Sun 10.00–18.00 |

| | | |
|---|---|---|
| Chiado Museum (Modern art) | Rua Serpa Pinto 4–6 | Tues. 14.00–18.00 Wed–Sun 10.00–18.00/20.00 |
| City Museum (da Cidade) | Palácio de Pimenta, Campo Grande 245 | Tues–Sun 10.00–13.00 14.00–18.00 |
| Coach Museum (Coches) | Praça Afonso de Albuquerque, Belém | 10.00–13.00; 14.30–17.30 |
| Costume Museum (Trajo) | Largo São Joã Baptista | 10.00–18.00 |
| Decorative Art (Espírito Santo) | Largo das Portas do Sol 13 | Wed, Fri, Sun 10.00–17.00 Tues, Thur 10.00–20.00 |
| Ethnology, Museum of | Av. Ilha da Madeira | Tues14.00–18.00 Wed–Sun 10.00–18.00/19.00 |
| Folk Art Museum | Praça do Império, Belém | Tues 14.00–18.00 Wed–Sun 10.00–18.00 |
| *Gulbenkian Foundation | Av. de Berna 45 The modern art collection is adjacent | Wed and Sat 14.00–19.30 Tues, Thurs, Fri and Sun10.00–17.00 from Oct–May Tues–Sun 10.00–17.00 |
| Marine Museum | Praça do Império, Belém | 10.00–18.00 |
| Military Museum | Largo do Museu da Artilharia | Tues–Sat 10.00–16.00 Sun 10.00–17.00 |
| Musical Instruments | Alto dos Moinhos underground station | Tues–Sat 13.00–20.00 |
| São Roque (Religious Art) | Largo Trinidade Coelho | Tues–Sun 10.00–17.00. The church open daily |
| Torre do Tombo (Nat. Archives) | Alameda da Universidad off the Campo Grande | temporary exhibitions |

For practical purposes the description of Lisbon has been divided into six sections: **A**, Central Lisbon; **B**, Eastern Lisbon, including the Castle of São Jorge and the Alfama district; **C**, Western Lisbon, including the Chiado and the district of Rato; **D**, the Museu de Arte Antiga; **E**, Belém, further west; and **F**, Northern Lisbon, including the Gulbenkian Foundation.

# A. Central Lisbon

## THE ROSSIO

The Rossio (officially the Praça de Dom Pedro IV), lying just south of the lower end of the Av. da Liberdade (see below), and north of the Baixa, or planned lower town, is still an important hub of activity. Until the 18C this rectangular square was the scene of public executions, *autos-da-fé*, bull-fights and carnivals. It was once known

LISBON
METRO

existing line

planned extension

Pontinha
Carnide
Colégio Militar-Luz
Alto dos Moinhos
Laranjeiras
Sete Rios
Palhavã
S. Sebastão
Parque
Rotunda II
Rato
Avenida
Restauradores
Campo Grande
Cidade Universitaria
Entre Campos
Campo Pequeno
Saldanha
Picoas
Rotunda I
Alvalade
Roma
Areeiro
Alameda
Arroios
Anjos
Intendente
Socorro
Rossio
Baixa-Chiado
Cais do Sodré

to the English as 'Rolling-Motion Square', from the undulating pattern of its tessellated pavement formed by small blocks of white limestone and black basalt, but this has been partly removed in the interest of traffic.

In the centre is a poor bronze statue 'of Dom Pedro IV' (1870; he was crowned king of Brazil as Dom Pedro I), which was in fact cast as a statue of Maximilian of Mexico, and was being shipped out to Mexico when he was assassinated. The boat from Marseille put in at Lisbon, and a deal was made with the authorities, who after making a few superficial changes, got a royal statue cheaply.

At the north end of the square is the Classical portico of the **Teatro Nacional de Dona Maria II** (1842–46, by Fortunato Lodi, an Italian), restored since gutted by fire in 1964, and surmounted by a statue of Gil Vicente, Portugal's earliest dramatist.

It stands partly on the site of the Paço dos Estãos, a royal palace built in 1449, near which was a point of assembly for Portuguese Jews in 1497 prior to their (partial) expulsion from the country. After 1571 it was occupied by the Inquisition, and later, until its destruction by fire in 1836, it was used as government offices.

The west side of the square, flanked by crowded cafés, provides a good view of the castle of São Jorge, while from the opposite pavement one can see the ruins of the Carmo.

Facing the west side of the theatre is Lisbon's main **railway station** (Estação do Rossio; 1891), a mock-Manueline construction by J.L. Monteiro (1849–1942), built on two floors. It immediately abuts the south end of a long tunnel, the line beyond its north end providing a view of the Aguas Livres aqueduct (cf.).

East of the theatre is the Largo de São Domingos, flanked by the **Paço dos Condes de Almada**, in 1640 the scene of the conspiratorial meetings of the 'Restauradores', before the overthrow of the Spanish establishment and their proclamation of independence after 60 years of occupation.

At the south-east corner of the square stands *****São Domingos**, almost entirely rebuilt by Carlos Mardel after 1755, in which victims of the Inquisition heard their sentences read, and which contains the tomb of the Spanish preacher Fray Luís de Granada (1504–88), whose *Guia de Pecadores* (sinners) was first published in Lisbon in 1556–57. The church, re-roofed since gutted by fire in 1959, is most impressive in its partly calcined state, but it would appear that further restoration is in progress. A few paces to the south is the smaller Praça da Figueira, with its statue of Dom João I.

Further to the north-east is the Largo Martim Moniz, a somewhat derelict area at the south end of the wide Rua da Palma and its extension north-east, the Av. Almirante Reis, which with its continuation, leads towards the airport.

From the south-west corner of the Rossio, the pedestrian Rua do Carmo climbs steeply up to the Chiado: see Rte 1C.

## THE BAIXA

The area immediately south of the Rossio and Praça da Figueira consists of the grid of streets laid out under the aegis of Pombal, assisted by military engineers and surveyors, principally Manuel da Maia (1672–1768), and Eugénio dos Santos de Carvalho (1711–60), succeeded by Carlos Mardel (1695–1763). It is generally known as the Baixa or lower town.

Its three main thoroughfares are the **Rua Augusta** (leading off the south-east corner of the Rossio towards a triumphal arch, only finished in 1873), and to the west and east respectively, the **Rua do Ouro** (officially Rua Aurea; of the gold-smiths), and the **Rua da Prata** (silversmiths), below which are the remains of a Roman *cryptoporticus*. The streets were originally allotted to separate trades, but this division is now hardly noticeable.

At the west end of the first transverse street (de Santa Justa) stands the incongruous Elevador, a passenger lift of 1903, said to have been designed by Eiffel, but in fact by Raúl Mesnier, providing a rapid ascent to the Carmo (see Rte 1C), and commanding a panoramic view from its summit.

From the east end of the fifth cross street (Rua da Conceição) one may ascend towards the cathedral and castle: see Rte 1B.

The three main streets shortly reach the riverside **PRAÇA DO COMÉRCIO**; perhaps more impressive when seen from the Tagus, but much spoilt since used as a parking site. Many would agree with Sacheverell Sitwell, who remarked that it 'does not deserve the encomiums that have been lavished upon it'. It is still widely known by its earlier name, Terreiro do Paço, after the 16C royal palace 'da Ribeira' (of the riverbank) here, destroyed in the convulsion of 1755, but it is even better known—at least to English visitors—as '**Black Horse Square**', from the effective but somewhat pretentious bronze equestrian statue by Joaquim Machado de Castro, erected in 1775 to commemorate the generosity of Dom José to the victims of the earthquake. The medallion of Pombal was replaced on the pedestal in 1833, having been removed on that minister's dismissal, and hidden by its designer. The horse and the elephant on either side (although done from life) are of equal size.

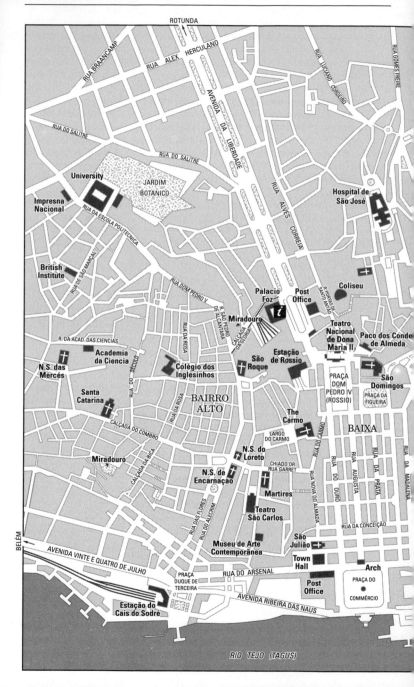

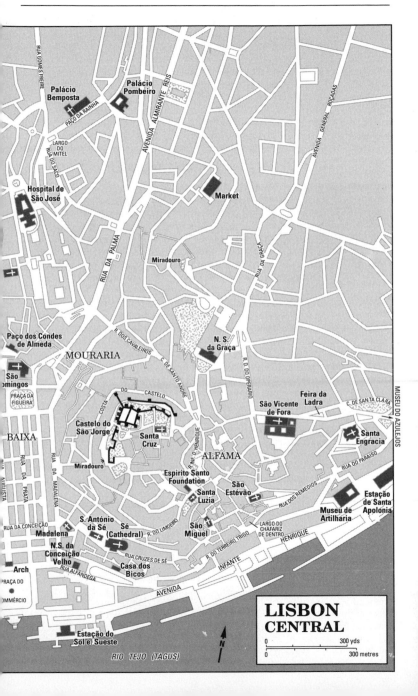

RUA GOMES FREIRE

Palácio
Bemposta

Palácio
Pombeiro

AVENIDA ALMIRANTE REIS

PAÇO DA RAINHA

LARGO
DO
MITEL

RUA DO SACO

AVENIDA GENERAL ROÇADAS

Hospital de
São José

Market

RUA DA PALMA

Miradouro

RUA DA GRAÇA

Paço dos Condes
de Almeda

R. DOS CAVALEIROS

MOURARIA

N. S.
da Graça

São
Domingos

PRAÇA DA
FIGUEIRA

C. DE SANTO ANDRÉ

R. D. DO OPERARIO

C. DE SANTA CLARA

MUSEU DO AZULEJOS

DO       CASTELO

Castelo do
São Jorge

Santa
Cruz

São Vicente
de Fora

Feira da
Ladra

Santa
Engracia

BAIXA

RUA DA PRATA

RUA DA MADALENA

Miradouro

R. NF. D'HENRIQUE

ALFAMA

RUA DO PARAISO

Espirito Santo
Foundation

Santa
Luzia

São
Estévão

RUA DOS REMEDIOS

Estação
de Santa
Apolonia

AUGUSTA

S. António
da Sé

Sé
(Cathedral)

R. DO LIMOEIRO

São
Miguel

LARGO DO
CHAFARIZ
DE DENTRO

Museu de
Artilharia

RUA DA CONCEIÇÃO

Madalena

N.S. da
Conceição
Velho

RUA CRUZES DE SÉ

R. DO TERREIRO TRIGO

HENRIQUE

Arch

RUA ALFANDEGA

Casa dos
Bicos

INFANTE

PRAÇA DO

COMMÉRCIO

AVENIDA

Estação do
Sol e. Sueste

N

RIO   TEJO (TAGUS)

# LISBON
# CENTRAL

0       300 yds

0       300 metres

*Bronze equestrian statue of Dom José in the Praça do Comércio*

Three sides of the arcaded square are lined with yellow-painted 'Pombaline' façades of government offices, designed by Eugénio dos Santos. At its south-east corner stands the Bolsa or Exchange, adjoining which is the Alfândega or Custom House, while opposite is the **Estação do Sul e Sueste**, or Fluvial, from which passenger and car ferries ply to and from the far bank of the Tagus (6.00–23.00) and to Barreiro, the terminus for trains to the Algarve.

A few paces to the west, a marble staircase descends between two columns into the river. It provides a view of the 'Sea of Straw' or Mar de Palha, as this stretch of the estuary is designated, and once familiarly called 'Jackass Bay' by English mariners. From here, on 23 April 1662, Catherine of Braganza and her suite sailed for England. She reached Portsmouth on 13 May, and married Charles II on the 21st. (She did not return to Lisbon until January 1693.)

From the north-east angle of the square the Rua Alfândega leads past the church of **N.S. da Conceição Velha** (of the Conception), built on the site of a synagogue. It is notable for its splendid Manueline *portal (c 1520), whose tympanum represents the Virgin sheltering with her mantle Dom Manuel and Dona Leonor (widow of Dom João II, and founder of the church), Pope Leo X, Miguel Contreiras, founder of the brotherhood of the Misericórdia, and other ecclesiastics.

A few paces beyond, on the north side of an open space, stands the so-called **Casa dos Bicos**, once a residence of the Albuquerque family, and adorned with diamond-shaped bosses. In 1982–83 it was gutted, and the restored lower two floors of the 16C building were provided with an additional two floors. The reconstruction faithfully copies the original façade as illustrated in several early engravings (in particular on an early 18C *azulejo*), which show in some detail the balustraded upper windows and balconies in the Manueline taste.

For the riverside district further east, see Rte 1B.

Leaving the Praça do Comércio at its north-west corner, where, by the post office (Correio), Dom Carlos I, penultimate king of Portugal, and his eldest son Luís Felipe, were assassinated on 1 February 1908, the small Praça do Município is shortly entered. In the centre stands a late 18C *pelourinho*, a twisted monolithic column surmounted by an armillary sphere, symbol of municipal authority (see Glossary). The east side is flanked by the town hall (Câmara Municipal) of 1865–75, from which the Republic was proclaimed on .5 October 1910. Adjoining is São Julião (1854), occupying the site of the former cathedral church of Western Lisbon.

The Rua Nova do Almada climbs north from beyond the church, providing an alternative approach to the Chiado: see Rte 1C.

Along the south side of the square extends the 18C Arsenal da Marinha, while the Rua do Arsenal leads west to the Praça Duque da Terceira, at the foot of the steep Rua do Alecrim (see Rte 1C), and to the Estação do Cais do Sodré (terminal for Estoril and Cascais). From the adjacent quay, Junot and his defeated troops embarked on British ships to be repatriated, sailing to La Rochelle as agreed by the Convention of Sintra.

The riverside road continues west to the suburb of Belém: see Rte 1E.

# B.  Eastern Lisbon

This area, only a part of which is known as the **ALFAMA**, some of it surviving the 1755 earthquake, is largely dominated by the Castelo de São Jorge, conveniently approached by the Rua de Santo António da Sé, climbing south-east from the Rua da Madalena, two streets east of the Rua da Prata (see Rte 1A).

The church of La Madalena (1783), incorporating the Manueline portico of its predecessor, is the first passed (right). Then (left) is **Santo António da Sé**, by Mateus Vicente, apparently paid for by alms collected in the streets, but not completed until 1812, and alleged to have been built on the site of the birthplace of St Anthony of Padua (1195–1231).

A few steps higher, overlooking a small square, stands the *SÉ or **cathedral**, its two low battlemented towers flanking a rose-window above a Romanesque portal. The building is still of some interest in spite of the damage caused by earthquakes, fires, and injudicious rebuilding, although its entire restoration is long overdue.

Although legend has it that the cathedral was used as a mosque by the Moors, there is no evidence of it existing before the time of Afonso Henriques. The original Romanesque edifice, of which the English crusader-priest Gilbert of Hastings was the first bishop, was largely rebuilt by Dom Afonso IV and his successors after the earthquakes of 1337–47. In 1388, the populace, infuriated by his Spanish sympathies, flung Bishop Martinho Anes from the north tower. In 1393 Dom João I raised the see to metropolitan rank. Philippa of Lancaster's English chaplain, Robert Payn, when canon of the cathedral, translated Gower's *Confessio Amantis* into Portuguese. The crypt served as an armoury for an abortive *coup* against the Salazar regime in March 1959.

Note, in the short barrel-vaulted **interior**, with its low lantern and plain capitals, the triforium and the rose-windows in the apses; and in the Gothic ambulatory chapels, the tombs of Lobo Fernandes Pacheco (14C), together with that of his wife, and of João Anes (died 1440), the first archbishop. The Capela-Mór, originally built by Afonso IV, but 'restored' in the late 18C, contains that king's tomb and that of his wife, Dona Brites, two late 18C urns, and Baroque organs of the same period.

Also to be seen is the elaborate *presépio* or crib by Joaquim Machado de Castro (1766). Also housed here are the relics of St Vincent (brought to Lisbon from Cape St Vincent in a boat miraculously guided by a pair of ravens, which now figure in the city arms). Three sides of the cloisters (late 13C, but much damaged; the north walk is being restored), entered from the N side of the ambulatory, extend round the apse. A 13C iron screen is notable.

From the south side of the cathedral one may follow the Rua Cruzes de Sé which leads towards the Largo do Chafariz de Dentro (see p 113) to enter the west end of the Alfama, but it is recommended that the visitor should first continue the ascent along the north side of the cathedral by the Rua do Limoeiro, passing (left) near the slight remains of a 1C Roman theatre (in the Rua São Mamede) and the Aljube, once the archbishop's palace, and later a women's prison. On the right is the ruinous **Limoeiro**, once a royal palace, later the Mint, and since the late 15C a men's prison, named after a lemon-tree which stood in its courtyard. It was here that late in 1383 João, the Master of Avis, assassinated Andeiro (lover of Leonor Teles, the widow of Dom Fernando), and standing at one of the windows, was acclaimed regent by the populace.

Continuing uphill, Santa Luzia is passed on the right, adjacent to which one may obtain a good view over the Alfama, into which steps descend. A better view is commanded by the neighbouring Largo das Portas do Sol.

To the left is the entrance to the **\*ESPÍRITO SANTO FOUNDATION** (trams 28 or 28B; bus 37), established in 1953 by Ricardo Espírito Santo Silva, the banker, with the intention of preserving the traditional skills of Portuguese craftsmanship in the decorative arts, and providing the city with a **Museum of Decorative Art** (Wed, Fri, Sun 10.00–17.00, Tues, Thur 10.00–20.00).

The 21 workshops may be visited during weekdays, and orders may be placed for the restoration and fine quality reproduction of fabrics, furniture, book-bindings (some examples of which are displayed in the museum), and iron-work, etc. The foundation also provides a three-year course in interior decoration.

The museum, accommodated in a 17C palace of the counts of Azurara, preserving some good *azulejos* and ceilings, contains a remarkably fine collection of Portuguese furniture and silver (some showing English influence), displayed in a series of rooms built round a courtyard. Note the blue and white *azulejos* in the portária; the Directoire furniture, and a remarkable rosewood card-backgammon-and-chess-table; the Indo-Portuguese tapestries; Arraiolos carpets; and embroidery from Castelo Branco; and on an upper floor, the Jacaranda and boxwood cupboard; the doors of sicupira wood; the japanned furniture; the painted ceiling, and the silver in the dining-room; and the model for the 'Black Horse' (see Rte 1A). Notable among paintings are the two views of Lisbon by Alexandre Noël (1752–1834) and that of Oporto by Carlos van Zeller, those of the sieges of Lisbon, and Santarém (17C), and portraits of Dom Pedro II and Dom João V.

From here, an easy ascent to the castle may be made by retracing one's steps down-hill and taking the first turning on the right, which leads in a few minutes' to the Porta de São Jorge (1846), the main entrance to the precinct of the **Castelo de São Jorge** (bus 37), the Moorish citadel occupying the centre of the Phoenician and Roman settlements of Lisbon. Its tree-shaded terraces, rampart walks, and ten old towers, command extensive \*views over the city, but the municipal 'restoration' of the site is suspect, to say the least.

On its south side stood the Paço de Alcáçova, the Moorish Kasba, converted into a palace by Dom Dinis, which remained the principal residence of the king until the time of Dom Manuel. Dom João I died here in 1433, and it was the birthplace of Dom João II (1455) and Dom João III (1502). By the 17C it was largely a neglected ruin, although the Torre do Tombo (cf. Rte 1F) still held archives, of which the chronicler Fernão Lopes was keeper from c 1418. It was later used as a prison, while restored dependencies now accommodate the *Casa do Leão restaurant*.

From the north-west corner a wall descends part of the way down the steep hill to an outlying tower; passing this, the north flank of the castle is skirted to make one's exit near the church of Santa Cruz.

Continuing downhill, the small Largo de Rodrigues de Freitas is shortly reached, near which is the church of Meninos-Deus (1711–37), attributed to João Antunes. Façade towers were planned but not executed.

Downhill to the left lies the unsavoury Mouraria (better avoided after dark), the district relegated to the Moors after the re-occupation of Lisbon, from which one may return to the Rossio.

Almost due north is the Calçada da Graça, with the Baroque church of the Augustinian convent of **N.S. da Graça**, the sacristy of which, with good *azulejos*, contains the tomb of Mendo de Pereira (died 1708).

From a left-hand turning a short distance beyond, a lane climbs steeply to approach the Miradouro de N.S. do Monte.

By following a lane to the right from the far side of the Largo de Rodrigues de Freitas, a few minutes' walk brings one to the imposing but frigid white limestone church of *****SÃO VICENTE DE FORA** (1582–1627) (tram 28), by Felipe Terzi and Baltasar Alvares, its name a reminder that one is now outside (*fora*) the medieval line of walls. It was later known as the Patriarchal church (of Eastern Lisbon). The square front, in the Italian Renaissance style, is crowned by short twin towers. The dome fell in the 1755 earthquake. The well-proportioned **interior** is notable for its coffered barrel vault, and its great 18C organ, sited behind the main altar.

The cloisters, entered from the south aisle, contain a wealth of most attractive 18C *****azulejos** depicting La Fontaine's *Fables*. A passage to the left leads to the Pantheon of the House of Braganza (the refectory being so-transformed in 1855), accommodating the remains—previously displayed in an embalmed state—of the majority of that dynasty from Dom João IV (died 1656) to Dom Manuel II (died 1932, in England), together with his widow (died 1951, at Versailles), and his brother Luís Filipe (assassinated 1908). Catherine of Braganza (died 1705, after 20 years of widowhood, the last 12 in Lisbon) also lies there; as do King Carol of Rumania (deposed in 1940, who spent part of his exile at Estoril, and who died in 1953) and Mme Lupescu, his morganatic wife.

Of more interest is the *portária*, to the right of the cloister entrance, with a ceiling by Vincenzo Baccerelli of Florence, dating from 1710, while scenes of the sieges of Lisbon and of Santarém are depicted in *azulejos*.

It was in São Vicente that the great retable of Nuno Gonçalves was found, and later translated to the Museu de Arte Antiga; and it was here in 1787 that Beckford first met his protégé and friend, Gregorio Franchi (1770–1828), who was then a choir-boy.

Passing under a bridge on the north side of the church, the Campo de Santa Clara, scene of a flea-market on Tuesday and Saturday mornings (Feira da Ladra), is reached, on the north side of which is an 18C mansion by Manuel da Costa Negreiros, containing some fine *azulejos*.

A short distance downhill to the south stands the ambitious church of *SANTA ENGRÁCIA (10.00–17.00, closed Mon), begun in 1682 by João Nunes Tinoco, and continued after 1690 by João Antunes to replace an older church apparently demolished in consequence of an act of sacrilege in 1630. The present building, once used as an artillery magazine, was only completed in 1966, with the addition of the balustraded cupola, thus invalidating the expression for never- finished work as being 'obras de Santa Engrácia'. Since its termination it has been proclaimed as being 'National Pantheon' (in the manner of dictatorships), and contains the modern cenotaphs of Vasco da Gama, Afonso de Albuquerque, Nun' Alvares Pereira, the Infante Dom Henrique (Henry the Navigator), Pedro Alvares Cabral, and Luis de Camões.

The plan is that of a Greek cross with rounded extremities and framed by four square towers. On the entrance front four huge Doric columns frame a triad of arches and pedimented niches. The splendid **interior**, with its four ribbed semi-domes of coloured marbles set in contrasting patterns, is spatially one of the hand-somest in Portugal.

Descending downhill to the south-west, one soon reaches the **Museu de Artilharia** (Tues–Sat 10.00–16.00, Sun 10.00–17.00; tram 3, 16, 24; bus 13a, 17, 35), a so-called Military Museum, accommodated in the Arsenal do Exército, with an imposing Corinthian façade by the French architect Larre. Unfortunately, it would seem that the collection, which includes some individually interesting pieces, has hardly been touched since first accumulated here.

To the left of the entrance are some early bronze cannon, some cast in Goa, including the 'Touro' (1518) and 'Tigre' (1549), but the most curious specimens are in the main courtyard, among them the enormous cannon taken at the siege of Diu (1539), cast in 1533. On the **first floor** (right) are two rooms devoted to the Peninsular War, specifically the battles of Roliça, Vimeiro, and Busaco, and the Lines of Torres Vedras, including a maquette of the last, showing the position of the lines of fortifications across the peninsula north of Lisbon; cf. Rte 18A. Arms, uniforms, and a poor collection of prints and maps are also on view. Other rooms concentrate on Portuguese military operations in the 19–20Cs, including the First World War. To the left of the landing, in a long gallery overlooking the courtyard, are an interminable series of rooms containing a depressingly displayed collection of uniforms, armour, weapons, and small-arms of all periods, together with daubs of generals, et al, hardly one of which is of any merit.

Just east of the museum is the **Estação de Santa Apolónia**, the main station for trains to Spain, France, and Oporto.

The road flanking the north side of the station, leading east to the Museu do Azulejo (see below) passes close to the Museu do Agua within the Barbadinhos Pumping-station of 1880 (at Rua do Alviela 12), which is a well-preserved example of industrial archaeology.

It is advisable to take a taxi (or tram 3, 16, 24, 27; bus 13a, 18, 42) from the station to the secularised *CONVENT OF MADRE DE DEUS or **Museu do Azulejo** (Tues 14.00–18.00, Wed–Sun 10.00–18.00) in the nearby suburb of Xabregas. The convent was founded by Dona Leonor, widow of Dom João II, in 1509, and later enlarged and embellished.

The **church**, to the right of the entrance, is resplendent with gilt Baroque wood-work surrounding paintings of the Life of St Francis attributed to André Gonçalves (1687–1762), below which are rustic scenes in Dutch tiles (c 1710), and a richly carved pulpit of c 1730–50. The sacristy contains *azulejos* from the factory of Rato

*Detail from the azulejos 'Panorama of Lisbon' in the Convent of Madre de Deus*

(c 1780). Steps descend to the lower part of the nave, in fact the floor of the earlier church, from which the main cloister is entered. Off this are rooms displaying other examples of *azulejos*, among them some from the Lisbon factory (mid 16C), and including caricature *singeries*. Stairs ascend through a patio, and further steps (note the 18C *azulejos*) climb to an upper gallery.

The **\*Chapel of Santo Antônio** retains its *azulejos* depicting the life of that saint (c 1780), together with a series of canvases. From here the richly gilt Coro Alto is entered. Above the stalls are numerous reliquaries, while among the paintings are an anony-mous Portuguese Annunciation (16C), Adoration (15C), and a curious Flemish Panorama of Jerusalem in which are set scenes of the Passion (15C). The famous Panorama of Lisbon, an early 18C tile picture, some 36m long, possibly painted by Gabriel del Barco, can hardly be overlooked.

Some distance further north, flanking the west bank of the Tagus estuary, there at its broadest, will be the 1998 Exhibition site, beyond which a new road and rail bridge and viaduct will span the river to a point not far north of Montijo. This will provide direct communication with the new highway being laid out between Setúbal and Elvas, and ease the flow of traffic crossing the Ponte 25 de Abril. These will be described in the next edition of this guide.

Return past the Military Museum to the **Largo do Chafariz de Dentro**, the main lower square of the Alfama. This is a convenient base from which to explore the characteristic maze of narrow alleys (bright with hanging washing) and breakneck flights of steps threading the lower slopes of the hill, which have changed little in recent centuries, and recall the Moorish occupation. But **caution** is advised if exploring the area: beware of bag-snatchers.

At a higher level to the north-east is Santo Estêvão, containing a wooden high altar carved by José de Almeida, which was originally at Mafra. To the west is São Miguel.

On regaining the Largo, follow the Rua do Terreiro do Trigo (corn market), shortly passing (right) the Chafariz de Dentro, a 17C fountain, and the Casa dos Bicos to reach the Praça do Comércio; for both see Rte 1A.

The area between the Av. da Liberdade and the Rua da Palma, lying on the hill immediately north of the Rossio, on which several medical and scientific institutions are concentrated, is of comparatively little interest.

The **Hospital de São José** contains some fine *azulejos* of c 1730 in its courtyard and staircase, and retains a sumptuously fitted sacristy, having been until 1769 part of the former Jesuit monastery of Santo Antão o Novo, or do Tojal. Camoens is believed to have died in 1579 in a house on the site of Nos. 139–141 in the neighbouring Calçada de Sant' Ana.

In the Paço da Rainha, further north, stands the **Palácio da Bemposta**, over the entrance to which are carved the arms of England. It was built after 1693 for Catherine of Braganza, the widowed queen of Charles II of England, who residence it was after her return to Portugal. Here in 1704 she entertained the Archduke Charles (the Habsburg claimant to the Spanish throne), and died the following year. Dom João VI also lived here before his death in 1826. It has been in military hands since 1851. The chapel was designed by Manuel Caetano de Sousa (1742–1802), with a chancel decorated by Pedro Alexandrino de Carvalho (1729–1810).

A short distance beyond is the 18C Palácio Pombeiro, now the Italian Embassy.

The **AVENIDA DA LIBERDADE** (like the Champs Elysées in Paris, with which some have compared it) is not what it was in its heyday, the principal promenade of Lisbon. Extending north-west from the Praça dos Restauradores to the Praça do Marquês de Pombal or Rotunda (see Rte 1F), it was laid out in 1879. Almost 1.5km long and some 90m wide, the thoroughfare is lined by rather commonplace buildings, many of them now put to commercial use, and few are of any interest. An exception perhaps is the once-magnificent **Palácio Foz** (1755–77), built for the Marquês de Castelo-Melhor by Francesco Saverio Fabri, on the west side of the Praça dos Restauradores, named in honour of the leaders of the anti-Spanish revolution of 1640. The commemorative obelisk in the centre was only erected in 1886.

The Palácio Foz now accommodates Lisbon's main **tourist office**; also the important Duarte de Sousa Library, and a valuable photographic library.

From the north-west corner of Praça dos Restauradores a funicular ascends the steep hillside to the west (the Calçada da Glória) to the Miradouro de São Pedro de Alcántara: see Rte 1C. On the east side of the square is one of the main Post Offices.

Parallel to and east of the Avenida, and also approached from the Largo de São Domingos, is the entertaining Rua das Portas de Santo Antão, thronged with restaurants and bars. At No. 100 is the Museu Etnográfico do Ultramar and the **Sociedade de Geografia**, founded in 1875. The latter contains an early astrolabe, and a research library; also relics of famous explorers (including David Livingstone's travelling-chair and telescope) and products of Portugal's late colonies. (The collections are normally open to view on Wednesdays only.) Here also is the huge **Coliseu** of 1890, designed by Cesar Yans, an Italian. Seating 8000, it has been restored recently.

The narrow street continues north, off which a funicular climbs the hill to the east.

# C. Western Lisbon

## The Chiado

There are at least four not-so-tiring approaches to this area from the Cidade Baixa: the most rapid is by taking the Elevador (see Rte 1A), which deposits one near the entrance to the Carmo (see below). The most convenient route for pedestrians is the Rua do Carmo, climbing from the south-west corner of the Rossio, which leads into the lower end of the **CHIADO**, officially Rua Garrett, along one of the main shopping streets.

Regrettably, in August 1988, a ravaging fire caused widespread damage in the area, gutting a number of old houses, and although their restoration is under way, progress so far has been slow.

Ascending this fashionable promenade, the first turning on the right leads shortly to the Largo do Carmo, with its curious fountain. To the right is the ruined church of the **Carmo**, founded by the Constable Nun'Alvares Pereira in 1389 in fulfilment of a vow made at Aljubarrota, and shattered by the earthquake of 1755. By 1855 it was harbouring a chemical manufactory. The west front retains its Gothic doorway, and its graceful re-erected nave arches now span a garden. Both this and what remains of the edifice have been laid out as a **Museu Arqueológico** (not to be confused with the Arqueológica and Etnologia Museum; May–Sept 10.00–18.00; Oct–April 10.00–13.00 and 14.00–17.00; closed Sun and hols), but its re-arrangement is overdue.

Among various tombs is the canopied tomb of Rui de Meneses (1528), with a recumbent effigy, while in the north transept is a Manueline window from the Jerónimos at Belém. The first south apse-chapel contains the tombs of Dona Constança, mother of Dom Fernando, and of Fernão Sanches, son of Dom Dinis. The Capela-Mór retains the tomb of Dom Fernando I (died 1383), and a model of that of Nun'Alvares, who took the Carmelite habit in 1423 and died here in 1431, but his remains have been translated to Santa Engrácia (see Rte 1B). A miscellaneous collection of artefacts (some from Vila Nova de São Pedro), Roman epigraphical and other archaeological and architectural remains, four Nottingham alabasters, and various azulejos and ceramics, lie scattered about. The former dependencies to the north, in which two companies of British riflemen were quartered during one period of the Peninsular War, are now occupied by the police.

Regaining the Chiado and turning right, the first left-hand street, the Rua Ivens (commemorating the late 19C African explorer Roberto Ivens), leads to a small square (view) in which stood the Biblioteca Nacional until its removal to the Campo Grande; see Rte 1F.

Next passed on the south side of the Chiado is *Bertrand's bookshop*, which is part of a firm established in Lisbon c 1732. In young Southey's opinion, Jorge Bertrand was 'the only civil and reasonable man in the trade'. Almost opposite stands the *Brasileira Café*, on the pavement beside which is sculptured the seated figure of Fernando Pessoa (1888–1935), this being one of the poet's favourite haunts.

The **Mártires** church (1769–84), dedicated to the English and other Crusaders who fell when wresting Lisbon from the Moors in 1147, is next reached, but the site of the earlier church of this name stood further south. A relief over the portal depicts Afonso Henriques giving thanks to the Virgin for the delivery of the city.

To the left, the Rua Serpa Pinto (commemorating the late 19C African explorer Alexandre Serpa Pinto) leads down past (right) the restored **Teatro São Carlos**, the largest theatre in Lisbon. It was built in 1792 by José da Costa e Silva

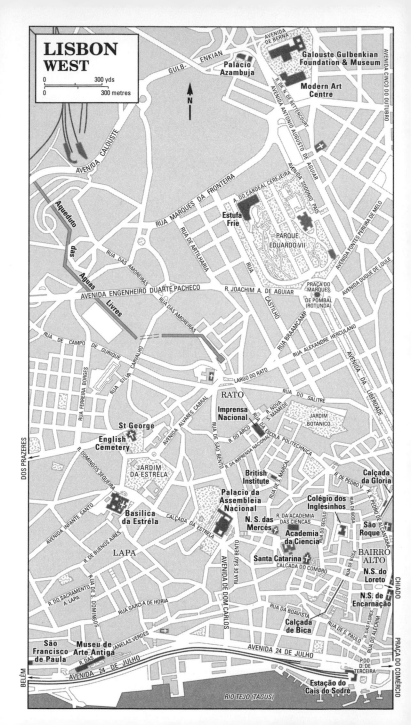

(1747–1819), who had previously spent some years in Rome, on the lines of the San Carlos theatre at Naples, while the rusticated *porte-cochère* and pilastered façade are very similar to Piermarini's La Scala theatre in Milan (1776–78). It replaced the opera-house designed by Giovanni Carlos Bibiena, destroyed seven months after its inauguration in 1755. The oft-repeated story has it that it was outside this theatre that Lord Byron was struck by an irate husband for making unwelcome advances to his wife.

Further downhill on the left is the entrance to the **\*MUSEU DO CHIADO** (Tues 14.00–18.00, Wed–Sun 10.00–18.00/20.00). (This was formerly known as the Museu Nacional de Arte Contemporânea, although the majority of its contents, despite its name, dated from the late 19C.) It is housed in part of the dependencies of the ancient Convento de São Francisco, which, having been entirely gutted and then imaginatively remodelled by the French architect Jean-Michel Wilmotte, was inaugurated in 1994. Between 1855 and 1894 the building had been used as a biscuit factory, and the ovens constructed there by Abraham Wheelhouse and his son George remain in situ. What is virtually an entirely new museum, much of it now devoted to temporary exhibitions of contemporary art, it will display a permanent collection of Portuguese 19–20C art, including representative works by Tomás Anunciação, Miguel Angelo Lupi, Teixeira Lopes, Prieto, Henrique César Auguste Pousão, António Carvalho Silva Porta, Amadeo Ferreira Sousa Cardoso, Almada Negreiros, Julio Pomar, Vieira da Silva, et al, together with sculptures by António Soares dos Reis, among others.

The Rua Garrett shortly widens into the **Largo do Chiado**, named after the satirical poet António Ribeiro (c 1520–91; 'O Chiado'), with his seated statue. Flanking its north side is the church of N.S. do Loreto, that of the Italian colony, rebuilt in 1785 by José da Costa e Silva, and preserving over its main doorway a 17C group by Francesco Borromini. Opposite stands N.S. de Encarnação, by Manuel de Sousa. Neither building is of great interest, although the west exterior wall of the latter is decorated with blue *azulejos*. To the west is the small Praça Luis de Camões.

From here, the wide Rua do Alecrim (meaning 'rosemary' in Arabic) descends steeply towards the river and the Estação do Cais do Sodré, passing (right) a statue of 1903 by Teixeira Lopes of the novelist Eça de Queirós (1845–1900), tempted by his slightly veiled muse. In the mansion opposite, the residence of Géneral Junot in 1808, the so-called 'Convention of Cintra' was probably signed.

The British Factory assembly rooms may have then stood in the Rua do Alecrim, and at an earlier date on a site at the lower end of the Rua das Flores, parallel to the west. They were certainly in this quarter of the town.

From the Praça Luis de Camões, a variety of routes may be followed to the west or north, depending on the visitor's interests and stamina. The latter area, and a shorter tour taking in São Roque, a short distance uphill, is described below.

A circuit to the west may be made by following the Calçada do Combro. At the third left-hand turning a funicular runs downhill; the following turning leads shortly to the Miradouro Alto de Santa Catarina, providing a good view of the Ponte 25 de Abril; see Rte 1E.

Further downhill and to the right in the Calçada do Combro is **Santa Catarina**, or dos Paulistas, founded in 1647 and largely rebuilt after the great earthquake. It contains a vault over the chancel decorated c 1730 by António Pimenta Rolim; the plaster ceiling of the nave, attributed to João Grossi (Giovanni Grossi;

1719–c 1781), an Italian stuccatore; and decorative sculpture and woodcarving in the apse by Santos Pacheco de Lima (active c 1717–55). Note the Baroque organ.

A recommended short detour may be made by retracing one's steps and following the Rua do Século to the north, skirting (right) two semi-circular levels, to reach (left) the Travessa das Mercês, in the chapel of which the tomb of Pombal stood neglected from his death until 1923. The house in which he was born in 1699 lies a short distance beyond. Turning here under the Arco do Jesús, the wide Rua da Academia das Ciéncias is entered, in which that institution (founded 1779), with its important library, is housed in a former convent of the Third Order of Penitents. On the floor above is an extensive, but old-fashioned, **Geological and Anthropological Museum**, also including prehistoric and Roman antiquities. By turning left and then right, the Largo de São Bento is shortly reached: see below.

Continuing downhill, one may take the next right-hand turning, ascending towards the façade of **N.S. das Mercês**, a handsome building of c 1760–70 by Joaquim de Oliveira, from which the lower Largo de São Bento is approached.

This is dominated by the **Palácio da Assembleia da República** (or Houses of Parliament), which since 1834 has occupied the 17C dependencies (much extended after 1876) of the older convent of São Bento da Saúde or dos Negros, where in 1552 the humanist George Buchanan spent four months after his trial by the Inquisition. The official residence of the Prime Minister stands in grounds behind the palace. Its Parliamentary Archives, containing a wealth of information from 1821 on, may be consulted on prior written request. The assembly rooms of the 'Commons' and former Câmara dos Dignos Pares do Reino (Lords) may be visited by appointment. The National Archives, known as those of the Torre do Tombo (having been preserved, until c 1757, in that tower of the Castelo de São Jorge) are now housed in a new building near the Biblioteca Nacional; see Rte 1F.

Bearing round the west side of the building—from which the Av. Dom Carlos I descends to the river—ascend the Calçada da Estrela, which passes (right) public gardens.

By turning left at the next crossroad (Rua Borges Carneiro) and its continuation (Rua da Lapa: the name Lapa serving to describe this sequestered diplomatic enclave), some minutes' walk will bring you to the **Rua São Domingos à Lapa**, in which No.37, formerly the Palácio Porto Covo, had been the Chancery of the British Embassy from 1941 until late 1995 (when, regrettably—owing to the prohibitive cost of rehabilitating the most attractive but increasingly dilapidated structure—the Embassy was moved to Rua São Bernardo 33, just east of the Jardím da Estrela). The palace, completed in 1790, was constructed for Jacinto Fernandes Bandeira, who, having made a fortune trading in tobacco with Brazil, in 1794 became a peer. The ambassador's Residence since 1875, a short distance further south-west (Rua São Francisco de Borja 63), dating in part from the late 17C, was once a convent.

No. 25 in the Rua do Sacramento à Lapa (the first right-hand turning on bearing downhill) is probably the house in which Byron briefly resided in 1809. The kitsch Campolide ceramic decoration of the Casa de Visconde de Sacavém (1900) at No. 25 can hardly be avoided. Southey lived with his uncle in the Rua Buenos Aires, parallel to the north (see p 98; this district of Lapa is approximately co-extensive with that previously known as 'Buenos Ayres'.)

By continuing downhill from the former Embassy, a small square off the Rua das Janelas Verdes is reached, opposite which is the north façade of the Museu de Arte Antiga: see Rte 1D.

## ESTRELA

The Calçada da Estrela continues to climb towards the Praça da Estrela and adjacent gardens, overlooked by the conspicuous **Basílica da Estrela** (tram 25, 26, 28, 29, 30; bus 9), built by the devout and melancholy Maria I in 1779–90 in fulfilment of a vow depending on the birth of an heir (cf. Mafra). It was designed by Mateus Vicente de Oliveira, and after his death in 1786 completed by Reinaldo Manuel dos Santos. Although some critics have been fulsome in their approval of the well-proportioned but frigid Baroque interior, it is perhaps the decorative appearance of the exterior which is the more effective, with its two tall belfries and dome (from which panoramic views may be obtained), which copy the proportional faults of Mafra. The painting in the retable is by Pompeo Batoni; the tombs of Dona Maria (died 1816, in Rio de Janeiro), by Faustino José Rodrigues, and that of her confessor, Fr. Inácio de São Caetano (died 1788), may also be seen. The Estrela Convent was used as a military hospital during the Peninsular War.

Adjacent are the offices of the Instituto Geográfico e Cadastral, where a wide variety of maps of Portugal may be obtained.

By bearing round the west side of the gardens, on crossing the street, the entrance (ring) to the umbrageous **\*English Cemetery** is reached: 'a most lovely place, sweet with flowers, & so hot and shady & green that we stayed there a long time', wrote Virginia Woolf when visiting it in April 1905. Permission for its establishment was granted to Consul-general William Poyntz in 1717 on condition that it was called the 'Hospital of the English Factory', although in fact the Treaty of 1654 had allowed the Factory to have their own cemetery. The Dutch Factory acquired an adjoining plot, and the two were united and enclosed by a wall. The first interment took place in 1725. In 1728 Tyrawley, the ambassador, was complaining at the expense to which he was put in maintaining a chapel for some 700 British Protestants, 'such a bigoted mob'. The avenue of cypresses (which caused the Portuguese to call the Cemitério dos Ingleses by the name 'Os Ciprestes') leads to the church of St George (1885, replacing one of 1815 which had burnt down). Off to the left is the tomb (replacing one erected by the Factory) of Henry Fielding (1707–54)—'on a spot selected by *guess*', according to Mrs Quillinan (Wordsworth's daughter), who visited the site in 1846. Fielding, the celebrated author of *Joseph Andrews*, *Jonathan Wild*, and *Tom Jones*, had made an unavailing voyage to Lisbon, to recover his health, and died only two months after his arrival; his *Journal of a Voyage to Lisbon* was published posthumously.

Among the many other burials here are: Dr Philip Doddridge (1702–51), the eminent Non-conformist divine and hymn-writer, who survived only 13 days in Lisbon; Abraham Castres (died 1757; the British Envoy at the time of the Great Earthquake); Thomas Barclay, born in Strabane (Ireland) in 1728, and killed in a duel in Lisbon in 1793, whom Washington had made American consul in Morocco in 1791 at the request of Jefferson; Daniel Gildemeester *père* (cf. Seteais, Sintra); Thomas Horne (1722–92), Beckford's agent and banker in Lisbon; Admiral Miklós Horthy (1868–1957), Regent of Hungary (1920–44), who died in exile at Estoril; and a number of Dutch and Scandinavian Protestants, apart from members of the Anglo-Portuguese community and other non-Catholics.

A building of c 1730 bearing the name of the Hospital, and used as such until c 1843, which is now the adjacent parsonage, was rebuilt in 1793 by Gerard de Visme (1713–95; cf. Quinta de Monserrate, nr Sintra), a wealthy merchant. The present Hospital (1910) stands to the north of the cemetery, above the old Jewish graveyard.

In Rua Coelho da Rocha, leading north-west from the cemetery, lived Fernando Pessoa (1888–1935) during the latter years of his life; it has been renovated to display mementoes of the poet.

The cypress-shaded **Cemitério de Prazeres** (Cemetery of pleasures!; further west), approached by the Rua Saraiva, deserves a visit.

It was between this and the Tagus that Dom Antonio, Prior of Crato, before going to ground, attempted in June 1580 to stop the advance from Cascais of the Duke of Alba's army, a brief encounter known as the battle of Alcântara.

The new premises of the British Embassy and Consulate are at Rue de São Bernardo 33, skirting the east side of the Jardim da Estrela.

A few minutes' walk to the north-east along the Av. Pedro Alvares Cabral brings one to the Largo do Rato, a busy road junction, from which nine streets radiate. It was in this district that the former Royal Factory of the Rato operated until 1835. It had been created by Pombal in 1767 (in emulation of the porcelain factory of Buen Retiro, established in Madrid in 1759), with Tomás Bruneto of Turin as its first director, but the production of porcelain in Portugal was not firmly established until 1824, when José Ferreira Pinto Basto founded the factory of Vista Alegre, near Aveiro; see Rte 20.

A few paces to the north is the Casa das Águas Livres, or Mãe (mother) d'Agua, the old reservoir of the aqueduct of Águas Livres (Free Waters), with a capacity of 1.25 million gallons, and the starting-point for the various channels feeding the city's fountains. The **\*Aqueduct das Águas Livres** itself, of which the most conspicuous part—the Passeio dos Arcos, of 14 pointed arches—strides across the Alcântara valley to the north-west, is borne on a total of 109 arches of *pedra lioz*. It was constructed in 1729–48 by the engineer Manuel de Maia and the architect Custódio Vieira to bring water from Caneças, some 18.5km north. One of the 'lions' of Lisbon, it was visited by most travellers in the past as it still deserves to be, although one need not 'devote an entire morning to inspecting it', as George Borrow had over-enthusiastically suggested.

At Praça das Amoreiras 58, not far north of the Largo do Rato, the restored building of the former Real Fábrica dos Tecidos de Seda (The Royal Silk Factory) houses the Arpad Azenes-Vieira da Silva Foundation, devoted to their work, and of other contemporary artists

The Rua Alexandre Herculano leads east from the Rato to the upper part of the Av. da Liberdade, off which the Rua Braamcamp forks left direct to the Praça Marquês de Pombal, while the Rua do Salitre bears south-east downhill to the centre of the Avenida.

Our route turns south down the Rua da Escola Politécnica, passing (right) the Imprensa Nacional, the successor of the royal printing-press founded in 1768, and (left) some University faculty buildings in the old Colégio dos Nobres, an aristocratic foundation dissolved in 1837. Adjacent is the entrance to the **Jardim Botânico**, a luxuriant sub-tropical garden founded in 1874, also containing a Meteorological Observatory of 1863.

Opposite, the Rua São Marçal leads downhill to the buildings of the **British Institute**, the first of its kind established abroad by the British Council (1938), which moved to its present address—Rua Luís Fernandes 1–3—in 1943. Branches had been opened at Coimbra and Oporto in 1939 and 1941 respectively. Previously it had been known as the Palácio do Menino de Oiro ('the Golden Boy'), after its builder Luis Fernandes (1859–1922), who devoted his fortune largely to the acquisition of works of art: his ceramic collections may be seen at the Museu Nacional de Arte Antiga.

On his death the mansion was bought by Francisco Alves dos Reis, who gained notoriety as 'the man from Lisbon' in the financial scandal known as the 'Portuguese Bank-note Case' (1925), in which Waterlow, the printers, were involved. When raided by the police, cases full of crisp 500-escudo notes were found in the basement. The building also contains a general library, but the important Anglo-Portuguese Collection—built up over the years by Dr Carlos Estorninho under the auspices of George West—is at present housed in the library of the Gulbenkian Foundation (see Rte 1F).

The Praça do Príncipe Real is next skirted, in the gardens of which is a remarkable cedar with branches trained to form a huge arbour. On its south-west side are the offices of the Instituto de Cultura Portuguesa.

## THE BAIRRO ALTO

The northern end of the Bairro Alto proper is now reached. This network of characteristic streets, only slightly affected by the earthquake of 1755—although parts are now little less than tenements—contains a number of restaurants.

An alley half-way down the Rua da Rosa, which bisects this district, leads up to the often restored buildings of the '**Colégio dos Inglesinhos**', founded in 1628, during penal times, for the education of English seminarists, and only closed in 1973.

In May 1671 Consul Maynard, reporting to Lord Arlington in London, refers to the 'implacable malice of the English Seminary to our Religion'. Among its professors was Richard Russell, who partly negotiated Catherine of Braganza's marriage with Charles II, taught her English, and accompanied her as almoner; he later became Bishop of Portalegre, and then of Viseu. Dr Godden, President of the College, became her chaplain and preceptor. Fr Edmund Winstanley offered his services to Wellington as chaplain to the military hospitals around Lisbon during the Peninsular War. It was visited out of curiosity by George Borrow, who had to admit that the view from its roof was 'very grand and noble'.

From 1634 there had also been an Irish Dominican community in Lisbon, that of Corpo Santo, one of whom, the devious Fr Daniel O'Daly, was the queen's confessor. More popular were the English Brigittine nuns, whose convent, rebuilt in 1760 after its destruction in 1755, stood at the corner of the Rua das Francesinhas and the Travessa do Pasteleiro (a short distance south-west of São Bento). They had moved to Lisbon in 1594, and remained there until 1861, and were referred to by many travellers, among them Baretti, who remarked that visitors were 'used by them with such endearing kindness, that their parlatory is in a manner never empty from morning till night. The poor things are liberal to every body of chocolate, cakes, and sweetmeats...'. A certain Thomas Robinson, who had been 'secretary' there some 150 years earlier, chose to abuse them in '*The Anatomie of the English Nunnerie at Lisbon in Portugall*' (London, 1622).

The Rua Dom Pedro V is continued by the Rua São Pedro de Alcântara, on the east side of which is an extensive terrace and Miradouro, immediately beyond which a funicular descends to the Praça dos Restauradores; while just opposite, at No. 45, in a palace of 1747 by Ludovice, are the offices of the Lisbon branch of the **Port Wine Institute**, with a bar in which most varieties of port may be sampled, at a price, in comfort.

A few paces beyond brings one to the outwardly unpretentious Jesuit church of *SÃO ROQUE (open daily), begun by Afonso Alvares in 1567, followed after his death in 1575 by his nephew Baltasar Alvares, while Felipe Terzi was active there from 1582. Its interior is more impressive, and surprisingly well kept. Notable are the *azulejos* by Fr de Matos (1584) in the third right-hand chapel. To the right of the altar is the Baroque Chapel of the Assumption.

To the left is the sumptuous *chapel of St John the Baptist, commissioned by Dom João V in 1742, and designed and erected in Rome by Luigi Vanvitelli (1700–73), the architect, and Niccolo Salvi. After being blessed by Benedict XIV, it was dismantled and shipped to Lisbon, where it was installed in 1747 under the supervision of the Italian sculptor Alessandro Giusti (1715–99). This opulent confection of lapis lazuli, agate, porphyry, and ormolu, etc., which survived the earthquake of 1755, is also notable for the mosaic picture of the Baptism in imitation of oil-painting, while the hanging lustres are also remarkable examples of Italian craftsmanship of the period. The effect caused a sensation, even if the cost was crippling, and its artistic value is still much exaggerated by the Portuguese.

Adjacent is another chapel rich in inlaid marbles, while nearer the entrance is a long inscription in memory of Sir Francis Tregean (died 1608), a Cornish recusant, who is buried upright near the pulpit. Father Henry Floyd, SJ (also known as Fludd), a zealous converter of souls, and chief visitor of the Inquisition for the English, resided here at the turn of the 17C. Above the chapels is a series of paintings of the Life of St Roche, while the flat wooden ceiling is painted to give the impression of a vault, a form of *trompe l'oeil* noticeable elsewhere in the church. Note also the 18C German organ. The sacristy, with its blue and yellow *azulejos*, contains a number of paintings of the Lives of St Francis Xavier by Andrés Reinoso, and of St Ignatius Loyola.

Just to the right of the church is the **Museu de São Roque** (Tues–Sun 10.00–17.00), containing an impressive collection of vestments, frontal hangings, etc., many of gold and silver filigree-work, and in a remarkable state of preservation. Also a collection of silver-gilt altar-furniture, etc., mostly Italian, including two paschal candlesticks. In a vestibule are portraits of Dom João III and his wife Catar first passing (left) a shopping precinct in which part of the late 14C city wall is displayed in situ; and right, the long-established Tavares restaurant—the Chiado is regained.

# D. The Museu Nacional de Arte Antiga

This important *MUSEUM, a visit to which is essential for an appreciation of Portuguese painting and decorative art, is perhaps best approached by taxi (from the Praça do Comércio or elsewhere), or alternatively by tram 19 and buses 27, 40, 49, and 60 travelling west along the Rua das Janelas Verdes ('Green Windows')—pronounced Yanells Verds—which skirts the building. The museum was for some time named after this street, although the main entrance is now at its west end.

(A short distance east, at No. 32 in the street, is the long-established hotel of York House, installed in the dependencies of a former convent of Discalced Carmelites, dating from 1606. It was so-named by two ladies from Yorkshire who in 1880 had rented part of the building and converted it into an inn. No. 46 was the residence of the British consul in 1811.)

The museum is partly housed in the 17C palace of the Condes de Alvor, in which two mutilated ceilings by Vincenzo Baccerelli survive. This had been extended to the west by a chapel, part of the former Carmelite convent of Santo Alberto. The whole was radically reconstructed internally in the 1980s, when a mezzanine floor was incorporated, providing 50 per cent more display space; since when the distribution of the permanent collections has been entirely rearranged.

These collections, based on material accumulated after the suppression of the monasteries in 1838, and which have grown considerably since, enriched by numerous donations, were opened to the public in 1884.

Steps, and a ramp, ascend from the Jardin 9 de Abril to the main entrance hall, on the left of which a gallery overlooks the chapel (Room 31). This remains largely intact, retaining its richly carved and gilded woodwork, paintings, and *azulejos*. Note the huge *presépio* or Christmas crib. Adjacent are a collection of copes, etc., two anonymous 16C paintings of St Vincent and St John the Evangelist, and a polychrome statue of St Michael weighing souls.

Rooms 33–35, adjacent, contain a changing display of Portuguese tapestries, Arraiolos carpets, brocades and other delicate fabrics, etc.

Rooms 36–43, right of the entrance, are devoted to a representative collection of furniture, both Portuguese and foreign, much of it made of lignum vitae, mahogany.

Left of the staircase hall (Room 44) is Room 45, containing a Greek male torso of Parian marble (4C BC), and a grey basalt Lion, a Graeco-Egyptian work of the Ptolemaic period, among other objects donated by Calouste Gulbenkian (cf. Rte 1F).

Beyond the hall is the museum shop and a coffee lounge (Rooms 46–47).

Stairs between Rooms 65 and 66 descend to the restaurant and garden, providing a fine Tagus-side view. Also approached from here are rooms for temporary exhibitions, the library, an auditorium, and the **Department of Prints and Drawings** (seen by appointment). Among the drawings are many by the Bibiena family (fl. 1665–c 1780); João (Giovanni) Carlos Bibiena, son of Francisco, who died in Lisbon in 1760. Also several by Jean Pillement (1728–1808), who visited Portugal on three occasions, the longest in 1780–86; and numerous examples by Domingos António de Sequeira (1768–1837).

Rooms 48–65 display **European paintings**, roughly in chronological order. Among outstanding works, the following may be mentioned:

**Dutch and Flemish Schools**: *Hans Memling*, Virgin and Child; *anon. 15C Dutch*, Mystic Marriage of St Catherine; *anon. 16C Flemish* Virgin and Child; *Jan Provost*, Triptych; *Jan Gossart (Mabuse)*, *The Holy Family, with SS Barbara and Catherine; *Gerard David*, Rest on the Flight into Egypt; *Hieronymus Bosch*, *The Temptation of St Anthony; *Patinir*, Landscape with St Jerome in adoration (note camels); *Isenbrandt*, St Jerome; *Cornelius van Cleve*, The Virgin; *Quentin Metsys*, The Virgin of Sorrows, The Presentation, Jesus disputing with the doctors, and a Calvary; *anon. 16C Flemish* St Luke painting the Virgin; *attributed to Eduardo, o Portuguese* (a disciple of Metsys), Virgin and Child; *Brueghel the Younger*, Acts of Mercy; *H.-C. Vromm*, Naval Battle; *David Vinckeboons*, Kermes; *Antiveduto Grammatica*, St Cecilia and two angels; *attributed to P. Snayers*, Sack of a town; *Jacob-Adriaensz Backer*, Courtesan; *Van Dyck*, Portrait of Lucas Vosterman, the Elder; *António Moro* (Anton van Dashorst Mor), Male Portrait; *anon. 16C Flemish* Portrait of Jean de Luxembourg, a knight of the Golden Fleece; *attributed to A.-F. van der*

*Meulen*, Equestrian portrait of Louis XIV offered to the king by the Portuguese ambassador, the Conde de Atalaia; *Pieter Fransz de Grebber*, Family Group; *Wouwerman*, two Landscapes with figures; *David Teniers, the Younger*, Weapons' store; *Pieter de Hooch*, Conversation piece.

**Spanish Schools**:*Bernat Martorell*, Triptych of the Descent from the Cross; *Bartolomeo Bermejo*, St Damian; *attributed to Ramón Destorrents*, St Anne and the Virgin; *Morales*, Virgin and Child; *Velázquez da Silva* (he is usually known by his mother's name; his father's family, of Portuguese origin, had only settled in Sevilla in the 16C), Portrait of Mariana de Austria, wife of Philip IV of Spain; *Zurbarán*, a group of Twelve Apostles (1633), commissioned for the patriachal palace of São Vicente de Fora); *Ribera*, Martyrdom of St Bartholomew, St Peter's Denial, and *attributed to Ribera*, Vision of St Francis of Assisi; *Murillo*, Mystic marriage of St Catherine.

**Italian Schools**: *Piero della Francesca*, St Augustine; *anon. 15C* Battle of Darius; *Raphael*, St Eusebius bringing three men back to life; *Andrea del Sarto*, Self-portrait; *Luca Giordano*, Vision of St Francis of Assisi; *Pannini*, Ruins of ancient Rome; and examples of the work of *G.-B. Tiepolo*.

**German Schools**: *anon.* (School of Cologne) Triptych of the Calvary (c 1500); *Dürer*, *St Jerome (1521; offered to Rui Fernandes de Almada, then living in Antwerp, but later it was seen hanging in the library of the convent of the Jerónimos at Belém); *Cranach the Elder*, *Salome, and St Catherine (*attributed to Cranach*); *Master of the Morrison Triptych*, Virgin and Child, with SS. John the Evangelist and John the Baptist; *Hans Holbein, the Elder*, Virgin and Child with saints (presented by Christina of Sweden to Dom João IV, who in turn gave it to his daughter Catherine of Braganza).

**French School**: *Hubert Robert*, The Mill, and Ruined Temple; *Largillière*, Portraits of Mme Largillière. and of M. de Noirmont (?), and attributed to him, of the Marquis d'Argenson,; *Rigaud*, Cardinal de Polignac; *anon.* Portrait of the sculptor Jacques Buirette (1631–99); and examples of the art of Claude Joseph Vernet.

**English School**: *Romney*, Capt. Sir John Orde, Bart.; *Reynolds*, General William Keppel, and of Dr Duheney; *John Russel*, pastel of Sir Richard Clode d'Orpington; *Hoppner*, Country woman.

Also, among *anon.* portraits, those of Dom João I; and a (sour-faced) Infante Don Carlos (1607–32).

On crossing a landing, the first of a series of rooms (66–70) is entered, devoted to the decorative arts. Among a resplendent display of **French Silver** is the (so-called) Duque de Aveiro's Banquet Service, made by François Thomas Germain of Paris and his assistants; a remarkable *epergne* by Thomas Germain, his father; and 16 silver-gilt figures (1757–58) by Ambroise-Nicolas Cousinet.

They also contain collections of **French Furniture, and porcelain**, and a carved wooden font attributed to Grindling Gibbons. Another room, with panelling of 1769 from a palace in Vienna, has furniture by Louis Charles Carpentier (active 1752–88), covered with Beauvais tapestry.

A broad flight of stairs ascends from the hall to the **second** (mezzanine) **level**, on which Rooms 26–30 (ahead) display the art of the **Goldsmith**: reliquaries, chalices (including a 16C English example), salvers, processional croziers, and other cult objects. Note also the rock-crystal crosses. Remarkable are the Monstrance of Belém or Custodia dos Jeronimos (1506), made by Gil Vicente from the first gold sent back from the Indies by Vasco da Gama; the so-called Cross of Dom Sancho I (1412); and the Cross of Alcobaça (14–15C). The collection—

enriched by the donation of numerous pieces by Francisco de Barros e Sá—contains numerous examples of 17–18C silver, including a monstrance said to have been designed by Ludovice; a sumptuously chased late 16C silver-gilt salver; and 18–19C silver from Oporto, showing English influence in the tankards and tea-service. Adjacent are cases displaying jewellery.

Rooms 20–25 display the collections of **Portuguese Ceramics and Glass**, the latter largely from the factories at Marinha Grande and Vista Alegre (cf.). The ceramics include several of Oriental origin; the Portuguese were also the first Europeans to import and copy in faïence the porcelains of the East, much of it from Goa, and therefore known as '*porcelana da India*'; from Japan between c 1550–1640; and Macau. The main Portuguese factories were those of Rato established 1767) and Bico do Sapato (1796), both in Lisbon; that of Miragaia (Oporto; founded 1775), and Massarelos (1783; although operating from c 1730); and Santo António do Vale da Piedade (1785) and Cavaquinho (1789), both at Vila Nova de Gaia; at Darque (Viana do Castelo; 1774); at Rocio de Santa Clara (Coimbra; 1784); apart from others at Caldas da Rainha; Brioso, and Vandelli (Coimbra; 1784); and Vista Alegre (1824), Estremoz, etc.

In Rooms 15–19 are collections of **Furniture** from Portugal's former possessions, particularly Goa, including several fine examples in ebony with bone or ivory inlay; a remarkable Indo-Portuguese hunting-scene in cotton and raw silk (16–17C); and full-length Indo-Portuguese portraits of Francisco d'Almeida (1505–9), and Afonso de Albuquerque (1509–15); and several carved ivory boxes, Virgins, and the Infant Christ (Bom Pastor).

Outstanding among the Oriental collections are several Japanese screens **\*Biombos Namban**, depicting the arrival and disembarkation of the Portuguese at Nagasaki, where they were known as the Namban-jin (barbarians from the south). The first one of a pair of large six-fold screens (*honken* in Japanese) was made in Kyoto, and is attributed to Kano Domi (1593–1600); the second pair—in which the Portuguese are shown setting sail from Goa (?) to Japan, and their landing—is by Kano Naizen (c 1603–10). A third screen (or *ho-byobu*), of which the musem has only one of a pair, is later in date, perhaps between 20 and 30 years after the Portuguese were forced to leave Japan (1639). The detail is not so well characterised, for the artist had probably not seen the Namban-jin in person, nor their ships. (An informative and well-illustrated catalogue is available.) Note also the large 7C bronze statue of Bothisava.

Stairs ascend to the **third level** (good view from its south-west windows), its landings (Rooms 13–14) devoted to a remarkable collection of polychrome wood or stone **Sculpture**. Notable among the former are a Santiago, St Jerome with his lion, and a Virgin and Child (reading); and among the latter, a Virgin and Child with St Anne, Sta Ana, Sta Lucia, Sta Caterina, the Baptist, and a Pietà; also a late 15C English alabaster of St Catherine, etc.

Rooms 1–11 contain the masterpieces of the **Portuguese School of painting**, among them several works by *Frei Carlos* (active 1517–40) or from his studio, including Christ appearing to the Virgin, Annunciation, Assumption, Ascension, and (notably) a Resurrection; also a Descent from the Cross by the *Master of the Tabulo da Capela-Mór*, and a copy of a Flemish Apparition of an angel to SS. Coleta, Ines, and Clara.

Remarkable are the **\*Retable of the Infante** by *Nuno Gonçalves*, an artist worthy of comparison with the foremost figures of his age, and who died before 1492. The polyptych was painted c 1467–70 for the altarpiece of the chapel of

St Vincent in the Sé, and later moved to São Vicente de Fora. It consists of six panels representing the youthful St Vincent, patron of Lisbon, receiving the homage of the king, court, and various national communities, and many of the 60 faces have been variously identified. A statue of the saint probably once separated the two central panels, and it is likely that the whole was a votive picture offered by Dom Afonso V, 'the African', in gratitude for his victories in Morocco, in particularly that at Alcaçer in 1463.

The panel on the extreme left depicts Cistercian monks from Alcobaça, possibly including Vasco Tinoco, the king's Grand Almoner; beside it are a group of fishermen. On the extreme right is a rabbi, representing the important Sephardic community, which, before its forcible conversion by Dom Manuel, made an important contribution to the prosperity and culture of Portugal, together with a beggar or pilgrim, and clerics. The lower figure is displaying the saint's relics (part of his skull). Adjacent are armed nobles, who have been identified as Fernando, 2nd Duke of Braganza (brother of Dom Afonso V), with behind him, (left) João, his youngest son, and (right) Fernando, his eldest; and abgure thought to be Queen Leonor (died 1455), and behind her is probably the widowed Duchess of Braganza; while in the upper left-hand corner is what may be a self-portrait of Nuno Gonçalves.

Also remarkable are an Adoration of the Magi from the *studio of the Master of Sardoel* (early 16C); an anonymous early 16C painting of the Apostles; a Martyrdom of the eleven thousand virgins, by the *Master of the retable of Sta Auta* (early 16C), and an anon. Portrait of a Knight; *Francisco Henriques* (fl. 1500–18; Master of the Retable of São Francisco at Evora), Our Lady of the Snows; Christ appearing to Mary Magdalen; SS. Cosmas, Thomas, and Damian, and eight other panels.

*Gregório Lopes* (active 1513–c 50), Martyrdom of St Sebastian; *Cristóvão de Figueiredo* (active 1515–43), Entombment; *Cristóvão Lopes* (1615–94), Portraits of Dom João III and his wife Catherine of Austria; *Cristóvão de Morais* (active 1557–71), Portrait of the ill-fated king, Dom Sebastião; panels by the *Master of the Retable of São Tiago* (St James); the *Master of the Paradise*, Retable of the Life of the Virgin; *Master of the Arches*, Presentation in the Temple (1538), and a St Jerome; *Master of the Retable of São Bento*, Adoration of the Magi, and Presentation in the Temple; and six panels by the *Master of the Retable of Santos-o-Novo*.

Among several anonymous paintings are a lurid Vision of Hell (16C); St Anthony preaching to the fishes; Martyrdoms of St Hippolytus, and of St Andrew; Virgin and Child with angels (probably from Tomar, and showing German influence); Birth of the Virgin; Portrait of a Nun with a rosary; and a Portrait (c 1524), perhaps of Vasco da Gama.

Other sections contain later 17C and 18C canvases of the Portuguese School, among them a selection of paintings by a master of European significance, *Domingos António de Sequeira* (1767–1837). It was Sequeira who in 1813–16 was commissioned by Dom João VI to design the silver service offered to the Duke of Wellington, now in Apsley House, London. His paintings include one of Mariana, his daughter, playing the piano, and one of the family of the 1st Viscount of Santarém. Other artists whose works are displayed here are Josefa de Ayala (or de Óbidos; 1634–84), Francisco Vieira, Portuense (1765–1805), Francisco Vieira de Matos (Vieira Lusitano; 1699–1783); and José António Benedito de Barros (c 1750–1809; better-known as the Morgado de Setúbal).

Other paintings include an anonymous View of Goa, of c 1600; *Domingos Vieira* (c. 1600–78), Portrait of Isabel de Moura; and *Felipe Lobo* (1650–73), View of Belém.

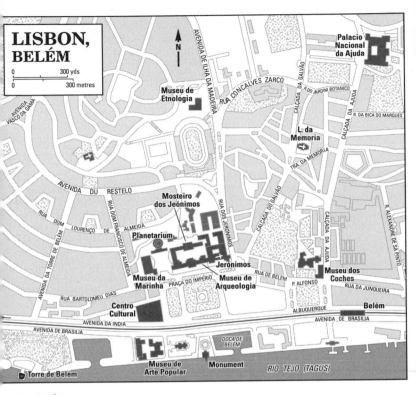

# E. Belém

Driving west (tram 15, 16, 17; bus 14, 27, 28, 43, 49 and 51) from the Museu de Arte Antiga (see above) by the upper road (Rua Presidente Arriaga; the continuation of the Rua das Janelas Verdes) one shortly passes (right) **São Francisco de Paula** (founded 1719), with a ceiling by Inácio ·de Oliveira Bernardes (1695–1781). The Av. Infante Santo, with a view of the Ponte 25 de Abril spanning the Tagus (see below), skirts the Doca de Alcântara and Gare Marítima before bearing towards the riverside Av. da India from the Praça da Armada, which is soon reached.

Up to the right, standing in its gardens (the 'Tapada') is the pink **Palácio das Necessidades** (no admission), a royal palace of 1745–50, designed by Caetano Tomás de Sousa, and built on the site of a chapel dedicated to N.S. das Necessidades. It was the Lisbon residence of the royal family from the time of Dona Maria II, who died here in 1853, until October 1910, when Dom Manuel II was driven out by shells from rebel warships in the Tagus. In 1916 the building became the Foreign Office, and its valuable contents were largely dispersed among museums, including the Museu de Arte Antiga.

The main riverside thoroughfare now leads below the huge **\*Ponte 25 de Abril**, the longest suspension bridge in Europe, commenced in 1962. Its present name commemorates the Revolution of April 1974, although it was known as the

'Salazar Bridge' when inaugurated in 1966. The central span is 1013m long, and some 70m above water-level. The total length of the structure above the river is 2300m, extended on the north bank by a viaduct some 950m long. It is doubtful whether there will be much decrease in the amount of traffic crossing it once the new bridge and viaduct spanning the wide estuary east of Lisbon is completed.

Beyond, to the right, are International Trade Fair Grounds, replacing old rope-walks. Uphill stands the chapel of **Santo Amaro** (1549), with a circular domed nave, round part of which extends a vaulted porch of seven bays, and containing *azulejos* from the Rato factory.

After some little distance the Praça Afonso de Albuquerque is reached, immediately to the north of which is the *****MUSEU DOS COCHES** (10.00–13.00 and 14.30–17.30). This is accommodated in the *Picadeiro* or riding-school (by Giacomo Azzolini; died 1781) of the Palácio de Belém, or Quinta de Baixo. The palace was bought by Dom João V from the Conde de Aveiras in 1726, and under the monarchy it was used mainly for the reception of royal guests. It was also known as the Quinta 'dos Bichos' (beasts), as at one time Moroccan lions were mewed up in cages in one of its courtyards. The palace itself is now the offical residence of the President of the Republic.

The collection of extravagantly carved and gilded coaches, which bear comparison to the collection at Schönbrunn, Vienna, and the actual quantity still preserved, is impressive; and certain of them, such as the plain travelling-coach (No. 1; 1619) of Philip III of Spain (II of Portugal), are of historical interest, but few will want to give this display of cumbersome and creaking vehicles more than a cursory inspection. Among the more notable examples are that of Dom João V (No. 3), and the elaborately carved ambassadorial coaches of the Marquês de Fontes, envoy to the Vatican in 1716; and in the adjoining room, an 18C *sege* (No. 50); a carriage constructed in London in 1825 (No. 51); and in the entrance hall, one of 1824 made for Dom João VI. A collection of livery and harnesses is also on view (including some of the 5th Marquês de Marialva's, Beckford's friend, who had the hereditary title of Master of the Horse), together with bull-fighting costumes, etc.

Another extensive collection of carriages may be seen at Vila Viçosa.

The adjacent Calçada da Ajuda climbs steeply to the **Palácio da Ajuda**, a vast and pretentious edifice begun in 1802 by Dom João VI on the site of a wooden palace built to shelter the royal family after the 1755 earthquake; this even had an opera-house, damaged by fire in 1787, and the rest was burnt down in 1795. The plans for its replacement were by José da Costa e Silva, collaborating with Francisco Saverio Fabri. It was continued by António Francisco da Rosa, but never completed. The north wing now houses the Instituto Português do Património Arquetectónico e Arqueológico; the south, the Instituto Português de Museus.

The **interior**, entered from the east, may be visited by those curious to see the sumptuous furniture and decoration, but decadent taste, of the time of Maria II and her second husband, Ferdinand of Saxe-Coburg-Gotha (a cousin of Prince Albert), of Dom Pedro V, married to Stéphanie of Hohenzollern-Sigmaringen, and of Dom Luís, married to Maria-Pia (daughter of Victor Emmanuel II of Italy), who, as Queen-Dowager, lived here until her death in 1911.

The important **library**, of which Herculano was once librarian, is on the ground floor and may be visited by appointment. It includes scores by João de Sousa Carvalho (died 1778).

Visitors are escorted in small groups through a series of rooms, some of which, such as the **Jardin d'Hiver**, faced with light brown marble, are of interest; likewise the Private Dining-room, with tapestries after Goya, and a silver service by Thomire; the Chinese Salon; the set of naval chairs, etc. Impressive are the Oval

Room, and the State Dining-room, still occasionally used, with its three huge lustres, and silver by François Thomas Germain (1757–64). Most of the rest is an ostentatious collection of inferior objects selfishly acquired at the expense of the Portuguese people in an epoch that could ill afford such extravagance.

Just south-east of its west end are gardens laid out on two levels.

The Rua do Jardim Botánico leads west to the church of the **Memória**, founded in 1760 in thanksgiving for the escape of Dom José from an attempted assassination on this spot in 1758, and designed by João Carlos Bibiena. The alleged conspirators, the Duke of Aveiro, the Marquês of Távora and his wife, and the Conde de Atouguia, among others, were executed at Belém in 1759 (where a rusticated Pelhourinbo is almost hidden from sight). Pombal, himself suspected of instigation, took advantage of the outrage to accuse the Jesuits of complicity, and had them driven from the country that same year. In 1923 Pombal's remains were transferred here from the Mercês.

The Calçada do Galvão descends to the main road and the monastery of Belém, passing (left) the entrance to the **Jardim e Museu do Ultramar**. At one time linked with the Institute of Hygiene and Tropical Medicine, the gardens contain plants mostly gathered from Portugal's former colonies, and also an Agricultural museum and herbarium.

The next main street to the west, ascending steeply past the square apse of the Jerénimos, is the Rua dos Jerónimos; it later skirts (left) a stadium, and is extended by the Ave Ilha da Madeira. To the west stands the *Museu de Etnologia (Tues 14.00–18.00, Wed–Sun 10.00–18.00/19.00), containing the extensive collections of the Instituto de Investigacao Científica Tropical. Although there is no permanent exhibition, it is the site of regular important temporary exhibitions from Portugal and from its former empire and colonies, including Brazil, Mozambique, Angola, Goa, Macao, and from other areas. The complex comprises four exhibition galleries, a library and archive, and study rooms.

## MOSTEIRO DOS JERÓNIMOS

A few minutes' walk to the west from the Museu dos Coches brings one to the *Mosteiro dos Jerónimos, or of Santa Maria, at Belém, one of the most beautiful and accessible of Lisbon's monuments (winter 10.00–13.00 and 14.30–17.00, summer 10.00–18.30; closed Mon and hols). An excellent example of the exuberant Manueline style of architecture, it has impressed most travellers to the monastery in the past.

### History

The site, occupied in the 15C by the Ermida de Restelo, a mariners' chapel founded by Henry the Navigator and served by the Order of Christ, was chosen by Dom Manuel in 1496 for the foundation of a monastery of Hieronymites. The name was changed to Belém (Bethlehem), and the Order of Christ was compensated with the church of N.S. da Conceição Velha; see latter part of Rte 1.

The departure from Belém of Vasco da Gama's fleet in 1497 and his successful return in 1499 inspired the king to expend every effort to make the new monastery a splendid memorial of Portugal's thanksgiving, and the first stone was probably laid in 1502. The first master of the works was Diogo Boitac, succeeded c 1517 by João de Castilho. Nicolas Chanterène, a French sculptor, was also working here. Suspended for a while in 1551, the work was later continued by Diogo de Torralva and Jerónimo de Ruão (from 1571), son of the better-known Jean de Rouen. The 1755 earthquake caused only slight damage, but extensive 'restorations' were undertaken in the 19C, when a

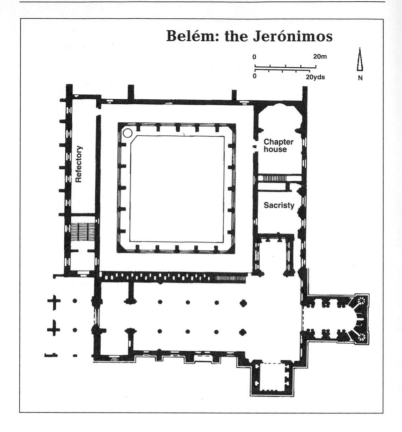

# Belém: the Jerónimos

dome was added to the south-west tower. The western extension of the building, in a pseudo-Manueline style (largely reconstructed since its partial collapse in 1878), dates from 1850.

The magnificent **\*south portal**, constructed by João de Castilho, consists of two doors enclosed within a deep round archway between buttresses, and is surmounted by a statue of N.S. de Belém. A figure on the central pillar is said to represent Henry the Navigator. Over all is a canopy, with a hierarchy of statues in niches, crowned by a top-heavy niche above which is the cross of the Order of Christ. The two large windows on either side and the elaborate roof balustrade harmonise with the design. The Mannerist chancel was built by Jerónimo de Ruão.

The **west portal** has suffered by being at various times overshadowed by bridges built to connect the monastery with its more modern extensions, but, in spite of mutilations, preserves the portrait statues of Dom Manuel and Dona Maria, his second wife (daughter of Fernando and Isabel of Spain), with their patrons SS. Jerome and John the Baptist, by Chanterène (1517); above are the Annunciation, Nativity, and Adoration of the Magi.

The general effect of the **interior** (91m long; 25m wide; 25m high), with its soaring columns and bold vault, is both delicate and imposing. The nave has six lofty columns, with Renaissance decoration in low relief, but with empty niches, supporting a vault of uniform height extending over the aisles. Beneath the Coro Alto, with fine stalls of c 1550, above which are 17C panels, are two dark chapels, one used as a baptistry. In the north wall of the nave are confessionals, alternating with others facing the south walk of the cloister. On the north-west pier of the crossing (completed 1522) is a medallion with the alleged portrait of Boitac or João de Castilho. Note the ornate pulpits built into the eastern shafts.

The Renaissance **Capela-Mór**, completed by Jerónimo de Ruão in 1572, contains the tombs of Dom Manuel I and Dona Maria, and Dom João III and Dona Catarina, plain sarcophagi borne by elephants, as is that of Dom Sebastião in the south transept, while in the north is the tomb of Dom Henrique, the Cardinal-King. From here one may enter the sacristy, a Renaissance room vaulted from a single central pier.

On leaving, turn right to visit the *****cloisters**, with a lion-fed fountain at the north-west corner, surrounding the garth. The lower storey, contemporary with the church, was elaborately decorated by João de Castilho and his assistants, each bay being divided by three columns supporting traceried arches. Note also the unusual corner canopies. The upper storey, each bay of which contains a single supporting column, was not finished until 1544.

On the east side is the chapter-house, not completed until the 19C, containing the tomb of Alexandre Herculano (died 1877), the anti-clerical historian. Opposite is the **refectory**, a long hall with a good depressed vault and containing 18C *azulejos* illustrating the story of Joseph.

To the north of the monastery are the Manueline chapels of Santo Cristo and São Jerónimo; the latter, commenced c 1514, with a portal possibly designed by Boitac, was probably completed by Rodrigo Afonso.

Beyond the west portal is the entrance to the *****MUSEU NACIONAL DE ARQUE-OLOGIA E ETNOLOGIA** (Tues 14.00–18.00, Wed–Sun 10.00–18.00/19.00), installed here in 1903, an extensive and interesting collection of objects illustrating prehistoric and primitive Portugal. Since its thorough reorganisation in 1980 the museum has become the principal institution for Portuguese archaeological research, and includes interdisciplinary units concentrating on paleo-ecology and underwater archaeology. A series of archaeological guides, with English summaries, is in the process of publication.

Bronze Age objects include bracelets, collars, and other artefacts from sites such as Vale de Viegas (Serpa), Arnozela (Fafe), Cabeceiras de Basto, Sobreiral (near Castelo Branco), and Herdade do Alamo (Moura); Iron Age artefacts include the remarkable gold bracelet from Torre Vã (Grândola); the Roman collections include sculptures, mosaics, cameos, bronzes, coins, inscriptions, weapons, jewellery, and a stone statue of a Lusitanian warrior. There is also a small collection of Egyptian antiquities.

At the far end of the long 19C façade of the western extension to the monastery is the entrance to the **MUSEU DA MARINHA** (10.00–18.00), containing collections describing the seafaring exploits of the Portuguese over the centuries. It is particularly rich in ship's models.

It is convenient to start on the **first floor**, passing on a landing a room devoted to the Far East, containing Oriental furniture, a 17C screen showing a plan of Nagasaki (Japan); a painting depicting the Action of Bocca Tigris against Chinese pirates (1810), and mid 19C Chinese views of Macao, etc. On the upper landing are seen some 18C Indo-Portuguese sculptures of St Francis Xavier; St Philip Neri; Luis Frois, a Jesuit missionary who died at Nagasaki in 1597; and of Santa Isabel (1271–1336), queen of Dom Dinis, all from the Oratory at Goa founded in 1682. A large room on the right displays numerous models and half-models; ship's furniture; paintings; models of slipways; guns, and decorations, photographs of the Lisnave and Setenave shipyards, etc.

On the **ground floor** (note the display cases decorated with rope-work) are larger models; uniforms; navigational instruments; and among the miscellaneous paintings, one of Admiral Sir Charles Napier at the Battle of Cape St Vincent (5 July 1833, against Dom Miguel), by Morel Fatio (1842). The north wing contains further models (19–20C), models of river-craft, and furniture from the royal yacht 'Dona Amélia' (1900; dismantled 1938), in which Dom Manuel II set sail from Ericeira in 1910.

A modern extension to the museum, in the form of a large hangar, has been built on the far side of the adjacent square, its north side flanked by the Calouste Gulbenkian Planetarium (1965).

In the entrance-hall of this extension is an interesting collection of portolanos, charts and maps, mostly in facsimile, including José da Costa Miranda's map of the Atlantic, of 1681. Also here is the Fairey 17 sea-plane 'Santa Cruz', which, with Gago Coutinho and Sacadura Cabral as pilots, was the first plane to cross the Atlantic, in 1922 (from Lisbon to Rio); also a Schrenck F.B.A. hydroplane of 1917. Also protected here are two ceremonial oared Royal Barges or *galliotes*, that of Maria I dating from 1785, and embellished by Pillement; and some Merryweather fire-engines.

Turning south towards the Tagus, one passes the recently completed Cultural Centre, and may descend into a pedestrian tunnel below the main road to approach the **Museu de Arte Popular** (Tues 14.00–18.00, Wed–Sun 10.00–18.00), opened in 1948, illustrating the folk art of the provinces of Portugal, with a representative range of ceramics; metal, wood, and leather-work; costumes; fabrics; carpets; domestic utensils, and farm implements; toys; musical instruments; basketry; and jewellery. Many of the objects displayed deserve the more sophisticated presentation which is planned.

To the east stands an ill-conceived monument erected under Salazar in 1960 to commemorate the quincentenary of the death of Henry the Navigator. On its north side is carved a huge sword, the hilt of which is in the form of the Cross of Avis.

Some distance further west, partially hidden beyond trees, and adjacent to the coastal Fort of Bom Sucesso, is the splendid ***TORRE DE BELÉM***, its bold silhouette familiar as the much-illustrated classic example of Muslim decoration applied to Manueline architecture. As the Bulwark of Restelo, this defensive tower was originally designed for Dom João II by Garcia de Resende, the historian, but was constructed of *pedra lioz* on another plan by Francisco de Arruda between 1515 and 1520, and dedicated to St Vincent. At the time it was entirely surrounded by water, until stranded on a sandy beach. Some idea of its original state is provided by the recently erected retaining wall, which is covered at high tide. It served as a state

*The Torre de Belém, a classic example of Muslim decoration applied to Manueline architecture*

prison from 1580 until 1828, when opponents of Dom Miguel were incacerated in its water-lapped dungeons.

Its main external features are the square tower adorned with *ajimece* windows and Moorish balconies, and the advanced platform whose battlements bear the shield of the Order of Christ. At each corner of its landward side and on the summit of the tower itself are circular casemates or sentry-boxes topped by segmented or melon-shaped domes; others line the platform. Between and below these are rope-mouldings.

The tower is open from 10.00 to 18.30 in summer, and until 17.00 the rest of the year. A cat-walk leads to the main entrance. The ground floor contains a series of gun-emplacements approached by a wide vaulted passage lit by an interior patio, while below were the magazines and store-rooms. Steps to the right of the entrance ascend to a terrace. On the seaward side of the interior balustrade is a richly carved niche protecting a statue of the Virgin holding the Child and a bunch of grapes. On either side are columns topped by armillary spheres, the device of Dom Manuel. Note also the delicacy of the carving of the balustrade of the long gallery on the side of the tower, which we now enter, the first level of which provides entry to the corner casemates. A spiral stair ascends to the second level, with a corner fireplace, and balconies, and up again to another room with window seats set into the thickness of the wall. Above is the oratory, a well-vaulted room (note the face carved on a corbel), off which is a wall-walk. Stairs climb to the flat roof, providing a fine panoramic view of Lisbon and towards the mouth of the Tagus estuary.

For the coast road, the Avenida Marginal, to Estoril and Cascais, see the latter part of Rte 2, in reverse.

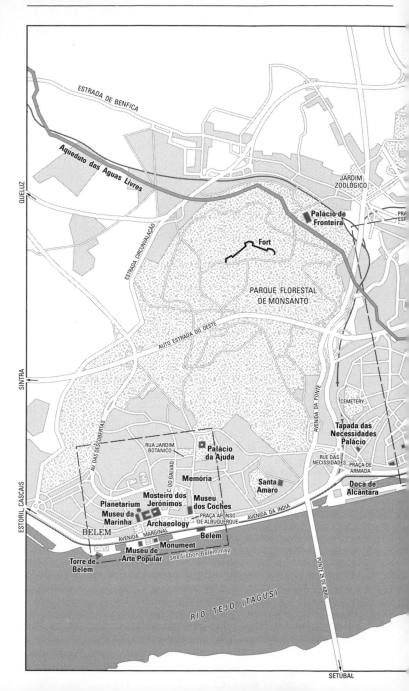

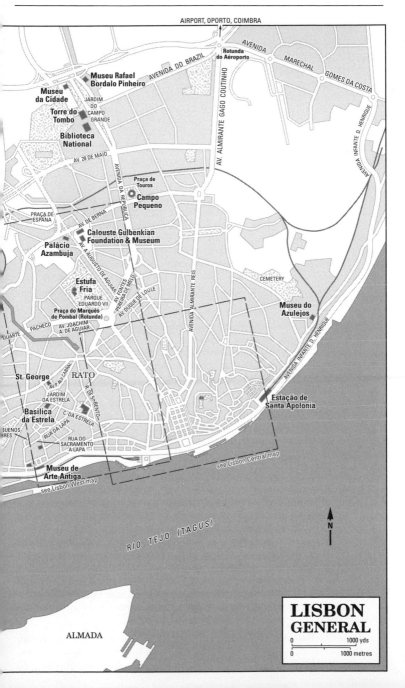

AIRPORT, OPORTO, COIMBRA

AVENIDA

Rotunda
do Aéroporto

MARECHAL

GOMES DA COSTA

AVENIDA DO BRAZIL

AV. ALMIRANTE GAGO COUTINHO

AVENIDA INFANTE D. HENRIQUE

**Museu Rafael
Bordalo Pinheiro**

**Museu
da Cidade**

JARDIM
DO
CAMPO
GRANDE

**Torre do
Tombo**

**Biblioteca
National**

AV. 28 DE MAIO

AVENIDA DA REPÚBLICA

Praça de
Touros

**Campo
Pequeno**

PRAÇA DE
ESPANA

AV. DE BERNA

**Calouste Gulbenkian
Foundation & Museum**

**Palácio
Azambuja**

AV. A. AUGUSTO DE AGUIAR

**Estufa
Fria**

PARQUE
EDUARDO VII

AV. FONTES
PEREIRA DE MELO

AV. DUQUE DE LOULE

AVENIDA ALMIRANTE REIS

CEMETERY

**Museu do
Azulejos**

**Praça do Marquês
de Pombal (Rotunda)**

PACHECO

AV. JOACHIM
A. DE AGUIAR

DUARTE

**St. George**

AV. P. AV. CABRAL

RATO

R. DE S. BENTO

AVENIDA INFANTE D. HENRIQUE

JARDIM
DA ESTRELA

C. DA ESTRELA

**Estação de
Santa Apolonia**

**Basilica
da Estrela**

BUENOS
AIRES

RUA DA LAPA

RUA DO
SACRAMENTO
A LAPA

**Museu de
Arte Antiga**

see Lisbon Central map

see Lisbon West map

RIO TEJO (TAGUS)

N

**LISBON
GENERAL**

0                    1000 yds

0                    1000 metres

ALMADA

# F. Northern Lisbon and the Gulbenkian Museum

At the north end of the wide Avenida da Liberdade (see last page of Rte 1B) is the Rotunda, or **Praça do Marquês de Pombal** (Metro Parque), dominated by a statue of that dynamic but dictatorial statesman, unveiled in 1934 in the centre of a busy roundabout.

A wide street (at first called the Rua Joaquim António de Aguiar) leads steeply uphill almost due west from the Rotunda, and is later continued by the Auto-estrada do Oeste, bearing west towards Sintra (see Rte 2), off which forks the Av. da Ponte, the most direct approach to the Ponte 25 de Abril.

Immediately north of the Rotunda extends the large **Parque de Eduardo VII**, laid out in honour of Edward VII and Queen Alexandra's visit to Lisbon in 1903 (he had been in Lisbon in 1876, when Prince of Wales), and now overlooked from the west by the *Ritz Hotel*.

Near its north-west corner is the **Estufa Fria** (or 'cool' greenhouse) built into a quarry in 1910, later enlarged, and opened to the public in 1930. Supported by columns of rusticated masonry is a roof constructed of bamboo slats through which the sunlight filters. At a higher level is the Estufa Quente (or 'hot' glasshouse), with a glass roof. Together, they protect an extensive and varied collection of tropical and sub-tropical plants, those in the Estufa Fria being comprehensively labelled. Both the botanist and casual visitor will find this curious garden—almost a jungle—with its rivulets, flamingo pool, ferns, banana trees, cacti, etc., a place of pleasure and interest.

A good view down the Avenida towards the Tagus is commanded from a central point on the north side of the park; while further north is a prison (Penitenciária) of 1874, and conveniently near, the Palace of Justice (1970).

The Av. Fontes Pereira de Melo leads north-east from the Rotunda to the Praça Duque de Saldanha, passing near (left) the small Casa-Museu Dr Anastácio Gonçalves (8 Av. 5 de Outubro), with collections of furniture, ceramics, and 19–20C paintings, etc. For this district see below.

The Av. António Augusto de Aguiar, the first thoroughfare forking left from the Av. Fontes Pereira de Melo, climbs for some distance before descending to the Praça de Espanha.

On the south-west corner of its junction with the *praça* stands the **Palácio Azambuja** or dos Meninos de Palhavã, dating from 1660, in which Maria-Francesca of Savoy died in 1683. It was later the gloomy residence of Dom João V's bastards (cf. Odivelas), and since 1918 that of the Spanish Embassy. It has been restored since being severely damaged by fire in anti-Spanish demonstrations on 26 September 1975.

## CALOUSTE GULBENKIAN FOUNDATION

To the south-east, in part of the gardens of the palace, stands the Calouste Gulbenkian Foundation (Metro S. Sebastião, Palhava, tram 24, 27, and bus 16, 26, 30, 56). Its museum, inaugurated in 1969, comprises one of the more important collections of art in the world, considering its size and that it constitutes the lifetime's accumulation of one man, whose eclectic tastes it reflects (Wed and Sat 14.00–19.30, Tues, Thur, Fri & Sun 10.00–17.00; Oct–May Tues–Sun 10.00–17.00).

**Calouste Sarkis Gulbenkian** (1869–1955) was born at Scutari, Turkey, into an already wealthy Armenian family, and studied at King's College, London. Although he acquired British nationality by naturalisation in 1902, he later resided for some years in Paris, but spent most of the last 13 years of his life in Portugal. Here his Foundation has its headquarters, with an important branch in London (at 98 Portland Place). To this Foundation he left his collections of art, and substantially the whole of his very considerable estate, largely based on his five per cent interest in the Iraq Petroleum group of companies. The offices of the Foundation, established in 1956 to further work of a charitable, artistic, educational, and scientific nature, is adjacent to the museum.

The main building, of four storeys above ground, stands in landscaped gardens, and comprises an administrative block; three auditoriums, one seating 1400, where numerous concerts take place (the Gulbenkian Orchestra was established in 1962); lecture-rooms, and a library; adjacent is an open-air theatre. (See below for the Centre of Modern Art.)

The *MUSEUM itself is located to the east of the main block, with the entrance to the library, and a bookstall for the sale of the Foundation's publications, on the floor below. There are cafés here and at the Modern Art Centre.

The museum is laid out as a series of open-plan sections built around two interior patios, and divided into two main groups: Oriental Art and Classical Art; and European Art. The whole is well planned and tastefully decorated, and the exhibits well labelled although some deserve better lighting (such as the Japanese boxes). Explanatory notes are at hand in each section. A complete illustrated catalogue is available.

**A. Egyptian Art**: 14, Statuette of the Lady Henut Taoui, of polychromed wood and gold (18th Dyn.); 23, Bronze statue of the Lady Chepes; 24–26, Bronze cats; 28, Silver-gilt mask for a mummy (30th Dyn.); 29, Sun-boat of Djedher (bronze; 30th Dyn.); 32, Bas-relief study for a portrait of a pharaoh (early Ptolomaic period); 35, Head of a priest (?; green shist; middle Ptolomaic period).

**B. Graeco-Roman Art**; largely devoted to Greek coins, for which Calouste Gulbenkian had a passion; jewellery, and Roman glass; notable are a gold Winged Victory (51), and 50, a silver two-handled bucket.

**C. Middle Eastern and Islamic Art**; 85, Urn with two handles from Mesopotamia or Persia (2–3C BC), and 86, Alabaster bas-relief (Assyrian; 9C BC). A long room is now reached containing an extensive display of ceramics, *azulejos*, glass, rugs and carpets, costumes and brocades, lacquered doors, illuminated Armenian MSS, Persian book-bindings, and Syrian mosque lamps; notable among a remarkable collection are 282, a pale green jade jar (15C Persian), and the miniatures on six 17C Persian screens (284).

**D. Oriental Art**: an extremely fine collection of Chinese porcelains; carved jade and rock crystal objects; and a 12-panel Chinese screen (411; ? 18C). A collection of gilt Japanese lacquer boxes, etc.; *inros* and *netsukes*; and Japanese prints (displayed in rotation), by such artists as Utamaro (1735–1806), Hokusai (1760–1849), Hiroshige (1797–1858), et al.

A series of rooms devoted to **European Arts** is now entered.

**E.** A collection of French ivories (14C), notably 630 and 632, Scenes from the Life of the Virgin, and from the Life of Christ. Also several illuminated MSS, including (497) the Book of Hours of Margaret of Cleves (early 15C), and a late 13C English Apocalypse (498).

**F. Paintings and sculpture**: 899, anon. Portrait of a young couple (16C); 892, *Lochner*, Presentation in the Temple; 894, anon. Virgin and Child (Flemish; 15C); 896, *Van der Weyden*, St Catherine; 895, *Dirk Bouts*, Annunciation; 981, *Cima da Conegliano*, Holy Conversation; 980, *Carpaccio*, Virgin and Child, with donors; 979,

*Ghirlandaio*, Portrait of a young girl; 898, *Gossaert (Mabuse)*, Virgin and Child; 983, *G.-B. Moroni*, Portrait of Marco Antonio Savelli; 984, *Giuliano Bugiardini*, Portrait of a young woman; 964, *Hals*, Portrait of Sara Andriesdr. Hessix; 900, *Van Dyck*, Portrait of a Man; 904, *Paul de Vos*, Cock-fight; 969, *Ruysdael*, Landscape, 968, View of the coast of Norway, and 970, View near Haarlem; 965, *Jan van der Heyden*, Dutch landscape; 905, *Sébastien Bourdon*, Portrait of Colbert; 603, *Coysevox*, Bust of Maréchal de Turenne (bronze); 903, *Rubens*, Portrait of Helen Fourment; 966, *Rembrandt*, Pallas Athene, or Alexander, and 967, Figure of an old man; 921, *Hubert Robert*, Le Tapis Vert, and 922, Le Bosquet des Bains d'Apollon; 910, *Fragonard*, Fête at Rambouillet; 914, *Lépicié*, The Astronomer, and 915, Self-portrait; 916, *Nattier*, Portraits of a noble, and 918, of Louis Tocqué; 911, *Lancret*, Fête galante; 604, *Caffieri*, Terracotta bust of Molière; 606, *Lemoyne*, Terracotta bust of Robbé de Beauveset; 912, *Maurice-Quentin Delatour*, pastel Portraits of Mlle Sallé, and 913, of Duval de L'Epinoy; 924, *François-André Vincent*, Portrait of Mlle Duplant; 609, *Houdon*, Marble statue of Diana. (See below for other paintings.)

**G. Furniture and furnishings** (together with some paintings, etc.): most of the furniture is by French *ébénistes*, including Nicholas Blanchard, Charles Cressent, Jean Desforges, Jacques Dubois, George Jacob, Jean-François Oeben, Jean-Henri Riesener, J.-B.-C. Sené, M.G. Cramer, and Martin Carlin. Also 909, *Fragonard*, The Regatta; 626, *attributed to Antonio Rossellino*, marble bas-relief of the Virgin and Child; 627, *Luca della Robbia*, Ceramic plaque of Faith; 601, *anon.* St Martin dividing his cloak (French; 1531); 701, an eight-panel lacquer screen (18C); 1004, Brussels tapestry (mid 16C); and 1005, three Italian tapestries, probably after cartoons by *Giulio Romano* (Ferrara, c 1540); 1015, a 15C Venetian velvet parasol.

A collection of Italian bronze **medals** (15–16Cs), some designed by *Pisanello* (648–54).

A collection of 18C **French book-bindings**, several attributed to binders such as Derôme and Padeloup.

607, *Clodion*, terracotta Nymph and Satyr; 917, *Nattier*, Portrait of Madame de la Porte; 906, *Largillière*, Portrait of M. et Mme Thomas Germain; 1012, Beauvais tapestry, after Boucher (1755); and 1008–11, four Aubusson Chinoiserie tapestries, after Pillement.

A collection of French snuff-boxes, and **silver** and silver-gilt, elaborate and massive, by *orfèvres* such as Auguste, Biennais, Durand, F.-T. Germain, Lehendrick, Mongenot, Roettiers, and Spire. The following section contains **paintings** of the English School, among others: 971, *Gainsborough*, Portrait of Mrs Lowndes-Stone; 973, *Romney*, Miss Constable; 972, *Hoppner*, Miss Frances Beresford; 974, *Lawrence*, Lady Elizabeth Conyngham; 976, *Turner*, Quillebeuf, and 975, Shipwreck; also 941, *Diaz de la Peña*, Forest of Fontainebleau; and representative works by *Daubigny* (936–40), and *Lepine* (947–50); 19 paintings by *Guardi* (985–1103); several works by *Corot* (929–35); 954, *Millet*, Winter; 951, *Manet*, Boy with cherries, and 952, Blowing bubbles; *Fantin-Latour*, Still-lifes (942–45); 893, *Mary Cassat*, Maternal attention; 960, *Monet*, Boats, 961, Still Life, and 962, The Thaw; 963, *Renoir*, Portrait of Mme Claude Monet; 958, *Degas*, Man and puppet, and 959, Self-portrait; 977–8, *Burne-Jones*, The Mirror and Bath of Venus; and (unnumbered), *Boldoni*, The artist ? Brown and family.

Several **bronzes** by Barye, Rodin, Carpeaux, and Dalou.

The visit ends with a large and varied collection (742–849) of the exotic art of René Lalique (1860–1945) displayed in a suitably designed *art nouveau* room. On making our exit, a bronze statue of Apollo, by Houdon (610), is passed to the left.

An extension of the Gulbenkian Foundation's activities is the **\*MODERN ART CENTRE**, inaugurated in 1983, and approached through the gardens of the Foundation or from the Rua Dr Nicolau Bettencourt, immediately to the west. It is an attractive stepped structure sustained by reinforced concrete ribs, the overall design of which was entrusted to Sir Leslie Martin. It has a roomy, well-lit interior with a main exhibition room on three levels.

The larger area (1800 sq m) is devoted to temporary (one to two year) exhibitions of Portuguese art (from 1911), selected from its extensive reserves; an upper gallery displays contemporary foreign art, and below this is a section for exhibiting prints and drawings. The collection includes paintings, sculptures, installations, drawings, photographs and graphic works. It features work by Amadeo de Souza-Cardoso, Paula Rego, Júlio Pomar and Fernando Dacosta. There are also pieces by artists who have a strong connection with Portuguese art, for example Sonia and Robert Delaunay, Vieira da Silva, Arpad Szénes, Candido Portinari, and Torres Garcia. The collection of British art from the 1960s to the present day includes work by Peter Blake, Howard Hodgkin, Hamish Fulton, Julian Opie and Rachel Whiteread. A selection of Armenian art includes work by Arshile Gorky. In the vestibule there are two triptychs by Almada Negreiros (1893–1970), a forerunner of Portuguese modernism. The building also contains other temporary exhibition rooms, experimental studios, and a documentation and research department. The park has a number of sculptures, including works by Henry Moore and Ruben Nakian.

A small Children's Pavilion, reached from the Rua Marquês Sá da Bandeira, to the east, has been opened to promote an interest in the arts amongst the young.

Approximately 1km north-west of the museum lies the **Jardim Zoológico** (metro Ríos); while further west, in the Largo São Domingos of the suburb **Benfica**, is the church and convent of São Domingos, containing the tomb of João das Regras (died 1404), who secured the election of Dom João I. In the cloister is a chapel in which is the tomb of João de Castro (died 1548; Viceroy of Portuguese India).

Nearby is a *quinta* built by Gerard de Visme; and a short distance beyond are the attractive gardens of the *Quinta* or **Palácio do Marquês de Fronteira**, its formal gardens containing *azulejo*-panelled basins, their tiles of c 1670 depicting knights on prancing chargers similar to Velázquez's equestrian portraits in the Prado, Madrid.

*Detail from azulejo panel in the gardens of the Palácio do Marquês de Fronteira*

Check with a tourist office for times of admission, which are variable.

Also in this area, by the metro station of Alto dos Moinhos, is the **\*Museu da Música** (Tues–Sat 13.00–20.00), an important collection of musical instruments, inaugurated here in 1994. Among c 500 instruments of interest and quality, many restored for performance, is a double virginal by Ruckers of 1620.

At **Carnide**, c 1km north, is the monumental church of N.S. da Luz (1575–96).

From the Praça Duque de Saldanha (see above) the wide Avenida da República leads due north, passing (right) the Campo Pequeno, off the centre of which is the **Praça de Touros** (bull ring; 1892), which seats nearly 8500 spectators.

At the far end of the avenue extends the elongated Jardim do Campo Grande. To the west rises a tasteful if bunker-like building, inaugurated in 1990, protecting the national archives and known as the *****Arquivo da Torre do Tombo** from the name of the tower in the Castelo de São Jorge where the archives were kept before the earthquake of 1755. It provides the latest research facilities, and there is usually an exhibition of MSS and books on view, although no permanent exhibition.

Among the earliest and more interesting items which have been on display, and which give some slight idea of the range of its holdings, are: a grant founding the Church of Lodosa (882); the *Apocalypse of Lorvão* (1189); the first document in which Afonso Henriques is mentioned as king (1140); *Bull of Alexander III* conceding the title 'King' to Afonso Henriques, and recognising the Independence of Portugal (1179); an illuminated Book of Hours from Alcobaça (late 13C?); a Flemish Book of Hours of c 1436; the *Hours of Dom Duarte* (French; 15C); a missal printed in Naples (1487); a document founding a School at Alcobaça (1269); Treaty ratifying the division of the Atlantic and adjacent territories between Spain and Portugal (Tordesillas, 1494); Testament of the Infante Dom Fernando (1437); Fernão Lopes, Crónica de Dom João I (16C), with a view of Lisbon; the *Livro das Fortalezas* of Duarte Darmas (early 16C); Bulls creating bishops for Baia (1555) and Rio de Janeiro (1676); João Teixeira, Plan of the coast of Brazil (1640); Plan of Goa by Gaspar Correia, from his *Lendas da India* (1538); the illuminated Florentine Bible given to the Jerónimos of Belém by Dom Manuel (c 1500; 7 volumes); letters signed by Vasco da Gama, and Magellan; the *Livro da Nobreza* of António Godinho (16C); a copy of the *Nuremberg Chronicle* (1493); João de Lisboa, *Livro da Marinharia* (16C), depicting the coast of Africa; early Views of Portuguese castles; Fernão Vaz Dourado, *Atlas* (1571); Bull of Clemente VI nominating Frei Diogo da Silva Inquisitor in Portugal (1531); Peace Treaty between Dom João IV and Oliver Cromwell (1654); and a copy of the first Portuguese Constitution (1821).

Further west are the buildings of the Cidade Universitária and the unimaginative block of the **Biblioteca Nacional**. Inaugurated in 1969, it looks more like the mammoth Hospital further to the west than a library, but no doubt it is more practical than its predecessor. It was founded in 1796 and these functional new premises with all their modern facilities now preserve as *Reservados* its chief treasures, among which are numerous incunabula and MSS, none of which is at present exhibited, which is a pity.

At the north-west end of the Campo Grande, standing too near an overpass for comfort, is the Palácio Pimenta, an attractive mansion attributed to Carlos Mardel, and traditionally built as a residence for Madre Paula (cf. Odivelas). Since 1979 it has housed the municipal *****MUSEU DA CIDADE** (Tues–Sun 10.00–13.00 and 14.00–18.00), a visit to which is essential to a proper historical perspective of Lisbon. It is reached by metro Campo Grande and bus 1, 3, 7, 7a, 17b, 33, 36, 36a, 46a, 47, 50.

Its archaeological collections are displayed on the ground floor, and include artefacts found when the Casa dos Bicos was gutted in the early 1980s. Its ceramic collection includes numerous examples from the Fabrica do Rato, among other rare pieces (boar's head, and Negro heads). Another room contains a set of 17C bronze weights. Several rooms are devoted to an extensive collection of views of Lisbon, including engravings by Dirk Stoop (1610–80) depicting the Embarkation of Catherine of Braganza from 'Black Horse Square' (then with a fountain in the centre), escorted by the Earl of Sandwich; views of Lisbon before 1755, including some of the Aqueduct, and designs for fountains; a copy of a Panorama of 1763, and a vista by C. Lemprière (1756); watercolour plans for the reconstruction of the city after the earthquake; an anonymous Portrait of Pombal; views by J.P. Lebas (1757); a view painted on glass of the Praça do Comércio; views by Henry L'Evêque (1816), Alexandre Noël (1780), J.C. Stadler, and Albert Dufourcq; Delarive. The Feira da Ladra; J. Pedroso (1825–90), The Tobacco Factory; Robert Batty (c 1830), sepia wash views; and watercolours by George Atkinson (1838); Maps of Lisbon of 1837 and 1884; Isaias Newton (1838–1922; who was born in Lisbon and died there), views of the Ajuda Palace; also a vista of the city; and James Holland (1800–70), The church of N.S. da Conceição Velha.

At the north-east corner of the Campo Grande is a small **museum** devoted to the curious ceramic art (much of it carried out at Caldas da Rainha) of Rafael Bordalo Pinheiro (1846–1905), together with examples of his caricatures.

The right-hand turning at the far end of the Campo Grande leads shortly to the airport (Portela).

Approximately 2km north, in the suburb of **Lumiar**, perhaps best approached by the Av. Padre Cruz, is the ***MUSEU DO TRAJO** (costume), installed in the Quinta Palmela, off the Largo de São João Baptista (bus 1, 7, 7a, 17b, 36). It retains most of its original decoration and *azulejos*. It was here that Mrs Norton (the author, and Richard Brinsley Sheridan's granddaughter) met Almeida Garrett, the Liberal politician and author. Opening times are Mon–Fri 10.00–18.00.

The collections of costumes (over 5000 items, and being extended continuously by donations) are displayed in rotation, not only for reasons of space, but in the interest of the preservation of the many fragile fabrics. It is therefore impossible to describe in detail any specific section. Nevertheless, the museum is of importance for an understanding of Portuguese dress, and a visit is recommended to all interested in the history of costume. There is a small restaurant, and the gardens are attractive. In out-houses (once a cow-shed) are looms, dyeing baths, etc., where the processes of hand-blocking, etc. may be seen.

Nearby, at Estrada do Lumiar 12, the restored Quinta do Monteiro-Mór ('Master of the Hounds') accommodates the **Museu Nacional do Teatro**, containing extensive archives, and exhibitions of material illustrating the history of the Portuguese stage from the early 19C to the present. It is open daily except Mon, 10.00–13.00, 14.30–17.00.

For the Convento de Odivelas, further to the north-east, see Rte 18A.

# 2 · Sintra: Cascais: Estoril

The circuit (from Lisbon) of approximately 90km described below is a convenient form in which to point out the main sights en route, but of course it may be followed in the reverse direction. Rte 3 might be considered a pendant, but Queluz may also be seen on the way, while Mafra may be visited directly from Sintra, or alternatively by turning off the A8 driving north from Lisbon.

It was the excursion to Sintra and Mafra which almost all past visitors to Lisbon would make, even if they got no further afield, and the excursion is still recommended. Avoid making it at weekends and holidays, and likewise avoid certain well-sited cafés and restaurants in Sintra whose rapacity has given the place a bad name.

■ **By train from Lisbon**. These are frequent to Sintra via Queluz from Rossio station; those to Estoril and Cascais leave from Cais do Sodré station.

From the Rotunda in Lisbon (see p 134), bear uphill to the west onto the A5, with a good view to the right of the Águas Livres aqueduct (see Rte 1C) from a viaduct spanning the Alcântara valley. The road briefly traverses the thickly wooded Monsanto park, on the far side of which, on making the descent, bear right onto the N117 and then the IC19 dual carriageway. To the north extends the huge suburb of **Amadora** (122,106 inhabitants).

Those intending to visit the palace at Queluz en route (see Rte 3) must keep a sharp look out for the turning off the IC19.

The main road (later the N249) drives north-west, running the gauntlet of gross urbanisation which has proliferated in this area within recent years, now leaving the palace at Queluz isolated within a concrete jungle. The 'protected' Serra de Sintra rises ahead, and the village of **Ramalhão** is bypassed, where from July to October 1787 Beckford, in his 18C *quinta*, would trifle away the whole morning 'surrounded by fidalgos in flowered bed-gowns and musicians in violet coloured accoutrements, with broad straw hats...'. In 1794 this was acquired by the intriguing Carlota Joaquina, who retired there in 1822 on having refused to take the oath to the Constitution, and would have been expelled from the country had not ten doctors declared that she was unfit to travel! Not surprisingly, she survived for another eight years, continuing to plot meanwhile. From here, in 1833, Don Carlos of Spain, her reactionary brother, proclaimed against his niece Isabel II, thereby precipitating the First Carlist War.

## SINTRA

Sintra (equally well known to the English as **Cintra**), and formerly sometimes Cyntra, beautifully sited on the north slope of its *serra*, has had its praises sung over the centuries, often being described both in poetry and prose. While its main attractions may be seen in a day, the proper exploration on foot of its wooded heights and many *quintas* requires, and deserves, more time. Unfortunately, although it is delightfully cool in summer, the views are often obscured by sea-mists, which cling to the higher summits of the range.

Roy Campbell, the reactionary South African poet, lived here during his later years (1952–57). He had written *Flowering Rifle* in Portugal in 1939, was killed in a car crash near Setúbal, and is buried in the São Pedro cemetery here.

■ The **Tourist Office** is at 23 Praça da República, near the Palácio Nacional.

Of its monuments, the most interesting is the \***PALÁCIO NACIONAL**, long a royal summer residence, which, with its two conical oast-house-like chimneys, dominates the main square. The opening times are 10.00–13.00, 14.00–17.00; closed Wed and holidays.

### History

Dom João I set about enlarging the palace which already existed on this site at some time before 1415. The central block dates from this period, although its *ajimece* windows and arabesque balustrading are of c 1500–20, when the right wing was added by Dom Manuel; the buildings on the left are 18–19C

*View of the beautifully-sited, largely fifteenth century, Palácio Nacional, Sintra*

additions. It was here that Dom João I decided on the Ceuta expedition (1415), and received the Burgundian envoy in whose train came Jan van Eyck (1429). (He painted a portrait of the Infanta Isabel for Philippe le Bon, who married her next year at Bruges.) Dom Afonso V was born and died in the palace (1432–81). Dom Sebastião, who was proclaimed king here when three years old (1557), held his last audience here before starting on his disastrous African expedition of 1578; and Dom Afonso VI spent his last impotent years here, his brother's prisoner (1674–83). The palace was damaged in the earthquake of 1755; and the entrance courtyard was cleared of buildings in the 19C.

Steps ascend to the entrance vestibule below a plain Gothic arcade, where a guided tour is awaited. The **Sala dos Archeiros** and then the **kitchens**, with their pale grey tiles and two huge chimneys, are seen first. From here steps ascend to the **Sala dos Árabes**, attractively tiled with green, blue, and white *azulejos* (15C), and with a marble fountain. The adjacent chapel, with an *artesonado* roof and a late 15C *azulejo* pavement, was redecorated in the last century in an execrable style. Dom Afonso VI died of apoplexy in the gallery while hearing mass, terminating his imprisonment in the so-called **Sala de Dom Afonso VI**, whose *azulejo* floor he is said to have worn away by his incessant pacing. The **Chinese Room** contains an ivory pagoda presented to Carlota Joaquina in 1806 by the Chinese emperor, Chippendale chairs, and attractive black, pink, and white *azulejos*.

A clumsy Manueline doorway leads into the **Sala dos Brasões**, named from the 74 blazons of the noble Portuguese families of the years 1515–18 which decorate its impressive *artesonado* dome. One blank space is pointed out, incorrectly, as being that from which the arms of the Aveiros were erased after their participation in a plot against Dom José in 1758: in fact it once held the arms of the Coelhos. Prancing stags support the blazons, while blue and white *azulejos* below depict hunting scenes. Descending, and passing through a charming patio and other rooms, including **Dom Sebastião's bedroom** (with 16C vine-leaf *azulejos*), the **Sala das Sereias** (sirens or mermaids, playing musical instruments) is entered, containing Indo-Portuguese furniture.

*A panel of the magpie ceiling in the Sala dos Pêgas*

The adjacent **Sala das Pêgas**, much restored, is named after the numerous painted magpies inhabiting its compartmented ceiling, each bearing in its beak the device '*Por Bem*', that of Dom João I. He suggested this decoration to satirise the chattering gossip of the court after he had been surprised by Queen Philippa surreptitiously embracing one of her ladies-in-waiting while presenting her with a rose: so the story goes. Note also the 16C Hispano-arab *azulejos*, the marble chimney-piece (from Almeirim, near Santarém), and the *contadores* or *bargaños*.

From here one passes through the central patio overlooked by *ajimece* windows, to enter the Manueline **Sala dos Cisnes**, with its fine doors and shutters, green and white *azulejos*, and magnificent polychrome roof panelled in octagons and adorned with the 27 gold-collared swans which gave the room its name. Also shown is the private **study of Dom Manuel I**, with its *azulejos*, and a tapestry displaying the armillary sphere, that king's device.

Those pressed for time are recommended to continue the circuit of the range by car via the palace of Seteais and the Quinta of Monserrate, although on a clear day the excursion up to the **Pena Palace** may be made, if only for its gardens and for the extensive views it commands, but these are often obscured by sea mists.

- The excursion to the Pena Palace may be made from the upper end of the main street of Sintra. For those without transport it is possible to walk up to the palace, but you should allow an hour to get there. Alternatively, take a taxi or horse-drawn carriage. There are guided tours of the palace between 10.00 and 13.00, 14.00 and 17.00, closed Monday.

From the upper end of the main street of Sintra, continue uphill, passing (right) the former Hotel Lawrence (Estalagem dos Cavaleiros), where Byron put up in 1809 and is said to have conceived *Childe Harold*, and perhaps that referred to some 50 years earlier as 'an English inn kept up by a society of English merchants'. Turning sharp left, the road zig-zags steeply up through the thickly-planted hillside, with its moss-covered rocks, to a ridge separating the Pena from the **Castelo dos Mouros**, or Moorish Castle, which rises boldly to the left. It is open daily, between 10.00 and 18.00 in summer, 17.00 in winter.

This castle, commanding fine views, and standing at 450m, is an imposing ruin of undoubtedly Moorish foundation, although its battlements were restored in the mid 19C. The remains of Moors and Christians slain in 1147 when the fortress was taken by Afonso Henriques were unearthed during restorations, and reburied. From here a steep path descends directly to Sintra via the Trinidad convent and Gothic Santa Maria.

The road continues the ascent towards the main entrance to the **CASTELO DA PENA**, built on the site of an Hieronymite monastery founded by Dom Manuel I in 1509, which was certainly superbly placed and provides splendid views. Unfortunately, the picturesque position of this eyrie prompted Ferdinand of Saxe-Coburg-Gotha (consort of Maria II and a cousin of Prince Albert) to commission a certain Baron von Eschwege (1777–1855) to design a suitably 'Romantic' or 'Gothick' baronial castle amongst its dank and horrid crags. This pile, begun c 1840, is among the most extraordinary architectural confections imaginable, and should be seen to be believed.

It is approached by passing over a drawbridge and through a tunnel. From a small cloister of the original monastery, the **chapel** may be visited, containing an alabaster altarpiece carved by Chanterène for Dom João III in 1532, and a Nottingham alabaster of the Crucifixion. The *azulejos* date from c 1620; the vaulting is Manueline. From here one is escorted through a series of rooms whose only interest is that they are preserved in almost the exact condition in which they were left by the royal family on 4 October 1910, before their flight to Mafra and Ericeira, and thus remain a monument to their taste.

To the south-west is a peak crowned with a statue of Von Eschwege in armour, to the left of which is the Cruz Alta, the highest point in the Serra de Sintra (529m). Further to the west is the Feteira da Condesa, a fern garden above which is a rustic cottage surrounded by rhododendrons, erected by Ferdinand for the Condessa d'Edla (a German singer named Haensler, who was his mistress after the death of Maria II in 1853). Perhaps the best way to get an idea of the surprising mixture of temperate and sub-tropical vegetation characteristic of the park and of Sintra itself, is to descend through the Jardim das Camélias to the Fonte dos Passarinhos, a tiled Moorish pavilion, from which walkers may climb down to regain the main road. Regrettably, the gardens have been allowed to run wild.

Motorists descending from the Pena Palace may follow a number of routes:

**A**. The first right-hand turning leads down steeply to the village of **São Pedro** towards Ramalhão (see p 142), there forking right for **Linhó**, on the direct road to Estoril, 11km south, or Cascais, to the south-west (passing a monument to the Arab poet Ibn Muqana, born at Alcabideche c 1042). From Linhó an attractive road leads to Malveira (see below), skirting the lower slopes of the range, shortly passing (left) the former Hieronymite monastery of **Penha Longa**, founded by Dom João I in 1355, but rebuilt in the mid 16C, with a charming cloister and garden-chapel. In 1879 it was used as a farm; and in 1988 acquired by a Japanese corporation, who have turned the place, now the Quinta da Penha Longa, into a luxury golf-hotel complex.

**B**. The first left-hand turning on descending from the Pena leads round the south side of the higher slopes of the massif, dominated by the peak of Peninha (490m), after 4km passing a turning (right) to the **Convento dos Capuchos** (open daily summer 10.00–18.00, winter 10.00–17.00). This was founded in 1560 by Alvaro de Castro, and long known to the English—many of whom visited its hermits (according to Baretti, who did so in 1760)—as the 'Cork Convent', from the slabs of cork which line the damp walls of the rock-cut atrium; the 12 cells are merely cavities cut into the rock. At a lower level is the cavern in which the 95-year-old hermit Honorius died in 1596 after 36 years as a recluse. The Colares road (see below) is met 4km further west.

**C.** On regaining the village of Sintra near the Hotel Lawrence, turn left onto the narrow Estrada Velha de Colares (N375), skirting the north flank of the range, and passing several *quintas*; firstly the **\*Palace of Seteais** (seven sighs)—now a luxury hotel—with its grandiose entrance arch (c 1802). The main building was virtually completed by 1787 for Daniel Gildemeester *père*, the Dutch Consul in Lisbon, and a diamond merchant. His son, also consul, sold it a decade later to the 5th Marquês de Marialva. It was long supposed to have been the scene of the signature of the reprehensible 'Convention of Cintra' (30 August 1808), by which General Hew Dalrymple allowed Géneral Junot and some 24,000 French troops, recently defeated at Vimeiro (cf.), to evacuate Portugal, even providing transport to La Rochelle in British ships, and allowing them to carry off most of their spoil. The document, although despatched from Sintra, was actually signed in Lisbon, but the name has been thus associated with the Convention since the publication of Byron's vitriolic lines in *Childe Harold* (I, 24–26).

Further along on the same side is the *Quinta* of *Penha Verde*, where João de Castro (1500–48), viceroy of India, retired in 1542 and died in comparative poverty. In the garden here he planted the first orange-trees in Europe.

After c 2km the entrance to the **Quinta de Monserrate** is reached, built by James Knowles for Sir Francis Cook (Visconde de Monserrate since 1870). Opening times are 10.00 to 18.00 in summer and to 17.00 in winter, every day. It is famous for its **\*gardens**, covering 30 hectares, laid out in the 1850s by William Stockdale, the artist, with the advice of William Nevill from Kew. The collection of exotic plants, trees, and shrubs, is possibly unparalleled in Europe.

The tree-ferns and the sub-tropical garden at the foot of the hill are remarkable, and the eucalyptus trees are the descendants of the first of their kind brought to Portugal, where they are now ubiquitous. There are some 25 species of palm, and some huge conifers, among a variety of other trees, and a Bog Garden, most of which can be seen by following the signs. Slowly, starting a decade ago, the gardens are being restored to their former splendour, since 1994 being taken in hand by the Instituto da Conservação da Natureza.

The *quinta* itself takes its name from the vanished chapel of N.S. de Montserrat, and once belonged to Gerard de Visme, a wealthy English merchant. William Hickey, who visited it in 1782, was entertained by De Visme 'in a manner never surpassed and seldom equalled'. It was described by Beckford, who rented it in 1794 (the year he made his excursion to Alcobaça and Batalha) as 'a beautiful Claude-like place, surrounded by a most enchanting country'. Lady Craven, three years previously, had remarked on its glorious situation, even if it was 'a Vile Planned house'—for De Visme was 'Gothicizing' it. Beckford may well have continued to dabble in 'improving' the villa, and landscaping. Nevertheless, to quote Rose Macaulay: 'Both at least are absolved from the barbarous orientalism of the Monserrate of today, constructed in a Moorish delirium by the Visconde Cook of 1856'. The contents of the house were auctioned off in 1948, and the property sold to the State. There is also a project to restore the house, the structure having been long in a sorry state of abandon.

The road goes on past several other *quintas* before descending through the village of **Colares**, famous for its red wine: 'a sort of half-way excellence between port and claret' to Southey's taste. The valley here was already (in 1760) being compared to the Garden of Eden, according to Baretti. Both here and in nearby **Penedo** the parish churches contain *azulejos* of interest.

From Colares a road leads north-west to reach the coast shortly at **Praia das Maçãs**, beyond which is the former fishing-village of **Azenhas do Mar**, while inland, at **Janas**, is the curious circular 16C church of São Mamede.

3.5km beyond this turning, the road from the Cork Convent (see above) is met, and after another 3km, a turning leads towards the Atlantic, dominated by the precipitous Cabo da Roca, the western extremity of continental Europe—Ireland is further west—a tall slender mass of granite, often misnamed the 'Rock of Lisbon' by English mariners. The main road now descends to **Malveira**, where one may either drive direct to Cascais, 7km south, or, by turning right prior to the village, follow the coastal road via the beach of **Guincho** and the so-called 'Bóca do Inferno' (where the sea roars at high tide when entering a cavern in the cliff). On entering Cascais from here, the Castro Guimarães museum is passed to the left, and then the old Citadel (right), in which Dom Luís died in 1889.

**CASCAIS** (18,962 inhabitants), attractively sited among pines and eucalyptus woods, has grown considerably since 1870, when first patronised by the Court. It is now both a fashionable dormitory suburb of Lisbon and a summer resort at the terminus of the railway from the Cais do Sodré station, Lisbon (frequent trains taking half an hour). It has few attractions in itself, apart from the church of N.S. da Assunção, which contains a series of paintings by Josefa de Óbidos.

■ The **Tourist Office** is at 25 Alameda Combatentes da Grande Guerra.

### History

An old seaport, Cascais was the birthplace of Afonso Sanches, the pilot who in 1486 was driven westwards by a tempest to an unknown land, and contriving to return to Madeira, was there entertained by Columbus (cf. Cuba). The town was sacked in 1580 by the Duke of Alba, when advancing on Lisbon to enforce the Spanish claim to the throne of Portugal; and in May 1589 (after the Spanish Armada's failure) by a retaliatory expedition from England commanded by Drake, who landed there in an unsuccessful attempt to sack the capital.

Cascais now merges with **Monte Estoril** and **ESTORIL** itself, the latter with a casino, and both with luxurious villas—the residences in recent decades of miscellaneous monarchs and pretenders in exile, among them Carol of Romania, Umberto of Savoy, and Juan de Borbon of Spain. The **Tourist Office** is in the Arcadas do Parque.

The area has long been popular with retired or invalid Britons, who have congregated on this Portuguese 'Costa do Sol', with an equability of climate unrivalled in Europe, and luxuriant sub-tropical vegetation. Aubrey Fitz Gerald Bell (1881–1950), the author of many books on Portugal, first settled here in 1911.

The coast road (N6), running parallel to the railway, skirts several minor resorts, later passing the dismantled 16C Fort of São Julião da Barra, a political prison during the Miguelite wars, and containing impressive vaulted cisterns, opposite which is the Fort of São Lourenço or Torre do Bugio, marking the sand bar at the mouth of the Tagus.

**Carcavelos**, on the inland road, is reputed for its wine; while further east, at **Oeiras** (10,277 inhabitants), once a village of ancient origin, is a Baroque church

(1744) and the *quinta* built for Pombal by Carlos Mardel, its gardens decorated with sculpture by Silvestre de Faria Lobo and Joaquim Machado de Castro, and preserving a charming fishing pavilion.

Before reaching the present approach to the auto-estrada (N7; avoiding the built-up riverside suburbs west of Lisbon), **Caxias**, with a former royal residence among 18C gardens, is skirted; and c 1km inland, the dependencies of one of the two Carthusian monasteries in Portugal (the other being near Évora), founded in 1595 by Simoa Godinho, a negress. It was here that the artist Domingos António de Sequeira (1768–1837) was a novice during the years 1798–1802.

In the suburb of **Dáfundo** is the Vasco da Gama Aquarium (founded 1898); while a short distance inland is the well-designed stone-built National Sports Stadium (1944).

Shortly beyond, with a distant view of the Ponte 25 de Abril spanning the Tagus, the Torre de Belém is passed on the right; see Rte 1E.

# 3 · Lisbon to Queluz and Mafra

*Total distance, 40km (25 miles).*
*For an alternative direct road to Mafra, see Rte 18A.*

## QUELUZ

Follow Rte 2 as far as the right-hand fork for the former royal palace at Queluz (42,885 inhab.), now an unattractive dormitory-suburb of Lisbon.

■ Queluz can be visited by **train** from the Rossio station in Lisbon. The **Tourist Office** is in the Palácio Nacional de Queluz.

The \***PALACE**, one of the more remarkable monuments of Rococo architecture in the vicinity of the capital—indeed, in Portugal—was built for the Infante Dom Pedro (1717–86) in 1747–52 by Mateus Vicente de Oliveira (1706–86). Opening times are 10.00–13.00 and 14.00–17.00, except *Tues* and holidays.

It is an irregularly planned two-storey edifice of *pedra lioz* and rose stucco, entered from a courtyard emulating in miniature that at Versailles, in which stands a Neo-classical statue of Maria I (1797) surrounded by Four Continents, by F.S. Fabri and João José de Aguiar (1769–1841).

In view of the too recent experience of earthquake, only single storey extensions were started in 1758 by Jean-Baptiste Robillon (or Robillion; who at one time had worked with Thomas Germain, the Parisian silversmith), who also laid out the gardens just prior to Dom Pedro's marriage to his niece, the future Dona Maria I. Géneral Junot stayed here briefly in 1808 until obliged by Wellington to decamp, naturally removing all that was valuable.

The north wing incorporates the former kitchens and a luxurious restaurant known as the **Cozinha Velha**. Opposite the south wing are the restored royal chapel (open for mass on Sundays), decorated by Silvestre de Faria Lobo (1750–60); and the Pousada Dona Maria I.

The **interior** of the palace (guided tour) contains some imposing rooms, many preserving furniture showing English influence, among them the Sala do Trono (throne room), decorated by Antoine Collin and Silvestre de Faria Lobo (died 1769); a richly gilt oval Hall of Mirrors; the Music Room, containing an anonymous portrait of Maria I; the Sala dos Azulejos, containing a Mafra-like bird-cage, red lacquer screens from Macao, and childrens' furniture; the Sala dos Embaixadores (1757–62), damaged by fire in 1934; the council-room, with a fine hardwood floor; the mirrored Queen's dressing-room (1774–86); the circular King's bedroom (completed 1768), in which Dom Pedro IV was born and died (1798–1834), with a series of scenes by Manuel da Costa depicting the exploits of Don Quixote; and the coffered Sala das Merendas, or breakfast-room, with charming Goyaesque picnic scenes.

The heavily-swagged west front overlooks the *gardens, with their formal parterres, in which Beckford ran a race with one of the maids of honour to Carlota Joaquina in 1796. They are particularly attractive, with box hedges, urns and topiary, cypress avenue, fountains, colonnades and steps, lead statuary by John Cheere, shipped out from London (regrettably burnished), and *azulejos*, some of maritime scenes.

Follow the N117 to the north through **Belas** (where the Infante Dom Manuel held court after 1735 on his return from 20 years of self-imposed exile in Austria) to traverse undulating country before meeting the N9 from Sintra at **Pero-Pineiro**, with its quarries of pink marble, seen in so many Portuguese churches. After descending to **Cheleiros**, in a deep valley with a small bridge (restored) probably of Roman origin, the road makes a circle to the east, and after skirting part of the stone wall of the park, bears right, with the immense bulk of the convent-palace of Mafra rearing up ahead.

## MAFRA

The small town of Mafra—entirely dwarfed by the convent, but which once surrounded the vanished castle—is of little interest except for the **Casa de Brasão**, and the church of **Santo André** (c 1400), containing the tomb of Diogo de Sousa and his wife. Pedro Julião, better known as Pedro Hispano, was priest here before his election to the papacy in 1276 as John XXI. A small local museum may be visited.

■ The Tourist Office is in Av. 25 de Abril.

The *CONVENT DE MAFRA, impressive by its sheer size, has little similarity in plan with the Escorial (near Madrid), with which it has been occasionally compared. Its main west front, 220m long, is some 12m longer than the Escorial, but the whole is slightly smaller in area. The extremities of the main façade are terminated by square corner pavilions (which Beckford described as 'pagodas') crowned by squat onion-domes and lit by a series of oval windows. They have certain similarities with the towers of the royal palace in Lisbon destroyed in 1755. The long, flat, indeed ponderous, façade between the two pavilions is relieved by tall twin steeples (68m high) and an Italianate portico, while over the crossing is a Baroque dome. The church, lateral pavilions, and aperture frames, are of the local limestone, which, exposed to Atlantic storms—the sea is only 11km distant—has been darkened by lichen. The rest of the building is mainly of brick, plastered over. It is open from 10.00 to 13.00 and 14.00 to 17.00; closed *Tues* and holidays.

### History

The present convent was erected by Dom João V, who in 1708 had married Maria-Ana of Austria. Although their first child, Maria Barbara, later to become queen of Spain, was born in 1711, the anxious father had meanwhile taken a vow that on the birth of a male heir to the throne he would found a church and convent to replace the Capuchin friary at Mafra. But Pedro, born in 1712, survived only two years; and it was not until 1714 that José, Dom João's actual successor, was born 1714.

Work began in 1717, and the design entrusted to Johann Friedrich Ludwig (Ludovice; Ratisbon 1670–1752), a German trained in Augsburg and Rome, who had come to work for the Jesuits in Lisbon. He was assisted by an Italian, Carlo Battista Garbo (a Milanese settled in Portugal since c 1698, who died in 1724). Senior to Garbo were the architect-engineers who worked immediately under Ludovice, namely his son Antonio Ludovice, Custodio Vieira, and Manoel da Maia. The original scheme was gradually enlarged, and absolutely regardless of expense, some 15–20,000 labourers and craftsmen being employed on the erection and decoration of the edifice, rising in the peak years 1729 and 1730 to 45,000, while a special hospital for their care, and a military force of c 7000 for their control (when not assisting with the actual construction), were established.

The church was consecrated in 1730, and by 1735 the building was completed—large enough to house not 13 (as had originally been intended), but 280 friars and half as many novices in addition. The cost has been variously estimated: it was certainly sufficient to hasten the financial ruin of the country in spite of the riches of Brazil flooding in.

Within 73 years Géneral Junot was in occupation; to be followed soon after by seven British regiments (all at once), and here in November 1810 Wellington gave a dinner for 200 and a dance on the occasion of Marshal Beresford being invested as a Knight of the Bath. In 1827 Lord Porchester found Sir Edward Blakeney and a British expeditionary force quartered here. Since the dissolution of the monasteries—by 1835 Borrow found it 'abandoned to two or three menials'—it has been intermittently used as a military school: indeed half the building is again in military hands. Dom Manuel II and his suite passed their last night in Portugal here: see Ericeira, below.

The *church is remarkable for its excellent proportions and comparatively sober ornament, the main decorative scheme consisting in the skilful use of red, black, blue, and yellow marbles, among which the rose-coloured Pero-Pinheiro is easily identified. Only the statues of saints in the vestibule, the imported work of Italian sculptors, are of Carrara marble. Among sculptors working in the church were Claudio de Laprada (Claude de Laprade, of Avignon; 1682–1738) and, later, the Italian Alessandro Giusti (1715–99), who in 1753 commenced the replacement of the painted altarpieces, which had already deteriorated in the damp coastal climate. Beckford was impressed by the carving of the capitals and *dessus des portes* decorations. Note the cases of the six organs, which were not completed until c 1807.

The guided tour of the **monastery-palace** takes the visitor along an interminable series of galleries with their well-polished hardwood floors, and up numerous flights of steps. The circuit includes the *hospital, infirmary, and hospital kitchens; collections of models for the sculptures, and relics; the audience chamber, with its *tromp l'oeil* panelling; the principal corridor along the west front, providing a good plunging view of the church from the royal oratory; and a collection of incunables and illuminated books of hours. The 'palatial' apartments are of slighter interest.

One of the finest rooms is the *library, a well lit Baroque hall, 88m long, in the central wing (behind the church apse), and containing some 40,000 volumes.

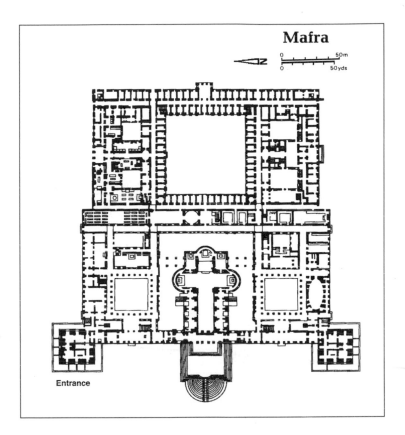

# Mafra

0 _____ 50m
0 _____ 50yds

**Entrance**

However, in opulence of decoration it hardly compares with the abbatial libraries of Austria. Southey reported that the friar who accompanied him suggested that 'it would be an excellent room, to eat and drink in'; while when Byron was visiting the monastery in 1809 (an example of 'magnificence without elegance' in his opinion), the monks asked him 'if the *English* had any *books* in their country?'.

A visit may also be paid to the **towers** and dome, the former containing over 50 bells each, including carillons cast at Malines, near Brussels, in 1730. It is said that when the Flemish bell-founders expressed a doubt as to Dom João's ability to pay their price, the king reacted by sending double the required amount, and in advance. One is shown the clock mechanism, tools and machines used in the construction of the immense building, together with a fine balance of 1697.

The original kitchens and refectory are unfortunately still in military hands, and cannot be visited.

Those wishing to continue north from Mafra to Torres Vedras, may rejoin the N8 to the north-east: see Rte 18A.

It was from **Ericeira**, some 12km north-west, that in October 1910 the king and queen-mother embarked on the royal yacht *Dona Amélia* (cf. Museu da Marinha, Belém) on their flight from Portugal, first to Gibraltar, later being escorted to England. Dom Manuel II, the 'Unfortunate', settled at Twickenham, devoting himself to his library (cf. Vila Viçosa), and died in 1932.

What was then a small fishing village with a hexagonal hermitage (São Sebastião), is no longer of any interest, for the coast has now been overwhelmed by villa development.

The coast road leading south from Ericeira to Sintra, skirts **Odrinhas**, where remains of a Roman villa below the chapel of São Miguel, and an archaeological museum displaying a good mosaic, may be visited; while in the vicinity are several menhirs. For Sintra, see Rte 2.

# 4 · Lisbon to Setúbal: the Serra da Arrábida

*From Lisbon to Setúbal is c 46km on the A2 motorway.*

The south bank of the Tagus estuary, known as the Outra Banda, is not now of great beauty (and since 1959 dominated by an offensive monument of Christ), but it commands magnificent *views of Lisbon. For the Ponte 25 do Abril itself, see Rte 1E.

On the cliff to the west are the buildings of the Lazareto, or quarantine station, where until a century ago many passengers arriving by ship were first obliged to spend several days. **Trafaria** (some 5km west of the bridge), at that time a small fishing village of rush-roofed huts, was burnt to the ground in January 1777 on Pombal's orders, for harbouring those resisting press-gangs, an unnecessarily Draconian act which was later held against him. Even decades later, when officers of the law visited the spot (which they seldom did, except perhaps in search of some delinquent) they were accompanied by a military force. To the south-west are the beaches of the **Costa da Caparica**. A rebuilt mid 16C Capuchin friary is conspicuous.

To the east of the motorway is industrial **Almada** (22,550 inhabitants), with the Convent of São Paulo, founded in 1568. Further east are the Lisnave shipyards, etc. on the many-armed south bank of the estuary, beyond which is **Barreiro** (47,901 inhabitants), with its railway terminus adjoining the quay, from which ferries ply to the Terreiro do Paço station in Lisbon.

The motorway traverses pine forests, skirting **Coina** (where in 1719 John Beare founded the first mirror factory in Portugal) and provides intermittent views ahead of the castle-crowned hill of Palmela, which it is convenient to approach by turning off at c 35km.

**Palmela** (5553 inhabitants), with the exception of the 18C *azulejos* in São Pedro, is of little interest although finely sited, with views south from the esplanade and from the commanding height of the castle itself.

This was taken from the Moors in the mid 12C, and from 1288 was the head-quarters of the Portuguese Order of São Tiago, but it was seriously damaged in the 1755 earthquake, and abandoned. In recent years it has been extensively restored to accommodate a luxurious *pousada*, and is a pleasant centre from which to explore the area. One church, on the site of a mosque, was destroyed in the earth-quake; the other (1443–82) contains the tomb of Jorge de Lencastre (died 1551), the last Grand Master of the Order, and son of Dom João II. A megalithic necropolis was discovered 3km to the west about a century ago.

## SETÚBAL

One may descend directly by the N252 to Setúbal (83,220 inhab.), a thriving commercial and fishing-port and industrial centre, although no longer quite the 'terrestial Paradise' described by Hans Andersen, who visited it in 1834. Nevertheless, its animated older streets retain one or two buildings of interest, and its museum an important series of paintings. Long famous for the export of salt—obtained from the marshes of the Rio Sado, on the wide estuary of which it stands—and reputed for its sardines, rice, oranges, and muscatel grapes, Setúbal was once familiarly known to British sailors as 'St Ubes'. The extensive Setenave shipyards are close by.

■ The **Tourist Office** is on Rua do Corpo Santo. There is a ferry from Lisbon's Terreiro do Paço to Barreiro and **trains** from there to Setúbal.

### History

Setúbal takes its name from the Roman *oppidum* of Caetobriga, long believed to occupy the site of Tróia (cf.), on the far side of the estuary, but ceramics characteristic of Phoenician and Carthaginian settlements in Iberia have recently come to light on its site. In 1979 hoards of 4C coins were found in two amphorae here. The present town was founded in the 12C. Dom João II, who married Leonor de Lencastre here (1471), frequently favoured the town with his presence. Its medieval walls, of which little survives, were in the 17C superseded by a second line of defences, part of which is preserved to the west of the town. Setúbal suffered severely in the 'Lisbon' earthquake of 1755, and again in November 1858.

Its most famous natives were the opera singer Luisa Todi (1754–1833), and Manuel Maria de Barbosa du Bocage (1765–1805), the poet, a 'pale, limber, odd-looking young man' whose compositions apparently 'thrilled and agitated' Beckford in 1787.

A few minutes' walk north from a central point in the wide Av. de Luisa Todi, between the older centre and the river, brings one to the *\*Igreja de Jesus* and its adjacent museum. The hall-church, with its six thick spiralling cable-like breccia columns, and rope-like ribs of the apse—all to become characteristic of the Manueline style—was begun in 1494 by Diogo Boitac. A better view of the interior may be obtained from the shuttered grille of the *coro alto* (also containing a good Flemish primitive), entered from the *\*museum*, installed around the monastic cloister. Outstanding in the Sala dos Primitivos is the series of eight 16C paintings by the Master of Setúbal, among them the large Annunciation and the Calvary; and the Saints of Morocco; also notable are the anonymous 15–16C Flemish paintings of Santa Clara, Santa Inês and Santa Coleta, and an Ascension. The museum contains a good numismatic collection. It is open Tues–Fri 9.00–12.00 and 14.00–17.00; 9.00–11.00 and 15.00–17.00 at weekends; closed Mon and holidays.

A short walk to the south-east lies the Praça do Bocage, at the far corner of which is São Julião, with a Manueline north portal of 1513, and 18C *azulejos* within, depicting the life of the saint. From here one may explore the narrow streets of the old town, before regaining the Av. de Luisa Todi further east.

*The charming fifteenth century Quinta da Bacalhôa*

Here (at No. 181) is the small Museu Oceanográfico e de Pesca and, adjacent, an **Ethnographical Museum**, largely devoted to the fishing industry, with ship models (including working models of dredgers, etc., which the guardian enjoys setting awhir); also collections of agricultural implements and a section concerned with lace-making, spinning, etc.; and some naïve ex-voto paintings. It is open from 9.30–12.30 and 14.00–17.30; closed Mon and holidays.

A street almost opposite leads to the riverbank and to the point of embarkation for the regular Tróia ferry (approx. every 45 minutes) and hovercraft (when functioning): see below. Note that the car and passenger-only ferries embark from different points.

Immediately to the west of Setúbal rises the **Castelo de São Filipe**, attributed to Filippo Terzi (1590), and built by Philip II of Spain (I of Portugal) to cow the local inhabitants and as a defence against projected English attempts to make a landing in the vicinity. Converted to accommodate the *pousada* São Filipe, it commands a good view over the town, estuary, and across to the Tróia peninsula.

**Tróia** was formerly assumed to occupy the site of Caetobriga, possibly of Phoenician foundation, said to have been overwhelmed by a tidal wave in the 5C. The *ruins* opposite the marina, including tanks for salting fish, may be visited. Some important finds have been made since excavations began in 1850, but the area described half a century ago as 'now a wilderness of sand, gay with flowers in spring' is unfortunately again overwhelmed, this time by tall blocks of flats described as a 'Tourist Complex'.

For the excursion along the Arrábida ridge to Vila Nogueira de Azeitão, see below; but it may also be approached directly by the N10 from Setúbal, climbing up the north flank of the Serra da Arrábida, and descending past (right; hidden behind a thick hedge just before meeting the N379 from Palmela), the **\*Quinta da Bacalhôa** (for admission, apply to the caretaker during normal working hours).

This small palace was built in 1480 for the Infanta Brites (Beatriz), possibly—as suggested by Sacheverell Sitwell—by Sansovino, who spent six years in Portugal at about this time. The gardens were begun after 1528, when the property was acquired by the son of Afonso de Albuquerque (first viceroy of India). He built the pavilion with its three towers, where the *azulejo* depicting Susanna and the Elders (1565) is the earliest dated tile picture in Portugal. The palace was much neglected from 1650 until 1890, when inherited by the Conde de Mesquitella, and again from 1910 until 1936, when it was bought by a Mrs Herbert Scoville (née Zabriskie) from Connecticut, who brought some order to the garden, with its topiary hedges, water-tank, orchard, melon-domed towers, etc. Its boxwood parterre has been restored; and it is hoped that it will not be allowed to deteriorate again. The garden may be visited between 13.00–17.00, except Sun and holidays.

At adjacent **Vila Fresca de Azeitão**, just to the west, is the 16C *Quinta das Torres* (transformed into a hotel and restaurant), its small formal garden with *azulejo* panels. The church also contains early *azulejos*.

At **Vila Nogueira de Azeitão**, an attractive village some 2km further west, is the Távora Palace, its coat of arms erased by Pombal after the arrest here of the then Duque de Aveiro for his alleged complicity in the plot against Dom José in 1758.

For the road on to Cabo Espichel, and/or back to Setúbal over the Arrábida range, see below. Those returning to Lisbon may continue north on the N10.

# Setúbal to Vila Nogueira via the Serra da Arrábida

25km. There are two alternative routes, the lower road skirting the coast via **Portinho da Arrábida** being slightly shorter, but not so impressive. It first passes the old fort of Albarquel, and the 14C tower of Outão. The stalactite cave of Lapa de Santa Margarida may be visited.

The upper road turns right after 4.5km past a cement works, and climbs steeply towards the summit of the limestone ridge (which rises to 500m at the Formosinho), on which a number of belvederes have been built, providing a distant panorama of Lisbon. The road descends past (left) the **Convent of Arrábida** (founded 1542), a beautifully sited group of buildings, with little hermitages and chapels scattered over the steep seaward slope.

The road then descends, bearing away to the north, and after meeting the lower road, reaches a junction 2km west of Vila Nogueira: see above.

The excursion may be continued to Cabo Espichel, c 20km south-west, by turning left onto the N379, passing north of **Calhariz**, where the 17C palace of the Palmela family, contains late 17C *azulejos*. At **Santana**, where the N378 leads 21km north to meet the motorway to Lisbon, the left-hand turning descends steeply to **Sesimbra** (7320 inhabitants), a fishing-port and resort, defended by the 17C fort of São Teodósio, among others. The 15C Misericórdia contains a painting attributed to Gregório Lopes (1531/40); the Igreja Matriz is 16C.

A minor road leads south-west just beyond Santana to the restored castle of Sesimbra, of Moorish origin, providing a wide view, and preserving a church rebuilt in 1721. Here also is a small archaeological collection.

On regaining the main road, continue west to approach the pilgrimage church of N.S. do Cabo (1701), in a semi-derelict condition, at the end of a long forecourt flanked by ranges of equally derelict pilgrim accommodation built over arcades. There is a project to convert it into a *pousada*. Beyond lies **Cabo Espichel**, the Roman Promontorium Barbaricum, with its lighthouse, providing plunging views of the Atlantic far below, of the coast below the Serra da Sintra to the north-west, and south-east towards Sines.

# 5 · (Badajoz) Elvas to Lisbon

## A. Via Estremoz

*Total distance, 200km (124 miles). N4. 39km Estremoz—43km Arraiolos—25km Montemor-o-Novo—23km Vendas Novas—13km Pegões crossroads—N10. 12km Marateca junction—A2. 45km Lisbon.*

*It is planned to improve this main route into Portugal by building a dual carriageway from Badajoz to meet the new extension of the motorway north of Setúbal near the Marateca crossroads. This will at first run roughly parallel to the road described, but will bear south-west from Estremoz to veer west some distance north of Évora.*

*The construction by 1998 of a new bridge and viaduct across the Tagus from a point north of Montijo to meet the A1 at Sacavém, immediately north-east of Lisbon, will provide an alternative direct approach to the capital.*

*For Badajoz, see Blue Guide Spain, 6th ed.*

Those wishing to make the **excursion** to the former Portuguese fortress of **Olivenza**, 25km south-west of Badajoz, may take the C436 there, and back. It was occupied by the Spanish in 1801, but despite provision in the 1814 Treaty of Paris for its return to Portugal, this was never implemented. Some of its architecture is distinctly Manueline. The castle dates from 1306. The Misericórdia contains good *azulejos* of 1723; and La Magdalena, some impressive spiral pillars. Sta María is late 16C. The former Hospital de la Caridad, founded in 1501, and the late 15C portal of the Municipal Libarary, are also of some interest.

Having (preferably) bypassed Badajoz, the frontier is reached shortly after crossing the Guadiana (in the Roman period called Anas, later arabised as Wadi-anas), and is formed by its tributary, the Caia, beyond which the road ascends gently, with a view ahead of Elvas and its hill-top forts on the approach.

### ELVAS

Elvas (13,190 inhabitants; *Pousada de Santa Luzia*), strategically sited, was once one of the strongest fortresses in Portugal, and still retains its circuit of walls. A characteristic frontier town, commanding a distant view of modern Badajoz across the border, it would provide a pleasant introduction to visitors to Portugal, if they did not have to run the gauntlet of two narrow streets leading to its centre, which are entirely devoted to selling trash to trippers. It is reputed for its olive oil, plums, and striped blankets.

■ The **Tourist Office** is in the Praça da República. Infrequent **trains** to Lisbon are not direct.

#### History

Elvas was finally recaptured from the Moors in 1230, when a band of Portuguese knights found it abandoned. A bishopric was founded here in 1570 but was abolished in 1882. In June 1580 Elvas gave way to the invading Spanish troops after the death of Henrique, the Cardinal-King, and it was here that Philip II first briefly established his court; but in 1644, under the Count of Alegrete, it successfully resisted a retaliatory Spanish attack, and by 1644 the Portuguese were actually threatening their late rulers. In 1658 they routed another Spanish incursion. Elvas also saw some fighting during

*A sixteenth-century pelourinho at Elvas*

confused campaigning early in the War of the Succession (1705). It was an important base of operations, and hospital, during the Peninsular War, particularly before the sieges of Badajoz in 1811 and 1812.

The composer Manuel Coelho Rodrigues (c 1555–c 1635), was born here; Maj.-Gen. Daniel Hoghton (1770–1811), killed at Albuera, was buried here (monument in St Paul's Cathedral, London).

A convenient entrance to the town from almost opposite the *pousada* is the **Porta de Olivença** (1685) in its Vaubanesque fortifications, from which the Rua de Olivença ascends directly to the Praça da República. Halfway along this street (known to have been so-called since 1435) a right-hand turning leads shortly to the conventual church of São Salvador (17C), adjacent to which, its entrance below a characteristic porch covered by a cupola of *azulejos* (1715), are the library and an apology for a museum. An alley runs downhill from here to **São Domingos** (13C), with a good Gothic apse.

At the upper end of the Praça de República, with the Town Hall (Câmara Municipal), and Tourist Office, stands the former **cathedral** (1517–37), by Francisco de Arruda, but much altered since, preserving part of a 13C tower. The nave and sacristy contain early 17C *azulejos*, and the carved and gilded rococo organ-loft was completed in 1777. (The cathedral is frequently closed.)

*A section of the Aqueduto da Amoreira*

Behind, to the right, is the curious octagonal church of the **\*Freiras de São Domingos** (or N.S. da Consolação; 1543–57), built on the plan of a Templars' church on this site destroyed in 1540. It contains beautiful mid 17C *azulejos*, and its vaulted lantern is supported by elegant marble pillars, with gilt and polychrome carving.

Uphill to the right is a *pelourinho*, and an ancient archway, beyond which, adjacent to the Moorish castle, its Torre de Menagem, commanding an extensive view, added in 1488, is the oldest part of the town. By following alleys skirting the walls one may descend south-east to São Francisco (1761) and São Pedro (1227, but much altered), from there working one's way back to the centre.

The arcaded Rua da Cadeia, below the central square, overlooked by a medieval tower, leads down towards the Porta de São Vicente and the marble Misericórdia fountain (by Diogo Marques; 1622).

The most imposing individual monument of Elvas is the **\*Aqueduto da Amoreira** (1498–1622), strengthened by huge cylindrical buttresses, which, bringing water from a distance of c 7km, rises just west of the town. There is a good view of the aqueduct from the Lisbon road.

The road leading through the aqueduct circles to the north, providing a view of the fortifications. Also to the north is the outlying **Forte N.S. da Graça** (1763–92), its terrace commanding a wide view. It is also known as the Forte de Lippe after its designer, Count William (Wilhelm von) Schaumburg Lippe-Bückeburg (1724–77), an English-born German, who did much to reorganise the Portuguese army in the early 1760s. Elvas is overlooked from the east by the older Forte de Santa Luzia (1641–87).

For the roads to Portalegre and Castelo Branco, and to Abrantes, see Rtes 14 and 15 respectively; and for Vila Viçosa and Évora, Rte 5B.

## To Alandroal and back via Vila Viçosa

34km. The N373 leads south-west to (18km) the village of **Juromenha**, once an important frontier station and probably of Roman foundation, on a height overlooking the sluggish Guadiana. It was captured briefly from the Moors by Geraldo

Sem-Pavor in 1166, but not definitively until 1230. It capitulated to Don Juan of Austria after a short siege in 1662. The river here was crossed by William Beresford's troops on a bridge in April 1812, prior to the siege of Badajoz. The deserted ruins of its castle (rebuilt 1312), severely damaged by an explosion in 1659, provide a good *view towards Olivenza; see above.

The road continues south-west to (16km) **Alandroal**, with remains of a large late 13C castle, and a charming fountain, from which the N255 leads south via (10km) **Terena**, also with a castle and fortified church (14C), to (27km) Reguengos-de-Monsaras: see Rte 7. Redondo, on the road to Évora, lies 12km south-west; see Rte 5B. Turning north from Alandroal, after 12km **Vila Viçosa** is reached, 5km beyond which, at Borba, the N4 is regained 30km west of Elvas. For both places, see Rte 5B.

---

Driving west from Elvas through attractive rolling country and with good retrospective views, the road bypasses **Vila Boim**, later passing (right) a lake, and skirting the *tapada* or estate of Vila Viçosa, for which, and for Borba, see Rte 5B.

### ESTREMOZ

Fortified Estremoz (6746 inhabitants), an attractive, well-sited garrison town, important enough to have been granted a *foral* in 1258, is seen some distance ahead. It is reputed for its earthenware and white marble, the latter featuring in numerous houses.

The main feature of the lower town is the Rossio or Praça Marquês do Pombal, the large central square, where there is a market on Saturday mornings.

■ The **Tourist Offices** are at 26 Largo da República.

Facing the Rossio are the **convents**, one of 1698, now the Town Hall; the other, formerly that of the Order of Malta, with two cloisters and a church of c 1540, which since 1880 has been the Misericórdia, preserves *azulejos*. Adjacent is a small regional handicraft museum. Close by is the Largo General Graça, with São Francisco (founded in the 13C, and now in military occupation), but one may enter the Senhor dos Passos chapel, with a Manueline window. Near is the 17C Tocha Palace, containing contemporary *azulejos*.

A street ascends to the upper town clustering within the walls erected by Dom Afonso VI to the 13C *Torre de Menagem** (a keep 27m high, and similar to that at Beja), abutted by part of the palace, severely damaged by an explosion in 1698, but rebuilt by João V. It now accommodates the luxuriously appointed *pousada* da Rainha Isabel. Adjacent is the stark façade of Santa Maria do Castelo (commenced 1559, by Afonso Alvares), replacing part of a Gothic church built on the site of a mosque. Beside it is a relic of the earlier palace, with its Gothic arcade, in which Isabel, the 'Rainha Santa', wife of Dom Dinis, died in 1336, and where their grandson died in 1367. In 1380 the abortive Anglo-Portuguese alliances of 1372 and 1373 were formally renewed after secret negotiations here between Don Fernando and Richard II.

Opposite, in the old Hospício de Caridade, is the Municipal **Museum** of Archaeology and Ethnography, containing collections of popular painted ceramic figures (*bonecos de Estremoz*), stelae, furniture, carved and gilt woodwork, a reconstructed kitchen, firearms, a plan of the town in 1758, etc. It is open 10.00–12.00 and 14.00–18.00; closed Mon and holidays.

For routes from Estremoz to Portalegre, and via Sousel to Crato, see those included in Rte 16, in reverse.

## Estremoz to Évora

46km south-west. Fork left onto the N18 not far west of Estremoz, which shortly climbs into the wooded Serra de Ossa and to (11km) **Évoramonte**, a village retaining a recently restored *castle of 1306 damaged in the earthquake of 1531, with a 16C keep, imposing cylindrical towers and decorative stone knots, and containing Manueline piers in each of its three storeys. The roof provides extensive views. Its name is famous for the Convention signed here in May 1834 by which Dom Miguel ostensibly abandoned all claim to the throne. Although he sailed from the country, on reaching Genoa he denounced the agreement as being signed under duress, but he no longer played any active part in peninsular politics. The road then descends into the rolling plain of the Alentejo, after 28km entering Évora: see Rte 6.

The main road under construction will run south-west likewise before veering west towards Montemor-o-Nova before reaching Évora.

---

An alternative, longer but attractive, road is that via Redondo (See Rte 5B). This, the N381, leading due south from Estremoz and climbing over the Serra de Ossa, on its descent passes (left) the former **Convento de São Paulo**, now a luxurious hotel. Among notable features of the convent, founded in 1376 and in the late 17C–early 18C much enlarged and baroquised, are two Baroque fountains, and a superb collection of *azulejos* attributed to Oliveira Bernardes flanking its main stairs, corridors, etc.

---

The N4 leads due west from Estremoz, after 24km bypassing (right) **Vimieiro** (not to be confused with Vimeiro, north-west of Torres Vedras).

---

From here the N251 diverges north-west to (18km) **Pavia**, said to have been colonised by Italians under Roberto de Pavia after its reconquest in the 13C. Its church has cylindrical buttresses similar to that of São Bras at Évora, while the minute 16C chapel of São Dinis in part envelopes a megalithic tomb. **Mora** lies 16km beyond, to the south of which, 3km from **Brotas**, is the imposing Torre das Aguias.

---

High-lying **Arraiolos**, bypassed, is a very ancient town dominated by a ruined castle (early 14C; views). It was once famous for its blue and red embroidered carpets, many late 18C examples of which embellish the walls of Portuguese museums. The 16C **Convento dos Lóios**, beautifully sited in a valley to the north-east, is in the process of being converted to house a *pousada* (which may be completed by the time of publication). The *azulejos* of 1700 in its church, the work of Gabriel del Barco y Minusca, depicting the life of San Lorenzo Giustiniani, are remarkable.

About 3km south-east, some distance to the left off the Évora road, is the **Solar da Sempre Noiva** (c 1500), the former country-house of Archbishop Afonso de Portugal, retaining deteriorated relics of Manueline *ajimece* windows.

At **Montemór-o-Novo** (6758 inhabitants), the old centre of which is bypassed, is a ruined Moorish castle rebuilt in the late 13C). It was the birthplace of St John of God (Juan de Díos, or de Robles; 1495–1550), of Jewish lineage, and the founder of the Order of Charity. He devoted his life to the care of captives, foundlings, and the sick, and died at Granada. The Inquisition was active here in 1623.

To the left of the N2 on approaching **São Geraldo** (c 12km due north), is the dolmen of Comeda.

Alcácer do Sal (see Rte 11) is 44km south-west of Montemór on the N253.

## Montémor-o-Novo to Santarém

85km. The N114 leads 85km north-west to Santarém (see latter part of Rte 16), traversing uninteresting country via (47km) **Coruche**, a large agricultural town on the Rio Sorraia, spanned by several bridges. It was rebuilt in 1181 after its destruction by the Almohads. A small Misericórdia preserves curious *azulejos*, some suggesting Oriental influence.

Another 31km brings one to **Almeirim** (10,038 inhabitants), once a favourite residence of the Avis dynasty from 1411, the remains of whose palace, the scene of several *cortes*, was demolished in 1889. The Cardinal-king Dom Henriques (1512–80) was born and died here. For Alpiaça, 7km north-east, see sub-route of Rte 16.

---

The N4 leads west across the lonely undulating plain of the Alentejo, with plantations of cork-trees and evergreen oaks extending on either side, sheltering an occasional isolated *monte* or farmstead of the region, before entering **Vendas Novas** (8481 inhabitants), an agricultural centre which grew up round a palace built in 1728 by Dom João V in one of his many fits of extravagance, merely to house the bridal cortège of the Infanta of Spain, Mariana Victoria, wife of Dom José.

A sandy region is now entered to approach the crossroads of **Pegões**—turn left there. The new main road will veer further south towards the Marateca junction to join that part already completed.

---

An alternative, but not particularly recommended route from here to Lisbon is that via Vila Franca de Xira, 45km north-west on the N10, where the Tagus is crossed: see Rte 18B. This was the main motor road from 1951, when the Maréchal Carmona bridge was inaugurated, until 1966, when the Ponte 25 de Abril, spanning the Tagus at Lisbon, was opened.

However, this is likely to be superseded with the completion in 1998 of the projected new bridge and viaduct extending across the wide estuary from a point between Montijo and Alcochete to Sacavém, immediately north of Lisbon and near its airport. **Montijo** (23,247 inhabitants), reputed for its oysters, was until 1930 known as Aldeia Galega, and it was from here that ferries formerly would ply to the capital. Its 15C and 17C Igreja Matriz contains *azulejo* panels. The much restored church at **Alcochete** preserves a Gothic rose-window, while paintings of 1586/88 by Diogo Teixeira may be seen in the church of the Misericórdia there, also said to contain a Virgin and Child attributed to Lucas de Leyden.

---

Bearing south-west through scattered pine woods, the motorway to Lisbon may be entered on reaching the Marateca road junction. From here the N5 turns south towards the Algarve (see Rtes 11 and 12), while the older main road leads west to skirt an arm of the Sado estuary to approach Setúbal, with the Arrábida range beyond, and dominated by the hill and castle of Palmela to the north-west, see Rte 4.

The motorway drives through a wooded area, bypassing the worst of extensive industrial and ship-building districts on the south bank of the Tagus estuary.

Although vehicles are prohibited from stopping on the Ponte 25 de Abril (see Rte 1E), it is worthwhile to make the crossing at a leisurely pace for the impressive *panorama of Lisbon ahead. (First study an up-to-date map, to make the requisite exit on the far bank—traffic flows fast once across the bridge.)

For Lisbon, see Rte 1.

# B.   Via Vila Viçosa and Évora

*Total distance, 211km (131 miles). N4. 29km Borba—N255. 5km Vila Viçosa—N254. 20km Redondo—34km Évora—N114. 30km Montemór-o-Novo—23km Vendas Novas—13km Pegões crossroad—N10. 12km Marateca junction—A2. 45km Lisboa.*

For the road to Borba, see Rte 5A.

**Borba**, a pleasant little white town, was twice occupied by the Spaniards in 1662/3. The place is noted for both its wine and its neighbouring quarries of white marble, which is ubiquitous.

It preserves an imposing fountain (das Bicas) of 1781, slight remains of its walls and 13C castle, while the only church of any interest is that of São Bartolomeu (late 16C). The large Renaissance cloister of the Convento das Servas no longer has its walls and central fountain plastered with 17C *azulejos*. The arcades have been bricked up, the fountain removed to embellish some *quinta*, and there is not a tile to be seen in the ruinous relic of a cloister, long put to commercial use: and all this happened, so confirmed the local priest, almost half a century ago.

A monument c 4km south-west commemorates the battle of **Montes Claros** (June 1665), in which the Count-Duke Frederick of Schomberg finally defeated the Spaniards under the Marquês de Caracena. Colonel Sheldon, a commander of the British contingent, which had a principal share in the battle, was killed.

## VILA VIÇOSA

By bearing south-east through the glistening marble quarries bristling with derricks, Vila Viçosa (5048 inhabitants) is shortly entered. It is an attractive town, dominated by its bastioned **castle**, built by Dom Dinis, and the original *solar* or seat of the ducal family of Braganza. For the first half of 1382 it was Edmund of Cambridge's HQ during the fecklessly led Anglo-Portuguese campaign of that year, in which Sir John de Southeray (a bastard of Edward III and Alice Ferrers) led a mutiny of English troops against Cambridge. The marquisate was bestowed on Fernando, the second duke, beheaded at Évora in 1470.

Adjacent to the castle (in which it is planned to install an archaeological museum) is the church of the **Conceição**, lined with 17–18C *azulejos*. To the south is the wide Praça da República, at its far end São Bartolomeu (1636–98). The main street leads off the north side of the square to approach the **Terreiro do Paço**, flanked by the huge and monotonous Classical façade of the Ducal Palace (see below), the Chagas convent of 1530 (in which lie the tombs of the Braganza wives), and **Santo Agostinho**, founded in 1267 and rebuilt in 1634 as a ducal pantheon. The high-arcaded cloister is in the Tuscan style, with later additions. It is planned to convert the convent into a *pousada*.

Note, before visiting the palace, the **Gate of Knots** (Porto dos Nós) on the left side of the road leading north from the square.

The **Paço Ducal**, mainly 17C, was begun in 1501, and its façade was faced with Montes Claros marble in 1601–02. It now contains the Braganza archives and collections. The palace is open from 9.30–13.00 and 14.00–18.00 (17.00 in winter); closed Sun, Mon and holidays.

Here, in 1512, the duke stabbed to death his wife and her page, with whom he assumed she was having illicit relations. It was a residence of the kings of Portugal of the House of Braganza after 1640; here the future Dom João IV (more interested in music and the chase than politics) received the first over-tures of the nationalist party, which brought about his accession. Among composers of music for the chapel have been Gines de Morata and António Pinheiro. Catherine of Braganza was born here in 1638, where she is said to spent her youth 'bred hugely retired', indeed virtually uneducated.

Joseph Baretti, who passed through the place in 1760, was not impressed, remarking: 'The furniture is rather mean than old, and there are a hundred houses at Genoa incomparably better'. Dom Pedro (who later married Dona Maria I) occasionally visited the palace, but preferred to lodge in a small house adjoining, which, Baretti was assured, was 'elegantly fitted up'. Here Dom Carlos I (an amateur artist) and his eldest son passed their last night before their assassination in Lisbon in 1908.

The guided tour starts with the kitchens (glittering with copper pans), an impor-tant part of the establishment, if one is to judge from Dom Carlos's appearance; then the important *Library of Early Portuguese Books, accumulated by Dom Manuel II during his long exile at Fulwell Park, Twickenham. Its catalogue of three handsome volumes, limited to an edition of 698 copies, containing over 1000 facsimiles, and published by Maggs Bros in 1929–35, has been described as 'one of the few really great books ever prepared by a monarch'.

The tour continues through the chapel, in Pompeian style; the music room; the Sala Hércules; and Sala dos Duques, etc. Apart from a triptych once attributed to Cristóvão de Figueiredo and now to Jorge Afonso, and a portrait of Dom Manuel by Laszlo, some tapestries after Rubens, one or two items of furniture and porcelain, and some 16C Dutch tiles, the palace and its contents are disappointing. Of more interest are the rooms in the older palace, and the gardens.

A *Collection of Carriages, some 70 in all, complementing those in the Museu dos Coches at Belém (see Rte 1E), may be seen in the three adjacent ranges of stables (separate admission). Notable are one made for the Conde dos Galveias (No. 18; London, c 1820); No. 29, the square landau in which Dom Carlos I and his son were riding when assassinated (see above); No. 31, belonging to the Távora family; No. 51, a charabanc (by Thrupp of London; 1850); and No. 70, the mail-coach, made in England in the second quarter of the 19C. Almost all are in perfect condition.

The Tapada, a walled hunting chase of considerable extent (some 18km in circumference) is close by, and it was while on a hunting expedition here in 1861 that Dom Pedro V, and a younger brother, Fernando, were taken fatally ill with typhoid fever.

Turning south-west, the wooded Serra de Ossa is crossed, passing near a series of dolmens, to **Redondo**, an old town, retaining some of its fortifications, but its churches are of no great interest. See Rte 5A for the Convento de São Paulo, c 10km north beyond Aldeia da Serra. From Redondo the road veers due west through attractive undulating country towards Évora: see Rte 6, below.

The road then continues west, shortly bearing north-west to bypass (left) **Guadalupe**, near which are the 2.5m high menhir, and nearby cromlech, of Almendres. (A useful booklet in English, containing detailed maps, *A Guide to the Megalithic Monuments of the Évora Region* is available from the Tourist Office in Évora.) To the left of the next right-hand turning (on approaching **Valeira**) is the dolmen of Silval. The course of the new highway under construction is passed to regain the present main Lisbon road (N4) at Montemór-o-Novo, for which, and the road beyond, see Rte 5A.

# 6 · Évora

Évora (38,005 inhab.), the ancient walled capital of the Alentejo, and one of the most picturesque and interesting towns in Portugal, stands on a low hill among rolling plains, for which it is an important market. Remains of every age from Roman times onwards survive, and the windings of its narrow streets preserve more of a medieval aspect than in many other towns; and much also recalls its long Moorish occupation, while numerous prehistoric remains survive in the vicinity (see above).

■ The **Tourist Office** is at 71 Praça do Giraldo. The **railway station** is on the line between Lisbon and Estremoz, changing at Casa Branca.

### History

Celtic Ebora may have been a headquarters of Quintus Sertorius (c 80 BC); it was later awarded the title of Liberalitas Julia by Julius Caesar. A bishop of Évora (its name with the same origin as Eboracum or York, in England) attended the Council of Elvira (near Granada) in 300. It was in Moorish hands from c 715 until c 1160, largely controlled by the Ibn Wazir family, when it was taken by surprise by the outlaw knight, Geraldo Sem-Pavor (Gerald the Fearless), who thus regained the favour of Afonso Henriques, and it remained a Christian bastion in the Alentejo until 1211. With the accession of the House of Avis in 1385, Évora became a frequent residence of the kings, and the Cortes were often summoned here. By the end of the 15C its population had grown to some 25,000. A Jesuit university was established here in 1559. The Holy Office was suppressed by Pombal 200 years later. The Cardinal-King Dom Henrique was archbishop of Évora before his accession in 1578; it had been an archbishopric since 1540.

The first serious outbreak against the Spanish domination occurred at Évora (1637–38); and in 1663 the town was briefly occupied by the besieging army of Don Juan of Austria until relieved by the victory of Ameixial (8 June). In 1750, at the accession of Dom José, Pombal exiled Dom João V's bastards, the Meninos of Palhavã here (cf. Odivelas). In July 1808 it was brutally sacked by Géneral Loison after its defending forces had been massacred.

On 9 September 1973 the Roman temple was the rendezvous of disillusioned junior officers, who were to precipitate the Revolution of 25 April 1974.

Évora was the birthplace of Garcia de Resende (1470–1536), poet and architect, and André de Resende (1498–1573), the antiquary; the architect Diogo de Torralva (1500–66), and the Arruda family of architects (16C); and Pedro Fernandes de Queirós (1563–1615), discoverer of Australasia.

Luis António Verney (1713–92), known as 'El Barbadiño', author of the influential *Verdadeiro Método de Estudar* (1746), was Archdeacon of Évora. Gil Vicente, the dramatist, died here c 1540.

Perhaps the most convenient entry into the upper town is that from the north-east (Rua Cordovil), which after a short climb brings one to a high wall (left), immediately beyond which turn left to gain the highest point, dominated by the remains of the **\*Roman Temple**. It is arbitrarily known as that 'of Diana', and dates from the 2C or 3C AD. The best preserved of its type in the Peninsula, it was apparently hexastyle and peripteral, but only 14 survive of the original 26 columns: the south colonnade has vanished. Most of the podium remains. The existing granite columns have only 12 rather than the normal 24 flutes, and they are crowned with white Vila Viçosa marble Corinthian capitals. The building was once 'fortified', and long used as shambles; indeed it was not cleared of centuries of accretions until 1870.

Opposite its east side is the former **Monastery dos Lóios**, the dependencies of which have since 1965 accommodated the luxurious *pousada*. The Gothic *cloister (with a Renaissance gallery above) preserves the beautiful Luso-Moorish doorway of the chapterhouse of two granite horseshoe arches supported by delicate twisted marble columns with curious capitals. Beneath the crowning ogee of the doorway is a carved stockade, which may represent either that of Arzila in Morocco, captured by Rodrigo Afonso de Melo in 1470, or of Azammur, where the 1st Earl of Tentugal was wounded in 1513.

Tombs of the Tentugal family may be seen in the adjacent church of São João Evangelista (1485), generally known as **Os Lóios**, notable for its Flamboyant entrance portal and the *azulejos* of 1711 by António de Oliveira Bernardes (1684–1732) depicting the Life of St Laurence Giustiniani, patriarch of Venice. Note also the *trompe l'oeil azulejo* window.

A few paces downhill stands the old **Palace of the Melos**, also known as that of the Cadavals, with two tall towers. Opening times are 9.00–12.00 and 14.00–17.00. Its terrace is built above a massive stretch of Roman wall, parts of which may be discerned between this point and the Praça do Giraldo. A small 'museum', to the left inside the entrance, contains an equestrian portrait of the 3rd Duque de Cadaval, by Pierre Antoine Quillard (1701–33), and two Flemish brasses, etc.

Return past the *pousada* to skirt the *library (established 1805), now containing the important collection of c 33,500 volumes donated by its founder, Archbishop Manuel do Cenáculo Vilas-Boas (1724–1814; see below), among others. A copy, by Isaias Newton (1872), of his portrait, hangs in the main reading-room. The collections—increased by those of conventual libraries after 1834—include some 250,000 volumes; 500,000 MSS, and 660 incunabula.

Facing the south side of the temple stands the former Archbishop's Palace (late 16C–early 18C), bearing the arms of Archbishop Luís da Silva (1691–1703), and now housing the **MUSEUM** which, under the aegis of Mário Tavares Chicó (director in 1943–66), grew to become one of the most important in Portugal.

It is open 9.00–12.30 and 14.30–18.00; closed Mon and holidays.

The basis of the collection was formed by Vilas-Boas, who in 1801 had been described by young Southey, who met him in Beja (where he was then bishop), as 'a little, cheerful, large-eyed man'. He was apparently the only person who bought a book in Beja, so the bookseller complained to Southey, to whom the bishop also hospitably gave 'cheese and incomparable wine' for his journey on. In 1808 Géneral Loison plundered the palace, when 'heaps of MSS were destroyed', and 'Loison *himself* stole from a table whilst the Archbishop was sleeping his episcopal ring', and pocketed it. By the time Borrow visited the building, in 1835, and saw its 'superb library' and 'a collection of pictures by Portuguese artists, chiefly portraits', it was the residence of the Governor.

The archaeological collections ranged around the central cloister contain several examples of Roman sculpture and stelae excavated in the neighbourhood, but also include a female head from Tavira. Notable are a frieze from a Roman temple; the bas-relief of a diaphanously draped lower half of a bacchante or Vestal Virgin; a barrel-shaped tombstone; and the sepulchres of Fernão Gonçalves Cogominho

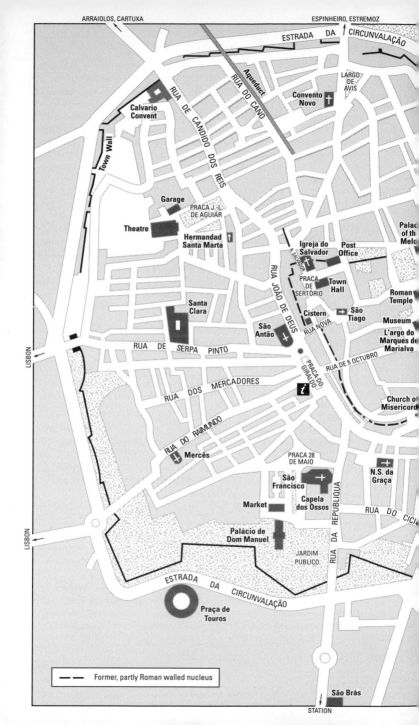

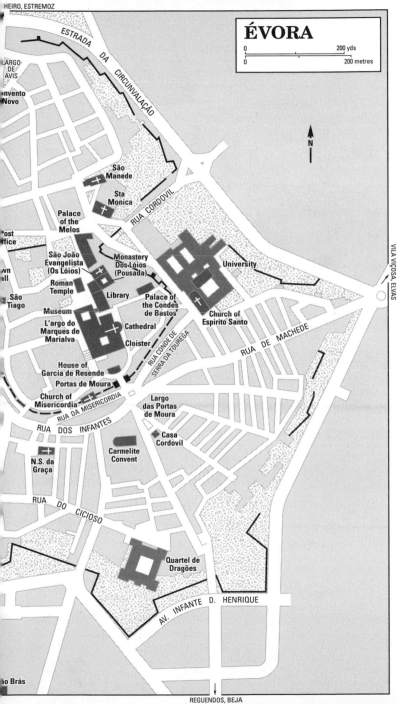

ÉVORA

HEIRO, ESTREMOZ

ESTRADA DA CIRCUNVALAÇÃO

LARGO DE AVIS

Convento Novo

São Manede

Sta Monica

RUA CORDOVIL

Palace of the Melos

Post Office

São João Evangelista (Os Lóios)

Monastery Dos Lóios (Pousada)

University

Town Hall

Roman Temple

Library

São Tiago

Museum

Palace of the Condes de Bastos'

Church of Espirito Santo

L'argo do Marques de Marialva

Cathedral

Cloister

House of Garcia de Resende

RUA CONDE DE SERRA DA TOUREGA

RUA DE MACHEDE

Portas de Moura

Church of Misericordia

RUA DA MISERICORDIA

Largo das Portas de Moura

RUA DOS INFANTES

Casa Cordovil

N.S. da Graça

Carmelite Convent

RUA DO CICIOSO

Quartel de Dragões

AV. INFANTE D. HENRIQUE

São Brás

REGUENDOS, BEJA

VILA VIÇOSA, ELVAS

N

0        200 yds
0        200 metres

*A view in Évora*

(1364), a hero of the battle of Salado; the cenotaph of Rui Pires Alfageme (14C); a marble relief of the Annunciation (1382); and the monument to Bishop Fernando Martins (mid 14C).

Adjacent is the escutcheon of Évora, and an *ajimece* window from the old town hall (1516), destroyed in 1895 to be replaced by the new (at the south end of the Praça do Giraldo); the Tomb of Alvaro da Costa (1535), by Nicolau Chanterène, who worked in Évora between 1533 and 1540; two marble pilasters from the Monastery of Paraíso (1533), likewise attributed to Chanterène, and also the cenotaph of Bishop Afonso of Portugal (1537); and a basalt *Allegory of the Portuguese Discoveries* (16C; from the Palace of the Earls of Unhão). The *azulejos* displayed on this floor should not be overlooked.

Stairs ascend to the **first floor**, where outstanding among the paintings are: *Master of Sardoal*, Portraits of two bishops; *Master of the Retablo of Evora Cathedral*, Life of the Virgin, a series of 13 paintings (Flemish; late 15C): the central panel of the Virgin surrounded by angels playing musical instruments is attributed to *Gerard David*; and six smaller paintings of the Life of Christ (Flemish; early 16C); *Frei Carlos*, Nativity; also an early 16C Triptych of the Calvary in Limoges enamel; anonymous Portraits of Joana de Bragança, and Catherine of Braganza in her youth; and several portrait miniatures; The Lamb of God and several still lifes attributed to *Josefa de Obidos*, and others attributed to *Sanchez Cotan*; *Hendrick Avercamp*, Skating scene; and *A. de Vris*, Male portrait (1631). Other rooms display furniture, most of which originated in this building, when it was the archbishop's palace, much of it of fine quality (note the desk or *escrivaninha*), and a collection of ecclesiastical silver, including a remarkable silver and gilt chalice, and silver mitre (17C). Archaeological collections are displayed in the basement.

The church of Mercês (see below), in which ecclesiastical treasures may be seen, serves as an annexe to the museum.

The granite *CATHEDRAL or SÉ, abutting the museum, and one of the largest and finest churches in the south of Portugal, is believed to have been begun in 1186, possibly on the site of an earlier mosque. It was consecrated in 1204 and virtually finished by c. 1250. The chancel was rebuilt in the 18C but the rest remains almost in its original state. It is open from 9.00–12.00 (Sun to 11.00) and 14.00–17.00; closed Mon and holidays.

The west front consists of a deeply recessed ogival porch protecting a series of sculpted Apostles of local workmanship (14C), built between two dissimilar towers, and approached by a flight of steps. The north tower, containing a number of irregularly placed windows, is surmounted by a conical cap covered with *azulejos*; the buttressed south clock-tower and belfry is topped by a series of turrets surrounding a cone, somewhat resembling the central octagonal lantern or *zimbório*, which with its scale-like tiles and eight subsidiary turrets, is of the Salmantine type (like the lanterns of the *old* cathedral at Salamanca, Plasencia, Toro, and Zamora).

In the **interior** (70m by 22.5m) the eye is immediately drawn to the disconcerting accentuation of the mortar-joints, a peculiarity of Évora: see São Francisco, below. Note the curious 'rosary-like' chains supporting the chandeliers. The nave, with seven rectangular bays, lower lateral aisles, and a triforium, is lit by a curious west window and by rose-windows in the transepts. At the end of the north transept is a Renaissance portal ascribed to Chanterène. The incongruous *Capela-Mór*, previously—until 1717—embellished by the retable now in the museum, was entirely rebuilt in vari-coloured marbles by J.F. Ludwig, the architect of Mafra, in 1718–46. In the south transept is the tomb of André de Resende (died 1573). The **treasury**, reached by steps in the south tower, contains an unusual ivory figure-triptych of the Virgin (13C) with a later wooden head; a silver-gilt monstrance (16C); an early 16C Bishop's crook; the Reliquary of St Lenho; several copes, and a collection of plate. Adjacent stairs ascend to the flat roof, which is worth the climb for the panorama it provides and for a closer view of the lantern.

Request entry to the Gothic **cloister** dating from c 1325, which the south transept abuts, and to which two flights of steps descend. Figures of the Evangelists stand at the corners, while in the south-east corner is a chapel containing the tomb of the founder, Bishop Pedro. Some of the openings pierced above the main arcade are markedly Moresque in pattern, and suggest Mudéjar influence.

Facing the cathedral, on the north-west side of the Largo do Marquês de Marialva, stood the Court and Palace of the Inquisition, the first branch of the Holy Office to be established in Portugal (1536), occupying part of the earlier house in which Vasco da Gama lived before his appointment as Viceroy of India in 1524.

Returning towards the library, one may pass below the archway connecting it to the old archbishop's palace and, turning left, shortly reach a tower, next to which is the entrance to the **Palace of the Condes de Bastos**, originally a Moorish palace built on the Roman walls adjacent to the so-called Torre de Sertório, which later became a royal residence. Much of its exterior decoration is of c 1500; admission to the interior may be granted on application.

On regaining the cathedral apse and bearing left, descend towards a block of buildings consisting of the **old university** (see History), containing a refectory vaulted from a central line of columns, a restored Sala dos Actos, with good *azulejos*, and an imposing arcaded courtyard, seen through a gateway at a lower level than the porch of the severe church of **Espírito Santo** (by Afonso Alvares and Manuel Pires; 1567–74). The latter preserves a tomb intended for the Cardinal-King Dom Henrique, who founded the university, but which in fact contains the remains of Duarte, Duke of Guimarães (died 1576).

Turning south-west along the Rua Conde de Serra da Tourega, overlooked by a belvedere, the Largo das Portas de Sol is shortly reached, with another belvedere on the right, just south of which is a spherical fountain (1556). Beyond the latter is the 16C Casa Cordovil, with a delicately columned belvedere. Steps nearby descend to the former Carmelite convent, with a strange 17C portal, a Baroque version of the Manueline style. Further south is the large Quartel de Dragões (Dragoon Barracks; 1736–1803), built on the site of the early 16C castle erected by Diogo de Arruda.

Just within the Portas de Moura is the Manueline mansion of Garcia de Resende (see History), a few paces beyond which steps ascend to regain the cathedral.

To the west, in the Rua da Misericórdia, is the church of the Misericórdia (1554, with a portal of c 1767), its interior baroquised.

By crossing to the left at the next road junction, and turning down an alley, the monastery of **N.S. da Graça** is approached. Its church of 1524–37, attributed to Diogo de Torralva (but also ascribed to Francisco de Holanda), has a striking but ill-designed Mannerist façade, added c 1550, displaying two huge 'rosettes'and crowned by four colossal figures supporting globe-like grenades. The interior is of little interest, and the nave has collapsed three times in the past. Its former dependencies, with a small cloister, now accommodate an officers' club.

Continuing west, cross the Rua da República, and turn left and then right, to pass (right) a vaulted building once a royal grain-store, and later a hostelry, probably that at which George Borrow put up when visiting Évora in January 1836. It has recently been used as a display centre for handicrafts, etc.

The adjacent Praça 28 de Maio is dominated by **São Francisco** (1480–1500), a large aisleless Gothic edifice crowned with battlements and pinnacles. It is open Mon–Sat 8.30–13.00 and 14.30–18.00; Sun 10.00–11.30 and 14.30–18.00. The narthex combines semi-circular, horseshoe, and pointed arches in one arcade. The interior is remarkable for the scarcity of windows and for the accentuation of the lines of mortar (as in the cathedral). Off the south side is a gruesome 17C charnel-house (Capela dos Ossos), lined with human bones, and with the much-quoted inscription over its entrance: '*Nós, ossos, que aqui estamos, Pelos vossos esperamos*' ('The bones here are waiting for yours'). Additional curiosities are the numerous recent photographs left on an adjacent altar as ex-votos (or ex-photos, if you will).

In the nearby gardens overlooking the mid 17C bastions of the **town walls** (designed by Nicolas de Langres) stand the disfigured relics of the Palácio de Dom Manuel, so-called because that king enlarged it, adding a brick arcade on granite piers, but it was begun earlier in the 15C.

From here one can see, a short distance to the south, the curious battlemented hermitage of **São Brás**, its 14 cylindrical buttresses crowned by conical caps, but otherwise of little moment, and except as an architectural curiosity it hardly merits the detour. Very similar is that of Santo André, at Beja.

Ascend the Rua da República to enter the south end of the **Praça do Giraldo**, the main centre of activity in the town, with a low arcade over the pavement on its east side, from which the Rua 5 de Outubro ascends towards the cathedral. Here in 1484 Dom João II watched the beheading of his over-mighty brother-in-law, the Duke of Braganza; while at an auto-da-fé here in 1573, in the presence of Dom Sebastião, some 17 victims of the Inquisition were burnt alive.

At the north end of the square, beyond a fountain of 1571, stands **Santo Antão**, a hall-church of 1557 begun by Manuel Pires and completed by Miguel de Arruda. Large drum pillars support its lofty vaulting, but otherwise the interior is of no great interest except for the wooden tomb-covers in the nave.

On the west side of the square is the tourist office (where one may acquire a useful *Guide to the Megalithic Monuments of the Évora Region*), besides which the Rua do Raimundo descends towards the late 17C church of Mercês, containing subsidiary collections of ecclesiastical art not housed in the Museum, *azulejos* of 1773, etc.

Between this street and the Rua de Serpa Pinto (leading north-west from the square) was the *Judiaria* of Évora, in which a number of old houses are preserved. In the latter street stands the church and convent of **Santa Clara**, founded in 1452, later enlarged, and a cloister added. Juana, 'La Beltraneja' (daughter of Enrique IV of Castile and Joana of Portugal), who had professed at Coimbra in 1480, may have resided here for some time. The derelict interior is now of slight interest.

From the east side of Santo Antão, one may continue north along the arcaded street to the Largo Luis de Camões (or Porta Nova) to reach the gardens of the Praça J.-L. de Aguiar, by the near corner of which is the little church of the Hermandad, Santa Marta (1698). Adjacent to the theatre at the far end of the square is a garage built into part of the old convent of São Domingos.

Continuing down the main street (Rua de Cândido dos Reis), a few minutes' walk brings one to (left) the **Calvário convent** of 1570, with a small cloister, where Juliana de Sousa Coutinho retired after refusing to marry Pedro de Carvalho e Melo, Pombal's son.

Just beyond this point is a good stretch of the 14C outer **\*town wall** (left), while to the right is the 9km-long **\*aqueduct**, known as that of 'Água de Prata', constructed in the 1530s by Francisco de Arruda, most probably on the site of a Roman one.

On regaining the Porta Nova, bear left to pass below two low arches of the aqueduct, then right along the Rua Salvador—on the left of which is the **Igreja do Salvador** (1605; its interior plastered with *azulejos*)—to enter the Praça de Sertório. The right-hand lane at the far end of this small square passes on the next right-hand corner a cistern (*caixa*) of 1536.

Turn left here to skirt **São Mamede** (15C, but modernised in the late 17C), containing Dutch tiles of 1700, bearing round which, continue uphill to regain the Roman temple.

A few steps north-east, at a lower level, stands **São Tiago** (c 1566), with a Classical porch, Dutch tiles, and a profusely decorated ceiling to its vaulted nave.

Three convents of comparatively slight interest may be conveniently visited from Évora, of which the **Cartuxa**, to the right of the Arraiolos road, c 2km north-west beyond a stretch of the aqueduct spanning the road, is one of the two Carthusian monasteries in Portugal, and remains *in clausura* (closed order). One may only glimpse its somewhat derelict 17C church, with a Classical façade attributed to Terzi.

A short distance beyond, on a hill to the left, and now a school, is the former Benedictine convent of **São Bento de Cástris**, founded in 1274, with a 16C cloister showing Mudéjar influence, and a 14C chapterhouse, etc.

The former convent of **N.S. d'Espinheiro**, c 4km north of Évora, now a farm, dates from 1458, although later altered. Frei Carlos, the artist of Flemish origin, professed here in 1517. The dependencies are private property, but one may walk through the farmyard to approach a small chapel in which lies the tomb of Garcia de Resende (1520; see History).

# 7 · (Jerez de los Caballeros) Mourão to Évora

*Total distance, 116km (72 miles). C4311. 61km Mourão—N256. 19km Reguengos-de-Monsaráz—N256 and then N18. 36km Évora.*

From Jerez de los Caballeros (see *Blue Guide Spain*, 6th ed.) follow the slow winding road west and then south-west to Oliva de la Frontera, there bearing north-west along a new road undulating through more open country to cross the Portuguese frontier beyond Villanueva del Fresno.

**Mourão**, a charming and characteristic Portuguese village and old frontier fortress (not to be confused with the town of Moura), has an early 14C castle abutted by its Igreja Matriz.

Some 6km south-west, near **Luz**, is the Roman fortified villa of Castelo da Lousa (1C BC).

On crossing the Guadiana, the short **detour** should be made to Monsaraz, 7km north. (The road passes near the cromlech of Xarez/Xeres, a square of stones in the centre of which is a 4m-high menhir. There are two other menhirs below the fortress-hill of Monsaraz: that of Bulhoa, engraved with symbols; and the 5.6m-high example of Outeiro.) The picturesque ridge-top village of *Monsaraz, largely unspoilt, was reconquered by Geraldo Sem-Pavor in 1167, given to the Templars, and later passed to the Order of Christ. It is said to have been sacked by the unpaid English archers of Edmund of Cambridge in 1381. It preserves extensive fortifications, commanding wide views, including Vaubanesque outworks added in the 17C. Park outside the entrance gate. In the narrow cobbled Rua Direita a Gothic house preserves a 15C fresco. The 16C Igreja Matriz contains the marble tomb of Gomes Martins (late 13C). The N256 may be regained at Reguengos, 16km west.

The main road continues west through rolling country through **Reguengos-de-Monsaraz** (5214 inhabitants), lying among its vineyards. 20km beyond this, it meets the N18 from Évora to Beja via Portel; see Rte 9B.

For Évora itself, see Rte 6. A bypass now circles south of the town to reach the N114 for Montemor-o-Nova, for which see the latter part of Rte 5A.

# 8 · (Sevilla) Rosal de la Frontera to Lisbon via Serpa and Beja

*Total distance, 214km (133 miles). N260. 37km Serpa—28km Beja—N121/IP8. 24km Ferreira do Alentejo—N259. 44km Grândola—N120/IP1. 23km Alcácer do Sal— 33km Marateca junction—A2 motorway. 45km Lisbon.*

For the road from Sevilla climbing through the Sierra de Aracena to Rosal de la Frontera, see *Blue Guide Spain*, 6th ed. The first town of any consequence entered after traversing ancient olive groves is **Serpa** (*Pousada de São Gens*, 2km south, with an extensive view), an agricultural centre with a reputation for its cheeses.

■ The **Tourist Office** is at 2 Largo Dom Jorge de Melo (at the bottom of the steps to the citadel).

Known to the Romans by the same name, Serpa was conquered by Geraldo Sem-Pavor in 1166, retaken by the Moors, and finally regained c 1232; but owing to Castilian claims, the frontier here (including Moura) was not settled until 1297, and was again briefly occupied by the Spaniards in 1707–08.

The old town, on the slope of a spur of the Serra Abelheira, retains stretches of walls, a ruined castle and, among medieval gateways, the Porta de Beja, abutted by remains of a huge *nora* or chain-pump and aqueduct. An ethnographical museum is housed opposite the gateway. The only ecclesiastical buildings of interest are the convent of Santo António (1463; rebuilt 1502), with a church similar to Santo André at Beja, and a small cloister; and Gothic Santa Maria, containing mid 17C *azulejos*.

## Serpa to Mourão via Moura and Amareleja

81km. Follow the N255 north-east through olive groves to (29km) **Moura** (8279 inhabitants), reputed for its olive oil. The history of what was the Roman Civitas Aruccitana is very similar to that of Serpa, but the romantic legend of its capture from the Moors is without foundation. Its most eminent native was Afonso Mendes (1579–1656), Patriarch of Ethiopia in 1623.

The **castle**, rebuilt by Dom Dinis, and again in 1510, and partly restored in 1920, commands an extensive view. The Manueline doorway of the Igreja Matriz is notable. The convent of N.S. do Carmo, the first Carmelite house in Portugal (c 1251), and now a hospital, contains a debased Classical cloister.

Bear north-east on the N386 to (28km) **Amareleja**, from which those wishing to explore the remotest recesses of the Alentejo may make the expedition to **Barrancos**, 27km further east, and the abandoned village and castle (1308) of **Noudar**, some 10km beyond to the north-west, overlooking the Rio Ardila, here marking the frontier. For Mourão, 24km north-west of Amareleja on the N385, see Rte 7.

For the road from Serpa to Mértola, see sub-route in Rte 9A.

A rough road leads directly south from Serpa via **São Brás** to (c 18km) the 'Pulo do Lobo' (Wolf's leap), a waterfall almost 60m high.

The Guadiana is crossed some 7km beyond Serpa, to approach Beja, the tall keep of its castle prominent: see Rte 9A.

The N121 leads west across undulating corn lands past **Ferreira do Alentejo**, an agricultural centre of slight interest, and descends into the valley of the Sado to meet the main road from Lisbon to the Algarve. **Grândola** (5122 inhabitants), with cork factories, is bypassed shortly. The town played a small part in history on 24/25 April 1974, as the broadcasting of the old popular song entitled *Grândola vila morena* was the pre-arranged signal confirming that the military coup was on (see Introduction to History, p 33).

The road now veers north through pine woods towards Alcácer do Sal (see Rte 10), also bypassed by a new bridge over the Sado, later bearing north-west to approach the Marateca junction, where one may enter the extension of the A2 motorway for Lisbon; see last paragraphs of Rte 5A.

# 9 · Évora to Vila Real de Santo António via Beja and Mértola

## A. Via Viana do Alentejo and Beja

*Total distance, 203km (126 miles). N254. 31km Viana do Alentejo—10km Alvito—18km Cuba—20km Beja—N122. 53km Mértola—65km Castro Marim—6km Vila Real de Santo António.*

The N254 leads due south (retrospective views) and veers west towards **Viana do Alentejo**, on the north slope of a range of hills. It preserves the walls of its castle (rebuilt 1482), with pepper-pot corner towers, and a wall-walk providing attractive views. Within the enceinte stands the well-buttressed granite *Igreja Matriz (16C), with a notable Manueline portal, surmounted by a wealth of conical pinnacles and crenellations, and retaining several features of interest. East of the town stands the pilgrimage church of N.S. de Aires, rebuilt between 1743–90, with twin belfries and an octagonal cupola, and an interior plastered with ex-votos.

Some 5km beyond is the **Solar de Aguas de Peixes**, a Mudéjar mansion of the Dukes of Cadaval, with a simple Renaissance courtyard.

The road climbs through the hills to **Alvito**, with a half-Moorish late 15C castle, begun by Diogo Lobo, baron of Alvito, preserving moulded brick horseshoe arches typical of the district. It has recently been restored to house a *pousada*. The 16C Igreja Matriz, higher in the town, contains good mid 17C *azulejos*.

Bearing south-east, **Vila Ruiva**, with a Roman bridge over the Odivelas, is entered, where one may either turn south through (10km) Cuba to approach the N18 7km beyond; or, preferably make a short detour by continuing east via Vila de Frades, with its Roman villa, to meet the main road at Vidigueira: see Rte 9B.

**Cuba**, a village of slight interest in itself, has an unlikely historical association. In his *The Portuguese Columbus* (1992) Mascarenhas Barreto has convincingly argued that, in spite of numerous contrary claims, either Cuba or Vila Ruiva was the birthplace of Salvador Fernandes Zarco (1448–1506; better known as Cristóbal Colón or Christopher Columbus), who was the bastard son of Fernando, the youthful Duke of Viseu and Beja (1433–70). His mother was Isabel Gonçalves de Câmara, a New Christian of the locality, who later married Diogo Afonso de Aguiar.

## BEJA

The country becomes more open on approaching Beja (19,212 inhab.), capital of its district, an ancient episcopal city, dominating the rich rolling wheat-belt of the Lower (Baixo) Alentejo, and long an important centre of communication (on the direct road between Sevilla and Lisbon, and between Évora or Lisbon and Faro).

- The **Tourist Office** is at 25 Rua do Capitão J.F. de Sousa. The **train station** is in the north-eastern part of town; the **bus station** is on Rua Cidade de São Paulo.

### History

Founded by Caesar or Augustus, Pax Julia (whose name refers to its pacification), later corrupted by the Moors to Beja, was the capital of one of three Roman *conventus* in Lusitania, the others being Santarém and Mérida. The Moors walled the town, and it remained in their hands until 1162. In 1252 it was refortified. Its history since—apart from its sack by Colonel Maransin during the French occupation (June 1808)—has been comparatively uneventful. In recent decades it has had a reputation as a stronghold of Communism, while still a thriving agricultural centre, this largely in reaction to centuries of exploitation by the large landowners of the Alentejo. A NATO air base was constructed to the north-west in the 1960s. An abortive revolt against the Salazar regime took place here on 1 January 1962, planned by General Humberto Delgado, who was assassinated near Badajoz three years later by secret police.

Beja was the birthplace of Jacinto Freire de Andrade (1597–1657), author of a famous *Life of João de Castro* (1651); and Agostinho de Macedo (1761–1831), the writer and pamphleteer.

From the main road junction west of the town, turn in to approach the conspicuous keep of its castle, first passing (left) the 15C Ermida de Santo André, with cylindrical buttresses similar in outline to those of São Brás at Évora.

The **castle**, whose 40m-high limestone keep or **\*Torre de Menagem** dominates the area, abuts a surviving stretch of town wall. It was built in 1272–1310 by Dom Dinis on foundations probably Roman, and was restored in 1940. It is open 10.00–13.00 and 14.00–18.00. Some 200 steps ascend through its three floors, each with a vaulted room, and providing progressively wider views, the panorama from the summit being bounded on the north-west by the Serra de Sintra, by Évora to the north, and to the east by spurs of the Spanish Sierra Morena. A small military museum has been installed off the courtyard.

Immediately east of the castle is the Renaissance São Tiago (1590), while a short distance downhill to the north-west stands the deconsecrated pre-Romanesque church of **\*Santo Amaro**, recently restored to house a lapidary museum, and containing Visigothic columns and capitals, etc. of interest.

Turning south-west from the castle, a hospital is shortly passed (right), with relics of two cloisters, beyond which is a small square, with the chapel of N.S. dos Prazeres (1672).

Turn left uphill to approach the hall-church of the Misericórdia (1550), with a rusticated porch, and said to have been built as a covered meat-market, which faces the Praça da República, the site of the Roman forum. Follow a lane beyond the far end of this long square (off which, in another street to the right, a fine Manueline window is preserved ) to reach the entrance to the former **\*Convent of N.S. da Conceição**, founded in 1467, and once amongst the richest in Portugal. It now

*The Torre de Menagem at Beja*

accommodates the Regional Museum (open 9.45–13.00 and 14.00–17.15; closed Mon and holidays).

It was from here, it has been assumed, that Mariana Alcoforado (?1640–1723) may have written the five reproachful letters to the Chevalier de Chamilly (Colonel Noël Bouton, Comte de Saint-Léger, later Marquis) who had made her his lover during the latter part of the Portuguese war with Spain of 1661–68, and then deserted her. The letters were published in a French version in 1669 and in an English translation nine years later, which gave the reputed 'Portuguese Nun' some notoriety. Spurious letters were added to later editions.

The exterior copings are crowned by balustrades influenced by Batalha, and above the west door is a charming *ajimece* window brought from the palace of the Dukes of Beja (once the title held by the king's second son). (The palace, destroyed in 1895, stood further east, joined to the convent by a brick gallery.) The Baroque chapel is richly gilt, while the whole interior is remarkable for the *azulejos* with which both the cloister and chapterhouse are covered (16C and earlier; some Mudéjar).

The contents of the **museum** are miscellaneous, and include archaeological collections; costumes; and, among paintings, a Flemish Virgin and Child, and three saints attributed to Ribera, an anonymous Martyrdom of St Vincent, a Decapitation of St Barbara, and a portrait of that bibliophile bishop, Manuel do Cenáculo Vilas-Boas.

To the north-east, at a lower level, is Santa Maria, with a 15C narthex and apse, but largely rebuilt.

Downhill to the south-east, beyond a junction of streets, steps descend to the former convent of **São Francisco**. Although dating from the 13C, since 1834 it served as barracks and was seriously mutilated; but its chapel and imposing cloister were tastefully restored recently when the whole was converted to house a luxurious *pousada*.

Some 7km south-west, approached by a track leading to the right off the Aljustrel-Faro road, lie the extensive remains of the 1–4C Roman villa of **Pisões**, preserving baths, mosaic pavements, etc., but much excavation remains to be done. (The interested visitor is advised to contact the tourist office in Beja before making the excursion.)

Those intending to drive direct from Beja to Lagos or Faro will follow the N391/IP2 to the south-west, crossing the N2 near (46km) Castro Verde, there turning south for Faro (see below), although the faster road is the N264, some 12km further west, entered near Ourique; see Rte 12.

## Castro Verde to Faro via São Bras de Alportel

99km. The N2, a slow and winding road beyond Almodôvar, was until comparatively recently the main highway south to Faro, and those following it will soon understand why the Algarve was for so long isolated from the rest of the country. At **Castro Verde**, now with a bypass, a well-sited agricultural centre of ancient origin, the Igreja Matriz contains *azulejos* of 1713 imaginatively depicting the Battle of Ourique, while the Igreja das Chagas preserves others of Dutch inspiration.

The 'battle' of the **Campo de Ourique** (25 July 1139) may have taken place near by, but its site is in dispute, for it is as likely that it was fought at Chão de Ourique, near Santarém. Afonso Henriques defeated five Moorish 'kings' in this skirmish, afterwards adopting as his coat of arms their five shields ('as cinco quinas'), each charged with the five wounds of Christ, in memory of a vision of the Crucifixion which he had the night before the engagement.

Beyond **Almodôvar**, where the church in the main square has a Manueline window, the road starts to climb over the convoluted Serra do Malhão, providing several extensive views, eventually descending through woods to **São Bras de Alportel**, on the inland road between Tavira and Loulé; see Rte 13. The *pousada* here is passed to the left on climbing down to the town. The only monument of note between here and the coast at Faro is at Estoi; see paragraphs after Faro in Rte 13.

The main road between Beja and Mértola, 51km south-east, is of slight interest.

The more interesting alternative, but longer and slower route, is that via Serpa, 28km south-east, and from there to Mértola, 53km south on the N265. This lonely twisting road first leads south-east past Serpa (see Rte 8) to (36km) **Minas de São Domingos**. Known to the Romans, and an extension of those at Tharsis and Rio Tinto (beyond the Spanish frontier, which here follows the course of the Chança), these copper mines were only re-discovered in 1857, and then exploited by a British company, who constructed a mineral railway down to Pomarão, on the Guadiana. A small reservoir among eucalyptus woods is skirted as the road bears west before descending steeply (views) to cross the river at (17km) **MÉRTOLA**, impressively sited beneath its Moorish castle, which commanded the highest point to which the Guadiana was navigable.

- **Buses** occasionally run to Vila Real de Santo António and Beja.

### History
Founded in remote antiquity, Mértola was known to the Romans as Julia Myrtilis, and was one of their four *municipia* in Lusitania. By 440 it was in Suevic hands (who here seized Censorius, the Roman legate), until occupied by the Moors in 712. It was later captured by Ibn Qasi, when rebelling against the Almoravids in 1143/4. He in turn was ousted in the Almohad invasion of 1146 (whose forces wintered here before marching on Sevilla), but it was eventually lost by them in 1238.

On the river-bank—the Guadiana was the Roman Anas, later Arabic Wadi-Anas— is a curious pier-like structure, probably part of a *nora*, as at Serpa, incorporating Roman masonry, but dating perhaps not earlier than the Moorish occupation. Below the castle is the battlemented *Igreja Matriz, where the discovery of a *mihrab* confirms that it was a converted mosque, as suggested by its square plan. Its fine vault is probably contemporary with the castle keep (1292). A tombstone from Mértola (now in the Ethnological Museum at Belém), dated AD 525, displays the horseshoe 'Moorish' arch, an additional confirmation that it was in use in the Peninsula *before* the Moslem invasion of 711.

Both a forum and cryptoporticus have been uncovered not far west of the church.

At a lower level is the **Town Hall**, below which are the foundations of a Roman villa, with a small museum. Other museums are devoted to Mértola's successive eras of occupation: that illustrating the Islamic domination being near the southern prow of the enceinte, and Palaeo-Christian remains are displayed *in situ* towards the north end of the town.

Climbing out of the Guadiana valley, with impressive retrospective views, the road crosses the deserted cistus-covered hills of the eastern Algarve (the Serra do Malhão, the western extension of the Spanish Sierra Morena), described by Southey as 'great waves' when he crossed them, which here run parallel to the coast, their valleys threaded by tributaries of the Guadiana.

At 34km a left-hand turning leads 6km to **Alcoutim**, an ancient river-port with a ruined castle and a Renaissance church, facing the Spanish town of Sanlúcar del Guadiana.

The right-hand turning here leads via (25km) **Martim Longo** to meet the N2 35km further south-west, some 13km north of **São Brás de Alportel** (see Rte 12), and provides several extensive views.

The main road continues to wind south, descending steeply into the valley of the Ribeira da Foupana, and climbs again before reaching lower land on approaching **Castro Marim**, Roman Baesuris. It was also the first headquarters of the Order of Christ (1319), before its transfer to Tomar (cf.). The huge castle, built by Dom Afonso III, but damaged by the earthquake of 1755, contains the ruins of the 14C church of São Tiago.

After crossing the flooded estuary of the Guadiana—spanned a short distance upstream by the new international bridge—Vila Real de Santo António, the easternmost town of the Algarve, is shortly entered: for which see last paragraphs of Rte 13.

## B. Via Portel and Beja

*Total distance, 202km (126 miles). N18. 16km, there bearing right for (24km) Portel—15km Vidigueira—24km Beja—N122. 51km Mértola—71km Vila Real de Santo António.*

The rather dull road reaches more attractive wooded country on approaching **Portel**, dominated by its late 13C castle of the Dukes of Braganza, reconstructed by Dom Manuel I.

There is a well-preserved castle of c 1350 at **Amieira**, 14km due east; and at **Vera Cruz**, 9km south, a 13C church on earlier foundations which once belonged to the Order of Malta; while not far north-west of Portel is the hermitage of São Pedro, commanding a panoramic view.

At **Vidigueira** (bypassed) the neighbouring Carmelite church contained from 1539 until transferred to Belém in 1898 (since when they have been moved to the pantheon of Santa Engrácia, Lisbon) the remains of Vasco da Gama, Conde de Vidigueira. The Marrano family of Baruch Spinoza (Amsterdam 1632–77) may have lived here before the expulsion of the Jewish community from Portugal a century earlier.

In idyllic surroundings some 4km to the west, on the Alvito road beyond the village of **Vila de Frades**, a signposted lane to the right leads to the imposing remains of the mid 4C Roman villa of **\*São Cucufate**, later used as a monastery. Work is being carried out to consolidate the brick-built structure and preserve its fading murals.

For Alvito and Cuba, see Rte 9A.

The road continues south from Vidigueira, cross the rolling Alentejano plain to Beja; see Rte 9A, and for the remainder of this route.

# 10 · Évora to Odemira via Ferreira do Alentejo, for Lagos

*Total distance, 158km (98 miles). N380. 32km Alcáçovas—N2. 14km Torrão—30km Ferreira do Alentejo—24km Aljustrel—N263. 58km Odemira.*

From Évora (see Rte 6), follow the N380 south-west, off which after 11km a right-hand turning leads shortly to the *Quinta de Valverde*, or Mitra. This was once a country seat of the archbishops of Évora, where the church of the Capuchin monastery founded in 1544, known as that of **\*Bom Jesus**, is of architectural interest, despite its diminutive size, for its widest dimension is merely 6.5m. It has been ascribed to both Manuel Pires and Diogo de Torralva, the latter being more likely. Its plan consists of five domed octagons separated by four squares, with eight free-standing marble columns supporting the central dome, with its clerestory, and 24 others abutting the walls. Admission should be requested at the adjacent house.

Beyond the village of **Valverde** is the chapel of São Brissos, abutting a megalithic tomb (cf. Pavia); also in the neighbourhood is the dolmen of Zambujeiro. (The guide in English to the Megalithic monuments of the Évora region, available at the Tourist Office there, will be found useful.)

On regaining the tree-lined main road, continue south-west. From just beyond the second railway crossing a road leads 12km south-east to Viana do Alentejo: see Rte 9A.

**Alcáçovas**, an ancient town, which gave its name to the peace treaty with Spain of 1479, retains the palace of its counts, and that of the Barahonas, with curious towers, and a Manueline hall-church. It was the birthplace of the composer Duarte Lobo (c 1565–1646). Some 3km to the west is the 16C chapel of N.S. da Esperança, surviving from a Dominican monastery, with *azulejos* of interest.

**Torrão**, near the head of the Xarrama reservoir, and the birthplace of the poet Bernardim Ribeiro (1482–1552), preserves slight Roman remains, and a small Manueline church containing 16C *azulejos*. The Pousada de Vale de Gaio is c 8km south-west, approached from the north side of a reservoir.

Turn south past **Odivelas**, near the dam of another reservoir, to bypass **Ferreira do Alentejo** (see Rte 8) and on to approach or bypass **Aljustrel** (5208 inhabitants), pre-Roman Vispasca, whose copper-mines were known as early as the 2nd millennium, but only actively exploited by the Romans (whose shafts descended to a depth of 120m). The extent of the slag heap gives some idea of their former importance, but apart from the small Museu da Mina, with archaeological collections, the place is now of slight interest.

For Castro Verde, 24km further south, see Rte 9A.

The N263 leads south-west from Aljustrel, beyond **Messejana** descending into the upper valley of the Sado, crosses the N264 and, rising again, reaches crossroads some 4km beyond the village of **Santa Luzia** (right).

### Santa Luzia to Portimão via Monchique

About 90km. This is a difficult winding road through the Serra de Monchique. The left-hand turning at the above-mentioned crossroads leads south to **São Martinho das Amoreiras**. Then bear south-west to meet the N266 north of **Santa Clara-a-Velha** and a bridge over the Rio Mira. Immediately beyond, a road to the left leads to the huge reservoir—Barragem de Santa Clara—overlooked by the Pousada de Santa Clara. The narrow road shortly starts to climb into the thickly wooded Serra de Monchique to the high-lying village of **Monchique** (458m), the Igreja Matriz of which has a Manueline portal. To the south-east rises the peak of Picota (773m; view); while a road ascends west to the summit of Fóia (902m), the highest peak in the range, commanding extensive panoramic *views. Another road turns right off the N266 further south, skirting its upper southern slopes via **Marmelete** to meet the N120 at Aljezur; see Rte 11.

The main road descends past **Caldas de Monchique**, the waters of which—known to the Romans and Moors—Dom João II took in 1495 in a vain attempt to relieve his dropsy, soon after which he died. The road continues to climb down the flank of the range (views) past **Porto de Lagos** (some 11km east of which is Silves (cf.) to meet the new bypass north of Portimão: see Rte 13.

The N263 continues south-west from the crossroads near Santa Luzia along a bare ridge providing distant views towards the Atlantic, and gently descends to Odemira, on the Rio Mira, where the N120 from Lisbon to Lagos is met: see Rte 11, below.

# 11 · Lisbon to Lagos (or Sagres) via Santiago do Cacém

*Total distance, 257km (160 miles). A2 motorway to (45km) the Marateca junction, there bearing right onto the IP1 for (33km) Alcácer do Sal—at 18km fork right onto the IP8 for (34km) Santiago do Cacém—N120. 56km Odemira—48km Alfambra—23km Lagos. Sagres is 36km south-west of Alfambra on the N268.*

See the latter part of Rte 5A in reverse as far as the Marateca junction, from which the improved highway, here of slight interest, veers south-east over low-lying sandy tracts and through the pine and cork-oak woods in the neighbourhood of the Sado estuary, to approach or bypass **ALCÁCER DO SAL**, on the north bank of that river. With rice fields and salt marshes in its vicinity, it was once of considerable importance, but is no longer so.

Known to the Romans as Urbs Imperatoria Salacia, it was later a strong Moorish fortress (Qasr Abi Danis), and Afonso Henriques was wounded here in an unsuccessful attempt to capture it soon after the fall of Lisbon. After repeated assaults it was taken in 1158, but fell into Almohad hands in 1191, and was eventually recaptured after a long siege in 1217, with the help of a contingent of crusaders who had anchored off the estuary. It was then handed over to the Order of São Tiago. Alcácer was the birthplace of the mathematician Pedro Nunes (c 1492–c 1577).

The ruined Moorish **castle** in the upper town, which is to be restored to house a *pousada*, encloses a Romanesque church (Santa Maria), near which are the ruins of the Convent of Aracoeli (founded 1537). Below the castle is the Renaissance church of Santo António (1524). In the former church of **Espírito Santo**, with a Manueline window, and in which Dom Manuel I married his second wife, Maria of Castile, in 1500, is a small archaeological collection. The Paços de Concelho also has Manueline features. About 1km to the west is the Gothic church of Senhor dos Mártires, with an octagonal chapel of 1333, near which is a pre-Roman burial-ground.

The monotonous road undulates almost due south through pine forests, and at 18km bears right onto a new stretch of road leading to Sines; see below. For the IP1, veering left to bypass Grândola (see latter part of Rte 8) and then up the Sado valley—for Albufeira in the Algarve—see Rte 12.

The Serra de Grândola, crossed by the winding but attractive old direct road from Grândola to Santiago do Cacém, is skirted by the new road, which provides a more convenient approach.

**Santiago do Cacém** (Pousada de São Tiago) is pleasantly sited on a hill slope dominated by its ruined Moorish castle, rebuilt by the Templars, the walls of which now enclose a cemetery (views). On an adjacent hill to the north, a turning (right) off the Lisbon road not far from the *pousada* leads shortly to the extensive site of Roman *Miróbriga Celticum. Only partly excavated, it also commands a fine view east towards Beja, the castle keep of which may be discerned in clear weather. The pre-Roman *oppidum* was in occupation since the 8–9C BC.

23km south-west of Santiago do Cacém is **Sines** (9772 inhabitants), some 65 years ago described as 'a remote little town', with a sheltered fishing harbour, its only claims to fame being the birthplace of Vasco da Gama (1469–1524) and the port from which Dom Miguel sailed to exile after the Convention of Evoramonte in 1834. It has recently been transformed into a tanker terminus, and is the centre of vast oil refineries (Petrosul), the whole area being wreathed with pipelines and new roads, making it a sinister tubular jungle into which only the most intrepid traveller will want to penetrate.

The old road continues south from Santiago do Cacém to **Tanganheira**, some 13km west of which is the small fishing-port of **Porto Covo**, and the offshore islet of Pessegueiro, with ruins of a fort and old church.

At **Cercal** a detour may be made to **Vila Nova de Milfontes**, 15km south-west, at the mouth of the Rio Mira, and formerly an important harbour. Its striking castle, which had been once sacked by Algerine pirates, was later 'half converted into a poor dwelling house', as described by Southey. One may now cross the estuary of the Mira here to regain the main road 23km south-east.

The N120 skirts **Odemira**, repopulated by Dom Afonso III in 1252. The town is pleasantly sited on the Rio Mira, but is of slight interest in itself.

On crossing the river, the road ascends the south side of the valley, later running along a ridge (views), to approach **Odeceixe**, the first village in the Algarve. The river here separating it from the Alentejo could only be crossed 'in a square boat pulled by a rope', when Southey passed this way in 1801. It is now spanned by a bridge, beyond which the road winds through a district in which wild geraniums flourish, with a view east towards the Serra de Monchique, before descending to low-lying **Aljezur**, conquered in 1246. The ruins of a Moorish castle crown the hill. When Francisco Gomes de Avelar, Bishop of Algarve (1739–1816) began to build a church on higher and healthier ground to the east, the locals showed scant interest, and at his death the project was abandoned.

From here a new road climbs east along the southern flank of the range to Marmelete to meet the N266 between Monchique and Caldas de Monchique; see latter part of Rte 10.

At **Alfambra** the main road bears left across a shoulder of the Serra de Monchique directly to Lagos; see Rte 13.

---

## Alfambra to Lagos via Sagres

70km. The recommended detour may be made by taking the right-hand fork (N268), which leads through lonely country broken up by humpy hills to **Carrapateira**, protected by a ruined fort, before turning away from the sea to (27km) **Vila do Bispo**. Before 1515 known as Santa Maria do Cabo, and once of importance, it was severely damaged in the 1755 earthquake. The church contains 18C *azulejos*.

**Sagres** (*Pousada do Infante*), 10km south-west, now a windswept resort and small fishing-port, lying to the left at a T-junction, is in danger of over-exploitation.

Ahead at the junction is an old fort and more modern *rosa dos ventos* or wind-compass. The former preserves a house claiming to have been occupied by the 'Infante de Sagres' (Henry the Navigator), but this was more certainly at Cape St Vincent, 5km to the west. Known as Vila do Infante, it was sacked by Drake and further damaged in the earthquake of 1755. It was here that Prince Henry founded a school of navigation and set up an observatory, and here he died in 1460, after which the place decayed, with the centre of maritime studies moving to Lisbon.

There remain on *****Cape St Vincent** (Cabo São Vicente) a ruined 16C monastery and a lighthouse. This barren south-west extremity of mainland Europe is certainly majestic in its desolation. The Atlantic heaves on three sides of its high rockbound promontory, on the precipitous edge of which the local fishermen calmly perch.

This Promontorium Sacrum of the Romans takes its present name from the legend that the relics of the martyred saint were brought here in the 8C, from which, guided by a pair of ravens, they were in 1173 miraculously translated to Lisbon. Several naval engagements have been fought off this cape, among others the defeat of Sir George Rooke by Admiral Tourville (1693). Rodney attacked a Spanish fleet here in 1780; while on 14 February 1797 Admiral Jervis (later Lord St Vincent) and Nelson with 15 vessels defeated 27 Spanish men-of-war; Sir Charles Napier defeated a small Miguelite squadron here in 1833 during the War of the Two Brothers.

On returning to Vila do Bispo, bear right onto the N125 through **Raposeira**, where Henry the Navigator resided before setting up his headquarters at Vila do Infante, 'being remote from the tumult of people and propitious for the contemplation of study'. Its church has a Manueline door. The hermitage of N.S. de Guadalupe, with capitals of interest, dates from the 13C.

The dull road runs parallel to the coast through cistus-covered hills, off which a number of resorts such as **Praia da Luz** may be reached, to (23km) Lagos. A good view of the walls of Lagos may be had by turning right at the crossroads when approaching from this direction. For Lagos itself, see Rte 13.

# 12 · Lisbon to Faro via Alcácer do Sal and Ourique

*Total distance, 283km (175 miles). A2 motorway to (45km) the Marateca junction, there turning onto the IP1 for (33km) Alcácer do Sal. 23km Grândola—77km Ourique—53km Bartolomeu de Messines—15km N125, there turning left to bypass Albufeira, 4km south—37km Faro.*

*This main road to a central point on the Algarve coast, although the most rapid approach, has its hazards, as too many cars drive along it at high speed, and caution is advised.*

For the first part of this route see the latter part of Rte 5A, in reverse; and from the Marateca junction to Grândola via Alcácer, Rte 11.

At 15km beyond Grândola (see latter part of Rte 8) the road bears south—the left-hand turning here leading via Ferreira do Alentejo to Beja; see Rte 9A—bypassing most villages as it ascends the upper valley of the Sado to skirt **Ourique**. For the site of the legendary battle, see Castro Verde (14km north-east; Rte 10). There is a good Manueline church at **Garvão**, 15km north-west.

From a point some 6.5km south of Ourique, a track leads right off the main road for c 4km to the well-sited Luso-Roman camp of **\*Castro dos Palheiros** or **da Cola**, with its rectangular walled enclosure, before starting to climb between the eastern foothills of the Serra de Monchique and those of the Serra do Caldeira.

From **São Marcos de Serra**, which is skirted, a good road leads 13km north-west to **Nave Redondo**, 12km south of Sta Clara-a-Velha; see Rte 10.

**São Bartolomeu de Messines**, later bypassed, has a late 14C church containing spiral columns and a carved marble pulpit.

From here the N124 leads south-west along the sunny south flank of a ridge to Silves (28km south-west; see Rte 13); and south-east to (10km) **Alte**, where the 16C church preserves interesting early *azulejos*. There are some bat-haunted stalactite caves in the neighbourhood known as the Buraco dos Mouros and the Igrejinha dos Soudos. South of Alte, on the N270, is **Paderne**, with a ruined Moorish castle, captured in 1248.

The IP1 continues south past São Bartolomeu to approach the transverse dual carriageway, only the eastern half of which—from here to the Guadiana—has been completed, and then the N125, which was until recently the main highway running parallel to the southern coast of the Algarve. Albufeira is entered by turning right 2km east of this latter junction, for which, and for Faro, 35km further east; see Rte 13, and likewise for the N125 leading west to Portimão and Lagos.

# 13 · Lagos to Faro and Vila Real de Santo António: the Algarve

*Total distance, 136km (84 miles). N125. 18km Portimão (also bypassed)—9km Lagoa. Silves is 7km north.—21km. Albufeira is 4km south. 8km. From here the N270 (inland road) forks left via (13km) Loulé and (13.5km) São Brás de Alportel to (22km) Tavira. The N125 continues east to (27km) Faro—8km Olhão—22km Tavira—23km Vila Real de Santo António.*

*The dual carriageway has now been completed, leading off the IP1 north of Albufeira and driving east roughly parallel with the coastal road to approach the international bridge spanning the Guadiana north of Vila Real. This should ease the flow of traffic between the Spanish frontier and the central Algarve. There are plans to extend it to the west, and a stretch bypassing Portimão has already been finished.*

*This route may be followed by train, calling at all the main centres: Lagos, Silves, Albufeira, Faro, Tavira and Vila Real de Santo António.*

For Sagres, and the coast between the Cabo de São Vicente and Lagos, see the latter part of Rte 11.

**LAGOS** (11,746 inhabitants), the most westerly town of any consequence on the Algarve, and once its capital (from 1578 to 1755), lies on the west bank of an estuary sheltered from the south-west by the promontory of Ponta da Piedade. This fishing-port with its sardine-canning factories has been developed as a holiday resort in recent years, and much of its charm has evaporated.

■ The **Tourist Office** is in the Largo Marquês de Pombal.

### History
The successor of Roman Lacobriga (possibly at adjacent Monte Molião) was bypassed by the Crusaders in 1189, who rather than attacking the Moorish capital at Silves, proceeded to sack the neighbouring stronghold of Alvor. Lagos itself was not captured from the Moors until 1241. It later became a favourite residence of Henry the Navigator (cf. Sagres), who formed a company here for trading with the newly discovered African territories; while in 1574 and 1578 it was one of the main ports of assembly for the ill-fated expeditions of Dom Sebastião.

A decline set in after it was laid in ruins by the 1755 earthquake. It was off the coast here that in 1759 Admiral Boscawen defeated a French squadron commanded by De La Clue, who lost five ships. It was visited by Southey in 1801, who was arrested for not having 'waited on' the Corregedor on his arrival. Here he bought a work-bag of aloe fibre for his wife: one of the first tourists to patronise the local handicraft industry.

A stretch of the mid 14C walls (restored) flanks the Av. dos Descobrimentos, skirting the waterfront. Another extends from the seaward end, where the walls are set off by gardens. The defensive towers on the landward side are well seen from the main road climbing north-west. Near here is a fort, and an aqueduct of 1490–1521, while overlooking the harbour is the Fort of Pau da Bandeira.

In the Praça da República, half-way along the promenade, is the old custom House, below the arches of which African slaves were once auctioned, and **Santa Maria**, with its Manueline windows, from which it is said Dom Sebastião harangued his troops in June 1578 before embarking on the disastrous Moroccan campaign.

Beyond (left) is the chapel of **\*Santo António** of c 1710–20, richly embellished with carved and gilt woodwork above *albarrada azulejos*. The painted vault was added after the 1755 earthquake, probably replacing a ceiling of framed paintings. Here too is the grave of Hugh Beatty (died 1789), a colonel of the Irish Regiment.

Adjacent is the local **museum**, containing miscellaneous collections, the most interesting of which are those of ethnography and archaeology, deserving more scholarly attention. It is open 9.30–12.30 and 14.00–17.00; closed Mon and holidays.

Turn right along the Rua de Silva Lopes—less narrow than many of the lanes leading off it—to reach the Largo de Marquês de Pombal, and the central Praça Gil Eanes.

There are some curious rock formations to the south of the town, beyond the Ponta da Piedade. For the excursion to Sagres and Cape St Vincent, see the latter part of Rte 11, in reverse.

Shortly after leaving Lagos the N125 skirts **Odiáxere**, 9km north-west of which is the attractively sited reservoir da Bravura.

Circling to the east, **Alvor** is bypassed, an ancient port (assumed to be the Carthaginian Portus Hannibalis), which was sacked and plundered by a crusading fleet in 1189, when the few thousand Moors who had taken refuge there were massacred. Dom João II died here in 1495, after taking the waters at Caldas de Monchique in a futile attempt to obtain relief for his dropsy. It has a good Manueline church. There are slight remains of Roman origin at **Abidaca**, on a slope to the east. A minor road leads directly east to Praia da Rocha; see below.

A bypass now spans the Arade north of **PORTIMÃO** (previously Vila Nova de Portimão; 16,786 inhabitants), a fishing-port with canning factories. Most of its older buildings were destroyed in the 1755 earthquake, while the slight interest it may have had formerly has been entirely dissipated by recent speculative development, making the place an ugly and charmless resort. It lies on the west bank of the Arade estuary, its mouth defended by two old forts, where, in July 1189, another force of Crusaders (including some English), led by Dom Sancho I, landed to besiege Silves; see below.

Now contiguous to the south is the resort of **Praia da Rocha**, promoted on account of the erratically shaped rocks and caves of this indented coast, and for its sandy beaches.

The main road shortly bypasses **Estombar**, birthplace in 1031 of the poet Ibn 'Ammar, with a Manueline church containing a curiously carved column, beyond which **Lagoa** (6570 inhabitants) is skirted. A left-hand turning here leads north to Silves, the best view of which may be had from this approach road.

**SILVES** (6048 inhabitants), once, as Shalb or Xelb, the capital of the kingdom of Algarve, lies on the north bank of the Arade, spanned by a new bridge parallel to the old. The town retains little but its ramparts, a ruined red sandstone castle, and a cathedral, to remind one of its illustrious past.

### History
The Arab chronicler Idrisi reported that it was protected by a strong wall, possessed a port and shipyards, and was 'of fine appearance, with attractive buildings and well-furnished bazaars. Its inhabitants are Yemenite Arabs and others, who speak pure Arabic, compose poetry, and are eloquent in speech and elegant in manners, both the upper and the lower classes'. In the mid 12C it was the centre of Ibn Qasi's revolt against the Almoravids.

In 1189, after a terrible three-month siege by Dom Sancho I, assisted by the above-mentioned Crusaders, the starving citizens opened their gates to the Christians, who proceeded to sack the place, but by 1191 it was again in Moorish hands, and they were not finally driven out until c 1249.

Until 1579 the city was a bishopric, which was then transferred to Faro, for a decline had set in with the silting up of the river-port, and in 1755 what remained of the then depopulated city was severely damaged in the earthquake, so much so that it was described a century later as 'one of the most desolate and deserted places in Portugal'.

The upper town is approached through a Moorish gate in the walls, which themselves deserve inspection, to reach the **cathedral** of dark sandstone, probably erected on the site of a mosque. In 1596 the building was sacked by Essex, and it has been largely spoilt by restorations since the earthquake. Its west portal, flanked by two towers, the plain octagonal piers, and vaulted chancel, are its main architectural features.

Above stands the Moorish **castle**, 'the colour of congealed blood', as well if clinically described by Sarah Bradford. Its interior, now laid out with gardens, contains little of interest apart from the huge vaulted cisterns, but its parapet walk commands pleasant views of the orange-groves and almond orchards in the vicinity. A municipal museum may be visited.

A pleasant drive is that leading 17km north-west on the N124 to São Bartolomeu de Messines: see latter part of Rte 12.

The main road continues east through (11km) **Alcantarilha**, reputed for its tangerines, and with a Manueline church. 3km to the south is **Armação de Pera**, a resort sited near more tooth-like rocks; on the east bank of its estuary is an 18C fort. From adjacent **Pêra** one may follow a minor road directly to Albufeira, the main approach to which turns right 10km east of Alcantarilha, before meeting the IP1, where turn left to reach the present entrance to the new dual carriageway driving east; see below.

**Albufeira**, now a popular resort, preserves the remains of a Moorish castle (Tourist Office: Rua 5 de Outubro). Its beach is reached from the lower town by a tunnel pierced through the cliff in 1935. There are several rock outcrops and caves in the vicinity.

At (7km) **Boliqueime**, to the left of the N125, Henry the Navigator is said to have made the first plantations of sugar-canes in Portugal, having introduced them from Cyprus; they were later transplanted to Madeira, and Brazil.

The N270, the old inland road to (48.5km) Tavira forks left here, also providing another entrance to the dual carriageway, before climbing up to (13km) **Loulé**, a well-sited and thriving town of 9105 inhabitants, with remains of Moorish ramparts, and an interesting 13C Igreja Matriz (behind the market), recently restored. The large open-work chimneys of Loulé are a characteristic feature, but are perhaps better seen in some of the smaller towns and villages of the Algarve. The road, providing occasional distant sea views, continues east through (13.5km) São Brás de Alportel (sub-route on p 177), later descending through attractive hilly country to regain the coast at (22km) Tavira: see below.

The dual carriageway (IP1) also provides a convenient approach to Estói and the Roman remains at Milreu (see below) and, later, to Tavira.

---

The coastal road (N125) shortly passes a turning to **Vilamoura**, with a marina, where adjacent to the resort of **Quarteira** (8284 inhabitants) are the important remains of a *__Roman villa__: excavations continue. From here one may work one's way north-east through a maze of lanes flanked by modern villas among trees to regain the main road.

Beyond **Almansil**, the church of *São Lourenço is passed to the left, its interior and dome entirely covered with blue *azulejos* of 1730, attributed to Policarpo de Oliveira Bernardes.

Several golfing resorts have been established during recent decades between here and the coast, among them **Vale de Lobo** and **Quinta do Lago**.

## FARO

Faro (31,619 inhabitants; airport), the most southerly town in Portugal and the flourishing capital of the Algarve, while long famous for its figs and almonds, cannot on any account be considered a place of much architectural attraction, preserving few relics of antiquity, while its modern buildings are of no consequence.

■ The **Tourist Office** is at 8–12 Rua da Misericórdia. The **train station** faces Largo da Estacaõ; the **bus station** is on Avenida da República.

### History

It was long assumed that Milreu (c 8km north; see below) was Roman Ossonoba, but it is now ascertained that this was in fact Faro, although few remains of that city can be seen. Faro (also once known as Santa Maria de Harune) was taken from the Moors by Dom Afonso III in 1249, and increased in prosperity, having a large Jewish colony, who in the late 15C established a printing press here. In 1596 (when under Spanish domination), an English force under the Earl of Essex, finding Loulé and Faro deserted, sacked and burnt the latter. Essex had the forethought to carry off the well-bound theological library of some 200 volumes (already mutilated by the Inquisition) belonging to Bishop Osorio (known as the 'Portuguese Cicero'), and later donated the indigestible tomes to the Bodleian Library, which was considered a generous gesture from a Cambridge man. The city suffered severely in the earthquakes of 1722 and 1755, and its rebuilding was largely due to its energetic bishop, Francisco Gomes de Avelar (1739–1816). Another loss to Faro was the destruction of the musical archives of the composer Sousa Carvalho, whose son, the cathedral organist, had his house sacked by partisans of Dom Miguel.

The only area of interest in the straggling modern town is the walled enceinte ('Vila-a-Dentro'), just south-east of the harbour (*doca*) and yacht basin, with a

Maritime museum to the north. It is not the easiest part to approach, owing to a confusing system of one-way streets.

The area may be entered from the adjacent Jardim Manuel Bivar by the 18C Arco da Vila, with its statue of St Thomas Aquinas, a few paces from which is the tourist office, where enquire if the miniature Teatro Lethes, a converted chapel, may be visited. On passing through the gate, a short walk brings one to the **cathedral** or *Sé*, a Renaissance building damaged by earthquakes, and retaining the squat 13C tower of an older church, which had been built on the site of the Roman forum. It is open from 10.00–12.00 daily. The interior, embellished by *azulejos*, contains the 18C tomb of Bishop Pereira da Silva, supported by two lions, a 17C altar in the sacristy, and a red and gilt chinoiserie organ painted in 1751 by Francisco Cordeiro. The old Episcopal palace stands to the west.

Facing a small square just south of the cathedral apse is the former convent of N.S. da Assunção (1539), restored and transformed into a **museum**, most of the rooms of which surround an attractive two-storeyed cloister by Afonso Pires. (Opening hours are Mon–Fri 9.00–12.00 and 15.00–17.00.) Notice the roof (cf. Tavira). The archaeological collections are important, including material from Roman Milreu, a mosaic being prominent. The church contains a 14C Nottingham alabaster. The paintings, among them *Four Doctors of the Church* by Vieira Portuense, are of less interest. Note also the 16C chest (? from Goa) of mother of pearl (*madrepérola*), and some Mudéjar *azulejos*.

Turn right on making one's exit, pass through the old Arco de Repouso, and bear diagonally across a deserted square to reach, adjacent to barracks, 17C **São Francisco**, with *azulejos* of 1762 and a richly gilt *capela-mór*.

From here, turning due north, the Praça Alexandre Herculano is approached, and just beyond, the Rua de Santo António (a continuation of one of the main thoroughfares). Immediately to the right is the Ethnographical Museum, with displays of models of chimneys, costumes, old photographs, etc., and sections devoted to fishing, basketwork, etc. It is open Mon–Fri 9.30–12.30 and 14.00–17.30.

The street is continued by the tree-lined Av. 5 de Outubro, beyond the far end of which is the high-lying chapel of **Santo António do Alto**, commanding the best view of Faro and its lagoon.

Some minutes' walk to the north-west of the latter museum, via the Ruas Vasco da Gama and José Estêvão, brings one to **São Pedro** (16C; rebuilt), which escaped the fire of 1596, containing a well-carved polychromed and gilt Last Supper. Behind the church is the Largo do Carmo, dominated by the two belfries of its early 18C church, with an attractive 18C organ, and a macabre ossuary.

Ferries to the resort of **Praia de Faro**, on a sand-spit to the south-west, leave from a jetty just south of the harbour. This beach is one of several sand bars, that known as the Cabo de Santa Maria, with a lighthouse, being the southernmost extremity of Portugal.

---

At **Estói**, 8km inland and just east of crossroads, a turning (left) leads immediately to the extensive ruins of the Roman villa of *\*Milreu*. It was visited by Southey in 1801, but most of the 2–7C ruins were not excavated until 1877. These include a temple converted into a Palaeo-Christian basilica, and 3C baths ornamented with mosaics. Some of the latter, and other finds from this site may be seen in the gardens of the neighbouring Palace of the Condes de Carvalhal, Viscondes de Estoi (18C, with 19C additions).

---

From Faro, the N125 continues east, at 8km skirting **Olhão** (24,607 inhabitants). The older cubist quarters of the fishing-port, with its marshmallow-like dwellings inviting comparison with North Africa, has been engulfed by recent and unattractive development. It was one of the first towns in the Algarve to rise against the French in 1808, and it is said that its fishermen conveyed the news of their expulsion to Dom João VI in Brazil.

Near (16km) **Luz**, where the church has a good Manueline portal, stood the ancient city of Balsa, but excavations have revealed little of interest so far. The outskirts of Tavira, also bypassed, are shortly entered.

## TAVIRA

Tavira (8892 inhabitants), although damaged in the 1755 earthquake, remains one of the pleasantest towns on the Algarve, and was so described by J.M. Neale in the 1850s, and earlier by Southey as 'clean and opulent'. It lies in well-cultivated country on the river Gilão, spanned by a 17C bridge in the town centre, and lined by 18C houses with unusual Oriental-looking triple-gabled tiled roofs. It has a reputation for its figs and almonds, and its mullet are particularly succulent.

■ The **Tourist Office** is in the Praça da República.

### History
Although a 1C Greek inscription has been found in the vicinity, Tavira's early history is vague. It may have been Roman Balsa, but this is now thought to be further west near Luz. It was captured from the Moors in 1239 by Paio Peres Correa, and raised to the rank of a city in 1520. With the silting up of the port (dredged in 1932), and visitations of plague, a decline set in, although it was briefly reputed for its tapestries in the late 18C.

From the arcaded central Praça da República (its medieval arches replaced by modern copies) adjacent to riverside gardens, one may ascend into the old walled town, passing the church of the **Misericórdia**, with a fine portal of 1541 and well-carved *altar-mór*. Beyond (left), adjacent to the ruins of the castle, is **Santa Maria do Castelo**, traditionally on the site of a mosque, rebuilt after 1755, but retaining a 13C Gothic doorway. In its chancel are the tombs of Correa (died 1275; see History), and an inscription recording the 'Sete Caçadores', seven Christian knights treacherously slain by the Moors during a truce, while they were out hunting, and whose death precipitated the final successful assault on the town.

From here the main road continues east, after **Conceição**, its church with a Gothic portal, providing intermittent sea views, to bypass **Cacela**, a decayed port of ancient origin, where the church has a fine Renaissance door. It was here that the Duque da Terceira disembarked in June 1833 with 2500 men before his march on Lisbon (abandoned by the Miguelites on 24 July).

**Monte Gordo**, a recently developed resort, is passed on approaching **Vila Real de Santo António** (8151 inhabitants), at the mouth of the Guadiana facing Ayamonte, to which plies a ferry, although partly superseded by the new international bridge spanning the river a short distance upstream. Huelva is some 60km further east of Ayamonte, and Sevilla another 95km beyond, for which see *Blue Guide Spain*, 6th ed.

Vila Real was run up in some five months in 1774 by Pombal near the site of Santo António de Arenilha, an ancient town, possibly a Phoenician settlement, which had been engulfed by the sea c 1600. This 'new' town is laid out on the rectangular grid plan he had chosen for the rebuilding of the Baixa quarter in Lisbon, and apparently all the ashlar used in its construction was brought here from the capital at a ruinous expense, *after* which stone quarries were 'discovered' only a few miles away.

Apart from a small museum devoted to printing, there is little to see in Vila Real, which is important as a tuna-canning centre, and for the export of the copper ore of São Domingos; see Rte 9A.

For adjacent Castro Marim, and the roads climbing through the hills to Mértola, Beja and Serpa, see the latter part of Rte 9A, in reverse.

# 14 · Elvas to Abrantes

## A. Via Portalegre

*Total distance, 156km (97 miles). N373. 19km Campo Maior—N371. 27km Arronches—N246. 23km Portalegre—IP2. 26km Alpalhão—15km N118—46km Abrantes.*

Although the direct road (N426) from Elvas north to Arronches is 14km shorter, the more interesting route is that via Campo Maior, to the north-east, an old frontier town which in 1811–12 was the centre of Wellington's defensive position facing Badajoz. The left flank was at **Ouguela**, some 8km beyond, with a ruined castle of 1310 (views); while there is an Iron Age site at Castro de Segóvia, 5km south.

**Campo Maior** (7135 inhabitants), of Roman origin, was taken from the Moors in 1219. In 1310 it was fortified, but the castle was enlarged at a later date, and provided with Vaubanesque outworks under the direction of Nicolas de Langres. Its two churches are of slight interest.

> In 1732 the powder magazine within the fortress was struck by lightning, the explosion not only destroying most of the citadel, but also numerous houses, and killing 1500 people. Nevertheless, during the Peninsular War it successfully withstood minor attacks. The position was strong but unpleasant, according to Commissary Schaumann, who was stationed here, for 'All day long we were infested by snakes, blowflies, and other vermin, while our water came from a dirty stream known as the River Caya, in which the whole army bathed, the cattle went to drink, and dirty clothes were washed. At night we were plagued with scorpions, mosquitoes, and a piercingly cold wind'.

The Caia has been dammed to form a reservoir to the west of the town, from which the road bears north-west, with views to the east, to approach **Arronches**, Roman Plagiaria, which (like **Assumar**, 9km west, Roman Ad Septem Aras), with ruined walls, lay on the direct Roman road from Mérida to Lisbon. The area was then perhaps more populous. **Alegrete**, c 12km north of Arronches, preserves the ruins of an early 14C castle on the site of an earlier fortress.

### PORTALEGRE

Continue north-west, parallel to the Serra de São Mamede, to Portalegre (15,383 inhabitants), capital of the Alto Alentejo and since 1545 an episcopal city, standing at the foot of the Serra de São Mamede, the highest range in Portugal south of the Tagus. The district was well described by Huldine Beamish in her study *The Hills of Alentejo* (1958).

■ The **Tourist Office** is at 25 Estrada de Santana. There are **trains** from Elvas. The **bus station** is on Rua Nuno Álvarez Pereira.

### History
Its long history has been unexceptional. It was besieged for five months in 1299 by Dom Dinis during the dynastic feuds of the period, and was attacked by the Spanish in 1704, when Stanhope's regiment was captured. During the Peninsular War it was often the winter quarters of British troops: military bands played in the outer cloisters of nunneries to entertain their inmates; races were organised; and occasional hunts took place between here and Castelo de Vide. The town contains cork factories, among them that developed by George Wheelhouse Robinson in the late 19C; and once had a reputation for its textiles, and a much publicised tapestry factory still exists in an abandoned Jesuit convent of 1695.

The older walled town stands on a height to the south-west, dominated by the **cathedral**, with its twin pinnacled towers, commenced in 1556, but mainly 18C. It is a plain building, with massive pilasters. Its architectural retables (c 1590) are by Gaspar and Domingos Coelho, with paintings possibly by Simão Rodrigues. Also notable are the *azulejos* in the sacristy, and the pediment to its cloister.

Adjacent is the **municipal museum**, pleasantly installed in one of the few remaining 18C mansions of Portalegre, containing small collections of furniture, ceramics, fans, silver snuff-boxes, a Chinese silver tea service, worn Arraiolos carpets, and paintings and sketches by Abel Santos. It is open 9.30–12.30 and 14.00–18.00; Sat 9.30–11.30 and 15.00–18.30. To the north is the yellow-painted Palace of the Abrancalhas (*Palácio Amarelo*), in a poor state of repair, but preserving ornate 17C ironwork.

There is a good small **museum** in the house of the poet José Régio, a short distance south-east, with collections of folk art, crucifixes, ironwork, etc. (Open 9.30–12.30 and 14.00–18.00; closed Mon and hols.)

Perhaps the most impressive monument surviving is to be seen in the convent of **\*N.S. da Conceição**, a short walk east of the Largo A.J. Lourinha, the main square of the lower town. The convent (also known as that of São Bernardo), now a training school for military police (who on application at the gate will courteously escort visitors round), was founded in 1518 by Jorge de Melo, Bishop of Guarda, whose **\*tomb** (c 1540), attributed to Chanterène or a pupil, is seen in the church. The building itself, with a good portal of 1538 in its porch, is decorated with very fine \**azulejos* of 1739; but its two cloisters have not been improved by the military presence.

For Crato and Flor da Rosa, 20km or so due west, see Rte 15B.

## Portalegre to Marvão
22km. (Buses run between the two.) The direct road (N359) veers north-east just north of Portalegre, shortly climbing over the Serra de São Mamede, off which, at **São Salvador de Aramenha**, is the site of the Roman *oppidum* of Medobriga or Ammaia, but most of its scanty remains have been removed to Lisbon. The road descends to meet that from the Spanish frontier some 7.5km south-east of Castelo de Vide, and 6km south of Marvão, crowning its mountain: for both, see Rte 16.

A slightly longer road (29km) climbs due east from Portalegre, off which a track to the right approaches the summit of the range (1025m), commanding extensive \*views.

Castelo de Vide may be approached more directly by driving north from Portalegre on the N246 (off which a minor road crosses the Serra) after 18km meeting the main road just west of the town.

The IP2 leads north to a junction of roads at **Alpalhão**.

### Alpalhão to Castelo Branco via Nisa

58km. The N18, the former main road (see below) leads due north to (12km) **Nisa**, with remains of fortifications and gates; and 3km away, relics of the older settlement. Hillier country is entered before descending steeply (views) into the Tagus valley.

The river is crossed just east of the **\*Portas de Ródão**, where it forces its way through a narrow gorge between high perpendicular cliffs, of which the bridge commands a good view. The crossing here was of vital importance during the Peninsular War, and provided with a bridge of boats by Wellington. 'The Passage of the Tagus' at this point was reproduced in a number of contemporary prints. On the far bank is **Vila Velha de Ródão**, with remains of a castle and a small museum in the Largo do Pelourinho, partly devoted to the archaeology of the area, together with replicas of Palaeolithic engravings from now-submerged sites near the banks of the Tagus.

The N18 turns north-east through the rolling country of the Beira Baixa, with occasional distant views of the Serra da Estrela ahead beyond the nearer Serra da Gardunha, at 14km meeting the completed part of the highway between Castelo Branco and Abrantes (see below). For Castelo Branco, see Rte 17.

A new highway (IP2)—faster, but longer—has recently been completed, which circles to the north-west from Alpalhãa to a junction 11km west of Nisa, crossing the Tagus near the Barragem de Fratel to reach the start of the IP6 under construction, which will provide direct communication north of the river between Castelo Branco and Abrantes. Until its completion, one must turn west at the abovementioned junction for Abrantes, described in the latter part of Rte 22A.

# B.  Via Monforte, Alter do Chão, and Ponte de Sor

*Total distance, 128km (80 miles). 32km Monforte—N369. 28km Alter do Chão— N369 and N119. 34km Ponte de Sor—N2. 34km Abrantes.*

Passing under the aqueduct of Elvas (see Rte 5A), the N246 is briefly followed before forking left for **Barbacena**, with relics of a 16C fortress, and crossing rolling country to **Monforte**, with a ruined castle of 1309. It was the birthplace of Manuel Barradas (1572–?), the Jesuit missionary.

The road descend into a small valley dotted with chapels, and over a medieval bridge. After c 4km a left-hand turning leads 1km to the well-sited *Quinta da Torre de Palma*, from the main gate of which a muddy track leads south-west to the extensive remains of a \*Roman villa, Palaeo-Christian basilica (c 4C) and burialground.

Regaining the main road, continue north-west through **Cabeço do Vide**, with castle ruins and—just north of crossroads—**Alter do Chão**, of Roman foundation and probably the Abelterium of the *Antonine Itinerary*. In the central square rises the restored \*castle of 1359; here also is the 18C Solar de Vasconcelos, and a Renaissance fountain.

Some 4km east, at **Alter Pedroso** is another ruined fortress (views); while 3km north-west is the Estação Zootécnica, replacing a stud farm established here in 1748 by Dom João V. For Crato, 12km north, see Rte 15B.

The road now veers west, off which at 9km a left-hand fork leads to (16km) Avis (see Rte 15B) via **Seda**, with remains of walls, later skirting the picturesque Ribeiro de Seda, now part of a reservoir.

The right-hand fork descends into the valley of the Seda, crossed by the imposing six-arched *Roman bridge of **Vila Formosa**, beyond which a Roman road is followed to **Ponte de Sor**, now an important cork centre. After 12km the road veers north-west towards Abrantes, commanding the far bank of the Tagus; see Rte 16.

## C. Via Monforte and Avis

*Total distance, 139km (86 miles). 31km Monforte—N243. at 22km Fronteira is 2km north.—24km Avis—N224. 28km Ponte de Sor—N2. 34km Abrantes.*

For the road to Monforte, see Rte 14B, above. There turn south-west to follow an attractive road parallel to the south bank of the Ribeira Grande to bypass **Fronteira**, founded in 1226 by the Master of the Order of Avis, Fernão Rodrigues Monteiro, and the birthplace of the composer Manuel Cardosa (1566–1650). Near here the battle of Atoleiros (1384) took place, in which Nun' Alvares Pereira defeated a superior Spanish force (traditionally 'without loss'), the first engagement in the campaign terminating at Aljubarrota (cf.).

The road continues due west to **Avis**, an attractively situated village on a height above the confluence of the swollen Ribeiras de Avis and de Seda.

In 1220 it was granted to the Spanish military order of Calatrava, referred to in Portugal as the Knights of Évora, who built a castle, and settled in the area, soon becoming known as the Knights of Avis (or Aviz), and later as the Order of São Bento. Dom João I (son of Dom Pedro I and Teresa Lourenço) was Grand Master of the Order before he acceded to the Portuguese throne in 1385 and married Philippa of Lancaster in 1387: the Avis dynasty survived until 1580.

The monastery of São Bento was frequently transformed, the last time in 1711, but the church preserves a good Baroque retable, and a large 16C sacristy; while three imposing towers remain of the original fortress.

A rough road bears north-west to Ponte de Sor (see Rte 15A) and on to reach the Tagus below Abrantes; see Rte 16.

# 15 · (Cáceres) Valencia de Alcántara to Estremoz

## A. Via Portalegre and Monforte

*Total distance, 98km (61 miles). 12km to the frontier at Galegos—10km to the cross-roads below Marvão, 6km north—N239. 17km. Portalegre—N18. 29km Monforte—30km Estremoz.*

Rtes 15A and B describe two alternative roads to Estremoz (for Lisbon, or Évora) if entering Portugal from Cáceres in preference to Badajoz.

For the road from Valencia de Alcántara to the crossroads below Marvão, and Marvão itself, see Rte 16, and for the roads climbing over the Serra de São Mamede from that junction to Portalegre, the paragraphs, in reverse, after Portalegre itself; see Rte 14A.

From here, the improved N18 drives due south to bypass Monforte (see Rte 14B) and then veers south-west to skirt **Veiros**, with a church of 1559 and castle of 1308, partly destroyed in 1662. There is an Iron Age site some 2km south.

The hilltop fortifications of Estremoz, dominating the area, shortly come into view. See Rte 5A for this and for the main road on to Lisbon, and also for the continuation of the N18 to Évoramonte and Évora.

# B.  Via Flor da Rosa, Crato, and Alter do Chão

*Total distance, 127km (79 miles). 12km to the frontier at Galegos—10km to the crossroads before Marvão, 6km north—N359. 17km Portalegre—N119. 21km Crato. Flor de Rosa is 3km north. N245. 12km Alter do Chão—18km Fronteira—13km Sousel—18km Estremoz.*

*If making the alternative approach to Flor da Rosa via Castelo de Vide and Alpalhão, the distance will be only 5km longer.*

For the road to Portalegre, and Portalegre itself, see Rte 14A; for Castelo de Vide, Rte 16.

From Portalegre, the N119 shortly turns off the IP2 (leading north-west) and leads directly to Crato, but it is worth making the short detour to the neighbouring village of **Flor da Rosa** if only to visit the recently restored dependencies of the large fortified *convent founded there in 1356 by the prior Alvaro Gonçalves Pereira (father of Nun' Alvares). It now accommodates a *pousada*.

**Crato**, an ancient little town, was a headquarters or *Grão Priorado* of the Order of Crato, a branch of the Knights Hospitallers, transferred here from Leça do Bailio (near Oporto) in 1350. The last of the Grand Priors was Dom António, in 1580 a rival to Philip II of Spain in his claim to the Portuguese throne. António (1531–95; died in Paris) was the bastard son of the Infante Luíz and Violante Gomes, known as 'the Pelican'. Little remains of the once powerful 13C castle, destroyed in 1662 by Don Juan de Austria, but the Igreja Matriz (rebuilt in 1456, and later altered) contains some pleasant 18C *azulejos*, and good altars.

From here the road climbs south, later passing (right) a tumulus, to Alter do Chão (see Rte 14B) and then Fronteira; see Rte 14C. From **Sousel** a byroad leads some 4km south-west to an attractive modern hilltop *pousada*), providing a panoramic view to the south, while the main road continues south past (Santa Vitória do) **Ameixial**, where in May 1663 Don Juan de Austria was decisively defeated by the Conde de Vilar Flor and Schomberg, with a contingent of English troops under the command of Colonel Thomas Hood. It is said that Dom Afonso VI, on hearing of the gallantry of the English, sent each company a present of snuff, which they threw away in disgust; while Charles II of England ordered 4000 crowns to be distributed among them.

For Estremoz, see Rte 5A.

# 16 · (Cáceres) Valencia de Alcántara to Abrantes, and Santarém, via Alpiarça

*Total distance, 178km (110 miles). 12km to the frontier at Galegos—10km the Marvão crossroads: Marvão is 6km north.—N246. 8.5km Castelo de Vide—17km Alpalhão—IP2. At 15km turn left onto the N118 for (46km) Abrantes—N3. 27km Entroncamento crossroads (19km south of Tomar)—N365. 7km Golegã—N243. 26km Alpiarça—N368. 10km Santarém.*

The N118, referred to above, will be superseded by the IP6 under construction along the north bank of the Tagus, which, when completed, will branch off the IP2 circling north-west from Alpalhão to Castelo Branco just after spanning the river at the Barragem de Fratel. (A left-hand turning before the road descends to the river, and leads shortly to **Amieirado Tejo**, with a 14C castle.)

Driving from east to west, the IP6 will bypass **Envendos** and **Mação**, near both of which are Roman bridges, and (left) **Belver**, with ruins of a late 12C *castle, restored in 1390, surrounded by towers, and later, Abrantes, to meet the completed stretch at the Entroncamento junction, which joins the A1 motorway for Lisbon, west of Torres Novas, for which see the sub-route below, after Abrantes.

The main road (N521) from Cáceres leads through (30km) Aliseda for (93km) Valencia de Alcántara, from which a recommended detour (only 12km longer) is that turning off onto the C521 at Aliseda for Alburquerque, there bearing north-west on the C530 to Valencia de Alcántara: see *Blue Guide Spain*, 6th ed.

From Valencia de Alcántara, the road turns south-west to the frontier at **Puerto Roque/Galegos**, situated in a narrow wooded valley between a serrated ridge of the Serra de São Mamede (south-west) and the Serra de Marvão (north-west).

On approaching the Marvão crossroads, the fortress of Marvão itself is seen crowning a commanding height to the right, well worth climbing to unless visibility is bad.

Turning right, the road climbs steeply for 6km to *\**MARVÃO** (*Pousada de Santa Maria*), passing the convent of N.S. da Estrela (founded in 1448 as a Franciscan monastery) on approaching the summit. The village, sited on this outcrop of the Marvão range, known to the Romans as Herminius minor, has been fortified from remote antiquity. Its 13C ramparts remain practically intact, but outworks were added in the 17C.

■ The **Tourist Office** is in the Rua Dr. Matos Magalhães.

There is a small museum near the castle, which commands very extensive *views (to the summit of the Serra da Estrela to the north-west, and east over Spain).

For the roads from the junction below Marvão to Portalegre, see Rte 14A in reverse. (There are buses to Portalegre.)

The main road continues north-west to **CASTELO DE VIDE**, an attractive and beautifully situated old spa on the slope of a spur of the Serra de São Mamede, was the birthplace of José Xavier Mousinho da Silveira (1780–1849), the Liberal statesman, and possibly of Garcia da Orta (1500–c 1570), the natural philosopher, physician, and traveller.

■ The **Tourist Office** is at 81 Rua Bartolemeu Álvares da Santa. By **bus** from Marvão, change at Portagem; buses also to Portalegre.

The central Praça de Dom Pedro V is flanked by the 17C Torre Palace (now a hospital), and Baroque Santa Maria. Numerous smaller chapels, mansions (including the Town Hall of 1721), and fountains are to be found throughout the place, which also preserves its medieval *Judiaria*. The large castle, successfully defended by an Anglo-Portuguese force against a Spanish incursion in June 1704, but which later surrendered, was seriously damaged by an explosion the following year. The chapel of N.S. da Alegria here is lined with 17C *azulejos*, more of which may be seen in São Tiago.

Dotted over an area to the north, between Castelo de Vide and Castelo Branco, are a number of circular stone edifices or 'beehive' huts, similar to those at the Citânia de Briteiros, known as *chafurdões*.

From **Alpalhão** the old N18 to Castelo Branco turns to Nisa; see Rte 14A; for Flor da Rosa, to the south, see Rte 15B.

The IP2 circles north-west to meet the N118, which winds west parallel to the Tagus.Near the ancient village of **Alvega** stood Roman Aritium Vetus (beyond which the view is spoilt by a power-station), while several medieval towers and walls survive in the vicinity of **Rossio**, from which a byroad continues to skirt the south bank of the Tagus to Chamusca; see below.

From Rossio a long bridge crosses the river, on a height above which stands **ABRANTES** (5504 inhabitants), not obviously a town of great attraction.

■ The **Tourist Office** is on the Largo da Feira.

### History
It resisted an Almohad attack in 1179; was a headquarters of João de Avis in 1385, prior to the battle of Aljubarrota; was captured by Géneral Junot in 1807 in his advance on Lisbon (for which facile exploit Napoleon created him Duc d'Abrantes); and was briefly Wellington's HQ before his march on Talavera in 1809, and remained an important base throughout the war, even passing into proverb: '*Quartel General em Abrantes, tudo como dantes*' (Headquarters at Abrantes, everything as before).

The narrow lanes of the older town are conveniently explored on foot from the Largo de Santo António, at the top of the long ascending approach road. Follow the short Rua do Montepio and bear right to the Jardim da República and the 16C convent of São Domingos, with a large cloister. Flanking the neighbouring Largo Motta Ferraz is the church of the **Misericórdia**, dating from the 16C, containing eight paintings by the 16C Master of Sardoal and panels attributed to Gregório Lopes. The Rua de São ascends towards the partly restored **castle**, preserving good brick vaulting, and commanding a wide view. Santa Maria do Castelo (1215, but rebuilt in the mid 15C) houses the **Museu Lopo de Almeida**, with tombs of several members of the Almeida family, counts of Abrantes, early Sevillian tiles, paintings and sculpture, etc. (The museum is open 10.00–12.30 and 14.00–17.00; closed Mon and holidays.) Among other churches which may be visited are pinnacled São Vicente, a spacious 16–17C edifice; and São João Baptista, founded in 1300 by Santa Isabel, but rebuilt in the 16C, with a coffered ceiling. Several cobbled lanes in the upper town are flanked by characteristic mansions deserving a brief glance.

At **Sardoal**, 10km north-east of Abrantes, both the Igreja Matriz and the Town Hall preserve paintings by the 16C Master of Sardoal.

The main road descends west from Abrantes running roughly parallel to the IP6 under construction, at the confluence of the Tagus and Zêzere reaching **Constância**, Roman Pugni Tagi (from which came the name Punhete, by which it was known until 1836).

A right-hand turning here ascends the left bank of the Zêzere to **Castelo de Bode**, and the Pousada de São Pedro, overlooking a huge reservoir, to meet the N110, where turn right for Tomar: see later part of Rte 18B.

On crossing the Zêzere (over which a French bridge-of-boats was destroyed in March 1811, and where a British bridge-of-boats was thrown across the Tagus when in pursuit of Masséna's army in retreat) the important military and air base of **Tancos** is approached, which played its part in the 1974 Revolution.

A lane to the left here leads to a viewpoint overlooking the *Castle of **Almourol** on its picturesque island site, rebuilt in 1171 by Gualdim Pâis on the foundations of an earlier fortress. The tall central keep is surrounded by a rampart with nine other towers, including the square gate-tower on the south. A boat (*abrangel*) may be hired to circle the island. (It is referred to in the 16C romance of *Palmeirim de Inglaterra*, by Francisco de Moraes Cabral, translated by Southey in 1807.

---

Crossroads are met before reaching the railway junction of **Entroncamento** (13,925 inhabitants), while an entry to the completed stretch of the IP6, leading west to meet the A1 motorway for Lisbon (with an exit for Santarém), may be approached by turning right here onto the N110 for Atalaia and **Tomar**, 19km north; see Rte 18C.

The left-hand turning leads to Golegã; see below.

One may turn off the IP6 to visit **Torres Novas** (9802 inhabitants), a small industrial and agricultural town which was the birthplace of Carlos Reis (1863–1940), the artist. It is commanded by a ruined late 14C castle, while its Misericórdia has a Renaissance portal and contains *azulejos* of 1674. In the vicinity are the remains of the Roman villa of Cardílio.

The road system in this area is confusing. Check a map carefully if intending to follow the N243 north-west across the Serra de Aire (views) towards Batalha via Porto de Mós (see Rte 18A), which passes near several stalactite caves; and also if taking the attractive N361, leading south-west towards Rio Maior via **Alcanena** (near which is the Bronze Age necropolis of Marmota) and Alcanede; see Rte 18B.

---

At **Golegã**, the site of an important horse fair in early November, the Igreja Matriz preserves a very fine *Manueline portal incorporating several characteristic ornaments of the period (1510–20), surmounted by a bull's eye window decorated with two armillary spheres, etc. The Galeria Carlos Relvas (a collection of early photographs), and a museum devoted to the sculptor Martins Correia, may be visited.

The Tagus is shortly re-crossed (where in 1385 it was forded by a force under João de Avis in the expectation of an invasion from the south-east), to enter the market-town of **Chamusca**.

At **Salvador**, some 25km south-east, is a large church of interest, founded by Dom Afonso III, but much altered and restored.

The main road continues south-west to (17km) **Alpiarça** (6110 inhabitants), where the 'Casa dos Patudos', just south of the village, formerly the home of the politician and collector José Relvas (1858–1929), is now a museum. It is occasionally open on afternoons, but if closed, apply to the secretary of the old peoples' home across the road, which Relvas also founded.

One is guided round the collections, among which are several items of interest, although some attributions are doubtful. Apart from numerous Arraiolos carpets (including a silk embroidered example of 1761), English grandfather clocks, objects pertaining to Portuguese bull-fighting, ceramics, etc., among the paintings are: *Van Dyck* (?), Portrait of Anne of Austria; anon. Portrait of Domenico Scarlatti (said to be the only one known of the composer); anon. Portrait of Henriette of France; *dessus des portes* by *Vieira Portuense*; four panels by *Francisco Henriques* (fl. 1500–18); anon. Flemish Virgin; Portrait of a Young Man, *attributed to Reynolds*; works by *Silva Pôrto*, and a painting of that artist in his studio, by *João Columbano*, and *Columbano*'s Portrait of Carlos Relvas; representative works by *Carlos Reis*, *António Ramalho*, *the Marquês d'Oliveira*, and *Alberto de Sousa*; three Still lifes by *Josefa de Óbidos* (and also in the dining-room, some interesting *azulejos*); School of *Sanchez Coelho*, Portrait of Juana of Castile; Virgin and Child *attributed to Perugino*; anon. Tobias and the Fish; anon. Portrait of Pope Clement XIII; and examples of the art of Constantino Fernandes; and also in the library, a collection of enamelled watch-cases.

In the vicinity is a large earth-work identified as Moron, which Decimuus Junius Brutus made his military base c 138 BC before leading his troops north to the Lima.

The N368 turns south-west to cross the Tagus below Santarém, for which see Rte 18B, and also for the former main road (N3) and the A1 motorway to Lisbon.

---

The road continuing south-west from Alpiarça along the left back of the Tagus and crossing the river at Vila Franca de Xira is of slight interest. Beyond Almeirim (see latter part of Rte 5A) the N118 leads through **Muge**, where numerous Palaeolithic artefacts have been discovered, and **Salvaterra de Magos**, damaged by an earthquake earlier this century, but preserving the slight remains of a royal palace of the Avis dynasty. The river Sorraia is crossed at **Benavente** before meeting the N10 and turning right for Vila Franca de Xira and the A1; see Rte 18B.

---

# 17 · (Cacéres) Alcántara to Coimbra via Castelo Branco, and Serta

*Total distance, 241km (150 miles). C523. 11km Piedras Albas—9km Segura—N355. 13km Zebreira—N240. 46km Castelo Branco—IP2. 31km Perdigão—N241 45km Serta—IC8. 20km Pedrogão Grande—23km Pontão—N110 and N347. 33km Condeixa-a-Nova—N1. 10km Coimbra.*

*This distance is likely to be reduced before long, with the extension south-east from Serta of the IC8, which will much ease communications in the beautiful but mountainous area between the Tagus valley and that of the Mondego.*

---

**Alcántara**, 62km north-west of Cáceres, is described in detail in *Blue Guide Spain*, 6th ed. It takes its name (*el kantara* being the Arabic for bridge) from the immense bridge of six arches of uncemented granite spanning the gorge of the Tagus built in c AD 105 by Caius Julius Lacer. Unfortunately, the site is spoilt by the huge dam and electrical installations a short distance upstream at the confluence of the Tagus and Alagón.

After some 16km the Rio Erges (a tributary of the Tagus), which here forms the frontier with Portugal, is crossed on a bridge of Roman foundation to enter **Segura**, with slight remains of a fortress.

The N240 leads right at the next T-junction to (24km north-east) the isolated spa of **Termas de Monfortinho**, passing a turning for **Salvaterra do Extremo**, with ruins of a frontier castle overlooking the Erges. From Monfortinho the N239 bears north-west to (26km) Monsanto, which may be approached more directly via Idanha-a-Velha—for both see Rte 22B—from **Zebreiro**, passed by the main route leading west from the above-mentioned T-junction. The next right-hand turning off the N240 leads 14km north-west to hill-top **Idanha-a-Nova**, a small agricultural centre, founded in 1187 by Gualdim Páis, with ruins of a Templar castle, providing a wide view, and relics of one or two 18C mansions.

## CASTELO BRANCO

Castelo Branco (26,146 inhabitants) is the administrative and commercial capital of the Beira Baixa. Since the late 18C it has been known for its embroidered *colchas* or bed-spreads, a variety of which may be seen in the museum.

■ The **Tourist Office** is in a kiosk in the Alameda da Liberdade. The **bus station** is on the corner of Rua Rebelo and Rua do Saibreiro; the **railway station** on Avenida de Nuno Álvares.

### History

Of ancient origin, it was refounded by the Templars in the early 13C, and a century later passed into the hands of the military Order of Christ. Remains of its walls and castle are still evident. The area is said to have had a large crypto-Jewish community in the 16C. Being at no great distance from the Spanish frontier, it has often been subject to attack, both in 1704 and 1762. The French under Junot, briefly quartered here in November 1807, proceeded to sack the place; in April 1809 Marshal Victor held it momentarily; Wellington passed through on 1 July 1809 when advancing on Talavera; and in April 1812 Général Marmont captured the place, only to retreat shortly after.

The town's few monuments of interest lie some short distance to the north of the central Alameda da Liberdade. São Miguel, which served as a cathedral from 1771 to 1881, when the diocese became extinct, is passed. Beyond arcaded steps bridging the street is the entrance to the elaborate formal *gardens of the former Bishop's Palace, laid out in the mid 18C, with a profusion of ornamental Baroque statuary, balustraded steps surmounted by naïve statues of Portuguese kings, a water-tank lined with *azulejos* and surrounded by urns and obelisks, and a parterre of box arabesques embellished by topiary.

Adjacent is the *Museu Francisco Tavares Proença Júnior*, accommodated in the former palace, undergoing restoration, and containing important archaeological, ethnographical, and ceramic collections; some representative Portuguese 16C paintings; 16C Flemish tapestries; and an extensive series of *colchas de Castelo Branco*, some showing Persian, Indian, or Oriental influences. At the time of writing the museum was closed for restoration. The building also houses a school of embroidery to carry on the strong tradition, and work may be commissioned here.

For the N18 leading north to Fundão and Covilhã, see Rte 22A, in reverse.

## Castelo Branco to Coimbra via Góis

155km. The N112, a slow, serpentine, road, winds north-west towards and over foothills of the Serra da Gardunha, crossing the Zêzere at **Cambas**, and then weaves through the wild broken country of the Serra da Lousã to (70km) **Pampilhosa da Serra**, and after another 35km reaches a junction.

In the valley 5km to the right lies **Góis**, a small agricultural centre, beautifully situated, with a Manueline bridge over the Rio Ceira, and in the church the Renaissance tomb of Luis da Silveira by Diogo de Torralva (1531).

The road then climbs over two ridges to meet the N17. Penacova (see Rte 23) is 13km north-west on the Mondego, from which a new road circles west to approach Coimbra from the north.

Turning left onto the N17, the winding valley of the Rio Ceira, a tributary of the Mondego, is followed to Coimbra: see last part of Rte 21, and Rte 25.

The left-hand turning at the junction west of Góis climbs over a ridge to (16km) **Lousã**, a pleasant town with old paper factories, beneath the range named after it, which rises to 1202m, forming the south-west extremity of the Serra da Estrela. It has a castle, 18C mansions, and a Misericórdia with a Renaissance portal of 1568. **Casal Nova**, to the south, was the site of a spirited action on 14 March 1811 during Masséna's retreat, after which the French burned several houses in Lousã. From Lousã, one may descend north-west via (7km) Foz de Arouce (see last part of Rte 21) to meet the N17, there turning left for (20km) Coimbra: see Rte 25.

An alternative approach from Lousã may be made by continuing west on the N342 via Miranda do Corvo (see Rte 18B), and then climbing over a ridge to *Vila Seca*, to meet the N1 just beyond (26km) Conímbriga (see latter part of Rte 18A), 15km south-west of Coimbra.

---

From Castelo Branco, the IP2 drives south-west, off which at 17km the old road south (N18) forks left for Vila Velha de Ródão and Nisa; see Rte 14A. Another 14km bring one to the N241, leading west over the Rio Ocreza and through undulating country, passing few villages, among them **Proença-a-Nova** (some 15km south-west of which, at **Cardigos**, is a Roman bridge). To the north rises the thickly wooded Serra de Alvelos—the road (and the IC8 under construction) now crosses a shoulder of this range to approach **Sertã**, a small market-town with a Gothic church on the site of an earlier edifice.

### Serta to Tomar

52km. The N238 leads north-west to (9km) the high-lying village of **Sernache do Bomjardim**, birthplace of the Constable Nun' Alvares Pereira (1360–1431), the victor of Aljubarrota, and one of the 32 illegitimate children of Alvaro Gonçalves Pereira, Prior of the Portuguese branch of the military Order of the Hospitallers of St John. The road then descends steeply to cross the Zêzere, where, some 2km to the right on the far bank, on a meander of the river, is the picturesquely sited village of **Dornes**, with a medieval tower and 14C church with a pulpit of 1544. It later winds down (views) to meet the N110 7km north of Tomar: see Rte 18B.

---

From Serta, the IC8 veers due north to cross the deep valley of the Zêzere near the Barragem do Cabril to **Pedrógão Grande**, well sited on a height and an ancient town, probably of Roman origin, with a 12C church rebuilt in 1537. At 11km a left-hand turning leads to **Figueiró dos Vinhos**, picturesquely sited among the wooded hills, in the Igreja Matriz of which, with a Renaissance portal, are some 16C paintings and an organ of 1689; the convent of N.S. do Carmo dates from 1601. The N110 is met 12km beyond this crossroads, where turn right. For the road from here via Penela and Condeixa-a-Nova for Conímbriga, and Coimbra, see latter part of Rte 18B.

The IC8, on crossing the N110, leads due west towards (27km) Pombal (see Rte 18A), meeting the A1 motorway a short distance beyond.

# 18 · Lisbon to Coimbra

## A. Via Torres Vedras, Óbidos, Alcobaça, Batalha, and Conímbriga

*Total distance, 225km (140 miles). A8 motorway and N8. 57km Torres Vedras — 35km Obidos—8km Caldas da Rainha—26km Alcobaça—N8 and N1. 20km Batalha—10km Leiria—27km Pombal—29km Condeixa-a-Nova, for Conímbriga— 13km Coimbra.*

*The A1 motorway now provides the most rapid direct route (c 210km) to Coimbra, and on to Oporto, with exits some 18km east of Batalha, and close to Conímbriga. An alternative road to Alcobaça is that via Rio Maior, leading off the A1 56km NE of Lisbon; see sub-route of Rte 18B.*

*Until the old main road (N1) was made tolerable for motor vehicles, the overland journey from Lisbon to Oporto took at least four days, and as much as seven in more leisurely times. The sea route was faster.*

From the far end of the Campo Grande, the dual carriageway drives due north past Lumiar (see last part of Rte 1F) to meet the entrance of the A8.

A left-hand fork leads shortly to **Odivelas** (48,774 inhabitants), where the portal and apse is preserved of the church and convent built by Dom Dinis in 1295–1305. The rest of it was destroyed in the earthquake of 1755. It contains the founder's tomb (much restored), and that of his natural daughter, Maria Afonso (died 1320). Queen Philippa of Lancaster died here of the plague on 18 July 1415, and in October the following year was buried at Batalha (cf.).

> In what was then a fashionable convent resided Madre Paula (1701–68), who, among other inmates, was a mistress from 1718 to 1728 of Dom João V, the *freiratico* (nun-lover). The philoprogenitive king had the right of entry to the nunnery, and the results of his peculiar penchant (as commented on by Voltaire) were three bastards, known as the *Meninos de Palhavã*. They were Dom José, born 1720 to Madre Paula (Teresa da Silva; 1701–68), and later an Inquisitor-general; Dom Gaspar, born 1716 to Magdalena Máxima de Miranda, and later Archbishop of Braga; and Dom António, born in 1714 to a French nun. Sacheverell Sitwell suggested that Madre Paula, who when not otherwise occupied—for the nuns also had a reputation for their *marmelada* or quince jam—was an excellent musician, and may have been a pupil of Domenico Scarlatti, who was active in Lisbon in 1721–29. But in general they were a turbulent lot. In October 1713 there was even a rebellion of nuns here, 'only subdued by the Duke of Cadaval after a pitched battle', so reported the British consul.

**Loures** is bypassed, to the west of which is the 18C *Quinta do Correio-Mór* (Postmaster General), erected for Luís Gomes da Mata, with features of interest, but suffering from decades of neglect.

The A8 merges with the N8 near **Malveira**, from which a road leads west 11km to Mafra; see Rte 3.

**Turcifal**, with a large 18C church, is skirted on approaching **Torres Vedras** (13,394 inhabitants), an important wine-growing centre, and frequently a royal residence until the 16C. Elenore of Portugal (1436–67, at Wiener Neustadt), wife of the Emperor Friedrich III and mother of Maximilian, was born here. Although it was the scene of fighting during the troubles of 1846, its name is more famous as being the headquarters of Wellington's lines defending Lisbon during the early stages of the Peninsular War: see below.

The town itself is of slight interest, preserving the fort of São Vincente; a ruined castle; a Gothic fountain, the Chafariz dos Canos; the Manueline church of São Pedro, and that of Graça, containing some *azulejos* and Portuguese primitives.

---

Some 4km west is the hamlet of **Varatojo**, where the large convent of Santo António (late 15C, with later additions), has a Gothic cloister, and a sacristy lined with 17C *azulejos*.

Some 3km east is the complex of prehistoric fortifications known as the Castro do Zambujal, which probably gave the town its name (Turres Veteres).

The N248 leads east and then south-east from Torres Vedras past **Matacães**, with a well-carved retable and *azulejos* of 1736 in its church, to (6km) **Runa**, with the Asilo dos Inválidos, founded for old soldiers in 1792. At **Dois Portos** (5km beyond), the church preserves a 16C *artesonado* ceiling; and 5km further, south of **Sobral de Monte Agraço**, the church of São Quintino has an unusual baptistry of 1592.

The so-called **'Lines of Torres Vedras'** were basically Wellington's two bands of hill-top redoubts and batteries extending across the neck of the wide peninsula on which Lisbon stands, which were some 40km in length. The first ran from the mouth of the Sisandre on the Atlantic c 12km west of Torres Vedras, to Alhandra, on the Tagus just south of Vila Franca de Xira. The second line of defence extended from Ribamar and a point just north of Mafra through Bucelas, to just north of Póvoa de Santa Iria, on the Tagus.

The remains of what were some 126 masonry redoubts and earthworks, which contained 249 guns and were manned by almost 30,000 Portuguese militia and *ordenanza*, are still recognisable, particularly along the more northerly line, and their exploration provides interesting excursions for the energetic. In certain areas the defensive positions provided what is virtually a third line.

> Wellington, traversing the area after the battle of Vimeiro (see below) had already remarked on its suitability for defence, and the construction of these extensive works were in progress secretly since October 1809 in preparation for any eventual retreat necessary in the face of superior French armies. The area enclosed behind the Lines was over 500 square miles (1300 sq km). Wellington had also ordered a 'scorched earth' policy to be put into effect north of the Lines. The local population, with their livestock, was moved south, so that when in October 1810, after the battle of Busaco (see Rte 24), the British retired into secure and well-provisioned territory, Masséna and his huge army found themselves in a comparative desert. But he had learnt his lesson, and warily did not even attempt to attack the Lines. The fact that the French were able to subsist near them for so long, being cut off from their supplies, is remarkable, but in the following March sheer starvation forced them to retreat from their own positions between Rio Maior and Santarém, closely followed by Wellington's Anglo-Portuguese army. This continued until 3 May, when just across the Spanish frontier, between Vilar Formoso and Fuentes de Oñoro (see Rte 21), they turned on their pursuers. It has been estimated that Masséna lost between 25,000 and 30,000 men, 9000 horses, and his entire waggon-train during this disastrous campaign.

Detailed maps and descriptions may be found in Wyld's *Atlas* (1841), William Granville Eliot's *Treatise on the Defence of Portugal*, and Jones' *Journal of Sieges, etc.*, and in *The Lines of Torres Vedras* by A.H. Norris and R.W. Bremner (3rd ed. 1986, published by the British Historical Society of Portugal in Lisbon.); while maquettes of the ground may be seen in the museum at Óbidos, and the military museum at Lisbon.

## Torres Vedras to Óbidos via Vimeiro and Peniche

69km. Follow the N8-2 north-west towards Lourinhã for 7km, where, after climbing down through woods, turn left for **Vimeiro**, with its monument to the battle: see below. It is worthwhile making the short detour to the mouth of the Maceira (unfortunately spoilt by the erection of an ugly hotel), and the Praia do Porto Novo, where one can well imagine the British troops and their mounts struggling ashore through the breakers, in which several were drowned, as so brilliantly described in Commissary Schaumann's *On the Road with Wellington*.

Wellington, after the engagement at Roliça (see below), had originally taken up a defensive position along the hills just south of the Maceira river, at the mouth of which his reinforcements were to disembark. He later transferred them to other hills south and north-east of the village of Vimeiro, where they awaited the combined French armies of Junot, Delaborde, and Loison advancing from Torres Vedras. The resulting battle of 21 August 1808 was the first and a classic example of Wellington's defensive tactics, which were later to serve him in good stead at Busaco and in other battles during the Peninsular War (and at Waterloo). The massed French columns, which for years had been successful elsewhere in Europe, disintegrated before the superior firepower of the sheltered, extended lines of their disciplined foe, whenever the two formations came together. The French were heavily defeated, their casualties being 2000 compared to some 720 British, and they also lost at least 13 pieces of artillery. Géneral Kellerman proposed a truce, to which Wellington was obliged to agree by his elderly superior, Sir Hew Dalrymple, who with Sir Harry Burrard had just landed to supersede him in command of the victorious army. They preferred to draw up the unpopular 'Convention of Cintra' rather than risk further fighting.

The main road may be regained at **Lourinhã**, where the restored Igreja Matriz preserves a Gothic portal and rose-window, while the Misericórdia has a Manueline portal and contains paintings by the early 16C Master of Lourinhã of St John on Patmos and St John the Baptist. N.S. da Anunciação retains a small cloister.

**PENICHE** (15,304 inhabitants), whose name, a corruption of the Latin for peninsula, well describes its rock-bound site, was once a rabbit-infested island, isolated from the mainland except for a narrow sandy isthmus, and protected by a line of 16C fortifications. The place was raided by Drake, Sir John Norris, and the Earl of Essex on 16 May 1589, when in Spanish hands, before they marched on Lisbon.

Several fish canneries may be seen, but the recent building boom on the approach and in the vicinity of the isthmus has destroyed much of its former attraction.

Passing through the gate, turn left to skirt the walls and gardens, to reach the deep-sea fishing harbour and dockyard and nearby **Fortaleza**. During the Salazar regime this fortress was one of the main prisons of the repressive secret police, the PIDE, from which the Communist leader Alvaro Cunhal escaped in 1960. The Rua José Estevão leads to São Pedro (16C), some distance to the west of which (behind the apse) is **N.S. da Conceição**, with *azulejo* panels and a painted ceiling. The

**Misericórdia**, adjacent to the gardens, contains 55 painted panels on its ceiling of scenes from the Life of Christ, etc.

A road leads across the peninsula to the chapel of **N.S. dos Remédios**, lined with *azulejos*, and providing a good view of the **\*Berlengas**, an offshore archipelago lashed by the Atlantic. The largest and nearest of these rocky islands (12km out), has a lighthouse and fort, while ruins of a monastery founded in 1513, but later abandoned owing to its inaccessibility, may be seen. The island may be visited by ferry in summer, and is now a bird sanctuary. There is another lighthouse on Cabo Carvoeiro, the western headland of the peninsula.

From here, the N114 leads east through **Atouguia da Baleia** (of the whale), once of importance, with a Gothic fountain, and early Gothic \*São Leonardo, its belfry topped by twin pyramids, containing Romanesque capitals, a stone Nativity (14C), the tomb of the 1st Count of Atouguia (1452), and relics of murals.

Beyond **Serra d'El Rei** (retrospective views), which has relics of a palace of c 1360 built for Dom Pedro I, the road approaches the walls of Óbidos, and provides a good view to the south of the battlefield of Roliça; see below.

---

The N8, long in a deplorable condition here, and full of pot-holes, but in the process of being upgraded, after 24km bypasses **Bombarral**, 7km south-east of which, at **Cadaval**, is the Iron Age fort of Castelo de Pragança. The next right-hand turning beyond Bombarral leads to **Carvalhal**, with a quaint Mannerist retablo in the Igreja do Sacramento, and good *azulejos* of 1733 in N.S. do Socorro.

Continuing north, the N8 descends from the rim of hills defended by the French at the battle named after the village of **Roliça** bypassed to the left before meeting the road from Peniche.

> The engagement which took place here on 17 August 1808 was the first of the Peninsular War fought by British troops, who, commanded by Wellington, had landed some days previously at the mouth of the Mondego; see latter part of Rte 24. Géneral Delaborde's small force was at Roliça, a short distance south of Óbidos and within a horseshoe of low hills; while Loison, with a larger army, was approaching from Abrantes. Had they joined forces, they would well outnumber the British. Wellington therefore decided to attack immediately, obliging Delaborde to withdraw to a ridge further south to avoid being outflanked by the two wings of his army, which, divided into three columns, was making a pincer movement. But when they repeated the initial manoeuvre, at the same time advancing up the gullies of the hillside in a frontal attack, the French had little alternative but to give way again, and although the fighting was hard, Delaborde was forced to retire south-east, his position having been carried. Colonel Lake, who had led his men up one of these gullies, was buried where he fell (monument).
>
> Next day Wellington proceeded south-west towards the mouth of the Maceira, near the village of Vimeiro, the site of a more serious engagement on the 21st: see above.

## ÓBIDOS

The ancient walled town of \*Óbidos (provided with a bypass) is seen ahead. Captured from the Moors by Afonso Henriques in 1148, and once marking the southern extremity of the domains of Alcobaça, it remains one of the most attractive and picturesque sights in Portugal. It is therefore best visited when not overrun by groups on the Alcobaça—Batalha—Nazaré circuit.

■ The **Tourist Office** is on the Rua Direita. Infrequent **trains** run from Lisbon; **buses** from Peniche and Caldas da Rainha.

Unless staying at the *pousada* in the castle, it is preferable to leave one's car near the Porta da Vila (note its tiled oratory) at the south end of the walled enceinte, close to which is the aqueduct, built at the instigation of Dona Catarina, queen of Dom João III.

The Rua Direita leads ahead to approach the imposing *castle, built by Dom Dinis on a height dominating the north end of the town. Pedro López de Ayala (1332–1407?), the Spanish chronicler, while imprisoned after the battle of Aljubarrota, wrote here his *Libro de las Aves de Caça* (or *Libro de la Cetrería*), a treatise on hawking. Adjacent is the uninteresting church of São Tiago.

The main square is flanked by restored *Santa Maria* (late 17C, with a Renaissance portal), on the site of an earlier church. The interior contains *albarrada azulejos* (early 18C); the fine Renaissance *tomb of João de Noronha, by Chanterène (1526–28; left-hand wall); good retables, that over the *Altar-Mór* with late 17C paintings by João da Costa; to the right are others depicting the mystic marriage of St Catherine, by Josefa 'de Óbidos' (Josefa d'Ayala, born in Sevilla c 1630, who spent much of her life in a convent here, where she died in 1684, and was buried in São Pedro). Note also the series of paintings (School of Josefa de Óbidos) around the ceiling, and the organ.

Adjacent is the **museum**, established in the former town hall by the Gulbenkian Foundation. Opening times are 9.30–12.30 and 14.00–18.00; closed Mon. Among the somewhat miscellaneous collections of paintings, mostly 15–16C martyrdoms, are an anon. St Francis (late 17C Portuguese); N.S. de Misericórdia (School of Bento Coelho da Silveira); and a Portrait of Faustino das Neves, attributed to Josefa de Óbidos. A collection of polychromed statuettes; a room devoted to the Peninsular War, specifically Roliça, with a maquette of the 'Lines of Torres Vedras', and French and English arms, etc., and architectural and archaeological relics are also to be seen.

About 1km to the north, beyond a bridge and to the left of the main road, standing rather like a huge white elephant, is the curious hexagonal church of Senhor da Pedra (1740–47), left unfinished at the death of its builder, Rodrigo Franco. It was intended as a stopping-place on the road north, where Dom João V could attend mass. Incorporated in the design are two three-storey pavilions which would also provide shelter for his carriages and entourage.

**CALDAS DA RAINHA** (21,070 inhabitants), with warm sulphur springs reputed for centuries, is now approached, but its monuments, near the centre, are few, and the place has not been improved by recent urbanisation, seen from the new bypass.

### History

The town grew up round the hospital established in 1486 by Dona Leonor, queen of Dom João II, and restored in 1747 by Dom João V, who, it is said, derived much benefit from its waters. Southey found it a 'little clean town on sand amid fir groves' in 1801. It was a temporary forced residence of refugees from occupied Europe during the Second World War. On the 16 March 1974 a detachment from its garrison marched prematurely towards Lisbon, only to be turned back. The factory of the artist and potter Rafael Bordalo Pinheiro (1846–1905: see latter part of Rte 1F) was established here.

The chapel of the hospital, **N.S. do Pópulo**, has a curious Manueline cupola, 14C font, 17C *azulejos*, and a triptych attributed to Cristóvão de Figueiredo cut to fit the chancel arch. In the park stands the **Museu de José Malhôa**, named after the local artist (1855–1933), containing paintings by him and his contemporaries, including João Columbano (1857–1929).

On the coast 10km north-west is the beach of **Foz do Arelho**, at the mouth of the Lagoa de Óbidos, a salt-water creek famous for its eels.

The N8 veers north-east past **Alfeizerão** (from which a road leads towards Nazaré; see below) and starts to climb the flank of a range of hills. It then leads through attractive country, with the bald Serra dos Candieiros to the east, before winding down to Alcobaça; see Rte 19, and likewise for the 20km stretch of road between there and Batalha.

## Alfeizera to Al cobaça via Nazaré

31km. Turn left to **São Martinho do Porto**, on a land-locked bay, beyond which bear north-east along an inland road. At **São Gião**, near by, is a church said to be of Visigothic origin. Later skirting the shore, the road approaches the often-photographed village of **NAZARÉ** (9908 inhabitants). Its fisherfolk, possibly of Phoenician descent, unconcernedly carry on their hard life in spite of the tourists who infest the place during the season. The larger fishing boats, with their crescent-shaped prows (*meia-lua* or half-moon) and painted eyes, are indeed picturesque, even if they are now hauled up the beach by tractors rather than by teams of oxen. The sardines drying on their wire frames; the chequered shirts and black stocking caps of the men; the impassive groups of black-shawled women, with their thickly pleated skirts and gold earrings: the scene is curious and the impact great.

■ The **Tourist Office** is on Avenida da República.

The buildings are of very much less interest than the local life. In the Praia or lower town, the narrow lanes of fishermen's dwellings lie at right-angles to the beach, near the north end of which a funicular ascends to the *sítio* or upper town on the 110m-high cliff top (view), also reached by a road. The 17C chapel of N.S. da Nazaré replaces the hermitage founded in 1182 by Fuas Roupinho, the mayor of Porto de Mós, to contain an image of the Virgin, who had miraculously saved him from riding headlong over the cliff when stag-hunting in a fog. On a promontory is the fort of São Miguel Arcanjo.

Marinha Grande (see below) is 21km north-east on the N242, off which after 13km the N356 turns right for Batalha, 13km east; see Rte 19.

From Nazaré, bear south-east to approach Alcobaça (see Rte 19), at 10km passing a left-hand turning for **Coz**, where the convent of Santa Maria, founded c 1279, but much transformed since, has *azulejos* illustrating scenes from the Life of São Bernardo de Claraval.

The N1 leading north from Batalha (see Rte 19) shortly bypasses **Azoia**, near which was the Roman station of Colipo, to approach the Leiria bypass.

## LEIRIA

Leiria (27,758 inhabitants), an episcopal city (from 1545) and capital of its district, lies among attractive country on the river Lis (or Liz), crossed by an ancient bridge, and is dominated by its imposing castle. Its recent growth has not improved its appearance.

- The **Tourist Office** is in the Jardim Luís de Camões. There are **trains** from Caldas da Rainha; the station is north of the town.

### History

Situated on the road between Roman Olisipo and Bracara (Lisbon and Braga), it superseded Azoia in importance. In 1135 Afonso Henriques set up an advance post here, but it was recaptured by the Moors and its garrison massacred. It changed hands several times during the next few decades, being rebuilt by the Portuguese in 1144 and again in 1191. In 1254 Dom Afonso III held a *Cortes* here, the first such assembly in Portugal at which the Commons were represented, and later Dom Dinis (who is claimed to have promoted the afforestation of the area to the west) and his wife St Isabel chose it as a residence. A printing press established here in 1492 (or possibly earlier, in 1466) was noted for the printing of works in Hebrew.

A rising in 1808 against the French was savagely repressed by Géneral Margarot. English troops retreating through Leiria after the battle of Busaco broke down the doors of a convent, as the French were close, and out came the nuns 'as thick as a flock of sheep and set off for Lisbon', some of them jumping up behind the dragoons, clasping their saviours tightly round their waists. The town was then sacked by the French during Masséna's retreat (March 1811). In 1827 it was briefly Sir William Clinton's HQ during the British intervention in Portugal's chaotic internal affairs. The town was the scene of Eça de Queroz's novel, *The Sin of Father Amaro*, and the birthplace of the poet Francisco Rodrigues Lobo (1590–1621).

From the central Praça Rodrigues Lobo one may approach the plain **cathedral** (1550–74), attributed to Afonso Alvares, its vault borne on flat ribs resting on square piers. The cloister lies behind the apse, as with the Sé at Lisbon.

Steps mount from its west front past a detached belfry to the gateway of the older town. Beyond is the 18C Bishop's Palace, now containing a library and museum (an Ethnographical Museum may also be visited); a municipal museum is to be installed in the former convento of Santo Agostinho.

Near the ascent to the castle is the Romanesque portal of São Pedro (c 1140).

Passing through the main outer gate of the curtain wall of the **\*castle**, and climbing left, the apsidal chapel of N.S. da Penha (c 1400), is first reached, erected by Dom João I and bearing his monogram, a crowned 'Y'. To the left is the restored Royal Palace, with an imposing hall and loggia; and higher up, the *Torre de Menagem* (1324), providing an extensive view of the Serra de Monte Junto to the south, and west across the Pinhal Real (or d'el-Rei; see below) towards the coast.

Just outside the town is the high-lying chapel of N.S. da Encarnação (early 17C), with a large porch, approached by a monumental flight of steps.

For the road from Leiria to Figueira da Foz, see Rte 20. The A1 may be entered 6km east of Leiria.

---

The great **pine forest** (*Pinhal Real*) to the west of Leiria (enquire at Leiria tourist office for directions) was first established in the 13C to anchor the encroaching sand dunes, and now covers an area of almost 10,000 hectares. 11km west of Leiria, and almost surrounded by the forest, lies the straggling industrial district of **Marinha Grande** (21,984 inhabitants), with the glass-works founded in 1748 by John Beare, an Englishman, and from 1769 developed by William Stephens, subsidised by Pombal. Stephens died in 1802, and his brother bequeathed it to the State in 1826. Stephens fitted up an opera-house here, where performances were given each month, many of the parts sung by his employees, whom he had instructed in music and dancing.

---

Shortly after leaving Leiria, a left-hand turning leads to the Baroque church of Milagres, of 1732, with *azulejos* of 1795. The architect was José da Silva, of Juncal, and his grandson designed the tiles, which depict the miracle of a local peasant restored to health after being paralysed by a fall.

The A1 passes below the motorway to approach and bypass **Pombal**, an old market town with a partially restored castle built c 1174 by Gualdim Pais. It is famous principally for having given a title to the '*Gran Marquês*', Sebastião José de Carvalho e Melo (1699–1782) (see History). He retired here in disgrace in 1777 on the accession of the reactionary Maria I. He died bed-ridden at his residence in the main square, and his remains were first buried in N.S. do Cardal (1703). The town was sacked by the French on their retreat in 1811.

An earlier peculiarity of Pombal was the fact that one of each of its three parish churches concentrated on baptism, marriages, and funerals.

At **Santiago da Guarda**, c 20km north-east, the 3rd Conde de Castelo-Melhor (1636–1720) was born. He was minister of Dom Afonso VI for five years, until his temporary disgrace in 1667.

A left-hand turning 15km north of Pombal leads to **Soure**, with the ruins of the Knights Templar's first castle in Portugal (1128), and a 17C Misericórdia. It was briefly in Spanish hands prior to the battle of Aljubarrota; and was later reputed for its hat manufactory.

**Redinha**, to the right at this turning, was attacked on 12 March 1811 by Ney's Corps in retreat.

The main road continues to undulate towards **Condeixa-a-Nova**, a pleasant small town preserving among other mansions the 17C Casa Sotto Maior, almost opposite the new *pousada* Santa Cristina. **Ega**, c 3km south-west, just beyond the motorway, contains a small Manueline church with a Renaissance pulpit, and a good anonymous 16C triptych.

## CONÍMBRIGA

3km south-east of Condeixa is the site of ancient *Conímbriga, the largest Roman settlement excavated in Portugal. It is open 15 Mar–14 Sept from 9.00–13.00 and 14.00–20.00; and to 18.00 the rest of the year.

■ There is a **bus** (every day) from Coimbra to the site, and a frequent service to Condeixa-a-Nova, 3km away.

### History

Although a pre-Roman site (from c 800 BC), it lay on the Roman road from Lisbon to Braga via Tomar, and as such it became a station of importance, remaining so until its destruction by the Suevi in 468, after which the Visigothic kings transferred their seat to the more easily defended town of Aeminium, present-day Coimbra, as did its bishops between 572 and 589, although they still retained the name of Conímbriga.

While the presence of ancient remains had been previously noted, it was not until 1898 that any survey was undertaken, and in 1912 the first diggings were carried out by Dr Virgílio Correia, who was also responsible for the more systematic excavations of the extensive site after 1930.

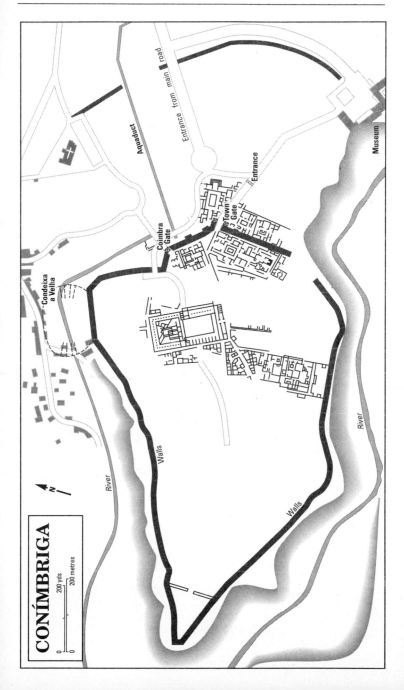

CONÍMBRIGA

0 — 200 yds
0 — 200 metres

N

Museum

Entrance from main road

Aquaduct

Entrance

Coimbra Gate

Town Gate

Condeixa a Velha

River

Walls

Walls

River

It is convenient to visit first the **museum** (with a restaurant). (Opening hours between 15 Mar–14 Sept are 10.00–13.00 and 14.00–18.00. It closes at 17.00 the rest of the year, and is closed Mon.) Near the entrance vestibule are rooms concentrating on the smaller objects found on the site. The collection of coins, glass, ceramics, domestic utensils and tools, cameos, jewellery and metalwork, is extensive. Other rooms are devoted to epigraphical collections, stelae, sculpture (or fragments; much of it carved from Estremoz marble), bronze statuettes, mosaics (one of the Minotaur in his labyrinth, and another geometrical composition), carved capitals and architectural elements, including decorative stucco-work, etc. Larger sculptures and a huge capital found in the Flavian forum may be seen in the patio.

Conímbriga lies on a triangle of land between two gorges, and much of the walls (some 1500m in extent), circumscribing this area of 13 hectares, still exist, with an outer defensive wall further to the east, crossed by the approach road and an aque-duct, which provided the city with water from a reservoir at **Alcabideque**, some 3km distant.

To the right of the irregularly flagged Roman road leading to the main town gate is the site of a large villa surrounding a peristyle, retaining a number of mosaic pavements, now protected by a tasteless roof. In the centre is a large pool, with numerous fountain jets of bronze (reconstructed by copying surviving pieces, and again in working order). To the left of the road are some smaller houses, also preserving mosaics and *thermae*.

Pass through the gate and bear right to reach the entrance of the aqueduct into the walled enceinte, which leads to a distribution cistern, beyond which is the

*Partial view of the Roman remains at Conímbriga*

'Coimbra gate'. To the left of the main gate is another villa containing more than one ornamental pool, in the largest of which five skeletons were found when it was excavated, probably of men slain there when the place was sacked in 468. Further south are its private baths with the usual arrangement of *frigidarium, tepidarium,* and *caldarium* over a hypocaust. Beyond are more skeletons (in situ) of the Visigothic period. Further west is the recently excavated Flavian forum, partly overlying that of the Augustan period, south of which is a commercial area abutting the Temple of Flavius. On the slope beyond, reached by a flight of steps, is the buttressed palaestra and the public baths of the Trajan *thermae*, etc., which await consolidation. Slight remains of an amphitheatre, just beyond the north wall, may be excavated, while excavations in other areas are continuing.

Another Roman villa is in the process of excavation near **Rabaçal**, some 10km south-east of Conímbriga.

Shortly after regaining the N1 (near which is an entrance to the motorway, which bypasses Coimbra and also provides an approach from the west before driving north towards Oporto) the village of **Cernache**, with a Nottingham alabaster of the Coronation of the Virgin in its church, is passed to the left.

The south-west outskirts of Coimbra are entered on descending towards the Mondego, with a good view of the older town rising above the far bank: see Rte 25, while this near bank is described in Rte 25C.

# B.  Via Santarém and Tomar

*Total distance, 213km (132 miles). A1 motorway. 23km Vila Franca exit—21km Aveiras de Cima exit (for Rio Maior)—17km Santarém, 5km south-east—26km to meet the IP6.—17km Atalaia exit—N100. 16km Tomar—52km Penela—N347. 14km Conímbriga—2km Condeixa-a-Nova—N1. 15km Coimbra.*

The motorway is followed past (left) the airport of Portela, and (right) the future approach to the new bridge and viaduct over the Tagus (see Rte 5A), and bears north-east parallel to and above the west bank of the river through a scruffy industrial area. An exit for **Bucelas** (8km west), well-known for its wine, is passed, and then that for Vila Franca; see below. At **Arruda dos Vinhos**, 15km north of Bucelas, the church preserves a good Manueline portal of c 1530. To the northwest, between the two exits, the internecine battle of Alfarrobeira (1449) took place, in which Pedro, Duke of Coimbra was killed, his nephew Dom Afonso V being victorious.

**Alhandra** (7120 inhabitants), bypassed, the birthplace of Afonso de Albuquerque (1453–1515), viceroy of India, marked the eastern flank of the 'Lines of Torres Vedras'; see Rte 18A. It was here that a British naval contingent, with their gun-boats, were stationed, and where the French Géneral La Croix was killed by a random shot.

**Vila Franca de Xira** (17,191 inhabitants) is said to have been founded by French followers of Afonso Henriques c 1200. The military *pronunciamento* (or 'Vilafrancada') of the reactionary absolutists against the liberal government of the time took place here on 27 May 1823. The British-built Maréchal Carmona Bridge (1300m long) spanning the Tagus here, was inaugurated in 1951.

An exit is provided for **Alenquer**, 6km north-west on the N1, an old town once famed for its paper factories, but sacked by the French during Masséna's occupation in 1810–11. It is said to derive its name from its foundation by the Alans (Alanokerkae), and claims to occupy the site of Roman Jerabrica, but the origin of its name may as easily be Arabic. São Francisco, founded c 1222 by Dona Sancha, daughter of Dom Sancho I, preserves a 13C portal and Manueline cloister. Close by is the ruined castle (13C), while in the lower town the rebuilt Santa Maria da Várzea contains the tomb of Damião de Góis (1501–74), the humanist, a friend of Erasmus, and a victim of the Inquisition. He was probably also born here, as was Pêro de Alenquer, a pilot with both Bartolomeu Dias in 1488 and Vasco da Gama in 1497.

In the neighbourhood is the prehistoric Castro da Pedra de Ouro; while at **Aldeia Galega da Merceana**, c 14km north-west, are the churches of N.S. da Piedade, with a sumptuous interior, and N.S. dos Prazeres, both altered in the 18C.

From Alenquer, the N1 ascends north over the Serra de Montejunto, passing (left) a TV station, to reach a junction, where the left-hand fork leads north-west towards Óbidos (see Rte 18A), and the right joins the N366 just north of Alcoentre; see below.

From the Alenquer exit one may also follow the N3 north-east to (38km) Santarém, first skirting **Azambuja**, beyond which passing a right-hand turning to the ruined monastery of Santa Maria das Virtudes, where Dom João II was visited briefly by Columbus in 1492 after his first voyage of discovery (cf. Cuba) when en route to report to the Catholic Kings.

**Cartaxo** (8363 inhabitants), a wine-growing centre, contains several *quintas*, among them that of Dos Chavões. Note also the Manueline *cruzeiro*. The Marqués de la Romana (1761–1811), the Spanish patriot, died here suddenly during the Peninsular War. Some 7km north-west, beyond the motorway, at **Vila Nova de São Pedro**, is an important prehistoric fortified *castro*, c 40m in diameter, discovered in 1936. 4km further west is **Manique do Intendente**, with a huge derelict palace of great pretension erected by Diogo Ignácio de Pina Manique (1733–1805), the Intendant of Police during the reign of Dona Maria I. The key to this architectural curiosity may be found at the adjoining *venda*.

An area occupied by Dom Pedro's forces prior to the evacuation of Santarém in the spring of 1834, at the close of the Miguelite War, is crossed between Cartaxo and Santarém; see below.

## Aveiras de Cima to Alcobaça (53km) and Batalha

64km. The next exit from the A1 turns onto the N366 to skirt (10km) **Alcoentre**, of slight interest in itself, but only 5km east lies Manique do Intendente; see above. **Rio Maior** (6686 inhabitants), an agricultural centre of very remote origin, is later bypassed. Numerous prehistoric artefacts have been found in the district, while speleologists will be rewarded by a visit to the Cave of Alcobertas, 9km north.

A pleasanter, but longer, alternative to the main road to Batalha is the ridge road (N362) leading north from **Alcanede** (15km north-east of Rio Maior, but also approached direct from Santarém), with a partly restored castle and a Roman bridge. This climbs (retrospective views) to (12km) **Mendiga**, with a church containing unusual late 18C *azulejos*, beyond which it winds north along the flank of the bald Serra dos Candeeiros before descending past (12km) Porto do Mós for Batalha; for both, see Rte 19.

The N1 leads along a wide valley parallel to the *serra*, off which the N8-6 forks left along a ridge (views) direct to Alcobaça (see Rte 19) via **Turquel**, with a

Manueline church, and **Évora de Alcobaça**, where the Igreja Matriz preserves a bas-relief of an armoured knight above a side door.

## SANTARÉM

The A1 continues north-east to an exit for Santarém (23,678 inhabitants), once one of the strongest fortresses in Portugal, built on a commanding height overlooking the Tagus. Although it is the capital of a rich agricultural district, the venue of the Ribatejo Fair in June, and the centre of Portuguese bull-fighting, it is now of more interest for its historical associations than for the majority of its surviving monuments.

■ The **Tourist Office** is at 63 Rua Capelo Ivens. **Trains** run from Lisbon and to Coimbra; and there are **buses** from Lisbon. The train station is to the north-east of the town.

### History

Roman Scallabis, dignified by Julius Caesar with the title of Praesidium Julium, and one of three *conventus* in Lusitania (the others being Mérida, and Beja), derives its present name from Santa Iria (Irene), a nun of Tomar, who, accused of unchastity, suffered martyrdom in 653. Her body (some say in its marble coffin) was flung into the Nabão, and after floating down the Tagus was here washed ashore, her innocence being then indisputably established by miraculous apparitions. They were a credulous lot, and were singled out in the proverb: 'Quem burro vae a Santarém, burro vae e burro vem' (The ass who goes to Santarém, ass he goes and ass returns). Others have suggested that this referred more specifically to the seminarists.

Santarém was a Moorish stronghold (Shantariya) from 715 to 1093, when it was taken by Alfonso VI of León, whose son-in-law (in 1095) called himself 'Lord of Galicia and Santarém'. But the Moors recaptured the place. It was not finally regained until 1147, by Afonso Henriques (who founded the Abbey of Alcobaça in gratitude), in a night attack. Dom Sancho I held the place against a desperate attempt by the Almohads to reconquer it in 1181. In 1223 Dom Afonso II died here, a leper and excommunicate. Dom Dinis also died at Santarém, in 1325; and the executions took place here of the murderers of Inês de Castro (cf. Alcobaça, and Rte 25C) in 1357.

It was the scene of many gatherings of the Cortes in the 14–15Cs, being conveniently near Almeirim (cf.), a summer residence of the Avis dynasty, near which in 1491 the Infante Dom Afonso, only son of Dom João II, falling from his horse, was drowned in the Tagus. In 1811 Masséna briefly held a line between Santarém and Rio Maior after retreating from before the Lines of Torres Vedras (see Rte 18A), when it was sacked: '11 Convents and 8 Churches fell a Victim to the French, who have been guilty of the most wanton Mischief', recorded Captain William Bragge.

In 1833 it was the last stronghold of the reactionary Miguelites.

Among eminent Scalebitanos were the poet Ibn Sara (fl. 1095–1123); Fernão Lopes de Castanheda (c 1500–59), the historian; Frei Luís de Sousa (1555–1632), the chronicler; and the Marquês de Sá da Bandeira (1795–1876), the radical leader. Alexandre Herculano, the historian, spent the last ten years of his life on his estate of Vale de Lobos, in the vicinity.

The principal square of the old town, the Largo Sá da Bandeira, just south of the main junction of roads, is dominated by the many-windowed façade of the **Seminário**, built for the Jesuits in 1676 by João Nunes Tinoco.

To its north-east is São Francisco (c 1240), degraded to stable cavalry; and beyond the road descending steeply to the Tagus, **Santa Clara** (c 1258, but much altered since), with a long nave and containing the 17C tombs of Dona Leonor, daughter of Dom Afonso III, and her original tomb.

By following the Rua Serpa Pinto from the south-east corner of the square, a few minutes' walk brings one to the early 16C church of **Marvila**, with diamond-patterned *azulejos* of 1617/20, a notable pulpit, and coffin-lid wooden roof.

Take the next right-hand turning beyond the church to reach that of **Graça**, with a portal imitating Batalha, and with perhaps the finest *rose-window in Portugal. Steps descend into the restored nave, with the tombs of Pedro de Meneses (c 1437), governor of Ceuta, and his wife; and the tombstone of Pedro Alvares Cabral (Belmonte, c 1467–1526), the discoverer of Brazil.

Regaining the main street, turn right to reach—opposite the 15C Torre das Cabaças or Cabaceiro—13C São João de Alporão, perhaps on the site of a mosque, and now containing a lapidary museum, in which the over-restored *tomb of Duarte de Meneses (died 1464), governor of Alcácer-Ceguer, is outstanding. Crum Watson, the historian of Portuguese architecture, considered it the finest 15C tomb in the country. It is said to contain only a relic of the governor, killed in Africa: one tooth! The area behind the church was once the *Judiaria*.

The walk may be continued along a promontory towards the gardens of the Portas do Sol, laid out within the walls of the Moorish citadel (Alcáçova), which commands an extensive panorama over the Tagus valley and plain of the Alentejo.

At **Almoster**, 10km due west of Santarém on the N365, is the restored Bernardine convent of Santa Maria, founded in 1289, with remains of a later cloister. The church contains good Baroque woodwork, and a 14C carved crucifix.

For the road from Santarém to Tomar via Alpiarça (10km north-east) and Golegã, see the latter part of Rte 16 in reverse. See below for the N110 leading north to Tomar after crossing the N3.

The faster route from Santarém to Tomar is now the A1, regained north-west of the town, although the N3 passing through **Pernes**, formerly fortified, continues to be a reasonable road, which may be followed past Torres Novas; see Rte 16. From there, an alternative route is the N349 turning left at the foot of the hill beyond the town, off which fork right through **Paço**, with the 18C Casa de Vargas. The road later veers right through attractive country dotted with cypress trees, with a view (left) of the Convento de Cristo on approaching Tomar.

The motorway veers north from the Santarém entry, passing (right) **São Vicente de Paul**, with slight Roman remains, after 26km meeting the IP6. For the continuation north of the A1; see below.

Turn onto the IP6, with exits for Torres Novas and **Atalaia**, where take the N110 leading north. The 16C church here, its façade broadened by buttresses, has a rich Renaissance portal, possibly by Chanterène, dating from c 1545, while the interior contains interesting *azulejos*, notably those of angels playing contemporary musical instruments.

The N110 veers north-east and then north through undulating wooded country, passing a turning (right) for the Pousada de São Pedro, overlooking the Castelo do Bode reservoir on the Zêzere, to approach Tomar; see below.

The next exit on the A1 as it drives north towards Coimbra—with later exits for Leiria, Pombal, and Condeixa-a-Nova for Conímbriga (for all of which see the latter half of Rte 18A)—provides an entry to the N356, a convenient approach from this direction to Batalha (see Rte 19), some 17km west, with a wide view on the descent. It is also convenient for Fátima, only 3km east, to which few—having seen, or in expectation of visiting, Alcobaça, Batalha, or Tomar—will want to deviate.

**Fátima**, well-described as 'the Lourdes of Portugal', standing on a desolate high-lying plateau, is of little interest to the traveller unless curious to investigate the phenomenal growth of the religious souvenir industry and the massive commercialisation of the cult. The pilgrimage was described ten years after the apparitions occurred as being 'attended by real hardship, as the country is wild and accommodation practically non-existent'. The scene has changed. Under the Salazar regime, which imposed on the devout, vast sums were spent on the erection of a Basílica (consecrated in 1953). It is an affront to the instinct of veneration. Its tower (65m high) is buttressed by a hemicycle surmounted by statues of saints. Below this, in the huge esplanade, is a chapel on the site of visions of the Virgin claimed to have been witnessed on 13 May 1917 by three peasant children, two of whom did not survive the age of 12, and who are now buried within the basilica. It is thronged with pilgrims on the 12th/13th of each month, especially May and October.

## TOMAR

Tomar (14,022 inhabitants), although with some industry, is a charming small town on the Rio Nabão, overlooked to the west by the great convent-castle of the Knights Templar, for which it is justly famous.

- The **Tourist Office** is on the Avenida Dr. Cândido Madureira. (Enquire there for the key to N.S. da Conceição.) There are **buses** and indirect **trains** from Santarém; both stations are on Avenida Combatentes da Grande Guerra.

### History

Roman Sellium or Nabancia stood largely on the left bank of the Nabão, where St Irene was martyred in 653 (see Santarém, History), while the medieval town grew up between the right bank and the castle, its history bound up with the fortunes of the military and monastic orders which have been its overlords. In recognition of his services in expelling the Moors, in 1157 Gualdim Pais, Grand Master of the Templars, was awarded the site of a Roman villa on the left bank (some 2km downstream), of which only slight remains have been excavated. He is said to have begun a church (Santa Maria dos Olivais), and a castle, abandoned in 1162 for the better site on the hill opposite; and in 1190 this new fortress withstood the assaults of Almohad forces.

In 1314 the papal order for the suppression of the Templars was nominally enforced in Portugal; but Dom Dinis, mindful of their crusading enterprise in the past, decided to replace it in 1319 by founding the knightly Order of Christ, which succeeded to their extensive property. In 1356 its headquarters (transferred from Castro Marím, in the Algarve) were at Tomar, and in 1417–60 its Grand Master was Prince Henry the Navigator. In 1492 the mastership (which afterwards remained in the king's hands) fell to Dom Manuel I, who set about enlarging the church.

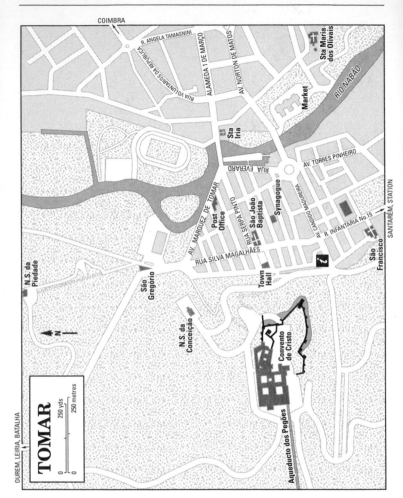

Further impetus was given to the building operations by Dom João III, who converted the Order into a monastic brotherhood, making the construction of living-quarters essential. The master of works (c 1523–51) was João de Castilho, who had already designed the south portal, and now added to the church and built the dormitories, and four additional cloisters. The main cloister, begun in 1558, was largely completed by Diogo de Torralva by 1564. In 1580 Philip II of Spain was proclaimed king of Portugal before the church door, and thereafter Tomar's political importance diminished, reflecting also the decline in importance of the Order of Christ. Attempts were made to revive the town's commerce and in 1759 a royal hat factory, and later a cotton-mill, were established.

In 1801 it was a military headquarters, and repeatedly sacked in 1809–10 by Masséna's marauding troops—'fine paintings in the chapel torn in pieces, and many carried away; the organ broken, and altars thrown down, fireplaces made in all the cloisters, and every thing broken and defaced.' So wrote Colonel Frazer of the Royal Horse Artillery. In 1834 the monastic orders were suppressed, and it long remained in a sorry state of neglect, although partially restored in 1843. Murray's *Hand-Book* of 1856 refers to the forecourt as being a wheat-field.

The *CONVENTO DE CRISTO (9.30–12.30 and 14.00–17.30), still in the process of a thorough restoration, is approached by ascending past the tourist office at the west end of the main avenue, and climbing in zig-zags to the hill crest, leaving on our right the chapel of N.S. da Conceição (see below). The precinct is entered through the old gate beneath the ruined castle. On the right of the terrace are the remains of the Palace of Prince Henry, where Dom Duarte died in 1438.

A flight of steps, dominated by the well-buttressed tower of the Templars' **Church**, ascend to the south portal, João de Castilho's addition of 1515, a brilliant combination of Flamboyant Gothic with Renaissance detail.

To the right on entering is the *Charola, the original 16-sided church of the Templars, with the high altar enclosed in a central octagon, the typical plan of the Order, modelled on the Rotunda of the Holy Sepulchre in Jerusalem. It has been and may remain closed for some time ahead, due to restoration. On the ambulatory wall (right) are some paintings in the Flemish style attributed to Jorge Afonso (c 1510–20), and against the much-worn painted piers of the octagon are poly-chromed wooden figures of saints, probably by Fernão Muñoz, and those remnants of Oliver of Ghent's choir-stalls of 1511–14 not destroyed by the French. Note also the faded coats of arms on the ceiling.

A passage on the east side leads to the **Claustro do Cemitério**, decorated with *azulejos*, and containing two 16C tombs, one of which is that of Baltasar de Faria (died 1584), partly responsible for introducing the Inquisition into Portugal. From here one has a view of the partially restored two-storey Claustro da Lavagem. Adjacent is the sacristy (1620).

Returning through the octagon, and to the vaulted nave added to it in 1510–14 by Diogo de Arruda, one may descend into the chapterhouse below the upper choir.

From the nave, the upper storey of the **Great Cloister** is entered, its design attrib-uted to Diogo de Torralva (1558–64), the Spanish son-in-law of Francisco de Arruda, but completed after 1584 by Filippo Terzi. Generally, though inappropriately, named the cloister 'dos Felipes', it is one of the more successful Renaissance works in Portugal, even if awkwardly abutting the chapterhouse, a window of which it partially screens. The main features of the design derive from two books of archi-tecture by Serlio published at Venice in 1537 and 1540. Two spiral staircases descend to the lower level, in the centre of which is a Baroque fountain built by Pedro Fernandes de Torres; while in the south-west corner is the unfinished 'New' chapterhouse (1533–45).

A gallery off the upper cloister, overlooking the Manueline Claustro de Santa Bárbara and the Claustro da Hospedaria beyond, commands a fine view of the extraordinary *west front of the church, whose sensational central window and supporting pinnacled buttresses comprise the outstanding example of the Manueline style at its most extravagant, an anonymous masterpiece designed while Diogo de Arruda was supervising work here (c 1510–14).

The Cross of the Order of Christ surmounting the royal arms and the armillary spheres of Dom Manuel are connected by a writhing mass of ropework, seaweed

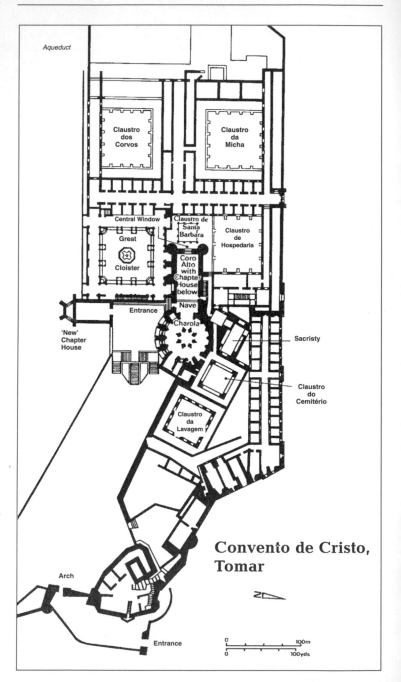

Convento de Cristo, Tomar

and coral-stems with a profusion of pattern and foliation. Original details are the transverse rope with cork floats; the chain round one buttress, and the colossal buckled garter which binds the other, possibly symbolising the Order of the Garter presented to Dom Manuel by Henry VII; and the head and shoulders of an old man supporting the roots of a tree-stump which protrudes from the base of the grated window. Above is a round window (or port-hole) representing swelling sails held by spirally arranged ropes.

Parts of the other dependencies may be visited once their restoration has been completed. These comprise the refectory and kitchen; the dormitory-corridors; and two further cloisters (Da Micha, and Dos Corvos), from the latter of which extends the aqueduct: see below.

Before leaving the convent, visitors are advised to enquire for the key to *N.S. da Conceição (of the Immaculate Conception), built on a spur overlooking the valley, on the left on descending the hill. This is a plain and perfectly proportioned cruciform building with a low dome, and lined with Corinthian columns supporting barrel vaults in both nave and aisles. Its construction (influenced by Serlio), attributed to Diogo de Torralva, dates from the 1530s, being completed by 1551.

---

The short **excursion** by car is recommended to view at closer quarters the **Aqueduto dos Pegões**, attributed to Terzi, and constructed in 1593–1614. This may be approached by following a track to the west along the north side of the convent and then turning left through an almost Tuscan landscape before descending into a valley, which is here spanned by some of the aqueduct's total of 180 ogival arches. By bearing left on climbing back, the N113 ascending northwest towards Vila Nova de Ourém from Tomar is shortly met, where turn right. A lane to the left leads to the chapel of N.S. da Piedade (1613; view), from which a long flight of steps descends to the porticoed octagonal hermitage of São Gregório (16C), near which convenient parking may be found.

---

Near the foot of the castle hill extends the attractive **Praça da República**, the main square of the old town, flanked by several 16–17C houses. The 17C Town Hall faces **São João Baptista** (1510), with Manueline doorways and an octagonal spire capped by an armillary sphere. Within are a carved stone pulpit, and 16C paintings, some attributed to Gregório Lopes (c 1460–1550), among them Salome with the head of the Baptist, and the Mass of St Gregory (1538/9).

At No. 73 in the adjacent Rua Dr Joaquim Jacinto is the 14C *synagogue, in use from the mid 15C until 1497, and the only one surviving in such a good state in Portugal. It was recognised as a synagogue by a Polish Jewish refugee during the Second World War, and now houses the Museu Abraham Zacuto (named after the astronomer and mathematician (1452–c 1515), who, on the expulsion of Jews from Spain in 1492, had taken refuge in Portugal, where he remained as Court astonomer until forced to seek asylum in North Africa after 1497). It is a square vaulted chamber sustained by four columns, and contains a number of tombstones and inscriptions in Hebrew collected from various sites in Portugal. The women's ritual baths were discovered below the floor of the adjacent house in 1985.

At the lower end of the street stand the late 18C buildings of a water- powered cotton-mill, which in the 1850s employed 300 people. Turn right here to reach the central roundabout, on the far side of which are remains of medieval structures, and bear left across the river.

Turn right at the next crossroads to approach, at a lower level, the much-restored church of **Santa Maria dos Olivais**, said to have been founded by Gualdim Pais (see History), but of this the basement of the detached belfry is probably all that remains. The present late 13C building, altered in the 15C, has a mutilated west porch surmounted by a large rose-window. Within are the graves of Pais (died 1195; 2nd south chapel), among other Templars; and the Renaissance tomb of Diogo de Pinheiro (died 1525; north side of chancel), the first bishop of Funchal, but who never visited his see.

On returning to and crossing the road junction, go through an arch abutting (left) the Renaissance doorway of Santa Iria (1536), on the alleged site of that saint's martyrdom, and turn left to cross a 15C bridge. Adjacent is a pleasant riverside restaurant; and ahead, the main street of the old town (Rua Serpa Pinto), while to the right are riverside gardens flanked by a huge water-wheel.

## Tomar to Batalha

About 50km. The N113 climbs north-east (views) through **Vila Nova de Ourém** (5772 inhabitants), an important but decayed market town, to the south-west of which stands the imposingly sited fortified enceinte of **Ourém Velha**, in which Dom Sancho II's queen was held captive when carried off from Coimbra in 1246 by a band of barons headed by Raimundo Viegas de Portocarreiro, a brother of the archbishop of Braga, very probably with her connivance.

The 15C Igreja Matriz (of Ourém Velha), rebuilt in 1756 and with a curious organ-loft, preserves in its crypt—similar to the synagogue at Tomar—the drastically restored tomb of its founder. The castle has unfortunately received modern additions, which have not improved its otherwise remarkable bastions.

At neighbouring Pinhel, the left-hand turning leads to Fátima, which may be avoided by continuing north-west for 6km to crossroads (from which the N113 descends through woods to an entry to the A1, and beyond to Leiria) where turn left onto the N357 and, after 4km, right onto the N356 for Batalha, with wide views ahead on the descent into the coastal plain; see Rte 19.

---

The N110 leads north-east from Tomar, at 7km meeting the N238 from Sertã (see sub-route in Rte 17, in reverse), later bypassing (right) **Areias**, with a church attributed to João de Castilho (1548), and the ruins of a medieval tower.

The road goes on to pass near (left) the ancient town of **Alvaiázere**, probably of Roman origin, with relics of a fort.

The junction with the new IC8 (see sub-route in Rte 17) is crossed at Pontão, as the N110 continues north through attractive country to skirt **Penela**, an old town with a *castle claimed to have been erected by 1087, but later rebuilt.

---

The right-hand turning here leads across country to Lousã via **Miranda do Corvo**, an old town receiving its *foral* from Afonso Henriques in 1136, but much damaged by the French in the Peninsular War (March 1811). From Miranda, the road continues north over a ridge to **Semide**, with the monastic church of Santa Maria, founded by Afonso Henriques. Rebuilt in 1697 after a destructive fire, it is lined with 18C *azulejos* and contains a large organ.

---

From Penela, the main road climbs north-west over a ridge, later descending towards Condeixa-a-Nova, first passing a turning for the important Roman site of Conímbriga, for which and for the rest of the route to Coimbra, see the last part of Rte 18A.

# 19 · Alcobaça, Aljubarrota, and Batalha

*Total distance, 20km (12 miles). For the road from Lisbon to Alcobaça, and its continuation from Batalha to Coimbra; see Rte 18A.*

## ALCOBAÇA

Alcobaça (5121 inhabitants) is a pleasant little town in the centre of a rich fruit-growing district at the confluence of the rivers Alcoa and Baça. It once had a reputation for its cotton chintzes. In the mid 18C the manufacture of cambrics had been promoted there under the guidance of Scottish and Irish managers.

■ The **Tourist Office** is in the Praça 25 de Abril. There are **buses** from Lisbon (infrequent) and from Leiria; the bus station is just outside the town.

The magnificent although mutilated Cistercian **\*ABBEY OF ALCOBAÇA** is considered by many to be the finest surviving example of medieval architecture in Portugal. Even Lady Holland, who visited it in 1805, remarked: 'by far the best and least disgusting convent I ever saw'.

The whole façade is some 220m long. The Baroque west front of the church, with its two cupola-topped towers, retains a deep-set but worn Gothic portal and rose-window, below which is a wide terrace. The two ranges of dependencies flanking it once housed guest rooms (north) and to the south, the cells, formerly accommodating some hundreds of monks.

### History

The abbey was founded by Afonso Henriques c 1153 as a thanks-offering for the capture of Santarém, and the original structure, started in 1178, was completed in 1223. Its mitred abbot, the senior of his rank in Portugal, held great influence, being ex-officio high almoner and precentor to the king. One of the abbots, depicted in the São Vicente altarpiece in the Museu de Arte Antiga, Lisbon, has been identified as Vasco Tinoco. The west front was cloaked by indifferent Baroque reconstruction in 1725, and in 1770 the interior was embellished with rococo woodwork by William Elsden, responsible for several buildings in Coimbra.

*Recollections of an Excursion to the Monasteries of Alcobaça and Batalha*, Beckford's description of his visit there in June 1794, was not published until 1835. Here he found some 300 monks including servants 'living in a splendid manner', which is confirmed by his contemporaries. Twiss dined and supped with above 20 of the superiors in a private room, 'and in the evening the bottle went as briskly about as ever I saw it do in Scotland; so that with the aid of some musical instruments, we spent a very agreeable day'. The ill-informed and anti-clerical Major Dalrymple, having accepted their hospitality, ungratefully commented that it was a shame 'that the celestial pastors should possess so much worldly wealth, thereby wallowing in sloth and idleness, a nuisance to society'. In fact they were very good and 'improving' landlords.

In 1810 the French pillaged the place; the library, which was important— 'splendid', according to General d'Urban, was ransacked. William Tomkinson, a cavalry officer, passing the monastery on 7 March 1811, described the scene: 'They [the French] had burnt what they could, and destroyed the remainder with an immense deal of trouble. The embalmed kings and queens were taken out of their tombs, and I saw them lying in as great preservation as

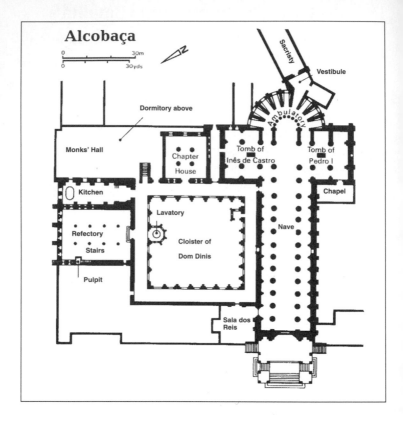

the day they were interred. The fine tessellated pavement, from the entrance to the altar, was picked up, the facings to the stone pillars were destroyed nearly to the top, scaffolding having been erected for that purpose...'. It was again sacked during anti-clerical rioting in 1834, and has since been the object of the equally rigorous attentions of 'restorers', who in an attempt to re-convert the interior to its original Cistercian purity, have stripped it bare.

Nothing can now detract from the imposing interior of the church, massive and austere, remarkable for its great length as compared with its width (109m by 23m; and 20m high), an impression accentuated by the great girth of the piers and the narrowness of the spaces between them, while the pier shafts stand on bevelled corbels some distance from the ground throughout its length. The general plan is modelled on the French Cistercian church of Cîteaux. Light is admitted only by the aisle windows and the rose-windows of the west front and transepts.

In the north and south transepts respectively are the **tombs of Inês de Castro** (died 1355) and **Dom Pedro I** (died 1367), whose romantic tragedy is celebrated in Portuguese literature and history (see Rte 25C). They had been placed foot to foot, as it was traditionally said that the king had ordered this disposition so that at the Resurrection the first object before his eyes would be the form of his beloved: on their tombs are inscribed the words 'Até ao fim do mundo' (until the end of the world).

Although damaged by D'Erlon's troops in search of treasure, they survived gross mutilation. Both are designed in the best traditions and with the highest crafts-manship of the 14C, and show the richness of imagination characteristic of Portuguese sculpture at its zenith. They are embellished by intricately carved scrip-tural scenes, martyrdoms, the Passion, etc. Note the line of musicians along the top of one side of that of Inês, and the Day of Judgement at the foot. The Wheel of Fortune is seen at the foot of Dom Pedro's. Both are attended by six angels.

Off the south transept is a neo-Gothic **chapel** designed by Elsden for the tombs of Dom Afonso II and Dom Afonso III and their respective queens, Urraca and Brites. Here also is a mutilated terracotta group of the Death of St Bernard, attrib-uted to Frei Pedro (c 1687–90), which Southey, much prejudiced, condemned as one of 'the most execrable puppet shows of modern popery;—angels playing the fiddle at the nativity, and Portuguese washer-women coming to see the infant Jesus!'

From here one may cross the ambulatory, off which is the vestibule, to the sacristy (damaged by the earthquake in 1755), approached by a beautiful foliated Manueline doorway (c 1520) giving access to the circular Chapel of the Relics (1669–72), containing numerous painted reliquary busts, etc., long despoiled of their contents. Beyond the vestibule is the early 18C chapel of N.S. do Desterro, with Salomonic pillars.

A door in the north aisle admits to the **cloister of Dom Dinis**, the lower storey of which, with double and triple arches surmounted by traceried circles, dates from 1308–11. The upper storey, with graceful arches, was added by the Cardinal-infant Dom Afonso (1509–40), son of Dom Manuel.

Off the east walk is the **chapterhouse**, notable for its fine round-arched door-ways and windows. A staircase adjacent ascends to the monks' dormitory, its vaulting sustained by two rows of ten columns, extending over the chapterhouse and Monks' Hall, the latter adjacent to the kitchen.

The **\*kitchen**, with an immense oblong pyramidal chimney, and tiling of 1752, similar to those in the kitchen of the Palace of Sintra, has the rivulet (a branch of the Alcoa) mentioned by Beckford running through its conduit. While still impres-sive in size, Beckford's 'most distinguished temple of gluttony in all Europe' now lies silent and empty; yet one can still imagine the pastry-making scene he so well described, when 'a numerous tribe of lay brothers and their attendants were rolling out and puffing up into a hundred different shapes, singing all the while as blithely as larks in a corn-field'.

Adjacent is the huge vaulted **refectory**, with a flight of steps built into the thick-ness of the wall ascending to the lector's pulpit. This was the 'immense square of seventy or eighty feet; linen foul and greasy', which Beckford noted in his Journal of 1794. Earlier this century it was temporarily transformed into the local theatre. Opposite its entrance is a charming 14C lavatory containing an hexagonal Renaissance fountain.

Continuing the circuit of the cloister, the 16C **Sala dos Reis** is reached, displaying royal statues and a group representing the Coronation of Afonso Henriques, *azulejos* illustrating the Life of St Bernard and the history of the monastery, and a huge cauldron said to have been captured from the Spanish at Aljubarrota.

*The kitchen with its huge pyramidal chimney at Alcobaça*

The rest of the much-debased monastic dependencies (including four other cloisters) has now been put to a variety of mundane uses, but entry may be gained to some parts by the persistent.

A little to the north is the attractive Praça da República and, beyond the converging rivers, a wine museum (right) on the Leiria road.

There is little else of interest in the immediate neighbourhood, except the remains of a Moorish castle. Baron Taylor was informed by an old woman, when he was sketching it early in the 19C, that the Moorish chief to whom it belonged returned on one night of every year 'for the purpose of keeping a kind of witches' Sabbath, and of demanding twelve virgins as an annual tribute. 'However', she continued, 'there is not much danger in him now, for the *frades* prevent his injuring us; but still any young woman who visits the ruins by herself runs the risk of losing her senses, and I have even known some who have died from so doing.'

At **Vestiaria**, some 2km west, off the road to Nazaré (see Rte 18A), the early 16C Manueline portal of N.S. da Ajuda is remarkable.

The N8 climbs east and bears north-east through **Aljubarrota**, with a 13C church. It gives its name to the decisive battle of 1385, which in fact took place some distance further north-east. In the village centre stood the house of Brites d'Almeida, the baker's wife, who, it is said, laid low seven Spaniards with a baker's oven-peel or shovel during the battle, thus the proverb: *'Endiabrado como a padeira de Aljubarrota'* (as full of the devil as the baker's wife of Aljubarrota).

The **Battle of Aljubarrota**. At dawn on 14 August 1385 the Portuguese army heard mass at Porto de Mós before following the track from there and taking up a strong defensive position facing north. This lay between the hamlet and restored chapel of São Jorge (bypassed by the main road) and Batalha. It was here, in an area not then encumbered by pines, that João, Master of Avis, together with the Constable Nun' Alvares Pereira, redeployed their waiting troops, which included a small contingent of English archers. This movement had become necessary because the Spaniards, originally advancing from Leiria, had made a flanking march to the west before turning here for the attack, which in the event did not start until the late afternoon of that hot August day.

Although caution had been agreed, individual hot-heads amongst Juan I's undisciplined army forced the issue by indulging in harassing attacks, and soon both sides were generally engaged. The battle lasted hardly an hour, for although the Castilians were superior in numbers, they faltered when they saw their royal standard go down, the whole army disintegrating, Juan himself galloping off the field towards the castle at Santarém. Dom João I was able to make the claim that 2500 enemy men-at-arms had been killed, apart from numerous members of the landed aristocracy of Portugal who had opposed his recent succession.

The N1, the old main Lisbon—Coimbra road is met (see sub-route in Rte 18B), off which the N243 shortly turns right to nearby **Porto de Mós**, with potteries and a 13C castle on a Roman site, altered in the mid 15C, but preserving a richly decorated balcony similar to that of the castle at Leiria (see Rte 18A).

## BATALHA

A right-hand turning off the main road leads to the west front of the magnificent 'Battle-Abbey', Santa Maria da Vitória, in Batalha (*Pousada Mestre Afonso Domingues*), a small town in a fruitful valley. Unfortunately, the immediate vicinity of the abbey itself has not been improved by the erection of 'model' houses largely devoted to selling souvenirs.

■ The **Tourist Office** is in Largo Paulo VI.

The *****ABBEY OF BATALHA**, once served by Dominicans, lacks the austere grace of Cistercian Alcobaça, but is undoubtedly one of the masterpieces of Portuguese architecture. Some details recall the English Perpendicular style, and the nave reminded Beckford 'of Winchester in form of arches and mouldings, and of Amiens in loftiness' although he had reservations concerning the 'scollops and twist-ifications' of its exuberant ornamentation.

### History

The abbey's construction dates from 1388, in consequence of a vow made by João I, Master of Avis, prior to the Battle of Aljubarrota (15 August 1385), fought not far away, if he should gain a victory over the Spaniards. Dom João's building comprised the church, the founder's chapel, the first cloister, and the chapterhouse, and its masters of works were Afonso Domingues (1388–1402), and Huguet (or Ougete; 1402–38). In 1437 Dom Duarte (the king's eldest son) commissioned the erection of an octagonal chapel behind the apse, while Dom Afonso V commissioned the construction of the second cloister (1438–77), built by the Alentejanos Martim Vasques and Fernão de Évora. Work on the pantheon was resumed during the reign of Dom Manuel, executed by Mateus Fernandes the Elder (1480–1515), who is buried here; and intermittently between 1509 and 1519 by Diogo Boitac. But this was finally abandoned when Dom Manuel (died 1521) turned his attention to his own mausoleum at Belém.

An additional cloister, dismantled in 1811, was built by Dom João III c 1550. The whole was only comparatively slightly damaged by the earth-quake of 1755 and during the Peninsular War, although General Picton's Division was briefly quartered here in October 1810. Since 1839 the care of its fabric has been in the hands of the State, who chose to place here the Tomb of Portugal's Unknown Soldiers, apart from gutting the building almost as dras-tically as they have done at Alcobaça. On at least three occasions James Wyatt used architectural designs based on drawings of Batalha published in 1795 by James Kavanagh Murphy (1760–1814).

The exterior lacks major vertical accents in its composition, and there is no impor-tant tower or central feature to hold the eye. The details of the many-pinnacled **west front** are of interest, notably the statues of the Evangelists in the tympanum. In the centre is Christ in Majesty, surrounded by saints, etc. The apostles on the splay are modern copies. The traceried limestone above the portal, weathered to a honey tint, is surmounted by a fine Flamboyant window. To the right rises the octagonal lantern of the founder's chapel, once capped by an openwork spire, which fell in 1755. The plainer south doorway is likewise of interest.

Like Alcobaça, the church is long and high in proportion to its width (80m by 22m, and 32m high). The nave consists of eight bays separated from the aisles by plain piers, while the small apsidal choir is flanked by two chapels on either side. The transepts are 32m across. A few steps within the west door is the tomb-slab of Mateus Fernandes, the master of works (see above).

The **Capela do Fundador** (1426–34), entered from the south aisle, is 20m square, and roofed by an octagonal lantern 12m in diameter; the delicate clustered columns and arches and the elaborate star vault with its central rosace are all remarkable. In the centre is the double **tomb of Dom João I and Philippa of Lancaster** (transferred here from the Capela-Mór on the completion of this chapel). The recumbent effigies of the king (died 1433), armoured, and of his English wife (died 1416; cf. Odivelas) lie hand in hand, each beneath an octagonal canopy on which is carved the arms of Avis and Lancaster (also carved above the south door), while around the margin of the tomb their mottoes '*Por Bem*' (Pour Bien; cf. Sala das Pêgas in the palace at Sintra) and '*Yl me plet*' (Il me plait) are many times repeated. The carved insignia of the Order of the Garter, founded by Philippa's grandfather, Edward III, will be noted. (Colonel Leach admitted to having cut off a button from the royal robes, when the embalmed body of the founder had been exposed by troops during the retreat from Busaco in 1810.)

On the south wall are the restored **altar-tombs** of their four younger sons (Duarte, the eldest, lies in the Capelas Imperfeitas; see below), each decorated with their individual devices. Farthest to the left lies Fernando, Master of the Order of Avis, the 'Infante Santo' (died 1443), rashly left as a hostage for the surrender of

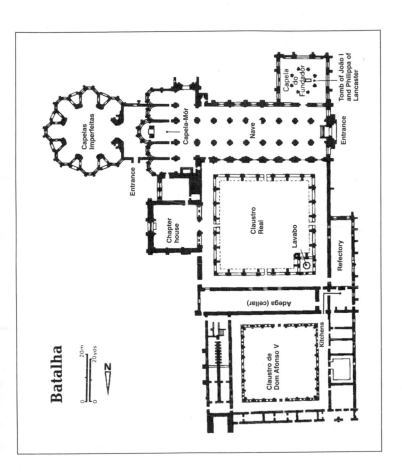

**Batalha**

Capelas Imperfeitas

Capela-Mór

Nave

Capela 'do' Fundador

Tomb of João I and Philippa of Lancaster

Entrance

Entrance

Chapter house

Claustro Real

Lavabo

Refectory

Adega (cellar)

Claustro de Dom Afonso V

Kitchens

Ceuta, which was never made, by the ill-fated expedition against Tangier in 1437; his remains were brought back from Fez and interred with great pomp in 1472. That of João, Master of the Order of São Tiago (died 1442) has a representation of the Passion behind. The tomb of Henrique, Duke of Viseu and Master of the Order of Christ, and better known to the English as Prince Henry 'the Navigator' (died 1460) bears an indifferent effigy. Next to it is that of Pedro, Duke of Coimbra and Regent of Portugal (died 1449; at Alfarrobeira).

The tombs on the west wall are modern imitations: they contain the remains of Dom Afonso V (died 1481); Dom João II (died 1495), and his only son, Afonso (died 1491; cf. Santarém).

The apsidal **Capela-Mór** is notable for its early 16C stained-glass windows (ascribed to Francisco Henriques), which represent the Visitation, Adoration of the Magi, the Flight into Egypt, and Resurrection.

*Sculptural detail in the Abbey of Batalha*

From the north aisle one may enter the **\*Claustro Real** (55m by 50m), originally built by Afonso Domingues, the arches of which were later embellished for Dom Manuel (attributed by some to Mateus Fernandes, by others to Boitac) and were filled with elaborately convoluted 'vegetable' tracery of varied patterns (in which Sacheverell Sitwell observes the poppy, cardoon, and artichoke), including Dom Manuel's emblem, the armillary sphere, and the Cross of the Order of Christ. The supporting colonettes are likewise lavishly adorned.

Off the east walk opens the **\*chapterhouse**, entered through a massive yet graceful arch between two fine double windows. The east window, also of good design, contains 16C glass, while the vault, 19m square and without any central support, is remarkable.

On the north side is the Tomb of the Unknown Soldiers (one from Africa, and one from the Flanders front), perpetually guarded, above which is the shattered crucifixion known as the 'Christ of the Trenches', found at Neuve-Chapelle.

Continuing round the cloister, an elaborate Manueline door to the long vaulted cellar is passed. At the north-west angle of the cloister projects the **\*well-house**, or *lavabo*, where the foliation of the tracery surpasses itself. The diagonal view across the cloister, with its four secular cypresses, to the upper parapet and to the clerestory of the church, and of the small spired tower (rebuilt in the mid 19C), is memorable. Adjacent is the refectory, now containing a miscellaneous military museum and objects left at the Tomb of the Unknown Soldiers.

From here, passing the kitchens (left), one may enter the Claustro de Dom Afonso V, austere in comparison to the Claustro Real. Follow its south walk and continue ahead to reach the vacant site of Dom João III's cloister, cleared after its virtual destruction by French troops in the Peninsular War, and turn right to approach the entrance to the **\*Capelas Imperfeitas**, which have no direct communication with the church.

The original plan of Dom Duarte's mausoleum can be seen in the comparative simplicity of the main arches of the seven chapels which surround the central octagon, now open to the sky. Note also the descending keystones over three of the chapels. Mateus Fernandes, Dom Manuel's master of works, planned an upper octagon with a vault supported by massive buttresses built up from the six smaller intervening pentagonal chapels, but work was abandoned before the piers had risen more than a short distance above the rich cornices of the main storey. Part of the latter, which had not been commenced on some chapels, was added in the late 19C.

Some idea of the intended elaboration may be gauged from the profuse ornamentation of the truncated bases of the upper storey, and from that of the exotic west portal (1509), 15m high, a masterpiece of lace-like tracery in stone. The obsessively repeated inscription on the arch is the motto of Dom Duarte: '*leauté faray tam yaserey*' ('loyal I shall ever be'). Above is a double- bayed Renaissance loggia or tribune, added c 1533, attributed to João de Castilho.

The chapels now contain the tombs of (left) a Duke of Aveiro, whose escutcheons have been effaced; that of an infant son of Dom Afonso V; and, opposite the portal, those of Dom Duarte (died 1438), and of his queen, Leonor of Aragón, which were mutilated by the French in 1810. These lay originally in the apse chapels, which have been attributed to both João de Castilho and Boitac.

Santa Cruz, south-east of the town centre, preserves a fine Manueline portal.

# 20 · Leiria to Oporto via Figueira da Foz and Aveiro

*Total distance, 186km (114 miles). N109. 54km Figueira da Foz—55km Vista Alegre—8km Aveiro—IP5. and N109. 20km Estarreja—15km Ovar—18km Espinho—16km Oporto.*

This route provides an alternative to the frequently congested N1, although the A1 motorway is faster.

From Leiria (see Rte 18A) the N109 leads almost due north parallel to the railway, at 32km passing a right-hand turning for **Louriçal**, with a mid 18C conventual church of some interest, to bypass **Marinha das Ondas**, with the ruins of the monastery of Ceiça, of ancient foundation, largely rebuilt in the 17C, beyond which the improved road bears north-west to cross the estuary or mouth (*foz*) of the Mondego.

On the far bank lies **FIGUEIRA DA FOZ** (25,929 inhabitants), an important fishing-port and popular resort, but of slight interest except for its sands, casino, and museum.

■ The **Tourist Office** is on Avenida 25 de Abril. **Trains** run here from Leiria, and there are **buses** to Aveiro.

### History
It was off the coast here that a British convoy on its way to the West Indies was wrecked in April 1804, when HMS Apollo split in two with the loss of 150 lives. And it was on the extensive beaches on both sides of the river-mouth that during the first five days of August 1808 Wellington's expeditionary force disembarked from its transports, with some losses of men and equipment in the pounding surf, preparatory to marching south towards Lisbon and its first encounter with the French at Roliça; see Rte 18A.

Wellington briefly occupied the late 16C fort of Santa Catarina at the south-west corner of the town, built to defend the bar. Before reaching this the Jardim Municipal is passed, just behind which, to the right, is the Casa do Paço, its walls covered with several thousand 18C Dutch tiles said to have been unloaded here from a shipload destined elsewhere.

Some minutes' walk inland from this point is the ***Museu do Dr Santos Rocha**, installed in a modern building overlooking a park, and under the auspices of the Gulbenkian Foundation. The archaeological collection is important, with finds from dolmens in the region, funerary stelae (some from Faro in the Algarve), Phoenician inscriptions, and ceramics, etc. Other sections are devoted to furniture, numismatics, ethnography, and paintings (the last disappointing, except for the naïve ex-votos); and in a covered courtyard, a marine section, describing the fishing industry, salting, etc.

For the road from here to Coimbra, 44km east, see the latter part of Rte 24, in reverse.

Skirting the east flank of the Serra da Boa Viagem to the north of Figueira, the site of Neolithic settlements, the road descends to a low-lying dune-flanked plain, and continues north through (24km) **Tocha**, with good *azulejos* of 1763 in its church, from which, and from **Mira** and **Vagos** further north, byroads approach the coast.

On the far bank of the Rio Boco is **Vista Alegre**, with deposits of china clay in its vicinity, and a village of workers' cottages. The factory was founded in 1824 by José Ferreira Pinto Basto (1774–1839), whose wife, Bárbara Inocéncia Allen, was of English descent. It is said that the fragile china was at one time carried to Oporto and Lisbon on camel-back.

Adjacent to the large factory is a museum, well displaying the extensive range of glass and porcelain that has been produced here. Although glass is no longer made, Vista Alegre porcelain may be bought or ordered at the showroom next door. The museum is open on weekdays 9.00–12.30 and 14.00–17.30.

Opposite is the chapel of N.S. da Penha, containing the dramatic *tomb by Claude de Laprade of Manuel de Moura Manuel, Bishop of Miranda do Douro (died 1699).

At neighbouring **Ilhavo** (13,144 inhabitants), an ancient fishing-port now virtually stranded by shifting sands, is a museum containing models of fishing-boats, local costumes, examples of *moliceiros* (designed to harvest seaweed), etc., and a conchological collection.

## AVEIRO

Aveiro (32,847 inhabitants), an episcopal city and district capital, is sited on the edge of dull mud-flats adjoining the east bank of the marshy lagoon or Ria de Aveiro, fed by the Vouga, Agueda, and Antuã. It is an important fishing-port with a considerable trade in salt, obtained by evaporation, and with its few canals, dykes, and humpbacked bridges, its centre has a slightly Dutch appearance. The recent completion of the transverse IP5 highway from Spain via Guarda and Viseu, which terminates at Aveiro, promises future prosperity.

It contains a museum of some interest in the Convento de Jesús, and there are shipyards in the area; it is also noted for its *ovos moles* (an egg sweetmeat), sardines, and *mexilhões* (preserved mussels).

■ The **Tourist Office** is at 8 Rue João Mendonça. There are **buses** from Figueira da Foz and **trains** to Oporto and Lisbon.

### History

Perhaps Roman Talabriga—but this is unconfirmed—it flourished in the 16C with the exploitation by João Afonso of the cod-banks of Newfoundland, and its fishing fleet at one time counted 60 vessels. The fish used to be taken into the interior in baskets carried on women's heads, many of them from the village of Ovar (see below), at the north end of the lagoon. In 1575, a year of drought, a violent storm closed the mouth of the Vouga with a sand bar, causing it to overflow its banks during winter floods, which inundated the low-lying area parallel to the coast, and formed fever-breeding marshes, which reduced Aveiro's population from some 14,000 to 5000. In 1808, a canal, the Barra Nova, was cut through to drain the marshes, and only the salt lagoon now remains. In May 1809 General Hill, by transporting one brigade at a time by boats from here to Ovar, partially outflanked the French retreating on Oporto.

Its most eminent native is José Estevão Coelho de Magalhães (1809–62), the political orator.

Roads converge on the town centre, the Praça Humberto Delgado, in fact a widened bridge across the central canal, near which is a car park. The tourist office (at which trips on the lagoon may be arranged, and boats hired) is a short distance to the south-west, opposite the 16C Misericórdia. The house of the Harbour Master (*Capitania do Porto*), to the east, appears to be built over an open drain.

To the south-east, a road leads up to the Praça do Milenário, with a Manueline Calvary and (left) the church of **São Domingos**, described as 'a squalid and tawdry room' in the 1850s by J.M. Neale. Raised to the rank of cathedral, it has recently been monstrously 'modernised'. Its only objects of interest are the ten paintings of the Life of St Dominic placed over the choir-stalls, and an 18C organ.

To the west of the square is the former Convento de Jesus (15C; altered in the 18C), now housing the **Museu Regional**, which although extensive, contains little of great merit. The principal objects are the richly decorated *chapel of Princesa Santa Joana, named after the daughter of Dom Afonso V, who spent the last 14 years of her life here, dying in 1489; she was unaccountably beatified in 1693, and it is recorded that her capacity to suffer the lice bred in her chemise was greatly admired by her hagiographer. A charming series of naïve 17C paintings describes her life from the moment of leaving her father's palace. Her tomb, an ugly confection of marble marquetry completed in 1711 by João Antunes, stands in the lower choir. Note the *talha dourada* by António Gomes and José Coreia (before 1725) and, in the upper choir, the Chinoiserie panelling and ceiling (1731), and the portable organs. The *azulejos* in the refectory, the 16C Albuquerque tomb in the cloister, and the *presépio* or crib attributed to Machado de Castro, are notable; and among paintings, one attributed to Vieira Portuense on copper, a Sienese Virgin and Child, and a portrait of Santa Joana attributed to Nuno Gonçalves, are of interest in an otherwise miscellaneous collection of ecclesiastical paintings and sculpture, etc.

A few minutes' walk to the west brings one to the Praça do Marquês de Pombal, with a Carmelite church of c 1650, preserving rich gilding; while further to the south, adjoining a park, stands Santo António, founded in 1524, with an 18C façade.

By turning left on crossing to the north bank of the canal, and then over a hump-backed bridge, the site of the daily fish auction is reached. It takes place between 6.00 and 9.00.

The only other building of interest is best approached by road, turning right on crossing the canal and following the main Av. Dr Lourenço Peixinho to the railway station, continuing past which, turn left at the next T-junction. Below gardens on the right stands the restored octagonal chapel of **Senhor das Barrocas** of 1722–32, the design of which has been attributed to João Antunes, and which contains sculptures by Claude de Laprade.

From the west end of the IP5, which skirts the lagoon, one may drive past shipyards to approach a rash of buildings flanking the coastal dunes at **Praia da Barra**, where at least the pounding Atlantic breakers are impressive, but beware the strong undertow.

On leaving Aveiro, follow the IP5 north-east past a particularly evil-smelling cellulose factory and turn left onto the N109; an entrance to the A1 motorway for Oporto is a short distance further east, beyond which is the old N1.

At **Estarreja** is the 17C Casa da Praça.

---

An **excursion** may be made from here to the *Pousada da Ria*, 22km south-west, by turning left through the fishing village of **Murtosa** and across an arm of the Ria d'Aveiro to reach the long peninsula cutting off the lagoon from the Atlantic.

The left-hand turning here—a humpy road—leads past (13km) the Pousada da Ria, overlooking the lagoon, occasionally dotted with the seaweed-harvesting *moliceiros*, and continues on to (7km) **Praia da São Jacinto**, on the north bank of the Vouga estuary. To the west, at the south end of a sandy beach over 40km long, the Atlantic breakers, with a strong undertow, crash against the shore. The right-hand turning skirts the north arm of the lagoon to regain the main road just north of Ovar. The small resorts on the west side of the peninsula are sad little places, however much sand and sea they have to offer.

---

The main road continues north from Estarreja through **Avanca**, with a large mid 18C church, to skirt **Ovar** (11,476 inhabitants), an agricultural centre with light industries, once of importance as a fishing village. It lies in a somewhat sombre district, described at the turn of the 19C as being a wilderness 'so perfect and so destitute of any trace of civilization, that no part of Siberia or Africa could exhibit greater solitude'! Its short-skirted big-boned fishwives, known as *'varinas'*, sometimes still seen barefooted, made a living by taking their catch to sell in the hinterland, and even in Lisbon the local itinerant fishwives are still so named. There is a small ethnographical collection near the town centre. In 1809, Major Alexander Dickson, superintending Wellington's artillery, was quartered in the town hall briefly, before moving on towards Oporto.

From just north of the town, which contains an ethnographical museum, the N223 bears north-east towards an entry to the A1, and to (11km) Vila da Feira; see Rte 26.

A right-hand turning off the coastal N109, here recently converted into a dual carriageway (IC1), leads shortly to **Rio Meão** (not to be confused with Rio Mau), with an early church remodelled in the 15C, and again later.

**Espinho** (11,888 inhabitants), with canneries, but more recently developed into a seaside resort, is now skirted. It boasts a casino; and its streets are merely numbered, not named.

For Grijo, 6km north-east, see Rte 26.

Several smaller resorts are bypassed before the road turns inland to approach the A1 bypassing the expanding conurbation of Vila Nova de Gaia and spanning the mouth of the Douro to enter Oporto; see Rte 33.

# 21 · (Ciudad Rodrigo) Vilar Formoso to Coimbra via Guarda

*Total distance, 207km (129 miles). Fuentes de Oñoro—Vilar Formoso—N16. 44km Guarda—25km Celorico da Beira—N17. 39km Seia is 2km south.—19km Oliveira do Hospital is 3km north.—53km. Penacova is 13km north-west.—27km Coimbra.*

For Ciudad Rodrigo (27km east), the *old* village of Fuentes de Oñoro, site of the critical battle between Masséna and Wellington of May 1811, and Fort Concepción, see *Blue Guide Spain*, 6th ed., and the first paragraph of Rte 22B.

For the road from Vilar Formoso to Castelo Branco via Sabugal, see Rte 22B; for those to Vila Real, see Rte 27 (and Rte 27B for Almeida).

The faster new road (IP5), running roughly parallel to the old, which it now largely supersedes as part of the transverse highway to Aveiro via Viseu, may be followed past Guarda to Celorico. The adventurous may prefer to take the slower old road (N16) to Guarda, which enables one to visit several smaller places (bypassed by the new road) en route, and continue on it to make the steep descent from Guarda to Celorico.

The N16 is entered just beyond **Vilar Formoso**, skirting the former frontier fortress of **Castelo Bom** before crossing the rocky valley of the Coa. This whole area served as a base for a large part of Wellington's army during the months prior to the siege of Ciudad Rodrigo in January 1812, and the battle of Salamanca in that June. Their lines of communication and supply passed through here during the winter of 1812/13, and before their triumphal advance on Vitoria.

During two successive winters Wellington himself lived in a house opposite the church at **Freinada** (5km south of Castelo Bom), where he kennelled his pack of hounds and hunted two or three times a week, while his headquarters staff were distributed among surrounding villages.

**Castelo Mendo**, an old town with relics of its fortifications, is just south of the road on the far bank of the Coa valley, beyond which bare undulating country is crossed before hill-top Guarda is discerned in the distance. The Romanesque church of **Póvoa do Milea**, with a small rose-window, is passed (right) on approaching the town, while adjacent is the site of an ancient settlement and Roman villa, the objects excavated from which are in the museum at Guarda.

## GUARDA

Guarda (17,877 inhabitants), standing bleakly on a ridge commanding the entrances to the upper Mondego valley (west), and the Zêzere (south-west), and with a wide view to the east towards the wind-blown plateau of Spain, at 1000m is the highest and coldest town in Portugal: indeed, it was known as the city of the four Fs: *Fria, Farta, Forte, e Feia* (cold, well-supplied, strong, and ugly).

- The **Tourist Office** is in Praça Luís de Camões. **Trains** run on the Vilar Formoso line.

### History

Guarda has always been of strategic importance, and its name alludes to its foundation by Dom Sancho I in 1197 as a bastion against Moorish incursions. Sir John Moore's army passed through in November 1808 when pushing into Spain prior to their forced retreat to Corunna. It was also a base of Wellington's operations in 1811–12, after being pillaged by the French, who converted the cathedral into stables. In April 1812 it was briefly in Marmont's hands after a surprise raid.

The partially arcaded Largo Luis de Camões in the centre of the old town is over-looked by the grey granite fortress-like *cathedral, which replaced an earlier church on a different site, demolished c 1375 as being too near the walls for secu-rity.

The new building, not completed until c 1540, is to some extent inspired by Batalha (cf.), being the only other church in Portugal with a clerestory and flying buttresses. Note the gargoyles (those facing Spain simulating cannon), and trefoil ornamentation. The narrow west front is constricted by two octagonal towers. The interior, in spite of the thick ribs of the vault, is imposing. Boitac worked on the building in 1504–17, and Manueline influence is seen in the pair of twisted colonettes near the crossing, and the keystone above. The somewhat static four-tiered retable, with its details and statues picked out in gilt, is attributed to Jean de Rouen (1550–52). In the Capela dos Pinas is an unusual late Gothic bishop's tomb. (Admission to the cathedral may be difficult to obtain on Tuesdays.)

From behind the apse, pass through the Torre dos Ferreiros, a medieval town gate, beyond which, by bearing right and then left, the Bishop's Palace (rebuilt in 1601) is reached. After being gutted, it is now partly occupied by the **regional museum** (closed Mon), its collections well displayed in a series of rooms round the courtyard and in the open-plan first floor. Sections are devoted to the geology, flora and fauna of the area, together with archaeological collections, and Roman, Suevic and Visigothic artefacts. Other sections concern the life and productions of the District. Among paintings are several by Eduardo Malta, Eduardo Lapa, and T. Victoriano. Among militaria are relics of the Peninsular War period, etc.

To the north is the Baroque façade of the Misericórdia (17C), with a good Renaissance tomb to the left of the chancel. Continuing north, the Porta da Estrela and a stretch of the town walls are reached (view), but only ruins survive of the castle which once commanded the place. One may re-enter by the Porta do Rei to regain the central square, a short distance north of which stands 18C São Vicente, containing contemporary *azulejo* panels.

For the road from Guarda to Miranda do Douro, see Rte 28, in reverse; to Viseu, Rte 23; and for Castelo Branco via Covilhã, Rte 22A.

Shortly after driving west on leaving Guarda, the old main road bears round to the north, descending steeply into the upper valley of the Mondego, providing magnif-icent *views across to the north spur of the Serra da Estrela and into the valley itself. The scenery and vegetation also changes once the high central plateau of Castile and León is left behind as the road drops some 500m in 10km, and indeed appears to be entering another country. The village of **Aldeia Viçosa**, down in the valley, was until half a century ago known as 'Porco' after the wild boar that infested the area; while at **Açores**, to the right of the road, the church contains some 16C paintings and a Latin funerary inscription referring to a Visigothic princess who died there in 666.

The IP5 is regained 5km north of Guarda, which then starts to descend steeply north-west, providing very similar views to those described immediately above, and flattens out on reaching the valley floor. It then veers left, bypassing Celorico, which may be approached by keeping right and crossing an old granite bridge.

**Celorico da Beira**, long at an important junction of roads, is dominated by the ruins of its castle, possibly of Roman origin, which was besieged by the Spanish in 1385. The Igreja Matriz (18C; replacing one of the 13C) was used as a British hospital during part of the Peninsular War.

For the road from here to Trancosa (19km north) and Lamego, see Rte 27A; for that to Viseu, Rte 23.

The N17 leads south-west parallel to the great dividing range of the Serra da Estrela, the Roman Herminius Major.

A worthwhile **detour**, at the same time providing several wide views to the north, may be made by turning left before or at **Carrapichana** for (6km) hill-top *Linhares, a village of ancient origin largely composed of 15C houses. The façade of a gutted mansion is passed near the village entrance. A narrow street leads up to the partly restored castle ruins, displaying some remarkable masonry. (Return by the same street.) Linhares, formerly Leniobriga, was the seat of a Visigothic bishopric, and it would appear from what monuments remain on the narrow road winding along the valley side here that it was formerly on the 'main' road, later superseded by the present highway.

One may continue along the older road by turning left before regaining Carrapichana. This enters **Melo**, with the desecrated remains of a medieval palace, above which is **Folgosinhos**, with relics of fortifications, and continues south-west through Gouveia to Seia (for both see below), close to the N17.

The main road now leads through a particularly beautiful part of the country, with its orchards, and vineyards characterised by their granite props, through **Vila Cortes da Serra**, with a number of old stone houses, to reach crossroads 9km beyond.

To the south-east is **Gouveia**, above which towers the peak of Santinha (1593m). Although a very ancient town, its main surviving monument is the 16C Casa da Torre, briefly Wellington's HQ before retiring on Busaco (September 1810). Near **São Paio**, to the north-east, stood a monastery, plundered by the French and used later as a British hospital. From Gouveia, the N232 ascends to cross the range, passing the source of the Mondego before climbing steeply down to Manteigas, 38km south: see Rte 22A.

The main road later bypasses **Seia**, taken from the Moors by Afonso Henriques c 1055 (then known as Sena). This is an attractively sited town preserving several old houses, including the Casa dos Obras (18C), and on the site of its castle, the Igreja Matriz. It was the birthplace of the politician Afonso Augusto da Costa (1871–1937).

From here the N339 ascends steeply to the south-east to (29km) Torre (1991m), the summit of the **Serra da Estrela**, and the highest peak in Portugal, commanding—in good weather—superb panoramic *views. The road descends even more steeply to Covilhã (18km beyond: see Rte 22A), passing the source of the Zêzere. In winter, it is as well to check on road conditions before crossing the range. A longer road (80km) climbs south from Seia through **São Romão**, and likewise commands extensive views both on the ascent and as it winds down to the east towards Covilhã via (59km) the tiny spa of **Unhais da Serra**.

13km **Póvoa das Quartas**, a hamlet of stone houses with exterior steps, lies to the right of the road, immediately beyond which (left) is the Pousada de Santa Bárbara, providing a fine *view across to a shoulder of the Serra da Estrela, and a convenient base from which to explore the district.

At 6km a right-hand turning leads shortly to **Oliveira do Hospital**, a beautifully situated market town at the head of a valley settled since Roman times; a number of buildings in the vicinity appear to incorporate Roman masonry, while at neighbouring **Bobadela** (8638 inhabitants; 3km west) a Roman arch survives. Oliveira, as its name implies, belonged to the Hospitallers. Its Igreja Matriz (13–14C; later remodelled) contains tombs of the Ferreiros, above which a carved equestrian knight has been placed (cf. that in the Museum at Coimbra); note also the 14C altarpiece. The church of São Gião, near Oliveira, has a painted ceiling.

After regaining the main route, a left-hand turning leads to **Avô**, with the ruins of a castle built by Dom Dinis, and the Manueline house of the poet Bras Garcia de Mascarenhas (1596–1656). To its south-east is the hamlet of **Aldeia das Dez**, probably built on the site of a Roman *castro*.

A track ascending from Aldeia das Dez, off which another turns to climb to the ancient village of **Piódão**, below the Serra de Açor (rising to 1340m) commands extensive mountain views, and later joins the N344 leading south to **Porta da Balsa**, among numerous small reservoirs in the centre of this remote and beautiful district.

Many of the village churches between, and including, Avô, Arganil (see below), and Góis (46km south-west; see sub-route of Rte 17), along the south side of the luxuriant valley of the Alva, contain medieval remains. If following this road, the main route may be regained from either Arganil or 24km north-west of Góis.

A rewarding detour off the N17 may be made at the next left-hand turning which leads shortly to **Lourosa** (8063 inhabitants), an old village, where the church (request entry at a neighbouring house) of *São Pedro is the only one of its kind surviving in Portugal. It dates from 912, the year Ordoño II had ordered that the limits of the ancient bishopric of Dume should be delineated by the erection of several churches. Presumably built by Mozárab workmen, it consists of a central nave with shorter aisles divided from it by broad horseshoe arches. The *ajimece* windows and the typical Visigothic decoration of the period in the entrance porch will also be noticed; while a baptismal stone and confessional seat are pointed out. The 15C belfry was removed to its present position when the church was restored in the early 1930s.

The main road continues west along a ridge between the valleys of the Alva and Mondego, and provides several extensive views.

At 5km a right-hand turning leads c 10km north-west to **Tábua**, with a large 18C church, overlooking the Mondego, which is crossed to approach Santa Comba Dão, at the junction of the old road to Luso and Busaco with the IP3 from Viseu, to meet the A1 north of Coimbra: see Rte 24.

At 17km a left-hand turning off the N17 leads directly to (8km) **Arganil**, with the late 13C chapel of São Pedro. The church at **Pombeiro da Beira**, to its west, contains the Manueline tomb of Mateus da Cunha, attributed to Diogo Pires the Younger.

The IC7, the next right-hand turning off the N17, winds 12km north-west to meet the IP3 7km east of Penacova, also approached by another turning 20km further south-west, beyond the Rio Alva, and winding down into the Mondego valley. The IC7, and the IP3, which beyond Penacova circles to the north, now provides a more rapid, but still attractive, alternative approach to Coimbra from the north. For Penacova itself, see Rte 24.

Continuing west on the N17, **Foz de Arouce** (frequently mis-spelled Aronce in contemporary descriptions), is bypassed, where in March 1811 Marshal Ney narrowly escaped capture. At least 500 of his troops, forming Masséna's rearguard, were killed or drowned in their precipitate retreat under strong British pressure, and over 200 mules were left hamstrung; the British loss was about 65. Not long after this event Ney, insubordinate to Masséna, returned to France in disgrace.

For Lousã, 7km south-east, see Rte 17.

The N17 now threads the winding valley of the Rio Ceira, a tributary of the Mondego, to approach Coimbra: see Rte 25.

# 22 · Vilar Formoso to Castelo Branco, for Abrantes

## A. Via Guarda and Covilhã

*Total distance, 143km (89 miles). IP5. 42km Guarda—N18. 20km Belmonte exit— 18km Covilhã exit—17km Fundão—12km Alpedrinha—34km Castelo Branco.*

*For the IP2, and the extension under construction to Abrantes and beyond to meet the A1, and the alternative N118, see Rtes 17 and 14A.*

For the roads to Guarda, see Rte 21, where turn south onto the N18.

### Guarda to Covilhã via Manteigas

75km; the excursion up to Torre will add 12km to the route. Those wishing to visit this highest peak of the **Serra da Estrela**—also the highest in Portugal—may conveniently make the ascent by this sub-route, should visibility be good, and the road not snowbound, as it occasionally is in winter.

To do so, bear right off the N18 some 5km south of Guarda onto the N18.1 to follow a parallel valley to (23.5km) **Valhelhas**, with a church of 1262, and an old bridge in the valley to the south-east. Turn onto the N232 here, veering west to (17.5km) **Manteigas** (Pousada de São Lourenço), an old town reputed for its butter (as its name implies), cheese, and trout. The main road climbs steeply in hairpin bends across the range, later descending to (38km) Gouveia: see Rte 21. Bear south-west via the small spa of **Caldas de Manteigas**, 6km to the east of which, approached by a rough track, is the cascade of the Poço do Inferno (Hell's Well). After 11km the N339 is reached. The Torre (previously called 'O Malhão'), rising to the right to a height of 1991m (6532ft), commands wonderful panoramic views. Seia, on the far side of the range, is 29km north-west: see Rte 21. Descending from Torre, the road climbs steeply down through the winter-sports and mountaineering centre of **Penhas da Saúde** to Covilhã: see below.

The improved N18 shortly reaches a watershed, and commences the descent into the upper valley of the Zêzere (views). On approaching Belmonte, on its height, a byroad to the left leads to the granite ***Torre Centum Cellas**, a curious and interesting ruin in a good state of preservation and almost certainly of Roman origin, but with medieval alterations to its upper storey. No convincing answer has yet been advanced as to its precise purpose, but it may have been part of a villa.

The ascent to **Belmonte** itself, commanded by its granite castle (late 13C; and at various times restored, the most recent being the most inept), and providing extensive views, forks off to the left. Opposite are the remains of perhaps a *domus municipalis* or council-house (cf. Braganza), and near by is the old church of São Tiago, containing a 14C pietà, and the chapel of the Cabral family. Pedro Alvares Cabral (c 1467–c 1526), the 'discoverer' of Brazil (1500), which he named Vera Cruz, was born at Belmonte (and is buried at Santarém). The image of N.S. da Esperança, which travelled with Cabral round the Cape of Good Hope on his expedition to India, is preserved in the more modern church at the far side of the village. Belmonte had long been the centre of a crypto-Jewish community, a descendant of one of whom was Francis Schonenberg (alias Belmonte; 1653–1717), the Dutch minister in Madrid, and in Lisbon, and an important figure in the War of the Spanish Succession.

There are traces of a Roman road at **Caria**, 10km south, and further Roman remains at **Capinha**, some 12km beyond.

The Zêzere is crossed as the main road continues due south-west to bypass Covilhã, on the steep lower slopes of the Serra da Estrela.

**COVILHÃ** (21,836 inhabitants), a surprisingly large town to find in this once isolated area, but long an important textile centre known for its woollen blankets, has been developed as a resort for winter sports and excursions into the range.

■ The **Tourist Office** is in the Praça do Município. The **train station** is 4km outside of the town; it is on the Guarda–Castelo Branco line.

### History

Dom Sancho I, in resettling the area in the late 12C, granted it a *foral* guaranteeing the liberty and freedom of all Christian captives after a year's residence, while Dom Afonso III encouraged trade by granting safe conducts on the roads to its August fair, where no fairgoer could be arrested for any past crime from a week before its commencement until 30 days after! Some crypto-Jews later settled in the district.

In 1677 the English consul in Lisbon was reporting to London that the Portuguese ambassador there had apparently lured over nine men and two women from Colchester 'to teach their people to card and spin in the English way', and that they had gone to Covilhã in spite of him trying to persuade them to return home. Looms were smuggled over, together with more English workers, and some months later the consul was reiterating that unless they were recalled the English exports of cloth to Portugal would soon be ruined. Colonel John Richards (who met his death at Alicante in 1709), when visiting Covilhã in 1704, observed that the industry was not flourishing because of the Inquisition's interference with the New Christian entrepreneurs and artisans. Nevertheless by the mid 19C some 150 looms were in operation, manufacturing brown woollen cloth.

It was a cavalry base during the Peninsular War, with Sir Stapleton Cotton in command, and many dances were got up to enliven the long cold winter evenings, the local women being passionately addicted to balls: indeed Commissary Schaumann refers to 'barbarously brilliant' balls, at the same time contending that 'As regards morals'...he had never come across 'such a Sodom and Gomorrah as that place was'.

It was the birthplace of Pêro de Covilhã, the late 15C explorer; who died at the court of Prester John in Ethiopia in 1526, and Hector Pinto (c 1528–c 1584), the mystic.

Its remaining monuments are of slight importance, among them the relics of a castle and, in the lower town (to the left of the road leading out to Castelo Branco, just before passing under a bridge), the Romanesque chapel of São Martinho.

The road descends to cross the Zêzere again and then a fertile region known as the Cova da Beira to **Fundão** (5900 inhabitants), pleasantly situated amidst orchards below the north slope of the Serra da Gardunha. It is likely that António Fernández Carvajal, a Marrano, spent his youth here before going to London in the early 1630s, where he was to become an influential (and at first covert) Jewish merchant, in 1659 being one of the first Jews to be buried in the Mile End cemetery. There are important wolfram ore deposits (from which tungsten is obtained) at **Panasqueira**, some distance due west, and the continuing export of that mineral to Germany by Salazar during the early years of the Second World War was a bone of contention between the Allies and Portugal.

An alternative to the main route is that turning south 6km south-west of Fundão, and passing through the ancient village of **São Vicente de Beira**, to which Dom Sancho I conceded a *foral* in 1195, still preserving a number of medieval houses.

Crossing the ridge of hills, which command some beautiful views, the main road bypasses (left) the village of **Alcaide**, with a 13C church, altered in the 16C. There are several chapels in its vicinity.

**Alpedrinha**, Roman Petrata or Petratinia, shortly entered, was the home town of the notorious 15C pluralist Jorge da Costa, Cardinal of Alpedrinha, Archbishop of Braga, Lisbon, and Évora. He also took under his capacious wing the bishopric of Coimbra, the priories of Crato, and Guimarães, the abbacies of São José de Tarouca, and even Alcobaça. The town retains a number of old houses, a ruined 18C palace, an 18C fountain, and a stretch of Roman road. The 16C Igreja Matriz largely replaced the Romanesque original; the Capela do Leão is early 16C.

After 3km a lane to the right leads to *****Castelo Novo**, an attractively sited village refounded in 1202, containing 17C houses, and castle ruins.

The N18 continues south, following the line of a Roman road, to approach Castelo Branco (see Rte 17), also bypassed by the IP2.

For the old N18, which 17km south-west of Castelo Branco, turns south off the IP2 to Portalegre via Vila Velha de Ródão, Nisa, and Alpalhão, see sub-route in Rte 14A, in reverse.

The longer but faster IP2 circles further to the west, crossing the rocky gorge of the Tagus near the Barragem de Fratel, to meet the N118 11km west of Nisa, for Abrantes, some 46km further west: see Rte 16.

The IP6, still under construction, will turn west off the IP2 from a junction immediately north of the Tagus to bypass Abrantes and meet the A1 motorway for Lisbon. When completed, this highway from Guarda to Abrantes for Lisbon via Castelo Branco will provide a rapid alternative approach to the capital from southwest France via Burgos and Salamanca, in preference to the longer route via Madrid and Badajoz.

# B.  Via Sabugal and Penamacor

*Total distance, 132km (83 miles). Immediately on crossing the frontier, turn south onto the N332.—48km Sabugal—N233. 34km Penamacor—50km Castelo Branco.*

*The recommended detour to take in Monsanto and Idanha-a-Velha will add 40km to the route.*

The N332 crosses part of the battlefield of **Fuentes de Oñoro**, where on 3 and 5 May 1811 a French force of 48,000 men under Masséna made two powerful attacks in an unsuccessful attempt to dislodge Wellington (with 34,500 men), losing some 2200 men compared with 1550 of the Allies, who nevertheless were temporarily forced to withdraw the right flank of their line from **Nave de Haver**, which is shortly skirted. The road continues south parallel to the frontier over an area frequently contested during that period of the war, before veering south-west through **Alfaiates**, with a ruined castle, to Sabugal.

**Sabugal**, an early frontier fortress on the Coa, with a medieval bridge and an early 14C castle, was the scene of a meeting in 1230/1 between Fernando III of León/Castile and his cousin Dom Sancho II. It was for some time under Spanish control, not being returned definitively to Portugal until 1393. Masséna withdrew through Sabugal when retreating from Guarda in 1811, and in a confused action here on 3 April, Reynier's rearguard was badly mauled (losing 760 men compared with the Allied loss of 180), and would have been annihilated but for the incompetence of Sir William Erskine's command. Relics of another castle (13C) may be seen at **Sortelha**, 11km due west.

The road descends into the Valle da Senhora da Póvoa, and veers south to (20km) **Penamacor**, on a commanding height, retaining some of its ramparts and gates, remains of a castle keep, and a Misericórdia; while Manueline windows are occasionally seen in the dwellings flanking its steep lanes. The 16C convent of Santo António, just off the Castelo Branco road, which retains a two-storeyed cloister, is of some interest. It was among the superstitious peasantry of Penamacor that the first of the false Sebastian pretenders briefly held court in 1584. It was also the birthplace of António Nunes Ribeiro Sanches (1699–1783), of Jewish origin, who became physician to Catherine II of Russia.

## Monsanto and Idanha-a-Velha

This detour may conveniently be made from here, the main road being regained 20km south-west. Follow the N332 due south to (16km) **Medelim**, repopulated in 1200, but probably once a Roman station. *\***Monsanto**, with a *pousada*, some 9km to the east, is a quaint village of granite dwellings built into a boulder-strewn castle-crowned height (views), below which is the relic of a Romanesque church. There is one early morning bus from Castelo Branco, returning mid-afternoon.

From the crossroads below the village, the N239 continues east to (10km) **Penha Garcia**, on another rocky outcrop, anciently fortified, to Termas de Monfortinho; see Rte 17.

On returning to Medelim, turn left to (7km) *\***Idanha-a-Velha**, the site of Roman Egitania, and the legendary birthplace of Wamba, elected king of the Goths in 672. (As the crow flies, it is only 45km north-west of the important Roman bridge over the Tagus at Alcántara, in Spain; see start of Rte 17.) It was also the seat of a bishopric from 569 until transferred to Guarda in 1199. Previously sacked by the Moors, Idanha was given to the Knights Templar in the 12C. The present village takes up only a part of the massive walled enceinte, with its rebuilt Roman doorway. A medieval watch-tower has been erected on the podium of a Roman temple. The key should be requested from a villager living near this tower, who will escort one through a partially excavated area to the restored Paleo-Christian *\*basilica or cathedral, its three naves containing a number of carved and inscribed stones from the site, which is undergoing further excavation. A ruined baptistry and bishop's palace may also be seen, while from just without the walls a ramp descends to a Roman bridge over the river Ponsul. For Idanha-a-Nova, 13km south-west, see Rte 17. On returning to Medelim, turn left through the characteristic village of

**Proença-a-Velha**, with a partly Romanesque Misericórdia, to regain the N233 further west.

This leads south-west through (17km) **Escalos de Cima**, which like **Escalos de Baixo** to the south, and **Alcains** to the west, was once a Roman settlement (substantiated by the discovery of hoards and artefacts in the area, although little remains above ground to suggest so), to approach Castelo Branco: see Rte 17.

# 23 · Guarda to Aveiro or Oporto via Viseu

*Total distance, 152km (94 miles). Those making directly for Oporto will turn onto the A1 motorway 12km before Aveiro, from which junction Oporto is 56km (34 miles) further north.*

*The IP5 is entered 5km north of Guarda—22km Celorico crossroads—32km Mangualde exit—14km Viseu—N337 and IP5. 29km Cambra junction—33km N1 crossroad (between Albergaria-a-Velha and the Pousada de Santo Antonio)—5km A1 junction—12km Aveiro.*

The recently completed IP5, winding across very attractive wooded country, is a great improvement on the much slower old road, which may still be followed. Regrettably, some Portuguese drive along the new highway at too great a speed.

For Guarda and the descent to Celorico, see Rte 21.

The road shortly crosses the Mondego, bypassing (right) **Fornos de Algodres** (to the north of which are two dolmens) and, veering away from the river, leads along a ridge commanding extensive vistas, to approach crossroads just north of **Mangualde** (5113 inhabitants), containing a number of old houses, including the late 17C Palácio dos Anadia, and an 18C Misericórdia.

Near **Penalva do Castelo** (12km north-east; known as Castendo until 1957) stands the Baroque Casa da Insua, owned by the Albuquerque family.

## Mangualde to Santa Comba Dão crossroads

42km, for Coimbra. The N234 leads south-west through **Nelas**, a pleasant little town, later running parallel to the Mondego and bypassing (left) **Oliveira do Conde**, with the well-carved tomb of Fernão Gomes de Góis (1440) in its church, and the Solar dos de Albergaria. The new IP3 highway to Coimbra, 51km further south-west, is met just south of Santa Comba Dão; see Rte 24, and also for Busaco.

Near the road between Mangualde and Viseu, at **Fornos de Maceira Dão**, is a former royal convent, largely rebuilt in the 17C and later altered, but of much earlier foundation.

### VISEU

Viseu (20,659 inhabitants), flourishing capital of its district, and an episcopal city of very ancient origin, is attractively sited among wooded hills on the left bank of the Pavia, a tributary of the Mondego. It is a agricultural centre, and has grown considerably in recent decades (8250 inhab. in 1920). Its main points of interest are the Cathedral and the Grão Vasco Museum. It has a reputation for its Dão wines, its egg and chestnut sweets, and for the black pottery of Molelos, among other handicrafts of the region.

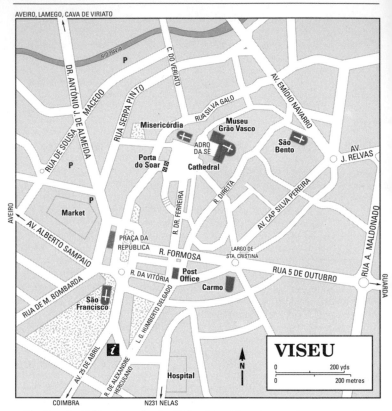

AVEIRO, LAMEGO, CAVA DE VIRIATO

RIO PAVIA

DR. ANTÓNIO J. DE ALMEIDA

RUA DE SOUSA ALMEIDA

MACEDO

RUA SERPA PINTO

C. DO VERIATO

RUA SILVA GALO

AV. EMIDIO NAVARRO

Misericórdia

Museu Grão Vasco

ADRO DA SÉ

São Bento

AV. J. RELVAS

Porta do Soar

Cathedral

R. DIREITA

AV. CAP SILVA PEREIRA

RUA A. MALDONADO

GUARDA

AVEIRO

AV. ALBERTO SAMPAIO

Market

PRAÇA DA REPÚBLICA

R. FORMOSA

LARGO DE STA. CRISTINA

RUA 5 DE OUTUBRO

R. DR. FERREIRA

RUA DE M. BOMBARDA

R. DA VITÓRIA

Post Office

Carmo

São Francisco

L. G. HUMBERTO DELGADO

i

AV. 25 DE ABRIL

R. DE ALEXANDRE HERCULANO

Hospital

**VISEU**

N

0    200 yds
0    200 metres

COIMBRA

N231 NELAS

- The **Tourist Office** is on the Av. Gulbenkian. There is no railway station but it can be reached by **bus** from Guarda, Oporto, or Coimbra. The bus station is on Avenida António José de Almeida.

### History

Although Viseu is traditionally connected with the last stand of Viriatus against the Romans (see below), there is no historical evidence for this, nor for the claim that Don Rodrigo, the 'Last of the Goths', was buried here in 711. In 1028 Alfonso V was killed when besieging the place, but it was not occupied until 1058, by Fernando I. Being on one of the main routes into central Portugal from Spain, it was taken by Enrique de Trastamara in 1372; and in 1810 by Masséna not long before the battle of Busaco.

Here were born Dom Duarte (1391–1438; the eldest son of Dom João I and Philippa of Lancaster); possibly Vasco Fernandes (c 1475–1541), the artist usually known as 'O Grão Vasco'; João de Barros (1496–1570), the chronicler of Portuguese conquests in Asia; the physician Gabriel da Fonseca (died 1668), and Baltasar Teles (1595–1675), the historian.

The older town lies huddled below a rock outcrop on which the cathedral stands, dominating the place. Although this may be approached by car (by the same route as described), it is perhaps preferable to park in the lower town somewhere near the central Praça da República or Rossio.

From here one may ascend the Rua Nunes de Carvalho, shortly passing (right; entrance round corner) the small **Casa Museu Almeida Moreira** (named after the first director of the Museu Grão Vasco), with good wooden ceilings, and his private collections of furniture, 18C 'Mandarin' porcelain, etc.

Beyond the Porta do Soar do Cima in the town walls, and (left) a chapel, the Adro da Sé is entered, its west side flanked by the remarkable and oft-illustrated *façade of the twin-towered **Misericórdia**, begun in 1775 to the designs of António da Costa Faro. The interior, except for its organ, is of slight interest. A painting of this church, made by Tristram Hillier in 1947, served as the frontispiece to Sacheverell Sitwell's *Portugal and Madeira*.

Opposite rises the **cathedral**, a late Gothic and Manueline edifice dating from 1513, probably replacing an earlier building on the site of a mosque. At a remoter period the church of São Miguel do Fetal, on the east side of the town, was perhaps more important, containing a tomb said to be that of Don Rodrigo (see History).

The west front, with its two towers (1641–71), which is undistinguished, was added by Juan Moreno, a Spaniard.

However cluttered the interior may once have been, it is still remarkable for its fine Manueline *vault, the ribs of which are carved to represent knotted cables. The paintings by Grão Vasco, which once embellished the main retable, are now in the adjacent museum; they were replaced by a retable of 1730 by Santos Pacheco. Good 18C *azulejos* decorate the north chapel; a portative organ is preserved, and the choir-stalls are well carved.

*The twin-towered façade of the Misericordia*

Stairs ascend off the north aisle to the upper choir, containing a large lectern of Brazil wood. From here the upper cloister (c 1730) is entered, retaining attractive late 17C *albarrada azulejos* in two walks, off which opens the chapterhouse, providing a view, and containing the treasury.

This includes a 13C Limoges enamelled coffer; a 12C Gospel, with a later silver cover; a 12C pectoral cross; a monstrance of 1533; a wooden box with a 12C painting in its lid; a 16C sculptured figure of Santa Isabel; a St Raphael and Tobias, by Machado de Castro; *azulejos* of 1721, and an octagonal wooden ceiling of the same date. In the adjoining room are anonymous paintings, a solid bronze pelican (16C Flemish), an 18C Bishop's sunshade (a rare survival), an altar frontal, etc.

Before leaving the cathedral, pass through the lower Renaissance cloister of c 1550, retaining a Romanesque portal, and with a carved Descent from the Cross of the Coimbra School. Note also the belvedere to the left on leaving.

To the right stands the granite four-square bishop's palace, now accommodating the *Museu Grão Vasco. This is open from 10.00–12.30 and 14.00–17.00; closed Mon. The paintings, recently restored, of *Vasco Fernandes* (c 1475–1541), who Viseu claims as her own, are now on the second floor, among them those which originally adorned the high altar of the cathedral, outstanding being the St Peter (in fact a copy of that at São João de Tarouca), also attributed to *Gaspar Vaz*. Adjacent are a Martyrdom of St Sebastian, and Pentecost (in which the knotted cables of the cathedral ribs are depicted), very similar to that in Santa Cruz, Coimbra. Below each painting is a series of half-lengths of apostles or saints, by an inferior hand. Other rooms contain a Death of the Virgin; Baptism of Jesus; and Crucifixion, with a predella of three small Passion scenes; and attributed to *Gaspar Vaz*, a Triptych of the Last Supper, and Christ at the house of Martha. Note also the remarkable series of 14 Scenes from the Life of Christ of the *School of Viseu* (c 1520), among them a curious Adoration of the Magi, in which the traditional negro has been replaced by a Brazilian Indian.

Collections of furniture are displayed on the first floor, together with later paintings, among them watercolours by *Alberto de Sousa*. On the ground floor are part of a retable from Oporto cathedral (1683); an anonymous Annunciation; a collection of sculptured Virgins; a damaged Nottingham alabaster; ceramics, including examples from Viana do Castelo; glass; and Arraiolos carpets.

There is a pleasant square behind the museum, and also another to the south of the cathedral square, from which, by descending behind the apse through narrow alleys and steps, one may reach the thronged Rua Direita traversing the old town. To the right at the north end of this street stands São Bento, containing 17C *azulejos* (apply next door), to the north-west of which is the Porta dos Cavaleiros.

From a central point in the Rua Direita, the Rua da Arvore leads south-east through a medieval arch to approach the Largo de Santa Cristina, with its fountain, and dominated by the **Igreja do Carmo** (1733–38), with 18C *azulejos* and Baroque carved and gilt woodwork. Behind it is the Seminary, with a 'suspended staircase' of which they are inordinately proud, but which is only of slight architectural interest.

The Rua Direita is regained by ascending the Rua Formosa. Just to the left in the former is the Casa de Cimo de Vila, with attractive *azulejos* of hunting scenes on its staircase. The Rua Formosa then passes (right) the colourful covered market before bringing one back to the Praça da República.

To the south, the square is dominated by the front and belfry of the **Igreja dos Terceiros**, or São Francisco (1773), approached by a flight of steps, and containing an octagonal chancel, *azulejos* illustrating the Life of St Francis, and an attractive organ.

> Off the N2 leading north-west, to the right just beyond the Rio Pavia and at a higher level, its edge defined by a line of trees, is the site of an octagonal fortified camp established here after the death of Viriatus in 139 BC—it was *not* his last stronghold, although still known as the **Cava de Viriato**. Its ditch could be flooded by adjacent streams.

For the roads from Viseu to Busaco, Coimbra, and Figueira da Foz, see Rte 24; and to Lamego, Rte 31, in reverse.

## Viseu to São João da Madeira for Oporto via São Pedro do Sul

90km. The N16 leads north-west through attractive country to (22km) **São Pedro do Sul**, at the confluence of the Sul and Vouga, where the cloister of the Baroque convent of São José abuts the Camara Municipal. From here the N227 climbs north-west along the steep north flank of the Vouga valley towards the Serra de Gralheira, after c 16km passing (left) **Santa Cruz da Trapa**, where the conventual church of São Cristóvão de Lafões survives among the ruins of a 12C Cistercian foundation, and relics of its aqueduct. The road later bears away to the north-west over wooded hills, passing near (right) **Roge**, with an attractive mid 18C church, to approach (40km) **Vale de Cambre**, a small industrial town, from which the detour to Arouca may be made; see sub-route in Rte 26, and also for São Jão da Madeira, 13km north-west. The N1 for Oporto is met just before entering that town.

## São Pedro do Sul to Albergaria-a-Velha

About 55km. The N16 bears south-west through (8km) **Termas de São Pedro**, whose hot sulphureous waters made it the site of Roman medicinal baths. The Vouga is crossed here to approach (8km) **Vouzela**, with a Baroque-façaded police station, 13C Igreja Matriz, and a Misericórdia, the interior of which has been variously described, by the 'Selective Travellers' as 'worth the visitor's while' to enter, and by Sitwell as 'creepily unpleasant...with horrid portraits of early 19C benefactors, fly- blown objects, and mange and ringworm in all around'. (A long but attractive detour may be made to the south-west through the high-lying village of **Vilharigues**, with slight remains of a castle, and impressive views over the wooded valley and of the Serra da Gralheira beyond.) An approach road now leads south-west to join the IP5 highway.

The N16 winds along the valley floor, later hugging the north bank of the Vouga gorge before turning north-west to meet the A1. Adjacent **Albergaria-a-Velha** was founded as a hospice in 1120. At the south end of the village is the mid 18C Casa de Santo António.

---

The IP5 may be regained 5km north or 9km west of Viseu. This continues to drive west, following a long ridge (wide views) and through impressive scenery until descending to cross the Vouga shortly before reaching the N1. The A1 motorway is met 5km beyond, approximately halfway between Oporto (56km north) and Coimbra. For the road between the two, see Rte 26.

For Aveiro, 12km west: see Rte 20.

# 24 · Viseu to Figueira da Foz via Busaco and Coimbra

*Total distance, 134km (83 miles). IP3. 41km Santa Comba Dão—N234. At 20km Busaco (Buçaso) is to the left.—2km Luso—7km Mealhada—N1. 19km Coimbra—N111. 27km Montemór-o-Velho—18km Figueira da Foz.*
*The IP3 between Santa Comba Dão and Coimbra is described in a sub-route.*

The IP3 leads south-west from Viseu (see Rte 23) parallel to but some distance west of the valley of the Dão, famous for its orchards and wines, to bypass **Tondela**, with a good Baroque portal to the Casa de Corso, and a convenient point from which to turn north-west into the Serra do Caramulo.

The N230 climbs north-west to (19km) **Caramulo**, passing en route the *Pousada de São Jerónimo*, a good centre for the exploration of the range, the summit of which, Caramulinho (1075m; extensive views) lies further to the south-west, now reached by road. The village surprisingly sports two *museums: one devoted to veteran cars; and the Fundacão Abel Lacerda, a miscellaneous collection of paintings, some attributed to Pourbus, Jordaens, and Rigaud, and containing minor works by Picasso, Dufy, Dalí, Léger, Sutherland, and Vieira da Silva; also five early 16C Brussels tapestries of the Portuguese in India.

The main road continues south-west to **Santa Comba Dão**, a small market town, where in the Largo Alves Mateus a plaque marks a house in which Catherine of Braganza stayed in 1692, and Dom Pedro II in 1704. António de Oliveira Salazar (1889–1970), the ci-devant dictator of Portugal from 1932 to 1968, was born and is buried in the neighbouring village of **Vimieiro**.

## Santa Comba Dão to Coimbra

53km. The IP3 winds south-west across the Barragem da Aguieira and then skirts and crosses the Mondego, at 28km bypassing Penacova (with an exit; see below), from there circling to the north-west along part of the Busaco ridge, before bearing west to meet the N1 7km north of Coimbra.

## Penacova to Coimbra via Lorvão

About 27km. It is worth entering **Penacova**, an ancient and picturesque little town, for the *views it commands before turning south-west onto the N110 skirting the north bank of the Mondego, off which a byroad shortly leads to **Lorvão**, a village which, with Penacova, is a centre of the tooth-pick (*palitos*) industry, much white wood whittling being done in the vicinity. It was once famous for the convent of Santa Maria, founded in the 12C and almost entirely rebuilt in the 18C; its dependencies are now a sanatorium. The huge church contains the repoussé silver tombs (1713, by Manuel Carneiro da Silva) of Teresa and Sancha, daughters of Dom Sancho I, who had been abbesses there in the 13C. The mid 18C carved stalls, the iron grill of the nuns' choir, and the portative organ, are noteworthy. The riverside road approaches Coimbra from the south-east.

From Santa Comba Dão, the N234 climbs west to bypass **Mortágua**, with a view of Wellington's 'damned long hill' of Busaco rearing up ahead, which may be approached by turning left off the main road not far beyond the hamlet of **Moura**, but perhaps more conveniently from adjacent **Luso**, an attractively situated spa, whose bottled mineral water, sold throughout Portugal, gushes freely from its fountains.

From Luso a byroad ascends to the Porta das Ameias (Battlement Gate), one entrance to the walled State Forest (the *Mata do Buçaco*), which covers the northern extremity of the **\*Serra do Buçaco**. It is remarkable for its magnificent trees, both native and exotic, and famous for the battle of 1810 (see below) in which the 'Valoroso e glorioso Duque de Wellington' inflicted serious losses on Masséna's army before retiring behind the defensive 'Lines of Torres Vedras'. In the centre of the park stands the Palace hotel (see below), which is shortly reached.

**BUÇACO** (also Bussaco; and Anglicised as Busaco), or at least the estate of that name, was presented by the Arcbishop of Braga to the Discalced (barefooted) Carmelites in 1626. They planted the area with a variety of trees, among them the rare Mexican cedar (*Cupressus lusitanica*), extinct in its original habitat. Some have grown to a height of 35m, and are best seen not far north-west of the hotel. The convent was completed in 1630. By 1643 Pope Urban VIII was issuing a bull excommunicating any person damaging the trees, while his predecessor, in 1622, had prohibited the entry of women into the precinct prior to the advent of the monks. In 1667 Castelo-Melhor, the disgraced minister of Dom Afonso VI, sought shelter here and hid in the forest, which his pursuers would have set alight was it not for the entreaties of the monks. He later escaped to England. While afforestation proceeded spasmodically during the next 160 years, the east slope of the ridge was still comparatively bare in 1810. At their dissolution, the conventual dependencies were handed over to a School of Forestry.

Between 1888 and 1907 a summer palace for the royal family was built adjacent, designed by one Luigi Manini, a scene painter for the São Carlos Opera-house in Lisbon. This pseudo-Manueline confection was later added to and, with the demise of the monarchy, in 1917 converted into an ostentatious establishment known as the Palace hotel, to which General Spínola retreated during a crucial stage in his presidency (August 1974).

On the north façade of the hotel—surrounded by gardens laid out amid the forest—its entrance porch encrusted with black and white pebbles, is the remnant of the convent, now totally engulfed, with its tiny church and few gloomy cork-lined cells, in one of which Wellington is said to have passed the night before his great defensive battle. There are a number of similarly decorated hermitages and 17C chapels dotted around in the surrounding forest, and flanking the numerous signposted footpaths radiating from the hotel.

Continuing through the forest, the Porta da Rainha (Queen's Gate), is shortly reached, not far beyond which is a small Military Museum devoted to the battle, containing British, French and Portuguese uniforms, arms, maps, prints, models, etc.

Just to the south is a commemoratory obelisk and \*viewpoint, commanding an even better view than the Cruz Alta (see below), and providing an extensive panorama over the area through which Masséna's army approached the ridge, with the Serras da Estrela and do Caramulo to the east and north respectively.

The **Battle of Busaco**. It should be emphasised that much of the mountain-side has since been afforested; it was still much more open earlier this century. Wellington, with some 49,000 men (including 24,500 Portuguese, largely untried recruits), and 60 guns, took up an almost impregnable position along the summit of the ridge (rising to c 550m), behind which they lay concealed, although deliberately showing a thin line of sentries. 'Every one expected and wished for a general attack at daylight. The army is in most beautiful order, and the Portuguese as fine-looking men and as steady under arms as any in the world', wrote William Tomkinson prior to the battle.

Wellington was faced by a force of 66,000 French, comprising three Corps, commanded by Junot, Ney, and Reynier, which had been deliberately deflected towards this point by the destruction of the road between Celorico and Abrantes. Masséna, as yet unbeaten, and undissuaded by the saner advice of his subordinates, on 27 September 1810 drove his columns in a frontal attack up the steep and broken slope in a thick morning mist. Not surprisingly, by using such tactics (cf. Vimeiro), they were repeatedly hurled down again in confusion, and with a total loss of at least 4600 men compared with the Allied loss of 1170.

Eventually the French, after working their way laboriously round beyond the northern edge of the ridge, turned on Coimbra, which they sacked. Wellington had meanwhile been able to retire undisturbed through the town, from there proceeding at leisure towards his prepared 'Lines' north of Lisbon: see Rte 18B.

## Busaco to Penacova

About 16km. From the obelisk one may follow a forest road leading south along the ridge top towards the Cruz Alta (c 530m), a good viewpoint, partly overlooking the coastal plain, with the Atlantic visible beyond a line of dunes. A left fork off this track leads to Wellington's vantage post during the earlier part of the battle, but now shrouded by pines. From here another forest road eventually descends towards the main Luso–Penacova road (N235), west of the ridge, on reaching which turn left below the IP3 to approach Penacova, for which, and for the roads beyond to Coimbra, see above.

From Luso, minor roads lead south-west through **Pampilhosa** and **Souselas** towards Coimbra, avoiding some traffic, while the N234 descends due west to **Mealhada**, where turn left onto the N1 (there is an entry to the A1 motorway further west), following a Roman road, to Coimbra: see Rte 25.

On approaching Coimbra, one may turn right towards the N111, which leads west parallel to bank of the Mondego to its mouth.

Just after passing under the motorway, the N234.1 turns north-west via **Ança**, whose quarries are the source of so much of the stone used by Portuguese sculptors in the past, particularly of the School of Coimbra.

The agricultural centre of **Cantanhede**, 10km beyond, was the scene of Dom Pedro I's solemn avowal of his marriage with Inês de Castro at Braganza in 1354. The Igreja Matriz contains a retable ascribed to Jean de Rouen. Another, attributed to the same sculptor, may be seen in a chapel at **Varziela**, 4km further north-west.

After c 4km a byroad climbs off the N111, passing through a hamlet to approach the church of *São Marcos, part of an Hieronymite convent (1452) burnt down in 1860; the present buildings, later Braganza property, are owned by Coimbra University. Behind a façade of 1510, it contains a wealth of sculptural monuments, among them the tomb of Fernão Teles de Meneses (1481), by Diogo Pires the elder, with its Gothic curtained canopy held aside by hairy men; two Manueline tombs of the Da Silva family, of 1522, and a Renaissance tomb by João de Ruão (1559); also the beautifully carved *retable by Chanterène (1522–23), unfortunately repainted about a century ago. Note also the domed chapel dos Reis Magos (1556) and the Renaissance pulpit.

On regaining the main road, continue west, bypassing **Tentúgal**, reputed for its cakes (*pasteis de Tentúgal*); the Igreja Matriz contains a carved Renaissance retable.

**Montemór-o-Velho** is now approached, commanded by its imposing *castle, the ascent to which is recommended. This fortress, rebuilt in 1088, once enclosed a royal palace. Its wall walks provide attractive views over the ricefields of the lower Mondego valley, and of the town below. The restored church of Santa Maria da Alcáçova, within the enceinte, contains twisted Manueline columns between its three aisles.

Montemor, of ancient origin, briefly recovered from the Moors by Alfonso V in 1017, was eventually reconquered in 1034. It was the birthplace of the poet and pastoral novelist of Jewish descent, Jorge de Montemayor (1519–61), author of *Los siete libros de la Diana* (Valencia, 1559?); the traveller and chronicler Fernão Mendes Pinto (1514–83); and the navigator, Diogo de Azambuja (c 1456–1518), whose tomb—ascribed to Diogo Pires the younger—lies in N.S. dos Anjos (1498, with a façade of 1692). Note also the domed chapel, similar to that at São Marcos; see above. The Misericórdia of 1555 contains a Mannerist high altar.

A dyke over the ricefields is crossed and the road ascend past the rebuilt Quinta da Foja, beyond which (left) an Iron Age site has been discovered near the chapel of Santa Olaia.

While a new approach road bears left, the N111 continues west past the 18C Paço de Maiorca before descending to Figueira da Foz: see Rte 20.

# 25 · Coimbra

Coimbra (89,639 inhabitants), an ancient capital, the main city of the Beira and, until the advent of the Republic, the seat of Portugal's only university, is an interesting and animated place. It contains many remarkable buildings, among them the magnificent University Library, while the Machado de Castro Museum is one of the finest in the country. Unfortunately much of the old university district, on a height overlooking the old town, was ruined during the Salazar regime by the demolition of old buildings and the erection of a number of vast architectural blocks which do little more than supply walls for the application of student graffiti.

At the foot of the hill of Alcáçova, on which the town was built, flows the Mondego, the entire course of which is in Portugal, unlike the Douro or Tagus, which have their sources in Spain. The Mondego is notable for the amount of sediment it carries, which has caused its bed to rise and, being subject to sudden floods, it has silted up several old buildings near its banks in the past, including, probably, the foundations of a Roman bridge.

■ The **Tourist Office** is in the Largo da Portagem. Coimbra is well placed for **trains**; there are three stations—A, B and Parque. The **bus station** is on Avenida Fernão de Magalhães.

### History

Coimbra has been identified with Roman Aeminium, but it took its present name from the formerly more important Conímbriga, near Condeixa-a-Velha, some 13km south-west (see last part of Rte 18A), when the country as far south as the Mondego was wrested from Moorish occupation in 872. Its arms, a crowned lady between a dragon and a lion, are supposed to symbolise the alliance of the Suevi and the Alani by a marriage between their royal houses. It reverted to the Moors from 987, when overrun and sacked by Almanzor, until 1064, when it was reconquered by Fernando I of Castile, aided by the Cid, during which period it was largely occupied by Mozárabs. In 1081, Paternus, its Mozárab bishop, gained control of the churches of Lamego and Viseu, much to the consternation of Braga. It was again briefly surrounded by the Almoravids in 1116.

Idrisi, a Muslim geographer writing in the mid 12C, records that it was then 'a small city, flourishing and well populated, rich in vineyards and orchards of apples, cherries, and plums. Its fields are very fertile...and the inhabitants, who are the bravest of the Christians, possess many cattle great and small: the Mondego moves many mills and bathes many vineyards and gardens'.

From 1139, when Afonso Henriques was proclaimed king of Portugal, until 1385, Coimbra was the capital, having supplanted Guimarães. As such it was the birthplace of six kings: Dom Afonso II (1185), Dom Sancho II (1209), Dom Afonso III (1210), and, although the latter had transferred the main royal residence to Lisbon c 1250, of Dom Afonso IV (1290), Dom Pedro I (1320) and Dom Fernando I (1345). Dom Duarte and Leonor of Aragón were married here in 1428.

But the town, dominated by its bishops, meanwhile stagnated, for the University founded in Lisbon in 1290 was only definitively established at Coimbra in 1537. At the same time, during the second quarter of the 16C, an important and influential school of sculptors had settled here, among them the French artists Nicolas Chanterène, Jean de Rouen, Jacques Buxe, and Philippe Houdart, apart from João and Diogo de Castilho.

After 1567 it was one of the three seats (with Lisbon and Évora) of the Inquisition in Portugal, who were particularly active here in the 1620s. The Jesuits (suppressed in 1759) controlled the place until 1772, when Pombal undermined their influence by reforming the University. In 1808 its students formed the 'Academic Volunteers', and taking over from the occupying French the small port of Figueira da Foz, near the mouth of the Mondego, enabled the British expeditionary force to land there prior to the battle of Roliça. Wellington and Beresford passed through the place in May 1809 en route to Oporto. It was brutally sacked by Masséna after the battle of Busaco (September 1810; see Rte 24), but the following March, when retreating from before the 'Lines of Torres Vedras' (see p 202), finding the bridge at Coimbra had been recaptured and held by Nicholas Trant and his Portuguese militia, the French veered north-east, when still south of the Mondego, crossing the tributory Ceira at Foz de Arouce (cf.).

Southey observed that, although on approaching it Coimbra had the appearance of a gloriously seated city, the delusion ceased on entry, when 'It was noise and narrow streets, and stink'. Until very recently, little had changed.

It was the birthplace of Francisco Sá da Miranda (1481/95–1558), the poet, and the eldest of five sons of a canon of Coimbra; the sculptor Joaquim Machado de Castro (1732–1822); Carlos de Seixas (1704–42), the composer; and Joaquim António de Aguiar (1792–1874), the radical statesman, whose nickname, 'Mata Frades' (kill-friars) exaggerates his measures for the suppression of the religious orders in 1833.

The main hub of traffic (which can make parking a problem) is just west of the triangular Largo da Portagem, which is opposite the north end of the Ponte Santa Clara, with the tourist office on its east side.

# A.  The Lower Town

The Rua de Ferreira, the narrow main shopping street, now a pedestrian precinct (along which trams ran until recently), is continued by the Rua do Visconde da Luz. Steps ascend on the right of the former to enter the upper town: see Rte 25B.

Further along, on the left, is the truncated apse of São Tiago, preserving little of its late 12C foundation but the south door and the west portal overlooking the Praça do Comércio, flanked by tall houses, to the west and north of which, among a maze of narrow alleys, some of the cheaper little restaurants and bars of Coimbra may be found, which formerly advertised their presence by a laurel branch above their entrances.

The street widens and ends at the Praça 8 de Maio, on the right of which, at a lower level, stands the church of *SANTA CRUZ, historically the most interesting building in Coimbra.

A priory of Austin canons was founded here in 1131 on a site known as the Banhos Reais, by Telo, archdeacon of the cathedral, and João Peculiar (later Bishop of Oporto and Archbishop of Braga), while St Teotónio, the confessor of Afonso Henriques, was appointed prior. In 1502, the dependencies no longer being adequate, Dom Manuel ordered its reconstruction, Marcos Pires (died 1524) being the architect, assisted by Diogo de Castilho, Jean de Rouen (João de Ruão) and Nicolas Chanterène, among others. In 1539 Dom João III made the priors perpetual chancellors of the University, a rank they retained until the Dissolution of 1834. Amongst its canons was Heliodoro de Paiva (1502–52), a composer of numerous masses and motets, etc. The building served briefly as a British HQ during the Peninsular War.

The west front, or Portal da Majestade, under restoration, is a somewhat clumsy work by Diogo de Castilho (1524), with sculptures by Chanterène and Jean de Rouen, the general effect being spoilt by the addition of an incongruous 18C doorway. Note also the vaulting in the abutting café.

The **interior**, lined with 18C *azulejos*, contains (left) a corbelled pulpit, now attributed to Chanterène (1522), with high reliefs of Saints Ambrose, Jerome, Gregory, and Augustine. In the chancel are the ornately carved Royal Tombs of (left) Afonso Henriques (died 1135), and (right) his son, Dom Sancho I (died 1211), reinterred here in 1520. Various attributions have been made as to their sculptors, but it is now thought that although Diogo de Castilho was responsible for the general design, Chanterène carved the recumbent figures.

The sacristan should be sought out for admission to the **sacristy**, south of the chancel, a Renaissance room of 1622 containing an Ecce Homo, and a Crucifixion, both by Cristóvão de Figueiredo; a St Vincent by García Fernandes; and a Pentecost by Grão Vasco.

To the north of the chancel is the entrance to the **cloister** of two storeys (by Marcos Pires: from 1517), weak in design (with 'mandorla-shaped' ribs), on three sides of which are worn altarpieces by Jean de Rouen. In its south-east corner is the Manueline Capela de São Teotónio, with that saint's tomb (by Tomé Velho; 1582), and those of other priors. Stairs ascend to the upper choir, with Manueline stalls of c 1518, surmounted by a carved and gilt frieze of ships, castles, etc.; and housing a red and gilt 18C organ.

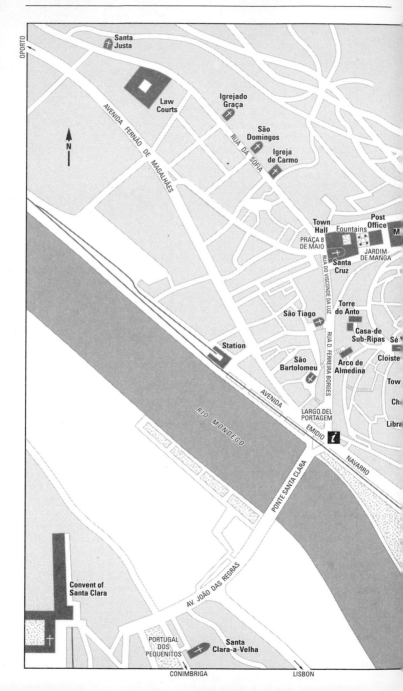

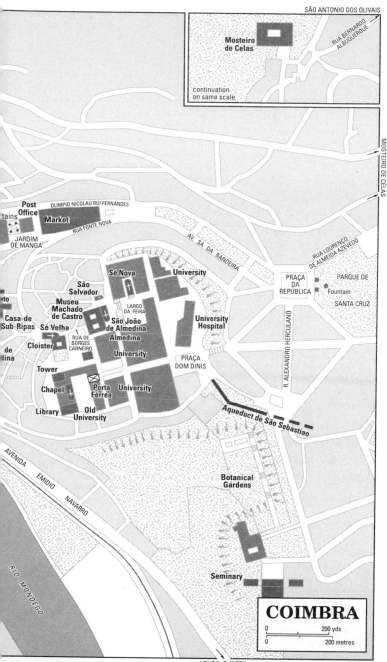

SÃO ANTONIO DOS OLIVAIS

RUA BERNARDO ALBUQUERQUE

**Mosteiro de Celas**

continuation on same scale

MOSTEIRO DE CELAS

Post Office

OLIMPIO NICOLAU RUI FERNANDES

tains

**Market**

RUA FONTE NOVA

JARDIM DE MANGA

AV. SÁ DA BANDEIRA

RUA LOURENÇO DE ALMEIDA AZEVEDO

PRAÇA DA REPÚBLICA

Fountain

PARQUE DE

SANTA CRUZ

**Sé Nova**

**University**

São Salvador

Museu Machado de Castro

LARGO DA FEIRA

e to

**Casa-de Sub-Ripas**

Sé Velha

São João de Almedina

Almedina

**University Hospital**

de lina

Cloister

RUA DE BORGES CARNEIRO

**University**

PRAÇA DOM DINIS

R. ALEXANDRO HERCULANO

Tower

Chapel

Porta Férrea

**University**

**Library**

Old University

Aqueduct de São Sebastiao

AVENIDA EMIDIO NAVARRO

**Botanical Gardens**

RIO MONDEGO

**Seminary**

# COIMBRA

0  200 yds

0  200 metres

LOUSA, GUARDA

From the adjacent Câmara Municipal, the Rua da Sofia leads north-west past a number of *convent-colleges* of comparatively little interest, some of which are at present in military occupation. Among them (right) is the Igreja do Carmo (1597), with an earlier cloister containing *azulejos*; the Igreja da Graça (1555); and beyond (left) the cloister of São Tomás (1540), now part of the Law Courts; and the unfinished and ruinous church of São Domingos, once serving as a garage. Santa Justa (1710; right) is further north.

Immediately behind Santa Cruz is the **\*Jardim da Manga**, formerly another cloister of the priory, in the centre of which is a curious domed fountain surrounded by four subsidiary chapels joined to it by buttresses (completed 1535).

The main road ascending to the east from Santa Cruz, after passing a market, is continued by the Av. Sá da Bandeira to the Praça da República, a hub of the upper town behind the university quarter: see last part of Rte 25B.

# B. The Upper Town

From the Arco de Almedina (*medina*, a city, in Arabic)—the main pedestrian entrance to the upper town, a gateway above which was the town hall until 1878—the steep ascent begins into the old university city of narrow alleys. Then bear left to ascend more steps.

From here a lane (left) leads shortly past the **Casa de Sub-Ripas** of 1547, with a Manueline doorway, now housing the Intitute of Archaeology.

This mansion was traditionally believed to be the scene of the murder of Maria Teles, who had excited the envy of her sister, Queen Leonor. She had also secretly married João (the eldest son of Inês de Castro), who was persuaded by the queen that Maria was being unfaithful, and that, if he had been patient, he might have married her own daughter. Without further enquiry, João rode to Coimbra and stabbed the unfortunate lady. He was then conveniently hounded from Portugal, much to the queen's satisfaction—she had no intention of offering her daughter's hand to him.

Beyond an arch studded with medallions is the Torre de Anto, part of the city wall. It contains a display of regional handicraft and local manufactures, among which was that of *palitos* or tooth-picks (cf. Lorvão), which had been remarked on as a flourishing industry over 200 years ago by Major Dalrymple: it has been suggested that it was the main occupation of the students.

Almost adjacent is the **Colégio Novo** (or of Santo Agostinho; from c 1590), with a cloister of 1598 designed by Filippo Terzi and inspired by that at Tomar, which survived a later fire; it preserves some 17C *azulejos*. The whole fabric has been restored to accommodate the faculty of Psychology; since 1842 it had housed the Misericórdia.

Return to the main ascending street to approach the **\*OLD CATHEDRAL**, or **Sé Velha**, one of the finest Romanesque churches in Portugal (c 1162), in which Dom Sancho I was crowned in 1185, as was Dom João I in 1385 after eloquently demonstrating his claim before the Cortes. The Sé Nova (see below) replaced it as the Episcopal cathedral in 1772.

The fortress-like **exterior** has three doorways of very different character. The west portal consists of a projecting bastion pierced by a deep round-arched doorway beneath a window almost equal in size. The Corinthian north portal is a Renaissance addition of the French School of Santa Cruz (see above), with a fine but worn Virgin in its tympanum. The door of the north transept was altered at the same time. The domed belfry dates from 1837. Above the apse is a Romanesque gallery.

The **nave** has massive square piers with semicircular pilasters, now stripped of the *azulejos* of 1508 once covering them. The bold triforium and central lantern should be noted. In the north aisle are the tombs of Bishop Tibúrcio (died 1246), and of Dona Vetaça, daughter of the Count of Ventimiglia and a Greek princess, who was governess to Santa Isabel.

The **Capela-Mór** has an elaborate late Gothic retable (1508) of the Assumption, by Olivier de Gand (Ghent) and Jean d'Ypres, presented by Bishop Jorge de Almeida (1483–1543), whose tomb lies in the chapel of São Pedro, in the north transept, beneath a retable depicting the history of St Peter, in the French style. On the left is the tomb of Bishop Egas de Faíes (1286). In the south transept is a semicircular retable containing figures of Christ and the Apostles, by Tomé Velho, presented by Bishop João Soares (1566), with a compartmented cupola above.

Beyond is the entrance to the **sacristy** (1593), erected by Bishop Afonso de Castelo Branco (died 1633), whose tomb, with that of Sisinando (died 1091; first Christian governor of the city, who is said to have been a converted Moor) lies in the chapterhouse. Steps ascend from the south aisle to the **cloister** (begun 1218) of the French Cistercian type, with canopied corners, which was at one time occupied by the university press. Here stands a mid 16C font.

Skirting the north side of the cathedral, the ascent is continued by the Rua de Borges Carneiro, overlooked by the two-storeyed loggia (built c 1592 under the aegis of Bishop Afonso de Castelo Branco) of the former Bishop's Palace, now housing the **\*MUSEU MACHADO DE CASTRO**, one of the more important in Portugal. It is open 10.00–13.00 and 14.30–17.00; closed Mon. Note the Moorish tower by the main entrance, facing the Largo de Feira, to the east.

Several departments of the museum are likely to be closed until the restoration of the entire building has been completed. Several floors have been excavated by archaeologists meanwhile.

Remarkable in the collection of medieval **sculpture** are: a Visigothic angel; Santa Comba; Santa Agada; a Mounted Knight wielding a mace; Santas Mães (15C); the Sepulchre guarded by three knights in chain mail; a Deposition attributed to Jean de Rouen; a retable from N.S. de Conceição; a Calvary and other works by Olivier de Gand; an early 16C Flemish carved and painted Nativity; and part of a terracotta group representing the Last Supper, by Philippe Houdart (c 1530).

Among the more important **paintings** are an *anonymous Flemish* Crucifixion of c 1525; *Monagramist MN*, Assumption (early 16C); examples of the art of the *Master of Sardoal*, including an Assumption of Mary Magdalen, a rare subject; *Master of Celas* (early 16C), Descent from the Cross, and Nativity; *Quintin Metsys*, Virgin (part of a triptych), Flagellation, and Ecce Homo; the Retable of Santa Clara, with a row of apostles below (15C); an anonymous Christ in the Garden; the Crucifixion of Santa Cruz; an emaciated black Christ (13–14C); an anonymous Santa Agatha (early 16C); *Garcia Fernandes*, Triptych of Christ appearing to the Virgin, Saints Cosmas and Damian; *Nogueira*, Repose on the Flight into Egypt (1590; note costumes); *Master of Santa Clara*, Christ appearing to the Virgin, and Deposition; *Morales*, Virgin and Child; *Cristóvão de Figueiredo*, Finding of the True Cross by St Helen, and The Exaltation of the Cross (showing German influence); also a Magdalen by *Josefa de Óbidos*, and a Vision of St Bernard.

Among other collections are those of dalmatics, pluvials, and other vestments and fabrics, and examples of Castelo Branco embroidery; furniture; and ceramics, including 18C Rocha Soares ware, and examples from Aveiro, Juncal, Brioso and Vandelli (both from Coimbra), from the Rato factory (Lisbon), and blue and white porcelain from Lisbon showing Oriental influence. Little of the important collection of gold and silverwork is at present on view.

One of the more interesting and surprising features of the museum is the Roman *cryptoporticus, a grid of subterranean passages forming the foundations to the palace. This displays a collection of Roman sculptures and stelae, and Visigothic artefacts found on the site; also some neolithic and Bronze Age implements and weapons, etc. Below this is another basement (no admission).

Admission should be requested to view the two attractive retables in the adjacent São João de Almedina, reached by a flight of steps to the right of the entrance hall, in which stands a bishop's coach. The church itself, although founded in the 12C, probably on the site of a mosque, was rebuilt between 1684 and 1704, but part of the Romanesque cloister is preserved.

In a side street to the left stands the small Romanesque church of São Salvador.

The north side of the Largo da Feira is dominated by the unwieldy Renaissance front of the Sé Nova (new cathedral), probably designed by Baltasar Alvares, and built from 1598–1698 by the Jesuits (suppressed in 1759) as a church for the Colégio das Onze Mil Virgens, but used as a cathedral since 1772. Note the ornate white marble font made for Bishop Jorge de Almeida, the coffered barrel vaulting and dome, the *reliquarios* in both transepts, a series of paintings of the Life of the Virgin (mostly copies of Italian originals) behind the choir stalls, and the repainted Baroque organs facing each other in the chancel.

To the north-east are the Natural History Museum (with a carved relief by Machado de Castro), and the Chemistry Laboratory, both designed by the English architect William Elsden and built during 1772–77. Elsden had taught mathematics at the Portuguese Royal Military Academy, and in 1771 was appointed Quartermaster-General in the Portuguese service. He also designed a chapel at Alcobaça. The Physics Laboratory here preserves an important collection of scientific instruments (580 were listed in the inventory of 1788), many of them sent out from London by João Jacinto de Magalhães (1722–90), a Fellow of the Royal Society in 1774, who had lived in London from 1764.

To the right, the former Real Colégio das Artes and the Colégio de São Jerónimo, both with degraded cloisters, accommodate other faculties.

Further south is the Praça Dom Dinis, the site of the castle, demolished in 1772, from which a flight of steps descends to the east. At the bottom, streets lead north-east to the Praça da República, and south-east to the Arcos do Jardim, flanked by the Aqueduct 'de São Sebastião'. See below for the Botanical Gardens and other monuments in this north-east part of the city.

Of the other modern university buildings, erected under the aegis of Dr Salazar, a former student, the less said the better. Writing in 1954, Sacheverell Sitwell succinctly condemned them as being 'shaming in their blatant ugliness', and their sculptures 'of an insulting hideousness'. (But of the previous view, Captain Bragge remarked in 1812, 'The Town and Students are equally dirty and the numerous Convents and Colleges built with no more Architectural Taste than our Manufactories at Chard...'.)

All that remains of interest, since the rebuilding under Salazar, is the main quadrangle of the *Old University, approached by a turning due west from the Praça Dom Dinis and entered through the Porta Férrea (Iron Gate) of 1634, in a wing formerly the Colégio de São Pedro. Before entering, first visit (a few steps to the right) the Casa dos Melos (16C), now the Pharmacy Faculty building.

The University, founded in 1290 by Dom Dinis in Lisbon, was transferred to Coimbra in 1308 and installed in a building adjoining the royal palace, or Paço de Alcáçcova. In 1338–54 and in 1377–1537 it was again in Lisbon, but Dom João III then established it definitively at Coimbra (inviting the humanist André de Gouveia, then at Bordeaux, to collect together a competent body of scholars for the purpose) and housed it in the royal palace on the present site. George Buchanan, the Scottish humanist and scholar, came to teach here in 1547; he was arrested and imprisoned by the Inquisition at Lisbon (1547–53). The University fell into the hands of mercenary priests in the 17C and doctorates were obtained for a 'fee' by students who never attended a lecture. In 1772 Pombal sensibly expelled the Jesuits who then controlled it, and established the system whose lines are largely followed to this day.

The head of the university, the rector (*reitor*), is assisted by the *Concelho dos Decanos* (deans of the faculties, and others), professors (*lentes cathedráticos*) and lecturers. Its students sport the following colours: violet (Pharmacy), yellow (Medicine), red (Law), light blue (Science), and dark blue (Philosophy).

The ***Praça das Escolas** is entered first, on the right of which is the Paço das Escolas, preceded by a covered gallery known as the 'Via Latina', which contains the rector's residence, the principal lecture rooms, and the **Sala dos Capelos**, which is approached through the imposing central portico of 1701, embellished with sculpture by Claude de Laprade. This room, in which degrees are conferred, has a notable panelled wooden roof of 1655. One is also shown the Sala do Exame Privado, hung with worthy portraits of rectors since 1537, and a guardroom with 17C *azulejos*. An exterior walk provides plunging views over the city.

At the north-west corner of the patio rises the Baroque clock-tower of 1733, known to the students as the *Cabra* (or goat) tower. In the west wing is the Manueline doorway (after 1517, probably by Marcos Pires) to the **University Chapel**, containing an impressive red and gilt Baroque organ of 1733, 17C *azulejos*, and a painted ceiling.

Adjacent is the imposing double-pillared entrance to the ***library**, or Casa da Livraria, a very fine example of the 'João Quinto' style (1716–28). Its designer is not known with certainty, but it may have been Claude de Laprade. For admission press the bell to the left of door. The interior is divided into three main sections opening off each other, each containing an upper gallery with tapering *gaine* supports. The bookshelves were designed and constructed by Gaspar Ferreira. The whole is richly gilt, which, with the 'chinoiserie' japanning, is the work of Manuel da Silva, and the rooms are decorated in light green, a darker green, and an orange. Notice also the ceilings painted in perspective by Vicente Nunes and António Simoes Ribeiro, and the rosewood and ebony tables. Its principal treasures are not at present on display.

At the far end (between carved wood curtains parted by putti) is the richly framed portrait of Dom João V (attributed to Giorgio Domenico Duprà)—who, although also responsible for the library at Mafra, was no great bibliophile—built the library here merely in rivalry with his brother-in-law, Karl VI, in Vienna, where J.B. Fischer von Erlach was building a sumptuous Hofbibliothek (completed 1737) abutting the Imperial Palace or Hofburg.

A view over the Mondego valley and of the hill-top convent of Santa Clara (see Rte 25C) is commanded by the adjacent terrace.

From the university, one may return to the lower town (if not visiting the district to the north-east, described below) by descending steps to the right, and then turning right, making one's way through a maze of narrow lanes, and keeping to the right, to regain the old cathedral.

### The Botanical Gardens: the Convent of Celas: Santo António dos Olivais

An addition to this route is the area to the east and north-east of the university, which may be more conveniently visited by car by the less energetic.

Immediately south-east of the Praça Dom Dinis are the first of the 21 arches of the Aqueduct 'de São Sebastião', begun by Filippo Terzi in 1568 on the site of a Roman aqueduct, which then crosses the Arcos do Jardim and an entrance to the **Botanical Gardens**. These were laid out by Pombal in 1774 on a site chosen by William Elsden (see above), and are the largest (20 hectares) in Portugal; the terraced gardens enriched with plants selected by Félix Avelar Brotero, the botanist, were only completed under Julio Henriques, director from 1873 to 1918.

On the far side of the gardens stands the seminary, the original part, designed by Francesco Tamossi, dating from 1748–65, to which additions were made in the late 19C. The octagonal domed church contains a fine organ of 1763 by Juan Fontana.

From the Arcos do Jardim one may descend the Rua Alexandre Herculano to the Praça da República, the main square of the district. On its east side is the Parque de Santa Cruz (or Sereia gardens), with an unusual fountain embellished by 18C *azulejo* panels.

The Rua Lourenço de Almeida Azevedo leads uphill, skirting the north side of the gardens, to approach in a side street to the left beyond the Largo de Celas, the **Mosteiro de Celas**. It retains the circular Manueline church and part of the 14C cloister of the ruined abbey founded in the early 13C by Sancha, daughter of Dom Sancho I (cf. Lorvão), but it is now of slight interest except for the capitals in the cloister. If shut, the key should be requested at the house opposite.

Regaining the main street, continue uphill along the Rua Bernardo Albuquerque to reach hill-top **Santo António dos Olivais**, approached by a short flight of steps flanked by chapels. The church, rebuilt in the 15C, is all that remains of the friary founded here in the 13C. Its terrace provides views over the surrounding country-side.

## C.  The convents of Santa Clara

Crossing the Mondego by the Ponte de Santa Clara, the third bridge on this site, and leaving the Lisbon road to our left, turn down the next lane to the left to the restored remains of **Santa Clara-a-Velha**, with its fine rose-window. Its floor had long been covered with silt by the Mondego in flood, and the church is all that has survived of the convent founded in 1286 by Dona Mór Dias, and refounded by St Isabel in 1330, six years before her death. Both she and Inês de Castro were buried here before removal to their present tombs in the new convent (see below) and Alcobaça, respectively. Juana La Beltraneja (1462–1530; daughter of Enrique IV of Castile and Joana of Portugal) professed here in 1480.

The murder of Dona Inês, the subject of numerous romances, is said to have taken place by a water-tank in the garden of the private property of the *Quinta das Lágrimas* (18C), some distance along the next left-hand turning.

**Inês Pires de Castro**, the daughter of a Galician nobleman, was brought up with her cousin Dona Constanza, daughter of the Duque de Peñafiel, and went to join her in Portugal after Constanza's marriage in 1340 to the Infante Dom Pedro, son of Dom Afonso IV. Dom Pedro, however, conceived an uncontrollable passion for Inês on first setting eyes on this 'heron-necked' beauty. She was later exiled, but on Constanza's death in 1345 returned to Portugal and set up house with Pedro at Coimbra.

During the next decade she bore him several children, and in 1354, to legitimise them, he married—or claimed to have married—Inês at Braganza. Meanwhile a court faction, jealous of the Spanish influence they considered she had on the heir to the throne (for her brothers had political pretensions), eventually extracted from Dom Afonso his tacit permission for her 'removal', but the king, then residing at neighbouring Montemór-o-Velho, riding over to the Quinta das Lágrimas to visit Inês, weakened at the sight of his grandchildren. The three nobles most concerned—Pedro Coelho, Diogo Pacheco and Alvaro Gonçalves—were not to be thwarted, and murdered her in cold blood on 7 January 1355.

Dom Pedro raised the standard of revolt, but, influenced by the Archbishop of Braga, was later ostensibly reconciled with his father. However, on his accession two years after, he had Coelho and Gonçalves executed at Santarém; Pacheco eluded him. At Cantanhede, Dom Pedro swore before the Cortes that his marriage with Inês was a reality, and had her body exhumed from her grave. According to Camoens, it was then enthroned beside him to receive the homage of his nobles before being placed in the royal tomb he had ordered to be constructed for her at Alcobaça (cf.).

The approach to the *new* convent of Santa Clara passes (left) a children's garden, beyond which a winding road climbs up to the early 18C chapel of N.S. da Esperança on the Monte da Esperança, passing (right) the former monastery of São Francisco (1602), long transformed into a factory, before reaching a esplanade providing a good view of Coimbra.

Here stands the barrack-like building—indeed much of it is now barracks, with a small military museum—of the **\*Convent of Santa Clara-a-Nova**, erected in 1649–77 by João Turriano, professor of mathematics at the university. The church contains, in the *Capela-Mór*, six charming paintings showing the translation of St Isabel's remains in 1696 to her new tomb, the adjacent silver shrine, and a display of her surviving garments. Incidents in her life are depicted in a series of carved and polychromed wooden panels in the aisles. The panelled apse is the work of Miguel Francisco da Silva (1730).

Near the choir are two Gothic tombs, containing the remains of Dona Isabel, daughter of Dom Afonso V; and Dona Maria, daughter of Dom Pedro I. In the lower choir is the original tomb of St Isabel (1271–1336), previously in Santa Clara-a-Velha, and surmounted by her effigy; also a red and gold portative organ of 1745; another is in the upper choir.

The large cloister, possibly designed by Carlos Mardel in 1738, and perhaps inspired by that at Tomar, was given to the Poor Clares by Dom João V, who (cf. Odivelas) had a penchant for nuns.

# 26 . Coimbra to Oporto

*Total distance, 116km (72 miles). N1. 19km Mealhada—23km Agueda—15km Albergaria-a-Velha—19km Oliveira de Azeméis—40km Oporto.*

*Although the N1 road is the one described here, it is occasionally congested, and passes through areas of ribbon development apart from more attractive stretches. The alternative is the A1 motorway, entered some 10km north-west of Coimbra, running through wooded country parallel to the N1, but 3–9km further west. The motorway provides a rapid route north, with exits for Aveiro, Vila da Feira, etc., and central Oporto.*

The N1 leads due north past **Mealhada**, centre of the Bairrada wine region—just beyond which the N234 climbs right to Luso and the long ridge of Busaco (see Rte 24)—and bypasses (left) the spa of **Curia**, and right, **Anadia**, with the 18C Paço da Graciosa.

From **Agueda** the N230 ascends the valley of the Agueda, climbing to (35km) Caramulo: see first part of Rte 24.

**Trofa**, its church containing tombs of the Coimbra Renaissance School (c 1535), is bypassed (left), and shortly after crossing the Vouga, the Pousada Santo António at **Serém** is skirted to approach an entrance to the IP5 highway between Viseu and Aveiro, just beyond which is Albergaria-a-Velha; see latter part of Rte 23.

**Oliveira de Azeméis** (9210 inhabitants), later bypassed, is an unprepossessing town of ancient origin (referred to in a document of 922), which in 1832 was a headquarters of Dom Miguel. It has an 18C church.

## Oliveira de Azemeis to Entre-os-Bios via Arouca

66km. Much of this sub-route is slow and winding, although passing through attractive country. The N224, the first 12km of which has a jolting *pavé* surface, winds round to **Vale de Cambra** and bears north-east to (20km) **Arouca**, a remotely sited town among wooded hills. The original Cistercian convent of Santa Maria, destroyed by the Moors, was refounded in the early 10C. After a fire it was entirely rebuilt on a much larger scale in 1704–18 by a Maltese, Carlos Gimac. It is interesting for its association with Dona Mafalda (?1194–1256), a daughter of Dom Sancho I. She retired here after her marriage (in 1215, when she was 21) to the 12-year-old Enrique I of Castile was annulled. He died accidentally in 1217. Her remains lie in a silver casket placed in the church in 1734 (not to be outdone by her sisters at Lorvão; cf.).

Notable are the 108 stalls in the lower choir, carved in 1722–25 by António Gomes and Filipe da Silva of Oporto; and the *organ of 1739. The stone figures of female saints, etc., carved by Jacinto Vieira of Braga, have not been improved by being daubed with coats of whitewash. The local museum contains 15–16C Portuguese paintings.

Returning to the main road, turn right to climb and wind across the hills to (22km) **Castelo de Paiva**, from there making the steep descent into the Douro valley. The river is crossed just west of Entre-os-Rios, and near the Roman *castro* of Eja; see pp 265 and 266.

The N1 bypasses (left) **Vila de Cucujães**, with a 17–18C monastery replacing an 11C foundation. Then **São João de Madeira** (18,452 inhabitants), a town of remote origin, from which a byroad leads north-west to neighbouring **Vila da Feira**, with a noble *castle, founded in the 11C but later much rebuilt.

Picturesquely sited on a leafy hill, with its four cone-capped towers, it contains an imposingly vaulted hall, formerly galleried. The 16C church of the monastery of Espírito Santo, its cloisters put to secular use, is of slighter interest.

The territory between here and Oporto was long known as the 'Terras de Santa Maria', and was the first to be wrested from the Moors by Afonso Henriques.

A turning to the left beyond Picoto leads shortly to the Augustinian monastery of São Salvador at **Grijó**, commenced in 1574 from the designs of Francisco Velasques. The two-storeyed cloister was completed in 1593; the hospice in 1605; but the *Capela-Mór* was not finished until 1629, with a *camarin* added later in the century. It was briefly Wellington's headquarters prior to his 'passage of the Douro' in May 1809 (see Rte 33, History).

The N1, continuing north, provides views to the east on approaching Oporto, and crosses the A1 before forking right to Vila Nova de Gaia, on the south bank of the Douro. The motorway bears north-west to cross the river by the Ponte da Arrábida (1963) before circling through the northern suburbs.

Those wishing to bypass Oporto are warned that the complex of roads attempting to ease communications is not yet completed, and bottle-necks may still be met.

For roads leading north to Viana do Castelo, and Braga, see Rtes 34A and B; for those to Guimarães, and Amarante, Rtes 37 and 29 respectively, all in reverse.

For Oporto, see Rte 33.

# 27 · Vilar Formoso to Vila Real

## A.  Via Celorico, Trancoso, and Lamego

*Total distance, 190km (118 miles). IP5. 39km. Guarda is 5km south-west.—20km Celorico da Beira—N102 and N226. 20km Trancoso—41km Moimento da Beira— 20km São João de Tarouca is 3.5km south.—12km Lamego—N2. 13km Peso da Régua—25km Vila Real.*

For the road to the crossroads just north-east of Celorico, see first part of Rte 21. From here the N102 bears north-east, crosses the Mondego and ascends the narrowing valley to (16km) crossroads, where turn left: for the road ahead see Rte 30, in reverse.

**Trancoso** is a walled town of some interest, well-sited for defence on a hill spur at a height of 900m. The ruined castle of 1160 was several times rebuilt, and its Romanesque churches have also been much altered, but the old town within the fortifications preserves several attractive corners.

### History
The town was of importance in the mid 12C and later. In 1283 Dom Dinis and Isabel of Aragón (St Isabel) were married here. In 1385 a battle took place here between the Portuguese and Spanish, when the latter were routed; and two years later negotiations were concluded here by which John of Gaunt agreed to let his daughter Catherine (Catalina) of Lancaster marry the future Enrique III of Castile, in return for a large indemnity in money, and surrendering his own claim to Spain.

It was at Trancosa in the 1580s that Gonçalo Anes, a local cobbler, composed his *trovas* under the name of Bandarra, describing the return of Dom Sebastião, which was one of the first popular verses propagating the messianic cult of Sebastianism. The Inquisition was active here in the early 17C. General Picton occupied what was known as the 'Casa Real' in March 1810. Later that year, after the battle of Busaco, General Beresford was given the title of Conde de Trancosa.

A 12C church and ruined castle may be seen at **Moreira de Rei**, 5km north-east. The main road shortly circles to the west, off which a track to the left leads to a neolithic site near **Carapito**. More interesting is **Aguiar da Beira**, approached by the next main left-hand turning. This is a pleasantly sited village with a granite clock-tower, what has been described as a medieval council-chamber (cf. Braganza, and Belmonte), and a curious dry-stone fortification known as the *castelo*.

Some 12km further west, approached by rough tracks, is **Ferreira de Aves**, with a Romanesque church and the later church of the ruined monastery of Santa Eufémia, founded in the 12C.

Continuing the descent of the Távora valley, the N226 bypasses (right) **Sernancelhe**, with a church of Romanesque origin, c 7km east of which, at **Guilheiro**, is a partly Romanesque church.

The south bank of the Barragem da Vigia is shortly reached, on skirting **Vila da Ponte**, Major Dickson's ordnance depot during part of the Peninsular War. During the summer of 1811 Wellington had ordered a train of heavy siege cannon, which had been disembarked at Oporto, to be transported on barges up the Douro to near Lamego, from where they were hauled south-east across country (by the road described below) towards Almeida (cf.).

17km north-west, at **Penedono**, is a well-machicolated 'toy' castle of triangular plan, and a *pelourinho*.

The main road runs through attractive country to **Moimento da Beira**, with a church of 1594 preserving 17C *azulejos*, and the 18C Casa dos Guedes or A Barros.

## Moimento to Tabuaço

27km. The N323 circles to the north-east, later descending the west bank of the steep valley of the Távora, and passing (right at c 18km) a lane climbing down to the well-carved Romanesque chapel of Granjinha or São Pedro das Aguias. Bearing north-west, at c 7km **Tabuaço**, its church containing carved altars and painted ceiling panels, is bypassed. To the west, at **Barcos**, are a Romanesque church and the hermitage of Sabroso. The road descends steeply from Tabuaço to meet the N222 skirting the south bank of the Douro some 19km east of the Peso da Régua bridge.

The N226 later passes a left-hand turning up a narrow valley to the extensive and impressive ruins of **São João da Tarouca**, the first Cistercian monastery in Portugal, founded in 1124, but not commenced until 50 years later. The *church (key from house opposite) contains the tomb of Pedro, Count of Barcelos (c 1280–1354), a bastard of Dom Dinis, and author of the *Livro das Linhagens*, the *Burke's Peerage* of its time. A fine painting of St Peter, similar to that at Viseu, ascribed to both Cristóvão de Figueiredo and Gaspar Vaz, may be seen here, among other works. Note also the organ.

A road opposite this turning leads down into the valley of the Barosa, where at **Ucanha** is a fortified 14C *bridge, to **Salzedas**, where an 18C church remains of a monastery founded in the 13C.

The main road passes (right) **Ferreirim**, with painted panels by Cristóvão de Figueiredo and others in the Igreja Matriz.

## LAMEGO

Lamego (9442 inhabitants), an attractive old episcopal city, is a pleasant centre from which to explore the region south of the upper Douro. It contains a wealth of Baroque architecture and an important museum. Its wines and hams are reputed.

■ The **Tourist Office** is in the Avenida Visconde Guedes Teixeira. There are **bus** services to Régua, Guarda and Viseu.

Lamego may have been Roman Lamaecum. In 1057 it was wrested from the Moors by Fernando I. It was later the residence of many New Christians, which later caused the Inquisition to be active in the vicinity.

Convenient parking may be found around the gardens in the lower town, but it is recommended that one first drives up to the pilgrimage church of **N.S. dos Remédios** (1750–60), overlooking the town to the south, standing near the head of a double flight of almost 700 steps, which invites comparison with Bom Jesus near Braga (cf.). Its architect is unknown; while the towers are a 19C addition. The octagonal granite platform of the upper terrace, the Largo dos Reis, is embellished by dramatically placed if inelegant statues, and obelisks, etc., below which, on lower landings, are fountains and pyramidal roofed pavilions. From the upper balustrade, the plunging *view of the town and of the hills above the Douro valley beyond, is very fine.

To the north of the gardens is the triangular Largo Camões, dominated by the **cathedral**. Little remains of the Romanesque original except the belfry. The fine Gothic west front dates from 1508–15; the restored cloister, with its belvedere, finished in 1557, is mainly Renaissance, with a few Gothic details. The interior preserves some damaged frescoes by Nicolau Nasoni (1734–40), better known as an architect (cf. Oporto). The retable painted by Grão Vasco in 1506–09 is now in the museum. The silver frontal (1758–68) by Master MFG in the chapel of the Blessed Sacrament is notable; and the two organs should not be overlooked.

Facing the main avenue is the *museum, installed since 1918 in the former episcopal palace, reconstructed in the late 18C and recently restored after a fire. Opening times are 9.30–12.30 and 14.00–17.00; closed Mon and holidays. It contains good collections of furniture, ecclesiastical plate, glass, *azulejos*, and 16C Flemish tapestries, including the Temple of Latona, Music, and an Oedipus series. Outstanding among the paintings of Vasco Fernandes ('O Grão Vasco'; cf. Viseu) are: Annunciation, Visitation, Circumcision, and Presentation, and his Creation of Animals.

On the ground floor is the chapel of São João Baptista; and on the floor above, that of *São João Evangelista, with its carved and painted panels and figures, which was previously in the Convento das Chagas (see below) and reconstructed here when that convent was demolished earlier this century. There are lapidary collections in the courtyard.

Several mansions may be seen nearby, including the adjacent Casa das Mores (17C), and Casa das Brolhas (18C), further along the street; and at the top of the Rua da Pereira (south of the cathedral), the Palacetes dos Vilhenas and de Santa Cruz; the neighbouring late 16C church and convent of that name are in military hands. Slightly further south at the next corner is the richly decorated Capela do Desterro (1640).

*The pilgrimage church of N.S. dos Remédios*

A lane leads downhill from this point to the picturesque riverside suburb of Balsemão; but see below.

Proceeding down the main avenue from the museum, the old hospital, now the theatre, is reached. From here climb right through the Porta do Sol to enter the walled enceinte, and bear left past an ancient vaulted cistern, beyond which (right) are relics of the 13C castle (views), and then the Porta dos Figos.

Further north is the 17C Casa dos Pinheiros, and at the far end of the garden square, the Igreja das Chagas (1588).

A few paces to the west of the Porta dos Figos is N.S. de Almacave, with worn Romanesque south and west portals. It is said to have once been a mosque, or at least abutting a Moorish cemetery (*macab*). The avenue is regained by following the Rua de Almacave downhill past (right) São Francisco (1599).

For the road south from Lamego to (76km) Viseu, see the latter part of Rte 31.

## Lamego to Entre-os-Rios (for Oporto) via the south bank of the Douro

93km. This slow road (N226 and N222), winding high above the Douro, occasionally provides impressive views, although the steep valley sides get increasingly built up on driving west. Bearing north-west past the Miradouro da Boa Vista (*view) the road shortly turns left through **Barrô**, with an unusual Romanesque church, to enter an area of Vinho Verde vineyards. Beyond, to the left, is **São Martinho de Mouros**, whose fortified Romanesque church has a superimposed belfry. Beyond **Resende**, where on a hill (views) stands restored Romanesque São Salvador, a left-hand turning climbs c 5km to Romanesque N.S. de Cárquere (late 13C), part of a convent founded in 1099.

On the far side of the Douro (which may be crossed before climbing steeply to Cinfães) is Ancede; see sub-route below. **Cinfães** is a centre for the production of Vinho Verde. To the south, the Bestança is spanned by the Roman bridge of Covelas. The N222 descends steeply, bearing left near the Barragem do Carrapatelo, to skirt **Tarouquela**, with the restored and partly rebuilt Romanesque church of Santa Maria Maior, once that of a Benedictine convent. Beyond **Souselo** is Romanesque São Miguel. Beyond the Paiva, the road ascends to **Castelo de Paiva** (or Sobrado), from which one may climb south across the hills to visit Arouca: see sub-route of Rte 26. The road descends steeply to cross the Douro just west of **Entre-os-Rios**, at its confluence with the Tâmega.

The main road north from Lamego (N2), in the process of improvement, descends steeply, passing a lane (right; signposted) to **Balsemão**, where the chapel of *São Pedro, a Visigothic basilica built in the 7C and remodelled in 1643, contains the tomb of Afonso Pires (died 1362), Bishop of Oporto. (It is advisable to enquire first for precise directions, and regarding admission, from the tourist office at Lamego.)

The road continues to climb down into the Douro valley (well-described by Somers Cocks during the Peninsular War, when heavy artillery was hauled up the rugged valley side here, as 'a superb *cabrazada*' or goat-track). The river is crossed by a comparatively new bridge adjacent to the rusting remains of the old, to **Peso da Régua** (5249 inhabitants), almost entirely devoted to the Port wine industry, being the westernmost town in the demarcated area, and the nearest river-port to Oporto. Here is the Casa do Douro, headquarters of the Port Wine Institute: see also p 287. Otherwise the town is of slight interest. To the west are the Casa dos Alambiques or Quinta do Salgueiral, bought by the Bearsley family (which later became Taylor, Fladgate and Yeatman) in 1744, probably the oldest English-owned property in the Douro. For more detailed information concerning them, see *The Port Wine Quintas of the Douro* by Alex Liddell (1992).

## Peso da Régua to Entre-os-Rios (for Oporto) via the north bank of the Douro

81km. The N108, a winding road providing a number of attractive views, leads west above the Douro, off which the N101 ascends north-west for Amarante (see sub-route below), before climbing away from the river and from the Port wine vineyards into those of the Vinhos Verdes. A byroad later descends to **Ancede**, with a ruined 13C convent. The main road climbs down to the river and continues west past the Barragem de Carrapatelo to **Alpendurada e Matos**, with a large convent of early foundation, much rebuilt after 1611 and again in the 18C, to reach **Entre-os-Rios**, just beyond which the Tâmega is crossed at its confluence with the Douro.

The N106 leads north past **São Vicente do Pinheiro**, with Roman baths, beyond which a byroad turns right to approach (c 6km) **Boelhe**, where 12C São Gens is a good example of rural Romanesque. The N106 continues through **Oldrões**, near which is the 1C fortified settlement of Monte Mozinho. A left-hand turning leads shortly to Paço de Sousa; see last part of Rte 29A.

From Entre-os-Rios the N108—deserving improvement—winds west, occasionally skirting the north bank of the Douro to (40km) Oporto.

## Peso da Régua to Amarante

38km. The N108 skirts the steep north bank of the Douro, off which the N101 climbs steeply to **Mesão Frio**, whose Igreja Matriz is embellished with numerous painted ceiling panels, and ornate carved and gilt woodwork. **Quintela**, with a 13C tower, is passed after c 6km before the road descends the Fornelo valley, bypassing (left) **Jazente**, with a late 13C church, to meet the IP4 from Vila Real to Oporto) on approaching the Tâmega at Amarante: see latter part of Rte 29.

At **Fonte do Milho**, some 12km north-east of Peso da Régua, reached by turning right off a road ascending parallel to the N2 (see below), and beyond **Canelas**, with the *solar* of the Condes de Resende, are the extensive remains of a 1C and 4C Roman villa, later fortified.

The N2 climbs steeply out of the Douro valley, passing (right) **Cumieira**, where the church of 1739 contains sumptuous carving, on approaching Vila Real: see Rte 31.

# B. Via Vila Nova de Foz Côa

*Total distance, 171km (106 miles). N332. 15km Almeida—20km. Castelo Rodrigo is to the right.—3km Figueira de Castelo Rodrigo—N332 and N222. 37km Vila Nova de Foz Côa—42km São João da Pesqueira—21km Pinhão—N322. 15km Sabrosa—18km Vila Real.*

*The second part of this route is slow going, particularly on the descent into and ascent from the Douro valley.*

Bear right immediately on leaving Vilar Formoso (see Rtes 21 and 22B for its vicinity) to **Almeida** (*Pousada Senhora das Neves*), long one of the strongest fortresses defending the Portuguese frontier, standing opposite its Spanish counterpart, Fort Concepción, c 10km east as the crow flies, on the far bank of the Tourões.

### History

Almeida was refounded by Dom Dinis, and received its *foral* in 1296, confirmed in 1510 by Dom Manuel, who strengthened its walls, which had not resisted Enrique de Trastamara in 1373, or Juan I in 1381. It was here that John of Gaunt and Nun' Alvares Pereira took leave of each other after their invasion of Castile in 1387.

It was briefly a base of operations against the Spanish in August 1704. In 1762 Almeida was obliged to surrender to a Spanish force, but during the 18C its fortifications were rebuilt on a Vaubanesque plan, with strong bombproof casemates, etc.

In June 1808, at the beginning of the Peninsular War, it was occupied by Géneral Loison, and the French remained there until forced to evacuate it by the Convention of Sintra. It was then garrisoned by Portuguese under the command of Colonel William Cox, who were isolated by Masséna's advance in 1810. Crauford's Light Division fought a bloody action against superior forces on 24 July just south of the town, before retiring. The French did not attack until 26 August, when a shell lit a powder trail from a damaged keg, causing the strongly vaulted main church, then used as a magazine, to blow up, killing some 500 Portuguese outright: Cox had no alternative but to capitulate. It remained a French outpost until after the battle of Fuentes de Oñoro (3 and 5 May 1811). On 10 May, before withdrawing, Géneral Brennier (with 1300 men) blew up more of the fortifications as a parting shot, together with their stores and artillery.

Here, in the 1840s, Barão de Bomfim briefly took up arms against Costa Cabral's administration. It was the birthplace of the historian Bernardo de Brito (1569–1617).

That there is still so much to see of the *fortifications, the main gate of which is dated 1797, is remarkable. The town itself has not much else to offer except for its *pousada*, and the views from its walls.

The road continues north through **Vilar Torpim**. It retains a Gothic church and an attractive mansion.

The heights of Marofa (left; 977m) are approached, beyond which (right) is **Castelo Rodrigo**, a decayed village, once of importance, with extensive remains of its circuit of bastioned walls, a castle, and the small church of Reclamador (sic: N.S. do Rocamador). The village commands panoramic views.

Neighbouring **Figueira de Castelo Rodrigo** has only one feature of architectural curiosity: the interior arch supporting the upper choir of its church is composed entirely of S-shaped stones.

At **Freixada do Torrão**, 5km west, are a medieval tower and a church with a Romanesque portal.

3km south-east are the imposing remains of the 13C Cistercian convent of **Santa Maria de Aguiar**, now a farm (to which apply), possessing a large Gothic *church and finely vaulted chapterhouse. Note the Renaissance loggia of the adjoining house. Some 3km further east, north of the Almofala road, are the partly reconstructed remains of a Roman temple known as the Casarão da Torre.

For the road north-east from Figueira de Castelo Rodrigo to Barca de Alva and Freixo de Espada à Cinta, see Rte 28, in reverse.

The N332 now bears north-west along a ridge (views) into 'Port wine' country and to (16km) **Almendra**, with a large Baroque mansion and fortified church, later passing (left) the ruined castle of **Castelo Melhor**, before steeply descending to cross the Côa at its confluence with the Douro (right; views). On climbing out of the valley, the N102 is met just south of **Vila Nova de Foz Côa**. The church here has a good Manueline portal; but note also the cant of its pillars, the stone pulpit, well-carved altar, and painted ceiling. Adjacent is a *pelourinho*. For the N102 cross road, see Rte 31.

The N222 bears right c 4.5km south of the town, and climbs north-west over the hills, shortly passing a right-hand turning to **Freixo de Numão**, taken from the Moors in 1055, with ruins of a castle (views) and a church of Romanesque origin, beyond which is the famous *Quinta de Vesúvio*, established by António Bernardo Ferreira in 1823. (On the opposite bank of the Douro here is the Quinta da Senhora da Ribeira.)

There is an 18C mansion at **Cedovim**, 4km south at the next junction, 4km to the north of which, at **Numão**, is an extensive circuit of fortifications.

The main road winds north-west to **São João da Pesqueira**, a large village on the plateau overlooking the Douro, surrounded by Port *quintas*. Pombal is said to have spent part of his youth here. The Baroque Casa do Cabo is notable.

---

A road leads steeply down to the river and the Barragem de Valeira at the Cachão de Valeira, where the narrow gorge was until 1792 the highest point of navigation on the Douro, being choked with granite slabs until cleared. Rapids still remained, and it was here that Joseph James Forrester (see p 67) was drowned on 12 May 1861, when his boat split on a rock or capsized. In 1988 a bronze plaque was fixed to the cliff by the Portuguese President to commemorate him, and a wreath cast on the river. High above the gorge is the shrine of São Salvador do Mundo, to the east of which is the Quinta de Vargellas.

---

The main road from São João climbs down to meet the Douro, first passing near (right) the *Quinta of Roriz* (originally owned by Robert Archibald until bought by Nicolau Kopke in the 1760s) and, nearer Pinhão, the 18C Quinta das Carvalhas. On the opposite bank north-east of that of Roriz are those of Tua, and Malvedos; opposite Carvalhas, those of Roêda (once owned by John Fladgate, created Barão da Roêda), and Bomfim.

To the left of the road on descending to the Duero is the Quinta do Bom Retiro. On reaching the river, turn right to cross it at **Pinhão**—this and Peso da Régua are the most important river-ports and transport centres of this region.

The N222 skirts the south bank of the Douro, off which the N323 ascends to Tabuaço; see Rte 27A, and for (23km) Peso da Régua. On the opposite bank here is the *Quinta da Boa Vista*, its vineyards possibly planted by J.J. Forrester himself.

The N322 climbs steeply north-east from Pinhão up a valley of the same name and past (right) the Quinta do Noval to (16km) high-lying village of **Alijo** (*Pousada Barão de Forrester*), and as the N212 continues north to meet the N15 (and the IP4 under construction) after 20km; see Rte 29.

The N323 ascends steeply north-west from Pinhão to **Sabrosa**, the birthplace of Fernão de Magalhães (Magellan; c 1480–1521). One ship of his fleet of five (commanded by Juan Sebastián de Elcano, a Basque) was the first to circumnavigate the globe (1519–22), although Magellan himself had been killed in the Philippines.

2km to the north is a Bronze Age site, while there is a Luso-Roman rock sanctuary at **Panóias**, to the right of the main road some 8km north-west. This shortly enters Mateus, passing (left) its *solar* on the outskirts of Vila Real: for both, see Rte 31.

For the road to Amarante and Oporto, see Rte 29.

# 28 · (Zamora) Miranda do Douro to Guarda

*Total distance, 193km (120 miles). N221. 48km Mogadouro—46km Freixo de Espada à Cinta—42km Figueira de Castelo Rodrigo—20km Pinhel—37km Guarda.*

The N122 from Zamora, 56km east (see *Blue Guide Spain*, 6th ed.), is followed to cross the boulder-strewn valley of the Esla, here dammed, at (24km) Ricobayo, where fork left. This byroad then descends to cross another dam over the Douro (Duero in Spain) just west of its confluence with the Esla, and drives west across a wide meander of the Douro, climbing down to re-cross the river (which here forms the frontier) immediately below Miranda.

**MIRANDA DO DOURO** (*Pousada de Santa Catarina*, with impressive plunging views of the Douro), once an isolated frontier outpost overlooking rapids, is now—with the construction of its dam across the gorge—one of the more important crossings from Spain into the Trás-os-Montes; but regrettably it is already being spoilt by a rash of shops selling trinkets to Spanish trippers. Here, and in adjacent villages, a dialect known as Mirandés, in fact a Leonese *patois*, is spoken.

■ **Buses** run here from Braganza and Mogadouro.

### History

Miranda was raised to a bishopric in 1545, but in 1782 the see was transferred to Braganza. It was attacked by the Spaniards under O'Reilly in May 1762, when the castle blew up, killing some 400 people. On 28/29 May 1813 Wellington, having ridden from Salamanca, was slung across the gorge here in a 'kind of hammock' suspended by ropes, to inspect 60,000 Anglo-Portuguese troops, assembled within Portugal in previous weeks under the command of General Graham. This composed the heavy-weight left wing of his army, which, crossing the Esla by pontoon bridges near Carbajales de Alba in Spain, surprised and outflanked the French. It was perhaps the most successful single offensive manoeuvre on the part of the British army during the Peninsular War, the immediate campaign culminating in the great victory at Victoria only three weeks later, on 21 June.

The walled town consists largely of 16C houses or earlier. At its far end, beyond the central square, stands the former **cathedral**, overlooking the ravine of the Douro. The edifice, ith its severe west front, was built between 1552–76 by a Spaniard, Francisco Velázquez, to the designs of Gonçalo do Torralva and/or Miguel de Arruda. The retable of the *Capela-Mór* was carved in 1610–14 by Juan de Muniátegui at Valladolid and transported here. Note also the well-carved furniture in the sacristy; the choir-stalls and gutted organ-case; the rich carving (of boys, birds, and grapes, etc.) of another altar (left), and (right) the curious puppet-like 'Menino Jesus da Cartolinha', the local cult figure, dressed in an opera-hat and white bow-tie!

Behind the cathedral, where an arcade survives of the unfinished cloister, stands the ruined Bishop's Palace.

The town has a small ethnographical museum 'da Terra de Miranda', which is open 10.00–12.15 and 14.00–16.45; closed Mon and holidays.

## Miranda do Douro to Braganza

84km. The N218, bearing north-west, shortly bypasses (right) **Malhadas**, an old village with a partly 13C church, and leads over the undulating country to bypass (left at 29km) **Vimioso**, known for its marble, frequently used for tombstones in north-east Portugal. Its Igreja Matriz, on the south slope of the village, dates from the 17C. Between its towers is an unusual cruciform window.

At **Algosa**, 14km south, beyond **Campo de Viboras** (vipers), is an early 13C castle once belonging to the Order of Malta (views).

The N218 continues to wind north-west to (22km) **Outeiro** (where the twin-towered 17C Igreja Matrix has a curious façade) before it meets the main road from Zamora to Braganza; see Rte 29, and also for Braganza itself.

---

The N221 bears south-west from Miranda to **Duas Igrejas**, 3km south of which is a rock shelter with late Palaeolithic carvings.

Two turnings lead left off the next stretch of road, both descending to the Douro: the first to the Barragem de Picote, the river at this point passing through a precip-itously walled gorge; and then the Barragem de Bemposta (just above the conflu-ence of the Tormes and the Duero, crossed by a road to Fermoselle in Spain), but the views are less impressive.

Later passing a turning for **Algozinho** (c 8km south-east), with a 13C church, the road bears south-west and then west through open country to **Mogadouro**, a market town formerly an important frontier fortress, retaining ruins of a strong-hold of the Távoras until that family was crushed by Pombal. The 16C Igreja Matriz contains some good carved and gilt woodwork (18C); the conventual church of São Francisco is of the same period.

At **Azinhoso**, 6km north, is a 12C church, 3km north-east of which, at **Penas Roias**, are a medieval tower and ruined Templar castle.

---

## Mogadouro to Macedo de Cavaleiros

49km. The N216 winds across country to the north-west, climbing down into the valley of the Sabor and ascending its far bank. 5km east of **Chacim**, formerly known for its silk production, and with a good *pelourinho*, is the abandoned convent of Balsemão, founded in the 18C by Frei Casimiro Wiszynski, a Pole. The N102 is met at **Macedo de Cavaleiros**, a small agricultural centre, in which stands the *solar* of the Morais Sarmento de Vasconcelos family. The IP4 may be entered some 6km north-west.

---

From Mogadouro the N221 climb south over the hills through the village of **Castelo Branco**, with the deteriorated Solar dos Morais Pimentéis, 20km beyond which reaching crossroads high above the Douro valley (views). The right fork leads due west, later along a ridge (views) to (26km) Torre de Moncorvo: see Rte 30.

Bear left, with the peak of Pocinhella (821m) on the right, to **Freixo de Espada à Cinta**, an old frontier fortress preserving the tall heptagonal tower of its castle, and remains of walls. It may take its curious name—'ash-tree of the girt sword'—from a gesture of Dom Dinis, who, when he founded the town, buckled his sword round an adjacent ash-tree, but there are alternative theories. It was the birthplace of Jorge Alvares, the navigator and mid 16C chronicler of Japan, and of the regional poet Abilio Manuel Guerra Junqueiro (1850–1923). Its cheeses are reputed.

Lanes flanked by medieval houses lead towards the main square overlooked by the *Igreja Matriz, an imposing Manueline rebuilding of a 13C church, its retable of c 1520–35 displaying 16 paintings ascribed to 'Grão Vasco' (cf. Viseu). Note also the tomb, and a figure of St Peter to the left of the altar, the pulpit, and the lateral portal. Opposite is the tower of the 16C Misericórdia.

On leaving Freixo, a ruinous church is passed to the right, and shortly the road winds round the Durão (727m) the summit of which may be reached by a right-hand turning on approaching the mountain. There are good views here, and where the road descends towards the Douro at the Barragem de Saucelle.

The N221 circles to the west above the north bank of the river and through a forest of almond-trees to **Barca de Alva**, at one time the upper limit of navigation, and the terminus of the railway up the valley of the Douro, which is crossed here. Ascending the steep far bank, with the Garganta de Agueda on one's left, **Escalhão** is approached, some 5km south-east of which, at **Mata de Lobos**, is a monument recording the Portuguese victory here in July 1664 over a Spanish force led by the Duque de Osuna.

For Figueira de Castelo Rodrigo, shortly entered, and (left) Castelo Rodrigo on its fortified height, see Rte 27B. Skirting the foot of Marofa (976m), which may be climbed for the view, the road winds south-west, crossing the rocky gorge of the Côa and ascends to **Pinhel**, an attractive old town and seat of a bishopric until 1882. It is dominated by its castle (1312), the interior of one tower of which is supported by a single column, while high on its eastern wall are two gargoyles offensively relieving themselves towards Spain. Nearby stands Santa Maria (14C), containing a series of 17C paintings of the Life of the Virgin. In the central square is the 18C Paço do Concelho, with a small archaeological collection. The Misericórdia has a Manueline portal; the Igreja Matriz (São Luís), Baroque woodwork and 18C *azulejos*. The former Bishop's Palace housed the headquarters staff of Generals Graham and Picton at various times during the Peninsular War.

Continuing south-west, at **Malta** a right-hand turning is passed for neighbouring **Souro Pires**, with the 15–16C Solar dos Távoras, from which the N226 goes on to (27km) Trancoso; see Rte 27A.

The IP5 is met on approaching Guarda, on its height ahead; see Rte 21, and also for the road on to Coimbra. For those to Castelo Branco, and for Viseu, see Rtes 22 and 23 respectively.

# 29 · (Zamora) Braganza to Oporto via Vila Real and Amarante

*Total distance, 232km (144 miles); but this figure is approximate, for a central section of the highway is not yet completed, although it will be shortly. IP4. 34km exit for Macedo de Cavaleiros—24km exit for Mirandela—70km Vila Real exit—36km Amarante exit—30km Penafiel exit—38km Oporto.*

What was a tortuous cross-country route has been greatly improved by the construction of the IP4.

The N122 leads north-west from Zamora through Alcañices (see *Blue Guide Spain*, 6th ed.) to approach the frontier, there formed by the Rio Maçãs. The present convoluted road between here and (30km) Braganza will be replaced in due course by a new road, which will circle north of the town.

The N218 from Miranda do Douro (see Rte 28) is shortly met and, 15km beyond, crosses **Gimonde**, with a medieval bridge.

At **São Julião de Palácios**, a hamlet 10km north-east, John of Gaunt confirmed the abrogation of all rights he and his wife might have to the throne of Portugal (1387; his daughter Philippa having married Dom João not long before).

The next right-hand turning leads to **Sacoias**, where the church (ask anyone near where the key is hidden) contains some damaged paintings formerly ascribed to 'Grão Vasco'; note also the naïve ceiling paintings. The neighbouring village of **Baçal** was the parish of the Abade of Baçal, who devoted his life to the archaeology of the region: cf. the Museum at Braganza.

The main road descends south-west, with a view of its ancient citadel on a height to the left, to enter Braganza.

## BRAGANZA

Braganza (**Bragança** in Portuguese; 15,624 inhabitants; *Pousada de São Bartolomeu*), a high-lying district capital (680m), and ancient capital of the Tras-os-Montes, was the Celtic Brigantia. It has long remained a provincial backwater, but its name, widely known as the surname of Charles II's queen, Catherine, has perhaps conjured up a different image, and some may be disillusioned. Its isolation has been largely due to bad roads, which have hampered both the sale of its produce and the movements of foreign invaders. It is also certain that in these remote districts some crypto-Jewish communities survived the persecutions of earlier centuries. (However, a synagogue was opened in Braganza in 1927.)

Change, not always for the better, is already noticeable, partly due to the construction of the IP4, which has improved communication in this district.

■ The **Tourist Office** is in the Av. Cidade de Zamora. **Buses** run from Zamora, or to Vila Real.

### History

John of Gaunt and Dom João I passed through in 1387 before the Anglo-Portuguese attack on León. The title of Duke of Braganza was created in 1442 for Dom Afonso, natural son of Dom João I. His family, whose seat was at Vila Viçosa (cf.), and whose rights of succession were ignored by Philip II of Spain in 1580, came to the throne in 1640 in the person of Dom João IV, the eighth duke. The male line became extinct in 1853, but descendants in the female line ruled until the end of the monarchy in 1910.

A small square in the town centre is flanked by the nondescript little **Sé**, from 1545 the church of São João Baptista, but a cathedral since 1770, when the seat of the bishop was transferred here from Miranda do Douro. It contains a gutted organ-case and, in the sacristy, 17 painted panels.

From here, follow a street downhill to the right to the Largo de São Vicente, overlooked by **São Vicente**, on a Romanesque base, and with a curious naïve ceiling of 1886. Traditionally it was here that the future Dom Pedro I was clandestinely married to Inês de Castro (cf. Cantanhede).

A cobbled lane ascends to gardens below the main entrance to the **\*walled upper town**, commanded by the keep or *Torre de Managem* of its **\*castle**, erected in 1187 by Dom Sancho I and besieged, unsuccessfully, in 1199 by Alfonso IX of León. It houses a small military museum. Adjacent is a *pelourinho*, its base driven through the back of an ancient granite boar (cf. Murça); and near by is 18C Santa Maria, containing a painted ceiling. Abutting the church is the over-restored and incongruously-roofed **\*Domus Municipalis**, a rare surviving example of Romanesque civic architecture, built over a cistern, and perhaps dating from the early 13C. The key may be obtained at a house opposite.

The present municipality has a well-conceived plan to clear this quarter of its hovels—there were formerly many more—and generally to improve its appearance. It looks well from a distance, preferably from the hill to the south-west, on the slope of which stands the *pousada*.

Turn right on leaving the enceinte to approach **São Bento** (1590), with a Mudéjar ceiling in the *capela-mór*, a painted barrel-vault of 1763, and a sumptuous retable. Access is not easy to obtain, the ecclesiastics of Braganza keeping up a running fight with the civic authorities over such matters as admission to its churches. São Francisco, a few paces to the right, is of slight interest.

Bearing downhill to the west, an attractive old mansion (No. 39) is passed before reaching, in the former Bishop's Palace, the *Museu do Abade de Baçal, named after its instigator, Francisco Manuel Alves (1865–1947), who dedicated most of his life to the study of the region.

On the ground floor are three bishop's litters, and smaller objects from the important archaeological collection. Larger artefacts, including numerous stelae, may be seen below the porch and in the garden; some of the more curious have unfortunately been imbedded in a wall to the right.

Stairs ascend to a landing below a cupola, off which, below carved compartmented ceilings (some of the gilt of which has been overpainted), opens a series of rooms, including a private chapel (with a painted wooden ceiling, and displaying vestments, plate, etc.). Other rooms contain miscellaneous paintings, among them Orpheus, by Roelland Savery; the Marquês d'Oliveira's Study of a boy's head; an anonymous Annunciation; Henrique Tavares, Portrait of the Abade de Baçal; works by Abel Salazar (1889–1946); and watercolours of *pelourinhos* by Alberto de Sousa (died 1961). Among books and manuscripts on display are some early 16C charters, including that of Braganza (1514; the first had been issued by Dom Sancho I in 1187), and Bulls of the foundation of the diocese of Miranda do Douro and Braganza (1545). Other rooms are devoted to a numismatic collection, and to ethnography: local costumes, including that of the 'Pauliteiros', or stick-dancers of the region; metalwork, including a scold's bridle, weights and measures, etc.; and ceramics.

At the corner of the second right-hand turning stands the **Misericórdia**, with a charming carved retable of the Virgin with her arms protectively extended. Opposite the end of this short street is the restored Santa Clara (16C), with a painted ceiling.

For the road south to Celorico da Beira, see Rte 30.

## Braganza to Chaves via Vinhais

96km. The N103, a beautiful but slow and tortuous road, occasionally impassable, veers north-west. Even in the 18C it was avoided by travellers from or to Chaves, who preferred to make the detour via Mirandela. It shortly passes **Castro de Avelas**, with the ruined 12C church of a Benedictine monastery, of interest as being the only one in Portugal built of brick and with blind arcading in the style of those at Sahagún, in Spain. After 30km **Vinhais** is entered, well-sited on the southern slope of a range of hills, its summit being the Coroa (1272m), and formerly 'much infested by custom-house officers', as being close to the border. Remains of fortifications survive, and the two churches of the convent of São Francisco, the best features of which are their organs and carved and gilt pelmets, etc., although the upper also has a painted ceiling. Another 25km, after following a ridge providing wide views, brings one to **Rebordelo**, where the road bears west to skirt **Lebução**, with an old church, and then the 12C castle of Monforte de Rio

Livre, probably erected on the site of a Roman fort, before descending towards Chaves: see Rte 31.

---

The IP4 drives south, later veering south-west, off which, at 34km, the N102 bears left for Macedo de Cavaleiros; see p 270 and Rte 30.

**Romeu**, one of the 'restored' villages of the Vale de Couço, with a small museum of mechanical curiosities, lies to the south before the highway descends to bypass **Mirandela** (7862 inhabitants), on the Rio Tua, there spanned by a medieval bridge of 17 arches, probably on Roman foundations. The town is dominated by a late 17C Palace of the Távoras, now the town hall.

From here the N213 leads 53km north-west to Chaves (see Rte 31) via **Valpaços** and **Vilarandelo**, with the Solar dos Calainhos of 1745 and 17–18C São Vicente, before crossing the Serra da Padrela. This was formerly the route used during winter, when that between Chaves and Braganza (see above) was likely to be impassable.

The IP4 starts to climb, skirting the southern slope of the Serra do Vilarelho to bypass **Murça**, in the municipal garden of which stands the 'Porca de Murça', a roughly sculpted boar of pre-Roman origin. To call someone such implies that he is a political turncoat. The Misericórdia retains a typical Baroque façade of 1692.

The Rio Tinhela, also spanned by a Roman bridge, is crossed (from which the old N15 climbed in steep zigzags) to a point from which the N212 bears north-west to Vila Pouva de Aguiar (see Rte 31) and south via (20km) Alijó to Pinhão, on the Douro; see Rte 27B.

The IP4 continues to wind across the hills before descending and crossing the valley of the Corgo just north of **Vila Real**; see Rte 31, and for the road south from there to Lamego and Viseu; and likewise for Mateus, which may be approached by turning left off the N15 as it climbs down towards Vila Real.

From Vila Real the IP4 climbs west over the Serra do Marão, at the Alto de Espinho (895m) passing a turning (the old N15) to the Pousada de São Gonçalo, with a plunging view down into a valley, before steeply descending into the Tâmega valley to meet and cross the N101 3km south-east of Amarante.

## AMARANTE

Amarante (7720 inhabitants), a straggling wine-growing town on the steep banks of the Tâmega, here spanned by a handsome three-arched obelisk-embellished bridge of 1790 by Carlos da Cruz Amarante (1740–1815), has a reputation for the curious phallic cakes baked there during the festival of its miracle-working patron, São Gonçalo, protector of marriages (13C; but only beatified in 1561).

- The **Tourist Office** is in the Rua Cândido dos Reis. The **train station** is north-west of the town centre.

### History

The name of Amarante is said to be derived from the Latin *Ante Moranam* (in front of the Serra do Morão), although there are no Roman remains there. Others have preferred an origin in its fertility cult! The Romanesque bridge is said to have been reconstructed by Gonçalo himself, but this collapsed in 1763.

In mid April 1809 General Silveira (later Count of Amarante: cf. Vila Real), holding the left bank of the river, effectively stopped a much superior force of French, having precipitately abandoned Oporto, from actually crossing here. In the face of reinforcement under Beresford advancing from Lamego, Loison evacuated Amarante on 12 May, jettisoning his wheeled transport and artillery, and clambered north-west to joined Soult at Guimarães. But with Wellington entering Braga on the 15th, and Beresford moving on Chaves to cut off their retreat east, the French had no alternative but to struggle north-east across country towards Salamonde and Montealegre (see Rte 32) in retreat.

The main monument of Amarante is the church and convent of *São Gonçalo, by the bridge. This was begun in 1540 under the supervision of Frei Julião Romero, architect of the Dominican Order, but was not completed until 1620. Its most obvious exterior features are its entrance façade; the arcaded loggia with its sculptures; and the cupola above the crossing. The interior contains some richly carved and gilt woodwork, particularly in the *Capela-Mór*, and the gutted organ-case with its supports is also notable; while to the left of the high altar is the tomb of the saint (c 1262), against which—so they say—husband-hunters past their first youth have only to rub their naked flesh to be granted one within the year. Its two Renaissance cloisters (partly in use as pigsties in the 19C) have been restored, and its dependencies now house the town hall and the **Albano Sardoeira museum**, largely devoted to modern art and concentrating on that of the local artist Amadeo de Sousa-Cardoso (1887–1918). The adjacent belfry will be noted.

Steps climb to São Domingos (18C), a cylindrical building (closed, but said to contain a fine organ-case and rococo woodwork). Further up the hill is São Pedro (1727), with a good sacristy.

On the far bank is a restored arcaded building of character.

For the road north-west to (33km) Guimarães, see the latter part of Rte 35, in reverse.

The deep valley of the Tâmega may be explored to the north-east by following the N210, skirting its north (or right) bank through **Gatão**, with the church of São João, of Romanesque origin, to **Celorico de Basto**, with an early castle (?11C), partly restored, and 17–18C mansions.

The same tortuous road leads south-west above the south (or left) bank of the Tâmega to a crossroad between **Tabuado** (left), with a good late Romanesque church, and on a height to the right, **Marco de Canaveses**, with a small Romanesque church and the 17C Casa da Ribeira. Roman remains are being excavated in the neighbourhood at **Freixo**, Roman Tongobriga. Also of interest are **Vila Boas de Quires**, with a 12C church (interior modernised), and in its vicinity, the extraordinary 18C façade of the so-called *Casa das Obras (or Obras do Fidalgo, or dos Portos Carreiros): the rest of the building, by an anonymous Spanish architect, was never completed. **Travanca** may also be approached from here, where the 12C church of the monastery of *São Salvador (founded 970–1002) has two good Romanesque portals. Note also the apse and a separate tower.

**Penafiel** (6886 inhabitants), founded in the 9C, and until 1770 known as Arrifana de Sousa, is later bypassed by the IP4. It retains a mid 16C Igreja Matriz on the site of an earlier building, a Doric Misericórdia, and in the Rua Direita, several old granite mansions, some with Manueline features; other may be seen in the Rua Serpa Pinto.

From just beyond Penafiel, the N106 bears left towards Entre-os-Rios via Oldrões (see sub-route towards the end of Rte 27A), off which a lane shortly turns right, passing (right) **Cabeça Santa**, with a good 12C church, to **Paço de Sousa**, where the fine 12C Romanesque monastic church of *São Salvador contains the tomb of Egas Moniz (died 1144), on which his legendary exploits are carved in high relief.

Adjacent are two charmingly sited 18C *quintas*. The IP4 may be regained via neighbouring **Cete**, with a Benedictine monastery retaining both Romanesque and Manueline features.

The IP4 circles to the south and then north as increasingly populous districts are traversed on approaching Oporto, which is entered from the north-east; see Rte 33. Although many roads eventually converge on the centre, it is preferable to check first exactly where in the conurbation one is heading for, as the road system is confusing, and not all bypasses have been completed.

# 30 · Braganza to Celorico da Beira, for Guarda, Viseu or Coimbra

*Total distance, 170km (105 miles). IP4. 34km—N102 (IP2). 7km Macedo de Cavaleiros—49km. Moncorvo is 9km south-east.—18km Vila Nova de Foz Côa—41km. Trancoso is 5km west.—21km Celorico da Beira.*

For Braganza, and for the first 34km of this road, see Rte 29.

The N102 turns left through Macedo de Cavaleiros (see sub-route of Rte 28), beyond which the road crosses the Serra de Bornes (Ladaino; 1174m) and descends the valley of the Vilarica to enter the Port wine region.

A right-hand turning (N215) climbs north-west to (8km) **Vila Flor**, with the 18C Solar de Diogo do Lemos, a 17C church, and one remaining gate of its fortification.

20km south-west of Vila Flor, approached by the N214, is **Carrazeda de Ansiães**, c 6km south of which, at **Ansiães**, are remains of its walls, and the ruins of Romanesque *São Salvador, with a good portal, among other Romanesque chapels in the vicinity. The road from Carrazedo later descends steeply to **Tua**, at the confluence of the Rio Tua with the Douro. From Tua the N212 climbs as steeply to Alijó; see Rte 27B.

The main road, running parallel to a rocky ridge, off which a byroad leads left to **Adeganha**, with an isolated 13C Romanesque church, turns to cross the Rio Sabor, a tributary of the Douro.

The N325 here climbs tortuously to the left to **Torre de Moncorvo**, among orchards on the north slope of the Serra do Roboredo (906m). It derives its name from an 11C *senhor*, Mendo Curvo, although the site of Roman Valarisa is in the neighbourhood. It retains slight ruins of its fortifications; a massively buttressed Manueline Igreja Matriz, its imposing interior containing a polychromed triptych; and a Renaissance Misericórdia with a well-carved granite pulpit. The town itself, once described as 'very ill-built and filthy', has not changed that much. There are some iron-mines near the N220, leading 26km east to meet the N221 14km north of Freixo de Espada à Cinta; see Rte 28. The N220 descends south-west to regain the main route skirting the Douro, which is crossed at **Pocinho**, to the north-west of which, within a meander of the river, is the *Quinta do Vale do Meão*, reputed for its red table wine apart from its port.

Vila Nova de Foz Côa is shortly bypassed, for which, and for the road to Vilar Formoso, 75km south-east, see Rte 27B, in reverse.

At 16km **Longroiva** (right), an ancient town with slight remains of its castle, is bypassed as the road drives south up a long valley, some 8km beyond passing another ruined castle at (right) **Marialva**, a long-abandoned but now partly repopulated walled village.

At 17km a right-hand turning leads shortly to Trancoso; see Rte 27A. For the N226 (turning left at the next crossroads and winding across the hills to the south-east to meet the N221 between Pinhel and Guarda) see the last part of Rte 28.

The N102 descends into upper valley of the Mondego to approach Celorico da Beira; see Rte 21, and also for the road from Guarda to Coimbra. For that to Viseu, see Rte 23.

# 31 · (Verín) Chaves to Viseu via Vila Real and Lamego

*Total distance, 172km (107 miles). N2. 36km Vila Pouca de Aguira—28km Vila Real—25km Peso da Régua—13km Lamego—33km Castro Daire—37km Viseu.*

■ **Buses** connect Chaves, Vila Real, Lamego, and Viseu.

From Verín (see *Blue Guide Spain*, 6th ed.), the N232 leads due south for 16km to cross the frontier at **Feces de Abaixo**, 10km north of Chaves.

**CHAVES** (11,708 inhabitants), its canting device being keys (*chaves*), was long a frontier fortress guarding this entry into northern Portugal. It has been less successful in defending itself from Spanish influence in recent decades, and its former attractions are being eroded. It is reputed for its smoked ham (*presunto*).

■ The **Tourist Office** is in the Terreiro de Cavalaría.

### History
Roman Aquae Flaviae, known for its hot springs, was a station on the road between Braga and Astorga. Hydatius, its bishop in the 5C, compiled annals describing the Suevic occupation. It later was occupied occasionally by invading forces, among them those of the Spanish General O'Reilly in 1762. In the spring of 1809 it fell to the French, but was recaptured by General Silveira. In mid May Soult's retreating troops were followed this far by Beresford, when some 1200 of them were forced to surrender. As recently as 1912 it was occupied briefly by a monarchist faction rising against the infant Republic.

The Tâmega is crossed here by a Roman bridge of 16 arches (AD 104), spoilt by the addition of a metal parapet. The bridgehead is commanded by a castle of the Dukes of Braganza, the imposing *keep of which now houses militaria. Adjacent is a miscellaneous archaeological collection, including Roman stelae, artefacts from the *castro* of Carvalhelhos, columns, carved escutcheons, etc.

Facing the Praça de Camões is the church of the **Misericórdia** (late 17C), with an attractive façade and porch, ornate retable, painted ceilings by Jerónimo da Rocha Braga (1743), and *azulejo* panels.

The adjacent **Igreja Matriz**, entirely rebuilt in the 16C, and since over-restored, retains part of its Romanesque portal below the belfry, also with Romanesque features, while the interior contains relics of an organ. Afonso de Braganza (died

1461), natural son of Dom João I and founder of the ducal dynasty, was buried here originally.

To the north is the fort of São Francisco, part of the 17C Vaubanesque fortifications; and further north, that of São Neutel.

To the left of the south end of the bridge stands the 18C Igreja da Madalena, with an octagonal nave.

---

Some 4km north, at **Outeiro Seco**, approached by a road leading off the north end of the bridge, is the restored Romanesque church of N.S. da Azinheira, with interesting exterior corbels and faint 16C frescoes (enquire at adjacent house for key).

West of **Abobaleira**, 4km north-west of Chaves, at **Outeiro Machado**, is a large rock covered with prehistoric carvings, reached by a track (30-minute walk).

For the cross-road from Braganza to Braga, see sub-route of Rte 29.

---

On leaving Chaves, the left bank of the Tâmega is skirted by a completed stretch of the improved road, with the Serra da Pedrela rising to the south-east, to **Vidago**, a small spa.

**Sabrosa** is shortly bypassed (right), where a small ruined chapel commemorates General Ranald Macdonald (or Macdonnel) of Glengarry, a reactionary Scot who met his death here in 1847 during a skirmish.

**Pedras Salgadas**, another spa, is passed on approaching **Vila Pouca de Aguiar**, with castle ruins, and two or three old houses of interest.

In the hills to the east, at **Tresminas**, are relics of the most extensive Roman gold workings in Portugal.

---

## Vila Pouca to Guimarães

80km. Several isolated settlements retaining medieval characteristics may be found in this trackless region, among them one near the Castelo da Pena de Aguiar, in the granite hills to the south-west, apart from the dolmens of Carrazedo on the slope of the Serra de Alvão, artefacts from which were the subject of academic discussion among archaeologists at the turn of the century. The N206 descends to cross the Tâmega, and at Arco de Baulhe reaches a turning for neighbouring **Cabeceiras de Basto**, with the large Benedictine monastery of **Refóios**, founded in the 12C, but rebuilt in the 18C, with a large cupola and twin towers, and containing two organs. The N206 continues west to bypass **Fafe** (11,584 inhabitants), a growing town on the site of an ancient fortified settlement, from which artefacts and some primitive statuary have been removed to the Museu Martins Sarmento in Guimarães. **Arões**, with the church of São Romão (1237), is entered before meeting the N101 and turning right to approach Guimarães; see Rte 37.

---

The Port wine region is shortly entered as the N2 continues south-west to approach **VILA REAL** (13,809 inhabitants), the largest town of the Trás-os-Montes and the capital of its district. Already at a hub of communications, with the completion of the IP4 between Braganza and Oporto (see Rte 29A), it promises to grow in importance but not in attraction, and is provided with a bypass to the west.

■ The **Tourist Office** is at 94 Av. Carvalho Araújo.

## History

Vila Real was granted royal rights by Afonso III in 1272. Here the reactionary Count of Amarante established the headquarters of an insurrectionary movement in February 1823 prior to the *pronunciamento* at Vila Franca de Xira (cf.). It was the birthplace of Diogo Cão, the first navigator to reach the mouth of the Congo (1482).

From the north end of the wide central avenue, a lane leads east to (right) the Capela Nova, or Clérigos, at the junction of two streets, its curious narrow façade framed by a set of twin columns. Further north is São Pedro (from 1528), the interior of which contains some good Baroque gilt carving. At the south end of the avenue, retaining a few 17–18C mansions, is Gothic São Domingos, a monastic church now raised to the rank of cathedral, but of slight interest.

Some 3km due east, at **Mateus**, stands the Baroque finialed *Solar* built for António José Botelho Mourão in 1739–43, probably by Nicolau Nasoni. It is open 9.00–13.00 and 14.00–17.00. Its theatrical façade has illustrated certain rosé wine labels during recent decades (see p 70). It has been restored and refurbished in recent years. The adjacent chapel has been ascribed to José de Figueiredo Seixas.

The church at neighbouring **Mouçós** contains the well-sculpted tomb of Fernão de Brito (1483).

For the IP4 driving west past Amarante to Oporto, see Rte 29.

The N2 descends steeply from Vila Real, winding down parallel to the Corgo into the deep valley of the Douro, crossed at Peso da Régua: see the latter part of Rte 27A, and also for roads winding west high above both banks.

The far bank is ascended in steep curves—but improvements are promised—to Lamego (see also Rte 27A), a good plunging view of which is commanded by N.S. dos Remédios, overlooking the town from the south. A turning to it is passed (left) as the N2 climbs south onto a high-lying plateau, with the Serra do Montemuro rising to 1381m to the south-west.

It later descends to **Castro Daire**, a small town of ancient origin but of slight interest; but at **Paiva**, 6km west on the north bank of the river Paiva, is a 12C hermitage.

From the south bank of its romantic gorge the N228, turning right, climbs south-west to (25km) São Pedro do Sul (see latter part of Rte 23). The improved N2 leads south through attractive and thickly wooded country before descending to cross the Vouga, just before which, at **Almargem**, near **Calde**, is a well-preserved stretch of Roman road.

The transverse IP5, swinging north of the town, is met 5km before entering Viseu itself; see Rte 23.

For roads on to Busaco, and Coimbra, see Rte 24.

# 32 . Chaves to Braga

*Total distance, 127km (79 miles). N103. 41km Montalegre is 8km north-west—57km Gerês is 15.5km north—13km Póvoa do Lanhoso is 3km south—16km Braga.*

On leaving Chaves (see Rte 31) the N103 crosses onto the right bank of the Tâmega, shortly passing (left) the site of the Roman *castro* at **Curalha**, and traversing the bald Terras do Barroso, the original home of the lyre-horned oxen known as *'barrosã'*, ubiquitous in the Minho.

At **Sapiãos** a byroad leads left via **Boticas**, to pass near the ancient bridges over the Rio Beça, to (11km) the *castro* of **Carvalhelhos**, beyond which, at **Covas de Barrosa**, is a Romanesque church.

On approaching the Barragem do Alto Rabagão, a byroad bears right to **Montalegre**, a small walled hill-top town with a restored 14C castle, standing at 966m below the Serra do Larouco, rising to 1525m.

> Here Wellington spent the night of 18 May 1809, on giving up the pursuit of Soult's army retreating in confusion from Oporto. Wellington's forces were then led south to Abrantes (see Rte 16) to re-group before the commencement of the Talavera campaign.

On regaining the N103, the *castro* of 'dos Mouros' or 'dos Duques' is passed near **São Vicente de Chã** as the road skirts the north bank of the huge reservoir before descending the valley and circling the south side of the Barragem de Venda Nova, to reach the village of that name.

The road improves on entering the Minho, and continues to wind above the south side of the Cávado valley, deep in which lies the ancient Misarela bridge (restored).

At the east end of the Salamonde reservoir is the confluence of the Rabagão and the Cávado. Further west is the many-armed reservoir of Caniçada, while to the north rises the Serra do Gerês.

A right-hand turning descends steeply past (right) the *Pousada de São Bento*, providing extensive mountain views, with the reservoir in the valley below.

At the crossroads on the valley floor, the N308 leads up a narrowing, thickly-forested, side valley to the village of **Gerês**, a small spa. Since 1970 the whole district to the north of the Cávado, abutting the Spanish frontier, and including Castro Laboreiro (see Rte 34B), an area of c 70,000 hectares, has been a nature reserve (or Parque Nacional da Peneda-Gerês). The track beyond Gerês continues to and beyond the frontier (for Bande, Celanova and Ourense), here the Portela do Homem, to which a Roman road, retaining an unexplained concentration of milliary columns, ascends from the south-west, above the south bank of the Barragem de Vilarinho. For the roads descending west from this crossroads down the Cávado valley and the parallel Homem valley from Covide (9km to the north-east), see sub-routes off Rte 34B, in reverse.

The N103 continues south-west to the turning for **Póvoa do Lanhoso**, passing (left) the well-preserved remains of a largely dismantled 12C castle and, to the south-east, the Romanesque church of a Benedictine monastery founded in 1067 at **Font' Arcada**.

This village probably supplied the title for the reactionary insurrection against the government of Costa Cabral in April 1846. This began with a conflict between village women (personified by 'Maria da Fonte') and the local civic authorities over the (insanitary) right to be buried *in* churches rather than in consecrated ground away from villages.

At **Taíde**, some 7km south-east, to the right off the N205 for **Arosa**, and on the north bank of the Ave, is the sanctuary of N.S. do Porto de Ave (1736), containing twin organs, painted ceilings, and an octagonal chancel. Above it rises a series of garden terraces and chapels in the style of Bom Jesus at Braga. The N310 descends the Ave valley from Póvoa. At 9.5km a right-hand turning leads up to the Citânia de Briteiros: see last part of Rte 36. At Caldelas das Taipas the N101 is met between Braga and Guimarães: see Rte 35A.

The N103, continuing west from the Póvoa do Lanhoso turning, winds along a ridge above the Cávado, later passing (left) the road ascending to the sanctuary of Bom Jesus, to approach Braga itself: for both see Rte 36.

# 33 · Oporto

The second city of Portugal, known as **Porto** by the Portuguese, but to the English as **Oporto** (*O Porto*, the port), is famous for the export of the wines of the upper Douro, the business of which has been largely in English hands for the last 300 years. The episcopal see is of very ancient origin, but the university dates only from 1911. In 1994 the estimated population of Oporto itself was 302,467, and that of transpontine Vila Nova de Gaia was 68,302, but the conurbation of which Oporto is the hub contains in the region of one million.

Like Lisbon, it is favoured by a magnificent site, rising on the steep north bank of the rock-bound gorge of the Douro near the river mouth; but likewise much of it is very hilly: indeed 'Arthur Costigan' remarked some 200 years ago that 'To walk about this city is, I assure you, rather a violent exercise, not one street in it being on a level excepting that where the most part of the English inhabit'. The sprawling city is ill planned; nor does it contain very many buildings of great architectural importance; nevertheless it is a thriving place, full of vitality and character.

Part of the population still lives in squalid '*ilhas*'—badly ventilated alleys leading off the main streets, particularly between the cathedral and the riverside; and yet, earlier this century it was stated that 'great progress has recently been made in the cleanliness of the place'.

The Douro, unlike the Tagus, has no wide estuary, its narrow mouth being partially blocked by a sand bar, and in the past Oporto was liable to sudden destructive floods in winter, the water rising some 4.5m above its normal level. In 1909 it rose to within 10cm of the lower level of the Ponte de Dom Luís, causing immense damage in the inundated lodges.

On the south bank is **Vila Nova de Gaia**, where most of these *armazéns* or lodges of the wine-shippers are to be found (see Rte 33D, and the Introduction to Port and the Wines of Portugal).

Pleasant central accommodation at a reasonable price is not too easy to find, a situation it is hoped will be improved; but see below. Most of the monuments of interest are within walking distance of the city centre, once this has been reached, approached through a confusing maze of one-way streets. Regrettably, at the time of writing, many of the museums are partly or entirely closed for an indeterminate period, but it is hoped that new accommodation will be found for that of Ethnography and History, and that the restoration of the Soares dos Reis museum will be completed before too long.

### History, and the English in Oporto

The name *Portucale* appears for the first time in the *Chronicle* of Bishop Hydatius of Chaves (456), and is applied to the site of Miragaia, near the present Custom House. A ferry crossed the Douro from here to Cale, a Roman *castro* said to have been established by Decimus Junius Brutus, and mentioned in the early 3C *Antonine Itinerary* as a strengthened Lusitanian fort on the road from Olisipo (Lisbon) to Bracara Augusta (Braga). To defend this crossing of the Roman Durius, a castle was later erected on the dominating Pena Ventosa (where the Bishop's Palace now stands), and in the 6C a church was built alongside it by the Suevi.

The town which grew up around it, the Burgo do Porto, was razed by the Moors in the 8C, but in 868 it was in the hands of a certain Vimara Peres, who held the line of the Douro, although not definitively recaptured by the Christians until 982. Rebuilt, it became the capital of the county of Portucalia and of the 'Terras de Santa Maria', the newly-won area south of the great river towards Vila da Feira. Count Henry of Burgundy is said to have founded a cathedral, and his descendants granted many privileges, including the decree, which ostensibly remained in force until 1505, that no nobleman 'or powerful person' should own property, or stay for more than three days, within the town walls.

In June 1147 a fleet, which had assembled at Dartmouth, bound for the Second Crusade, landed here, including an expeditionary force of English, whose reputation as 'plunderers, drunkards and rapists, men not seasoned with the honey of Piety' had apparently preceded them. Having patiently listened to the bishop's proposal that they 'move on' to the assistance of Afonso Henriques, intent on the capture of Lisbon, they lurched back to their ships ten days later, no doubt fortified with good wine, to follow up what sounded like a profitable escapade. They took with them as hostages both the bishop (Pedro Pitões) and João Peculiar (Archbishop of Braga; died 1175), as a precautionary measure.

A later bishop (Martinho), who had incensed the populace of O Porto in 1209, remained penned up in his palace for five months. In 1237 the Dominicans established a monastery in the town. Another boundary wall, of which there are slight remains, was later built, being completed c 1376. In 1387 Dom João I and Philippa of Lancaster ('Filippa de Alemcastre'), daughter of John of Gaunt, were married in the cathedral. Their fourth son, Dom Henrique (Henry 'the Navigator'; 1394–1460), was born in the old palace. From this time on the life of Oporto became progressively and inextricably involved with the English, although their interest in the wine now known as 'Port' did not mature for another 300 years.

In 1415, when the fleet of Dom João was preparing for the Ceuta expedition, the people of Oporto considerately sent their best meat, suitably salted, to the ships, reserving the offal for themselves, thus earning the ungrateful nickname of *'tripeiros'* or tripe-eaters; but they retaliated by calling the inhabitants of Lisbon *'alfacinhas'*, lettuce-nibblers.

The Inquisition was only briefly established in Oporto, one *auto-da-fé* taking place in 1543, and it was discontinued four years later. But in 1618 many of its 'New Christians' were arrested. In 1628, in the 'Revolta das Maçarocas' (the spindles), the women of Oporto attacked the minister responsible for a tax on linen and woollen goods; in 1661 there was another anti-tax riot. They were an obstreperous lot.

Although in 1668 Robert Southwell, in Lisbon, was promising to send some 'white Oporto wine' to Lord Arlington in London after the vintage, it is unlikely to have been what is now known as 'Port'. The first British merchants in Oporto were not then engaged in the wine trade, the centre of which was at Viana do Castelo (cf.), and it was not until about a decade later that wines were being exported from here by the two sons of a Liverpool (or Yorkshire) wine merchant, being sent down the Douro from Lamego. Peter Bearsley (son of Job Bearsley of Viana) was one of the first shippers to move to Oporto, and he was visited there by Thomas Woodmass of Kettering in 1704, by which time the small English and Scottish community was well established under their consul, John Lee. Hunt, Roope and Company had had premises at both ports for some 50 years, shipping dried cod and oil from Newfoundland, and wheat and wool from England; and in exchange exporting wine, cork and fruit, etc.; but this bartering of cod and cloth for wine had been going on since the 15C or earlier.

Woodmass, who lodged with Mr Page in the Rua Nova, noted that the shippers kept very much to themselves, even employing English-speaking negro servants, some from Carolina, so that they didn't have to converse in Portuguese with their cooks. They were even said to compel the peasants to sacrifice the honour of their daughters if they wanted to sell their wine, for 'they...only bought from growers who allowed their daughters to dance with them', which Trend suggests was merely making political capital out of old-time vintage customs. In 1757 the 'Tipplers' Riot' was put down by Pombal with some ferocity. He claimed it had been instigated by the English, who opposed his wine monopoly.

Luckily, the Lisbon earthquake of 1755 did not physically affect Oporto. Building had gone on rapidly. Nicolau Nasoni, an Italian, did much to embellish the city during the years 1730 to 1763, when the bell-tower of the Clérigos was completed, and he died in Oporto (where he had married a local girl) in 1773. In 1770 work started on the new Hospital de Santo António. According to Alexander Jardine (1779), the author of *Letters from Barbary*, Oporto had been 'much improved and beautified' by João de Almada e Melo, the governor from 1765, 'with the assistance and advice of our good consul' (Whitehead).

In June 1808, Lisbon having been occupied by the French, Oporto defiantly proclaimed the Prince Regent; a provisional junta under its bellicose bishop was set up; and the Loyal Lusitanian Legion was raised there by Sir Robert Wilson. But in March 1809 Oporto was unable to resist Soult's assault, and many citizens were killed or drowned as they sought to escape across the bridge-of-boats which was then tethered to both banks. Within two months, however, Wellington's brilliant 'Passage of the Douro', took place, and they were relieved.

The French, warned to expect a seaward attack, and with no bridge, isolated themselves on the north bank, on which they secured all vessels, including barges. Their complete surprise was effected by Wellington, at first using one small skiff, which had slipped over to the south bank under cover of darkness, to ferry across a landing party. This, invisible to Soult's sentries, installed itself in the buildings of an unfinished seminary surrounded by a walled enclosure running down to the water's edge. Meanwhile, another force crossed the river further south-east, at Avintes. Several barges were then unobtrusively collected from the north shore, and further troops ferried across. A fortified foothold having been gained, there was little Soult could do in a hostile town to stem the tide, for the area to the west of the seminary was now raked by artillery fire from Wellington's commanding position near N.S. da Serra do Pilar. With increasing numbers pouring across on more craft ferried over by high-spirited civilians, and with their flank turned to the east, the French precipitately retreated, Soult himself hospitably leaving his dinner in the Palácio dos Carrancas to be consumed by Wellington and his staff before setting out in pursuit. Sir Nicholas Trant was later the military governor.

A revolt of radicals broke out in Oporto in 1820. In 1832–33, during the Miguelite War, the city was again besieged. On 9 July 1832 Dom Pedro, having sailed from the Azores, landed with some 7500 men at the mouth of the Mindelo, just north of the city, in the face of which its besieging force of some 13,000 Miguelites briefly retired. These 'Voluntários da Rainha' were welcomed with relief by the citizens, who had suffered three years of Miguelite oppression, their stubborn defence against the usurper's attacks in late September and October being stiffened by a motley 'international brigade'. This had consisted largely of out-of-work Glaswegian and Cockney contingents under the command of Charles Shaw, plus a sprinkling of Peninsular War veterans. After ten months the opposing forces had increased to 17,800 Liberals, closely invested by 24,000 Miguelites. Captain Nugent Glascock RN, with a small flotilla, patrolled the river-mouth, keeping a weather eye on British interests, while Colonel Lovell Badcock remained in Oporto as the British Government observer.

Cholera raged. Although a soup kitchen was set up by the British merchants, cats and dogs (including Colonel Shaw's pets) soon became the common ingredient of stews. The Miguelites continued to bombard the city in a desultory way, causing some damage and even hitting the British Factory house. The wine lodges stood in Miguelite territory. In June 1833 Captain George Rose Sartorius was replaced by Sir Charles Napier as Pedro's naval commander, who shortly after captured Miguel's 'fleet' at Cape St Vincent. Eventually the Miguelites retreated, but not before they had blown up and set fire to the stores of the Old Wine Company at Vila Nova de Gaia. Gallant Captain Glascock, with a party of marines, stopped the fire from spreading to other lodges, but some 27,000 pipes of wine ran into the river, turning it a muddy red.

Among those defending the lodges was young Joseph James Forrester (1809–61), later famous for his survey of the Douro within Portugal; but see below. He was also a fine amateur artist and, together with his contemporary Frederick William Flower (1815–89; resident in Oporto from 1834), a pioneer in photography.

Oporto was a stronghold of liberalism throughout the century, being the scene of opposition to reactionary regimes in 1846, 1851, 1890 and 1891, while in 1878 the first Portuguese Republican deputy was elected there. Its commerce and industry flourished, and its population continued to grow. In 1864 it was 86,750; in 1960, 303,400.

Among those born here, apart from Henry the Navigator (see above), were Pedro de Escobar (c 1465–c 1535), composer; Francisco Vieira ('Portuense';

1765–1805), artist; Almeida Garrett (1799–1854), poet, novelist and liberal statesman; 'Julio Dinis' (Joaquim Guilherme Gomes Coelho: 1839–71), novelist and author of *Uma Familia Inglesa* (1868), analysing Anglo-Portuguese relationships: a more anglophobe description was *Epístola a John Bull* (1887), by Ramalho Ortigão (1836–1915), also from Oporto. Antonio Teixeira Lopes (1866–1942), the sculptor, was born at Vila Nova de Gaia. Cpt. Edward Quillinan (1791–1851), the poet husband of Wordsworth's daughter, was at one time Commandant at Oporto.

- **Useful addresses**: British Consulate, Av. da Boavista 3072; British Institute, and Associação Luso-Britânica do Porto, Rua do Breiner 155; English Church (St James's), Campo Pequeno; Câmara de Comércio Luso-Britanica, Rua Sá da Bandeira 784; Oporto Cricket & Lawn Tennis Club, Rua Campo Alegre 532.

For details of the various cruises on the Douro, lasting from three hours to two days, apply to the **Tourist Office** at 25 Rua do Clube Fenianos, immediately west of the town hall, at the upper end of the Av. de Aliados; or at 43 Praça Dom João I.

- The Pedras Rubras international **airport** is north of the city. **Public transport** to Oporto is plentiful: there are trains and buses to and from all major centres. **Taxis** are inexpensive once there.

- Among the many **HOTELS** of Oporto, listed in descending order of expense, are the following:

**Near the centre:**
*Infante de Sagres*, Praça Dona Filpa de Lencastre 62 (also restaurant) (tel. 201 90 31, fax 31 49 37)
*Ipanema Park*, Rua Serralves 124 (tel. 610 41 74, fax 610 28 09)
*Batalha*, Praça da Batalha 116 (provides good view; also O Burgo restaurant) (tel. 200 05 71, fax 200 24 68)
*Pensão o Escondidinho*, Rua de Passos Manuel 135 (also restaurant at No. 144) (tel. 200 40 79)
*Castor*, Rua das Doze Casas 17 ( north-east of centre) (tel. 57 00 14, fax 56 60 76)
*Dom Henrique*, Rua Guedes de Azevedo 179 (north-east of centre; also Navegador restaurant) (tel. 200 57 55, fax 201 94 51)
*São João*, Rua do Bonjardim 120 (tel. 200 16 62, fax 31 61 14)
*Malaposta*, Rua da Conceição 80 (tel. 200 62 78, fax 200 62 95)
*Peninsular*, Rua Sá da Bandeira (old-fashioned; opposite São Bento station)
*Albergaria São Jose*, Rua da Alegria 172 (north-east of centre) (tel. 208 02 61, fax 32 04 46)

**At Foz**, *Boavista*, Esplanada do Castelo 58 (also restaurant) (tel. 618 31 75, fax 617 38 18)

And among **RESTAURANTS** (but also see above), in the centre:
*O Tripeiro*, Rua Passos Manuel 195
*Cunha*, Rua Sá da Bandeira 662
*Aquário Marisqueiro*, Rua Rodrigues Sampaio 179
*Abadia*, Rua Ateneu Comercial do Porto 22
*Brasileira*, Rua do Bonjardim 118, near São Bento station
*Café Magestic*, Rua de Santa Catarina 112
*Café Na Praça*, Praça de Lisboa
*Mesa Antiga*, Rua de Santo Ildefonso 208

**Among riverside restaurants:**
*Casa Vitorino*, Rua dos Canastreiros 44
*Chez Lapin*, Rua dos Canastreiros 40
*Dom Tonho*, Cais da Ribeira 13
*Mercearia*, Cais da Ribeira 32
*Taverna do Bebobos*, Cais da Ribeira 25
Opposite, at **Vila Nova de Gaia**:
*Maré Alta* (on a boat)
*Três Séculos*, Rua do Choupelo 250

**Away from the centre:**
*Portucale*, Rua de Alegria 598 (north-east of centre)
*Gambamar*, Rua do Campo Alegre 110
*Degrauchá*, Rua Afonso Lopes Vieira 180

**At Foz:**
*A Capoeira*, Esplanada do Castelo 63
*Foz Club*, Av. De Montevideu 866
*Panorâmica* (Hotel da Boa Vista), Esplanada do Castelo 58
*Portofino*, Rua da Padrão 103

**At Leça da Palmeira:**
*Casa de chá Boa Nova*
*A Cozinha da Maria*, Rua Fresca 187
*O Garrafão*, Rua de António Nobre 53

# A. Central Oporto

One of the main hubs of activity is the Praça da Liberdade (Pl.7), embellished by an equestrian statue of Dom Pedro IV (1866), which is a short distance north-west of the São Bento railway station. From here, the gardens of the Avenida dos Aliados slope uphill to the Town Hall (begun 1929), with its tall belfry. Immediately to its west is the tourist office and, behind it, the large 18C Igreja da Trinidade.

From the south-west corner of the Praça da Liberdade, the Rua dos Clérigos ascends steeply towards the church and Torre dos Clérigos (see Rte 33B), one of the more conspicuous landmarks of the city.

By descending to the left almost immediately, turn right on reaching the Rua das Flores, partly flanked by silversmiths. Towards its far end (right) stands the church of the **Misericórdia** (1559; but largely rebuilt in 1749–54 by Manuel Alvares Martins and Nicolau Nasoni).

At No. 15, adjacent, is the entrance to the Misericórdia offices, where one should apply to visit the council-chamber, containing one of the finest paintings in Portugal, the *Fountain of Mercy* (1520), by an anonymous Fleming of the School of Van Eyck. Beneath the central subject of Christ crucified between the Virgin and St John, are the kneeling figures of Dom Manuel, founder of the Misericórdia, and Dona Maria, with their family and a group of nobles and ecclesiastics. The ceiling is also notable, and a collection of silver may be on display.

On reaching the adjacent Largo de São Domingos, follow the ancient Rua de Belomonte (note No. 49) to the right to approach the **Palácio de São João Novo** (Pl.9), with its curiously shaped granite-framed mezzanine windows, built by Nicolau Nasoni in 1723–33 for Pedro da Costa Lima, a wealthy magistrate.

It had long accommodated the **\*Museum of Ethnography and History**, but at the time of writing no decision had been reached as to its new home. Among collections are those of Palaeolithic and Bronze Age implements; ceramics, including amphorae from Póvoa do Varzim; glass and amber objects from Monte Mozinho; and a gold diadem and ring from Beiral, Ponte de Lima; part of a statue of a warrior from Monte Mozinho, Oldrões (south of Penafiel), of the Castreja culture; stelae, sun-dials, etc.; ship models, including those of the various types of vessels peculiar to the Douro, formerly used to transport wine from its upper reaches to Oporto, among them the *barcos rabelos*; the *catraias*, single-sailed passenger-boats, sharp at both ends; the *barcos de toldo*, like clumsy gondolas; flat-bottomed *caíques*, for ferrying the Douro; also high-prowed *moliceiros* from Aveiro, and the three-masted *rasgas* from the south of Portugal. Among other collections are those of costumes; silver filigree work from Gondomar; naïve paintings; ceramics from Vila Nova and Massarelos; pharmacy vases; *presépios* (Christmas cribs); ox-yokes; arms; locks; fishing equipment; furniture and domestic utensils; and plans and prints of Oporto.

On the opposite side of the *praça* stands São João Novo, started in 1552 and completed a century later. Note the organ-case. The adjacent cloisters now accommodate law-courts.

From the south-west corner of the square a lane descends steeply to 18C **São Pedro de Miragaia** (ask opposite for key), with an elaborately carved and gilded chancel, and with a small 'museum' containing a 16C Flemish triptych.

By turning downhill from São João Novo to the east, and bearing right and then left, the north entrance of the glass-domed court of the **Bolsa** or Stock Exchange is reached. Built in 1834–42 on the site of dependencies of the former Franciscan convent, it contains a particularly hideous ball-room in a pseudo-Moorish style which cost a great deal to construct, and of which the commercial hierachy has therefore always been inordinately proud.

Uphill to the left, opposite a restored covered market, are offices of the **Port Wine Institute** (Instituto do Vinho do Porto), containing a portrait of Joseph James Forrester (born Hull, 1809–1861), whose influence on the production of Port—for he was a passionate advocate of the 'pure wine' school—has become legendary. Forrester was drowned near the Cachão da Valeira, on the upper Douro; see Rte 27B. This Intitute sets out to supervise and regulate the Port wine trade, instituting quality control, and issuing Certificates of Origin, etc.; cf. Peso da Régua.

Turning downhill beside the gardens of the Praça do Infante Dom Henrique, steps are reached (right) ascending to **\*São Francisco** (Open 9.00–17.00, closed Sun and holidays). This is a late 14C building with a good west window. In the mid 18C its interior was elaborately festooned with gilded carving in late Baroque and Rococo styles, including the ceiling. On the south side is the altar of the Martyrs of Morocco; to the north, a richly carved Tree of Jesse. Also noteworthy are the 18C organ and the Renaissance tomb of Fernão Brandão Pereira (1528).

Above the riverbank here is the Rua Nova da Alfândega, some distance along which stands the Customs House. To the left is a medieval tower-house.

Following the broad Rua do Infante Dom Henrique, formerly the Rua dos Inglezes (and previously Rua Nova de São Nicolau), to the east, with its shipping offices and warehouses, etc., the Rua da Alfândega Velha is passed, in which stands the heavily restored and rebuilt **House of Prince Henry the Navigator**, a former royal palace said, traditionally, to be the site of his birthplace on 4 March 1394. It formerly accommodated the Customs House, and now the city archives, and is the occasional venue of temporary exhibitions.

A well-restored 18C *bacalhau* warehouse at 37 Rua da Reboleira, in a lane leading west from the adjacent square, is now a Centre of Traditional Arts and Crafts of northern Portugal.

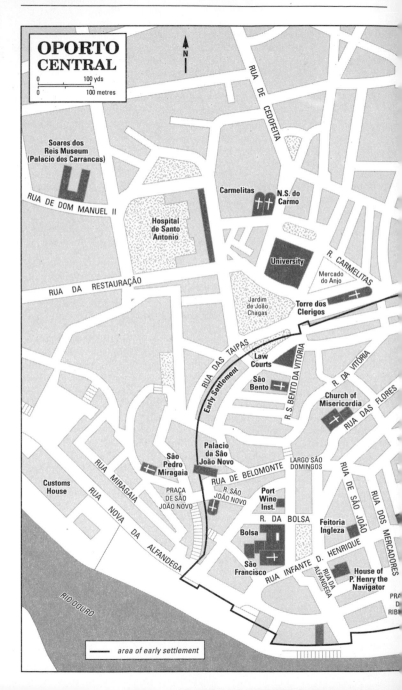

**OPORTO CENTRAL**

0        100 yds
0        100 metres

N

Soares dos Reis Museum (Palacio dos Carrancas)

RUA DE DOM MANUEL II

Hospital de Santo Antonio

RUA DE CEDOFEITA

Carmelitas

N.S. do Carmo

University

R. CARMELITAS

Mercado do Anjo

RUA DA RESTAURAÇÃO

Jardim de João Chagas

Torre dos Clerigos

RUA DAS TAIPAS

Early Settlement

Law Courts

Sâo Bento

R.S. BENTO DA VITORIA

R. DA VITORIA

Church of Misericordia

R. DA VITORIA

RUA DAS FLORES

RUA MIRAGAIA

Sâo Pedro Miragaia

Palacio da Sâo João Novo

RUA DE BELOMONTE

LARGO SÃO DOMINGOS

RUA DE SÃO JOÃO

RUA DOS MERCADORES

Customs House

RUA NOVA DA ALFANDEGA

PRAÇA DE SÃO JOÃO NOVO

R. SÃO JOÃO NOVO

Port Wine Inst.

R. DA BOLSA

Bolsa

Feitoria Ingleza

Sâo Francisco

RUA INFANTE D. HENRIQUE

RUA DA ALFANDEGA

House of P. Henry the Navigator

PRA D RIB

RIO DOURO

—— area of early settlement

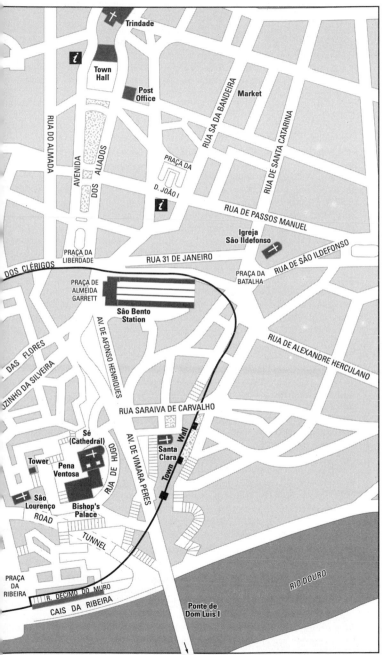

At the far end of the old Rua dos Inglezes stands the imposing granite façade of the *Feitoria Inglesa, or **Factory House** of the British Association, in 1787–90 erected on the site of previous buildings belonging to the association, which had been in existence since 1727 at least. Its architect was John Whitehead, the bibliophile Consul at Oporto from 1756 to 1802, possibly advised by John Carr.

Permission to visit the interior of the building, which is normally closed to the public, may be courteously granted by a member of the association of the British Port Wine Shippers, to whom interested parties may apply.

It was not *officially* opened until 11 November 1811. Most of the shippers had sailed for home with their valuables during the first few months of the Peninsular War, leaving Joseph Camo, an American citizen who remained in the town during Soult's brief occupation, to act as caretaker, and its confiscation was thus avoided. But it was requisitioned as a coffee-house and hostelry.

Major William Dalrymple, from the garrison at Gibraltar, who passed through Oporto in 1774 on his tour of the Peninsula, 'feasted most voluptuously with the consul and factory [presumably in the earlier building] who were remarkably civil and attentive; the only thing that I disliked amongst them'—he added—'was their supercilious treatment of the Portuguese, from whom they derive their wealth and opulence'. The consul would have been John Whitehead, who with his passion for the sciences and astronomy had erected a lightning conductor on his residence, which had caused consternation among the locals and even occasioned a visit from commissaries of the Inquisition. The Factory House still preserves his two globes. Whitehead's successor was referred to by H.F. Link, visiting Oporto a few years later, who commented that among the English merchants were several who possessed 'both knowledge and the love of science, particularly a gentleman named Warre'.

Consuls continued to be granted offices in the new building until c 1835. When not working, the British were playing, even indulging in a game called cricket on a field near the Palácio dos Carrancas, which quite bewildered the curious spectators.

Membership of the association has always been rigidly confined to firms which have been connected with the Port wine trade since the 18C, and the member firms (with the date of foundation of their original establishment in brackets) are: Warre (1670); Croft (1678); Taylor, Fladgate & Yeatman (1692); Offley Forrester (1729); Sandeman (1790); Martinez Gassiot (1790); W. & J. Graham (1814); Cockburn Smithes (1815); Guimaraens (1822); Silva & Cosens (1862); Delaforce Sons (1868); and Robertson Brothers.

Among these have been amalgamated a number of old firms, such as Quarles Harris (1680); Morgan Brothers (1715); Butler & Nephew (1730); Hunt Roope (1735); Smith Woodhouse (1784); Dow; Fonseca; and Gonzalez Byass. See also the Introduction to Port and the Wines of Portugal.

The loggia, some 24m long, contains seven openings, and leads to an entrance hall, from which a newel staircase ascends to the main assembly rooms, consisting of dining and dessert rooms, drawing-room, and ballroom. Also of interest are the old kitchen, and library (sadly diminished a decade ago, when some 2300 volumes, many of them rare three-decker novels, were sold via a London dealer to an American university), the collection of china, and much of the furniture.

Among portraits of Factory worthies are those of John Page (born in Oporto in 1699, whose father had also been in the wine trade), attributed to Richard Wilson;

of General Sir William Warre (1784–1853); Sir Robert Newman (1776–1848); George Glas Sandeman (1793–1868); Sir John Croft (1778–1862); and John Whitehead (1726–1802), together with others associated with the Port wine trade and the factory in previous centuries. Also to be seen is a painting by Francisco Vieira (Portuense) of Queen Eleanor sucking the poison from a wound inflicted on Edward I during the Crusades, being a variation on Angelica Kauffmann's study of the same theme.

From here one may descend the Rua de São João to the **Praça da Ribeira**, formerly the centre of the waterside traffic of Oporto, and still often providing an animated scene. Much of the area is being tastefully restored, not before time. The Cais da Ribeira (left) is flanked by an arcaded walk, housing shops and restaurants, built into the old town wall, above which runs the Rua Cima do Muro. It was from this quay that the old bridge-of-boats crossed to the far bank (see History).

It is now dominated by the **Ponte de Dom Luís I**, a two-storeyed bridge designed by Teófilo Seyrig, thrown across the chasm of the Douro in 1886. Its vertiginous upper span is some 172m long, and 60m above low water level.

The lower level is approached by traffic from a tunnel, the entrance to which is passed (right) on re-ascending the Rua de São João or Rua dos Mercadores. The former leads into the wide Rua Mouzinho da Silva, which bears north-east back towards the central station: the latter shortly enters a warren of steep and noisome alleys, of which the narrow Rua da Bainharia ascends to steps below the cathedral: see below.

A turning to the right off this latter alley leads to the Jesuit church of **São Lourenço**, better known as **Dos Grilos**, dating from 1577, and one of the earliest of its style in Portugal, attributed to Baltazar Alvares (who later built the new cathedral at Coimbra). Another flight of steps climbs past a 14C tower, above which stands the Sé.

Of the granite **\*Cathedral**, founded in the 12C by Count Henry and Dona Teresa, parents of Afonso Henriques, little remains except the foundations on which the church, with its high barrel-roof, was reconstructed in the late 13C, and in which Dom João I and Philippa of Lancaster were married in 1387. This was drastically and ineptly 'modernised' in the 18C by, among others, Nicolau Nasoni, who added the porch beside the north door in 1736. He also designed the grand staircase off the main cloister, and in part, the silver altarpiece (see below). The west rose-window (13C) and the west front generally, with its twin buttressed towers capped by cupolas, is typical of the medieval church architecture of northern Portugal.

The cathedral is open from 9.00–12.00 and 14.00–17.30. In the **north transept** is the silver altarpiece, largely composed by nine different silversmiths between 1632–83, but only completed after Nasoni's design in the 1750s. It is said to have been hidden behind a plaster wall in 1809 to protect it from Soult. It is likely that Nasoni was responsible also for the design of the railings and gates of the chancel arch. On either side of the Baroque altar, with its spiral columns of 1610, by Gonçalo de Morais, are the organs of 1727, the design of their cases also attributed to Nasoni.

In the **south transept** is the statue of the Virgin said to have been brought from France by the Bishop of Vendôme, when accompanying the Gascon fleet in 982, but probably of later date. Adjacent is the main cloister, of the French Cistercian type (1385), decorated with 18C *azulejos*. Off its south-east corner are the remains of the Romanesque cloister.

*Oporto Cathedral. Reconstructed in the late thirteenth century, it was 'modernised' in the eighteenth century.*

Immediately south-west of the cathedral, on the rock outcrop known as the Pena Ventosa, stands the former **Bishop's Palace**, with a façade 58m in length, designed by Nasoni before 1734, but which took more than a century to complete, before its temporary conversion into the town hall. It contains a fine granite staircase.

The esplanade provides a good view across the Douro to the *armazéns* of Vila Nova de Gaia, dominated to the east by N.S. de Serra do Pilar; see Rte 33D.

In a lane behind the cathedral apse is a house of 1730–46, attributed to Nasoni, containing a museum devoted to the poet Guerra Junqueiro (1850–1923), with collections of furniture, ceramics and silver, etc.

From the north side of the cathedral a few paces brings one to the Av. de Vimara Peres, leading south to the upper level of the Ponte de Dom Luís I (see above). Downhill to the north, skirting (left) a somewhat scruffy area, the railway station is approached, passing which and turning left the Praça da Liberdade is regained; for the area to the east of the avenue, see below.

## B.  Eastern Oporto

The Av. Dom Afonso Henriques leads south from the Praça da Liberdade towards the Ponte de Dom Luís I (see above) off which the Rua Saraiva de Carvalho turns left to reach, at the lower end of a small square, the convent church of **Santa Clara**, founded in 1416, but rebuilt in the 17–18Cs. It contains a wealth of carved and gilt woodwork of c 1730, by Miguel Francisco da Silva, but its cleaning is overdue.

Immediately to the east, approached from the next right-hand turning, is the best-preserved section of Dom Afonso IV's **town walls**, usually known as the 'muralha fernandina', of which several towers survive.

Bearing north-east, the ugly Praça da Batalha is entered, from which the Rua de Santa Catarina, one of the principal shopping streets, continues north. The Rua de São Ildefonso, passing the 18C church of that name, leads north-east towards gardens, flanked to the east by the monastic dependencies of São António (1783), housing the Municipal Library (with some rare illuminated manuscripts and incunabula); its cloister is lined with 16–17C azulejos. To the south, the gardens are overlooked by the façade of the orphanage and church of N.S. da Esperança (1724–31), by António Pereira, to which Nasoni added a portal in 1746–63.

Besides this, the Rua das Fontainhas descends towards the Alameda das Fontainhas, with a good view of the Ponte de Dom Luís I, and of the railway bridge of Dona Maria Pia (1876–77)—similar but without a lower level—which was Eiffel's first important construction. Beyond it, the gorge is spanned by the recently completed Ponte de São João, another railway bridge, and the Ponte do Freixo, a viaduct under construction, which will join a branch of the A1 with the A4 and A3, leading east and north-east from Oporto.

Close to Eiffel's bridge, but at a lower level, stands the seminary which played such an important part in Wellington's capture of the town in 1809; see History.

Some distance beyond, but now in a sorry state, is the relic of Nasoni's Casa do Freixo (1754), built for Jerónimo de Távora e Noronha, and sold by that family to the first Baron Freixo in 1850, who degraded it.

One may return towards the Praça da Batalha from the alameda by ascending the Rua de Alexandre Herculano.

From opposite the Igreja São Ildefonso, the Rua 31 de Janeiro descends to regain the Praça da Liberdade, with a good view of the tower of the Clérigos (see below), while from a short distance further north the Rua de Passos Manuel descends past the Praça de Dom João I, at the south-west corner of which is another tourist office (Pl.7), to reach the Av. dos Aliados.

# C. Western Oporto

The steep Rua dos Clérigos climbs from the south-west corner of the Praça da Liberdade towards the recently cleaned *Torre dos Clérigos (Pl.6; 75m high), which, together with the adjoining church, was designed by Nicolau Nasoni. The **church**, reached by a series of steps embellished with stone vases, and facing east, was the first part to be completed, in c 1750. It is an unusual oval-shaped, high-domed structure, to which a clergy house was added in 1754, linking it with the belfry, completed in 1763—described at the turn of the century by Crum Watson, the historian of Portuguese architecture, as 'vicious...not unpicturesque'. Those wishing to make the ascent (240 steps) should apply at the north entrance.

Immediately to the north of the Clérigos is the Mercado do Anjo, beyond which is the main building of the **university** founded in 1911, previously that of the Academia Politécnica. Facing it is the Jardim de João Chagas, flanked to the south by the imposing façade, with its trophies, of the former Cadeia da Relação (Law Courts) and prison, of 1766–96, by João de Almada e Melo.

In the neighbouring Rua São Bento da Vitoria stands **São Bento**, by Diogo Marques, erected between 1597 and 1646 on a site said to have been that of a synagogue. Remarkable are the high altar of c 1704, and its organs.

Beyond the north-west corner of the university are the twin churches of **N.S. do Carmo** (or Terceiras do Carmo, on the corner, of 1756–68), and the **Carmelitas** (1619–28, but remodelled after 1756 by José de Figueiredo Seixas).

To the west is the long colonnaded façade of the **Hospital de Santo António** (Pl.5), an unfinished edifice started in 1770 after the designs of John Carr of York (1723–1807). Alexander Jardine (visiting the place in 1779) rightly suggested it could not be finished 'in less than an hundred years; and perhaps never'.

Skirting its north side, continue west along the Rua de Dom Manuel II to approach (right; see Pl. 1) the former royal palace 'dos Carrancas' (by José Costa Lima Sampaio; 1795), headquarters of Soult in 1809, which he had to leave so precipitately; see History.

In 1942 the *SOARES DOS REIS MUSEUM was inaugurated here, named after the sculptor (1847–89). Many of the rooms are at present (early 1995) closed for a complete reorganisation of its important collections, which are described as when last visited by the author. It is open 10.00–13.00 and 14.00–17.00; closed Mon and holidays. Admission is free on Sun.

To the right of the entrance is the **ceramic** collection, including examples from the Fabrica do Cavaquinho (Vila Nova de Gaia); Bandeira; Fervença ware; from the Rato factory, Lisbon; and others from Coimbra, Viana, Estremoz, and Massarelos.

To the left are collections of **sculpture** and **painting**, including, among the former, an early Crucifixion. Among Portuguese primitives: St Helen and the discovery of the True Cross (anonymous early 16C), and other scenes from her life; *Frei Carlos*, a small Virgin and Child, and St Jerome with his lion; *Cristóvão de Figueiredo*, The Trinity; *Gaspar Vaz*, Annunciation; *Vasco Fernandes* (Grão Vasco), St Catherine, St Lucy, etc.

Stairs ascend past a landing, with views of the market of the Praça de Figueiroa, by *Delarive*, to the first floor, and a large room containing costumes and accessories. Among paintings are views of Oporto, by *Jean Pillement* (1727–1808); *Giuseppe Troni* (1739–1810), Portrait of Carlota Joaquina, and a Self-portrait; *Sequeira*, Junot 'protecting' the city of Lisbon, and other sketches; *J.G. Ströberle* (1708–92), Portrait of José Moreira da Cruz.

Rooms to the right concentrate on costumes of the Romantic period; and display further paintings by Pillement; and small anonymous paintings, among them a charming Holy Family; *Josefa de Óbidos*, Mystic marriage of St Catherine; an anonymous Calvary (? German); and two anonymous Adorations; *J.A. Backer* (died 1651), Male portrait; Portrait of Martin Rychaist, attributed to *Van Dyck*; *Vieira Portuense*, Landscape, Flight of Marguerite d'Anjou, and a copy of a Seascape (? by *Vernet*); *Domingos Vieira*, Pastoral Scene, and Latona and Metamorphosis; also furniture, including an ivory *contador* or box-of-drawers.

The **smoking room** is decorated by Pillement, contains more of his paintings, and a remarkable collection of *silver, including a 15C German silver-gilt chalice; a 16C Crucifix from Goa, and a filigree box; 18C silver from Oporto, among them two monstrances; anonymous French Portrait of a woman wearing a veil (18C); 26 Limoges enamels of the Life of Christ (late 16C); a watch, and a silver Triptych from Nuremberg (16C); tortoiseshell and silver boxes, and two jugs, from Goa; a coral, filigree, and gold pyx; an agate, jade, and gold Cross; the Reliquary of St Stephen; and other fine examples of English and Portuguese silverwork.

The **dining room** displays further collections of glass and ceramics, including Vista Alegre ware; Portuguese painted glass; and French opaline ware; also a Portrait of a naval officer, by Ströberle. Among the porcelain is a Bishop's service in green and gold; enamelled copper (Chinese; 16C); chinoiserie desk (English), surmounted by a figure on a frog (Japanese); collections of Worcester, Crown Derby, and Vista Alegre ware; a Japanese screen (17C); chest of drawers from Portuguese India, and further rare examples of Oriental porcelain.

Notable among 19C paintings are a Portrait of António Soares dos Reis by the Marquês de Oliveira, a Self-portrait by Henrique Pousão (1859–84), and a portrait by Aurelio de Sousa (1865–1922). Several of the miniatures painted on snuffboxes are of fine quality. The museum also contains Clouet's portraits of Marguerite de Valois and of Henri II.

Continue west to skirt the Jardim do Palácio de Cristal, named after a structure of 1865 replaced in 1952 by a domed sports pavilion.

Just beyond the gardens, turn left down the cobbled Rua de Entre-Quintas, in which No. 220 is the *Quinta da Macieirinha*, where Charles Albert, the abdicated king of Sardinia, died on 28 July 1849, four months after his defeat by Radetzky's Austrians at the battle of Novara (west of Milan). It houses an atmospheric **Romantic Museum**, containing furniture and decoration of the period, portraits of Admiral Sir Charles Napier and J.J. Forrester, and views of Oporto, etc. Opening hours are Tues–Sat 10.00–12.30 and 14.00–17.00, Sun 14.00–17.30; closed Mon and holidays.

At No. 219 are collections of archaeology, and numismatics; while close by is the *Solar do Vinho do Porto*, where Port wines may be sampled at leisure. It is open Mon–Fri 11.00–23.00, Sat 17.00–23.30; closed Sun and holidays.

The 'English' gardens of the adjacent Quinta do Meio, laid out after 1881 by Alfred William Tait (1847–1917), containing a huge tulip-tree and fine specimens of magnolia, japonica, wistaria, etc., may be visited by prior appointment.

The Rua da Boa Nova, at the corner of which is an old tower-house, leads north-east from the Jardim do Palácio de Cristal, shortly passing (left) the **Cemitério Inglês** (English Cemetery).

The first chaplain to the English community in Oporto, from 1671, was a Mr Brawler or Brawlard. A decade later, in 1682, the Rev. Samuel Burton was told that he must leave the country, as only one chaplain was allowed—at the Lisbon embassy. It was thought that this decision had originated with the Inquisition and four or five merchants who had turned Catholic (including Pickering and Wrothsly of Houblon's London-based firm), abetted by the Jesuits of the English Seminary in Lisbon. In 1685–87 Edward Hinde was chaplain, whose letters to the Bishop of Ely outlined some of the difficulties then faced by Protestants in Portugal.

However, by 1785 the situation had changed. In that year Consul Whitehead acquired a suitable site for a Protestant cemetery, inaugurated in 1787, in which he was buried in 1802; and a chapel was allowed to be erected in 1817–18 on condition that it had no external ecclesiastical appearance. Indeed it is of similar dimensions to the ballroom of the Factory House, in which church services may have well been held during the previous decade. The chapel, dedicated to St James, was not in fact consecrated until 1843, by the Bishop of Gibraltar. On this occasion the ladies of the community were for the first time condescendingly invited to dine at the Factory House.

According to Southey, writing in 1797, until ten years before that date the English clergyman at Oporto never officiated at a funeral, such were the prejudices of the natives. The body was carried about a mile along the Douro, and buried in a common grave on its banks without any monument.

Near the monument to Consul Whitehead are the graves of four members of the RAF and two of the Royal Canadian Air Force whose planes had crashed in Portugal during the Second World War.

From here, the Rua Maternidade, extended by the Rua da Boa Hora, leads north, where, approached by the dull Rua de Aníbal Cunha, stands the 12C church of **São Martinho da Cedofeita**, much altered and rebuilt, erected on the site of a mid 6C structure marking the place of conversion from Arianism to Orthodoxy of Theodomir, king of the Suevi. It was said to have been run up in a hurry (thus its name) to house relics of St Martin, sent from Tours. Some interesting capitals survive at the Romanesque west door, at the early Gothic north door, and in the modernised interior.

By turning to the right down the Rua da Cedofeita, a short distance to the east, the university and neighbouring Clérigos are eventually regained.

Several things of slighter interest may be seen some distance west of São Martinho, which are better approached by taxi or bus, found in the Rua da Boavista, a short walk north. This thoroughfare is extended beyond the Praça Mousinho de Albuquerque by the long Avenida da Boavista. The *praça* is an important road junction providing access to the Ponte da Arrábida (1960–63; designed by Edgar Cardoso) spanning the Douro between Oporto and its mouth.

Some 2km north-west of the *praça* is the restored Casa de Ramalde, where it was planned to open a literary museum. Whether this will happen is still doubtful.

South of the *avenida*, between the Rua do Campo Alegre and the Cintura Interna, is the 'Dr Gonçalo Sampaio' botanical garden.

At 977 Rua de Serralves, further west, is the **Casa de Serralves**, built in the 1930s, and in recent years displaying collections of modern art (but check first at a tourist office to see if there is any exhibition on).

The Av. da Boavista continues west to meet the Atlantic at the Praça de Gonçalves Zarco, and the restored 17C Castelo do Queijo. There is another fort further south-west guarding the entrance to the Douro opposite the sand bar. The seaside residential district of **Foz do Douro** was referred to as 'the Brighton of Porto' in the mid 19C, but it was noted that 'The English ladies have a bathing-place to themselves at some distance from the rest'.

To the north, the Parque da Cidade partly isolates this district from industrial **Matosinhos** (29,798 inhabitants), on the south bank of the river Leça, and **Leça da Palmeira** (15,605 inhabitants) on its north bank. The former was the birthplace of the cellist Guilhermina Suggia (1878–1950). Two moles enclose the adjacent harbour and docks of **Leixões**. It was near **Perafita**, further to the north, that Dom Pedro landed to relieve Oporto (see History).

The church of Bom Jesus at Matosinhos was largely rebuilt by Nasoni in 1743–50, and contains the Saviour of Boucas, a cult image moved here from a neighbouring church c 1550. There are a number of *quintas* near the banks of the Leça attributed to Nasoni, among them those of Fafiães (1732–36), and Chantre (1743–46), which may be discovered by the persevering.

Further north, c 12km from the centre of Oporto, is the airport.

# D.  Vila Nova de Gaia

This suburb, opposite the city, with a population in the region of 68,302, is approached with ease along the lower level of the Ponte de Dom Luís I, its quays providing a good view of old Oporto. Here, among a warren of lanes, stand the numerous *armazéns* or wine-shippers' lodges, in which the Port is stored before its export. Many of the shippers—among them Kopke (1638); Ferreira; Osborne; Borges; Barros; Almeida; Ramos Pinto; Manuel Poças; and António José da Silva (Quinta do Noval, Van Zeller brothers), not members of the Association (see p 290)—advertise their whereabouts by painting their names on their roofs. Most of them may be visited, and many hospitably provide facilities for the tasting of the varieties of Port: see the Introduction to Port and the Wines of Portugal.

One may ascend from the quays (with a tourist office at 242 Av. Diego Leite) to **N.S. da Serra do Pilar**, which may also be approached directly by the upper level of the bridge (not recommended to pedestrians likely to suffer from vertigo). This secularised convent is now in military hands. It was Wellington's post of vantage at the taking of Oporto in 1809 (see History). In 1832 it was held against the Miguelites by Sá da Bandeira, who lost his right arm in the bombardment which shattered most of the building.

It claims descent from one founded at Grijó (see Rte 26) in 912. The present structure (1576–83; by João Lopes and Jerónimo Luís) occupies the site of an earlier church containing 13C tombs, and consists of a round church connected by a square chancel to a circular cloister with 36 Ionic columns. The adjacent terrace provides a good view over Oporto.

In the **gardens** of the Conde de Campo Bello in Vila Nova de Gaia (prior appointment essential) was planted the first Camellia japonica in Europe, brought from Japan in the mid 16C. Some fine specimens may be seen in flower in Feb/March.

At **Gondomar** (20,622 inhabitants), not far east of Oporto, is the *Quinta dos Capuchinos*, the gardens of which are said to have been laid out 'by correspondence' with Humphry Repton some time before 1816.

For roads from Oporto to Aveiro, and Coimbra, see Rtes 20, and 26; for those along the banks of the Douro, see the sub-routes in Rte 27A; for Amarante and Vila Real, Rte 29; for Guimarães, Rte 37; for Viana do Castelo, see Rte 34A; and for Braga, Rte 34B: all these in reverse.

# 34 · (Tui) Valença do Minho to Oporto

## A.  Via Viana do Castelo

*Total distance, 125km (77 miles). N13. 27km Caminha—24km Viana do Castelo — 24km Esposende—19km Póvoa de Varzim—4km Vila do Conde—27km Oporto.*

From **Tui** (see *Blue Guide Spain*, 6th ed.), now spelt thus by the Gallegos in preference to Túy, two bridges now span the Minho: the older 333m-long International Bridge of 1885, constructed by Eiffel, and that recently completed a short distance downstream, carrying the motorway from Santiago de Compostela and Vigo into Portugal. (It is hoped that resistance to its projected cross-country continuation direct to Braga has been sufficient to convince the authorities not to desecrate a particularly lovely district.)

Entirely enclosed within its 17C ramparts, which are in a perfect state of preservation, the ancient frontier fortress of **Valença do Minho** (*Pousada de São Teotónio*) commands the bank of the Minho (with its source, as the Miño, in the Sierra de Meira, north-east of Lugo, in Galicia). Until the earlier stronghold here was rebuilt in 1262, its name had been Contrasta. It sustained two minor sieges by the Decembrists, in 1837 and in 1847.

The old town retains some pleasant corners, while at the far end of the main street is the *pousada*, providing a good view across to Tui. The church is of slight interest.

For the road along the south bank of the Minho to Monção, see Rte 34B.

The main road circles to the south-west, bypassing (right) **São Pedro da Torre**, with a restored Romanesque (?) bridge, and passing (left) the road climbing across the hills to Ponte de Lima; see Rte 34C.

Beyond **Reboreda**, with the 14C Torre de Penafiel, is **Vila Nova de Cerveira**, its early castle, with later additions, now accommodating the luxurious Pousada Dom Dinis. The road continues south-west, skirting the Minho, through **Gondarém**, with the 18C Casa da Loureira, to **Lanhelas**, which with the Casa da Torre, and its partly 12C fortifications, provides a pleasant view across its widening estuary towards Monte Santa Tecla on the Spanish bank.

**Caminha**, once an important river-port at the mouth of the tributary Coura, still retains its fortifications and a number of 17C houses. It was the birthplace of João Soares Rebelo (1610–61), the composer. The attractive central *praça* is overlooked by a 16C clock-tower on an 11C base, and the Misericórdia, with a good portal (and an organ open to the wind, as seen from an exterior balcony). On passing through an arch under the tower, a gateway of the medieval enceinte, the Rua Direita leads towards the *Igreja Matriz (1488). This, the finest in the district, has a later tower (1556) and two good doorways with Renaissance carving suggesting the influence of the Coimbra School of sculptors, while the apse and gargoyles deserve inspection. The *artesonado* ceiling, the carved granite pulpit, the Tree of Jesse of 1704, its *azulejos*, and the organ-case, are likewise noteworthy features.

At the mouth of the Minho is the island fort of Insua (16C), and two 17C forts, passed as the road bears south through **Moledo do Minho**, and skirts the Atlantic shore, bypassing **Ancora**, north-east of which is a well-preserved dolmen, to approach the mouth of the Lima.

## VIANA DO CASTELO

Viano do Castelo (9007 inhabitants), whose brochures have boasted of 'unpolluted beaches with a high iodine content', is a well-sited fishing-port and prosperous holiday resort, retaining several old buildings of interest. It is dominated by Monte Santa Luzia, surmounted by an ugly early 20C neo-Byzantine Basilica of the Sameiro variety, and a 1920s hotel with a view of pine woods which extend along the far bank of the Lima.

■ The **Tourist Office** is in Rua do Hospital Velho. **Trains** (station on Avenida dos Combatentes da Grande Guerra) and **buses** run to Viana from Oporto.

### History

Its name may have been a corruption of Diana. It formerly traded in *bacalhau*, while a British community had been exporting Minho wines from here to England before 1580, when they were expelled by the Spanish. But they returned, and by 1700 a British Factory had been established, with Christopher Battersby as Consul, while John Page was building a house here in 1703. Coopers were even sent out from England to supervise the manufacture of casks. With the growth of the Port-wine trade, and the silting up of Viana's harbour, the community later moved to Oporto.

In 1847 it was raised to the rank of city for resisting the revolt of the Septembrists. Its most eminent native was the military engineer and architect Manuel Pinto de Vilalobos (died 1734).

The main street leading south from the railway station to the river bank is of slight interest, and it is better to follow the Rua Candido dos Reis, further east, with the **Palace of the Távoras** (or Condes da Carreira) on the corner, rebuilt in 1714 and decorated in 1720 with a painted ceiling by Manuel Gomes and *azulejos* by António de Oliveira Bernardes (1684–1732).

Santa Ana, just to the north, has a Manueline cloister, while further down the street is the entrance to the church of the \***Misericórdia**, a curious building of 1598 facing the triangular Praça da República, with a façade of three superimposed loggias, the upper storeys supported by caryatids of original design, by João Lopes the Younger.

Adjacent is the arcaded town hall (*Paços do Concelho*; 1502). The Rua de Sacadura Cabral leads south, passing an elegant fountain, to a small square retaining some 16C houses (right), and the **Igreja Matriz** or **Sé**, with a 15C Gothic west portal (between Romanesque towers), bearing figures on the archivolts. The sculptures on the towers are also remarkable.

The Rococo façade of the Capela dos Malheiros Reimões, in the nearby Rua 8 de Março, is notable, as is one in the Rua São Pedro, further south in this pedestrian precinct. Beyond is the river front.

Returning to the square, turn left to cross the main avenue and follow the Rua Manuel Espregueira, at the far end of which (right) is the **municipal museum**, installed in the 18C palace of the Barbosa Macieis family, attributed to Manuel Pinto de Vilalobos (died 1734), a local architect. The museum is open 9.30–12.00 and 14.00–17.00; closed Mon and holiday.

It contains some good furniture (notably a japanned *bufete*), a ceramic collection, naïve late 19C watercolours of Viana, and paintings on glass; examples of the work of Vieira Lusitano, and Vieira Portuense; and drawings by Sequeira, etc. The *azulejos* of hunting scenes by Policarpo de Oliveira Bernardes (1721) are attractive. Adjacent stands the large Classical church of **São Domingos**, built by Frei Julião Romero for Archbishop Bartolomeu dos Mártires of Braga (died 1590), who attended the Council of Trent, and is buried here. He was an indefatigable visitor of his diocese, penetrating into its wildest recesses where certainly no bishop had ever been seen before, and it is recorded that he once met a procession of villagers chanting 'Blessed be the most holy Trinity, and her sister the most pure Virgin', much to his consternation. The church also contains a retable by José de Alvares de Araújo (died 1762).

To the south-west, beyond the Praça General Barbosa and near the port, is the fort or **Castelo de Santiago da Barra**, built by Philip II of Spain to guard the mouth of the Lima and later strengthened. There is a project to house a museum of Minhoto folk art in its dependencies, together with a maritime museum. To the north-west is the small Baroque pilgrimage church of N.S. da Agonia, the scene of a *festa* during August, when Minhoto costumes are displayed.

From north-east of the railway station, a road and a funicular ascend to the above-mentioned basilica, behind which is the Hotel de Santa Luzia, and nearby, the Celtic **Citânia of Santa Luzia**, with its defensive wall, the foundations of circular stone huts, and paved alleys.

## Viana do Castelo to Ponte de Lima

23km. The N202 leads east above the north bank of the Lima, at c 7km passing near **Nogueira**, with a church dated 1183, to approach the 18C Solar de Lanheses, 5km beyond which is the imposing \***Solar de Bertiandos**, largely 18C, but with a tower of 1566. A modern bridge over the Lima is reached (providing a good view of the ancient Ponte de Lima which gave its name to the town; see Rte 34C), at the far end of which is 17C N.S. da Guia.

The main route continues south, crossing the Lima by a bridge of 1895 designed by Eiffel, at the far end of which (right) is the 18C Casa do Cais Novo, to skirt **Darque**. Another bridge is under construction further east, by which the new IC1 will cross the river, along the south bank of which the N203 leads to Ponte de Lima.

On reaching the junction for Barcelos (see Rte 35), the N13 bears right, later passing the ruins of a fort of 1704 converted into a lighthouse on approaching the small resort of **Esposende**. The Cávado, both sides of its estuary flanked by pinewoods, is crossed to **Fão**, bypassing the resort of **Ofir**.

The road traverses several villages before veering south-east behind **Póvoa de Varzim** (23,851 inhabitants), a fishing port and resort, and the birthplace of José Maria Eça de Queiroz (1845–1900), the novelist, who in 1874–88 was Portuguese consul in Newcastle upon Tyne among other English towns. It retains an 18C fort, an Igreja Matriz of 1743–57, and N.S. da Lapa (1772), but few other buildings of interest.

A worthwhile **detour** is that following the N206 turning inland here to to (4km) **Rio Mau** where to the right of the road stands *São Cristóvão (1151), with well-carved capitals and sculpture of the period; and 1km to the left some 2km beyond, **Rates**, where restored *São Pedro (12C) is one of the more impressive Romanesque churches in Portugal, with remarkable carved capitals, among other features. It may have been built by Count Henry of Burgundy on the site of the martyrdom of the sainted Pedro de Rates, first bishop of Braga (said to be a Jewish convert of St James the Greater) who was also born here.

Almost contiguous with Póvoa do Varzim is **VILA DO CONDE** (19,990 inhabitants), another resort and fishing port at the mouth of the Ave, with shipyards and other industries. It is also reputed for its lace.

■ The **Tourist Office** is at 103 Rua 25 de Abril. There are **trains** and **buses** from Oporto.

The town is dominated by the impressive bulk of the former **Convent of Santa Clara**, now a reformatory, approached by turning east on the north bank of the river. The present building was begun in 1777 by Henrique Ventura, although the convent had been founded in 1318 by Afonso Sanches, a natural son of Dom Dinis, whose elaborate tomb, together with that of his wife, Teresa Martins, and their family, and also that of Brites Pereira, daughter of Nun' Alvares Pereira and wife of the first Duke of Braganza, lie in the 16C church, with its panelled ceiling. (It may be difficult to gain entrance.) The organ is a fine example. In the cloister walk is a fountain formerly fed by a 5km-long aqueduct of 1705–14, now partially ruinous. Adjacent is an attractive 18C mansion.

Also of interest in the town is the **Igreja Matriz** (São João Baptista; c 1514), with a later tower and a portal by João de Castilho combining Plateresque and Manueline features. By the river mouth is the 17C fort, also dedicate to the Baptist.

Near the confluence of the Ave and Este, some 5km inland, is the site of **Bagunte**, a pre-Roman settlement abandoned by the 6C.

At **Azurara**, on the south bank of the Ave, is a large Manueline church, the vaulting in its chancel completed in 1552, abutted by a later belfry.

The road now veers away from the coast towards **Moreira**, with (right) an Augustinian convent (1588–1662) containing an elaborate *altar-mór*.

The N107 turns right here past the airport of Francisco Sá Carneiro, to cross the Douro by the Ponte da Arrábida; the N13 continues ahead into central Oporto (see Rte 33); while the left fork leads towards Leça do Bailio.

The Leça is crossed by several small Roman bridges, among them the Ponte de Pedra, the Carro bridge, and the Guifões bridge, but the most important monument on the river is the fortified Romanesque monastic church of **\*Leça do Bailio**, once the head-quarters of the Knights Templar in Portugal. The severe granite building, heavily restored in 1940, dates from 1336, but retains an earlier cloister. The crenellated parapet surrounding the church; the tower, corbelled at each corner; and the rose-window above the entrance portal, are obvious features. The well-proportioned interior, with well-carved capitals, contains the tomb of João Coelho and a font, both by Diogo Pires the Younger (1514–15); the tomb of Cristóvão de Cernache (1567), showing the influence of Philippe Houdart; and the brass epitaph of Estêvão Vasques Pimentel (died 1374), who was responsible for the rebuilding. It was here that Dom Fernando announced his marriage with Leonor Teles in 1372.

# B.  Via Monção and Braga

*Total distance, 144km (89 miles). N101. 18km Monção—39km Ponte da Barca—33km Braga—N14. 18km Vila Nova de Famalicão—36km Oporto.*

At the main crossroads at Valença do Minho (see Rte 34A), the road ahead climbs 7km to the summit of Monte do Faro (565m), commanding extensive views.

The N101 winds east, parallel to the south bank of the Minho, providing pleasant vistas across towards Spain, shortly bypassing **Ganfei**, with a Romanesque church (partly rebuilt), containing good capitals. The ancient monastery was rebuilt in the 18C.

Another turning leads shortly to the 12C church of **São Fins**, also with well-carved capitals. Beyond **Friestas** is **Lapela**, with a medieval defensive tower.

**MONÇAO**, founded by Dom Afonso III, and fortified in the 17C, is an attractive little town with a ruined castle of 1306 overlooking the Minho opposite Salvatierra de Miño in Spain (to which there is a ferry service).

### History
It is now better known for its *vinho verde* and *bagaceira* than for its red wines, exported at the turn of the 18C by English factors who settled there and called the place 'Monson'. It is also reputed for its medicinal springs, and lampreys. Among the tombs in its Romanesque Igreja Matriz is that of the local hero Deuladeu Martins, who successfully defended the town against the Spaniards in 1368 by the expedient, it is said, of lobbing them loaves of bread to prove how well supplied they were. It held out for four months in 1658, again besieged by its neighbours, commanded by the Marquês de Viana, when the starving inhabitants eventually capitulated on advantageous terms.

### Monçao to Melgaço
23.5km. It was at the neighbouring hamlet of **Ponte de Mouro**, that on 1 November 1386 John of Gaunt met Dom João I to discuss his proposed marriage with Lancaster's daughter Philippa, and to plan the invasion and dismemberment

of Castile. At **Longos Vales**, south-east of the main road, the Romanesque part of the church contains capitals and carvings of interest. Continuing along the upper slope of the Minho valley, **Barbeita** (right), with a Romanesque bridge, is passed, and then the 18C Casa do Amioso at **Valadares**, before reaching **Melgaço**, which in the mid 13C had the privilege of choosing its own governor. It is known for its hams and for the numerous mineral springs in the neighbourhood. It retains the keep of its castle, but of more interest is N.S. da Orada (1245), standing on the right of the road 1km further north-east, which goes on to meet the frontier, here the Rio Trancoso, a tributary of the Minho, at **São Gregório**. For Celanova, c 40km east, and Ribadavia, c 30km north, see *Blue Guide Spain*, 6th ed.

Some 5km south-east of Melgaço are relics of the convent of Fiães; and at **Paderne**, c 2km south-west, a Romanesque church containing 13C tombs.

The N202 climbs south from Melgaço to (28km) the high-lying and remote village of **Castro Laboreiro**, with relics of Roman occupation at neighbouring **Bico**. The ruins of its castle (1033) command extensive views, while the Romanesque church has features of interest. The district is known for a special breed of ferocious sheep-dog.

It lies within the nature reserve of Peneda-Gerês, with the Serra da Peneda (1335m) rising to the east, while to the south-west is the Outeiro Maior (1416m), the highest peak of the range. A mountain road leads south through a enclave of Spain to meet the N540 bearing south-west to enter Portugal at Lindoso (see below), from which a byroad (OR312) ascends to the Portela do Homem, for Gerês; see Rte 32.

From Monção the main road (N101) turns south, shortly passing (right) at **Pinheiros** the huge granite mansion of **Brejoeira** (1806–34), erected in the style of the Ajuda palace, Lisbon, with its own chapel, and gardens surrounded by vineyards.

The road continues to wind up the boulder-strewn valley, with attractive retrospective views, to the Portela do Extremo, commanding wide vistas over the Lima valley, approached by descending the side valley of the Vez to **Arcos de Valdevez**, where in c 1140 an inconclusive tourney took place between Afonso Henrique's knights and those of Alfonso VII, which was a presage of later claims to independence. It suffered a destructive fire in the 17C, and its most architecturally interesting buildings are now the 18C church of N.S. da Lapa and the 18C Casas da Andorinha and do Terreiro. To the east is **Giela**, with the 14C tower of the later Paço de Giela, and the remains of the 18C Casa do Requeijo.

## Arcos de Valdevez to Ponte de Lima

About 22km. The N202 winds above the north bank of the Lima, passing near the *castro* of Cendufe and a number of attractive *quintas*, among them, at **Jolda**, the Paço da Glória, and beyond, at **Calheiros** (right), its imposing *paço* of 1700. Before reaching Calheiros, the former convent of Refóios do Lima (1122, but modernised and restored to house a school of agronomy) is passed (left), containing good woodwork and *azulejos*. The road later bears left to Ponte de Lima (see Rte 34C.

The return journey—from Ponte de Lima to Ponte da Barca—may be made along the south bank of the river, providing several beautiful vistas, passing near, south of **Gândra**, the Torre de Beiral (1733), and through Bravães: see below.

The Lima is crossed by a ten-arched bridge of 1543 (restored 1761 and 1896) to **Ponte da Barca**, the birthplace of the poet Diogo Bernardes (c 1530–c 1595) and his brother Agostinho da Cruz (1540–1619).

From here the N203, in the process of improvement, ascends the south bank of the wild upper Lima valley to (25km) Lindoso, passing near the ancient monastery of Vila Nova de Muía, and a turning to **Ermelo**, on its far bank, its church retaining Romanesque features, and to **Soajo**, with a remarkable assemblage of *espigueiros*. Many more of these may be seen at **Lindoso**, below its much rebuilt but imposingly sited 14C castle guarding the frontier 6km further east. The road beyond leads to (32km) Bande, for Celanova; see *Blue Guide Spain*, 6th ed.

At **Bravães**, 6km west of Ponte da Barca on the N203, is a fine Romanesque *church (ask for key at a house near its apse), with well-carved west and south portals (note the griffons on the latter), while the naïve capitals on either side of the windows in the interior, the rose-window, and remains of murals (St Sebastian on the left; the Virgin and Child on the right) are all notable.

Near **Nogueira**, south of Ponte da Barca, are a number of *quintas* and *solares*, among them, to the left, the Casa da Agrela. At **Crasto**, beyond, to the right, is a church of Romanesque origin.

The N101 starts to climb, passing a left-hand turning to **Aboim da Nóbrega**, with a interesting church of Romanesque origin.

West of **Vila Verde**, at **Carreiras**, are the Torre de Penegate (1360) and a *citânia*.

From just short of Vila Verde a road climbs north-west up the thickly wooded Homem valley to **Covide**, and from there down to (c 40km) crossroads on the Caniçada reservoir south-west of Gerês (see latter part of Rte 32), first passing near (left) **Couceiro**, its Romanesque church preserving curious sculptures, to cross the river at **Caldelas**. To the south-west of Caldelas is the Benedictine monastery of **Rendufe**, largely 18C, with elaborate Rococo decoration and sculpture, some ascribed to Frei José de Santo António Vilaça.

Beyond Vila Verde, a right-hand turning leads south-west via Prado to (21.5km) Barcelos; see sub-route on p 308 in reverse.

The river Cávado is reached at its confluence with the Homem.

From its north bank a road ascends the valley to (31.5km) the Caniçada crossroads via **Carrazedo**, with the 15C Casa do Castro; **Besteiros**, with a number of 18C mansions; **Ferreiros**, with the ruined Solar dos Vasconcelos; **Amares**; **Figueiredo**, with the medieval Ponte do Porto, perhaps on Roman foundations, and old mansions; **Dornelas**, with the ruined Torre, possible birthplace of Gualdim Pais, and the late 17C Casa do Outeiro, before reaching **Bouro**, with a ruined Cistercian monastery (Santa Maria), which existed in 1148. It was transformed in the 17C, and more recently despoiled of its lead and ironwork, since when it has rapidly deteriorated, although there are plans to restore it as a *pousada*. Note the curious statues on its façade and the *azulejos* in the sacristy.

Above Bouro is the 18C sanctuary of N.S. da Abadia. The road continues up the valley, shortly skirting the Caniçada reservoir, to the crossroads below Caldas do Gerês, and (right) the *Pousada de São Bento*; see latter part of Rte 32.

On crossing the Cávado, to the right on approaching the northern outskirts of Braga, is the hamlet of **Dume**, where, in the mid 6C, Carriaric, the Suevic king (converted to Catholicism during the illness of his son, Theodomir), founded a church. Its priest eventually became St Martin of Dume, who directed the activities of the second Council of Braga in 572, and died in 579. Capitals and shafts of Roman columns are imbedded in farm buildings near the church.

A short distance further west stands the Visigothic church of São Frutuoso de Montélios: see Rte 34C, and likewise for the monastery of Tibães.

For Braga (first reaching its bypass) see Rte 36; and for the road on to Guimarães, Rte 35.

From **Braga** the N14 bears south-west, after c 12km passing (right, before reaching the entrance to the A3 motorway) **Arnoso**, where Santa Eulália (12C), on the site of a convent founded in 642 by St Frutuoso, is of interest.

While the motorway provides a rapid approach to central Oporto, with an exit for Santo Tirso (see last part of Rte 37), the N14 continues south-west through **Vila Nova de Famalicão** (7147 inhabitants), with paperworks, east of which is Romanesque Sant'Tiago d'Antas, containing some unusual pink 17C *azulejos*.

To the left on approaching **Trofa** is **Lousado**, with the medieval Ponte da Lagoncinha, possibly on Roman foundations. In the vicinity is the *castro* of Alvarelhos, where several hoards of denarii have been unearthed.

Not far south of **Maia** (left) is the Romanesque church of Leça do Bailio (see last part of Rte 34A), beyond which the northern outskirts of Oporto are entered: see Rte 33.

# C.  Via Ponte de Lima and Braga

*Total distance, 125km (77 miles). N13. 6km—N201. 32km Ponte de Lima—33km Braga—N14. 54km Oporto.*

For the first part of this route, see Rte 34A.

The N201 turns left 6km south of Valença do Minho, climbing steeply, with retrospective views, to crossroads at **São Bento**, 8km south-east of which is the high-lying village of **Paredes de Coura**, with an ancient church rebuilt in the 18C. The main road briefly descends to cross the Rio Coura, with its Roman bridge, and climbs again past **Rubiães**, its fine Romanesque *church displaying well-carved capitals and corbels. Note the adjacent Roman milliary column.

The long descent into the valley of the Lima, probably following the course of a Roman road, and providing several attractive vistas, leads past **Romarigães**, where the façade of the Capela do Amparo is notable, to cross the river at Ponte de Lima, well seen on the far bank. For the roads upstream along its north bank, see that from Arcos de Valdevez in Rte 34B, in reverse.

## PONTE DE LIMA

*Ponte de Lima has been praised by many travellers for its beautiful situation, and it is a pleasant centre from which to explore the area. It contains a number of characteristic houses and streets, and is a delightful place to wander through.

■ Accommodation is available in many private homes in the vicinity: see Turismo de Habitação (p 85); enquire also—preferably in advance—at the **Tourist Office** in the Praça de República. **Buses** from Viana do Castelo.

### History

The Lima itself was assumed by the Romans to be the Lethe, the River of Oblivion, its beauty having the effect of the lotus, in making the traveller forget his own country and home. It was at this point that Decimus Junius Brutus had such difficulty in persuading his troops to cross, having already traversed the greater part of Iberia. Seizing the standard, and once more exhorting them, he waded into the stream, and lemming-like, they followed. It was later known to the Romans as Forum Limicorum, and it is probably the Lemici where the Suevic annalist Hydatius was born in 394. A number of English archers played a vital role in Dom João I's capture of the place in 1385.

Its sandy river-side has been the site of a Monday **market** (now fortnightly), which is the oldest in Portugal, existing under a charter of Dona Teresa, Countess of Burgundy, in 1125. The lyre-horned cattle, ubiquitous in the Minho, are sold on the far bank.

The Quinta da Tapada, near here, was the home of the 16C poet Sá de Miranda (cf. Coimbra).

The ancient *bridge of 31 arches, of Roman origin (five arches of which survive), was rebuilt in 1360 and restored in the 15C. At its north end is the chapel of São António da Torre Velha (1814).

The riverside *alameda* of huge plane trees leads west to the Renaissance church of São António dos Frades, part of a convent founded in 1480, and adjacent São Francisco, containing a collection of cult objects.

Near the bridgehead are the remaining towers of the town's fortifications, and behind them the Igreja Matriz (Santa Maria dos Anjos; 1359). Among the more interesting mansions, some of which have been restored, are the Paço of the Marquês de Ponte de Lima, originally of 1464, but much altered since, with Manueline windows; the Paço da Alcaideira (overlooking the tourist office), and the former Paço do Concelho.

In the district are the 12C chapel of Espirito Santo at **Moreira**, reached by turning right off the N202 after **Santa Comba**, west of Ponte de Lima; Romanesque Santa Marinha at **Arcoselo** (off the N306, turning off the N202 north-east of the town), also with a bridge of Roman foundation, and further north, the 18C monastery of N.S. do Socorro at **Labruja**: but see also the roads to Arcos de Valdevez (on the north bank) and to Ponte de Barca (13km east) via Bravães, in Rte 34B.

The summit of Monte de Santa Maria Madalena, c 3km south-east, commands a fine panorama over the valley.

## Ponte de Lima to Barcelos

31km. The N204 leads south-west through **Correlhã**, near which are the 18C monastery of N.S. da Boa Morte and the Romanesque chapel of Santa Abdão, and **Facha**, with the 17C Casa das Torres, and São Estevão. At **Balugães** is a church dated 1162. The road later passes close to **Cossourada**, with a church of 1714; **Quintiães**, also with an 18C church, and the abandoned Torre de Aborim (1650); and to the east, **Couto**, the church of which contains 15–16C tombs, before entering Barcelos: see Rte 35.

From Ponte de Lima the N201 leads south-east, following the route taken by Major Dalrymple 200 years ago, who was enchanted that the vines 'twining round the oaks, and other trees in the hedges, formed most beautiful festoons', and across the hills into the Cávado valley, passing through attractive wooded country.

From **Prado**, near which a Miguelite force was severely defeated in 1826, the N205 turns south-west to Barcelos via Manhente; see Rte 35.

On approaching the Cávado, the former Benedictine monastery at **Tibães** is seen from some distance away, standing out against the wooded hillside to the south-west. It is best approached after crossing the river and the next village, and then turning right along a lane between high walls.

Of the huge and long ruinous monastery of *São Martinho, little remains of the Romanesque period. The present church, by Manuel Alvares, is dated 1624–61, and contains a mass of mid 18C gilt woodcarving by the *entalhador* André Soares, and a Baroque organ of 1785. (It is open 9.00–12.00 and 14.00–17.00; closed Mon and holidays.) Note the stalls of 1666–68 in the upper choir, with their misericords, and carved and painted half-figures, arm in arm; also the *azulejos* of 1785 in the chapterhouse. One of the four cloisters, long derelict, has been restored in the long-term project to restore the dependencies as a whole (parts of which house a school of restoration), including the water-staircase in the abandoned formal gardens behind, which, when visited by Lord Porchester in 1827, with its roses in full bloom, were described as enchanting. With a series of progressively simpler fountains on each landing as they rise to the Capela de São Bento, they are said to have inspired the more ostentatious stair at Bom Jesus, Braga. A few paces to the east, at a lower level, is a small artificial, obelisk-flanked, lake.

Very soon after regaining the main road, a left-hand turning leads shortly to the early 18C church of São Francisco, abutting which is the tiny Visigothic chapel of **São Frutuoso de Montélios**. Apply at adjacent house for key. Steps ascend from the church to the interior of the chapel (2nd half of 7C), built on a Greek Cross plan, with a reconstructed central dome and barrel-vaulted apsidal arms. The vaulting in each bay is supported by two marble columns. An ornamental frieze is preserved, but the whole was remodelled in the 11C, and has received the more recent attentions of restorers. The exterior is embellished by Lombardic blind arcades terminating in alternate pointed and semicircular sections, and is also surrounded by decorative bands of marble.

The main road climbs round a hill to enter Braga: see Rte 36.

For the road to Guimarães, see Rte 35, and from there to Oporto, Rte 37. For the road from Braga to Oporto, see the latter part of Rte 34B.

# 35 · Viana do Castelo to Amarante via Barcelos, Braga, and Guimarães

*Total distance, 109km (68 miles). N13 and N103 for (30km) Barcelos exit—23km Braga—N101. 22km Guimarães—34km Amarante.*

For Viana do Castelo, see Rte 34A.

The N103 forks left off the N13 through **Forjães**, with the ruined tower of the Casa dos Pregais (c 1100), possibly the birthplace of the 15C navigator Gonçalo Velho, to the east of which, at **Fragoso**, is the 18C Casa da Espragueira. On approaching Barcelos, **Abade de Neiva**, with a charmingly sited church of 1152 with good capitals, and a restored tower, is bypassed, to the north of which is the 16C chapel of the Quinta da Silva.

## BARCELOS
Ancient Barcelos, now with a bypass, is an attractive small town on the north bank of the Cávado, crossed here by a restored 15C bridge, below which swarm lampreys.

On the suburban bank at **Barcelinhos** it is abutted by a chapel capped by a pyramid and surrounded by a colonnaded porch.

It is noted for being the centre of handicraft in a region rich in such, while its Thursday *market is still one of the more characteristic in Portugal, selling everything from its regional pottery to its lyre-horned cattle. Unfortunately, little of the ceramic ware is of the imaginative quality of the productions of the late Rosa Ramalho.

■ The **Tourist Office** is in Largo da Porta Nova (Torre Nova, also called Torre de Menagem). **Trains** run direct from Viana and to Oporto. The station is in the north-east of the town. **Buses** run frequently to Braga.

Immediately above the bridge-head is the **Archaeological and Ceramic Museum**, installed in the ruins (retaining its chimney) of a palace built by Afonso, natural son of Dom João I.

> On his marriage in 1401 to Brites, daughter of Nun' Alvares Pereira (cf. Vila do Conde), Afonso received the county of Barcelos from the king, the last count of the old line (Meneses family) having been killed at Aljubarrota. (Another of Dom João's bastards, Beatriz (1392–1439), was married off by Philippa of Lancaster in 1405 to Thomas Fitzalan, Earl of Arundel (died 1415); she later married John Holland, Earl of Huntingdon.)

The museum is open 10.00–12.00 and 14.00–18.00. Among the crosses to be seen is that displaying the 'Cock of Barcelos' just below the 14C Crucifix O Senhor do Galo. The cock is associated with a legend in which a roasting rooster miraculously crowed in protestation of an innocent Gallego being sent to the gallows ('I'll be hanged if the cock don't crow'). It has almost been taken up as a national symbol: this gaily painted fowl is certainly reproduced often enough as a representation of Folk Art.

Behind the museum is the Igreja Matriz, rebuilt by Afonso, retaining the 13C portal of an earlier church, with a rose-window above.

Nearby is a late Gothic *pelourinho* and, to the west, the 15C Solar dos Pinheiros, with its twin towers. To the north of the church is the town hall, housed in an 18C palace, behind which, in a little square, is the Casa de Nun' Alvares.

From here the main street of the enceinte leads to the **Torre Nova**, a tower of the 15C ramparts, housing a Centro de Artesanato (regional handicraft), which may be bought here. Beyond, to the right, are the Baroque municipal gardens, embellished with a multitude of fountains and obelisks, etc.

To the left is the 'round' or octagonal church of *Bom Jesus (or Senhor da Cruz; c 1705), possibly designed by João Antunes on the site of an earlier chapel. The interior is of interest, with a ground plan combining a Greek cross with a cylinder; and it contains a good organ.

On the adjacent large open space known as the **Campo da República** (or Campo da Feira, or Praça da Feira), the animated and colourful market takes place. To the east is a wooded park, and a Misericórdia installed in a Capuchin monastery of 1649.

To the north stands **N.S. do Terço**, formerly the nunnery of St Benedict, whose life is illustrated on the ceiling panels and on the *azulejos* of 1713 surrounding the carved and gilt pulpit, which features the crowned double-headed Habsburg eagle. (The eagle remained a popular decorative element even after the Spanish domination.)

From the adjacent Campo 5 de Outubro, a lane leads north-west towards an imposing 18C mansion facing the decrepit Largo do Bonfim.

For the road from here to Ponte de Lima, see Rte 34C, in reverse.

At **Gilmonde**, 7km south-west on the N205, is the 17C Casa de Fervença.

The N205 leads north-west along the north bank of the Cávado (views) to join the Ponte de Lima—Braga road at (17km) Prado (see Rte 34C), passing at **Manhente** the Romanesque church of São Martinho (1117), with a well-carved portal, and a medieval tower adjacent. 4km beyond, at **Lama**, is another tower, 'dos Azevedos', of 1536; and to the left further east at **Cervães**, the ruined Torre de Gomariz (15C).

From the south bank of the Cávado at Barcelos the N103 bears east through attractive country, passing near **Vilar de Frades**, its Baroque church with both a Manueline portal and one which has survived of the former Romanesque church of c 1070. The conventual dependencies, damaged by fire in 1898, house an institution.

From Martim a byroad turns left to Tibães (see Rte 34C), shortly beyond which an entry to the A3 motorway for Oporto is passed on approaching Braga; see Rte 36.

Leaving Braga, the N101 climbs south over a ridge of hills before descending to (14.5km) **Caldas das Taipas** (or Caldelas), a pleasant little spa whose hot springs were frequented by the Romans, and by Dom João I.

From here the N310 leads north-east parallel to the north bank of the Ave to **Souto**, where the monastic church of São Salvador retains good Romanesque details, passing en route a turning climbing left to the Citânia de Briteiros: see last part of Rte 36.

For Guimarães, shortly entered, see Rte 37, and also for roads from there to Oporto.

The N101 circles to the east round the Penha (617m), after 11km reaching a right-hand turning descending to the twin-spired Romanesque church of **Pombeiro de Ribavizela**, partly rebuilt in the 18C and containing Rococo decoration, but an interesting relic of a Benedictine monastery, with a good Romanesque west door, although the cloister is largely destroyed. On approaching **Felgueiras** the road is dominated to the east by Monte Santa Quitéria.

## Felgueiras to Penafiel

21.5km. The N207 leads south-west, to the right of which after c 3km is the partly Romanesque church at **Sousa**; to the south, at **Airães**, is another Romanesque church. After c 8km a left-hand turning leads to the 13C church of **Aveleda**. Turn left at **Lousada** for **Meinedo**, site of the Visigothic settlement of Magneto, with a 13C church, and **Bustelo**, with a Benedictine convent founded in the 12C but rebuilt in the 18C, shortly beyond which the road climbs to enter Penafiel: see latter part of Rte 29.

The N15 is met 8km south-east of Felgueiras, and then descends steeply into the valley of the Tâmega, passing near (right) **Freixo de Baixo**, with the 12C church of São Salvador, and another of similar date at **Telöes**, left of the road, to approach or bypass Amarante: see Rte 29.

For the IP4 on to Vila Real, see Rte 29; to Peso da Régua, sub-route at the end of Rte 27A, in reverse; and from Vila Real to Lamego, Rte 31.

# 36 · Braga

**BRAGA** (86,316 inhabitants) is one of the most ancient towns in Portugal, which long disputed with Tarragona and Toledo the primacy of the Iberian Peninsula. It continues to contend with neighbouring Guimarães for being the most interesting large town north of Oporto. Braga is a straggling and rapidly growing industrial and agricultural centre, and seat of the University of the Minho.

Although the creation of the Lisbon patriarchate in 1716 reduced its ecclesiastical pre-eminence, it still retains some of the bigotry of an episcopal city, as reflected in the local proverb: 'Every good house has its cattle and its tonsure'. Regrettably, as most of its numerous churches were 'modernised' in the 18C by prelates with more money than taste, the interiors of comparatively few—apart from the cathedral—merit attention.

■ The **Tourist Office** is at 1 Avenida Liberdade. From Viana do Castelo or Barcelos, change **trains** at Nine. There are some direct trains, and frequent **buses**, from Oporto.

### History

Bracara Augusta, claiming to have been founded in 296 BC, was later the main Roman station in northern Lusitania, being an important hub of communication. In 411 it became the capital of the Suevian kingdom of Gallaecia. In 456 it fell to Theodoric II, and the conversion of the Visigoths later from Arianism to orthodox Catholicism at two synods held at Braga in 563 and 572 marked the beginning of its ecclesiastical hegemony. From c 730 until reconquered by Fernando I of Castile in 1040 it was under Moorish occupation, but later became virtually abandoned, the see only being restored in 1070.

In 1103 Diego Gelmírez, the ambitious bishop of Santiago de Compostela, determined not to be dependent on Braga, forcibly carried off the relics of St Victor and St Fructuosus. However, St Gerald, a Cluniac monk from Moissac, then metropolitan, after recourse to Rome, was confirmed in his supremacy over all sees in the west of the Peninsula as far south as Coimbra. Some stability was provided by João Peculiar, who was archbishop for 37 years from 1139, but ecclesiastical wrangles persisted over the centuries.

Significantly, it was from reactionary Braga that in 1926 General Gomes da Costa addressed an appeal to all citizens 'of dignity and honour' in his successful attempt to overthrow the Democratic regime, precipitating the quasi- hierocratic dictatorship which lasted for the next half century. And it was in Braga in August 1975 that the archbishop instigated a mob to attack the local Communist headquarters during the recent revolutionary period.

From the gardens (and underground parking) just east of the central Praça da República, providing a distant view of Bom Jesus on the hill to the east (see below), and with the Tourist Office adjacent, follow the Rua do Souto to the west past the Torre de Menagem, a relic of the fortress-palace of 1378 guarding the north-east corner of the medieval enceinte. This street later changes its name to the Rua Dom Diogo de Sousa (commemorating the archbishop from 1508 to 1532).

In the first lane to the left stands the 16C **\*Casa dos Crivos**, of interest in that its windows retain their latticed shutters (*mushrabiyas*), which are rare surviving examples.

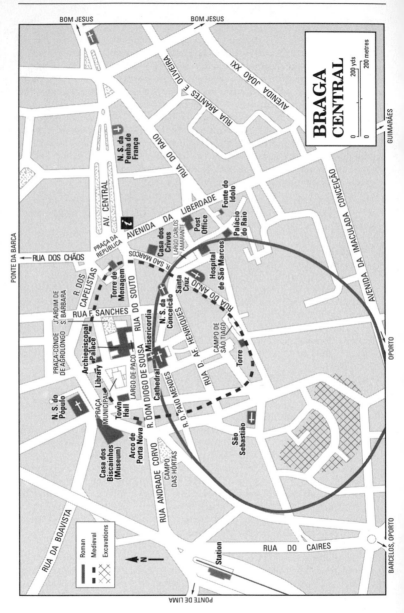

BOM JESUS

BOM JESUS

GUIMARÃES

AVENIDA JOÃO XXI

RUA ARANTES E OLIVEIRA

RUA DO RAIO

AV. CENTRAL

N. S. da Penha de França

PONTE DA BARCA

RUA DOS CHÃOS

AVENIDA DA IMACULADA DA CONCEIÇÃO

Fonte do Idolo

LIBERDADE

AVENIDA DA

Post Office

Palácio do Raio

LARGO CARLOS AMARANTE

Casa dos Crivos

PRAÇA DA REPÚBLICA

R. DE SÃO MARCOS

Hospital de São Marcos

OPORTO

R. DOS CAPELISTAS

Torre de Menagem

RUA DO SOUTO

RUA F. SANCHES

JARDIM DE S. BARBARA

Santa Cruz

RUA DO ANJO

PRAÇA-CONDE DE AGROLONGO

Archiepiscopal Palace

Library

RUA DE PAÇO

RUA DOM DIOGO DE SOUSA

N. S. da Conceição

Misericordia

N. S. do Pópulo

PRAÇA MUNICIPAL

Town Hall

Cathedral

RUA D. AF. HENRIQUES

CAMPO DE SÃO TIAGO

Torre

Arco de Porta Nova

R. DOM PAIO MENDES

RUA ANDRADE CORVO

Casa dos Biscainhos (Museum)

CAMPO DAS HORTAS

R. D. PAIO MENDES

São Sebastião

RUA DA BOAVISTA

BARCELOS, OPORTO

OPORTO

Station

RUA   DO   CAIRES

PONTE DE LIMA

N

BRAGA CENTRAL

200 yds

200 metres

Roman

Medieval

Excavations

Beyond the next cross street, the Largo de Paço, the courtyard of the former **archiepiscopal palace**, with its 18C façade, and a castellated fountain of 1723, is passed to the right. The building, part of which dates from the 14C, suffered a disastrous fire in 1866, and has been rebuilt and put to a variety of secular uses since, accommodating part of the university, and the important public library (formed from the spoils of 20 convents, and that part of the archbishop's collection not destroyed in the conflagration).

The **\*library**, one of the richest in Portugal, vying with that at Évora, now contains some 300,000 volumes and 10,000 manuscripts, among them one dated 1128 confirming Afonso Henriques as king, the Testament of Dom Afonso II (1218), the Codicil of Dom Dinis (1299), and an interesting topographical study of the city in 1750 entitled *Mappa das Ruas de Braga*.

Almost opposite are the miscellaneous dependencies (see below) of the **\*CATHEDRAL**, approached by bearing across the courtyard into the 18C cloister, there turning left. By turning left again, the north aisle is entered. Little remains of the original Romanesque building of c 1100 except the south portal and part of the west doors, now sheltered by a late Gothic porch (1532), added by Archbishop Diogo de Sousa when the east end was rebuilt, and later screened by a fine iron grille (1722). Above are two belfries, incongruously surmounted by basket-work pinnacles.

The **interior** was tastelessly modernised at the end of the 17C, although the chapel to the right of the *Capela-Mór*, and the crossing are not too spoilt, while some of the remining altars are well carved. Among those buried here are St Pedro de Rates, the first bishop (see the chapel of St Geraldo, below; and Rates), and the third, St Ovidius, a friend of the poet Martial. In the lower choir is the bronze tomb (damaged) of the Infante Dom Afonso (cf. Barcelos), son of Dom João I; the *Coro Alto*, containing some coarse but effective 15C stalls, is dominated by its magnificent carved gilt **\*organs** of 1737–38 (restored), played upon—according to Sacheverell Sitwell—by Carlos de Seixas (1704–42), a colleague of Domenico Scarlatti, and a composer of some 900 toccatas, largely unpublished.

From the south-west corner of the cloister, a flight of steps ascends to the extensive but badly displayed chestnut-floored **treasury** (fee), which should make the archbishop blush, for it deserves the attention given to the similar collection in the Museu de Alberto Sampaio at Guimarães. The treasures include the usual assortment of vestments, silver plate, crowns, crucifixes and other cult objects, among them an 11C Byzantine cross, a fine 12C Romanesque example, and another of ivory; a silver and gilt crozier of 1521, and another said to have been that of St Ovidius, but which is 11C; a Manueline chalice of 1509; and the 11C example 'of St Geraldo', said to have been used at the christening of Afonso Henriques; an Hispano-arabic ivory casket (10C), and other carved ivories; a painted Christ on the Cross (13C); and a japanned portative organ (17C), which the sacristan enjoys *kicking* into action, the pained groan then emitted proving that it still 'works'. On the stairs is an unusually sculpted tomb.

The sacristan will also escort the visitor across the cloister to the 14C **king's chapel** (*dos Reis*; or N.S. do Livramento), containing the tombs of the founder, Count Henry of Burgundy (died 1114; the legs of the count were once truncated to enable his tomb to enter a constricted space), and his wife Teresa (illegitimate daughter of Alfonso VI of León), parents of Afonso Henriques, the first king of Portugal; and the mummified body of Archbishop Lourenço who, after confessing Dom João I and his troops at Aljubarrota, took a prominent part in the battle, in which he was seriously wounded on the cheek: the scar was later carved on his effigy.

At the east end of the adjacent courtyard is the restored chapel of São Geraldo, containing the tomb of the first *Arch*bishop of Braga (died 1108), from which the **\*Capela da Glória** is entered. It was built in 1330 by Archbishop Gonçalo Pereira, whose tomb rests here. The *Mudéjar* decoration is noteworthy.

Making our exit from the courtyard, and leaving the Misericórdia of 1562 on the left, it is convenient to cross the road into the Praça Municipal, with the west façade of the Archbishop's Palace (see above) on our right, and left, the town hall (1753–56; attributed to André Soares), its staircase lined with *azulejos*.

Crossing the square diagonally, turn right towards N.S. do Pópulo (from 1596, but rebuilt c 1775–80 by Carlos Amarante).

Turn left to approach the **\*Casa dos Biscaínhos**, an imposing mid 17C mansion, now housing an interesting and charming museum. This is open 10.00–12.00 and 14.00–17.00; closed Mon and holidays. Off the entrance hall, embellished by statues, two of which are in 18C costume, are sections on ethnography and archaeology, displaying artefacts excavated from the Roman city (see below); while a passage to the left leads past stables to the gardens.

*The entrance hall of the Casa dos Biscaínhos*

Stairs ascend to a series of rooms, some with painted or plaster ceilings, and some containing *azulejos* of c 1725. The collections are mainly devoted to the decorative arts.

On turning right on making our exit, the pinnacled 18C Arco da Porta Nova is shortly passed. The street ahead ascends a gentle hill, forking right past São Sebastião to reach the present area of excavation of the **Roman city**, known as the Colina de Maximinos. Although over 60 years have elapsed since its probable importance was brought to public notice, it was not until 1977, after destruction had already been caused by the erection of blocks of flats, that the site of Bracara Augusta was first seriously excavated, and yielded numerous artefacts of interest. Meanwhile, an area between here and the Av. da Liberdade to the east is being protected from the further encroachment of property speculators. The ancient city, which is overlapped by the medieval town, is probably centred on the Campo de São Tiago, slightly to the east, now with a Archaeological museum, with the cathedral forming its northern boundary.

Three necropolises have been discovered to the south-west, north-east and north of this enceinte. The results of continuing excavations, which have already brought to light extensive thermae, are awaited with interest. Those wishing to study the site should apply to the Campo Arqueológico da Universidade do Minho.

While one may turn directly north-east via the Campo de São Tiago towards the Largo Carlos Amarante, perhaps the better approach is by returning downhill and then turning right along the Rua Dom Paio Mendes towards the west front of the cathedral, skirting its south side, and following the lane behind the apse (before 1511; by João de Castilho), which leads to a small square.

On its east side stands São João do Souto, abutted by the chapel of **N.S. da Conceição** (1525), with a well-carved Entombment and quaint statues of Saints Antony of Padua and Paul the Hermit. Adjacent is the relic of the Manueline Casa dos Coimbras, largely demolished in 1906, and reconstructed in 1924.

On the west side of the adjacent Largo Carlos Amarante stands Santa Cruz (1624), with a Baroque organ and loft; while the south side of the square is taken up by the unkempt 18C façade of the Hospital de São Marcos, with its twin belfries surmounted by statues, and containing a late 18C Baroque pulpit.

In the street flanking its east side is the Baroque mansion known as the **Palácio do Raio**, or do Mexicano (1754; attributed to André Soares), with a granite and too brilliant blue *azulejo* façade.

From here a street leads east to the Av. da Liberdade, the main thoroughfare, passing (right) a gate, beyond which, at a lower level, is the spring known as the *Fonte do Idolo*, of Roman date or earlier, with a figure wearing a toga, and a female bust carved into the rock.

Turn left in the avenue to regain the Praça da República.

Ardent ecclesiologists may also visit the churches of São Vicente (1691), with its scrolled frames, some distance to the north; the chapel of N.S. da Penha de França; São Vitor, east of the latter, with a façade of 1686, and superseding a Romanesque church: all contain *azulejos*.

Those with time on their hands may be curious to see the Museu Nogueira da Silva, named after that maecenas, and cynically preserved as a 'sociological warning'. Its entrance is a short distance along the north side of the gardens of the Praça da República.

# Environs

Apart from the excursion to São Frutuoso, and Tibães (see the latter part of Rte 34C), easily approached from Braga, two slightly longer excursions may as conveniently be made. The second excursion is an extension of the first, and may be followed as an alternative route from here to Guimarães. The main objects are Bom Jesus, and the Citânia de Briteiros. (There are buses to both from Braga.) It is best made in fine weather and in the late afternoon.

Turn left some distance down the Av. da Liberdade to enter the N103 (for Chaves; see Rte 32 in reverse), leading through residential suburbs, beyond which the road to the sanctuary of **\*Bom Jesus** climbs past the bottom of the monumental double flight of steps which ascend the thickly wooded slope of Monte Espinho (also approached by a funicular of 1882).

These steps were laid out in 1723 by Archbishop Rodrigo Moura Teles (1704–28), and each landing was subsequently embellished with grotesque wall fountains symbolising the Five Senses, and flanked by statues of biblical figures. The second section of the stairway, of the Three Virtues, is flanked by 12 chapels containing figures and fountains. Alexander Jardine, writing in 1779, remarked that the whole 'must have been attended with great labour and expence. Where despotism has left no other power but the church that is capable of great works, the public is obliged to her when she chuses to employ a numerous poor, though in useless labour: and still more, when she employs them in works of taste'.

The road climbs to gardens at the summit and the church of Bom Jesus (1784–1811) by Carlos Luís Ferreira Amarante (1748–1815), built on the site of a late 15C sanctuary. The adjacent esplanade commands a wide, but increasingly built-over, \*view. The *Hotel do Elevador* (named after the funicular) provides a similar panorama from its restaurant.

> Some 2km south-east, at a slightly higher level, is the ugly sanctuary of Monte Sameiro, attempting to vie with Bom Jesus, but which has nothing to recommend it except the views obtained by the lantern tower above the dome (613m; fee) of the church of 1904. The road from there follows the ridge of the Serra da Falperra to (4km) the church of Santa Maria Madalena (1753–55; designed by André Soares), from which one may return direct to Braga, or alternatively continue south-east towards Caldelas, on approaching which a track to the left leads to the *castro* of **Sabrosa**, excavated by Martins Sarmento in 1878. It is smaller than that at Briteiros (see below), is surrounded by a single but more massive wall, contains only 35 circular houses and three rectangular, and was probably abandoned at an earlier date.

The excursion from Bom Jesus should be continued by climbing south-east c 8km through attractive wooded hills to one of the most impressive archaeological sites in Portugal, the **\*Citânia de Briteiros**, approached by a path leading right from a lay-by.

From the guardian's house a succession of signs directs one round the extraordinary remains of the settlement, which straddles the slope of the boulder-strewn hill of São Romão. Dating back to 300–200 BC, it is supposed to have been the last stronghold of the northern Celtiberians against the invading Romans, but was probably abandoned by AD 300. Some 64 kinds of coin (from 149 BC to Constantine the Great), largely bronze and silver, were found on the site, mostly

*Part of the Citânia de Briteiros*

issued by the municipalities of Roman Spain, but also from the Lusitanian cities of Mérida and Évora.

The site was surrounded by terraces and three defensive walls, partly reconstructed, with an additional wall to the north across the neck of land connecting it with the adjacent hill. The ruined walls of over 150 stone huts, often with a vestibule or porch, survive, separated from each other by paved causeways, and skirted by stone conduits. A few houses contain more than one compartment, some rectangular; and a larger meeting-house is also seen. Towards the summit are some sarcophagus-like remains, together with two round houses reconstructed by Francisco Martins Sarmento, who was responsible for excavating the site in 1875. (He is buried in the churchyard of the hamlet of Briteiros.) Most of the numerous objects, artefacts, and ornamental portals, etc. discovered here may be seen in the museum named after him at Guimarães; see Rte 37.

The rebuilt hermitage commands fine panoramic views over the district.

A very short distance beyond the lay-by, to the right of the road, is a funerary monument in the form of a passage grave, discovered in 1930, with its 'house-shaped' portal stone.

The road descends towards Caldelas (Caldas das Taipas; see the last part of Rte 35). A right-hand turning just prior to the village provides and alternative approach to Sabrosa; see above. The N101 is met here some 7km north-west of Guimarães: see Rte 37.

# 37 · Guimarães to Oporto

*Total distance, 49km (30 miles). The A7, which nearly approaches the town from the west, and later joins the A3, is the most rapid road, but of more interest is the N105, further south, via Santo Tirso, just east of the A3, for which see the latter part of this route.*

## GUIMARÃES

Guimarães (47,435 inhabitants; *Pousada N.S. da Oliveira* is in the old town; *Santa Marinha da Costa* on the hill-side to the south-east), although it has doubled in size during recent decades, is attractively situated and retains several charming corners. It is known for its linen, cutlery, and other manufactures (apart from its football team), and contends with Braga as being the cradle of the Portuguese monarchy. The collections of the museums of Martins Sarmento and Alberto Sampaio are of particular interest.

■ The **Tourist Office** is at 83 Av. da Resistência ao Fascismo (also known as Alameda da Liberdade). Frequent **trains** and **buses** run here from Oporto. The train station is in the south of the town; the bus station in Av. Conde de Margaride.

### History

Alfonso II of León convened a council of counts and bishops here in 840, with a view to the restoration of Braga after its abandonment by the Moors, and 28 years later a certain Vimara Peres, calling it Vimaranes or Guimarais, established it as a centre for the reorganisation of the old Suevic territory: a burgh in the Germanic tradition. A monastery was founded, and a castle built; and in 1095–96 Henry of Burgundy, who made it his court, granted the burghers a charter of privileges.

It is likely that his son Afonso Henriques was born here in 1110, and it is in a document of 1127 that he was first referred to as king of Portucale. The following year he successfully defended—on the nearby field of São Mamede— his independent position against his mother and a faction supporting Alfonso VII. An alliance with England, prior to the Treaty of Windsor, was signed at Guimarães in July 1372.

It was the birthplace of St Damasus, Pope in 366–84; Gil Vicente (1470–1540), the dramatist; and the archaeologist Francisco Martins Sarmento (1833–99).

The curving gardens of the Alameda da Liberdade skirt the south side of the older enceinte. At a lower level stands **São Francisco**, one of the more interesting of the many churches in Guimarães (the *azulejos* in São Dâmaso, and *talha dourada* in São Sebastião are comparatively unimportant), founded in 1220 by Dona Urraca, wife of Dom Afonso II, reconstructed in the 18C, but much restored since. It retains little 13C work apart from the west door and the entrance to the chapterhouse off the Renaissance cloister (c 1600, by João Lopes) adjoining. To the right of the wide barrel-vaulted nave is a Tree of Jesse. The grisaille ceiling, the elaborately carved *Capela-Mór*, and the *azulejos* of St Francis preaching to the Fishes, are noteworthy.

Turning right on making our exit, a roundabout is shortly reached, where to the right, at the end of the leafy Largo da República do Brasil, is the **Igreja dos Santos Passos** (1767–89; by André Ribeiro Soares da Silva), with a bowed façade between

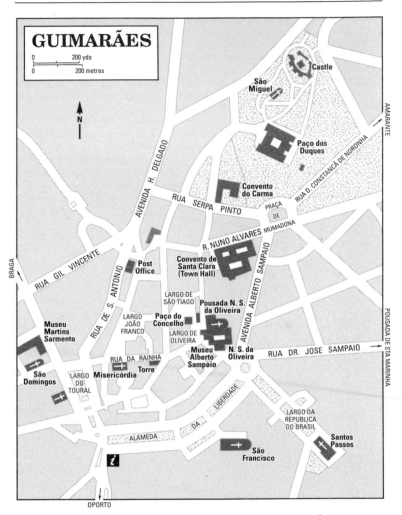

**GUIMARÃES**

0     200 yds
0     200 metres

N

Castle

São Miguel

Paço dos Duques

AMARANTE

AVENIDA H. DELGADO

RUA D. CONSTANÇA DE NORONHA

Convento do Carma

RUA SERPA PINTO

PRAÇA DE MUMADONA

R. NUNO ALVARES

BRAGA

RUA GIL VINCENTE

Post Office

RUA DE S. ANTONIO

Convento de Santa Clara (Town Hall)

AVENIDA ALBERTO SAMPAIO

LARGO DE SÃO TIAGO

Pousada N. S. da Oliveira

LARGO JOÃO FRANCO

Paço do Concelho

LARGO DE OLIVEIRA

Museu Martins Sarmento

Museu Alberto Sampaio

N. S. da Oliveira

RUA DR. JOSE SAMPAIO

POUSADA DE STA MARINHA

São Domingos

RUA DA RAINHA

LARGO DO TOURAL

Misericórdia

Torre

LIBERDADE

LARGO DA REPUBLICA DO BRASIL

ALAMEDA

DA

Santos Passos

São Francisco

ℹ️

OPORTO

two belfries surmounted by obelisks. The view of the exterior is of more interest than the interior.

By continuing uphill along the Av. Alberto Sampaio, flanked by medieval ramparts, the Praça de Mumadona is reached, where turn left. At the Convento do Carmo, on the next corner, bear uphill, passing the pretentious fake Paço dos Duques (see below) to the little Romanesque chapel of São Miguel (12C), containing a font in which, it is claimed, Afonso Henriques was baptised.

Beyond rises the **castle**, with its massive keep and granite towers with pointed monolithic battlements, emerging from a rock outcrop on the summit of a grassy hill. Count Henry reconstructed the original fortress c 1100, and this was later added to. In the early 19C, being still in a good state of preservation, it served as a debtors' prison. The whole was over-restored in 1940. It provides a view to the south-east of the former monastery of Santa Marinha da Costa (see below), above which rises N.S. da Penha, the north-west peak of the Serra de Santa Catarina.

Further north is 17C Sã Dâmaso, containing good 18C *azulejos*.

Returning downhill past São Miguel, some may wish to enter what *was* the **Paço dos Duques** (of Braganza), built c 1420 Dom Afonso (cf. Barcelos) for Constança de Noronha, his second wife, but abandoned c 1660. With its brick chimneys, this granite block, surrounding a large courtyard, was all too thoroughly reconstructed from 1930 as an 'official residence' for the Head of State, Dr Salazar, and VIPs. Most visitors are likely to agree that it would have been wiser to leave it as a 'Romantick' ruin than to have produced such a bogus building. It contains some good pieces of furniture and porcelain; canvases attributed to Josefa de Óbidos, and, among tapestries, modern copies of the famous late 15C series recording the Taking of Arzila by Portugal in 1472, the mutilated originals of which are at Pastrana, in Spain.

Continue downhill to follow the Rua de Santa Maria, which, leading ahead past (left) the façade of the 17C Convento de Santa Clara, now the town hall, and passing below an arch, enters the Largo de São Tiago. At its south end is the former Paço do Concelho, a battlemented structure built over massive arcades.

Beyond is the Largo do Oliveira (with the Pousada of N.S. da Oliveira), dominated by the *Colegiada de N.S. da Oliveira, founded in the 10C by Countess Mumadona, preceded by a curious Gothic canopy (c 1343) sheltering a *cruzeiro*.

The church takes its name ('of the olive tree') from the legend of Wamba the Visigoth, who when chosen king in 672, drove his staff into the ground here, swearing that he would not accept the office until it sprouted, which it did immediately, olive branches shooting out in every direction. All attempts at uprooting his potent staff being fruitless, Wamba fell on his knees and prayed for strength to govern, at least.

The west portal is surmounted by a door-like window (now blind), both dating from a rebuilding by Dom João I. The Manueline tower to the north, with a fountain at its base and plain grilles, was rebuilt after 1515 by Pedro Cogominho, whose tomb, with that of his wife (note head-dress) is in the chapel in its lowest storey. The interior, with fluted pilasters at the crossing, and a Classical organ over the entrance, was entirely modernised earlier this century.

Adjacent is the *Museu Alberto Sampaio, open 10.00–12.30 and 14.00–17.00; closed Mon. It is tastefully installed in the conventual dependencies surrounding a beautiful Romanesque cloister, rebuilt by Dom João I, well restored, and preserving good capitals. The chapterhouse, off the east walk, is lighted by a door with flanking windows all with slightly horseshoe-shaped arches; and at the south-west corner is the Gothic chapel of São Brás.

Among the well-displayed works on the first floor is the rich monastic treasure, with the usual cult objects, outstanding among which is the silver-gilt *triptych of Juan I of Castile. This was traditionally taken with that king's travelling chapel at Aljubarrota and given to Dom João I, but perhaps executed for the latter after the battle for presentation to this church in thanksgiving for his victory. Also of interest is the tattered *loudel* or tunic said to have been worn by Dom João at that engagement. The ceramic collection is notable, while among numerous paintings, those of Frei Carlos of St Vie, and of the Martyrdom of St Sebastian, and a Virgin and Child by António Vaz, should not be overlooked. Among the sculptures is the charming 18C group of the Flight into Egypt by Ambrosio Coelho.

Turn down the lane opposite the *colegiada* entrance, and at a tower (see below) bear right along the Rua da Rainha, towards (left) the imposing 18C Casa do Lobos Machados and, flanking the Largo de João Franco, the chapel of the Misericórdia, with a stucco ceiling of 1775 designed by Frei José de Santo António Villaça (1706–1809), executed under the direction of Paulo Peixote, a local goldsmith. At the north end of the square is the Casa dos Carvalhos.

The left-hand lane at the tower crosses the characteristic Largo de Condessa do Juncal to approach the southern end of the popularly known Largo do Toural, west of the Misericórdia.

Beyond the north-west corner of this square is the *Museu Martins Sarmento, named after the archaeologist who initiated the excavation of the Celtiberian settlements of Briteiros and Sabroso, some 12–15km north; see last part of Rte 36. It is open 10.00–12.00 and 14.00–17.00; closed Mon. While its collection of artefacts discovered on these sites and elsewhere are of particular importance to the specialist, the less informed visitor will also gain some insight into the culture of the peoples which occupied the area 2000 years ago. Many of the larger objects are to be seen in the 14C cloister of the adjacent secularised church of São Domingos, to which stairs descend (embellished by carved escutcheons from demolished mansions in the district). The floriated capitals of the cloister itself should be noted.

Among objects of interest to the non-specialist, apart from the collection of Roman votive altars, sepulchral and other inscribed stones, miliary columns, sarcophagi, etc., is the so-called *Pedra Formosa, a large carved stone slab curiously similar in shape to the traditional design of the *cangas* or ornamental wooden yokes of the lyre-horned Minho oxen. It undoubtedly served as a decorative front to a mausoleum, as with the Pedro Formosa-II, found *in situ* at the Citânia de Briteiros in 1930—*not* a sacrificial altar, as was once assumed. Also important are the two statues of headless Lusitanian warriors, protectively holding their round shields before them; the so-called Colossus of Pedralva; and the numerous geometrically ornamented door-jambs and lintels. Among the smaller objects on display are a bronze votive coach; bronze dolphins; a bull; a hermaphrodite figure holding a bunch of grapes; fibulae; and coins found on these sites.

The other collections, of slighter interest, include Chinese coins and, in the ethnographical section, an 18C litter, an 18C Psaltery made in Brazil, and costumes. Among the somewhat miscellaneous paintings, mostly 19C, are portraits by August Roquemont (1804–52), an artist of Swiss origin, who had taught J.J. Forrester painting, and died in Oporto. The important library of the Sociedade Martins Sarmento is also housed here.

São Sebastião, a short distance south-west of São Domingos, contains good *talha dourada*.

The Rua Dr José Sampaio leads east off the far end of the Alameda. A turning off it ascends towards the Penha (617m), overlooking the town to south, on the lower slope of which is the former monastery of **Santa Marinha da Costa**, founded in 1154, probably on the site of a 4C sanctuary. The prior of Crato (cf. Crato) was educated here. The whole was entirely rebuilt in the 18C and a new church was started in 1748. The *azulejos* by Policarpo de Oliveira Bernardes are notable, while the belvedere overlooking the garden known as the Varanda de Frei Jerónimo is most attractive, although the views towards Guimarães are no longer so. The well-restored dependencies now shelter the luxurious Pousada de Santa Marinha.

A minor road leads north-east from Guimarães via **Azurém**, with the medieval Casa de Pousada, and later passes a 19C church, beyond which at a higher level is the Igreja Matriz of **São Torcato**, retaining some 12C features, and the cloister of the Benedictine convent of Santo Agostinho.

For roads from Braga to Guimarães, and on to Amarante, see the last parts of Rtes 35 and 36.

The N105 leads south-west to enter the valley of the Vizela, where in the small spa of **Caldas de Vizela** Roman tessellated pavements have been found. At nearby **Vilarinho** is a good 12C church; but of more interest is that at **Roriz**, further west, reached by climbing left out of the valley, where the restored Romanesque *church of 1228 has a large rose-window above its portal.

Further south-west is the hill-top Iron Age *citánia* of **Sanfins de Ferreira**, preserving the walls of numerous stone huts and lines of defensive walls (cf. Citánia de Briteiros). The artefacts excavated here may be seen in the museum at **Paços de Ferreira**, further south, on the N207, with the Romanesque church (with a large apse, and separate belfry) of the monastery of São Pedro de Ferreira.

At **Santo Tirso** (12,321 inhabitants), a busy textile town on the river Ave west of Roriz, is the former Benedictine monastery of São Bento, the late 14C cloisters and other dependencies of which contain archaeological remains, etc. The church, under restoration, was rebuilt in 1659 to the plans of João Turriano of Coimbra.

The A3 may be entered a short distance west of the town. For Oporto, some 20km south-west, see Rte 33.

# Bibliography

The bibliography of books in English on Portugal is extensive. This revised selective list, concentrating on comparatively recently published titles, is by no means exhaustive. Many titles will contain bibliographies for further or more specialised reading. The Canning House Library (2 Belgrave Square, London SW1X 8PJ) produces an occasional *Bulletin of Publications*; a magazine entitled *Cultura* (241 King Street, London W6 9LP), which reviews new books on Portugal, may be subscribed to; while the Department of Portuguese at King's College, London, publishes *Portuguese Studies*, an annual journal containing reviews and a bibliography of new books. The British Historical Society of Portugal (13 Rua da Arriaga, 1200 Lisbon) can provide a list of their publications, many of which will interest readers of this guide. The Carcanet Press publish a growing series of books entitled 'Aspects of Portugal' in association with the Calouste Gulbenkian Foundation, Lisbon.

**Topographical and General**, some of which also cover the rest of the Peninsula; and some of which are now of interest as being 'dated':

Joseph Baretti, *Journey from London to Genoa* (1770; reprinted 1970)

Huldine Beamish, *The Hills of Alentejo* (1958)

William Beckford, *The Journal of William Beckford in Portugal and Spain 1787–1788* (ed. Boyd Alexander, 1954), *Recollections of Excursion to the Monasteries of Alcobaça and Batalha* (1835; reprinted 1972)

Ann Bridge and Susan Belloc Lowndes Marques, *The Selective Traveller in Portugal* (1949; last edition, 1967).

Adolfo Cabral (ed.), Robert *Southey: Journal of a residence in Portugal 1800–1801, etc.* (1960)

Roy Campbell, *Portugal* (1957)

Rodney Gallop, *Portugal, a book of Folk Ways* (1936; reprinted 1961)

Malcolm Jack, *William Beckford: an English Fidalgo* (forthcoming)

Harold V. Livermore (ed.), *Portugal and Brazil, an Introduction* (1953)

Rose Macaulay, *They Went to Portugal* (1946; since reprinted), and *They went to Portugal, Too* (1990); both being essential background reading

Henry Myhill, *Portugal* (1972)

Ian Robertson, *Portugal: a Traveller's Guide* (1992), more a 'companion' than a guide

José Cornélio da Silva and Gerald Luckhurst, *Sintra; a Landscape with Villas* (1989)

Sacheverell Sitwell, *Portugal and Madeira* (1954)

J. B. Trend, *Portugal* (1957)

*The Admiralty Geographical Handbooks of Spain and Portugal*, particularly volume II (1942)

Among earlier histories and descriptions of Portugal of some interest are: James Murphy, *Travels in Portugal* (1795), and *A General View of Portugal* (1798); Richard Twiss *Travels through Spain and Portugal* (1775); John Blankett, *Letters from Portugal* (?1777); H.F. Link, *Travels in Portugal* (1801); J.Fr. Bourgoing, *Travels of the Duke de Chatelet in Portugal* (1809); W.H.G. Kingston, *Lusitanian Sketches* (1845); Robert Southwell, *Letters* (1740); W.M. Kinsey, *Portugal Illustrated* (1828); Anon. (J.-B.-E. Carrère), *A Picture of Lisbon* (1809); 'Arthur Costigan' (James Ferrier), *Sketches of Society and Manners in Portugal* (1787); A.P.D. 'G'., *Sketches of Portuguese Life, etc.* (1826; with 26 plates); Robert Southey, *Letters from Spain and Portugal* (1797); Marianne Baillie, *Lisbon in the years 1821, 1822 and 1823* (1825); William

Dalrymple, *Travels through Spain and Portugal in 1774* (1777); Baron Fagel, *Account of the Campaign in Portugal* (1708); Gen. Dumouriez, *An Account of Portugal as it appeared in 1766* (1797); John Colbatch, *An Account of the Court under Pedro II* (1700); William Bromley, *Travels through Portugal* (1702); J.M. Browne, *An Historical View of the Revolutions in Portugal* (1827); Lord Porchester (Carnarvon), *Portugal and Gallicia* (1836); W.G. Harrison, *Jennings' Landscape Annual* (1839); Dora Quillinan (née Wordsworth), *Journal of a Few Months; Residence in Portugal* (1847); and J.M. Neale, *Handbook for Travellers in Portugal* (1855). For earlier books on the Peninsular and Miguelite wars, see below.

**History**, except the Peninsular War (for which, see below):
Harold V. Livermore, *A History of Portugal* (1947), the more compact *New History of Portugal* (revised ed. 1976), *Portugal: a Short History* (1973; concentrating more on the evolution of Portuguese society), and *The origins of Spain and Portugal* (1971)
Jorge de Alarção, *Roman Portugal* (1988; in 4 slim volumes)
P.E. Russell, *The English Intervention in Spain and Portugal in the time of Edward III and Richard II* (1955)
Fernão Lopes, *The English in Portugal 1367–87*, ed. by D.W. Lomax and R.J. Oakley (1988)
H.E.S. Fisher, *The Portugal Trade, 1700–1770* (1971)
C.R. Boxer, *The Portuguese Seaborne Empire, 1415–1825* (1969; reprinted 1991), and ed. with J.C. Aldridge, *Descriptive List of the State Papers Portugal 1661–1780 in the Public Record Office, London* (3 volumes; Lisbon, 1979–83)
A.J.R. Russell-Wood, *A World on the Move: The Portuguese in Africa, Asia, and America, 1415–1808* (1992)
David Francis, *The Methuens and Portugal, 1691–1708* (1966), *The First Peninsular War, 1702–1713* (1975), and *Portugal 1715–1808: Joanine, Pombaline and Rococo Portugal as seen by British diplomats and traders* (1985)
C. Hanson, *Economy and Society in Baroque Portugal, 1668–1703* (1981)
J.A.C. Hugill, *No Peace without Spain* (1991), on the War of the Succession
Sir Richard Lodge (ed.), *The Private Correspondence of Sir Benjamin Keene* (1933)
L.M.E. Shaw, *Trade, Inquisition and the English Nation in Portugal, 1650–1690* (1989)
Judith Nozes (ed.), *The Lisbon Earthquake of 1755: British Accounts* (1990)
Kenneth Maxwell, *Pombal: A Paradox of the Enlightenment* (1995); *The Making of Portuguese Democracy* (1995)
Douglas L. Wheeler, *Republican Portugal: A political history, 1900–1926* (1978), and ed. with L.S. Graham, *In Search of Modern Portugal: The Revolution and its Consequences* (1982)
Tom Gallagher, *Portugal: A 20C interpretation* (1983)
R.A.H. Robinson, *Contemporary Portugal: A History* (1979)
P. Fryer and P.McG. Pinheiro, *Oldest Ally: A Portrait of Salazar's Portugal* (1961)
D.L. Raby, *Fascism and Resistance in Portugal* (1988)
D.M. Machado, *The Structure of Portuguese Society: The Failure of Fascism* (1991)
José Hermano Saraiva, *Portugal: A Companion History*, ed., and with additional appendices, by Ian Robertson (1996)

**Peninsular War:**
C.W.C. Oman, *Wellington's Army* (1913); *A History of the Peninsular War* (1902–30). Its seven volumes are in the process of being reprinted (1995–97).
Jac Weller, *Wellington in the Peninsula* (1962; reprinted 1992)
Arthur Bryant, *The Great Duke* (1971)

Michael Glover, *The Peninsular War* (1974), and *Britannia Sickens: Sir Arthur Wellesley and the Convention of Cintra* (1961)
Elisabeth Longford, *Wellington, the Years of the Sword* (1969)
Julian Rathbone, *Wellington's War: Peninsular Dispatches* (1984)
Antony Brett-James, *Life in Wellington's Army* (1972)
David Gaters, *The Spanish Ulcer: A history of the Peninsular War* (1986)
Lawrence James, *The Iron Duke* (1992)
Thomas Henry Browne, *The Napoleonic Journal of*, ed. R.N. Buckley (1987)

Among earlier or contemporary narratives of the war, which are legion, some of which have been reprinted, apart from the multi-volume histories of Southey, Napier, and Oman, are Andrew Halliday, *The Present State of Portugal and the Portuguese Army* (1812); John T. Jones, *Memoranda Relative to the Lines thrown up to cover Lisbon in 1810* (1829); William Warre, *Letters from the Peninsula, 1809–1812* (1909); W.G. Eliot, *A Treatise on the Defence of Portugal* (3rd ed., 1811); George Landmann, *Historical, Military and Picturesque Observations of Portugal* (1818; for its illustrations); J.M. Sherer, *Recollections of the Peninsular* (1823); J. Leach, *Rough Sketches of the life of an old soldier* (1831); George Simmons, *A British Rifle Man* (1899); and A.L.F. Schaumann, *On the Road with Wellington* (1924).

Among those concerning the Miguelite War, or 'War of the Two Brothers': William Bollaert, *The Wars of Succession in Portugal and Spain* (1870); Lovell Badcock, *Rough Leaves from a Journal* (1835); Charles Napier, *Account of the War of Succession in Portugal* (1836); G. Lloyd Hodges, *Narrative of an Expedition to Portugal* (1833); Charles Shaw, *Memoirs* (1837); W.N. Glascock, *Naval Sketch Book* (2nd Series; 1834); Thomas Knight, *The British Battalion at Oporto* (1834); J.E. Alexander, *Sketches in Portugal during the Civil War of 1834* (1835); Hugh Owen, *The Civil War in Portugal, and the Siege of Oporto* (1835).

**Art and Architecture** (but not including works on specific artists or picture books):
Walter Crum Watson, *Portuguese Architecture* (1908)
Robert C. Smith, *The Arts of Portugal, 1500–1800* (1968)
George Kubler, *Portugues Plain Architecture, 1521–1706* (1972), and with Martin Soria, *Art and Architecture of Spain and Portugal, etc., 1500–1800* (1959)
James Lees-Milne, *Baroque in Spain and Portugal* (1960)
Julio Gil, *The Finest Castles in Portugal* (1986)
J.A. Levenson (ed.), *The Age of the Baroque in Portugal* (National Gallery of Art, Washington, exhibition catalogue, 1993)
Angela Delaforce, *A Aliança Revisitado* (Gulbenkian exhibition catalogue, 1994)
Alice Berkeley and Susan Lowndes, *English Art in Portugal* (1994) is a brief but attractively produced introduction to the subject.

Also of some interest are Anne de Stoop's *Stately Homes in the Vicinity of Lisbon* (1989), *Palais et Manoirs Portugais: Le Minho-1* (1995), and *Living in Portugal* (1995).

There has been a great improvement in recent years in the quality of catalogues in English produced by several, but by no means all, important museums, such as Silvana Bessone's *The National Coach Museum*, and José Luis Porfirio's *Museum of Ancient Art*, among others.

Spanish readers will find a useful reference book in J.-A. França, J.L. Morales y Marin, and Wilfredo Rincón, *Arte Portugués* (volume XXX in the Summa Artis series, Espasa Calpe, 1986).

Those with some knowledge of Portuguese will find *Arquitectura Popular em Portugal* (2nd ed. 1980; since revised), ed. by the Association of Portuguese architects, containing several hundred photographs, and with some English text, of interest; also the 3-volume Inventário published by the Instituto Português do Património Arquitectónico e Arquelógico entitled *Património Arquitectónico e Arqueológico Classificado* (1993).

## Other subjects:

David Francis, *The Wine Trade* (1972)

George Robertson, *Port* (1978)

Sarah Bradford, *The Englishman's Wine* (1969), revised ed. entitled T*he Story of Port* (1978)

Jan Read, *Wines of Portugal* (revised ed. 1987)

Alex Liddell, *Port Wine Quintas of the Douro* (1992)

Helder Carita and Homem Cardosa, *Portuguese Gardens* (1991)

Patrick Bowe, *Gardens of Portugal* (1989)

Aubrey F. Bell, *Portuguese Literature* (1922, reprinted, with a selective bibliography, 1970)

M. Barreto, *The Portuguese Columbus: Secret Agent of King John II* (1992)

D.J. Mabberley and P.J. Placito, *Algarve Plants and Landscape: Passing Tradition and Ecological Change* (1993)

J.M. Anderson and M. Sheridan Lea, *Portugal: 1001 Sights* (1994, largely archaeological)

David Corkill, *The Portuguese Economy since 1974* (1993)

Michael Gray et al, *Frederick William Flower: a Pioneer of Portuguese Photography* (Museu do Chiado exhibition catalogue, 1994)

Ana Margarida Arruda et al, *Subterranean Lisbon* (Museu Nacional de Arqueologia exhibition catalogue, 1994)

# A Note on Blue Guides

For thirty years prior to the First World War both James Muirhead (1853–1934) and his brother Findlay (1860–1935) had been employed by Baedeker's as editors of the English editions of their German series of guides. With the war, this association ceased. By 1915 Findlay Muirhead had acquired the copyright of most of the competitive Handbooks, published by John Murray. In 1917 an agreement between Muirhead Guide-Books Ltd and Hachette et Cie was signed, by which the two companies would collaborate, and on 31 May 1918 Findlay Muirhead's first 'Blue Guide', that to London, was published.

This was then translated and adapted for the French market as the first 'Guide Bleu'—Hachette had previously published the blue cloth-bound 'Guides Joanne', and that colour was chosen by the two publishing houses to distinguish them further from the red bindings of Baedekers and Murrays. In 1921 Muirhead published his translation and adaptation of Marcel Monmarché's Guide Bleu to Paris. The agreement continued in force until 1933, when it lapsed.

In 1931 Benn Brothers took over the Blue Guides, and in 1934 Russell Muirhead (1896–1976), Findlay Muirhead's son, and assistant since 1921, was appointed editor. He was succeeded in 1963 by Stuart Rossiter (1923–82), who had worked with Muirhead since 1954 and who compiled or revised a number of guides himself.

In 1984 A & C Black acquired the series from Ernest Benn, Ltd, carrying on the tradition of quality guide-book publishing which had begun in 1826 with 'Black's Economical Tourist of Scotland', among them several compiled by Charles Bertram Black, the eldest son of the firm's founder. The Blue Guide series had continued to grow spectacularly, now with over 50 titles in print, revised editions appearing regularly, and with new guides in preparation.

'Blue Guides' is a registered trade mark.

# INDEX